ALL DRESSED UP

Also by Jonathon Green

Chasing the Sun: Dictionary-Makers and the Dictionaries They Made

It: Sex Since the Sixties

Them: Voices from the Immigrant Community in Contemporary Britain

Days In The Life: Voices from the London Underground 1961–71

ALL DRESSED UP
The Sixties and the
Counter-culture

Jonathon Green

JONATHAN CAPE
LONDON

Published by Jonathan Cape 1998

2 4 6 8 10 9 7 5 3 1

Copyright © Jonathon Green 1998

Jonathon Green has asserted his right under the Copyright, Designs
and Patents Act 1988 to be identified as the author of this work

First published in Great Britain in 1998 by
Jonathan Cape
Random House, 20 Vauxhall Bridge Road,
London SW1V 2SA

Random House Australia (Pty) Limited
20 Alfred Street, Milsons Point, Sydney,
New South Wales 2061 Australia

Random House New Zealand Limited
18 Poland Road, Glenfield,
Auckland 10, New Zealand

Random House South Africa (Pty) Limited
Endulini, 5A Jubilee Road, Parktown 2193, South Africa

Random House UK Limited Reg. No. 954009

Every effort has been made to obtain the necessary
permissions with reference to copyright material. The publishers
apologise if inadvertently any sources remain unacknowledged

A CIP catalogue record for this book
is available from the British Library

ISBN 0-224-04322-6

Papers used by Random House UK Limited are natural,
recyclable products made from wood grown in sustainable forests.
The manufacturing processes conform to the environmental
regulations of the country of origin

Printed and bound in Great Britain by
Mackays of Chatham PLC

Contents

For Dan Franklin

Acknowledgements

My primary thanks go to all those individuals who ten years ago contributed their memories to *Days In the Life* and upon whose experiences I have once more allowed myself to draw. It is with great sadness that I have to record that of those people, David Widgery, Richard Trench, June Bolan, Derek Taylor, Peter Roberts and most recently Nicholas Saunders have all died in the interim. So too has Edward Barker, the underground's peerless cartoonist, who evaded an interview but whose presence was an integral part of many aspects of counter-cultural life.

In addition I would like to thank the staffs of the London Library, the British Library, the Special Collections department of the University of Edinburgh Library; Sue Jones of Blast! Films, Andrew Sclanders (who disinterred the cover picture), Jo Ellen Wisnosky of the Vintage Magazine Company Archives, and Rosie Boycott, Ian Buruma, Jenny Fabian, Dick Fontaine, Mike Hodges, David May and David Robins, all of who have let me air my theories and offered me their own.

Further thanks go to Charlotte Mendelson, who edited the text, and to Tristan Jones, who corrected my many errors; to my agent Julian Alexander and yet again to my publisher Dan Franklin who has allowed me once more to drag that most controversial of all modern decades back into the limelight it only reluctantly abandoned. The least I can do is make him my dedicatee.

Introduction

You can ask a dozen different people and you'll get a dozen different starting dates. The sixties, I always think, didn't really get going until about 1964, and didn't end until about 1972 or 1973. The early 1960s were, in every way, the fag end of the fifties – post-war austerity, drab, predictable . . . and not very imaginative or stylish. You see, the 1940s didn't end until about 1956. Then it was the 1950s until 1963 or '64 or so.
Anthony Frewin *London Blues* (1997)

We live in the shadow of the Sixties. Of all the artificial constructs by which we delineate our immediate past, 'the Sixties' have the greatest purchase on the mass imagination. They stand, rightly or not, as the dominant myth of the modern era. That one might have been too old or too young to enjoy them, indeed, that one might not even have been born, is of marginal importance. Rightly or wrongly again, the great edifice casts its shadow and everything must seek its own light within it.

The Sixties are as much a state of mind as a chronological concept. And like all states of mind they are open to many interpretations. The very concept of the period has caused as intense a polarisation in retrospect as ever it did at the time. For some the Sixties remain 'the best years of their lives'; for others 'the end of civilisation as they know it'. Neither is right, but ignorance has never stood in the way of zealotry. For the dissenters, there is little to consider here. Not that their views should be dismissed – it is their belated triumph that, after all, has determined the direction of the western world in the years that have followed – but they are views which, at least during the period under review, represented little more than the impotent bleating of the fearful and the threatened. The point of the Sixties is change – realised or otherwise, feasible or foolhardy. Are you part of the problem, asked the slogan, or part of the solution?

As for the advocates: utopian, over-optimistic, naïve they may have been, but they offered hope. However inchoate their theories they looked forward to a possible future, rather than backwards to a long-dead past. As I wrote in the preamble to my oral history of the period, *Days in the Life*, to its primary movers and shakers the Sixties was an era of unashamed utopianism: 'Above all it believed that the world actually could be made a better place. Embarrassingly earnest at times, gleefully unimpressed by the trappings of economic stability and the bottom line, the "freaks" set determinedly about their regenerative task much as their mothers might take over the Oxfam bring-and-buy. Crusading zeal to the fore, they plunged in undeterred, taking full advantage of the optimism of the times. Much of it was naïve, a good deal simply psychedelic pipe-dreams, but much too was achieved. A more sceptical approach might have avoided the more ludicrous blunders, but a more sceptical approach would have missed out on the undeniable successes.' I see no reason to amend that view now.

There is, perhaps, another aspect to this optimism. The young of the period had been brought up by parents whose own formative experience had been the Second World War. Unlike many such conflicts, this was categorised as a 'good war'. Those who survived it came home as heroes: they had 'saved the world from fascism' and, willy-nilly, 'made it a better place'. Whatever the realities that followed, the Labour landslide in Britain's General Election of 1945 was a triumph of utopian belief. Despite the obligatory antagonism of the 'generation gap' (a concept that was first voiced in that *echt*-Sixties year, 1967), the young people who made the Sixties were infused with that same optimism. The *leitmotif* of post-war life has been the idea of endlessly unfolding progress. It was never so deeply believed as in that period. The struggle was different, the 'enemy' was much nearer home, but the bottom line seems strikingly similar: changing things for the better. It cannot be sheer coincidence that the word 'fascist' was disinterred from the text-books and brandished so enthusiastically by a generation whose parents had supposedly purged it from the modern political vocabulary.

It is dangerous to think in neat chronological divisons – history is a continuum, not a series of topped and tailed decades and centuries. But there is no doubt that the generation of the Sixties was quite genuinely something new. If the 'generation gap' was coined only in 1967, then 'teenager' itself was little more than a couple of decades older. 'Adolescence', teenage's predecessor, had existed since the early fifteenth century. It meant simply becoming an adult. It was a passage, not a status. 'Teenage' conferred that status; one lingered, indeed, moving on was a regret, and no reward. A word so emblematic of the modern world, it emerged in America, moved gradually across the Atlantic and had reached its fullest flower as the Sixties began. The years between thirteen and twenty had never existed in so totemic and autonomous a way. Now, in the post-war decades, teenage life began its gradual move to centre-stage. The teens of the Fifties were essentially aping the lifestyle of their parents. The most important goal was the gaining of one's own income – one spent it on consumption and on carving out a small corner of the world for oneself – but there was little impetus to change the overall culture, merely to colonise a small section of it. As the Fifties proceeded, that changed. Middle class teens, apostrophised conveniently as beatniks, began to shift into new preoccupations. It is as if there arose a gradual, ever-intensifying sense of one's own potential. And as the state of mind known as 'the Sixties' came up to speed, fuelled by that triumvirate of 'dope, sex and rock 'n' roll', plus the non-specific and never so popular concept of 'revolution', there developed an 'alternative' society.

That society, calling itself the 'underground', was not, by the standards of the larger world, either clandestine or revolutionary. None the less, compared with such synthetic labels as 'Swinging London' it did count. In an era of instant myth, the underground could claim genuine cohesion; of as much if not greater validity than that gaudy offspring of a magazine writer's fantasies or a caravan-borne procession of paisley-wearing aristos.

It was an educated movement, drawing on the alienated children of the comfortable bourgeoisie, from which background it drew its strength – the middle-class belief that the world existed for its convenience and should be treated as such, and its weakness – an inevitable élitism that put off many 'ordinary' youngsters. It chose to stand against the consumerism of the era, offering a parallel and quite contrary nirvana to the 'white heat' of Prime Minister Wilson's technological revolution. It was not overtly political, preferring to mock both the old and new left, but it adopted a predictable liberal platform, backing abortion law reform, the abolition of censorship, sexual freedom, banning the Bomb and of course the legalisation of soft drugs.

It had its own media – newspapers, magazines, film, theatre and even fledgling video. Much of the rock industry was targeted straight at it. It had advice centres and self-help groups. There was the world of drug selling for those who fancied an alternative brand of 'venture capitalism' and for those more respectful of the law, a whole range of craft and cottage industries. It had restaurants, food shops, clubs and outfitters. And at its tribal gatherings, the great rock festivals, tens of thousands claimed allegiance to its ranks.

None of which was exactly 'teenage' – the hippie hardcore were in their early twenties and the feel was student rather than schoolchild – but the prevailing ethos was undeniably geared towards the desire to oust the adult world. Even the mainstream developments – a Labour government, the liberal social legislation on abortion, obscenity, homosexuality and capital punishment, all pioneered by Home Secretary Roy Jenkins, changes in music, in fashion, in architecture – are rooted in the desire for cultural patricide. But 'the Sixties' transcended mere teenage angst, however much that might have underpinned it. After all, the mere concept of such an 'alternative' (at least on so large a scale) had only just come into existence and the novelty of the idea in itself intensified what happened. Today's young may appear to have abandoned such efforts – but their task is so much harder. Three decades back it was very simple to shock. No so today. The idea that 'no one had done it before' is central to the impact of the Sixties. Taken individually, most of the cultural 'revolutions' had of course been carried out long before: one had been able to procure an abortion, to utilise contraception, to take recreational drugs, to read illicit literature, to divorce and to indulge in same-sex relationships. But one had not been able to do any of it very openly, and in most cases one had not been able to do it very easily without money. Contraception was not a matter of money: the exclusivity there came from gender rather than income. The complaisant doctor, whether wielding syringe or curette, the locked cabinet of *curiosae*, the discreet cohabitation of a pair of bachelors –

such things were the perks of the middle classes and above. There had also been vegetarians, feminists, British Buddhists, free lovers, communards and the like – but these were simply 'cranks'. This was the real world of 'Victorian values': a world of deference, of 'knowing one's place'. It lasted well into the Fifties and to some extent remains. Teen fantasies aside, what the Sixties brought was a democratisation of such things – the end of a value system which had stood in place for more than a century. It was that which created much of the hostility. In many ways the critics were right to worry; it was indeed the end of their ordered, hierarchical, deferential world.

The concept and the lifestyle that would become known as 'teenage' were not all that came from the US. Among the many currents running through the Sixties is that of American primacy. If the nineteenth century had offered Britain its imperial moment, then the twentieth passed it to America. That said, there was still a good deal of UK input. The 'Swinging London' label may have been coined by a bunch of *Time* editors, searching for a way of getting more mini-skirts and their wearers into the magazine, but it was London, not New York, they hymned. Then, as now, Britain offered a level of style that America would never attain. In addition there was British rock 'n' roll. The English invasion, as the media put it. Yet in the end even here America had the last word. For all the impact of the élite – Beatles, the Stones, the Who, and others – the pasty British white boys were in the end only recycling the music of the black American men, and making it palatable for the mass market.

The culture of the underground was a one-way street, and it started out in the States. Only the traditional lefties, undazzled by transatlantic charms, looked first to Europe; as far as America went, they might have puffed, but they rarely dared inhale. Perhaps they were right: there was something *ersatz* about Britain's espousal of the US scene. You could read *On the Road* but even Land's End to John O'Groats was hardly New York to San Francisco. But you could dream, and no one said Kerouac's Dean Moriarty had copyrighted craziness.

For those who position the period as the first step on some downward path, any thoughts of characterising it as a joyful, celebratory era are anathema. But whether looking back or experiencing it first hand, the party element is unavoidable. Thus, however he may have meant it, one need not see John Lennon's comment that gives this book its title as simply dismissive. After the self-denial of the Second World War and the period of austerity that followed, after the struggle towards mass consumerism that typified the Fifties (not quite so grey, perhaps, as they are traditionally painted, but hardly the most blithe of decades) there is an element of dressing up, of party-time about the decade that followed. For some it was 'party best', for others full-scale fancy dress, while for many, noses pressed to the window, it was merely the reflection, alluring or repellent, of those dead set on a good time. The 'long

Sixties', as it is best called, embraces a period from the chronological mid-Fifties to the early Seventies, if not even to 1979, when on 3 May the party came so abruptly to its end and the last diehard, desperate celebrants, puffing on their roaches, downing the very dregs of long-emptied bottles, were finally turfed out into the unwelcoming dawn of a very different day.

Any study of the period must take this lengthy overview – every party needs its preparation, none can avoid the clearing up – but the core period can be seen as running from the Albert Hall poetry reading of 1965, known as 'Wholly Communion', to the trial of *Oz* magazine in 1971. The first would see the gathering, the second the dispersal. And in between was a period of unprecedented intensity, the height of the party as it were, a glorious mêlée into which would be poured all the energies, all the creativity, all the hopes of a generation who foolishly but genuinely believed that they could change the world. If they failed, then it was not through lack of trying. And in some areas they did succeed, although not perhaps as they might have envisaged.

As the century draws to a close, it is hard not to see the Sixties as the pivotal decade. It was not the only momentous period and its perceived importance now may be ascribed to the current domination of the media by those whose youth was played out against its gaudy wallpaper, but for all the importance of the Twenties and the Thirties, the years of the two World Wars, and the grim, destructive Eighties, the Sixties seem to stand in the centre of it all, sucking in the influences of the past, creating the touchstones of the future. Certainly what has come since is consistently measured against the era – whether in the nostalgia it evokes, or in its demonisation. So much that has been suffered since can be seen as the revenge of the have-nots, the triumph of the grey: those who were either left uninvited to the party, or felt themselves unequal to its delights now finally, if perhaps temporarily, ascendant.

Perhaps, as Richard Neville was at pains to explain, although his emphasis was different, the 'alternatives' were never that important – merely one more example of the pleasure principle, and people were in fact 'playing at work' – but that didn't diminish their substance. The changes that took place in British society in the Sixties did not all spring from the underground, and certain purportedly underground figures capitalised even then on distinctly 'straight' business methods to found their fortunes, but many of them can be traced directly to hippie inspiration. There were many variations on the art of 'doing one's own thing' and 'getting one's shit together' in the face of Establishment society's obsessive cartelisation. At the time they seemed highly revolutionary, but today they have been absorbed into mainstream British life: fringe theatres, art centres, natural food stores, a host of 'cottage industries' and workers' co-operatives, a concern for the environment and its ecology, the 'personal politics' of gay liberation and the women's movement, the squatting movement and its legacy of housing action groups, the obsession with a clean, healthy body, the variety of alternative physical and mental therapies. Even the do-nothing hedonism has been perpetuated in the 'Slackers' of recent years.

We live today in a very different climate, for all the desperate re-creation of a new 'Swinging London', or the merchandising of that showman's slogan, 'Cool Britannia'. Today's government, Labour once more after so many years of Tory hegemony, is a very different creature from that which laid down the backdrop to the events that follow. The world is harsher, less optimistic; the idea of open-ended progress that lay beneath the counterculture's extemporising has been long buried in disillusion. Contemporary culture is no longer so open and the government, claiming to echo society at large, reflects it. What Roy Jenkins, then a reforming Home Secretary, termed the 'civilised society' has been replaced by a pervasive Sunday school morality, appeasing the worst national instincts rather than seeking to tease out and cultivate the best.

The conglomeration of events that have become known as 'The Sixties' made for a remarkable era. They changed, perhaps more than any decade of the century, the way that society works. For that they are both celebrated and excoriated and as such they are rapidly moving from fact to myth. In the pages that follow I have attempted to tell at least some of the story. Space, as ever, precludes the level of exploration one might have desired, but my intention has been, to reclaim a once-popular term, the 'demythologising' of the period. My own view is unlikely to be in doubt, but my aim here has been no more than to lay out what happened. As Lenny Bruce once put it, 'Everyone wants what ought to be, what should be. But there is no ought to be, no should be. There is only what is.'

Jonathon Green
June 1998

Chapter One

In the Beginning: Teenage Kicks

This teenage ball had had a real splendour in the days when the kids discovered that, for the first time since centuries of kingdom-come, they'd money, which hitherto had always been denied to us at the best time of life to use it, namely, when you're young and strong, and also before the newspapers and the telly got hold of this teenage fable and prostituted it . . . Yes, I tell you, it had a real savage splendour in the day when we found out that no one couldn't sit on our faces any more because we'd loot to spend at last, and our world was to be our world, the one we wanted and not standing on the doorstep of someone else's.
Colin MacInnes *Absolute Beginners*[1]

Of all the strands that weave together to make 'the Sixties', the concept of an autonomous teenage is perhaps the most important. The teenager, as Malcolm Bradbury has noted, is 'one of the most original of modern concepts'.[2] Bradbury, in an ill-titled but otherwise elegant essay 'The Pubertoids', published in 1961, sets out the situation very clearly. Once upon a time in the traditional, pre-1950s society, being mature was what mattered; being young was no more than an unfortunate period through which one had to proceed, best left behind as soon as possible. Not until one attained man- or womanhood, and even then not really until one reached middle and even better old age, could one really be said to have come to grips with life. Those who lived longest had to be the wisest, since they had worked out the various ways of best surviving in a world which was, in its essentials, pretty immutable. 'Authority *had* authority, and one of its tasks was naturally to repress, educate and control the feckless and expansive instincts of anyone younger than oneself.'[3] But what, under such a system, did one actually do with the young, whose only interests seemed to be fucking and fighting to their heart's content? One invented matrimony to geld sexuality, and sports to simulate less well-refereed violence. To top this off was the concept of original sin, which explained that children were *de facto* evil and should accordingly be squashed as rigorously as possible.

All of which collapsed in the face of a new phenomenon: the consumer society. The old, set in their ways, well aware that life, however much one garlanded it with distractions, was still essentially tedious, were the last people the merchants wished to consider. The young, on the other hand, still firmly of the belief that life was to be lived, that life was fun, that 'new' (like themselves) was what really mattered, were very much to their taste. Suddenly it was the young who 'always know best, and one of their tasks is to repress, educate and control anyone older than themselves'.[4] As for the idea that those who had learned the tricks of survival were the wisest: far from it – it was the young, as yet free from such pragmatic cynicisms, who were the wise. These 'absolute beginners' as MacInnes christened them, had the real knowledge. 'In consumer culture,' notes Bradbury, 'there are no fathers any more.'[5] The authority/father figure is dead. One need only check the US sitcoms: 'Dad', once paterfamilias, is reduced time and again to a buffoon. Youth has become 'a force, a peer-group, a self-contained domain that functions according to its own generational laws'.[6] The young socialise each other, helped by the 'endless boom of communications'[7] that feeds their self-image.

For Colin MacInnes, perhaps the one person who resisted pontificating on youth, but merely got down among them and started taking seriously what was going on, the situation was simple. He saw the new movement as a 'Children's Crusade' and declared that: 'We are in the presence, here, of an entirely new phenomenon in human history: that youth is rich. Once, the *jeunesse dorée* were a minute minority; now, all the young have gold . . . Farewell the classic century-old pattern of Youth, the industrious apprentice, penniless, nose glued to the grindstone, and Age, prosperous, authoritative . . . Today, Age is needy and, as its powers decline, so does its income; but fullblooded youth has wealth as well as vigour.'[8] Now all could ape Hogarth's 'Idle 'Prentice', lost to a world of hedonistic pleasure – and better still, with no fear of Tyburn's Triple Tree in the final frame.

For a polemicist such as Jeff Nuttall, what happened to the young during the Fifties, let alone beyond, was the direct product of the development and use of nuclear weapons. But fear of 'the bomb' is only part of the equation. The backdrop without which the whole show could never have been played out was a sense of economic stability. The statistics make it clear: from 1950–60 the number of cars in Western Europe doubled (and doubled again between 1960–70); in 1950 300,000 Britons owned a television set; a decade later ten-and-a-half million did so (in the US the figures go from 7,000,000 in 1946 to 50 million in 1960); by 1961 mass tourism, unknown a decade before, was taking four million Britons off on European holidays. Perhaps most important was the huge growth in university students: there were 60% more students in UK universities in 1964 than there had been in 1950. (In France the student population had tripled and in Germany it had doubled while in America numbers had risen by 200% between 1941–60 and by a further 70% by 1965 – five-and-a-half-million Americans, more than the nation had farmers, were in college). An economic boom, near full employment, a wealth of accessible, affordable consumer items – all this could be seen across the West. The mood was summed up on 20 July 1957 when Britain's Prime Minister Harold Macmillan appeared in Bedford marketplace and, borrowing from the US politician Adlai Stevenson who had campaigned (somewhat reluctantly) under the same slogan in the election of 1952, told the crowd, 'Let's be frank about it. Most of our people have never had it so good. Go around the country, go to the industrial towns, go to the farms, and you'll see a state of prosperity such as we have never had in my lifetime – nor indeed ever in the history of this country.' He went on to warn against the dangers of inflation, but the media ignored this, pouncing on his words as a glorious reflection of the nation's post-war prosperity. Certainly teenagers, newly freed by their own enrolment in the workplace, had more money than their pre-war peers might ever have imagined. And they weren't buying televisions and washing-machines, those 'white goods' which took pride of place in their parents' houses. Their money went straight to the new market that, with ever greater enthusiasm, had grown up to service their wants. In 1960 British teens spent £850 million – essentially on themselves. It was only 5% of the overall national spend but teens were responsible for buying 40% of the record-players, 30% of the cosmetics and toiletries and 28% of cinema tickets. It was a source of enormous and ever-increasing power. If earlier generations had not known what to do with their young, the entrepreneurs and the merchants of the 1950s certainly had no such problem: the answer was simple – sell to them. Their sheer numbers underpinned the new situation. The 'baby boom' of the immediate post-war period meant that by 1963 there were 800,000 more teenagers in the population than there had been a decade before. American figures, as ever, are even more dramatic. There, in 1956, the nation's thirteen million teens were spending $7 billion, a 26% increase on 1953 figures. The average teenager's weekly disposable income of $10.55 was almost equal to that of an entire family in 1941.

The world the teens occupied, however much it was dedicated to servicing their wants (and to creating them by skilful marketing and kindred exploitation of teen appetites) remained a top-down creation in the Fifties and early Sixties. The young were getting a parallel version of their parents' lifestyle – pop records for washing-machines, fashionable clothes for new cars – but as yet not an alternative one. The middle-class, educated teens might have been feeling their way towards some forms of inchoate social revolution, with the Beats and CND-ers leading the way, but for the vast majority these unformed theories were irrelevant. It would take such important developments as the gradual takeover of the music business by bands like the Beatles and Rolling Stones – who for the first time wrote their own lyrics, rather than parroting those created by Tin Pan Alley – to show that the young, and not just the young but the working-class and lower middle-class young, could strike out on their own. But even before that, music was immeasurably important as a unifier of the new young. Britain lacked the wonderful breadth and variety of the radio stations in the US but rock 'n' roll arrived nevertheless and the young could enter a new communality through buying records that increasingly reflected their emotions. Similarly, in the growth of the Mods, one would see a fashion autonomy, whereby the young didn't simply take on the grim 'teen casuals' that were being prepared for them, but asked for, and received, what *they* wanted. Carnaby Street, for all its increasing vulgarity and its gradual colonisation by tourism, made one thing clear from day one: its shops worked at youth's behest.

The impetus for all this came from America. However much their parents, and large chunks of upper and middle-class society, might deplore 'the Yanks' (still lost in wartime's 'over-paid, over-sexed and over here' sneers), the young knew where the cultural bread was buttered. The great heroes were American – Brando, James Dean, Elvis – rock 'n' roll was American, nascent counter-cultures – the Beats – were American. The best movies came from the States, the most interesting books, the best cartoons (Superman, not Battler Britain), the zappiest television shows (once independent television started importing them) and so on. The new Americana reflected almost exactly the artist Richard Hamilton's taxonomy of pop, laid out in 1957: 'Popular (designed for a mass audience), Transient (short-term solution), Expendable (easily forgotten), Low cost, Mass-produced, Young (aimed at youth), Witty, Sexy, Gimmicky, Glamorous, Big Business.' He called it Pop Art, the teenagers preferred Rock 'n' Roll.

Thus far the how, when and where but as for the why? To paraphrase another Richard Hamilton line, 'What is it that Makes Today's Teenagers so Different, so Unappealing?' The general view – and there were many variations – was that they'd had it too soft. Cosseted, indulged, infantilised *ad nauseam*, they had no discipline, no self-control. And really, other than the whinging adult, who cared? It was, apparently, all the fault of Dr Benjamin Spock, whose book *Common Sense Book of Baby and Child Care* (1946) sold tens of millions of copies in more than thirty languages. Spock's fundamentally liberal take on childcare, once the most rigidly policed of topics, made him a household name.

Children brought up according to Spock's precepts suffered from what Theodore Roszak called 'an anemic superego'.[9] Raised to demand and to expect (and to be assuaged in both categories), they did not reject such gratifying attitudes with the onset of pubic hair or menstruation. Instead they sought to prolong the pleasures and freedoms of childhood as long as possible. Once again, British boys and girls experienced a much-diluted form of the American situation – no cars for them in mid-teens, no drive-ins and double-dating – but the ethos was much the same. On both sides of the Atlantic the young, unlike their parents, had grown up against a background of economic security. The need to cast aside one's childhood, to 'knuckle down', to 'get one's nose to the grindstone', to accept discipline from others and impose it on oneself, was simply no longer there. Dissenters might deplore this wilful abnegation of 'the real world', but why buy into the 'real world' if its reality is, in the end, abhorrent? Why kow-tow to those for whom one has not the slightest respect simply to gain affluence if affluence is already there in abundance?

Chapter Two

Teds: Rock 'n' Roll Rebels

Don't step on my blue suede shoes.
Carl Perkins 'Blue Suede Shoes' 1956

It is unlikely that any party would willingly acknowledge the fact, but the Teddy Boys, the 'Edwardians' of the early 1950s, must be credited with starting what Colin MacInnes would term in *Absolute Beginners*, his stylised hymn to the new social confection, 'the whole teenage epic'. A lowbrowed mix of *declassé* Savile Row fashion and South London aimless thuggery, they dominated the media's coverage of 'the young' for most of the decade. With their greasy quiffs, their draped jackets and drainpipe trousers, their much-rumoured (and often actual) armouries of flick-knives, bicycle chains and worse, they provided a paradigm for the proper frisson that the unconforming young, hitherto unknown, now categorised as 'a problem', were to arouse in their elders.

The original name 'Edwardian' signposts the Teds' origins. With the end of the war, Britain's smart, upper-class young men, aided by their tailors, had made their own sartorial protest against the crowding limits of austerity. While the wider world, epitomised by a new name, Cecil Gee of the Charing Cross Road, responded by aping America (or at least the fantasised America of Warner Brothers' still-recent gangster epics), the customers of Savile Row preferred to link their raffish fantasies to an older England, the supposed decadence of the 'naughty Nineties' and the pre-First World War Edwardians. Many of them had already auditioned the style at Eton as the Thirties waned. Now, freed from school and from wartime khaki, they pushed it to new excesses. Starting with brocaded waistcoats, they moved into long, single-breasted jackets coupled with narrow trousers, velvet collars on their overcoats and occasionally silver-topped canes. The look lasted from around 1948 to the Coronation in 1953, but by 1954 no self-respecting guardee, however flamboyant, would have been seen dead in such a getup. By then the 'look' was no longer upper-class – it had been usurped, albeit in a down-market, cutprice version, by the proles, the nihilist, no-hope, layabout yobs of Tottenham, Highbury, Streatham, Shepherd's Bush and the rest of London's yet-to-be gentrified working-class suburbs.

Why the Teds adopted this fantasy Edwardiana is not proven. It's hard to believe that, like the style's first devotees, they had some platonic dream of an idealised social and sartorial world. Their grandfathers would have hardly been basking in the fantasy 'summer' before the 'Great' War. Yet, perhaps sub-consciously, they were none the less parading their own take on dandyism. And by the mid-Fifties, whatever their motives, they had transformed

their 'borrowing' into an easily recognisable uniform, a cross between the
Savile Row original and America's zoot suit, with its long and loose-draped
jacket. The critic Nik Cohn, writing in 1970, described the Teds thus:

> Drapes apart, they wore tight drainpipe jeans, tapered to the ankle, and lumi-
> nous yellow socks; creepers, large crêpesoled shoes like boats; brass rings on
> several fingers, worn both for ornament and for destruction; riverboat gam-
> blers' bootlace ties; and often, in the back jeans pocket, a flick-knife. They
> also had a standardised face, which was pinched and underfed, a bit ratty,
> and they tended to pimples and acne. But their greatest glory was their side-
> burns. . . and their hair, which was worn long and swept up in a quiff at the
> front, then dragged back at the sides and slopped down heavy with hair-oil.
> This style was known as the duck's arse and variations were a diamond-shaped
> crewcut on top, with the rest hanging down from the crown, and the Boston,
> cut straight across at the back, above a shaved white neck . . . Altogether, the ef-
> fect was one of heroic excess: garish, greasy and quite magnificent. None of
> this was cheap: a proper Ted suit would cost between £15 and £20, hand-
> made by a back-street tailor, and all the accessories would double that. If you
> wished to make top Ted, you had to be prepared to stroll into a dance hall
> with £50 on your back. This dedication was one of the things that made
> Teddy Boys so different from all that had preceded them. They had no con-
> cern with morals, politics, philosophies of any kind. Style was their only
> value and, about that, they were fanatic.

None of which, however garish, however exceptional in a world of baggy,
monochrome conformity, should automatically have qualified the Teds for
the fear and loathing they came to inspire. Nor was the fact that they were
bored corner-boys, up for 'giggles' and 'kicks' to help them while away the
time. The Teds, in their way, represent the first of the democratisations that
would rise in a crescendo during the Sixties. In time these would embrace a
variety of major social changes; at this stage it was merely clothing, and an attitude that related to the 'normal' world by showing it two be-ringed fingers.
The response to such class *lèse-majesté* was as might be expected. The garments, once seen as stylish when garbing the upper classes, became repellent,
threatening. The uniform personified its wearer: the Teds took on the character of the hooligan, the spiv, descendants of the razor gangs and the 'cosh
boys'. It took time for mere regret that a fashion had become so adulterated to
mutate into hardcore horror and condemnation, but by 1953 the process was
up and running. A story in the *Daily Express* noted that one Michael Davies,
convicted for a fatal stabbing near Clapham Common had spent 'nearly all
his money . . . on flashy clothes'. There was no mention of his being 'an Edwardian' but the link had been made. Soon the country's self-appointed
moral guardians, goaded and inflated by the media, would be able to parade
the 'obvious' connection. By March 1954, the first recorded use of 'Teddy
Boy' (replacing the dated 'Edwardian') described the breed as 'young thugs

who dress in Edwardian-style clothes'. A month later the provincial press was joining the furore. The Ted was becoming a major social problem.

The next month provided the final push that hurled the Ted towards universal obloquy. On 24 April, a Saturday night after the dancehalls had emptied, two gangs of Teds pitched into each other at St Mary Cray railway station in Kent. The machinery of fullscale moral panic, which would be seen again almost exactly a decade later when Mods and Rockers clashed on the South Coast beaches, and again with hippies, punks and the E generation, cranked itself into empurpled, spluttering expostulation. Cinemas and dancehalls began banning anyone dressed in Ted regalia; Scotland Yard demanded investigations of any incidents in which the dread uniform appeared; the press fulminated, MPs, safely distanced from the slightest personal involvement but quick to sense a possible vote-winning issue, demanded that 'something must be done', Sir David Maxwell Fyfe, the Tory Home Secretary, was suitably outspoken. The Ted, and his uniform, was branded as an evil outsider.

Not that the Teds should be represented as innocents. They were not. They did fight, they did kick and beat and slash, but it was – as is usually the way – an internal affair, a struggle for territory. Teds from one 'manor' trespassed on that of another group: they fought. It was ritualised, sometimes pre-arranged, and on the whole the 'innocent bystander' was excluded. This was carefully ignored by the commentators and pundits, who were quick to blame all manner of violence and hooliganism on this single, conveniently identifiable sub-group. And when, in 1956, Bill Haley's relatively quiescent rock 'n' roll movie *Rock Around the Clock* arrived in the nation's Odeons and Essoldos, an extra horror was factored into the equation. Rock 'n' roll! Haley may have been an anodyne, ageing substitute for the real thing, Elvis Presley, and his movies (this time all too like Presley's) formulaic dross, but no matter. The Teds slashed seats, jived in the aisles, and humiliated the hapless management. But for all the demonisation of 'Teddy-boy gangs', they were far less structured than the politicians and the media made out. Theory, however, was in no way constrained by reality. Those who manned what Vernon Bogdanor has typified as 'the public scaffold' were undeterred by reality. And as he further noted, 'Some of the popular attempts to explain the Teddy Boy at this time are most interesting in that they tend to reveal far more about those who explained than about those who were explained. They were, presumably, thought to be serious pieces.' There was, for instance, the family doctor, summoned to explain all to the readers of the London *Evening News*.

These deviant young people [are] all of unsound mind in the sense that they are all suffering from a form of psychosis. Apart from the birch or the rope, depending on the gravity of their crimes, what they need is rehabilitation in a psychopathic institution [sic] . . . [Lacking the 'mental stamina' to stand up as individuals, they preferred to huddle together in gangs.] Not only have these rampageous youngsters developed a degree of paranoia, with an inferiority complex, they are also inferior specimens apart from their disease. It is the desire to do evil, not the lack of comprehension, which forces them into crime. This is the real reason why they carry lethal weapons.

If there were experts better qualified to assess the evidence and offer a more reasoned, less hysterical response, they did not appear. Once branded, the Teddy Boy was relegated to the outer darkness. They had become fully fledged folk devils, and their name, like 'spiv' or 'hooligan' before it, had joined the list of figurative opprobria. Thus the 'Angry Young Man' play-wright John Osborne would find himself condemned as 'an intellectual Teddy Boy'. In time the opprobrium was extended to cover all teenagers, Teds or not. By the late 1950s, for all the efforts of such harmless family en-tertainers as Tommy Steele or Cliff Richard to present the 'acceptable' side of the young, teen equalled bad.

By then, of course, the original impetus, and many of the original Teds, had largely faded. The moralising wolfpack was still in full cry, but their tar-gets had retreated to the Teddy-come-lately provinces; Londoners had moved on – dividing gradually into what would become the new exemplars of teen horror: Mods and Rockers. Even the clothes had changed: the old drapes and drainpipes had been replaced by short 'Italian' jackets and pointed winklepickers. Jeans, the favoured garb of American cowboys and such Fifties teen idols as James Dean and Marlon Brando (in his *Wild One* mode), were taking centre stage as the ultimate symbol of teen apartness. And by the turn of the decade even the young rebels of the middle classes had joined in, declaring themselves beatniks, hitch-hiking across the country, congregating in their own clubs and festivals, and thronging annually along the roads between Aldermaston and Trafalgar Square. The Teds were dino-saurs, typified by Colin MacInnes's fictional 'Ed the Ted' of *Absolute Begin-ners*, a knuckle-dragging neanderthal roaming disconsolately along the Harrow Road, once Teddy Boy central, looking in vain for his long-dispersed 'click'. They staged one final, repellent flurry in 1958, featuring in a couple of especially unpleasant dancehall stabbings, and more importantly fronting the Notting Dale race riots, but like the fascist followers of Sir Oswald Moseley who joined them, they were throwbacks. Whether these riots, or their 'rock 'n' roll' predecessors were remotely political is unlikely. This was proper nihilistic, fuck-you violence; a way of saying, 'Look, I'm here.' At the same time it said, absolutely uncompromisingly, don't impose your middle-class values on people of whom you have not the slightest understanding or fellow-feeling. We don't want to know. Squash us, suppress our pleasures, limit our already limited options and we shall lash out.

The point of the Ted, however, is not what he or she did, but what they unwittingly created. As Nik Cohn has put it, 'In terms of English teenagers, Teddy Boys were the start of everything: rock 'n' roll and coffee bars, clothes and bikes and language, jukeboxes and coffee with froth on it – the whole concept of a private teen life style, separate from the adult world.' The word 'teenage' had been around since the 1920s. But teenagers as adult shorthand for a wholesale negative no-good group; the cultural connotations of teenage: this was a post-war phenomenon, cited first in the USA, around 1947, and spilling across the Atlantic to flaunt itself in powder-blue drapes and three-inch-high crêpe-soled brothel-creepers.

The placing of all teenagers in a single category – trouble-maker, juvenile delinquent – is absurd, but the attitude has yet to vanish. The ironic difference, perhaps, is that while the parents of the Fifties and Sixties stood aghast at what they had produced, unable to comprehend what was going on, those of the Eighties and Nineties, veterans of indulging their own teenage years at the height of youth fetishism, understand it too well. Absurd or not, the initial response to the idea of the adolescent as an entity in his or her right was condemnation. The American sociologist Edgar Z. Friedenberg, looking back from 1966, noted that

> Only as a customer and, occasionally, as an athlete are adolescents favourably received. Otherwise they are treated as a problem and, potentially, a threatening one. No other social groups except convicted criminals and certified lunatics are subjected to as much restriction . . . Willing as they are to trade with him [American adults] have no doubt that the 'teenager' is an enemy . . . Hostility does not come this easily to the middle class, which prefers to define any nuisance that it wishes to abate, or social situation that it finds threatening or embarrassing, as a problem. Our youth problem is a notable accomplishment. We have made it ourselves, out of little . . . Many adults seem to use the terms 'teenager' and 'juvenile delinquent' as if they were synonyms.

In England the 'superstar jock' has never achieved the same prominence – cosseted, fêted, deluged with money – that he (and more recently she) has in America; thus the role of customer/consumer is the only one cheerfully handed over to adolescence. And this is a role that the adult world was happy to acknowledge. The teenager, this freshly minted social group, was a new and extremely enthusiastic form of consumer, with money to spend on constantly-updated clothes and records. Other than what they might choose to hand over to Mum for board and lodging, teenage incomes were almost one hundred per cent disposable. But once step outside that social function and the teenager plummeted from grace. Quite why that step was taken would vary. For some it was politics, others utopianism, for many simple, all-encompassing disillusion – all versions of a 'better world'. For the Teds, less cerebral than those who followed them, it was a gut reaction to the denial of free choice. Unimpressed by education, unlikely to transcend the low-grade jobs for which they were destined, they sought release in the exploitation of their leisure time. That their greater disposable incomes could improve the quality of that leisure was not an option. Teenagers were not supposed to be so autonomous: the great youth leisure industry was still in its infancy. The adult response to the Teds (and to contemporary youth in general) was either patronising or downright hostile. As Bogdanor put it, 'To those who demanded the most of leisure, the least was offered.' That the Teds responded by turning to delinquency is hardly surprising.

As each successive youth cult – quite irrespective of its content, aims and philosophy, and indeed of its effect on the wider world – emerged, it was targeted, pilloried and condemned. While the idea that any society needs to define itself in terms of those outside its limits is understandable, the desire of America and Britain to consign to the outer darkness an entire segment of its own members was unprecedented. For the more aggressive of such groups – Teds, Mods and Rockers, Skinheads – the condemnation and exclusion was a self-fulfilling prophecy. Nor was there any form of reasoned response. As Bogdanor has said, in words that would stand for the treatment meted out to any 'problematic' youth group, 'Audiences did not react to the Teddy Boy; they reacted to their conception of him. This conception was largely founded on what they had been told by the newspapers and other media. This was true even of those people who had to cope with the problem. The ideas on which they had to act were often simplistic and misleading, and this distortion was sometimes aggravated by the reluctance of officials to wait and see what shape the . . . problem was going to assume.'

If the Ted was to serve as a paradigm for the 'teenager as problem' in adult eyes, he fulfilled an equally important role for other teenagers in the years to come. In the first place he emphasised the primacy of clothes as a way of defining one's difference. Your father might be a grey, baggy, faceless clone; you are not. The Ted uniform, whether the boys' drapes, creepers and drainpipes, or their girls' tight skirts and seamed nylons, performed a function that had never hitherto extended to the young, especially the working-class young: it defined them as a separate entity at odds with the mainstream.

This was no novelty – the élite had always had such options – but it had never before extended into the working classes. Subsequent generations would take on the same form of exhibitionist plumage as a means of asserting themselves. Some would be exotic – the hippies; some threatening – skinheads; and some a mixture of the two – punks; while others might emphasise clothes as clothes – the mods; but, nuance aside, the overall effect was always the same. As Nik Cohn summed it up in the Ted context, 'Clothes became slogans . . . clothes said just three things: I am different, I am tough, I fuck.'

The working-classness of the Teds was equally important. The realisation that fashion, far from necessarily coming from Savile Row or the catwalks of Paris, could – at least for the young – be created by the mass, was an invention of the early 1950s. That phenomenon that by the 1980s would be lauded as 'street' (and celebrated by the mass media as another glorious British export), emerged alongside the Teds. For the first time fashion showed its potential as a bottom-up rather than the older, top-down creation. Finally, while the Teds themselves were rarely objects of emulation – there was none of the class miscegenation that one would find on the way to Aldermaston, in the Tottenham caffs or the Hammersmith dancehalls – it became apparent to certain sections of the middle class, especially in the art schools, that this new explosion of the prole lifestyle had much to offer.

One cannot consider the Teds without considering their favourite music: rock 'n' roll. Once again the way in which a musical style could set one aside from the acceptable mainstream was established by these neophyte teens. For those, like jazzman George Melly, who had hitherto seen themselves as representing rebellion in its musical form, rock 'n' roll was at best incomprehensible, more often simply repellent. It was unsubtle, un-swinging, uncoloured. It was an 'incitement to mindless fucking and arbitrary vandalism: screw and smash music'. But as he and his peers came to realise, and as the Teds and later teenagers knew instinctively, 'the whole point of Rock 'n' Roll *depended* on its lack of subtlety. It was music to be used rather than listened to: a banner to be waved in the face of "them" by a group who felt themselves ignored or victimised.' Rock 'n' roll, like the clothes its main fans wore, was another way of making oneself felt, forcing one's individuality (albeit within the greater conformity of one's crowd) on those who would suppress it.

Looked at with a colder eye, the rise and fall of the Teds can also be seen as paradigmatic of teen 'cults' to come. A small in-crowd at first, fanatics with very specific and far from easily attained standards, they then expanded into the metropolis and thence to the provinces. At last noted (and vilified) by the media, arriving as ever too late to catch the true originals, they faded, diluted beyond any recognisable form, into insignificance. The Fifties, less sophisticated than the decades that would follow, were more inclined to savage the Teds than to exploit their money-making potential – they were, ultimately, too prole, too mindlessly violent – but one could see the emergent pattern.

And if one sets aside the manifest superficial differences, the well-educated, middle-class CND supporters, the art students and the beats were, when viewed from the outside, more like the Teds than they were different from them. Viewed from an adult perspective, a perspective formed in a society of 'knowing one's place', of 'seen and not heard', of 'following your father's footsteps', of stability, conformity and of repetition, they were all the same: wilfully, frighteningly different. Both groups could be seen as espousing a single philosophy: a complete lack of faith in the 'affluent society', its goals and its rewards. The Teds, inarticulate, lashing out at whatever they saw, had performed a vital, pioneering role. As the critic Maurice Richard-son put it in a review of a contemporary television play, the Ted was an 'existential storm-trooper in the age-war; he is coming for you as sure as Death.' By the end of the decade they would be virtually dead themselves, their clothes already in demand for collection by the fashion curators, while the young middle-class rebels were only starting to flex their muscles. But both had a role to play in prefiguring what was to come.

Chapter Three

CND: Questions of Morality

Suddenly, from 1956 onwards, there came a crack in the social-political situation that released old allegiances and left conventional parties frozen into postures that ignored these changes. There came Poland, Hungary, Suez, death of Stalin, rise of Africa, the New Left, the teenage phenomenon, the race riots, the teacher strikes, Osborne and the new-wave writers, and, for what it is worth, CND.
Colin MacInnes[1]

Forty years on, fortified by a knowledge of the development of the Cold War and its menacing avatar 'the Bomb', it is easy to agree with MacInnes's throwaway dismissal of what at the time was a major vehicle of protest. For all its sounds and furies, the Campaign for Nuclear Disarmament, even in its revivified pan-European format of the 1980s, had little impact. All the marches, sit-ins, protests both intra- and extra-parliamentary, even the momentary triumphs within the party political system itself, had no influence on any world leader. Defence is run on *realpolitik*, not emotion, and when the missiles would finally start to be removed from their silos it was for strategic, not moral reasons. Yet CND did have a profound social effect, and despite its image of jolly jazzers, happy-clappy clergy, grimy beatniks, earnest Quakers and Labour-party entryists, mingling in a sea of duffel-coats, it remains worthy of serious consideration. It may not have 'banned the Bomb', but its influence lies foursquare on the path that leads to 'the Sixties'.

The ultimate rationale of CND was a moral one. It was, as Vernon Bogdanor has put it, 'a protest against the immorality of defending the affluent society with nuclear weapons'.[2] Material life might be improving, as the government was keen to emphasise, but 'of what permanent significance were the social gains at home, if foreign affairs remained the domain of an unregenerate power politics based on nuclear calculation?'[3] CND would be pulled, as such moral protests tend to be, in a variety of directions, many of them increasingly unpalatable to its prime movers, and indeed to the tens of thousands who joined the great marches of the late 1950s and early 1960s, but the moral core would never wholly melt down. It was, perhaps, an unfocused, all-purpose morality – as would be seen when, briefly, CND seemed to have won what it desired (albeit in the parochial world of British left-wing politics) and then proved unable to push things further – but it informed its devotees, especially the younger ones; and it was these younger activists who would move on into the harder confrontations and the greater alienations of the new decade.

The first nuclear device had exploded over the Japanese city of Hiroshima on 6 August 1945. An explosion the equivalent of 12,500 tons of

TNT devastated the city and its population. Three days later a second bomb was detonated over Nagasaki. The bombs had their effect: Japan was brought swiftly to the negotiating table; but as details leaked out, an increasing number of people found themselves appalled by the effects of this terrible new weapon. Among them were many of the physicists who had worked on it, but their dissenting voices had little real power. By 1949 the Russians had their own weapon and as the Fifties dawned the primary weapons of the Cold War were in place. Humanity could now officially destroy itself.

Again, with hindsight, it is hard to appreciate quite how terrifying that prospect seemed. Jeff Nuttall, writing in his memoir-cum-manifesto *Bomb Culture*, enunciated the sheer intensity of feeling, especially among the young:

> We had espoused an evil as great as the Nazi genocide, we had espoused the instrument for the termination of our benevolent institution, society, and our certain identity, human. We had espoused a monstrous uncertainty both of future and of morality. If, besides the 'Nazi gangsters', we were also wrong, who was ever right? If no one was right, what was right, and was right anyway relevant, and what could guide us through the terrifying freedom such a concept offered?. . . We had driven honour away a few short months after finding it. Neither could we survive the next war, for the next wasn't going to be remotely like the one we had 'shown we could take'. The next war would certainly be more terrible than anything we had known, was probably more terrible than we could calculate, was possibly going to terminate the entire species. The first victory was a victory confirming our merits and security. The second victory destroyed them irrevocably.
>
> [In addition to fear was the bitterness of disillusion.] In the new world . . . moral values, thought absolute, were now seen to be comparative, for all social entities around which morality had revolved were now called into doubt and nothing of morality remained. The society for which we had more or less cheerfully fought and (some of us) more or less cheerfully died had dropped its mask and in doing so had robbed all its institutions of church, political party, social class, happy family, of moral authority. No longer could teacher, magistrate, politician, don, or even loving parent, guide the young. Their membership of the H-bomb society automatically cancelled anything they might have to say on questions of right and wrong.[4]

In 1950 Britain had what could at best be termed a nascent, if dedicated, anti-war movement. The veteran Peace Pledge Union, founded by George Lansbury, had survived the war, especially in its newspaper *Peace News*, but it harked back to an era blessedly free of such mega-weapons. Given the dedicated propagandising on behalf of nuclear arms – and the equally dedicated determination by governments to obscure or render inaccessible most of the detailed information on them – what would become a mass movement was still the province of a small, highly motivated group. In 1954 the Methodist minister Donald (later Lord) Soper joined his Anglican counterpart

Canon John Collins and six like-minded Labour MPs to create the Hydrogen Bomb National Campaign. A petition attracted a million signatories, all condemning the Bomb, but it had little or no real effect on policy. In a preview of things to come, the old pacifists ignored the petition: they distrusted what they saw as its overt politicisation. Shortly afterwards Gertrude Fishwick, a member of the Finchley Labour Party, pioneered the Golders Green Committee for the Abolition of Nuclear Weapons. Co-opted by Peggy Duff, a leading Labour activist, this was transmuted into the grander National Committee for the Abolition of Nuclear Weapons Tests, founded in February 1957. Earnest, enthusiastic, but ultimately impotent, the NCANWT found few supporters, especially powerful ones.

Simultaneously, and with equally little success, there had developed a more robust form of anti-bomb protest, relying on personal commitment rather than party politics. Operation Gandhi was founded in 1951, proclaiming the non-violent credo of the man for whom it was named. A sit-down protest was held outside the War Office in 1952, and there were further demonstrations at such bases as Aldermaston and Mildenhall (in Suffolk). Tom Driberg, the maverick Labour MP and fellow-traveller of a variety of liberal pursuits for the next quarter-century, suggested that in the face of upcoming British nuclear tests the most effective statement of opposition would be for people to sail into the test area. Two Quakers, Harold and Sheila Steele, volunteered; only Harold actually went, and he was quickly stopped from entering the high security zone. Back in the UK, he was just in time to join a greater movement, that which would become CND.

Nothing, as the cliché has it, can defeat an idea whose time has come, and in early 1958, that time had come for what would emerge as CND. But the forces that would lead to the first 'Aldermaston March' were not drawn only from the ranks of the pacifists or the pious. Vague fears of 'the Bomb' were hardened immeasurably when it was announced, in a Defence White Paper of 1957, that Britain would henceforth be adopting the US doctrine of 'massive retaliation', a nuclear strategy that at its crudest could be reduced to the threat: whatever you do to us we'll do back – and worse. Refined, three years later, as 'mutual assured destruction', rejoicing in the grimly apposite acronym 'MAD', it gave few people comfort. The White Paper also made it clear that Britain had 'no means of providing adequate protection for the people of this country against the consequences of an attack with nuclear weapons'. Mass fears were further prompted by news of radiation, popularly known as 'fall-out', which was known to kill long after the effects of the initial explosion had faded, and which could drift around the world on winds unfettered by political or national boundaries. The world lived, as Canadian Prime Minister Lester Pearson had put it in 1955, in a 'balance of terror'.

Of more immediate effect than these general fears, however, was a piece, 'Britain and Nuclear Bombs', published in the *New Statesman* on 2 November 1957. Written by the novelist J.B. Priestley, it suggested that Britain should abandon the nuclear nightmare and instead set itself at the head of a movement to see off the Bomb. It would be a moral crusade, and one that would not be dissimilar to the nation's much-mythologised 'Dunkirk spirit'. The British, declared Priestley, 'so frequently hiding their decent, kind faces behind masks of sullen apathy or sour, cheap cynicism, often seem to be waiting for something better than party squabbles and appeals to their narrowest self-interest, something great and noble in its intention that would make them feel good again. And this might well be a declaration to the world that after a certain date one power able to engage in nuclear warfare will reject the evil thing for ever.'

The response to Priestley's call was remarkable. So much so that the *New Statesman*'s editor, Kingsley Martin, summoned the great and good of left-wing politics to a meeting in early January 1958. Its purpose was the formation of an organisation to implement the piece, and channel the energies of what was still viewed with some surprise as a substantial anti-Bomb constituency. After the meeting, at the suitably named Amen Court in the City of London, the formation of the 'Campaign for Nuclear Disarmament' was announced. Its chairman was to be Canon John Collins, a former RAF chaplain, ardent anti-apartheid campaigner and now canon of St Paul's Cathedral. Bertrand Russell was to be honorary president, Peggy Duff to be full-time secretary, responsible for day-to-day organisation. Priestley, playing the grumpy Yorkshireman, opted out of hands-on involvement.

The most interesting and certainly the most intellectual of these figures was Bertrand Russell (1872–1970). His father, Lord Amberley, himself the son of two-term Prime Minister Lord John Russell, had been a high-minded agnostic and had passed on his refusal to accept easy conformity to his son. An outstanding undergraduate, and subsequently fellow of Trinity College, Cambridge, Russell's career was rooted in the principle that the scientific view of the world is largely the correct one. His aim was to pare down to an absolute minimum the range of human knowledge and to make his findings easily available. *The Principles of Mathematics* (1903) and the *Principia Mathematica* (1910–13 with A.N. Whitehead), the two ground-breaking treatises that made his name, were some way beyond the layman, but such works as *An Inquiry into Meaning and Truth* (1940) and his last major work, *Human Knowledge, Its Scope and Limits* (1948) proved more accessible.

At the same time Russell was moving into ever more intense conflict with the authorities. He refused to fight in the First World War, preferring to lecture against it. Lytton Strachey, a fellow member of 'Bloomsbury' attended one such talk: 'Government, religion, laws, property, even Good Form itself – down they all go like ninepins – it is a charming sight!'[5] He was fined in 1916, then lost his Trinity fellowship and was jailed for six months in 1918. He continued to write, mixing popular science – *The ABC of Atoms* (1923) and *The ABC of Relativity* (1925) – with provocative social commentary, notably *What I Believe* (1925) and *Marriage and Morals* (1929) (which won him the Nobel prize for Literature). In 1927 he and his wife Dora set up an experimental school at Telegraph House, near Petersfield; what critics termed its 'permissiveness' led to a good deal of media speculation. A brief spell teaching at City College in New York was terminated by the courts: the professor was apparently an advocate of sexual immorality.

Highly influential, Russell was not wholly consistent. An appeaser at Munich, he quickly turned against Hitler once war broke out. For all his later involvement with CND, he had allegedly claimed – he denied the story as a malicious smear – that under certain circumstances the bomb could and should be dropped on Russia. But his own philosophy was utilitarianism – whereby an action is considered 'right' if it confers the greatest happiness upon the greatest number of people – and he was sufficiently pragmatic to appreciate that different circumstances require different responses. His role in CND made him a hero to the young, but his position as a Nobel laureate and a lord made the authorities less than keen to pursue him, however keenly he goaded them. They did jail him, occasionally, but probably not as often, or as lengthily as he would have wished. In the end, as Richard Wollheim has noted, Russell was 'triumphantly right on nearly all the major issues of the day'. His views were 'correct and human . . . far in advance of thinkers no less liberal but ostensibly more expert than himself'.[6] He died in 1970, loaded with honours from the Establishment he had fought for so long, and celebrated as an unrivalled Grand Old Man of liberalism.

Barely a month after its initial, formative meeting, in February 1958, CND held its first public meeting; 5,000 people crammed Central Hall, Westminster. Alex Comfort, who would be infinitely better known as the author of *The Joy of Sex*, gave a keynote speech. In its earnestness, its belief in the efficacy of grass-roots action, its defiance of Establishment politics (whether of right or left), its call to action and above all in its stressing of the fundamentally moral basis of the cause, it can be seen as defining CND, in both its best and worst manifestations.

> That is the function of the campaign which we are launching here tonight: to make every individual reassume the moral responsibility for opposing public insanity. The issue is one for direct action by every one of us. We are not at the mercy of the Government, nor of events, nor of the policy of other nations, nor of the world situation, if we are prepared as a public to be sufficiently combative . . . Within the coming weeks we intend to raise throughout the country a solid body of opposition to the whole strategy of moral bankruptcy and ceremonial suicide which the hydrogen bomb epitomises, to all the mentally under-privileged double-talk by which it has been justified. I would urge every one of us at this meeting to go home determined to become

a living focus of that opposition . . . If there are no local committees in your area, keeping their eyes open for base building activity, form one.

If there is no focus for public opposition to nuclear tests and nuclear weapons in your district, in your church, among your neighbours, become one. If you are not already exerting pressure on your Member, on the Prime Minister, on the Press, on any scientists involved in unethical projects whose addresses you can get, begin to do so now, by letter and by lobbies. It is high time we held some atomic tests of our own – in Downing Street. Much has been said about a summit conference. Sanity is always hardest to restore at the summit – the air there is rarefied. It seems to affect the brain. We can re-assert it at the base. The people must take over – you must take over. We can make Britain offer the world something which is virtually forgotten – moral leadership. Let us make this country stand on the side of human decency and human sanity – alone if necessary.[7]

Other speakers were equally messianic. The playwright Robert Bolt spoke unashamedly of 'the brotherhood of man' and urged his listeners to 'live like Christians'. Fittingly the first Aldermaston March was scheduled for Good Friday. Collins did not march, but recalled later that the spirit of the marchers was: 'one of expectancy, of dedication and of hope, more religious and more reverent than many church services that I have attended'.[8] Talking to the 8,000 strong crowd he called for the 'symbol of the cross' to replace that of the sword. Reversing the route that would be taken in subsequent years, the marchers left Trafalgar Square and marched to, rather than from, Aldermaston, some fifty miles distant. There were no obviously political banners – the organisers had requested their absence – and as the marchers walked, they picked up new support. Some 10,000 arrived at the base. For them CND was more than just protest. It was, as Frank Parkin put it in *Middle Class Radicalism*, his study of CND, 'expressive politics', those very middle-class gestures of personal and moral purification which may have 'little or no practical consequence' but which do such wonders for the conscience.

Aside from the moral stars – other clergyman such as Trevor Huddleston and the Methodist Donald Soper backed Collins – the march attracted less ostensibly salubrious figures. The poet Christopher Logue had just returned from Paris where, *inter alia*, he had cranked out pornography for Maurice Girodias of the Olympia Press, signing himself as 'Count Palmiro Vicarion' as he put together such *minima opera* as *Lust* and the Count's *Book of Limericks*. For him, the idea of Aldermaston 'was just in the air, and a lot of people thought that this was the right thing to do . . .'

A lot of the population had only the most general idea about nuclear weapons and what they were about, and that we were manufacturing them and that we intended to use them. It was that kind of time. You could speak freely to people; it was the beginning of that free association between people. If you thought that you had something to offer, then you'd ring up somebody and you'd suggest it to them and you'd see what happened. And there it was. I found myself on the first day of the Aldermaston march in 1958. It was pouring with rain and there were about 150 of us, marching along by London airport in the most dreadful weather. And then of course the sun came out and the weather improved greatly and by the end of the afternoon there must have been 50,000 people. And by the middle of the next day there were 100,000.[9]

Poetic licence as regards numbers aside, the first march was hugely successful. Those who had seen it as a one-off event promised to meet again a year later. Back home they began setting up local CND branches; by March 1959 the movement boasted some 270. The joint universities branch became especially important, attracting many students (though they would never be a majority in their universities) and spawning much intellectual stimulus. Their elders were equally enthusiastic. Among the original sponsors were Philip Toynbee, Peggy Ashcroft, Doris Lessing, Herbert Read, Arnold Wesker and John Osborne. It was all very high-minded, although as march succeeded march, and the proportion of young people increased, the tone became somewhat less pious and a good deal jollier. The statistics underpin CND's growing popularity. The 1959 march attracted 50,000, that of 1960 75,000 and that of 1961 100,000.

CND now faced the question of where to go next. In a democratic country which still respected mainstream politics the logical route was through Parliament. Faced with this decision CND, hitherto neutral, and with a constituency that embraced a wide range of political standpoints, was forced to seek some form of political ally. The Conservatives, whose 'never had it so good' rhetoric jibed badly with the altruistic pronouncements of CND, were unlikely bedfellows. In any case those of the leadership who did espouse politics were firmly pro-Labour. Many of the Campaign's leaders were party members and Priestley's piece had appeared in the *New Statesman*, very much a Labour journal; its editor had no doubts: only through Labour, he declared, would there be a 'non-nuclear Britain'.

The Party itself, however, was less obviously enthusiastic. In the consensus politics of the period, the Opposition was as firmly committed to the Cold War *status quo* as the government. The leader, Hugh Gaitskell, was a right-winger; he was unlikely to bow to a movement that came from the left of his party.

In the event Labour had no need to worry: the party lost the 1959 General Election. The old magician, 'Supermac' Macmillan, had managed to charm the punters yet again. Far more surprising was CND's growing ascendancy. There were a number of reasons for this. In the first place the old Nonconformist morality, a bedrock of traditional Labourism, was far from dead and when the popular historian A. J. P. Taylor stated in 1958, 'We are not seeking to disrupt the Labour party nor to challenge its leadership. We are seeking to win it over. We offer it the moral leadership of the world',[10] he found an increasing number of believers among the members of that same party. Even more important was the gradual, but undeniable, conversion of the trade unions. In 1959 spectators crowding Trafalgar Square for the climax of that year's march could identify several union bosses, including the chairman of the TUC, mingling with the CND leaders on the plinth of Nelson's Column. In addition some sixty MPs had openly declared for the Campaign. Gaitskell remained unimpressed: a practical politician, he knew the extent to which *realpolitik* trounced the most impeccable of moralities; he also saw the unilateralists as pushing for a less obvious agenda: his own deselection as leader. This, equally vitally, determined his rejection of their claims.

None the less the drift continued, propelled by CND's leaders who, increasingly cut off from their members, saw an alliance with the mainstream party as the best way to achieve their demands. Their finest hour came at the Scarborough Conference of 1960, when, after a succession of impassioned speeches from both sides, the Party officially adopted unilateralism as its foreign policy. For the right it was a narrow defeat, an edge of just 297,000 votes out of six million cast, but defeat it was. The next year Gaitskell and his supporters fought to have the decision reversed. This time the votes ran nearly 3:1 in Gaitskell's favour. Unilateralism, dismissed as an insane policy that flew in the face of all that was sensible (and it was assumed electable) had been returned to its rightful place: on the back burner.

For the CND 'politicos' it was a crushing reversal. They had flirted with the mainstream and had been jilted once again. It was partly a disaster of their own making: after the Scarborough victory they had committed a major blunder; they had no plan of action. In the first place those CND members who had rushed to join Labour after Scarborough, swiftly decamped. Labour, seen briefly as saviours, were viewed with scepticism, a hangover that would carry on into the new decade (and which would be justified by the realities of Harold Wilson's unashamedly pro-American, and thus pro-Bomb foreign policy). For the younger CND people, this disillusion would bite even harder, and many would set themselves outside all forms of politics.

Rather more immediate was a split in CND's own ranks. Those who had advocated siding with Labour were seen as failures, trimming the movement's ethos to suit a misguided agenda. There had always been an element which, to reverse Macmillan's remark of 1958, preferred war-war over jaw-jaw. The advocates of civil disobedience had already, as early as 1954, formed the Direct Action Committee (DAC) and openly declared their belief in more militant activism. The DAC stepped aside with the formation of CND in 1958, but it did not disband. Now, with mainstream CND seemingly on hold, trying hard to resurrect itself after the Labour 'betrayal', the DAC pushed back to centre stage. It was announced that henceforth there would be a new movement, devoted to non-violent civil disobedience. Headed by Lord Russell, and backed by such DAC stalwarts as Mike Randle as well as a fair number of anarchists and libertarians, it would comprise a Committee of 100, which would begin by organising large-scale sit-down protests at 'strategic centres'. The old leaders were unamused: Collins condemned the Committee, as did his ally Commander Stephen King-Hall, one of a number of senior military men who had joined CND. Russell was particularly vilified – and duly resigned his CND presidency to head the Committee. Among those who joined him were John Osborne, Arnold Wesker, Vanessa Redgrave, Herbert Read and John Braine. More important than these celebrities, however, was the Committee's image in its supporters' eyes. The élitism of the Collinses and King-Halls had been abandoned; in its way this was 'power to the people'.

For many people the down-to-earth, genuinely impassioned oratory of a Mike Randle, Pat Arrowsmith or George Clarke was exactly what they wanted: as far a cry as possible from the empty platitudes of orthodox Labour. Politics it was clear, would never help, it was merely a means for its devotees to gain personal power. Something more immediate was needed. After all, there was no telling when the feared nuclear war might actually start. As for qualms about what might prove violent, or at least confrontational actions, what could be more violent than the threat of global destruction? The authorities, who might have chosen to defuse or at least debate such fears with open and factual information, remained as secretive as ever.

First on the Committee's hit-list was the Ministry of Defence in Whitehall. Here, on 18 February 1961, the day on which the first US nuclear submarine was due to arrive at its Holy Loch base in Scotland, 4,000 people sat down for two-and-a-half hours. In a preview of the much-heralded revolution of October 1968 (which ended not in blood and tears but in demonstrators and police linking arms for a chorus of 'Auld Lang Syne') the sit-in, while well-attended, failed to provoke the images its participants sought. There was no violence, no state overkill, no chance for what would come to be termed 'media manipulation'. Unlike their American cousins, whose demonstrations and Freedom Rides across the segregationist Southern states brought them all that and more, Russell and his companions found only striped-trousered civility. When, for instance, he attempted, Luther-like, to hammer a petition to the very door of the Ministry it opened before him, only to reveal an official replete with sellotape. The police watched with scarcely veiled amusement. Russell was furious, complaining like a child whose parents won't take his troubles sufficiently seriously, 'We do not want for ever to be tolerated by the police. Our movement depends for its success on an immense public opinion and we cannot create that unless we raise the authorities to more action than they took yesterday.'[11] Like SNCC, their counterparts across the Atlantic, the Committee had no wish for compromise. Both were infused with the 'anarchistic spirit of decentralism, direct action at centres of power, propaganda of the deed, non-co-operation with unjust laws, and symbolic revolution'.[12] Like so much else about the Committee, this mood laid down a basis on which the 'youth revolution' would find itself acting throughout the years to come.

Two months later, in late April, Russell had better luck. Another demonstration saw 800 people placed under arrest, and fined one pound apiece under the Metropolitan Police Act of 1889. Shortly afterwards another protest had Russell jailed for seven days (this time the law dated to 1361). Later still some thirty-six of the Committee, including Russell, Arnold Wesker, Robert Bolt and Christopher Logue, were jailed for up to two months – all resolutely refusing to be bound over to 'keep the peace'. The Committee's finest hour came on 17 September, Battle of Britain Day. This time 12,000 turned up in Trafalgar Square – the use of which had been forbidden by the police – and more than 1,300 were arrested. Even Canon Collins put in an appearance. And for those who yearned for police action, it finally came. Once the media, who had finally started to take notice, had left, the seemingly quiescent police moved in hard. In December five of the main Committee members were arrested and this time the sentences ran from a year to eighteen months.

The government, as Jeff Nuttall noted, was shaken. 'The police had been shown to be ineffectual, ridiculous and brutal. There was one thing that saved the squares and their death-wish in the months following the September sit-down and that was the squareness and death-wish of the demonstrators themselves.'[13]

The marches would continue, as would the demonstrations (though none would have the resonance of 17 September), but CND (and the Committee, tactics notwithstanding, remained a part of the main body) continued to sink into an inexorable decline. Aside from its increased in-fighting, its prime institution began to lose its way. The Aldermaston March, once portrayed as more a pilgrimage of dedication than anything so vulgar as a protest, had found itself gradually transmuted in the mass mind from irrelevance, to threat, to national institution, somewhere between the village fête and the cramming of students into a phone box. But with the Committee gaining more headlines, and the 'beatnik elements', with their weird clothes and weirder lifestyles, beginning to make themselves more and more apparent, the press, as ever, responded by turning nasty. By 1962 90 per cent of the marchers were under twenty-one; this was not the august body the media could accept.

A further intimation that CND might be more than a joke came in 1963. On that year's march activists (calling themselves 'Spies for Peace') distributed a detailed list of the nation's Regional Seats of Government, the bolt-holes set aside by national and local government for its own protection, were the bombs finally to fall. Passing that sited at Reading, a number of marchers promptly invaded. This was virtual treason. The march climaxed with a rally in Hyde Park, attended by 30,000 people. Some, prompted by a determinedly populist organisation named 'The March Must Decide', ran riot in the West End. Collins and his remaining supporters wrung their hands; the Labourites, unsurprisingly, simply quit. One last attempt to work within the system came with the founding of the Independent Nuclear Disarmament Committee (INDEC) in 1963. Its intention was to provide candidates to fight the 1964 election on the single issue of disarmament. The Committee was unimpressed and when the election came proposed a 'voters-veto', i.e. abstention. Traditional politics no longer mattered, although in some ways CND was just another organisation faced by the age-old clash: activism or acquiescence. As Sue Miles noted, 'It was about whether you actually rang up the police and were all terribly fair about it and said, "We're going to have a little demonstration in the Strand on such and such. . . " or whether you went "Right!" Suddenly thousands of hairy people show up outside this little suburban house that actually turns out to be an enormous bunker.'[14]

Finally, whether 'political' or 'activist', CND was in the end an amateur organisation. And for all the advantages gained from being free of party politics, that same 'outsider' status rendered the campaign's efforts increasingly impotent. Even the 'triumph' of Scarborough had been within an Opposition party; the government presumably viewed that year's shenanigans as yet another convenient example of Labour's unelectibility.

For all CND's well-aimed shots at its own feet, the most compelling reasons for its decline came from external forces. The most important of these, with suitable irony, came when the world approached nearer than it has ever (openly) done to actual nuclear holocaust. The resolution of the Cuba Crisis of October 1962 proved that whatever CND might wish to claim, the threat of 'massive retaliation' did work. Faced with America's demand that he remove Soviet missiles from Cuba, Khrushchev did not withdraw his supply ships on moral grounds – the vision of Soviet cities razed to radioactive ashes played a far more potent role in his backdown. It had also been shown that the politician's first recourse, say what the protesters might, was not to the button. Perhaps most telling of all was the Partial Test-Ban Treaty of July 1963, which forced all but the most hardline to admit that neither Kennedy nor Khrushchev seemed to be quite as psychotic as rumoured. In addition, in the wake of the Cuban scare, the Bomb was waning as a major threat. The superpowers would now prefer to tussle through proxies, such as the rival forces of North and South Vietnam. And there were other 'good brave causes': racism being among the most prominent. In medical terms the Bomb had become a chronic problem, a dull ache, and less and less of a sharp pain. Its novelty, and the terror that it had engendered, had worn off.

But if 'the Bomb' was no longer so acute a generator of anguish, however existential, CND remains absolutely vital in any consideration of the Sixties. Beyond anything else it provided the first public forum for youthful rebellion. CND, or more precisely its yearly marches, were an unrivalled source of excitement. Centuries earlier it was the passing circus or annual fair that swept young people away from their small towns and smaller villages. Now it was this parade of protest, this 'carnival of subversion'[15] as David Widgery, then a teenager, later a doctor, revolutionary and historian of the Left saw it. For the bright young members of the middle class – too upmarket to become a Ted, too straight to join the Mods (or indeed the Rockers), still a little too much a homebody to go on the road with the Beats – this was something you could join. It was 'something you could get into in your own right as a fifth former. You wore CND badges at school and had to take them off and wrote CND slogans on your desk and stuck Bertrand Russell pictures on the bottom of your desks and thought the Committee of 100 was absolutely heaven.'[16] For Widgery and many others, CND was 'a student movement before its time . . . in its midst could be found the first embers of the hashish underground and premature members of the Love Generation, as well as cadres of forthcoming revolutionary parties.'[17] The process worked the other way too. While the marches appeared solidly middle-class, there was a leavening of committed young workers. Politically, and perhaps even more socially it was eye-opening for both sides of the class divide.

And however serious the first couple of marches may have been, by the early Sixties, they had become as much spectacles and performances as the sort of unalloyed protests which the Establishment could comprehend. John Hopkins, co-founder of *IT*, the first British underground paper, took his first LSD just before the 1964 march. Instead of the usual banners he and his friends carried placards emblazoned with question and exclamation marks. This was hardly Canon Collins territory. Meanwhile, those who turned politicians were seen, at least by some, as playing into the authorities' hands. Once they declared themselves politicians they could be dealt with as such: granted access to the system if they accepted its rules, crushed or at best marginalised if they refused. For the pioneers of the 'counter-culture' this was not the way. Anarchism, libertarianism and subversion held a far greater appeal.

Simply joining CND was, for many young people, a means to that subversion. Pete Latarche, later chairman of YCND, explained, 'There was a kind of naïve socialism about the Aldermaston to London Easter marches . . . Everybody mucked in, everybody suffered the same discomforts, everybody shared, supported everybody else. It was very good humoured, people sang, there were endless political discussions as you walked along in this great caravan. It was an emotional blast to be among so many like-minded people. This, I thought, was how a civilised society would behave towards its members.'[18]

Above all CND was a political blooding for many of its younger members. As Nigel Young has written, 'for the young people who joined . . . participation was everything; the feeling of solidarity did not end when each particular project came to an end; it moved into other fields and other places. It represented a new synthesis, the beginnings of a visible social alternative – an imminent counter-culture, that merged personal expressiveness with political activism. In a partial merger of youth and working-class styles, they inherited a common rejection of inherited middle-class and middle-aged life patterns and styles. Aldermaston [was] a march of the dissenting young.'[19]

In the end, as the Cuba Crisis had shown, protest against the Bomb was largely useless. But it remained a potent symbol for the Establishment world of complacency, lies and misinformation, and it was that world that the young, slowly at first, but with increasing energy, would seek to 'ban'.

Chapter Four

Beatniks: America I Love You

A stench of fear has come out of every pore of American life, and we suffer from a collective failure of nerve. The only courage, with rare exceptions, that we have been witness to, has been the isolated courage of isolated people.
Norman Mailer '*The White Negro*'[1]

In the beginning was the word and the word, as it would be time and time again, was 'America'. Teds, Mods, Rockers: all these might be claimed as British inventions, but these were parochial phenomena, hugely dependent on dress, and primarily beloved of the working classes. Such pleasures were neither offered to nor especially desired by the young bourgeoisie. Class antipathies aside, they tended not to be in work yet, and could not afford the uniforms. Nor were they that keen on the rough and tumble that went with membership of such 'youth cults'. For them, or at least those of them who were disenchanted with the *status quo* and sought for ways to stand outside it, the stimuli were strictly American. Like other imports, the British version would be relatively anaemic, a diluted version of the real thing, but none the less sincere.

The word 'beat', essentially a contraction of 'beaten', had been used to mean exhausted or overcome by hard work or difficulty since the mid-eighteenth century. However its immediate origin, as would often prove the case with all sorts of aspects of the 'counter-culture', was in the world of black jazz musicians and hustlers. It meant down and out, poor or exhausted and had links to such slang phrases as 'beat up' or 'dead beat'. The term crossed over in 1944, used by a Times Square rent-boy, junkie, thief and con-man called Herbert Huncke (1915–96). Huncke had a friend, one William Burroughs, scion of the St Louis adding machine corporation and Harvard graduate, whom he had turned on to heroin. Burroughs, a dedicated student of America's seamier societies, started using the word with a couple of his friends – Allen Ginsberg, a student at Columbia University, and Jack Kerouac, a former Columbia football star who had dropped out and joined the merchant marine. In time, Ginsberg would recall the word as meaning 'exhausted, at the bottom of the world, looking up or out, sleepless, wide-eyed, perceptive, rejected by society, on your own, streetwise'.[2]

For Ginsberg and his friends, the aim was the creation of what they saw as a 'New Vision', a concept that played on W.B. Yeats's poem 'A Vision' and which Lucien Carr, another of the circle, later described as 'trying to look at the world in a new light, trying to look at the world in a way that gave it some meaning. Trying to find values . . . that were valid.'[3] Writing in his journal Ginsberg offered his own take: 'Since art is merely and ultimately self-expressive, we conclude that the fullest art, the most individual, uninfluenced, unrepressed, uninhibited expression of art is true expression and the true art.'⁴ Yeats spoke of a new society of 'artist-citizens', they would be its leaders.

The idea of a 'beat generation', a self-mythologising phrase that would add even more substance to their efforts, came in November 1948, the product of a late-night conversation between Kerouac and another aspirant writer, the New Yorker John Clellon Holmes. Discussing Kerouac's recent cross-country trip to visit a friend, Neal Cassady, and the short stories that had emerged from this, and other of Kerouac's adventures amidst America's lowlife, Holmes called on his friend to sum up this 'new stance towards reality',⁵ which he saw as embodied in this new lifestyle. Kerouac explained that: 'It's a kind of furtiveness . . . like we were a generation of furtives. You know, with an inner knowledge there's no use flaunting on that level, the level of the "public", a kind of beatness – I mean, being right down to it, to ourselves, because we all *really* know where we are – and a weariness with all the forms, all the conventions of the world . . . So I guess you might say we're a beat generation.'⁶ Ginsberg saw it, writing later, as a matter of seeing 'everybody lost in a dream world of their own making. That was the basis of the Beat Generation. That was the primary perception.'⁷ With a salesman's awareness of the phrase's potential Holmes grasped at Kerouac's image, seeing it as having 'the subversive attraction of an image that might just contain a concept, with the added mystery of being hard to define'. And, suitable to its inbuilt mystique, it was 'a vision, not an idea'.⁸ The coinage followed soon after the publication of Kerouac's first novel, *The Town and the City*, a *roman-à-clef*, drawn from his immediate circle. It also laid down one of the basic, nihilist beat credos, as enunciated by the Ginsberg character, 'Levinsky': 'Everybody is going to fall apart, disintegrate, all character structures based on tradition and uprightness and so-called morality will slowly rot away, people will get the hives right in their hearts, great crabs will cling to their brains.'

Holmes pushed the phrase along in his novel *Go*, when he re-created Kerouac's late-night theorising almost word for word and in 1952 wrote a piece, 'This is the Beat Generation' for the Sunday edition of the *New York Times*: 'It was John Kerouac . . . Who . . . several years ago . . . said, "You know, this is really a beat generation". The origins of the word beat are obscure, but the meaning is only too clear to most Americans. More than the feeling of weariness, it implies the feeling of having been used, of being raw. It involves a sort of nakedness of mind.' The *leitmotif* of the piece was that of disillusion and disaffection. The 'Beat Generation', according to Holmes, represented a group of young people who had looked at the post-Second World War, Cold War world and failed to find a set of spiritual values to which they could adhere. A culture which was happy to be overshadowed by the threat of nuclear war so long as it could pursue its materialistic ambitions was not worthy of positive consideration.

As David Halberstam summed their role up in his book *The Fifties*, 'The
Beats . . . revered those who were different, those who lived outside the system, and particularly those who lived outside the law. They were fascinated
by the criminal life and believed that men who had been to prison had experienced the essence of freedom from the system.' (To live outside the law, as
the hippies would intone, thanks to guru Bob Dylan, you must be honest.)

> In *Go*, Holmes described their world as 'one of dingy backstairs "pads" ',
> Times Square cafeterias, bebop joints, nightlong wanderings, meetings on
> street corners, hitchhiking, a myriad of 'hip' bars all over the city, and the
> streets themselves. It was inhabited by people 'hung up' with drugs and other
> habits, searching out a new degree of craziness; and connected by the invisible
> threads of need, petty crimes of long ago, or the strange recognition of affinity.
> They were going all the time, living by night, rushing around to 'make con-
> tact', suddenly disappearing into jail or on the road, only to turn up again and
> search one another out. They had a view that life was under-ground, mysteri-
> ous, and they seemed unaware of anything outside the realities of deals, a pad
> to stay in, 'digging the frantic jazz,' and keeping everything going.[9]

Or as Kerouac put it famously in *On the Road*, they were 'The mad ones, the
ones who are mad to live, mad to talk, mad to be saved . . . the ones who never
yawn and say a commonplace thing, but burn, burn, burn, like fabulous yellow roman candles exploding like spiders across the stars.'

And although they were mainly white middle-class, they adored Black
culture, using its slang, listening to its music, jazz, and taking its drugs. They
saw Blacks, with unconsciously patronising racism, as urban primitives, able
in their alienation from mainstream culture to indulge a freer, more spontaneous way of life. It was this concept that informs Norman Mailer's essay,
published in *Dissent* in 1957, 'The White Negro', a totemic figure further
apostrophised as 'the hipster', one of 'a new breed of adventurers, urban adventurers who drifted out at night looking for action with a black man's code
to fit their facts. The hipster had absorbed the existentialist synapses of the
Negro, and for practical purposes could be considered a white Negro.'
Mailer himself was never a beat: he was too old, he had already established
himself as an internationally celebrated writer with his debut novel *The Naked and the Dead* in 1947, but he was a connoisseur of the existential angsts
that fuelled the beats, and set them down. Mailer's piece holds theories that
would inform the next twenty years of 'counter-culture'.

For Mailer the post-war world offered two alternatives: the one to live
with death-in-life – whether the instant death of nuclear bomb, or the slower
one of conformity 'with every creative and rebellious instinct stifled' – the
other,

... the only life-giving answer, is to accept the terms of death, to live with
death as immediate danger, to divorce oneself from society, to exist without
roots, to set out on that uncharted journey into the rebellious imperatives of
the self. In short, whether the life is criminal or not, the decision is to encourage the psychopath in oneself, to explore that domain of experience where security is boredom and therefore sickness, and one exists in the present, in that
enormous present which is without past or future, memory or planned intention, the life where a man must go until he is beat, where he must gamble with
his energies through all those small or large crises of courage and unforeseen
situations which beset his day, where he must be with it or doomed not to
swing.[10]

Hip, he explains, is 'the affirmation of the barbarian for it requires a primitive passion about human nature to believe that individual acts of violence are
always to be preferred to the collective violence of the State; it takes literal
faith in the creative possibilities of the human being to envisage acts of violence as the catharsis which prepares growth.'[11]

Others might question his fine-tuning, but Mailer also differentiated between beat and hipster, 'white Negro and crippled saint', even though he almost immediately cancels it out, accepting that these are 'two types who
never exist so simply in the real life of any Village ferment. If there are hip-
sters and beatniks, there are also hipniks and beatsters.' (Among whom he
places Ginsberg and Kerouac.) As much as anything there is a class difference – the beat is often Jewish, usually middle-class 'and twenty-five years
ago would have joined the YCL'. The hipster 'comes out of a muted rebellion
of the proletariat, he is, so to say, the lazy proletariat, the spiv; nothing given
to manual labour unless he has no choice. The beatnik chooses not to work as
a sentence against the conformity of his parents. Therefore he can feel moral
value in his good-bye to society. The hipster is more easygoing about the
drag and value of a moneyless life of leisure.'[12] He is also, though Mailer does
not say so, 'blacker'. If Ginsberg can be cited as the *ur*-beat, then Lenny
Bruce is surely the hipster-supreme. Both would have their roles to play in
the years to come.

Of all Mailer's 'barbarians' and 'wise primitives' none would rival Neal
Cassady, the 'Dean Moriarty' of *On the Road* and the 'Cody Pomeroy' of *Visions of Cody*, *The Dharma Bums* and several more of Kerouac's novels. Looking like some young Paul Newman, Cassady had the credibility, the flawless
street-boy cool that the urban Jewish intellectuals like Ginsberg or the rich-
boy Midwesterners like Burroughs might desire but could never attain. He
also had the lifestyle. It was Cassady, the son of a wandering bum and
brought up on Denver's skid row, who fucked and fought and drove his way
back and forth across most of the forty-eight states, his friends marvelling at
his endurance and draining his experiences for their poems and novels. He
wrote himself – a fragmentary autobiography entitled *The First Third* – but

his genius was for movement, not prose. No one could have symbolised the Beat ideal more perfectly. As Ian Whitcomb put it, he was 'an unschooled boy-man sprite . . . a meaty model of Zen Buddhism in action, penetrating beyond the mundane logical mind into the true core of the human spirit. And that spirit – that all-knowing intuition – dicated the message: the only real goal in life was to be constantly celebrating the ecstasy of the passing moment.'[13] The others might write, Cassady did. Later he would move seamlessly from the Beats to the hippies, joining forces with Ken Kesey's Merry Pranksters, driving their acid-fuelled bus 'Furthur' along the same blacktops and highways down which he had taken Ginsberg and Kerouac.

'This isn't writing, it's typing,' spluttered Truman Capote at the publication of *On the Road*. Kerouac's manuscript, fuelled by benzedrine and composed on a huge roll of adding machine paper, marked a new development in counter-cultural progress. Kerouac was not alone. Burroughs had published his own *roman-à-clef*, *Junkie*, in 1953 while Ginsberg's magnum opus, 'Howl' had already appeared, in 1956, under the imprint of Lawrence Ferlinghetti's City Lights Bookstore. *Junkie*, published by Ace Books, a pulp imprint that hardly appealed to the literatteurs, made no great splash. 'Howl' was different. It appeared on 13 October 1955 when its author transfixed his audience at Gallery Six, a converted auto repair shop, with the words 'I saw the best minds of my generation | destroyed by madness | starving, mystical, naked, | who dragged themselves thru the angry streets at | dawn looking for a negro fix . . .'. It was all there, 'the Beat anthem' as David Halberstam characterised it. Kerouac sat in the audience with a jug of wine, exhorting his friend to ever-greater efforts. In the words of writer Ted Morgan, it had: 'an absolutely compelling incantatory quality, and seemed to be a manifesto for all the misfits of the fifties, the rejected, the deviants, the criminals, and the insane, who could unite under his banner.' From San Francisco Lawrence Ferlinghetti sent Ginsberg a cable paraphrasing what Emerson had said to their hero Whitman after reading *Leaves of Grass*: 'I greet you at the start of a great career.'

The authorities, unsurprisingly, hit back. *Go* had run into some trouble – six instances of 'Fuck you' had to be cut to three – but three years on, the beat phenomenon was mushrooming, and Ginsberg was chosen as a target. A year after the paperback version appeared two officers entered City Lights and bought themselves a copy. They arrested Ferlinghetti and his manager and laid obscenity charges. A few years earlier, and they might have succeeded; now it was too late. Ginsberg had had a number of positive reviews; as would happen in the great obscenity trials to come, the liberal intelligentsia were happy to appear for the defence. In October 1957 the poem was acquitted.

By then, the beats were a national phenomenon. Although Ginsberg, and the others, might protest that the group had never been especially large, and had mingled together for a relatively brief period of time, the image was fixed. As would be true of their successors – mods, hippies, punks – the idea of the beat lost its links to a specific sub-culture and became instead a catch-all synonym for anyone categorised as a 'bohemian' or 'rebel'.

These second generation beats cast their net somewhat wider than their mentors. In the words of David Halberstam, 'They were the first to protest what they considered to be the blandness, conformity, and lack of serious social and cultural purpose in middle-class life in America. If much of the rest of the nation was enthusiastically joining the great migration to the suburbs, they consciously rejected this new life of middle-class affluence and were creating a new, alternative lifestyle; they were the pioneers of what would eventually become the counter-culture.'[14] They were, to use another popular synonym, the 'dropouts'. For Jeff Nuttall this new generation were the descendants rather than the peers of the hipster. Confused and mainly middle-class, they might revere the delinquent but they could never hope to rival the purity of his lifestyle. And rightly or not Nuttall credits the hipster with another role: not just the fantasy rebel, but an individual whose existence defied the enormous public guilt engendered by the Korean war and the H-bomb. Crime was the truest example of an 'alternative society'. Such attitudes were, of course, in the time-honoured tradition of middle-class voyeurism. The ragged-trousered misanthropists who sipped coffee in the bars of the North Beach or Soho, and flocked to such jazz foci as 52nd Street or the Beaulieu festival, were essentially law-abiding. But in a conformist society, the outsider creates his or her own illegitimacy. Judged by the mass standards of conformism those same ragged uniforms, that same jazz, linked the middle-class drop-outs with hardcore villains. The simple act of rejection was enough.

The original beats were unimpressed by these *arrivistes*. In his piece 'The Origins of the Beat Generation', published in June 1959 amidst the pneumatic, airbrushed homecoming queens of Hugh Hefner's *Playboy* (itself another form of the 'revolution in manners', but in its hedonistic materialism quite antithetical to the beat philosophy), Kerouac pushed for a redefinition of the key term. Its source was the not the down-and-out but the term 'beatitude', itself meaning 'supreme blessedness or happiness'. It was hoped, presumably, that such revisionism would emphasise the Blakean, mystical aspect of the original 'New Vision' and the beats' affection for a somewhat Occidentalised version of Zen Buddhism, but *Playboy* was perhaps not the ideal forum. In any case, the old idea was much harder to displace, especially after yet another piece, published on 2 April 1958 by the *San Francisco Chronicle*'s columnist Herb Caen, gave the beats a new name which stuck. As he wrote it, taking 'beat' and the Yiddish suffix '-nik', '*Look* Magazine, preparing a picture spread on San Francisco's Beat Generation (oh, no, not AGAIN!) hosted a party in a North Beach house for 50 Beatniks, and by the time the word got around the sour grapevine, over 250 bearded cats and kits were on hand, slopping up Mike Cowles' free booze. They're only Beat, y'know, when it comes to work . . . ' Or as Mailer put it, in *Advertisements for Myself* (1961), '-nik being a pejorative diminutive [it] . . . gave a quality of condescension to the word which proved agreeable to the newspaper mentality.' In a subsequent column Caen noted that in North Beach, for many years the city's Bohemian enclave, the smell of marijuana was now more pervasive than that of garlic. Soon the nation's aspirant beats, small-town Bohos yearning for company, began turning up, forerunners of the hippie invasion of the city's Haight-Ashbury area a decade later. And after them were the tourists and finally, hard on their heels, their noses cocked for that new cultural odour, the police.

Many intellectuals were equally unsympathetic. For the archetypical scream of fearful incomprehension see Norman Podhoretz, the quintessential New York culture-maven, writing in 1958 of 'The Know-Nothing Bohemians' in the *Partisan Review*. At one minute patronising, at another disdainful, at a third terrified by something he cannot grasp, Podhoretz brands the Beat mindset as 'hostile to civilisation, it worships primitivism, instinct, energy, "blood". To the extent that it has intellectual interests at all, they run to mystical doctrines, irrationalist philosophies, and left-wing Reichianism.' Worse still, they like jazz, they admire criminality, they are promiscuous, which he accepts, but, unlike the older, 'proper' Bohemians of the 1920s and 1930s, they are condemned for failing to render it 'dirty'. Above all they are guilty of 'an anti-intellectualism so bitter that it makes the ordinary American's hatred of eggheads seem positively benign'. It goes without saying that they can't write: Kerouac, the best-known, is merely a solipsist, incapable of extending beyond his own inadequate limitations. But these are details. Podhoretz reserves his shrillest cries for his dismissal of the Beats' 'rebellion'. 'This is the revolt of the spiritually underprivileged and the crippled of soul – young men who can't think straight and so hate anyone who can; young men who can't get outside the morass of self and so construct definitions of feeling that exclude all human beings who manage to live, even miserably, in a world of objects . . . ' Ultimately he sees no difference between the Beats and the 'young savages in leather jackets who have been running amuck . . . with their switch-blades and zip-guns'. In short, he implies, the Beats are little more than fascists. To stand against them is 'to do with denying that incoherence is superior to precision, that ignorance is superior to knowledge; that the exercise of mind and discrimination is a form of death . . . It even has to do with fighting the poisonous glorification of the adolescent in popular . . . culture. It has to do, in other words, with being for or against intelligence itself.'[15]

As the Fifties drew to their close it was inevitable that this aspect of American culture would make its way beyond America. If television and refrigerators could cross the Atlantic, so too could *On The Road* and 'Howl'. But it was hardly welcomed. Britain had Bohemians too, or some variation on the theme. They had always existed, but had tended to come with class connotations. As the *Westminster Review* had pronounced in 1862, 'a Bohemian is simply an artist or littérateur who, consciously or unconsciously, secedes from conventionality in life and in art.' Within bounds they were quite acceptable: artists, thespians, essayists, men who could afford the Café Royal or Romano's, the twin centres of raffish 1890s London. One could find their descendants drifting through the inter-war years and beyond. By the late 1950s the current manifestations were dubbed the 'Angry Young Men'. They were an enormously disparate group, throwing together such figures as playwright John Osborne, novelists John Wain and Kingsley Amis and philosopher Colin Wilson. As the *Oxford English Dictionary* explains, 'the expression "angry young man" and variants of it became commonly used, especially by journalists, after the production of John Osborne's play *Look Back in Anger* (first performed 1956). The phrase did not occur in the play but was applied to Osborne by G. Fearon, a press reporter . . . thence used particularly of young writers, usually of provincial and lower middle-class or working-class origin, who denounced or satirised the "Establishment" and the abuses of the time; later applied by extension to any person, group, etc., in Britain and elsewhere who considered the times to be out of joint.' It was a slick categorisation that might not have reflected the complex reality, but served the cultural archivists quite satisfactorily. Once again the impetus was generational: as Fearon explained, 'I had read John Osborne's play. When I met the author I ventured to prophesy that his generation would praise his play while mine would, in general, dislike it . . . "If this happens," I told him, "you would become known as the Angry Young Man." In fact, we decided then and there that henceforth he was to be known as that.' In the years that would follow most of the Angries drifted increasingly rightwards (prescient Amis was already describing them as 'Solemn Young Men' before the decade was out).[16] Later ironically, Jack Kerouac, sickened by mass access to the 'New Vision', would follow a similar path; unsurprisingly, even in the Fifties they showed little sympathy towards the Beats. The nearest they came to the American group was by default, included as the British representatives in Gene Feldman and Max Gartenberg's 1959 anthology *Protest: The Beat Generation and the Angry Young Men*. Amis, Wain, Wilson, Osborne and, less obviously, J.P. Donleavy (in fact an American expatriate) were among those appearing for 'the Angries'; from America came Ginsberg, Kerouac, Burroughs (in 'William Lee' disguise), Chandler Brossard, and Mailer. The book positioned itself as a comparison of the two forms of rebellion, but it was easy to see which represented the genuine article. 'Howl' or 'My First Days on Junk' cut rather deeper than 'Socialism and the Intellectuals' or 'The Perils of Hypergamy'.

One more point cut the 'Angries' off from those who would embrace the 'youth cults' of the Fifties. Mostly born in the 1920s, they had no fellow-feeling with the new breed, the 'teenager'. In chronological terms they were nearer such panjandrums of the literary Establishment as Evelyn Waugh, John Betjeman or Anthony Powell than the relative 'babies' who would start emerging in the late Fifties. It was equally true that none of the *ur*-Beats – Kerouac, Ginsberg, Burroughs – had been teenagers either, but the sheer fact of being Americans gave them honorary membership of the young (whether they wished it, like the seemingly ageless Ginsberg, or, like the increasingly misanthropic Kerouac, did not).

Mainstream British poetry, which might have been expected to offer a degree of sympathy, if only on the grounds of fellow-feeling, was equally hostile. Writing in the literary magazine *X* in 1959, the poet George Barker penned his own satire under the title 'Circular from America'. In part it sneered 'O Kerouac Kerouac | What on earth shall we do | If a single Idea | Ever gets through? | . . . ½ an idea | To a hundred pages | Now Jack, dear Jack | That ain't fair wages.' He concluded, 'If you really think | So low of the soul | Why don't you write | On a toilet roll?' Barker and his editors preferred such writers as Joyce and Beckett, impenetrable but unsullied by the conceits of what they dismissed as 'an amusing phenomenon'. The celebrated expatriate W.H. Auden was more measured, but equally askance. When Ginsberg paid a pilgrimage to Auden, holidaying on the Italian island of Ischia, he expressed his disdain for Walt Whitman (and thence for his disciple Ginsberg) and described Ginsberg's work as being 'full of the author feeling sorry for himself' and devoid of any greater vitality or beauty. Ginsberg condemned Auden and his friends as 'a tableful of dull, chatty literary old fairies' and 'a bunch of shits'. And when Ginsberg arrived in England along with fellow beat poet Gregory Corso to give a reading in Oxford, Auden, currently in residence at Christ Church, gave orders that neither of the Beats was to be allowed near him. In the event they did meet and Ginsberg and Corso proferred their own little tease by attempting to kiss the turn-ups of the senior poet's trousers. Corso was a great prostrator: on being told that Shelley had been at University College he proceeded there, opened the first door he found, declared without the slightest foundation this must have been Shelley's sacred residence, and began kissing the carpet. Its occupant, Shelley devotee or not, was less than amused. Another British poet, Christopher Logue, whose own verses might have appeared more sympathetic, and who was contributing his own 'protest' poems to the *Universities and New Left Review*, had little time for the Beats.

I was already quite old for it, certainly ten years older than most of the people who were involved. I knew nothing about beatniks, nothing at all. I knew Ginsberg and I knew Corso, but I didn't have much sympathy for their aesthetic. I find Ginsberg's writing sloppy, I don't like Whitman's poetry very much so I don't really like Ginsberg's – it just goes on and on and on. Now and again, of course, it works very well and there are short sections of it which one is glad have been written and glad that you know. But in the end it's mostly slop. But Ginsberg was an inspiring figure – he [was] much more important as a figure than he is as a poet.[17]

However, there were others in Britain, not always poets, and not as respected as Auden or even Barker, but infinitely more attuned to Beat sensibilities. It began with 'Howl'. It was late, of course – until the advent of Better Books some time in 1958, beat bookshops were effectively nonexistent – but once the little black and white paperback had made its way across the Atlantic, the boom was on. Barry Miles, known universally as Miles, was at art school in Cheltenham when

> somebody showed me a copy of 'Bomb' by Gregory Corso which was first published as a long broadside, shaped like an H-bomb cloud. I was very knocked out, I thought it was a terrific poem and on the back it said write to City Lights for a catalogue so I wrote for a catalogue. And they sent back this postcard, 'cos they only published about eight books in those days, and I thought 'Howl' sounded a real interesting name for a book, so I got a copy of that, and one by Ferlinghetti, and a couple of others. All for two dollars. 'Howl' totally blew me away, I just thought it was terrific. When I started my little magazine, *Tree*, I wanted to publish these guys. So I wrote to Ferlinghetti and he actually replied, saying he didn't actually want to send anything but reprint whatever you want. So I did.[18]

Spike Hawkins, himself a poet, and a beatnik who for a while could be found living in a hedge somewhere in Buckinghamshire, was also drawn to Better Books, where he found the City Lights volumes, and a copy of *Protest*. A fan of Auden, he swiftly dumped the older master for a new one: Ginsberg.

Better Books, on Charing Cross Road just down from Foyles and across from Old Compton Street, cannot be underestimated as a disseminator of beat culture. Under a variety of dedicated managers Better Books provided an unrivalled source of material that was simply unavailable almost anywhere else. Only Jim Haynes' Paperback Bookshop offered the same range of stock – and for that one had to trek to Edinburgh. Its creator and owner was Tony Godwin, also managing director of Penguin Books, who encouraged his managers to import more and more American small press books and obscure beat publications. But he didn't know that much more about them than anyone else and it was up to individual managers to track them down. None would be more assiduous than Miles: 'no one told you what was going on, you just found out: it was what I was attracted to and if you're attracted to something you start to find out, like a groupie or something. I was some kind of cultural groupie on the American underground and wanted to promote it.'[19]

British beat, as Robert Hewison has noted, was 'a matter of style rather than content',[20] but for those who took to the lifestyle, that did nothing to diminish its appeal. It was chiefly the creature of universities and of art schools. Miles was an art school graduate, Jeff Nuttall, somewhat older, was an art teacher. Oxford had its own coterie: Michael Horovitz, who founded *New Departures*, Victor Schonfield, Robin Blackburn (although his devotion was to 'straighter' New Left politics), John McGrath, plus visiting firemen such as Johnny Byrne (later co-author of *Groupie*) and Pete Brown (songwriter-in-waiting for Cream).

Horovitz, however, was no instant convert. He had arrived in Oxford ready to do theses on Blake and Beckett, but that work lapsed and rather than produce what he saw as yet more arid criticism, 'I thought that the real work was to make poetry and to realise visions, in the way Blake realised his Jerusalem by putting his work together. I had a bit of humility and thought that my own work isn't that great shakes yet, but perhaps since I've got to know some of these writers and artists, many of whom had also just finished university, I could collect them together and publish them. Which turned into *New Departures*.' And although Horovitz included the first excerpts from Burroughs's *Naked Lunch* to appear in Britain (the book itself would not appear until 1964 and while causing some controversy, escaped the obscenity prosecution meted out – unsuccessfully – to the US edition of 1962), 'I didn't yet see myself as a beat. There were beats in America, but our awareness of them and communications with them only began in 1958–59. We'd only become aware of 'Howl' and *On the Road* in the later Fifties.'[21]

As noted above, Ginsberg and Corso visited Oxford in early 1958. Ginsberg had been invited to London by Thomas Parkinson, his former English professor at Columbia, who wanted to include his old student's work in a series he was preparing for the BBC. Ginsberg duly performed (his scheduled five minutes was hugely extended when the producer begged him to recite 'Howl' and 'A Supermarket in California' in their lengthy entirety). He paid a brief visit to Oxford for a small informal reading before moving on to Paris. Here he saw Burroughs and ran into Corso, the painter Larry Rivers, the author Mason Hoffenberg (like Christopher Logue an alumnus of the Maurice Girodias 'Dirty Books' factory at the Olympia Press, and co-author with Terry Southern of *Candy*) and other beat ex-pats. A new friend was a young Indian poet, Dom Moraes, who invited him back to England, promising a full-scale reading back in Oxford. Ginsberg and Corso duly appeared at Jesus and New Colleges – getting a less than friendly reception at the latter when Corso's poem 'Bomb' was considered by the local CND firebrands as insufficiently serious. He was accused of being 'a fascist' and responded by calling them 'a bunch of creeps'; Ginsberg preferred 'assholes'. The students, fortified by a number of local beats, retaliated by throwing shoes. A more civilised encounter was with the *grande dame* of English eccentricity, Dame Edith Sitwell, who fêted them at her London club. When the talk turned to drugs – specifically Aldous Huxley's experimentation with mescalin – it was alleged, in *Look* magazine, that Ginsberg offered Dame Edith some heroin. She declined, claiming, according to the magazine, that it brought her out in spots.

The Oxford event had been brief, but the American stars left the university's young poets in ferment. Horovitz himself was still holding out, as much through a young man's competitiveness as anything else, and attacked the Beats in his first editorial for *New Departures*, but gradually he came to see the light. Within a year he had become 'more or less converted'.[22] And where Horovitz had moved, so did increasing numbers of young people. It was hard to mimic the full *On the Road* wanderlust and the British poets were never going to unseat the American originals, but it wasn't for want of spirit.

Certainly the mainstream media were willing to do their bit. The *People*, a Sunday tabloid, headlined their exposé of 'this bizarre new cult' 'THIS IS THE BEATNIK HORROR', adding 'They don't care a damn for anyone or anything' and offered such titillatory crossheads as 'Uncombed', 'Pigsty' and 'Dope Fiends'.[23] These 'young followers of the cult' were 'on the road to hell', although the *People* (ironically echoing the British beats themselves) was forced to turn to America for supposedly hardcore revelations. The more salubrious side of Fleet Street weighed in with equal enthusiasm. The theatre director Charles Marowitz, with his quiff and goatee the very model of the young Fifties intellectual, urged the readers of the *Observer* to see beyond the 'frantic negativism, absence of moral fibre, and cultivation of eccentricity'.[24] In his way, however, Marowitz is as sensationalist as the *People*. With references to Antonin Artaud and Carl Solomon (both one-time inmates of mental asylums) and Norman Mailer (who had tried to kill his wife), Marowitz pictures the beats as driven half-crazy by the excesses and insights of their own chosen lives.

As with any 'youth cult' the bottom line for the beats was the belonging. As will be seen with the Mods, where any philosophical underpinnings were soon subsumed in the obsession with fashion, what mattered was being there. Given the heavy student/middle-class background of the beats, there was a good deal more fancy talk, but for the vast majority in the end it was simply fun. For the average beat it was a mixture of art college superheroes (Alfred Jarré, André Breton and Marcel Duchamp), of modern jazz, of (usually) soft drugs, of CND. As Sue Miles recalled, 'It was to do with words: it was to do with Kerouac, it was to do with beat poets and being cool. You wore black, white lipstick and long hair that you could sit on and couldn't see behind; long hair was a kind of ridiculously important, emotive subject. You were shouted at in the street. I had this little anarchist boyfriend who would put his filthy bare feet up on my parents' coffee table. I though this was wonderful.'[25] 'Protest' spelled festivity. CND was gradually colonised by beats, long-haired, weirdly costumed, clad in paint-stained jeans and ageing, filthy sweaters, blowing sousaphones and cornets, festooned in slogans, defiantly grimy. The strait-laced professional liberals who had set up the campaign were appalled, but impotent. By the time

CND moved into its final marches, the beats effectively ran the show, spreading the new gospel among the young.

And like so much of Fifties and later Sixties youth culture one cannot underestimate the charm of its origins: America. The art schools might celebrate the Dadaists and Surrealists, the most European of rebels, and proto-beats might have paid some homage to their existentialist peers clustered around Sarte and de Beauvoir in Paris, but the whole ethos looked West. Like some latterday 'lost generation', Burroughs, Corso and the rest set up shop for some time in the Beat Hotel at 9 Rue Git-le-Coeur in the Quartier Latin, but they were importing culture, not absorbing it. For all but a very few, America was the focal point of the Fifties. Britons of every sort found themselves seduced from the grim vistas of home by the technicolor fantasies of the States; the young beats were no exception. Aside from any specifics, European culture, whether mainstream or Bohemian, had always tended to élitism; democratic, self-confident America offered no such barriers to its devotees, described by the writer James Webb as 'a Beat "proletariat" '.[26] It didn't really matter that they failed to grasp the detail, they made the right noises and acted up on cue.

It was this gang of camp-followers, these 'existential window-shoppers'[27] who made this new Bohemia vastly more extensive than any predecessor, more visible, and ultimately more threatening. Yet it was not the duty of such acolytes to seek for perfect authenticity; chronology and (in Britain's case) geography militated against such ideals.

Certainly there were groups who did just that, classically Jeff Nuttall and his avant-garde acting troupe the People Show and his sTigma experiments in shock art, held in the basement of Better Books, or artists such as John Latham, burning his Skoob ('books' in reverse) towers. But these were the hardcore, more avant-garde artists than either beats or hippies. Nuttall was among those who opted out as the Sixties really came up to speed, publishing *Bomb Culture* in the hope that, alternative duty done, he could retire from the fray. To him, hippies were anything but authentic and, as such, an alien, less than appealing group. But as he discovered, publication by a major imprint at a time when there was precious little 'alternative' writing on offer, outside the 'little magazines' or the underground press, gave one a 'leadership' role that might far outstrip one's wishes.

All youth groups seek to *épater les parents*, but sometimes the nature of the beast transcends its more banal externals. For all the self-consciousness, the deadly earnestness and pretension, the beats, even in their British manifestation, could not be dismissed, however much the Establishment might patronise. Something was happening and the Mr Joneses did not know what it was. The phrase 'alternative society' was a figment of the late Sixties, but as a fact it was already in place a decade earlier. Indeed, the beat world, the parallel existence, was more truly alternative than much of the over-hyped and hugely overt 'underground' that would succeed it. It was not surprising that many British beats, witnessing the Albert Hall poetry reading of 1965, saw it as the culmination of that society rather than, as is popularly supposed, its inception. The true alternative thrives on exclusivity. The world of little magazines, of college poetry readings, of trips to Better Books to pick up brain supplies hot in from the States, of hitch-hiking around the way-stations of the beat existence, provided just that. As Spike Hawkins, at the very heart of things, recalled, 'There was this circle around which one wandered. We would be invited to various towns. The communication between the cities was very great. You would go up to Newcastle and you'd say "Right, we're doing a thing down in London, you must come along . . . We'll put you up. I don't know if there's any money involved . . ." There was this wonderful, virtually pre-pubic [sic] excitement over it. London was no more of the centre than anywhere else. There was constant movement. We were meeting people, communicating, establishing centres. We could all be cross-referred. There was a movement: letters would be exchanged. There was a cohesion, as if we had rubber bands stretched all over England and we could just pull one . . . It was as if we had a map that was shown to us, just for a second, but we knew it.'[28]

As the Sixties unrolled, that map would become clearer, more crowded, and more public. For the beats, however, it was less accessible. The 'spot marked X', where all things Beat might reach fruition, remained alluring but unsettled. Beat was, among other things, a rehearsal for hippie, and the move from one to the other is relatively seamless. But in quantity, rather than quality, there was no comparison. Beat was undeniably central to what followed, but it was a strand, not the whole weave. The Fifties and early Sixties saw what would become a giant of youthful self-expression starting to move, stirring itself, testing its limbs, stretching its muscles. The new decade would see it stand and move, expanding its kingdom, brandishing the club of its ever-increasing self-confidence. The times, too, were moving on. The backdrop less stable, more fissiparous, the lure of the mainstream becoming increasingly hard to maintain. Coming to the end of 'The White Negro' Norman Mailer laid down the next step. It was one, he assured his readers, that would be far harder, far more challenging:

> Hip may erupt as a psychically armed rebellion whose sexual impetus may rebound against the anti-sexual foundation of every organised power . . . and bring into the air such animosities, antipathies, and new conflicts of interest that the mean empty hypocrisies of mass conformity will no longer work. A time of violence, new hysteria, confusion and rebellion will then be likely to replace the time of conformity. At that time, if the liberal should prove realistic in his belief that there is peaceful room for every tendency in American life, then Hip would end by being absorbed as a colorful figure in the tapestry. But if this is not the reality, and the economic, the social, the psychologi-

cal, and finally the moral crises accompanying the rise of the Negro should prove insupportable, then a time is coming when every political guide post will be gone, and millions of liberals will be faced with political dilemmas they have so far succeeded in evading, and with a view of human nature they do not wish to accept.[29]

Chapter Five

Mods: I'm the Face

These long-haired, mentally unstable, petty little hoodlums, these sawdust Caesars who can only find courage like rats, in hunting in packs, came to Margate with the avowed intent of interfering with the life and property of its inhabitants. Insofar as the law gives us power, this court will not fail to use the prescribed penalties. It will, perhaps, discourage you and others of your kidney who are infected with this vicious virus, that you will go to prison for three months.
George Simpson, JP, sentencing a Mod involved in fighting on Whit weekend 1964

Of the three 'youth cults' that dominated the 1950s and early Sixties, and laid the groundwork for the greater upheaval to come, the Mods, arriving last, can be seen as the most widely appealing. They brought together the Teds' nihilism, the alienation from a life that in its traditional prescriptions offered them nothing but the dreary and mundane, and a bit of the Beats' philosophising (at least in the formative period). They also echoed the Teds' use of clothing to define themselves, but rather than create a single uniform and continue to wear it with relatively little alteration from thereon in, for the pioneer Mods it was all alteration. Clothes not as some kind of tribal totem, but clothes as clothes. Sartorial art for art's sake. Far more focused than the denizens of what would be known as 'Swinging London', the style obsession of these teenage exquisites undoubtedly prefigured that brief flare-up when London itself, alongside its young population, became for a moment the embodiment of dandy fashion. It was as if the group, apostrophised by Roger Daltry of the Who as 'the first generation to have a lot of money after the war', had heard Macmillan's much-touted 'Never had it so good' and taken it to heart.

Like Teds, the Mods emerged from the London outer suburbs: Tottenham, Ilford, Stamford Hill. But unlike the unlettered Teds they were more middle-class, often Jewish, the sons of middle-management, small businessmen or some equivalent. And whatever may have happened to them once the movement became diluted and commercialised, they began life as philosophers as well as dandies. One of them, Steve Sparks, later to move into the record business, recalled that 'Mod is always seen as this working class, scooter riding precursor of skinheads, and that's a false point of view. Mod before it was commercialised was essentially an extension of Beatniks. It comes from "modern-ist", it was to do with modern jazz and to do with Sartre. Amphetamine, Jean-Paul Sartre and John Lee Hooker. That was being a Mod. And the clothes. Church's brogues, silk and mohair suits.'[1] It was rock 'n' roll's 'Blue Suede Shoes' written infinitely large. Colin MacInnes, writing in

Absolute Beginners in 1959, saw the pioneers: 'Observe the Dean in the modernist number's version. College-boy smooth crop hair with burned-in parting, neat white Italian rounded-collared shirt, short Roman jacket *very* tailored (two little vents, three buttons), no turn-up narrow trousers with 17-inch bottoms absolute maximum, pointed-toe shoes, and a white mac lying neatly folded by his side . . .'[2] It was very much a boys together movement. There were girls, and they too had to dress well: MacInnes noted the 'short hem-lines, seamless stockings, pointed-toed high-heeled stiletto shoes . . . hair done up into the elfin style. Face pale – corpse colour with a dash of mauve, plenty of mascara.'[3] But they were secondary. There was an unstated camp streak running through all this masculine preening, although it was an auto-eroticism rather than any 'hands-on' activity. That said, it has been argued that Mod also saw the first real emergence of the working-class girl, who had been waiting somewhat longer for economic freedom than her brothers. She was certainly a regular presence at the clubs and the Bank Holiday weekends, but she remained tangential. Hardcore Mod was above all an incestuously, narcissistically male environment.

The first wave of Mods, scarcely more than one hundred purists, maintained impossibly high standards, hunting down the most creative, innovative tailors, spending every hoarded penny from their day-jobs on the latest suit or shirt. It was a group held together by the dynamic of its internal fetishistic rivalries. Its exclusivity could not last. By the first years of the Sixties, peaking in 1963–64, Mod had spread west, most noticeably to Shepherd's Bush, and south, to Richmond, and new elements of desire and stimulation had been introduced. Pills ('purple hearts' or 'French blues', properly known as drinamyl, a blend of dexamphetamine and amylobarbitone used as a stimulant), scooters, top heavy with chrome embellishment, and music, the newly discovered Rhythm and Blues or soul: still Black like Modernist jazz, but more accessible, less cerebral and, alongside rock 'n' roll, the elemental underpinning of Sixties 'rock'.

It was these Mods who crowded into the West End, to the Flamingo, the Scene or the Marquee, as well as more distant venues such as the Station Hotel, Richmond (for the nascent Rolling Stones – never a 'Mod band' but adopted none the less), the Crawdaddy, also Richmond (for Georgie Fame or Long John Baldry), the Noriek in Tottenham (Geno Washington) or the Goldhawk Social Club, Shepherd's Bush (for the High Numbers, soon to be rechristened the Who, the very ultimate in Mod musicians). Of the major clubs the Flamingo, already popular among expat black GIs, was the most exotic (Screaming Jay Hawkins, bizarre by any standards, chose it for a London gig), but the Scene, once home to the old Cy Laurie Jazz Club, was considered the apogee of Mod aspirations. Sited in Ham Yard, a tiny Soho cul-de-sac off Great Windmill Street, it drew Mods from across London and beyond. It was owned by Ronan O'Rahilly, whose Radio Caroline would be the

most successful of the offshore 'pirate radio' stations; its boss DJ was Guy
Stevens, an R&B and soul fanatic, later producer of Mott the Hoople and
even later the Clash. The walls were padded, the floor strewn with cushions,
the room filled with speeding Mods, gulping down 'French blues' at a shil-
ling a time – take ten and you were good for the night. There were regular police raids. The Marquee, owned by trad jazz musician Chris Barber, followed
the pattern. On Tuesday nights, at least in late 1964 and '65, you could see
the Who. There was no alcohol, but pillheads didn't drink. Nor was night-
time mandatory. On Oxford Street there was Tiles, hymned by a passing
Tom Wolfe as 'the Noonday Underground', where 'office boys, office girls,
department store clerks, messengers, members of London's vast child
work-force of teenagers who leave school at fifteen, pour down into this cel-
lar . . . in the middle of the day for a break.'[4] You could disappear down there
at one o'clock, bright sunshine outside and suddenly you're in pitch darkness
being a Mod. Unlike the Marquee or the Flamingo, where the environment
reflected the hard-edged music, Tiles aimed for something smoother. It had
proper bars, a good dance floor and a fancy stage; it was well decorated and
for the era, possessed a major sound system.

The beauty of Mod for many was its ability to set formal boundaries to the
world. For John Marsh, sometime lighting man for Pink Floyd, 'it provided
a first adult experience . . . What appealed to me was the physical, material
style. I was totally sold on the look. Among certain Mods a real dedication to
pleasure existed. As a Mod what was happening, and where it was happening
and where it was going and all the rest of it was all kind of understandable.
You were part of a certain sort of culture and group because of the possession
of so many suits, how much chrome there was on your scooter, how many
girls you'd had knee-tremblers with against the back wall of various West
End clubs, and all the rest. It was understandable: where you stood, who you
were, what you were was all fairly clearly defined.'[5] Such conceptions were
some way from Sartre, Camus and the rest of the existentialist reading list,
but they left their possessor with a satisfyingly black and white worldview.
'When you're a Jet you're a Jet all the way . . . ' sang the stage hoodlums of
West Side Story. The Mods understood. As one put it to the sociologists
Hamblett and Deverson, collecting material for their book *Generation X*, 'If
you're a Mod, you're a Mod twenty-four hours a day . . . ' The *hommage*
might have been coincidental, the emotion wasn't.

There was a subtext to all this formality: the fact that it all devolved on leisure, on free time. You worked, you needed the money, but the job itself had
precious little intrinsic importance. Tom Wolfe noted how 'it is the style of
life that makes them unique, not money, power, position, talent, intelligence.
So like most people who base their lives on style, they are rather gloriously
unaffected cynics about everything else. They have far less nationalistic
spirit, for example, than the orthodox English left-wing intellectual. They

simply accept England as a country on the way down, and who gives a damn, and America as a country with the power, money, and if you can get some, fine, and the music is good, and you can get that, and they couldn't care less about Vietnam, war, the Bomb, and all that, except that English Army uniforms are indescribably creepy.'[6] They were subversives, consciously or otherwise, who used the profits of their dead-end jobs to maximise their real lives: at play.

By the time Wolfe penned his essay Mod had reached its third, least perfectionist stage. What had been called the Shepherd's Bush Mod had been replaced (or at least paralleled) by his Carnaby Street successor. By 1964 Carnaby Street had been saddled with the 'Swinging London' persona that has yet, even in its pedestrianised, tourist-spattered latter days, fully to vanish. Running parallel with Regent Street, home of such traditional 'gents outfitters' as Aquascutum and Austin Reed, it was a block down from Newburgh Street where ex-photographer Bill Green, trading as 'Vince', had a decade earlier set up London's first ever outlet for chic young men. His original patrons were the gay musclemen, airing their pecs round the corner at the Marshall Street Baths, but Vince soon found itself selling to a wider market – not the teens (they couldn't afford its prices) – but Peter Sellers, Lionel Bart, John Gielgud and similar showbiz celebs. It was the start of something big. Green's star faded by the late Fifties (he moved into catering) but a replacement did all he had and more. John Stephen, a refugee Glaswegian who learned his trade in the military department of Moss Bros., set up his first business in 1957, working in Beak Street under the name of 'His Clothes'. When His Clothes was accidentally burnt down he shrugged, and moved round the corner to Carnaby Street. And where the older generation still went to Vince, Stephen attracted a new breed: Cliff Richard, Tommy Steele: the pop stars. He undercut Vince, putting immediacy and excitement in the place of traditional tailoring standards. Attuned to the ephemerality of 'youth culture' he drew in the young, including – at first – the Mod exquisites. As Nik Cohn explained 'There were . . . ploys, lots of gimmicks and publicity stunts. But this was all embellishment. Underneath the central equation was that every time you walked past a John Stephen window, there was something new and loud in it, and when you counted your money you found you could afford it.'[7] By the end of 1961 Stephen had four shops of his own and his imitators – Donis, Domino Male – had opened up in Carnaby Street. They had a new name: the boutique. Originally it had meant a store within a store, dealing the latest fashions. It was a bit Frenchified, a bit camp, but no one objected to this little tribute to Carnaby Street's gay origins.

Carnaby Street truly took off in 1963, the year of Beatlemania, a brief interregnum in which the Establishment believed that it could grab 'youth' and consign its eccentricities to the dump-bins of commercial exploitation. Two years later it was dead, a tacky carnival Midway full of Union Jacks and hucksters, inflated rates fattening the local council coffers, tourists blocking its passage as they searched for the real-life version of what they'd read in *Time*. But for a while it was a mecca. The original Mods disdained it, of course, but their coterie had long since been overwhelmed.

Although, with the Beats off fomenting the future underground and the Teds long vanished into rock 'n' roll preservation societies, the Mods were undoubtedly the predominant 'youth' group of the period – an assessment has put them at around half-a-million strong, numbers that made them a very large gang indeed – they were not quite alone. Antithetical to their neat, groomed style were a much rougher band, the motorcycling Rockers, also known (if only by the media) as 'ton-up boys'. They were the descendants of the Teds, and like them dedicated rock 'n' rollers. All leather jackets, light-blue skintight jeans, big boots, studs and greasy hair, they had elements of Ted style but their real influence was transatlantic and came via the movies: Marlon Brando in Laslo Benedek's *The Wild One*. Brando's movie mob had been modelled on California's Hell's Angels (specifically on the 1947 inci-dent when as many as 3,000 bikers rioted in a small town called Hollister); stripe-T-shirted Lee Marvin, Brando's rival in the movie, was far more like a real-life Angel, but Marvin was still just a heavy while Brando was a Fifties god. His leather jacket, white T-shirt and blue jeans (as recycled by James Dean and other *jeunes premiers maudits* of the era) was the chosen look. Like the Mods, the Rockers would one day delight the curators of fashion muse-ums. Aside from the jeans and jackets, 'accessories could include peaked cap . . . calf-length boots, neck bandanas, Nazi war relics, big brash colour trans-fers and . . . ornate patterns of brass studs, tiger-tails, fringes, chains and bells.' In Jeff Nuttall's opinion, 'Very little has come out of the whole teenage development that has more beauty than decorated rocker-jackets . . . they constitute tribal art of a high degree, symmetrical, ritualistic, with a bizarre metallic brilliance and a highly fetichistic power.'[8] Costumes aside, few if any British bikers could rival Brando, but that didn't stop them. In some ways no more than a reaction to Mod – when Mod faltered then died so too would the Rockers – and vastly fewer in number, they were sufficiently unified to set themselves as a rival teen powerbase. In convenient teen shorthand '"Mod" meant effeminate, stuck-up, emulating the middle classes, aspiring to a com-petitive sophistication, snobbish, phony. "Rocker" meant hopelessly naïve, loutish, scruffy, and, above all, betraying; for the mods, like the hep-cats, wanted a good image for the rebel group, the polished sharp image that would offset the adult patronisation by which this increasingly self-aware world of the adolescent might be disarmed. Rockers were so clearly "going through a phase". Mods, in whom alienation had become something of a de-liberate stance, were embarrassed and angered by this.'[9] The feeling was mu-tual. Buttons, later President of the Hell's Angels England chapter, recalled, 'I soon learned. The Mods were on one side. We, the Rockers, were on the

other and no one else seemed to matter. The Mods were our automatic enemies and we were theirs. Why it came about I don't know. It was the accepted
system – our code of ethics and we lived and breathed for it only.'[10] In due
course, much to the delight of those involved, and the predictable mouthings
of those who merely watched, the two sides clashed.

By 1964 Mod had reached the provinces, though its *ultima Thule* was
somewhere around Nottingham. Other conceits, as ever, divided off the
North from such southern poncing. Last to abandon their colonisation by
the Teds, Northerners were more likely to embrace the Rocker lifestyle than
that of the soft southern Mods who dyed their hair and (irrespective of sex)
wore makeup. The 'battlegrounds' on which the two sides met were however
as far south as one could go: the seaside resorts of Brighton, Margate and
Clacton. The fighting became almost fashionable and for a while between
1964 and 1966 most market towns would see bands of 'Mods' (very far from
the mohaired originators by now) wandering the dreary weekend streets in
search of 'Rockers' (as likely owners of pushbikes as the real thing). The real
flashpoints however were around the southern coastline.

The first notable battle came on the Easter weekend of 1964, 26–27
March. It was the coldest such holiday in eighty years, making the traditional
Cockney seaside refuge of Clacton even more than usually uninviting. That
did not deter the rival youngsters, quickly labelled as 'gangs' of Mods and
Rockers, who fought each other – as much perhaps to keep warm than out of
real, ideological hatreds – to the much-publicised horror of local and soon
national worthies. Later research pointed out that the fights were as much
territorial as anything: London Mods moving into 'turf' supposedly controlled by Clacton Rockers; not only that but when questioned a good many
of the scufflers claimed not to belong to either party; no matter – such details
were soon lost to view. It was also territorial in a different way: traditional
seaside resorts like Clacton and Margate were facing a threat infinitely
greater than a few rowdy kids. Their old constituency, the summer holiday-
makers of London's East End and working-class suburbs were abandoning
them. For them 'Never had it so good' didn't just mean a car or a washing-
machine; it meant holidays abroad, sea and sun that surpassed anything the
poor, windswept South Coast could ever offer. That they were replaced by
rioting youths who might have had full pockets but had no intention of emp-
tying them on pierhead cabaret or Palm Court orchestras merely intensified
the sense of loss and of bewilderment, and with them fury.

Had the authorities and the attendant media acted with the sort of adult
intelligence that they claimed so vociferously to embody, the whole thing
might have blown over. In the event the same efforts that were supposed to
quell the situation served only to widen the gap between the Mods and those
who sat in judgement over them. When the boys and girls congregated for
the second time, this time on the Whit weekend of May 1964, the attitude of

the local JP, Mr George Simpson, merely fanned the flames with his mantra of the need to 'teach a lesson' to the hooligan, his 'clever' remarks as he fined and jailed young offenders and his own smug self-satisfaction (echoed by a fawning press). The papers were especially exercised in their synthetic rage by seventeen-year-old James Brunton who supposedly responded to a £75 fine by a promise to pay by cheque. It turned out that Brunton had merely been attempting 'a pathetic gesture of bravado'.[11] He had no cheque book, nor yet a bank account; he had been making 'a little joke'.[12] If he was it totally misfired, and in any case ameliorating circumstances were uniformly irrelevant. The public *wanted* the Mods to come on cocky. Too much too young – that was their problem. How dare these people, these 'vermin' mock the consumerist society without which they could not exist. For all the expletives hurled from the nation's benches, these were not some nascent 'underclass'; these were average middle-class youngsters.

A year later and the whole cycle started again. The same towns, with a few extras – Brighton, Weston-super-Mare, Great Yarmouth – suffered the springtime invasion. This time the media, better prepared, were ready and waiting. The young duly obliged: plenty of broken deckchairs, fleeing grannies, stern-faced policemen, outraged councillors. Girls were thrown into the sea, teenagers were arrested with 'weekend packs' (or so said the *Daily Telegraph*[13]) filled with 'contraceptives and purple hearts'. But by now the event, like the rock 'n' roll riots of the mid-1950s, was becoming ritualised. Another year saw a few more 'invasions', but by now it was very half-hearted. The media was bored and so were the participants. The image of youth as a threat, however, had only been reinforced. That would not go away.

The very people who would vote Tory on the basis of Supermac's 'Never had it so good' sloganeering, were more than a little ambivalent about its application to those less restrained in their indulgences, in other words less middle-class. The sociologist Stanley Cohen recalled a magistrate explaining in 1965, 'Delinquency is trying to get at too many things too easily . . . people have become more aware of the good things in life . . . we've thrown back the curtain for them too soon.'[14] Youth was too good for the young. Establishment society as a whole saw the Mods and Rockers as emblems of decline, symbols that far transcended what little they actually did: a horribly three-dimensional example of a collapsing society. Mods and Rockers took on the role of 'folk devils' hitherto occupied by the Teds. That they were not as relentlessly downmarket as the Teds was more problematic. These were, one might almost say, one's own children. Mods would disclaim any link to the Teds, but observers drew kneejerk parallels. And like the Teds, the Mods and Rockers were pilloried not so much for what they actually did, but for the way in which they were perceived as doing it. Stanley Cohen, analysing the Margate 'riots' in the pioneering book for which he coined the phrase 'a moral panic', saw ten contributory factors. In every case the reality was a pale imitation of the myth. He found that there were no 'gangs' as such; very few people owned either a scooter or motorbike; the young were not especially rich, the average found in an arrested person's pocket was 15/- and most earned less than £10 a week; there was little evidence of planned violence – most participants had come as voyeurs, hoping that 'others' would set things going; despite the howls of local shopkeepers trade was not adversely affected, and while, for instance, the swimming pool receipts were down, those of the putting green and miniature railway were substantially up – effects of the unseasonably chilly weather rather than of rampaging youths. Finally, and most important, was that for all the reports of 'blood and violence' there was actually very little. Nor was there substantial vandalism.

For the media, however, the story was too good to miss. Calmer assessments would conclude that the events had been somewhat 'over-reported', but that was later. On Monday, the day after these events, every national newspaper with the exception of *The Times* ran a lead story on Clacton. They were predictably hysterical if slanted to readership: The *Daily Telegraph* offered 'Scooter Groups', the *Mirror* 'Wild Ones'. The Home Secretary (the viciously right-wing Henry Brooke) was 'urged' to take firm action to deal with the problem. Mods and Rockers were interviewed, delighted by the opportunity. This wilful plunge into panic was not merely homegrown. Major stories appeared in America, Canada, Australia, South Africa, and on the European continent, where a Belgian paper caught the mood with its caption 'West Side Story on English Coast'. What seemed to hurt the authorities most was the Mods' apparent rejection of everything that seemed valuable to non-Mod society. One could dismiss the Teds – gutter proles who would never make it anyway, direct descendants of uncompromising, easily categorised working-class hooligans – while the Beats, for all their ranting and raving, were at least educated. Even pop music, momentarily so unnerving, had been gelded. Tommy Steele was starring in musicals; what could be squeakily cleaner than Cliff Richard; even the Beatles – 'The Fab Four', 'The Moptops' – still seemed charming. You really wouldn't object were your daughter to bring one home. Mods, however, were less easily understood. The neatly combed, elegantly dressed, scooter-borne Mod, blank eyes distended with amphetamine overload: what was his problem? What did he want?

From mainstream society, the answer might have come, very little. The clothes, the pills, the music, for those who could afford them the chrome-bedecked scooters, all these were certainly necessary, but the basic irony, due to become even more pronounced over the next few years – that the young were decrying the very same world that provided them with the material pleasures they so obviously relished – was blithely ignored. At first the Mods had proclaimed a definite intellectual core, but by the 'Carnaby Street' generation that seemed to have gone.

If there was a rationale, a philosophy, then perhaps it lay in the music to which they listened. It may be, as Dave Marsh has noted, there was no Mod music as such, 'just music Mods liked',[15] but that can be extended forever, irrespective of sub-cult, and of all the bands 'Mods liked', none was so potent than the Who. The Who were products of the Shepherd's Bush scene, a mixture of the usual moonlighting semi-skilled workmen leavened by a little art school input in the person of Pete Townshend. They emerged through the local Mod scene, cutting their skills – as the Detours and later the High Numbers – at the Goldhawk Road Social Club. In the beginning they were not dedicated Mods as such, although their drummer Keith Moon, recruited to replace the ageing brickie of the original lineup, had serious pretensions, but the Mods had seen them first and adopted them as theirs. Townshend, lead guitarist and in time overall leader, was a total fan. 'The Mod movement . . . has always been one of the things that impressed me most in life . . . As individuals they were nothing. They were England's lowest common denominators. Not only were they young, they were lower-class young . . . As a force they were unbelievable. They were the Bulge, the result of all the old soldiers coming back from war and screwing until they were blue in the face. Thousands and thousands of kids – too many kids, not enough teachers, not enough parents, not enough pills to go round . . . It was the first move towards unity I have ever seen – unity of thought, drive and motive. If you were a Mod you liked the Who.'[16]

David 'Boss' Goodman, later road manager for the Deviants and the Pink Fairies, was an early fan.

> I was still a bit shy and the first time I came out of my shell was when I saw the Who at the Marquee. At the same time as there was the jazzy, bluesy stuff and the black soul at the Flamingo, up the road at the Marquee was this white Rhythm and Blues scene going down. The Tuesday night residency was the one to go to. I saw the Yardbirds with Eric Clapton there, and all that sort of stuff, but when I first saw the Who . . . I'd never seen anything like, I couldn't imagine that people could do such things. I went straight out and broke a window, I was that impressed. It broke down so many barriers for me, just that one evening of seeing the Who. The set was so fucking violent and the music so heady, it hit you in the head as well as the guts, it did things to you. Plus on top of that you'd never heard anything like it: Maximum R&B said the poster . . . and fuck me, was it! They used to do 'Smokestack Lightning', thirty minutes of it, and Townshend would go potty . . . That all really brought it home to me, what I'd been missing.[17]

Once they started making the charts the Who's manager unashamedly marketed them as super-Mods, especially Moon with his pop art 'target' T-shirts and Daltry, posing as a top face, but what mattered – Mod standards notwithstanding – was not so much the look as the lyrics. 'Can't Explain' in early 1965 was followed by a second hit, 'Anyway, Anyhow, Anywhere' and climaxed with the anthemic 'My Generation', 'Pete Townshend's battle hymn of unresolved and unresolvable tensions',[18] released fittingly on Guy Fawkes Night. It was, to ape the rockbiz cliché of the time 'the Brighton sound', not to mention the 'Margate sound' and the 'Clacton sound'. Daltry stutters out the words, his assumed speech problem a tribute to effects of 'leapers', throwing down the beliefs not just of the Mods but of more and more young people. As Nik Cohn has said, Townshend chronicled teen lives better than anyone since '50s rock's Eddie Cochran.[19] Whether Townshend intended to create the *leitmotif* of his era who knows; maybe, as he put it later, it was only 'some pilled-up Mod dancing around trying to explain to you why he's such a groovy guy but he can't because he's so stoned he can hardly talk'.[20] Maybe, as cynics might suggest, there was no real difference. Only in the Rolling Stones' 'Satisfaction' (a slightly earlier 1965 release) was teen angst so well addressed (and as commentators have noted, while Jagger, the performer, deals in the end with his own angst, Townshend, the populist, encompasses the *zeitgeist*).

> People try to put us down,
> Just because we get around . . .
> Things they do look awful cold
> Hope I die before I get old.
> Talking 'bout my generation.
> This is my generation, baby,
> My generation.[21]

Was there anything else to say?

Chapter Six

The Permissive Society: Do Your Own Thing

Permissive: having the quality of permitting or giving permission; that allows something to be done or to happen; not forbidding or hindering. In modern use ... tolerant, liberal, allowing freedom, spec. in sexual matters; freq. in phr. permissive society.
The Oxford English Dictionary

The image of the Sixties world as a 'permissive society' was coined in 1968, although the concept of 'permissiveness' had been gathering strength since the late Fifties when a number of commentators began debating the whole idea of a world in which hard-and-fast rules were starting to erode. Today the term is synonymous with 'anything-goes' liberalism, but as the dictionary definition makes clear, the term permissiveness devolves upon the ideas of permission: not what one wants, but what one is allowed. It is now generally assumed that such permission was automatically extended by the Labour government that took power in 1964, but like so many of the propagandist myths that have emerged since, this is far from wholly true. The concept of 'permissiveness' has become the dirtiest of words, a bogey to terrify the Thatcherite young, but the new government was hardly rushing headlong into some kind of libertarian free-for-all.

Those who voted Labour may have hoped for radical changes in the governance of the country, and, by extension, in the type of society in which they lived. However, the primary focus of those changes, much encouraged by Labour campaigning, was technological rather than sociological. Harold Wilson, who won the Labour leadership in the wake of Hugh Gaitskell's premature death in January 1963, posed as the representative of the thrusting younger professional, pushing the tired old country forward towards modernity and change. It was in fact the Tories who had pushed such genuine technological advances as the Comet jetliner, had raised the first tower block and built the first motorway – advances that however discredited they might become, were at the time lauded generally as the 'way forward'. But Conservative rule had gone spectacularly to the bad over the last two years, and Wilson was poised to snatch every advantage from the fact. He was, or at least carefully let himself seem to be, 'the technocrat in a white coat replacing the aristocrat in tweeds'.[1] Prefiguring Margaret Thatcher, Wilson positioned himself as the earnest, hard-working, up-from-nothing outsider, the tough-minded scholarship boy pitting his thrift, energy, self-determination and above all honesty against the corrupt indolence of an entrenched, and utterly out-of-date ruling class. He gloried in his isolation from the drawing rooms of Establishment power, salons of such upper-class political *grandes dames* as

Ann Fleming, in which fellow Labourites such as Richard Crossman or Roy Jenkins could be regularly found. He made it clear that he was a true man of the people, boasting famously that, 'My tastes are simple. If I had the choice between smoked salmon and tinned salmon I'd have it tinned. With vinegar. I prefer beer to champagne and if I get the chance to go home I have a North Country high tea – without wine.'[2] There was also much play made of a supposed affection for HP sauce; the Prime Minister enjoyed reciting, from memory, the French inscription that adorned this quintessentially proletarian condiment. Add to that his proven intellectual and political track-record – a bright young don at Oxford, the youngest ever Labour cabinet minister (President of the Board of Trade, aged thirty-two, in the post-war Attlee government) – and one had the ideal man for the job. Others might rail against it – when in 1948 Wilson boasted of attending 'a school where more than half the children in my class never had any boots or shoes to their feet' and let it be inferred that he was among that half, the Tory MP Ivor Bulwer-Thomas rejoined that, 'If ever he went to school without any boots it was because he was too big for them.' His headmaster also wrote to make it clear that Wilson was always adequately shod. But the public dismissed such attempts at deflation.

The truth was somewhat different. The 'plain man of simple tastes who in every respect except his ability and vocation resembled the average voter'[3] was a good deal more complex, not to mention élitist, than he chose to admit. He preferred brandy to beer; his children were privately educated; he and his poetry-writing wife Mary had a holiday home in the Scillies (though any privilege this might imply was quickly dashed by the release of his holiday snaps – Wilson posing with pipe and monster shorts, only the 'kiss-me-quick hat' was missing). Like any successful politician, he was very much the chameleon. Writing during the 1964 General Election campaign, *Daily Mail* journalist Walter Terry noted 'the ten faces of Harold' and listed them as 'Huddersfield Harold, American Harold, Basic Harold, "Nationalise 'em" Harold, Orthodox Harold, Intelligentsia Harold, Dynamic Harold, Little Englander Harold, Capitalist Harold and Russian Harold'.[4] His colleague George Brown was more acerbic: 'If the film of Walter Mitty [James Thurber's celebrated self-mythologiser] hadn't come first, Harold Wilson must have been the prototype on which that mythical character was based. His fantasies are endless. The roles he allots himself are breath-taking.'[5]

The public rolled happily with every punch. As the campaign proceeded the pollsters found him highly popular, outstripping Macmillan, scoring very high on personal trustworthiness, and even wooing unprecedentedly large numbers of the usually uninterested into watching Labour's party politicals. Indeed, on 27 February 1964 his appearance on one of these won the highest ratings for any TV programme to date, smashing through Macmillan's own record-breaking efforts of a month before.

In an era when party loyalty was not quite the shibboleth it would become, Wilson's greatest ability was in his balancing of his varied team. As befitted his technocrat mode he seemed an efficient problem solver; the less adulatory might prefer the less flattering 'good hustler'. He alone of Labour's leadership had managed to escape identification with either Left or Right in the squabbles that had divided the party for most of the 1950s. His forte was in manipulation rather than policy, and as his administrations passed, his inability to practise a consistent line, let alone to honour the promises that his campaigns proclaimed, made for a growing disillusion with his 'honest bluff Hal' approach.

What Wilson sold the voters was the future. He might have appeared at a rally in September 1964, kicking off the campaign proper with a 10,000 strong gathering at the Wembley Empire Pool, to declare that 'the spirit of 1945 is in the air again', but post-war austerity was not on the agenda. An earlier speech, delivered at the 1963 Labour Conference at Scarborough, set out the Wilson stall. Its theme was simple: science was the agent of social change. It was vital that Britain maintain its role in the scientific revolution that was dominating the developed world. Education would be revolutionised – the divisive 'eleven-plus' examination would go, there would be a 'tremendous building programme of new universities', there would be a 'University of the Air' (the Open University). Government-sponsored research would go hand-in-hand with economic planning, new investments in science and technology would bring new work to the country's depressed and run-down areas. Old industries would be kicked into shape. And, he declared, in a peroration that would enter the anthologies, 'In all our plans for the future, we are re-defining and we are re-stating our Socialism in terms of the scientific revolution. But that revolution cannot become a reality unless we are prepared to make far-reaching changes in the economic and social attitudes which permeate our whole system of society. The Britain that is going to be forged in the white heat of this revolution will be no place for restrictive practices or for outdated methods on either side of industry . . . In the Cabinet room and the boardroom alike those charged with the control of our affairs must be ready to think and to speak in the language of our scientific age.'

It was a speech that appealed not just to Labour stalwarts, but to young people of every political persuasion. Labour's image-makers had succeeded in identifying Wilson, who carefully bounded on to the podium at conferences, displaying his youthful sprightliness, with the vibrant future and Macmillan with the worn-out past. Labour's deliberately pacey campaign slogan, 'Let's Go with Labour' (with its images of 'on your marks, get set, go!', of 'get-up-and-go' and even a not-so-subconscious link to Rediffusion TV's recently inaugurated pop show *Ready Steady Go!*) struck a chord in many hearts. The same cross-party appeal that Thatcher manufactured in 1979 was Wilson's bonus in 1964. Even so, and despite facing Macmillan's successor Sir Alec Douglas-Home, a man even more imbued with the grouse-moor and the appurtenances of class than Macmillan himself, Wilson won but a narrow majority: just five seats, and in the seventeen months of his first government this would fall to a single MP. It did not deter Wilson, whom some observers felt might have been more prudent to suggest a Lib-Lab coalition, from forming his government. As the preface to Labour's 1964 manifesto had stated: 'The country needs fresh and virile leadership. Labour is ready.' Despite the miniscule majority, the electorate did not want Labour to fail. An air of enormous expectancy, and indeed relief, was apparent. In what Ben Pimlott has apostrophised as a 'democratic *coup d'état*: a symbolic shock that altered the way British people thought about themselves more profoundly than any other event since the Second World War'.[6] Labour had been given its chance – and not just by its traditional supporters, but by large tracts of the civil service and the business and industrial communities too. Now the country and perhaps especially those young people who had been happily seduced by Wilsonian oratory, waited to see what it would make of such an opportunity.

One area that escaped Wilson's campaigning rhetoric was the possibility of changes in the 'morality' laws that governed sexual preference, artistic censorship, personal relationships, and judicial punishment. For a traditional and instinctively puritan Nonconformist such as Wilson these topics were of little import. In the same way as he persisted in regarding Britain as a 'great power' (despite all evidence to the contrary), he saw the country's basic, long-lived social and moral standards as pretty much immutable. He cared about race relations – and would need to, given the increasing numbers of black and brown faces whom he governed – but topics such as abortion or homosexual rights left him cold. He might, for reasons of political expediency, tip his hat to current teenage preoccupations – notably in the granting of MBEs to the Beatles and in exploiting the photo-opportunity that went with the occasion (not to mention giving John Lennon a chance to introduce cannabis to the Buckingham Palace lavatories) – or attempt to ally the fact of a Labour government to England's winning of the soccer World Cup in 1966, but that was it. Had he been asked, his take on the more rebellious brand of 'teenager' would have probably resembled those of such figures as Richard Hoggart who saw them as the Huns at the gate of his beloved, if sentimentalised, working-class culture, or the National Union of Teachers, whose 'almost despairing papers',[7] published as *Discrimination and Popular Culture* in 1964, reflected what the earnest educators felt in the face of an incomprehensible revolution. Wilson's ministers, whatever their own background, tended to follow suit. Economics, education, the unions, foreign policy: these were the primary issues for such front-benchers as Richard Crossman, Anthony Crosland, Barbara Castle or James Callaghan. There was, however, one exception: Roy Jenkins. In time Jenkins would join the sorry ranks of the 'greatest Prime Ministers we never had' (around 1970 he had seemed a logical successor to Wilson and he has admitted how much he would indeed have liked the job), but in 1965 he took on his first senior post: as Home Secretary, and as such responsibility for those same 'moral' decisions. Of all the 'great offices of state' that of Home Secretary is perhaps the least glorious. It is hardly surprising then that for the most part those 'rewarded' with the post are either mediocre, malevolent or both. Jenkins would prove to be, and still remains, an exception.

In 1990 Lord Annan published a socio-political history of the century which he entitled *Our Age*. 'Our Age' defines not just a chronological period, but is the title (a liberal antecedent of the Thatcherite 'people like us') Annan gives to those who were born in the first two decades of the century and who went on to become the 'great and good' of the post-Second World War world. Born too late to fight in the First World War they were hugely influenced by it (and indeed helped create the myths that now surround it). Middle- or more likely upper-middle class, educated between the wars, and hugely influenced by the Bohemian standards laid down by 'Bloomsbury' (itself rebelling against the stuffiness of late-Victorian convention) they grew into *bien-pensant* liberals, running the great universities at which they had been educated, joining the ranks of civil service mandarins, taking over senior positions in the arts, providing the guiding lights on a succession of Royal Commissions and similar bodies. But their power, at least as portrayed by Annan, seemed not to corrupt. It tended, instead, to promote a paternalist liberalism. They had no desire to abandon their own well-upholstered lifestyles, they viewed the world very much from a privileged and patrician point of view, but they sincerely believed that the social rules they laid down for the conduct of other people's lives should reflect those by which they ordered their own. Why interfere with people's private lives when those lives – however alien to one's own predilections they might appear – caused no harm to others? And why not extend to others the pleasures that enhanced one's own existence? It was an attitude that one might find in more sophisticated countries, but Britain, after the long century of Victorian controls, was somewhat short on sophistication.

By the early 1960s, 'Our Age' was very much in control and Roy Jenkins was a prominent member. Educated politically by Hugh Gaitskell, he was of the party's right, and like Gaitskell unashamed of his cultural *savoir-faire*. A clever man, he infuriated such workaholics as Crossman with his ability to project an air of unbridled indolence, drawing what should have been hard-won, heavily worked-over conclusions with apparent insouciance. Most importantly, he had established unimpeachable liberal credentials. It is impossible to say whether Wilson appreciated what his appointment of Jenkins might mean, but that its effect was substantial – then and now – is incontrovertible.

'Our Age', viewed from a hostile standpoint, can be seen as complacent, patronising, arrogant and excluding – this was certainly the view taken by Margaret Thatcher, who would take spiteful revenge on them and all they

held dear. From a more favourable one their approach to the world was characterised as 'civilised'. Certainly that was their own view. No better example
could be found than in Roy Jenkins's pamphlet, published in 1959 to accompany that year's (unsuccessful) Labour election campaign. The climax of a
series of short essays on the state of the nation was one that asked 'Is Britain
civilised?', explaining that

> There are three aspects to the discussion. First there is the need for the State
> to do less to restrict personal freedom. Secondly there is the need for the
> State to do more to encourage the arts, to create towns which are worth living
> in, and to preserve a countryside which is worth looking at. Thirdly there is
> the need independently of the State, to create a climate of opinion which is fa-
> vourable to gaiety, tolerance, and beauty, and unfavourable to puritanical re-
> striction, to petty-minded disapproval, to hypocrisy and to a dreary, ugly
> pattern of life. A determined drive in these three directions would do as
> much to promote human happiness than all the 'political' legislation which
> any government is likely to introduce.[8]

Jenkins went on to greater specifics. He deplored 'the ghastly apparatus
of the gallows' and regretted that Britain, 'despite our much-vaunted social
and political maturity, still stands out as one of the few advanced countries
which retains this presumptuously final penalty'.[9] Among the other 'gross
restrictions on individual liberty' were 'brutal and unfair' laws on homosexuality, the Lord Chamberlain's censorship of the theatre, the continuing censorship of literature, the 'ridiculous and (fortunately) largely unenforceable'
Sunday observance laws, the betting laws (which militated against the small
punter while encouraging those who could afford a regular bookmaker's account), the 'unnecessary restriction' of the licensing laws (which would 'not
be tolerated by any other European country'), the divorce laws (involving 'a
great deal of unnecessary suffering'), the 'harsh and archaic' abortion laws,
the outdated treatment of suicide as a criminal offence and finally, 'the administration of the immigration laws . . . which would often be more suitable
to a police state, terrified of infection from the outside world, than to a Britain which is the traditional refuge of the oppressed'.[10]

Jenkins would not achieve everything – he could not have imagined the
government-fostered xenophobia which thirty years on would make those
immigration laws more rather than less savage, and there was no denying the
obsessions of those who sought to maintain the stultifying tedium of the English Sunday – but his aims were crystal clear. As he summed up, the overall
aim of all these reforms was:

> the need to campaign for a general climate of opinion favourable to gaiety and
> tolerance, and opposed to puritanical restriction and a drab, ugly pattern of
> life. It is not really a job for politicians, of course, although they, like any
> other leaders of opinion, can do something to set the tone . . . But the impor-

tant thing is to encourage them all, and to recognise that one form of intolerance breeds another and one type of drabness makes another more likely. Let us be on the side of those who want people to be free to live their own lives, to make their own mistakes, and to decide in an adult way and provided they do not infringe the rights of others, the code by which they wish to live; and on the side too of experiment and brightness, of better buildings and better food, of better music (jazz as well as Bach) and better books, of fuller lives and greater freedom. In the long run these things will be more important than even the most perfect of economic policies.[11]

In his two years as Home Secretary Jenkins actively promoted and encouraged measures to amend many of these anomalous, restrictive laws. The laws concerning abortion, homosexuality, capital punishment, suicide and theatre censorship all changed thanks to Jenkins's determination to make Britain a more civilised country. Of the principal targets only Sunday observance and the licensing laws resisted his advances. Indeed, Jenkins had not waited until taking office to institute reform. During his years at the Home Office, rather than simply place the government's imprimatur on one of these inevitably contentious bills, he would employ back-benchers to put forward the legislation in the form of private bills. He would then back them to the hilt, but the government would be far less imperilled. Such reticence might be mocked, but his strategy was politically sound. In any case, he knew that it worked. In 1958 he had taken on the back-bencher's role himself, championing the revised Obscene Publications Act, a piece of legislation that had not been touched since its original creation in 1857. The details of the new Act, and the campaign that put it in place, are best left until the discussion of censorship in general. What matters here is that Jenkins proved, five years before gaining office, his commitment to reform.

Jenkins's skilful and subtle work on the Obscene Publications Act had undoubtedly helped him gain his appointment to the Home Office. As will be seen in the discussion of individual reforms, he repeatedly used the same techniques. First of all the topic would be isolated, then the softening-up process would begin: a Royal Commission or some such agency would be established. After much debate, a suitable back-bencher would be chosen, then the bill, with maximum encouragement from the Home Secretary, would be ushered across the Parliamentary minefield. At the same time the relevant pressure group – the Abortion Law Reform Association, the Homosexual Law Reform Society, the Divorce Law Reform Union (many of which had been campaigning for years, even decades) – would step up its efforts in the public arena and in influencing individual MPs. There would inevitably be a good deal of opposition but as the record shows, the Home Secretary tended to get his way.

It would be wrong, however, to see any of these reforms as cut and dried successes. If, taken as a whole, they did indeed create a 'permissive society'

(Jenkins himself consistently preferred a 'civilised society'), then it was in the sense of what was permitted, not what was appropriated as a right. Rarely were they more than compromises, finding some middle way between the full scale demands of the pressurisers and the entrenched opposition of the traditionalists. The pragmatic need to see them on to the statute book meant that they were inevitably limited. The new laws left loopholes and opportunities for their liberal intentions to be bypassed. Homosexuality, for instance, was never properly legalised, just decriminalised in certain of its aspects; abortion was by no means 'on demand': the medical profession still had the right to grant or refuse. Nor, for all the subsequent demonisation of the era as a period of immorality run riot, was there some kind of coherent linkage between the various new bills. There was no conspiracy to corrupt. As Jenkins had made clear in 1959, there were many overdue reforms, but for all the chronological links, one cannot say that one reform followed logically upon another. Abortion, divorce, gay rights: each had to start the whole process afresh, calling upon a new set of supporters and fighting off the diehard resentment of a new set of opponents.

Yet it would be foolish to dismiss the reformer's achievements. However unsatisfactory, however disparate, the Jenkins package literally revolutionised the way many people lived their lives. And a final, less quantifiable effect should not be ignored. As the historian Jeffrey Weeks has noted, 'Their chief effect lay not so much in what they achieved themselves, as in the spaces they created through which more radical pressures were able to emerge. Almost despite themselves, the reformers of the 1960s wrought more than they thought – and often more than they desired.'[12] Quite what that meant will unfold in the chapters that follow.

There was also a degree of hardcore political pragmatism underpinning the advocacy of social change. The election of 1959, rather like that of twenty years later, had proved that relying on the traditional base of Labour supporters – the manual working class – was no longer sufficient. It was in decline, and old rock-solid Labour citadels – us vs. them, have-nots vs. haves – were crumbling. The consumer boom had trickled down and eroded old certainties, among them the moral givens that had underpinned the stability of Nonconformist working-class life. And hard as Labour might push the image of Macmillan (and later Douglas-Home) and his Cabinet as upper-class élitists, infinitely out of touch with 'real life', there was no denying that it had been Macmillan who had proclaimed, 'You've never had it so good', and Wilson who had spent thirteen years in opposition. That 'never had it so good' could also sound like 'I'm all right, Jack' (or to put it in its harsher, original form: 'Fuck you Jack, I'm all right') mattered very little to those enjoying their first foreign holiday or their first family car.

But ideals did have their place. Over the previous decade there had emerged a new generation of upwardly mobile young people, many of them products of the Butler Education Act of 1944, who wanted to vote Labour – their background would hardly have permitted them to do otherwise – but at the same time wanted to see the party they supported offer something more. Like the 'yuppies' of the 1980s these people represented a new class – the most successful of whom were apostrophised as the 'meritocrats' – but unlike yuppies this generation looked first to their social conscience, rather than their wallets. What they did not want was a perpetuation of the authoritarian standards that came with old, discredited Conservatism. Such meritocrats might not be *de facto* revolutionary, or even rebellious, but they believed firmly in the efficacy of change. Few of them would even consider joining the counter-culture, but their innate social liberalism and the atmosphere it promoted undoubtedly made it easier for that counter-culture to take root.

The positioning of Labour as an agent of liberal reform further appealed to the young people who were already impressed by the high-tech future that Wilson was promising. The idea of marrying economic improvement to greater individual choice seemed logical and attractive. While the more vociferous of the 'youth movements' – from Teds to Mods – were probably little interested in voting, their more established peers, who still saw a future within the mainstream, found such promises highly alluring. Britain's obsessive nannyism, the *leitmotif* of any Tory administration, pleased few of those who, like Wilson, wanted to be part of a new age. And after the election, hanging on by the merest thread of a majority, battered by increasing economic problems and the growing disappointment of an electorate who saw little sign of the promised new technological Jerusalem, Labour were delighted to have Jenkins, cutting his way through the old restrictions, opening up a more civilised society and, as a spinoff, enhancing their reputation.

Jenkins undoubtedly benefited from good timing – he arrived in office when the country had built up a whole shopping list of reforms – and had the courage, the enterprise and sheer political *nous* to put them into effect. It was the Tories who had put paid to the burden of National Service, and as for sexual depravity, it was high-living Tories, not grimly earnest Labourites, who stood at the centre of the Profumo Affair. The sound of cracking monuments was in the air. Professor George Carstairs, the 1962 Reith lecturer, made it clear that, 'Popular morality is now a waste land, littered with the debris of broken convictions . . . The confusion is perhaps greatest over sexual morality.'[13]

Morality, of course, was the traditional preserve of the Church, and by 1960 the Church was no longer presenting the united face that had once so comforted the socially repressive. The Anglican communion had been moving away from moral absolutism since the 1930s, and such publications as the Bishop of Woolwich's tract *Honest to God* (1962) showed that even within ecclesiastical ranks the old convictions, so simple, so productive of ideological comfort and so convenient for the suppression of independent thought, were toppling from their plinths. Roman Catholics were less doubtful: divorce, abortion and birth control elicited the predictably conservative response. The main defenders of the *status quo*, however, were the lower-middle and 'respectable' working-class ranks of Nonconformity – Methodists, Baptists and the like – who stood by the fundamentalist truths of Biblical proscription and would, as the 'permissives' gained more and more ground, form the bed-rock membership of such reactionary groups as Mary Whitehouse's Clean-Up TV (later the National Viewers' and Listeners' Association) campaign and the Society for the Protection of the Unborn Child, which sought to de-prive women of the right to abortion. Terrified by a world more subtle than their own parroted simplicities, such groups sought to reduce everyone to their own fearful level. Fortunately, for a while at least, such forces were treated with deserved contempt. Far more people agreed with Oscar Wilde's avowal that he had never met 'anyone in whom the moral sense was dominant who was not heartless, cruel, vindictive and entirely lacking in the smallest sense of humanity'. More important, however, was the revised attitude of the Church of England. Early Sixties Britain was still a place where the Church held some sway, at least on morals. If the established clergy were abandoning their old rigidity then the Establishment everywhere was likely to follow suit.

The most obvious example of this shift was the Jenkins programme of re-forms. But while the programme of legislation can be seen by some as a cause of 'permissiveness', it is equally possible to see it as an effect of a greater, less easily identifiable movement. The first important factor was money, the growth of what the Canadian economist John Kenneth Galbraith had chris-tened the 'Affluent Society'. The trickle-down effect of the consumer boom which, while most immediately noticeable in the 1950s, had been accelerat-ing since before the Second World War, gave the working class increasing in-volvement in the market. And since they were the principal consumers they began to dictate the terms of that market. According to Jeffrey Weeks this in-creasing influence made itself felt not merely in the variety and type of goods now available, but in a larger sphere: that of the attitude towards consump-tion as a whole. 'There is no doubt that the prolonged boom depended in part upon a switch in moral attitudes away from traditional bourgeois virtues of self-denial and saving ("prudence") towards a compulsion to spend ... these general moral characteristics – "saving", "spending" – have for long held strong sexual connotations.'[14] In the opinion of such Marxist analysts as Her-bert Marcuse, whose works *The One-Dimensional Man* and *Eros and Civiliza-tion* would become central manifestos of Sixties counter-cultural thought, while early capitalism demanded 'anal' attitudes (saving, the deferral of pleasure) mass consumption could permit the introduction of 'oral' ones, (spending, immediate gratification). A change in the basis of 'moral' legisla-tion was both cause and effect of that shift.

One last factor has to be mentioned here. Its efforts were among the most infuriating for the moralists, and a desire to counter what was perceived as its subversive effects would create the first of the anti-reform, pro-repression pressure groups: Clean-Up TV. The institution in question was of course the BBC, the national broadcaster, and in particular its director-general, Hugh Carleton Greene. Greene's attitude to broadcasting was not unlike Jenkins's to social reform; both men were very much 'Our Age'. It assumed a degree of sophistication, of maturity in the public at large, and determined to indulge it. For the devotees of control and of censorship this was of course anathema. The 'Wednesday Plays', especially the works of Dennis Potter, Nell Dunn's *Up the Junction* and Jeremy Sandford's *Cathy Come Home*, the new realism of the Liverpool-based cop show *Z Cars* (clichéd now, revolutionary then), the weekly excursion into satire *That Was The Week That Was*: such attempts by Greene to encourage what he saw as the essential pluralism of British life, made him into the moralists' chief object of hatred. To his enormous credit, unlike weaker successors, he chose to treat their whining with the disdain it deserved. The more feverish their attempts to promote themselves, the more Greene blithely ignored them. Twenty years earlier he had been among those who helped liberate the Nazi concentration camps: he needed no guidance as to the ultimate effects of 'true belief' and the tolerance of its ideologues. Unlike Lord Reith, whose rigid puritanism had made the BBC into some metropolitan extension of the harshest of Calvinist chapels, mixed with an automatic obeisance to his masters in Whitehall, Greene chose to make the corporation responsible and responsive to the widest range of those who paid their licence fees.

Greene was not perfect – against his better instincts he allowed himself to be persuaded to accept the censorship of Peter Watkins's *War Game*, a stark drama-doc laying out what would happen were a nuclear weapon to hit a town in the southern Home Counties. Whether nanny really had to be so protective of her charges remains in doubt.

Greene's credo is best seen in his own words, as expressed in a speech on 'The Conscience of the Programme Director' delivered in 1963 to the International Catholic Association in Rome: 'The main purpose of broadcasting, I suggest, is to make the microphone and the television screen available to the widest possible range of subjects and to the best exponents available of the differing views on any given subject, to let the debate decide or not decide as the case may be, and . . . "to emerge with a deeper knowledge".' The presentation of varying views, he stressed, did not mean that the BBC considered everything with an equivocal attitude, 'but it does mean, in my opinion, the BBC should encourage the examination of views and opinions in an atmosphere of healthy scepticism. I say "healthy scepticism" because I have a very strong personal conviction that scepticism is a most healthy frame of mind in which to examine accepted attitudes and test views which, in many cases, have hitherto been accepted too easily or too long . . . It follows that in its search for truth – indeed in whatever it undertakes – a broadcasting organisation must recognise an obligation towards tolerance and towards the maximum liberty of expression.'[15]

As far as the efforts of such censors as CUTV were concerned, he had no doubts. Quoting the academic Richard Hoggart, he cited two sorts of censors, the first of whom were the 'old Guardians': 'senior clergy, writers of leading articles in newspapers, presidents of national voluntary organisations, who like to think of themselves as upholders of cultural standards although, in many cases, they lack the qualities of intellect and imagination to justify that claim.' Alongside them come the 'new Populists', who 'claim to speak for "ordinary decent people" and to be "forced to take a stand against" unnecessary dirt, gratuitous sex, excessive violence, and so on. These "new Populists" will attack whatever does not underwrite a set of prior assumptions, assumptions which are anti-intellectual and unimaginative. Superficially this seems like a "grass-roots" movement. In practice it can threaten a dangerous form of censorship – censorship which works by causing artists and writers not to take risks, not to undertake those adventures of the spirit which must be at the heart of every truly new creative work.'[16] For Greene this populist censorship was to be resisted with even greater determination than that of the old guardians. They would always splutter on; the populists represented a far more insidious threat to freedom. 'I believe that broadcasters have a duty not to be diverted by arguments in favour of what is, in fact, disguised censorship. I believe we have a duty to take account of the changes in society, to be ahead of public opinion rather than always to wait upon it.'[17]

In answer to those who accused him of arrogance, he accepted (unlike his dogmatic opponents) that he was far from infallible. But in the end he vouchsafed one more personal conviction, 'one which I think one can support from the experience of history – it is better to err on the side of freedom than of restriction.'[18]

Greene's view undoubtedly appealed to the sophisticates (and as ratings proved, to a gratifyingly large section of the viewing public), but theirs was not the sole voice. Attacks on 'permissiveness' were launched almost as soon as the Sixties began and would continue long afterwards. Such landmark events as the trial of *Oz* magazine or that of the *Little Red Schoolbook*, and the various prosecutions brought under the Obscene Publications Act, will be addressed later. It is worth noting, however, the moving force behind this opposition, doyenne of the 'new populists' Mary Whitehouse. A Wolverhampton schoolteacher who combined invincible self-belief with equally invincible ignorance, she took it upon herself to act as the nation's moral watchdog, a self-appointed censor who, depending on one's point of view, would become a byword for rectitude and a bulwark against degeneracy, or a modern-day one-woman Savonarola.

Born Mary Hutcheson, she enjoyed a traditional middle-class upbring-
ing, and developed into what contemporaries recall as a 'lively sort of girl, not
at all academic but very energetic' and a born organiser. She did not, at that
stage, appear as an anti-smut crusader in embryo. That changed when in
1935 she joined the evangelistic Oxford Group, otherwise known as Moral
Rearmament (MRA). MRA was founded in June 1908 by an American Lu-
theran minister, Frank Buchman, who, on a visit to a church in Keswick, received 'a poignant vision of the crucified Christ' and a 'dazed sense of a great
shaking up'. On this basis Buchman created a major evangelistic movement
which, in its most extreme form proposes the establishment of a theocratic
state in which religion, in its most highly moral and restrictive version,
would dominate every aspect of life. The movement also embraced an obsessive anti-Communism in the 1950s and declared itself opposed in every way
to the 'permissive society' of the 1960s.

In January 1964, still working as a schoolmistress, Whitehouse helped to
launch the Clean-Up TV Campaign as an attempt to challenge the moral lax-
ity they felt to stem directly from the increasingly liberal standards of television in general and the BBC in particular. Their manifesto had exhorted the
'Women of Britain' to 'revive the militant Christian spirit' of the nation, and
a packed public meeting in Birmingham Town Hall proved that traditional
views still had a large constituency: CUTV would claim 235,000 signatures
on its Manifesto by August 1964. Some critics claimed otherwise, but the
movement was not simply a mouthpiece for Moral Rearmament, although
many early members did belong to both groups. However MRA's pro-
Christian and anti-Communist tenets certainly underpinned such minimal
intellectual framework as the campaign could offer. For CUTV, a distinctly
socialist devil was abroad and the BBC, under its unashamedly liberal
Director-General, was deliberately promoting his works.

'Men and women and children,' wrote Whitehouse in January 1964,
'listen and view at the risk of serious damage to their morals, their patriotism,
their discipline and their family life.' As a statutory body, the BBC was under
the control of Parliament, yet this institution seemed unwilling to check Corporation subversion. CUTV members determined to take the responsibility
on themselves. After monitoring 167 programmes, CUTV branded a large
proportion as 'objectionable'. Such programmes were those that included
'sexy innuendoes, suggestive clothing and behaviour; cruelty, sadism and
unnecessary violence; no regret for wrong-doing; blasphemy and presentation of religion in a poor light; excessive drinking and foul language; undermining respect for law and order; unduly harrowing and depressing themes'.
Programmes otherwise acceptable were ruled 'objectionable' if they included
any mention of homosexuality, abortion and similar topics. The royal family and
armed services were beyond comment. Then, in response to those who noted
that the campaigners always opposed, but never proposed, CUTV moved to

change its role. The National Viewers and Listeners Association (NVALA) was inaugurated in March 1965. CUTV was incorporated wholesale into the new pressure group, which acted not only to protest against the 'objectionable' but to represent and lobby for the views of Britain's silent majority.

Throughout the Sixties, and well beyond (when she would find in Margaret Thatcher a politician who appeared, if only for expediency's sake, to value her opinions) Whitehouse remained the classic self-appointed censor: deeply and undoubtedly sincere, but blinkered by her own beliefs into the assumption that she had the right and thus the duty to foist them on everyone else. Despite her much-publicised religiosity, it was clear that the concept of humility had been omitted from her catechism. She rejected the more extreme fantasies of some NVALA members, who would like to see any creative individual licensed before they are allowed to work, and believed only in a 'degree' of censorship, with exclusion for 'artistic creativity' (although the standards on which this would be based were not specified and may be assumed to be more stringent than any present definition). None the less, the idea of a world in which censorship did not exist was plainly terrifying and as a representative of 'the extremism of good' battling against 'the extremism of evil' for the allegiance of what she called 'the misty millions', she continued to champion it.

As a devoted opponent of censorship, both internal and external, Greene in 1963 abandoned the BBC's wonderfully outdated 'Green Book', in place since the Thirties and properly known as the 'Variety Programme and Policy Guide for Writers and Producers'. Among other restrictions this declared: 'Programmes must at all cost be kept free of crudities. There can be no compromise with doubtful material. It must be cut. There is an absolute ban upon the following: jokes about lavatories, effeminacy in men, immorality of any kind, suggestive references to honeymooning couples, chambermaids, fig leaves, ladies' underwear (e.g. winter draws on), animal habits (e.g. rabbits), lodgers, commercial travellers. When in doubt – cut it out.' There were also to be no mentions of drink or religion, the royal family was sacrosanct and while comedians might 'take a crack at the government', this must only be 'without undue acidity'. The term 'working class' was not to be used as a pejorative and there was to be no 'personal abuse' of politicians.

There would be a number of programmes that would benefit from this reform, but none rivalled *That Was The Week That Was* (soon abbreviated to *TW3*), a programme that in its heyday both delighted and appalled viewers in equal measure. For the young and sophisticated it was a blast of fresh air in a still stuffy world, for the self-proclaimed moralists it was the epitome of everything they hated about the BBC in general and its Director-General in particular. As Whitehouse summed it up, it was 'anti-authority, anti-religious, anti-patriotism, pro-dirt and poorly produced'. What was worse it seemed to bask in the approval of the BBC hierarchy and was as such 'impervious to discipline from within or disapproval from without'.[19] It did appear, however, that unlike the majority of the plays, books and programmes she attacked, she had actually watched the show.

TW3 was television's slice of the satire boom that had begun with the huge success in 1961 of *Beyond the Fringe*, an Oxbridge review turned international hit, and of such spinoffs as Peter Cook's Establishment Club and *Private Eye* magazine, founded in 1962 by old school pals Richard Ingrams, Christopher Booker and William Rushton (later joined by Cook as major shareholder). Like the Comic Strip performers of the 1980s, these early Sixties satirists were a tightly knit group, culled from the senior universities and in many cases already veterans of undergraduate revue. (The emergent underground would mock such élitist rebels, but it was surprising how many of the pioneers had been through the same cloister-bound mill.) But while they kept themselves to the clubs and the yellow pages of the early *Private Eye*, their audience remained relatively tiny. As would become more and more the norm, nothing mattered until it received the stamp of television, and when, on 24 November 1962, the BBC aired the first ever *TW3*, satire moved out of the smoky clubs and into the sitting room.

The format was supposedly that of the Berlin cabarets of the Weimar Republic; the tone was that of the Establishment satirists, some of whom were involved. Ned Sherrin, already established at the early evening TV current affairs show *Tonight* ('and the next *Tonight* will be tomorrow night'), and *TW3*'s inventor, was the producer and responsible for rounding up the cast. The core group included Rushton, David Kernan, Roy Kinnear, Kenneth Cope, Lance Percival and *chanteuse* Millicent Martin. To leaven the mix they recruited such figures as journalist Bernard Levin, still in *enfant terrible* mode (he was punched on-screen for his supposed disrespect to the Queen in one *TW3* slot) and the cartoonist Timothy Birdsall whose death that year of leukaemia, aged just twenty-six, robbed the show of one of its most sparkling talents. As a linkman Sherrin opted for John Bird, but he was already due to tour America with a review featuring performers from the Establishment club. Instead he turned to David Frost, seen as something of a hanger-on in the university milieu, but a man who, as his subsequent career would make very clear, was exceptionally attuned to the special demands of television. Frost's links were written by himself and Christopher Booker, who also wrote a couple of sketches in every show. Other contributors included future Labour front-bencher Gerald Kaufman, Keith Waterhouse and Willis Hall (already successful playwrights with *Billy Liar*), Dennis Potter, whose 'Nigel Barton' plays would prove among the most popular of the BBC's 'Wednesday Plays', and Peter Lewis (who would write the commentary for David Bailey's obituary for the Sixties, *Goodbye Baby and Amen*).

That *TW3* proved the huge success it did, came as a surprise, not least to Hugh Greene. Greene had carefully avoided viewing any of the pilots, and when he somewhat nervously watched the first live transmission was able to declare himself 'delighted: the programme sprang fully armed into life – almost every item seemed to be absolutely on the ball, and I thought, really, we have achieved something.'[20] Not only that, but it soon became clear that *TW3* was destined to be one of those programmes that could still unite the country as it settled to watch its favourite broadcasts. 'Those of us most concerned with the launching of *That Was the Week that Was* had thought that it would be a programme likely to appeal to a substantial minority rather than to a national majority audience. We were wrong. Its audience became national in every sense, both in size and in distribution. Women liked it as much as men; the old as much as the young; the provinces as much as London . . . It has been suggested that it matched the national mood of wry dissatisfaction. However that may be, it proved that an intelligent programme of sharp humorous comment on current affairs could hold an audience of many millions. *TW3* became the symbol for the BBC's new look. It was frank, close to life, analytical, impatient of taboos and cant and often very funny.'[21]

It also received a number of complaints. Politicians, especially Conservatives, who as the incumbent government were naturally faced with more criticism than a dormant Opposition, regularly demanded retractions or apologies, but Macmillan himself reportedly found it quite amusing. Harold Wilson also declared himself a fan, though Richard Crossman supposedly promised that, come a Labour government, such disrespect would be forbidden. But the main hostility came not from Parliament, but from Mary Whitehouse and her cohorts. She loathed the show, and never more so than its sketch 'Consumer's Guide to Religions', broadcast on 12 January 1963. Treated to a *Which?* magazine rundown of their various good and bad points, the Church of England was voted 'Best Buy'. Whitehouse, and many others, were not amused.

TW3 lasted for two series, one of 23 weeks, the second of just 14. It came off the air prematurely following the broadcast on 28 December 1963. The official reason was its clashing with the increasing likelihood of an upcoming General Election. The reality was that the BBC's governors were getting worried. The chairman, the liberal Sir Arthur fforde, was in favour of *TW3*, but he had fallen ill, and the more reactionary governors were pushing to have the programme withdrawn. In the end Greene concurred: above all its other duties the BBC was supposed to offer 'balance', and as its Director-General had to accept, 'You can't balance laughter.'[22] In the event there would be no election until the autumn; there would be no more TW3 ever. As Greene remarked wryly, the offence he had caused by permitting the show was equalled only by the opprobrium he earned for canning it. 'It was in my capacity as a subversive anarchist that I yielded to the enormous pressure from my fellow subversives and put *TW3* on the air; and it was as a pillar of the Establishment that I yielded to the fascist hyena-like howls to take it off again.' There would be more 'satire' shows but none of them lasted very long. Times changed, the youthful satirists lost inspiration, the Tory government, so fruitful a target, was overturned. But as Greene pointed out, there was more to satire than short-term deflation of the high and mighty. What it, and a number of other landmark programmes achieved was, as Greene put it,

> to bring out into the open one of the great cleavages in our society. It is of course a cleavage which has always existed: Cavalier versus Roundhead, Sir Toby Belch versus Malvolio, or however you may like to put it. But in these years was added to that the split between those who looked back to a largely imaginary golden age, to the imperial glories of Victorian England and hated the present, and those who accepted the present and found it in many ways more attractive than the past. It was not a split between old and young or between Left and Right or between those who favoured delicacy and those who favoured candour. It was something much more complicated than that, and if one could stand back for a bit as the brickbats flew it provided a fascinating glimpse of the national mood.[23]

Greene's tenure at the BBC lasted throughout the decade, but his authority began to wane in 1967 when Wilson, whose own reputation had never been sacrosanct among the satirists and who had no great affection for the Corporation, appointed Lord Hill, a former 'radio doctor' and Conservative Minister, as Chairman of BBC's governors. His last job had been running independent television, in the main a weakling institution compared to Greene's BBC. By the Director-General's standards Hill was a throwback, a cautious figure who was happy to take Whitehouse seriously and under whom such programmes as *TW3* would have been unthinkable. It is surely pertinent that the big comedy hit of the late Sixties was not satire, but surrealism, as offered by *Monty Python's Flying Circus*, which aired for the first time in 1969. Weird, wacky, utterly wonderful, and the brainchild of some of those post-*TW3* satirists whose efforts had failed properly to ignite, *Monty Python* might tease the *status quo*, but it would never trouble it. In 1963 *TW3*'s eulogy for the assassinated President Kennedy was read into America's Hansard, the Congressional Record; Monty Python's 'dead parrot sketch', mandatory source material for a million anorak-clad mimics, was unlikely to earn the same kudos.

Hugh Greene resigned in 1969. For the censors and moralists of NVALA, it was a victory over which to gloat. But if this was a battle won, the larger victory still went to the departing Director-General. Television, once so comforting and cosy, had entered the new world and would not return to the old. Indeed, if one believed Marshall McLuhan, the media guru of the decade, it was a revolutionary force in itself. Whatever the show might be, it bent to the same rule: unlike the linear, hierarchical culture that was the product of print, offering time for considered, distanced analysis, television's pictures promoted an egalitarian world of immediate sensation. Richard Hoggart and his peers might not like it, but it was the way ahead. As would be true of so many of the changes and reforms that went to make up 'the Sixties', Pandora's box had been opened and what emerged could not be easily shoved back in. And as classicists could point out, what the box contained was not evil, as the moralists might believe, but knowledge.

Chapter Seven

Swinging London: A Box of Pinups

England swings like a pendulum do
Bobbies on bicycles two by two . . .
Roger Miller 'England Swings' (1966)

Amongst the strands that go to make up 'the Sixties' there was more than merely the various brands of 'youth rebellion'. For many people those rebellions were almost irrelevant, an inconvenience when they spilled on to the streets, or a sideshow amusement when they did not. For them the Sixties were 'swinging London'. Decades, of late, have been gifted with their individual myths: in the Forties we stood on the White Cliffs of Dover, gave V-signs to Jerry, and did our bit, a united nation standing alone. In the Fifties we threw off austerity, embraced the concept of never having had it so good, and let ourselves be goaded by the Angry Young Men; in the Sixties, we swung.

It was a period when professions hitherto spurned as highly downmarket – hairdressing in the flamboyant person of Mr 'Teasy-Weasy' Raymond being an epitome – suddenly gained a new cachet. As Bernard Levin put it cattily, such formerly humble figures, once little more than glorified servants, now arbiters of social elegance, 'all jostled not only for money and fame, like other men, but for glory itself – and were not disappointed, their slightest activity being faithfully described in newspapers and magazines, several of the latter existing, on glossy paper, solely for this purpose, and their slightest word being no less faithfully recorded, the words of some of them being slight indeed.'[1] But if these few, plucked from their traditional obscurity, represented the successful, fashionable tip of the otherwise submerged lower or lower-middle-class iceberg, they were very much the exceptions. Perhaps Tom Wolfe was nearer to the truth when he talked of a 'New Boy network', a confection of the various stock 'swinging London' figures – 'young men and women in the commercial crafts, photography, fashion, show business, advertising, journalism'. But with the exception of a few real stars – the photographers David Bailey and Terence Donovan, the Beatles, Terence Stamp and Michael Caine – it was all very middle class, even upper-middle-class. 'There are no working-class boys in the New Boy Network.'[2]

Central to the greater legend that would become the 'swinging Sixties' was its very own creation myth: the fondly held belief that the whole idea was created three thousand miles to the west, in New York's *Time-Life* building. Like most of the myths that accrued to the era, this had a fair percentage of accuracy – it was undoubtedly the best-known journalistic evocation of the period – but while popularising, it did not in fact pioneer. The original piece predated *Time* by almost a year, appearing in the *Daily Telegraph*'s weekend magazine on

26 April 1965. Written by the urbane John Crosby, an American in London, it was headlined 'London, the most exciting city in the world'.

It's all rather wide-eyed, and far from all-encompassing. Despite a claim that 'suddenly, the young own the town', it focused firmly on a small, if highly visible section of those young: the rich, the successful and the well-connected. Two months later, for instance, would come the Albert Hall Poetry Reading, an assemblage of the counter-cultural hip that remains a focal point of the decade: there's not an inkling of that here. Instead Crosby polled such figures as Betty Kenward (the unassailably snobbish 'Jennifer' of *Queen* magazine), who informed him that, 'The young King and Queen of Greece may fly in for a ball and that brings in all those young princesses from Holland or Denmark. Then there are so many international marriages . . . We have charming young Italian wives, charming Spanish wives – and they all bring in their friends from their countries of birth.' He quoted the dicta of a few smart nightclub owners, mainly catering for the children of those same upper-class families who had, thirty years back, been 'Bright Young Things'. There is talent, of course: for instance Mary Quant 'and a bunch of other pretty Chelsea birds' have revolutionised fashion; Julie Christie gets her name-check, as do Bailey and 'Terry' Donovan and Carnaby Street entrepreneur John Stephen, obligatory proles on the make, although when it comes to fashion Crosby is soon out of Carnaby Street and even the King's Road, and heading back to the classier world of Blades, where Rupert Lycett-Green, the very model of a youthful upper-class dandy, set up to dress his peers.

As for the breakdown of the old establishment, Crosby was easily pleased. 'Another case [of youthful rebellion] is Noel Picarda, another Oxonian, who comes from a long line of lawyers. His father and brothers are barristers and they wanted Noel in the law firm, too. But he's in love with show business and he's performing at the Establishment, writing and appearing in sketches at the Poor Millionaire and has started a talent agency.' If, as he suggests, 'the caste system . . . is breaking down at both ends', it's hard to tell it from the piece. That the royals have allegedly become less stuffy – 'Not long ago, Prince Charles and Princess Anne gave a twist and shake party for their young friends at Windsor Castle. Princess Margaret is usually found with actors, writers or painters rather than Guards officers' – is hardly proof positive of a social revolution. And for all the 'explosion of creative vitality' and the 'muscular virility of England's writers and dramatists and actors and artists' such figures remain, as ever, mere walk-ons in England's hierarchical parade. They had, after all, been regularly absorbed, albeit as entertainers, into the upper classes; the process might seem to have paused during the Fifties, but that perhaps was because the 'Angries' had no time for the *jeunesse dorée*. The 'new aristocrats' , on the other hand, were quite happy to pick up tips.

Above all Crosby makes it clear that by swinging he means sexy and by sexy he means 'chicks'. Like some ageing medallion man, leering across a disco floor on which he's no longer young enough to dance, he positively sali-vates over 'a frenzy of the prettiest legs in the whole world belonging to mod-els, au pair girls or just ordinary English girls, a gleam of pure joy on their pretty faces, dancing with the young bloods, the scruffy very hotshot pho-tographers like David Bailey or Terry Donovan, or a new pop singer – all vi-brating with youth.' And in a paragraph that for pure, self-indulgent sexism would not be equalled until Richard Neville reminisced lingeringly in *Play Power* over his 'hurricane fuck' with some gullible fourteen-year-old, Crosby elaborates on 'The girls . . . They're more than pretty; they're young, appre-ciative, sharp-tongued, glowingly alive. Even the sex orgies among the sex-and-pot set in Chelsea and Kensington have youth and eagerness and, in a strange way, a quality of innocence about them. In Rome and Paris, the sex orgies are for the old, the jaded, the disgusting and disgusted. Young English girls take to sex as if it's candy and it's delicious.'

All of which, he concludes, after noting England's emergence from the long 'Dark Ages' of the last thirty years, and the dawning of this new 'swinging' ren-aissance, makes for a new London, 'the gayest, most uninhibited, and – in a wholly new, very modern sense – most wholly elegant city in the world'.

It is easy to mock Crosby's embarrassing enthusiasms, his unalloyed PR for a media myth. Yet the England of 1965 *was* a radically different place from its predecessor of, say, 1960. There was a Labour government; unem-ployment was low, exports high, the touted 'white heat of technological change' cast a morale-boosting glow in which the newly empowered 'young meteors' (as Jonathan Aitken, then a journalist, apostrophised the yuppies of the time) could caper unconstrained. Even the BBC, under Hugh Carleton Greene, was casting aside its Reithian hauteur, and not merely joining, but often hosting the party. Not everyone was in favour of the new society, but the old guard were definitely in retreat.

The myth gained even more power when *Time* magazine, a year behind the *Telegraph*, offered the world, and most particularly America, a vision of this new Britain. *Time*'s piece, published on 15 April 1966, was entitled 'You Can Walk Across It On The Grass' (a phrase that paid tribute to the city's many parks, although some detected a sly reference to the growing popularity of can-nabis), and was announced on the cover as 'London: The Swinging City', a headline that was backed by a collage mixing images of pop music and Pop Art. (Lurking rather less trendily among the minis – skirts and motors – the dollies and the op art T-shirts was the word 'Bingo!' Americans may of course have seen this as a shout of exultation; Britons knew rather better.) Its first sentence, 'In this century, every decade has had its city . . .' set the tone.

Andrea Adam, one of the team who assembled the piece, recalled,

The expression 'swinging London' just came out of the blue. One of the edi-tors used it jokingly. Somebody said, 'Oh hey . . . what about that?' Then it

became a working title . . . and then it was used for the cover. We were all totally riveted by London. London was special, it had a kind of mystique. But
what prompted the bloody cover story was not a fascination with a socio-
cultural phenomenon, it was the fascination among the senior editors for
mini-skirts. There was no more depth of emotion than that. They were a
bunch of the randiest pseudo-intellectuals you could ever have the misfortune to meet. Any opportunity to put legs, tits or bums in the magazine and
they would do it.

We knew that there actually was a phenomenon going on in London
which kind of differed from what was going on in the States and the London
Sixties had this mystique. I don't think we understood it. We felt that the way
in which England had adopted these new mores was based on some kind of
cultural maturity, England after all being an older culture, whereas in the
States it was yet another crazy fling. We felt that it had a legitimacy in London that we were uncertain about in the States. We perceived a kind of classlessness coming from the aristocracy, who were very heavily involved too,
that we found very attractive. We were fascinated. People would come back
from London talking about shops called Granny Takes a Trip and stuff like
that. Amazing, utterly exotic. For us it was where it was at.[3]

The idea that class stratifications had collapsed was central to the myth –
Londoners themselves knew how illusory the concept truly was. But the
myth was so alluring that even the most sophisticated either chose to let it en-
gulf them, or were genuinely seduced. The reality was that the country, London included, was indeed undergoing change, but rather than embrace it
wholeheartedly, there was a good deal of serious ambivalence. The 'baby
boomers' may have reached their teens and early twenties, and *Time* noted
that London boasted more young people than any other part of the country,
but that didn't mean that the change would be smooth. Like the 'Angries' before it, 'Swinging London' was heavily infused with media mythologising.
And like all good stories, why print the often pedestrian truth when the all-
singing, all-dancing legend was so much more exciting? The keywords are all
in place: 'kinky', 'uninhibited', 'new', 'a swinging meritocracy'. A typical interviewee was Peter Hall, then director of the National Theatre, who boasted
that, 'We've got rid of that stuffy middle-aged lot that go to the theatre as a
sop for their prejudices. We're getting a young audience who are looking for
experiences and will take them from the latest pop record or *Hamlet*.' Hall's
Hamlet, David Warner, who had already appeared in the movie *Tom Jones*
and would soon star as *Morgan: a Suitable Case for Treatment* (in their different ways both quintessential 'Swinging London' movies) was credited with
'a Carnaby Street slouch'. The city was seen as a 'sparkling and slapdash
comedy, switched on, a dazzling blur, buzzing, pulsing, spinning'. There
was a map, labelled 'The Scene', stretching from Notting Hill to Soho and
from the BBC in Portland Place to Cheyne Walk. It featured nightclubs, ca-
sinos, boutiques, galleries and theatres and an inset map of the whole coun-

try, notably 'Liverpool: the home of the Beatles' and a huge arrow illustrating the way in which the provinces were pouring into Town.

It was easy for the myth to take hold. Everyone seemed so keen to anoint it with their own enthusiasms. Jonathan Aitken, twenty years on a dedicated Thatcherite, then a bit of a raver, signing the Legalise Cannabis ad in *The Times* and even taking LSD on behalf of his readers, assessed the swinging scene in a series for the *Evening Standard*. Among his interviewees was twenty-eight-year-old Kevin MacDonald, nephew of press magnate Lord Northcliffe and co-owner of Sibylla's – along with the Ad Lib and the Scotch of St James, one of the smarter clubs. Rejecting journalism, he'd done a bit of advertising – 'some people don't understand me at all, and some people think I'm a genius' – before opening Sibylla's.

> I can't communicate with the squares, but when I can communicate with people I travel so fast that I'm flying. This club exists for people who can communicate with each other. A lot of people ring me up and say 'How do you become a member of Sibylla's?' Well, of course, anyone who had to ask how to get into Sibylla's wouldn't be a member. I mean, it's logical . . . This is Psychedelphia man, it's all happening. It's dreamland, and to enjoy it you have to be dreaming. Everyone here's in touch. Sibylla's is the meeting ground for the new aristocracy, and by the new aristocracy I mean the current young meritocracy of style, taste and sensitivity.
>
> We've got everyone here [he clicked his fingers to emphasise the point], the top creative people [click], the top exporters [click], the top artists [click], the top social people [click] and the best of the P.Y.P.s [swingingese for pretty young people]. We're completely classless. We're completely integrated. We dig the spades man. Relationships here go off like firecrackers. Everyone here's got the message [click]. Can you read it man? Sibylla's is the message. We've married up the hairy brigade – that's the East End kids like photographers and artists – with the smooth brigade, the debs, the aristos, the Guards officers. The result is just fantastic. It's the greatest, happiest, most swinging ball of the century, and I started it![4]

Mr MacDonald did not make 29: he killed himself later that year.

For all the endless bray of 'classlessness' this was a highly stratified world. At its pinnacle were the pop gods – the Beatles, the Rolling Stones – and around them a succession of lesser 'swingers', standing in widening circles through to the totally disenfranchised teen masses. Pop stars had always had a certain sway, but the Tommys and Cliffs had not, other than in the blandest of interviews, offered their opinions. Now the rock aristos could lay down the law, sharing airtime with the Establishment. John Crosby may have bracketed these 'swinging' upmarket nightspots with the Marquee ('young kids from the offices'), the Scene ('brings in the Mods'), Ronnie Scott's (home of 'classless' jazz fans) and the Flamingo ('caters to the West Indians') but they were worlds apart. Scott's aside, only the starriest of the young – the 'New

Aristocracy' – could have afforded them; and if Notting Hill's West Indians met the young swingers, it was on the latter's slumming tours to W11, up-market voyeurs, occasionally scoring 'charge'. The Ad Lib, another smart club, might have been fêted as 'classless' in the Sunday supplements, but it was hardly open to all. Classlessness was a convenient badge, like a faux-Cockney ('Mockney') accent, best heard from the remarkable lips of the son of a middle-class PE trainer and himself one-time student at the LSE: Mi-chael Philip Jagger. Ambition rides with pragmatism: if 'classlessness' was the flavour of the current month, then that was the way to go.

A sidebar to this new Jerusalem was the change in status of 'Mod'. The pure commercialism of 'swinging London' meant that 'Mod', once the most specific of descriptions, had long since been diluted almost to invisibility. What had been an English invention had taken on the appearance of its American equivalent. Mod in America had only ever meant 'modern'. It was applied slapdash to anything new and shiny and supposedly 'young'. Beatle boots were 'mod' as were the Beatles; Carnaby Street was definitely mod; Mary Quant was mod, models were mod, as were those who photographed them; even the royal family, or at least the polo-necked Lord Snowdon, were suddenly mod; indeed all the appurtenances of 'swinging London' – chic new restaurants, smart boutiques, trendy nightclubs, 'fab crimpers' like Vidal Sassoon – were mod. Original Mod, on the other hand, was nothing, and those Mods who remained true to the faith started calling themselves 'stylists', a desperate squeak of individuality that went largely un-noticed.

The more one reads these swinging Sixties lions, with their ever-present optimism and their unalloyed delight in their own success, the more one winces. Yet this was the way the times worked and there were plenty who were keen to benefit. The myth fed on itself and in so doing, grew in strength. It was not an era especially prized for its literary output, the main literary form was journalism, whether print or picture; the activist young wrote manifestos rather than fiction. Feature writers tumbled over each other to preach the word; the best were celebrated as 'new journalists' (their pieces as much autobiography as reportage), the rest churned out the usual dross. TV crews, from Japan, Scandinavia, continental Europe and the States, jostled outside the latest 'happening' venue. Symptomatic of the trend were a couple of the books that did come out, both by one of the sym-bols of the era. Each one featured the iconic black-and-white photographs of their creator David Bailey, for many contemporaries the masculine embodi-ment of the period, the Cockney shutterbug on whom Antonioni's *Blow-Up* was at least partially based, the sexual athlete ('David Bailey | Makes love daily' ran the couplet), the Matthew Brady of his particular social upheaval.

The first, *The Box of Pinups* appeared at the height of the boom in 1965. It really was a box, designed by Mark Boxer (first of the colour magazine edi-tors and creator of the satirical comic strip 'Life and Times in NW1', which charted the world – Islington gentrification, Habitat stripped pine – of the media-chic 'Stringalongs') and its aim was to capture the 'ephemeral glamour' of the era 'on the wing'. The pinups – 'the people in England who today seem glamorous' – were typified as 'isolated, invulnerable, lost' (the central adjective somewhat at odds with its bookends). The box held thirty-six captioned pictures, and on the basis of its selection, the 'New Aristocracy' was constituted primarily of two actors, eight pop stars, one pop artist, one interior decorator, four photographers, two pop group managers, one pop star's friend, one hairdresser, two photographer-designers, one ballet dancer, three models, one movie producer, one milliner, one disco manager, one dress designer, one ad man and a pair of villains. These 'lost' boys and girls were a pretty predictable lot: the top two Beatles, Jagger, Jean Shrimpton, Lord Snowdon, Michael Caine, Cecil Beaton, David Hicks, Rudolf Nureyev . . . Its inclusion of the criminal Kray Brothers – double-smart in twin black suiting – gained a good deal of notoriety: 'An East End legend . . .' breathed their caption, 'to be with them is to enter the atmosphere of an early Bogart movie'. Bailey too was an East End boy (the son of an East Ham tailor): respect, presumably, was due. (Reminiscing thirty years on, Bailey claimed, 'I scared them.') Four years later came its obituary edition, *Goodbye Baby and Amen*, burdened with the unfortunate subtitle, 'a saraband for the sixties'. (A saraband is 'a slow and stately Spanish dance in triple time'; in the eighteenth century it had been a regular feature of puppet shows, 'danced by a Moor'.)

The show business journalist Peter Evans ('young, strictly in vogue, very much in touch, but far removed from the herd' according to *his* profile) saw Bailey 'using his camera . . . to probe the shadows, expose the lie and fix forever the transient truth'. Hardly. If that was what you wanted, then his contemporary Don McCullin, the best-known newspaper photographer of the period, was a better bet. Bailey was the biggest myth-maker of the lot, but Evans is right to suggest that he 'caught the face of his own generation more accurately than any photographer'. Bernard Levin saw him as 'Virgil'[5] recording the period for posterity and in so doing establishing just who was in or out within that society:

> photographers . . . along with the models they photographed, the designers whose clothes the models wore, the singers whose records they played on their gramophones, the managers of the models, the gigolos, the younger sons of the nerveless aristocracy among whom they moved, the hangers-on of all these, and the vast penumbra of pimps and agents and tenpercenters, whores and pedlars and actors, film-makers and playwrights and decorators, all the froth and scum that, together with the chunks of real meat, bubbled and seethed in the stew of a society that was in the process of changing from what it no longer wanted to be into what it did not know whether it wanted to be or not.[6]

Of all of these the most iconic, treasured and lusted after for her youth
and (apparently) free-wheeling sexuality, was the 'swinging dolly bird'. The
dolly was not strictly a Sixties invention – the term had meant a slattern in
the eighteen and nineteenth centuries (the extended 'dollymop' had defined
an enthusiastic amateur tart), while it had referred to a pretty young girl since
the very early twentieth – but the Sixties gave it unparalleled popularity. The
ur-dolly was probably the contemporary supermodel Jean Shrimpton; her
infinity of clones would sport the same long straight hair (often ironed to im-
maculate flatness), the same long legs and tiny skirts. But unlike her predecessors in the Fififties, who had flaunted their hauteur and defied even the
richest to ape their arrogant posing, the essence of Shrimpton's look, like
Mary Quant's clothes, was its accessibility. You too could be a dolly bird, and
just as swinging (if only in your provincial fantasies) as 'the Shrimp' herself.
Linda Grant noted the dolly's role: 'Topless dresses, mini-skirts, hipster
trousers, edible knickers, seethrough blouses, nudity on stage, streakers, the
word "fuck" first heard on British television – all the ephemeral images of
Swinging London said that Britain had abandoned conventional morality
and replaced it with the most frivolous forms of hedonism. The culture of
fun cohered in the single icon of the dolly-bird. She symbolised everything
that was new, liberated, daring, sexually abandoned, independent and free.'[7]
Yet while she was presented as this paragon of new sexuality, popping her
pill, flaunting her nubile thighs, dropping her edible knickers, there was a
strange ambivalence. Her little mini-dresses, her round-toed shoes reminiscent of Fifties' schoolgirls, her obviously exaggeratedly painted lower eye-
lashes, her white lips (these last two creating a literally 'doll-like' or baby
face) all presented an image that while sexual, seemed at times to be geared to
the paedophiles. It was a soft sexuality, a passive acquiescence a million miles
removed from the mini-skirt's return in the late 1980s as a symbol of empow-
erment, not surrender.

She was also the creation of Mary Quant, as iconic a figure as a whole
disco-full of dollies. If Bailey committed them to posterity, then Quant had
already dressed them up for the experience. At first Quant was more Chelsea
set than swinging Sixties – her husband Alexander Plunket-Greene had gar-
nered a reputation as an upper-class iconoclast, earning for instance a small notoriety for appearing at Quaglino's (then somewhat faded from its Thirties'
heyday, rather than today's Conran makeover) in a suit, but no shirt, with
nothing but a row of buttons painted on his naked chest and stomach. She
opened Bazaar, her King's Road shop in 1955. (He ran Alexander's, a restaurant, in the basement.) In a world where 'design' was very much the province
of the rich and middle-aged, Quant had begun catering, if not to the mass-
market, then certainly to the daughters of these same well-dressed women.
She began wholesaling her designs in 1961 and two years later moved into the
mass-market. She based her 'look' on the kind of thing art students – she'd

been one herself, at Goldsmith's — were wearing. Like so many pioneers Quant began because she found herself unable to find something she wanted for herself, in her case 'absolutely twentieth century clothes'. Bazaar was a tiny shop, and the clothes that Quant designed and sold were tiny too, most obviously the mini-skirt, but also the clinging 'skinny-rib' sweater that accompanied it. As one King's Road resident recalled, the Quant woman, cat-walking her way up and down the King's Road, wore 'big floppy hats, skinny ribbed sweaters, key-hole dresses, wide hipster belts and . . . paper knickers. They had white lipsticked lips and thick black eyeliner, hair cut at alarming angles, op-art earrings and ankle-length white boots. They wore citron-coloured trouser suits and skirts that seemed daily shorter.'[8]

For the first time since post-war austerity plunged the country into monochrome conformity, England abandoned grey. What Quant did, in symmetry with fellow pioneers such as Terence Conran, whose first Habitat opened in adjacent Fulham Road in 1964 (selling furnishings to those same girls, now ensconced in student flats or if newly married, in their first homes in newly 'gentrified' Islington, Fulham or Notting Hill), was not only to start laying out the focal points of a typical Sixties' lifestyle, but also to change the geography of Bohemia. Fitzrovia was Forties, Soho Fifties, now Chelsea (with outposts in Notting Hill) became the contemporary equivalent.

In Quant one also sees another link, between the old Chelsea Set and what would be christened the Beautiful People or 'New Aristocracy' (well-fortified by large numbers of the old one), the sexiest, the most photogenic, the most 'happening' group around. The Chelsea Set, who could be catego-rised loosely as the older brothers and sisters of the BPs, represented a direct line that stretched back to the Bright Young Things of the Twenties: hedon-istic, rich (or due to be when inheritance or a 'good' marriage came around), apolitical, cheerfully convinced that pleasure, usually in the form of a good party, was the ultimate in human ambition. Gossip columns were courted; the middle classes offered up frissons of envious horror. MacInnes captured the female version in his fictional 'ex-Deb-of-Last-Year', sashaying blithely through the Notting Dale riots, reviling the racists as scum and dying 'to have a dance with someone African. They're the best dancers in the world!'[9] Unlike their Twenties' predecessors, the Chelsea Set were not always quite so rich, and often had to work, albeit in some 'amusing' occupation. While such amusements were usually advertising or perhaps work as an assistant director in the movies, there were also less respectable outlets: running dodgy games of 'chemmy', a little money laundering, some dope smuggling on the side. Robin Cook's novel *The Crust on Its Uppers* (1962) with its 'knoc-king morries' and 'slag punters', as central a work as MacInnes's teenage celebration, is the best guide.

On this basis Plunkett-Greene's restaurant and his wife's boutique were typical. In fact, as George Melly noted, 'it was a very Chelsea Set thing to do'.[10] Quant's skills, of course, were the exception. 'Bazaar was a banner, a battlecry, a symbol of the new sophistication, and above all news.'[11] Beyond that, and with greater long-term impact, Quant did for fashion what other of her peers would do for other areas of life: she exploded the old ways, casually dismissing a world in which 'fashion' was French (and *de facto* slightly suspect) and no one, other than gay men and 'working' girls, dared wear clothes that proclaimed just what they were. Quant created the 'dolly bird' in her own image and with her the whole apparatus. 'For good or ill the embryonic concept of "swinging London" was conceived in that small, disorganised shop in the King's Rd.'[12]

Deliberately or otherwise, the dolly (and her male cohorts) emphasised the increasing division between the generations. The *Guardian* agonised over the situation, noting that: 'the real point about very short skirts, white lace stockings and pantomime boots is that they separate the girls from the women.' Older versions of 'teenage' fashions had still been accessible for the over-twenty-fives; now that was over. The new designs – 'a dress with a black circle and dot directly over the stomach, with holes fretted Henry Moore-like in the most improbable places' – were right off-limits. The writer had no doubts what it all meant: 'Here was the first, final unanswerable way of proclaiming "I am young. Therefore I am different. I am special." ' Wearing such clothes stated one's membership of a closed group, whose membership extended only to the young. This was not a pretty prospect; indeed, it was 'a trend that must be defeated'. The writer suggested heavy taxes on teenage incomes, or perhaps the vote at eighteen. And concluded in a self-defeating paragraph that served only to underline his implicit lack of understanding: 'One thing is clear enough: mankind is already divided enough without perpetuating yet another schism that has no basis in history, or reason, or morality.'[13] One can still hear a youthful reader laughing.

It was not just the generation gap; Quant's clothes carried a heavy charge of sexual liberation. The mini-skirt, the fashion for legs over breasts (symbols of a motherhood that was no longer *de rigueur* once the contraceptive pill had become available), made it clear that clothes at least opted for greater sexuality. And the dolly, after all, was supposed to love it. Quant, whose husband would famously shave her pubic hair into a heart shape, exciting much ribaldry, had no doubts. Interviewed in 1967[14] she was convinced that the erogenous zone of the Sixties was 'the crutch. This is a very balanced generation and the crutch is the most natural erogenous zone. Clothes are designed to lead the eye to it. The way girls model clothes, the way they sit, sprawl or stand is all doing the same thing. It's not "come hither" but it's provocative. She's standing there defiantly with her legs apart saying, "I'm very sexy. I enjoy sex, I feel provocative, but you're going to have a job to get me. You've got to excite me and you've got to be jolly marvellous to attract me. I can't be bought, but if I want you, I'll have you." '

However, while Quant may have seen her clothes as sexy and provocative, the deliberate auto-infantilism, the refusal to 'grow up like one's parents', was quite conscious. Quant herself made clear her dread of 'looking like [my] mother'.[15] Growing up was no longer something to be looked forward to; rather it was to be postponed as long as possible. The mini-skirt, with its overtones of a little girl's pinafore, was designed to help girls stay exactly that: girls – and not women. The *Guardian* may have deplored it, the girls in question did not. Conversely, there was also a political side. The Second World War, like its predecessor, had liberated women, showing that they could do virtually any job that had hitherto been seen as a male preserve. Dior's New Look of the late 1940s had ostensibly returned women to 'femininity' and proclaimed an end to drab austerity, but in its yards of costly material, its corsets and swaying skirts, it also sent women back to a more traditional role. Now Quant and her peers were pushing for freedom once more. Fashion, once a badge of maturity, had reversed direction. Led by Quant it fêted immaturity, endless youth. As the decade proceeded this moved into pure dressing up – boys as toy soldiers, girls as fairy princesses: the upper-class nursery laid out for all to enjoy. Political change, the logical extension, would be a little longer in arriving.

Like her sexy role-model dollies, not everyone could 'have' Quant either. Bazaar was no bargain basement. But a little later, and a little further down the market, came Biba, the creation of Barbara Hulanicki and her husband, which opened in Abingdon Road, off High Street Kensington, before moving to Kensington Church Street (and thence, come the 1970s, to the High Street itself). Biba serviced those who saw themselves as peers of *uber*-dolly Cathy McGowan, presenter of Rediffusion TV's rock showcase *Ready, Steady, Go!* – straight hair, long fringe, those over-made-up eyes, the thinner the better. She offered shift-like dresses made from upholstery fabrics and large hats filled with holes. Once established on Church Street, she began pushing for the 'total look'. Alexandra Pringle, already a Quant fan, 'tried on clothes for the sinister and *louche*: slithery gowns in glowing satins, hats with black veils, shoes stacked for sirens . . . for real life there were raincoats to sweep the London pavements, tee-shirts the colour of old maids' hats, dusky suede boots with long zippers.'[16] Sludgy colours were especially popular. Later, in a succession of ever larger shops, would come home furnishings, makeup and other accessories; even later, after a final burst of over-extended hubris in which Biba took over that symbol of Kensington conservatism, Derry and Toms, food and drink.

Quant and Hulanicki were not alone. Aside from the mass-market outlets of Carnaby Street (and the increasingly common 'boutique' sections of otherwise traditional stores) the well-heeled dolly could take her choice from a variety of smart outlets. Of these the most celebrated was Quorum, creation of two northerners – Ossie Clark and his wife textile designer Celia Birtwell (best-known today from their portraits by another northern star, David Hockney – he and Clark had been at the RCA together) and their partner Alice Pollock. Clark, whose appearance moved a young Derek Jarman to note that 'Decadence . . . was the first sign of intelligence', was haute couturier to the swinging élite. He dressed models like Twiggy and Shrimpton, as well as such high-profile figures as Marianne Faithfull, Mick and Bianca Jagger, Jimi Hendrix and the then 'Mrs George Harrison' – Patti Boyd. Sadly, like so many of his peers the self-proclaimed 'master-cutter' lacked the slightest business sense and his career epitomised that cliché 'meteoric'. Talent, as an obituarist noted, was not enough and Clark, whose success had burned so very brightly, crashed out in the late 1970s amidst a welter of debts and drugs. When he was finally declared bankrupt, in 1981, he owed more than £200,000. Clark, who, for all his marriage and the two sons it produced, had always been candidly gay, died in 1996 aged 54, murdered by his live-in lover.

The dolly's boyfriend was equally well indulged. At the bottom end of the market was Carnaby Street, at the top Blades. Between were a variety of male 'boutiques': aristo Michael Rainey's Hung on You in Cale Street, Chelsea; John Crittall's Dandie Fashions on the King's Road, poster-artist Nigel Waymouth's Granny Takes a Trip at the World's End, Mr Fish (owned by ex-Savile Row salesman Michael Fish), I Was Lord Kitchener's Valet (on Portobello Road) with its selection of military jackets, Emmerton and Lambert's stall in the Chelsea Antique Market, selling 'sailor trousers' (precursors of 'loons') and crushed velvets. Boots came from the Chelsea Cobbler or showbiz specialists Anello and Davide, shirts from Deborah and Claire. Marginally less exotic was Just Men, just off the King's Road; and for the masses there was the chain of Take Six branches.

Of all such shops 'Granny's' was the exemplar. It was élitist, expensive, a shop in which the customer, far from being 'always right', was often made to feel somewhat less acceptable than those who ostensibly 'served' him or her. It was founded by Nigel Waymouth, girlfriend Shelagh York and John Pearce (who now runs a tailoring business in Soho).

> We used to go down to Church Street Market and Portobello Road, collecting these old clothes, and we thought that it might be a good idea to open a shop with all these things. I got the name when one night I sat down and I thought, well, Granny clothes, acid trips, it's obvious: Granny Takes a Trip, that's funny, let's do it. We used to change the windows every three months. We had black windows, a car coming out (that was about eighteen months after we started) . . . we did everything. The whole point was just to keep it change, change, change. We used to stay up all night and do it so that people would wake up the next day and it would be a different shopfront. We started off exclusively with old clothes: rather nice beaded dresses, blazers, all that sort of camp nonsense. That was fun.

Then we decided that we'd design our own clothes. It seemed fairly easy to do, but of course once we did that I began to lose interest in the manufacture of clothes, the rag trade. I lost interest in playing shops. I sold the shop to some Americans in late '69. It was part of this dressing up thing. Granny's and Dandie Fashions and Hung On You were the new alternative, we were definitely not Carnaby Street. I knew nothing about retailing or the clothes trade, nothing at all. We really did pioneer the idea of disposable clothes that you only wore for a while. People would come back and complain sometimes, but it was all part of the ethos of the new dressing up: not taking it quite so seriously. Of course it was terribly vain . . .[17]

Too vain, some would say. The critic Jonathan Meades, then at RADA, recalled visiting in search of a friend. 'I went down there to see him, and this was the first time I realised this extreme snobbery based on clothes, speech mannerisms and not so much vocabulary but lack of vocabulary. It was all extremely excluding. I dressed then very much as I do now [black suit and tie], and I certainly didn't have the hippie gear or the long hair. I remember Nigel Waymouth sneering at me – you could hardly see his face through this mass of Afro hair and this huge collar that came up to here and down to there and what the Americans call a "Windsor scarf". He obviously thought I was a jerk and I thought he was rather a jerk. I'd gone in to see my friend and Waymouth wanted me moved out of the way, because I was an extremely bad advertisement for his shop.'[18]

Meades should, perhaps, have known better. The hippies might offer an alternative posture, but for swinging London equality was never the point. Marianne Faithfull, a star in her own right, the girlfriend of Rolling Stone Mick Jagger, and a beauty whose looks, while conforming to the pattern, set her aside from any mere 'dolly', recalled a day in her life.

Everywhere I look there's some insane distraction; Bengalis selling scarves with magic signs on them, two buskers in Elizabethan rags playing hurdy-gurdies and tiny drums, a couple of hustlers selling knock-offs of those big plastic Biba bracelets. God, will you look at David Bailey with that little tart on his arm! Harrods looming up like a great liner, Walton Street with dozens of seductive boutiques. Shop windows filled with bright Smartie colours. Miniskirts, sequinned gowns, slinky thigh-high boots, brass earrings . . . Christ, better just duck in here and try on that velvet-and-pearl outfit. *Ready, Steady, Go!* tomorrow. Can't exactly be seen in this frumpy thing.

Courtfield Road . . . a veritable witches' coven of decadent illuminati, rock princelings and hip aristos . . . Peeling paint, clothes, newspapers and magazines strewn everywhere. A grotesque little stuffed goat standing on an amp, two huge tulle sunflowers, a Moroccan tambourine, lamps draped with scarves, a pictographic painting of demons (Brian's?) and decorously draped over a tatty armchair, a legendary leg, Robert Fraser's, I should guess. There's Brian [Jones] in his finest Plantagenet satins, fixing us with vacant, fishy eyes. On the battered couch, an artfully reclining Keith [Richard] is

perfecting his gorgeous slouch. The hand gesturing in the manner of Veron-
ese could only belong to the exquisite Christopher Gibbs, and hovering over
the entire scene with single-lens-reflex-eye the invisibly ever-present photographer, Michael Cooper . . . A dissolute 'Night Watch' of mid-sixties
Swinging London. Hipness, decadence and exquisite tailoring such as England had not seen since the Restoration of Charles II. We were young, rich
and beautiful, and the tide was turning in our favour. We were going to
change everything, of course, but mostly we were going to change the rules.
Unlike our parents, we would never have to renounce our youthful hedonism
in favour of the insane world of adulthood.[19]

Nowhere was the crossover between new and old aristos so visible as in
the Rolling Stones. The Beatles, still marshalled by Brian Epstein, may have
been emerging from the old pop style in private, but their public image had
yet to catch up. The Stones on the other hand, pushed ever further by their
manager Andrew Loog Oldham, had no such reticence. What you saw was
what you got – and everyone wanted it, from the children of the nation's
grandees downwards. They wore the clothes, walked the walk and talked the
talk. They, and few others, could outface the BPs. And for Jagger, if not the
others, the old aristos were equally alluring. According to Anita Pallenberg,
who shared the Courtfield Road flat with Brian Jones, it was the happiest of
situations: Jagger 'pretty quickly realised that those people all had something
that the Stones wanted, and the Stones had what all these kind of decadent
aristocrats wanted . . . so it was very compatible . . . and quite exciting really,
and very nice too.'[20] A mutual admiration society run riot: youth, beauty and
wealth, calling to each other across the class divide. Gradually the Stones
moved into a world that transcended the narrow confines of rock. Young
aristos such as Jane Rainey or Tara Browne (the Guinness heir who as John
Lennon would put it, 'blew his mind out in a car'), fashionable names like the
society photographer Cecil Beaton, art gallery owner Robert Fraser, antique
dealer Christopher Gibbs and designer David Mlinaric as well as more
louche figures, joined the cavalcade. But the Stones produced music too:
'19th Nervous Breakdown' a 1966 single, mocks the foolish deb who's 'seen
too much in too few years', while *Aftermath*, their album of the same year, is
pure, refined 'swinging London', with its sharp disdain for those who failed
the grade, whether through drugs that were less fashionable ('Mother's
Little Helper') or aspirations that could never quite maintain the pace
('Under My Thumb' and 'Play With Fire'). The word was overused, but
looking at Michael Cooper's pictures of the band, garbed in rich fancy dress,
surrounded by girls, high on pharmaceuticals, even, occasionally, playing
and singing, it is impossible not to think 'decadence'.
    But this was an élite, and there were many more voyeurs than participants.
Most were on the outside, gazing avidly in. The media were more than keen
to oblige. The *Sunday Times*, once a poor relation, had been taken over from

the Kemsley press by the Canadian Roy (later Lord) Thomson and soon began overhauling the *Observer* as the weekend's smartest liberal broadsheet. A
colour supplement, Britain's first, was launched in 1962. Its first feature offered 'A sharp glance at the mood of Britain' and a new James Bond story
from Ian Fleming. The cover featured a girl in a grey flannel dress: the pictures were taken by Bailey, the girl was Shrimpton and the dress designer
Quant. It also offered profiles of 'People of the 60s' – among them Quant
(again), her husband, painter Peter Blake, a footballer, a youthful industrial-
ist and an LSE sociologist. There was, presumably as a sop to the sticks, a
photographic portrait of the city of Lincoln, hitherto notable for its cathedral, now, apparently, a centre of vibrant culture. The magazine also asked
the question 'What do you need to be of the Sixties?' Its answer: be 'under 30'
and 'in tune with your times'. Just two years into its progress, the decade was
already embarked on building its myth.

Long before the phrase was coined, for the glossy youth magazines of the
Eighties, the *Sunday Times* supplement provided a 'style bible' for the aspirant. Philip Norman, a star of the paper, summed up the colour supplement's
appeal in his semi-autobiographical novel *Everyone's Gone to the Moon*
(1995). His alter ego 'Louis Brennan', still trapped in the provinces knocking
out obits and court reports, views the London paper with 'longing and frustration'. From an uninspired wallflower, the *Sunday Times* had blossomed
marvellously, re-created as an unrivalled 'mirror and chronicler of suddenly
stylish, affluent, double cream-gorging, "swinging" Britain. Whether one
sought enlightenment on the economic future of Ecuador, the potential of a
new cabinet minister, the direction of Parisian couture, the filming of the latest James Bond story, the durability of a French copper cooking pot, the
most pristine shade of white emulsion paint, the authentication and true nature of any of the thousand-and-one new "trends" which materialised each
week, there was only one possible authority.'[21]

Not everyone was so impressed. Bernard Levin saw the supplements as
'the nadir in the advocacy of conspicuous consumption' and saw such features as the *Sunday Times*'s 'Look' pages and the *Observer*'s similarly targeted 'Ego' as dedicated to the 'purchase of ephemeral rubbish . . . enough to
turn the stomach of the most materialist of their readers'. The description, in
an *Observer* colour magazine piece, of the Florentine ruler Lorenzo de Me-
dici as the 'inspiration of the affluent society' seemed to him the very ghastli-
est of such absurdity.[22]

Thirty years on, if one wants to wander down those swinging streets once
more, the best transport is possibly via Michelangelo Antonioni's contemporary film *Blow-Up* (1966). *Blow-Up* was not the only film to emerge from the
era: there was *Alfie* (Michael Caine as, in every sense, an 'old lad'), a variety
of spy thrillers ranging from the Bond canon (Sean Connery mode) to *Modesty Blaise* (a self-consciously camp send-up with Dirk Bogarde and Monica

Vitti, Antonioni's partner); there was *Darling* (1965), for many fans Julie Christie's apogee and a very successful movie, but that was basically a traditional morality tale – 'celebrity' ain't what it's cracked up to be – and the 'swinging' background was just that – background.

For the critics *Blow-Up* is not seen as a major work in Antonioni's oeuvre. Pauline Kael, in *5001 Nights at the Movies* (1982) for instance, dismisses it as a 'mixture of suspense with vagueness and confusion [which] seemed to have a numbing fascination for some people which they equated with art and intellectuality'. For Horace Ové, a film-maker himself, '*Blow-Up* made an attempt, but it didn't capture what was the mind of the Sixties people. [It] was an interesting movie, and people judge a certain part of the Sixties by it, but when it came out real Sixties people thought it was crap. Antonioni didn't know much about it.'[23]

Blow-Up, like its immediate successor, the California-set *Zabriskie Point* (a true failure to grasp the ethos of America's late 1960s radical spirit), came about as a result of Antonioni being invited to make two English-language movies. He chose as a source the exiled Argentinian writer Julio Cortazar's short story 'Las babas del Diablo' (1959, 'The Devil's Spittle'). Set in Paris it describes an amateur photographer whose roving lens captures a middle-aged woman and a young man, caught up in what seems a highly emotional conversation. A further watcher, an elderly man sitting in a car, appears to speak to the woman. The story focuses on the photographer's personal assessment of what he has seen and shot. To him the trio represent a pimp (the woman), a hustler (the boy) and a client (the older man). He then takes on the task, for his own amusement, of 'casting' and 'directing' what he sees as a single frame of what might be a full-length film. Its more immediate genesis, according to Gore Vidal[24] stemmed from Antonioni's own immersion in swinging London – bear-led by *Sunday Times* journalist Francis Wyndham (Bailey's caption-writer for the *Box of Pinups*) – during which he attended a party thrown by critic Kenneth Tynan, celebrating alongside such stars as Vidal and Marlon Brando, that day's general election (a Labour victory).

Transported to London by Antonioni, the story gained certain twists, the most obvious being the replacement of the amateur lensman by a professional, one of that iconic breed symbolised in the work and life of David Bailey. The Parisian *quai* on which Cortazar's action took place was replaced by South London's Maryon Park, which Antonioni had dressed – its grass, for instance, was painted a greener green – so as, it was claimed, to look more like itself. For his star he chose David Hemmings and to support him Vanessa Redgrave, Sarah Miles, Jane Birkin, the lanky model Veruschka and Peter Bowles. The English dialogue was by playwright Edward Bond whose play *Saved* would, two years hence, finally topple the 300 year-old system of censorship maintained by Britain's Lord Chamberlain.

For critics and *cinéastes* the key scenes were those in which Hemmings starts blowing up his negatives and discovers, or so he believes, that his pictures of a couple talking animatedly in a park in fact conceal a murder. For the general viewer Hemmings's frolic with a couple of teenage models ('a mini-orgy', noted Kael) provided greater excitement, as did Antonioni's travelogue of swinging London, taking in the Yardbirds, a 'spike' that wouldn't have surprised Orwell, and various episodes on a modern rake's progress, including what Kael dismissed as 'a pot party', the filming of which was an essay in Antonioni's subject matter. Then Oxford undergraduate Kieran Fogarty was summoned by a friend.

> I was flung into this bedroom in Cheyne Walk, hair parted, purple shirt with paisley motifs, black knitted Jaeger tie, square ended, black jacket. Plonked on the front of this bed with about another nine people on it and Antonioni tossed a couple of kilo bags of grass on the bed and said, 'Right, get on with it.' It took five days. It just went on and on. Nobody wanted to stop. Indeed they weren't to be stopped, no way. Meanwhile catering batted out more steaks, the wet bar off-loaded case after case of wine and scotch and anything else we could think of and the cameras just kept rolling. And it all ended up as about thirty seconds.
>
> It was a great party. Veruschka, the model, who was not actually being filmed, was at one point lying on the bed and getting very stoned. Because I was the nearest person to her . . . she got me to cover for her while she went off to Paris to fuck somebody. And she kept ringing up at four hourly intervals and the phone would ring and I'd pick it up – I was still in the same place, on this bed, and it would be Veruschka: 'Tell Michelangelo that my taxi crash . . .' This very surreal comment, and you'd say, 'Oh, it's Veruschka, her taxi's crashed, be here in five or six hours.' Most of swinging London was there, every deb that was halfway decent looking, and wild they were too. Outrageously dressed, superheavy makeup . . .[25]

As an essay in moralism – if indeed that was its director's intention – *Blow-Up* failed. Like many morality tales, the attempt to portray glamorous vice as wicked, diminishes the vice and upgrades the glamour. Few contemporary young men, for instance, watching Hemmings strip his giggling nymphets before plunging with them into a riot of backdrop paper, would have thought, 'This is the last thing I'd want to get mixed up in.' On the contrary, the ranks of aspirant photographers ballooned. The 'pot party', replete with beautiful people in a beautiful setting, hardly seemed the gateway to hell. Out in the sticks, *Blow-Up was* Swinging London – and didn't it look good.

Viewed from the past one can see Swinging London as a mass delusion, a world of endlessly self-aggrandising mythologies, each feeding off the next and replenishing the last. For Brenda Polan, writing twenty-five years on, it was 'the first example of the instant media myth, a combination of a new pop-sociology and that old propagandist's favourite, the big lie based on a small truth'.[26] The relentless intonation of 'young' or 'new' becomes increasingly irritating, even absurd. Reading the eulogistic reception offered the new Tory leader Edward Heath, by all acounts the vibrant, grammar-school educated new broom who would sweep away the stale fuddy-duddyness of traditional Conservatism, is to see the essential silliness. One might, carried away by superlatives, eulogise a rock star, model or restaurateur; to brand Heath, whose parliamentary career extended well back into the Fifties, as some kind of political equivalent was ludicrous. Yet even good writers seemed incapable of keeping their heads, so pervasive was the gospel. Did Heath appreciate, asked one of the best, Nicholas Tomalin, that he was the first Tory leader to boast that badge of modernity, wall-to-wall carpeting? It was not even as if the 'swinging' was universal. The best-selling single of 1966 came not from the Beatles or Stones, but from the mawkish American country singer Jim Reeves. Other chart-toppers that year included Northern comedian Ken Dodd and Cliff Richard, once a pop star but now locked religiously into 'family entertainment'. The masses might pay lip-service, but their real tastes remained predictable and grimly banal.

Yet if the numbers of 'swingers' were relatively small – and after all that's the way they wanted it – their influence was much greater. London, it seemed, had taken on the role traditionally ascribed to Paris: Sin City. The French *haute bourgeoisie*, for instance, took to sending their children to Ireland for their English lessons; London offered too many pitfalls. The wider world may never have been able, or invited, to join in, but the optimism, the excitement, the undeniable change in the way Britain saw itself, that all filtered through and had its long-term influence.

Swinging London lasted perhaps two years. Élitist, style-obsessed, hedonistic and apolitical, it was not destined to survive. The image, of course, has never gone. In 1996, carefully orchestrated by a London PR, the American magazine *Newsweek*, determined even after thirty years to catch up with its rival *Time*, launched its 'London Rules' issue, promising to take its readers 'inside the world's coolest city'. Two years on, a newly elected Labour government boosted 'Cool Britannia'. Now as then the trend-setters were unimpressed. Indeed, it was all rather embarrassing, more like Harold Wilson's pitiable 'I'm Backing Britain' campaign than anything remotely chic. The tourists, on the other hand, loved it.

Chapter Eight

Pop (Art): Young Contemporaries

There was this whole new thing going on. It was primary colours, it was hard-edge, it was crisp. It was 'Ready Steady Go', it was targets, chevrons, bright colours, crisp hard edges. There were fantastic art exhibitions in London. The '54-64' exhibition at the Tate had a whole room full of American pop art: Rauschenberg, Jasper Johns, targets and flags, what have you. Then you'd drift off to see the Who and you'd put two and two together. There seemed to be a direct line between what was on at the Tate gallery and what was on at the Marquee.
Pearce Marchbank[1]

In his study of Sixties' culture, *Revolt into Style*, George Melly noted that, 'If pop music is the centre of the working-class and more important wing of pop culture, pop painting seems to occupy the same position in relation to the intellectual development of the movement.'[2] And if pop informed many of the changes in the mass world, then pop art has to be recognised as a major impulse in the more cerebral assessments. The genesis of what came to be called 'pop art' is still debatable – and as Melly points out there were 'pop artists' who emerged before the term had ever been coined, just as there would be those who came later who claimed, all appearances notwithstanding, that their own development had in no way been influenced by the movement. But it can be taken as fact that sometime during the early 1950s the phrase entered common currency (at least in artistic circles).

The first sign of pop art in Britain came with the Independent Group, formed in 1952 by the critics Lawrence Alloway and John McHale, the architectural writer Reyner Banham, architects Alison and Peter Smithson and such artists as Eduardo Paolozzi and Richard Hamilton. Their initial fascination was with what Mario Amaya (in his book *Pop as Art*) termed 'the paradox of the creative individual in a mass-think society', but their focus moved from the generalised phenomenon of mass culture, to what could be seen as its most obvious manifestation, when in 1955 McHale returned from a trip to America bearing a collection of mass circulation magazines. Thereupon the group began looking at the culture those magazines reflected, the 'American dream', and incorporating it into aspects of their work. It was a move that more than coincidentally paralleled the arrival of the other sort of 'pop', rock 'n' roll music, on British shores. But while pop music went straight to the heart and the groin, pop art began in the head. As the art critic Robert Hughes has pointed out, they found 'the landscape of commercial America, that vast rain forest of signs and commercial messages . . . deeply intriguing. They saw the gross sign language of American cities with the kind of distant longing Gauguin felt for Tahiti – a mythical world of innocent plenty, far from the austerities of a victorious but pinched England . . . '[3] They also recognised what the young pop fans both knew instinctively, and made clear in their cultural tastes, that the old artistic standards had moved on: the 'canon' of high culture remained, but what mattered were new media: the movies, advertising, pop records and above all television.

The first reification of such knowledge came in 1956 when the Independents put on their exhibition 'This Is Tomorrow' at the Institute of Contemporary Arts (then in Dover Street). The 'star of the show' (or so it has come to be recognised) was Richard Hamilton's collage 'Just What Is It That Makes Today's Homes So Different, So Appealing?' It featured the very first appearance of the actual word 'Pop' in art: it is emblazoned on an unmistakably phallic lollipop protruding from the groin of a cut-out posing muscleman (the same lollipop would also appear, apparently coincidentally in an Eduardo Paolozzi collage). Other images, crowded into the picture, make up a virtual rollcall of what would be seen as definitive pop style: 'the framed *Young Romance* comic on the wall (Lichtenstein), the packaged ham on the table (Rosenquist), the TV set, brands like the Ford logo on the table lamp, the movie theatre with its cut-off kneeling Al Jolson billboard visible through the window, the brand-new vacuum cleaner and tape recorder, the harsh motel bed with its premonition of Oldenberg's zebra-striped motel suite of the sixties, and the Health and Beauty couple displaying their lats, pects [sic] and tits as Product.'[4]

The Independent Group's real significance was not so much its art but its happy embrace of America. Indeed even Hamilton, his ground-breaking collage aside, was not really producing 'pop art'. He was using the artefacts and symbols of mass culture, but still in an essentially traditional manner. This changed with the advent of two new names, Richard Smith and Peter Blake, students at the RCA when Hamilton, who had moved down from Newcastle, and Paolozzi were teaching at the college. Smith, who visited America, began creating works that reflected commercial packaging, while Blake, who had chosen Europe in his search for popular culture, began putting together 'paintings' that appeared to have been assembled from the contents of one of the 'camp' antique shops that would soon be luring visitors to an old West London market, Portobello Road. Even more important, and for some the 'true' birth of British pop – this certainly was the belief underpinning the Royal Academy's major restrospective of 1991 – was the Young Contemporaries show of February 1961, featuring the work of yet another generation: R. B. Kitaj, Peter Phillips, Patrick Caulfield, Derek Boshier, David Hockney and Allen Jones. Lawrence Alloway was on the selection committee; the name appositely combined two of the most currently popular adjectives. This group, celebrated in Ken Russell's 1962 television piece 'Pop Goes the Easel' took pop out of the still rarefied world of the Independent Group and introduced it to a wider, non-artistic audience.

It was swiftly assimilated, after due filtering through the media, as one more piece of the jigsaw of rebellion that typified the era. 'High' art had been too snotty for far too long; here comes pop art to blow it all to pieces. It was a deliberate thumbing of the nose, a clear V-sign to the old traditions. The critic John Russell, writing in 1969, described it as a 'classless commando . . . directed against the Establishment in general and the art-Establishment in particular . . .' It was the end of 'good taste'. On one level it could be seen as a continuation of the long development of the avant-garde, and some critics attempted to claim it as such, but they were grasping at straws. Unlike Dadaism or its immediate decendants, pop appeared to have no obvious political intent. It was instant, disposable, vulgar – in short, it was American. Ironically it would be something that fascinated Americans too; four years later 'pop art' would be one of the ingredients that spurred *Time* magazine to create the concept of 'Swinging London'.

By the time that celebrated, if mythologising feature appeared, 'pop', whether defining art or culture had become infinitely diluted, an all-purpose adjective that could embrace all manner of phenomena, from Union Jacks on coffee mugs to the quality of Mary Quant frocks, and the smashing of instruments by the Who to the posters on the walls of teenage rooms.

The use of pop art (itself dependent on a variety of 'found' images) to create a subset of images, best seen in the design of first magazines and subsequently record covers, began almost before the Young Contemporaries of 1961 had been taken down. The Royal College's in-house magazine *Ark* had, unsurprisingly, been among the first publications to pick up on the new trend. As its alumni moved into the larger world of commercial art direction, so did the style move with them. Barry Fantoni's cover for *Queen* magazine's May 1963 issue parodied what were already becoming pop art clichés; Mark Boxer, editor of the newly launched *Sunday Times* colour magazine, acknowledged pop's influence on its design; Alan Aldridge, the 23 year-old art director of Penguin books – not so much pop as such as pop-influenced – worked with editorial director Tony Godwin to set in motion the hitherto unthinkable: putting pictures on the covers of Penguins. The underground press, starting with the launch of the *International Times* (*IT*) in the autumn of 1966, absorbed the *leitmotifs* and styles of pop almost by osmosis. Pop-related galleries began emerging across London. The most important was owned by Robert Fraser, who had returned from America in 1962 and began exhibiting work by Claes Oldenberg, Jim Dine (to be the subject of a celebrated piece of Establishment censorship), Peter Blake, Richard Hamilton and Patrick Caulfield. Less grand, but enormously important to the nascent 'counter-culture' was Indica, in Mason's Yard, St James, opened in 1966 by John Dunbar (for a while married to Marianne Faithfull) and Miles. It was here that John Lennon would meet Yoko Ono. Other galleries included Kasmin, launched in 1963 and the Signals Gallery, run by Paul Keller and David

Medalla (later the mentor of the experimental troupe the Exploding Galaxy). Writing in the December issue of *Studio International* Patrick Heron, himself a painter, could declare London the 'art centre of the world', playing host to nearly a hundred commercial galleries (not all of them, of course, devoted to pop).

On a more immediate level, of course, it was not the galleries – the commercial conduits that rendered art as one more consumable – but the art schools that devoured pop. For an embryo graphic designer like Pearce Marchbank, then at the Central School of Art and a pop art enthusiast, they were the very fount of the new modes of society.

> If you want to try to find somewhere from which you could say the whole Sixties culture comes, it was the art schools. They really were the laboratories that were making rock musicians and designers and painters, they were the true universities of the Sixties. Hundreds of rock stars started off as art students. Lennon, Townshend, Clapton . . . loads. You could go to a university, but you wouldn't be in a capital city, you wouldn't be in the centre of what was going on. In an art school you were bombarded with a lot more than just a set syllabus. You had this thing called 'Liberal Studies' and the people who taught it were often very interesting. Art students had very open minds – we were interested in everything that was going on. The fact that they were technically being trained to design ceramic pots or books or theatre sets was irrelevant. You'd go to the canteen and you'd have a painter, a typographer, a film-maker, a graphic designer all at the same table, all talking, and you wouldn't get that anywhere else.[5]

For Marchbank, as for many others, pop was the perfect metaphor for the new world. One could appreciate the beats, but they were too soft, too blurred, in the end too 'Fifties'. Pop was 'bright and clean and new; Hockney wore a gold lamé jacket, and they were wearing seaman's sweaters, duffel coats, baggy trousers and sandals. The thing that first attracted me to CND was the logo, it's brilliant. But when you went on the marches, they weren't sharp enough. Listen to the first chords of "I Can't Explain" by the Who. One of the best openings of any pop song written and its absolutely clean and concise, just like the look of Robert Fraser's catalogues.'[6]

Pop's primary importance however, was not in its artefacts, commercially diluted to whatever extent they inevitably would be, but that it created what George Melly defined as a 'true culture, a direct expression of the aspirations and dreams of society as it is, rather than an attempt to impose a "desirable" culture from above'.[7] In this it found itself linked to the other, distinctly less intellectual side of pop, rock music. On a purely artistic level the most obvious manifestation was in the design of long-playing record covers: beneath the detritus of hashish, rolling papers and tobacco that often obscured the album, one could see definite inklings of pop influence.

The epitome of this came in 1967 when Peter Blake assembled a large collage, with the Fab Four plonked in its midst in the guise of Ruritanian bandsmen, for the cover of the Beatles' magnum opus: *Sgt Pepper's Lonely Hearts Club Band*. The original plans for the artwork, a psychedelic mish-mash thought up by the Dutch hippie designers The Fool, were scrapped, vetoed by Robert Fraser (their idea would turn up later the same year in a revised version adopted by the Incredible String Band for their album *5,000 Spirits*; in the short term they were given the 'consolation prize' of designing the bag that actually held the record). Instead Fraser suggested that the band turn to Blake, a senior pop artist, and one whose work had already paid due homage to such rock heavyweights as Bo Diddley and Elvis Presley. Blake and Fraser met with Lennon and McCartney. The basic image was a life-sized collage, based on head and shoulders pictures and photographed by Michael Cooper (more usually involved with the Rolling Stones), which would feature the quartet's favourite characters. Blake went for W.C. Fields, Dion, Tony Curtis, Sonny Liston and the inventor H.C. Westerman (a catalogue of whose work he had been given, some time earlier, by Lawrence Alloway). Lennon liked Oscar Wilde, Lewis Carroll and Edgar Allan Poe (he also asked for Christ but that was squashed: Lennon's previous entanglement with the Saviour, proclaiming a year earlier that 'We're more famous than Jesus', had caused enough trouble with the religious fanatics) while McCartney, always the autodidact, chose Stockhausen and William Burroughs. George Harrison opted for Indian gurus while Ringo just played along. There were also four waxworks of the Fabs themselves, Cardin-jacketed in their Beatlemania, 'mop-top' era. Other figures included but then dropped included Hitler, who had made the starting line-up but was removed on grounds of 'taste', Gandhi (the record company feared for sales in India) and Leo Gorcey, once hero of the 'Bowery Boys' Saturday morning movie series, who forfeited his chance for a comeback by demanding, with no success, to be paid (his fellow 'Boy' Huntz Hall did make the cut). Blank spaces were filled with musical instruments, a hookah, Lennon's TV and some plants, which Blake was informed (to his consternation) were marijuana; they were not. All in all the cover featured sixty-three images.

Andy Warhol, perhaps the best-known of all pop artists ('a baleful mimicry of advertising, without the gloss'),[8] entered the game with the peelable 'banana' used on the first Velvet Underground LP and (albeit a little later) his 'zipper' cover for the Rolling Stones. After Blake's colourful effort Richard Hamilton's 'white album' (the Beatles' follow-up sleeve to *Sgt Pepper*) was a failure (as in many eyes were the pair of albums it contained). The art had mistakenly transcended the pop. Equally 'pop-y', but less iconic, was a cover for another band, the Who, whose November 1967 release *The Who Sell Out* was described by one associate as 'a truly pop art album'. Their first album had already sported an Alan Aldridge cover; this record, which fea-

tured the four band members in cod-advertising displays, incorporated fake
pirate radio links and spurious 'advertising jingles'. Nik Cohn, writing in
Queen, disparaged it as a half-finished effort but for a band whose hype had
featured the words 'pop art' to a greater extent than any other, it did provide
a fusion between the two primary arms of pop culture.

If, in George Melly's words, the Who had succeeded in 'making the
Beatles sound precious and the Stones old hat'[9] the cause was not only their
music. More than any other band they nailed their colours to the mast of pop
art and for their first two years, the period of their greatest hits, they were,
rightly or not, identified with the movement. Ironically, given that
Townshend is invariably seen as the band's leader and primary innovator, it
was the quiet bassist John Entwhistle who made the start in adopting pop art
motifs. Townshend, in fairness, had draped a Union Jack (one of the most
clichéd of pop symbols, and a copy of Jasper Johns's use of America's 'Stars
and Stripes') over his amplifier, but Entwhistle started adorning his jackets
with badges and military insignia. It was also Entwhistle who was the first to
create a Union Jack jacket, a move that was swiftly imitated by his lead guitarist. At the same time drummer Keith Moon began adopting another classic pop icon: a target (another Johns creation, although Peter Blake had used
one too). Daltrey used electrician's tape to create geometric patterns on his
white sweaters.

Once the band had made their own moves, their manager Kit Lambert
saw the commercial possibility. The Who had already been positioned as
Mods, now they would be 'the first pop art band'.[10] Like any such image
there was a degree of hype and Townshend admitted that it was 'a bit of a
gimmick, but we felt it was necessary to bring colour to their image, to stop us
looking too sinister, too drab and overintense. Actually though there was
something in it, because pop art borrowed from real pop and we're taking it
back again.'[11] In addition Townshend, whose Belgravia apartment was wall-
papered with pop art images torn from a book stolen from his old art school,
threw in another art-derived gesture: auto-destruction. This time his source
was European rather than American/British: Gustav Metzger, an artist
whose philosophy centred on the principle of transformation by destruction.
You took an object – clothes, a typewriter, an armchair – smashed or ripped it
to pieces, then mounted the new 'sculpture' as a found object. However,
whatever the story might appear when the publicity got hold of it, as far as
the Who were concerned the whole concept was something of a 'found object' too: the first ever 'destruction' came in the low-ceilinged Railway Tav-
ern in Harrow, one of their earliest venues. Townshend's guitar was
suffering from feedback and in an effort to control it he started banging the
instrument around; one big lunge and the neck hit the ceiling. It looked good
and the audience loved it, so the next night he did it again. This time the guitar snapped. Townshend was less than happy, but the show must go on: he

went on to smash the entire instrument. The audience loved that even more. A week later he resisted temptation, but his audience was disappointed. To make up for Townshend's reticence, Keith Moon decided to make his own gesture – over went his drumkit. Increasingly often the band would smash all or part of their instruments in an orgiastic grand finale. (It was also mountingly expensive: at this stage the band's fee was £50 a gig, guitars were worth £200, and amplifiers twice as much). Quite when the Metzger connection was added to the band's self-definition remains somewhat nebulous, but the art undoubtedly followed the action. And the destruction itself, one must stress, was audience and not band-generated. Later, Metzger himself materialised at some of the band's shows. Watching his words made flesh he was, Townshend reported, really enthusiastic.

Lambert's hype was perfectly matched by Townshend's pronouncements. The manager admitted he didn't understand half of what his guitarist was saying. It barely mattered: Townshend himself talked an excellent game. 'We stand for pop art clothes, pop art music and pop art behaviour . . . we don't change offstage. We live pop art.'[12] What exactly he meant was better not queried – how exactly did one 'live' pop art? – but in any case, as Lambert noted, 'the theories would do for the press.'[13] Pop art was the image of the moment and the Who capitalised unashamedly. It was also helped that they were great rock 'n' rollers.

Another rock/pop fusion, and one that was even more easily accessible, was the television rock show *Ready, Steady, Go!* It was launched in August 1963 by Rediffusion and quickly made itself into an unrivalled vehicle for the cutting edge of music and all its auxiliaries – dances, clothes, gestures and hip 'young' slang to everyone who cared to turn on at 6:07 every Friday evening and hear the rallying cry of a generation: 'The weekend begins here!' Consciously or otherwise the young absorbed a broad band of information from the show, fronted by DJ Keith Forsythe and, far more importantly, Cathy McGowan – short skirts, long hair, the perfect dolly bird. Its backdrops were pure pop – the modified techniques of such pioneers as Boshier, Blake or Hamilton – and when a band like the Who were on stage, all Union Jack-ets and auto-destruction, even the most provincial young viewer could imbibe the pop message. *RSG* was infinitely superior to its rivals – ABC's *Thank Your Lucky Stars* or the BBC's chart-orientated *Top of the Pops*; it was perhaps inevitable that it lasted but a short time compared with such easy-viewing dinosaurs, with their patronising attitudes and unadventurous style.

The most commercialised and diluted aspect of pop was that found in Carnaby Street and in such shops as Portobello Road's I Was Lord Kitchener's Valet. Just as Mod, once it reached the mass-market, became an all-purpose label that could be attached to virtually anything as and when required, so for a period could pop. The ubiquitous Union Jack turned up not merely on mugs, but on T-shirts and knickers, on shopping bags and bikinis.

For a while the military badges and chevrons mutated into whole jackets, cast-offs of Her Majesty's guards' regiments. Jimi Hendrix, fittingly, wore the most gorgeous of all, and for a few months there were hundreds of recruits to the red-coated rank-and-file. Theory, already diluted in pop music and thinned further still by television, was lost completely by the time pop art reached the high street. By now, as George Melly noted, 'The expression "pop art" or "pop" implying "derived from pop art" became increasingly slapped on to all kinds of things. There were pop colours, for example, usually clear primaries or what would have been thought of as unfortunate or vulgar juxtapositions. Pop fashions also, the meaning here signifying anything either shiny or transparent and inevitably made from synthetic materials without any attempt to conceal the fact.'[14] For all intents and purposes pop, once so specific, was no more than a synonym for 'camp'.

There was, however, one last blast of a pop art that might claim a degree more validity. The poster had been fashionable in some quarters since the 1930s, notably in the form of those produced by London Underground; twenty years on and it was the bullfight poster which attained a brief period of chic before a million package holidays relegated it into vulgar cliché, no more stylish than the Tretiakoffs of the Seventies. For a while the Sixties poster, initially featuring a huge blown-up photograph of a movie superstar (Theda Bara, Marlon Brando astride his *Wild One* Harley), had a certain pop ethos. Its successor, the psychedelic poster, especially as created by Nigel Waymouth and Michael English (working as 'Hapshash and the Coloured Coat') or Martin Sharp (otherwise designer of *Oz* magazine covers and of its inimitable 'Magic Theatre' issue, perhaps the supreme example of the entire underground press), had its own moment. That said, such posters, especially Sharp's near-illegible, acid-soaked productions, were a million miles from the crisp, 'clean' imagery of quintessential pop. Either way it was a brief flowering and by the end of the decade the mass-market had seized the poster's time, one brand of cereal offering, for the requisite number of box-tops, 'Pop Posters in brilliant psychedelic colours'.

DOPE

Chapter Nine

Introduction: Drugs in History

A general view of the evidence relating to the question of prohibition of ganja and charas brings the commission to the same conclusion as that which they have framed upon a consideration of the evidence of the ascertained effects alone. The weight of the evidence . . . is almost entirely against prohibition.
Report of the Indian Hemp Drugs Commission, 1896

Oh the grave difficulty of the actual injection, the sterilizing in the dark and silence and the conflict of my hand and wish when it came to piercing our flesh. It was a grand night, and strange to feel so utterly self-sufficient – more like a Chinaman, or God before he made the world or his son and was content with, or callous to, the chaos.
Lady Diana Manners, in a letter recounting her morphine experiences, 1915[1]

In assessing the components of the counter-culture one aspect in particular demands attention. The consumption of drugs, especially cannabis and LSD, was a vital ingredient. Drugs had always been available to the avant-garde. The Romantics, typically Thomas de Quincey and Samuel Taylor Coleridge, had enjoyed opium; in France Baudelaire had luxuriated in his hashish-induced fantasies; Jean Cocteau was another, later, opium fan. Alcohol on the other hand, while running through the lives of hundreds of artists and writers, was an Establishment stimulant. Its consumers – Scott Fitzgerald, Dylan Thomas, William Faulkner and many, many more – may have led rackety lives and their creativity may have revolutionised the medium in which they worked, but rarely would they have been seen as looking to change the world. Drugs were quite different, and in the Fifties and particularly the Sixties their use assumed an importance that had never before been attained.

Those who take 'E', 'draw', 'trips' or 'whizz' today focus on the escapist or recreational aspects of their high of choice. Such pleasures were enjoyed in the Sixties too, but then drug use was as much symbolic and gestural as purely self-indulgent. The simple fact of smoking a joint, so matter-of-fact today, was sufficient to render oneself an outsider, a subversive, a rebel. If you escaped, then it was away from the mundane, quotidian world into the depths of one's innermost self. If there was pleasure, it was in the heightening of experience. That said, one should not promote an excess of piety – drugs were taken as much for simple enjoyment in the Sixties as ever they were – but it is an important appearance.

The primary drugs of Sixties choice, cannabis and LSD, with the odd excursion into uppers and downers and, as the decade waned, into cocaine and even heroin, were relatively new, but the idea of drug use was anything but.

It was not until the international community began falling prey to a series of usually ill-informed, hysterical and prejudicial 'drugs panics', and the first anti-cannabis law was passed in 1928, that things changed. Prior to that such drugs as pain-killing opium, its derivative morphine or the energy-boosting cocaine were part of the chemist's pharmacopoeia, and dispensed as such. Often they were incorporated without further comment into such proprietary medicines as Dr Collis Browne's (heavily opium-tinctured) Linctus, or an aperient composed mainly of opium, mixed with vinegar and spices and known colloquially among the poor to whom it was prescribed as the 'black dose', the 'black drop' or even the 'chimney-sweep'. Cocaine was less common, but Sigmund Freud, among others, had been an enthusiast for what was still seen as a purely beneficial drug. Cannabis itself was effectively unknown, at least in Britain – colonial administrators, especially in India, could hardly have ignored it – but in the compressed form of hashish it had gained, if only in literature and myth, a substantial reputation. The 'Old Man of the Mountains' and his 'hashishin' (the modern 'assassins') were exemplars of Oriental 'exoticism'.

The smokers and trippers of the Sixties were not, of course, taking drugs to 'feel better'. Not in the conventional sense, at least. The origins of their drug use went back to the early nineteenth century, and to a bonding of drugs and mental exploration, epitomised in de Quincey's *Confessions of an English Opium-eater* in 1821. It was published in the *London Magazine*, a journal dedicated to 'Principles of Sound Philosophy in Questions of Taste, Morals and Politics', whose contributors included Hazlitt, Charles Lamb, John Clare and occasionally Shelley, Byron and Walter Scott. De Quincey outlined both the pleasures of ingestion and the horrors of withdrawal, coming to the conclusion that the pleasures of the former outweighed the drawbacks of the latter. He spoke of his dreams – 'gorgeous spectacles' – and portrayed himself as a noble and courageous experimenter. He was quite pragmatic about the effects of the drug, noting that they were very much dependent on he whom it was affecting: 'If a man whose "talk is of oxen" should become an opium-eater, the probability is that (if he is not too dull to dream at all) he will dream about oxen.'[2]

Given the reception accorded a twentieth century equivalent of the *Confessions* – William Burroughs' *Junkie* (published under a pseudonym and eliciting shrieks of shock and horror) – there is a fine paradox in the reception that the supposedly upright Victorians gave de Quincey's essay. It was satirised, for his literary style rather than his drug-taking, and the general response was one of intelligent interest. Nor was de Quincy's career affected in the slightest. The *London Magazine* began by-lining his pieces 'by the Opium-Eater' but that was it. What the author chose to do with his own life remained his own business. In the event he remained an addict for forty-seven years, until his death in 1859. An unabashed libertarian, he declared publicly on his sixtieth birthday that since he had tried every available drug except 'bang' (cannabis) he was about to remedy the omission.

Most early English drug-takers began, as de Quincey claimed he had, by using opium to deal with some form of ailment. But de Quincey, Coleridge and others who appreciated the charms of opium could advocate it openly as a way of stimulating enjoyment, of sustaining energies that might otherwise flag. As de Quincey put it, 'What a man might lawfully seek in wine, surely he may lawfully find in opium . . . ' He also noted, laying down one of the pro-cannabis lobby's main contentions, that the effect of opium on a social level is far less noticeable than that of alcohol.

De Quincey was the most celebrated of 'opium-eaters', but he was hardly unique. In her study of contemporary opium use Virginia Berridge has amassed a substantial list of fellow-users. They include Dickens, Byron, Scott, Keats, George IV, William Wilberforce, Florence Nightingale, Wilkie Collins and Elizabeth Barrett Browning, for whom, as her husband Robert put it, sleep only came 'in a red hood of poppies'. In the nineteenth century drugs were one more part of life, their users tended to be literary, artistic and in the case of morphine and cocaine often aristocratic. But more importantly most drugs were a fad, a fashion, another form of fun.

It has been suggested that it was the innate 'antisocial' character of opium that so frightened its opponents. The opium den with its solitary smokers lacked the supposed conviviality of the good old pub. The essential 'alienness' of the drug – sinister 'yellow' Chinese slipping pipes between hitherto pure European lips, and in the very heart of Empire too – compounded the image. Opium, once lauded as 'God's own medicine', had moved through one hundred and eighty degrees.

However, just as the mood was beginning to turn against opium, and indeed any other form of drug (in 1908, a revised Pharmacy Act moved the hitherto freely available morphine, cocaine, opium and any derivatives, into Part One of the Poisons Schedule) so was 'recreational' use becoming more widespread. Once again the main users were élite or artistic groups; ostensibly focused on the occult and the paranormal, they often included drug experimentation in their 'researches'. In 1888 a group of Masons, Rosicrucians and others interested in changing society formed the 'Hermetic Order of the Golden Dawn', a self-proclaimed group of 'Christian cabalists', addressing its appeal to 'students of Zoroastrianism, Egyptology, Hermetism, Mystery Schools, Orphism, Pythagoreanism . . . etc.'[3] Its leaders were relatively anonymous, but among their recruits were such literary stars as W.B. Yeats and his lover Maud Gonne, and the self-styled 'Great Beast' and 'Wickedest Man in the World' Aleister Crowley. The Order also mixed with another group, the Rhymer's Club, one of the centres of Nineties 'decadent' London, much influenced by the French Symbolists, and home to such figures as Ernest Dowson (also an enthusiast of absinthe, not to mention 'the most degraded' of dockside prostitutes), Arthur Symons (author of *Confessions: a Study in Pathology*, in which he discussed his two years in an Italian lunatic asylum), the poet Francis Thompson and Richard le Gallienne (a friend, as was Symons, of Oscar Wilde, Aubrey Beardsley and other decadents). All these tried cannabis in its hashish form and, consciously or otherwise, paralleled a similar group across the Channel, the *Club des Haschischins*, in which Baudelaire, Rimbaud, Verlaine, de Nerval and others gathered to pursue similar interests. The practical link appears to have been Symons, whose studies of Symbolism, the movement to which many of the 'Haschischins' belonged, united the two groups.

One more drug counted in the recreational pharmacopoeia: mescaline, the chief active principle of mescal buttons; it had been synthesised in 1896. Once again the same group of experimenters took on this new source of inner adventuring. Symons, Ellis – who was especially interested in the connections between dreams, visions and drugs – Yeats and Dowson all tried it out. Yeats professed that he would rather take hashish; Dowson, who seemed to qualify as what later commentators would call a 'multi-drug abuser', was more enthusiastic.

None of this, while undoubtedly focusing on drugs as a pleasurable rather than a medicinal phenomenon, can really be said to describe a 'drug culture'. Ellis wrote a number of papers on his mescaline experiences and like Dowson, whose description of mescaline as a source of well-being included a comment on its 'beatitude', emerges as an unconscious prophet of the drug world of fifty years on. But as Berridge has noted, 'subcultures express violations of codes through which the social world is organised, and at this stage there was no self-defensive and self-conscious cohesiveness that might have arisen from a condemnatory reaction in society'.[4] The Victorian or Edwardian paterfamilias's own abstension did not mean that he automatically condemned as 'immoral' or 'wicked' the literary types who did experiment. Indeed, given the growing contemporary fascination with the workings of the unconscious, their experimentation – when it was even registered – was often greeted with interest. In any case, aside from their recreational potential, both opium and cannabis were still seen as capable of providing medicinal benefits. The *Club des Haschischins* had been formed against the background of a highly regarded study of the use of cannabis in the treatment of lunatics. A similar study, published in England in 1870, had won its author a Gold Medal from the Medical Society of London. Finally, as Berridge underlines, while there may have been links between drugs and the avant-garde, with their interest in the occult, in the inner self and other such esoterica, there was no link, as would be perceived (however erroneously) in the Sixties, between drug use and political radicalism.

The real importance of these decadent, mystic, literary drug-users was not in the fact of their consumption, but in its style. The image of what Blanchard and Atha christen the 'Wasted Artist', all pallor, sensitivity and substance abuse, would entrench itself in the popular mind. As yet the drug-user was not automatically equated with 'the deviant'. Instead they represented a bizarre coterie, their drug indulgences probably linked in some way to their supposed creativity, their tastes somewhat 'foreign', but otherwise harmless.

However, as recreational drug use gradually extended beyond small avant-garde circles and started to permeate the arts and the worlds of upper- and even middle-class Bohemia, what had been an oddity began to become a problem. The first major 'drug panic' came in 1916 when the authorities believed that soldiers on leave from France were taking the opportunity to indulge in an orgy of cocaine use. (Such indulgence was presumably encouraged by the fashionable chemist Savory and Moore who offered a small packet of drugs as 'a useful present for friends at the front'; the firm, alongside Harrods, was fined for such promotions under the Pharmacy Act.) It also appeared that dealers were targeting Canadian soldiers, billeted at Folkestone. In the event a report showed that the only habitual users were apparently 'a small number of broken-down medical men' and a few Canadians. Fanned by the tabloid press, however, the hysteria spread. First the Army Council banned the supply of opiates, cocaine, 'Indian hemp' and other possible intoxicants to military personnel. In 1916 the government, led by Sir Malcolm Delavigne, a Home Office Under-Secretary with responsibility for drugs, used Regulation 40B of the much-loathed Defence of the Realm Act (DORA) to tighten up controls. (40B was also responsible for the prohibition of 'Malthusian appliances', i.e. contraceptives.) DORA was the ideal means to fast-track legislation, permitting instant government interference, without possibility of redress or debate, in areas where such activity would have been stoutly opposed other than in wartime. Delavigne was well aware of its use, admitting that while 'the most convenient way of dealing with [the drug problem] would be by a Regulation under DORA, the difficulty of dealing with the question [of drugs] in this way is that its bearing on the "Defence of the Realm" is neither very direct nor important . . .' Still, given that the only alternative was controversial legislation, 'which may be difficult to get', the short-cut, justified or not, was the best way forward.[5] In another echo of the way that drugs seem to cloud the official mind, Delavigne would never publish the evidence upon which he claimed these new controls were so vital.

In 1920 Britain passed the Dangerous Drugs Act. Its passage was accelerated by an especially juicy scandal, starring the popular young actress Billie Carleton and a splendidly louche cast of characters led by one Reggie de Veulle, a theatrical dress designer and regular cocaine dealer. Miss Carleton, who had been introduced to cocaine and opium by de Veulle, was found dead in her bed in November 1918, the morning after appearing at the Victory Ball at the Albert Hall. As the investigation widened it revealed that drug use had become common among more raffish theatrical and cinema circles, and might even have ensnared the occasional passing subaltern.

By the 1920s recreational drug-taking, particularly of cocaine, with morphine almost equally popular, was a fact of artistic and aristocratic life. As the new decade passed there would be a steady flow of scandalous revelations, usually occasioned by court cases. This heady world of languid upper-class girls or glamorous *ingénues*, preyed on by sinister Chinamen who plied their vile trade from grimy Limehouse dens offered the great non-drug-taking public the most delicious of frissons. The press, who had picked up a strain of ill-informed, often fantastical anti-drug sensationalism from America, where it had begun appearing in the 1890s, intensified the situation with tales of black or yellow villains, sullied white flesh, 'foreign' substances and vice in high places. That such hysteria excited an ignorant public, and in turn led politicians influenced by 'public opinion' to abandon reason in favour of populist emotion (like his modern descendants one back-bencher advocated flogging for dealers – 'These aliens are frightened by nothing else'),[6] was as might be predicted. The whole scene was sensationalised in a variety of drug-related thrillers, the epitome of which was *Dope: a story of Chinatown and the drug traffic* (1919), by the pseudonymous Sax Rohmer (1883-1959). Rohmer's best-known creation was that exemplar of the 'yellow peril' 'Dr Fu Manchu', a figure who had come to Rohmer when in 1913 he was on assignment in Limehouse. Apparently there, amidst its teeming alleys, lurked a mysterious Oriental 'godfather', a Chinese super-villain named 'Mr King'. Rohmer searched in vain. There was no King, but he returned with the inspiration for a fictional Chinaman, more villainous by far than any supposed East Ender. The image of Fu Manchu, with his slit eyes, his drugs, his henchmen, his all-too-willing girls (both Chinese and, far worse, white) became the image of China for much of the Western public. *Dope* performed much the same role for drugs. It featured an out-and-out bounder, 'Sir Lucian Pyne', 'Rita Irvin', a young actress, a wicked Limehouse madame-cum-dealer 'Lola Sin', 'Mollie Gretna', 'a notorious society divorcee and Scotland Yard's stalwart 'Inspector Kerry'. Loosely based on the Billie Carleton affair and hugely melodramatic, *Dope* none the less gave – at least as to milieux – a reasonably fair picture of contemporary drug use. Such aristocratic superstars as Lady Diana Cooper enjoyed morphine and chloroform ('jolly old chlorers'[7]; drugs were available at fashionable venues such as the Café Royale and the Coq d'Argent in Soho. And both 'Rita Irvins and 'Lucian Pynes' were not hard to find.

Equally lurid was Aleister Crowley's *Diary of a Drug Fiend* (1922). Crowley, unlike Rohmer, was talking from experience, and he made no attempt to mask his own advocacy of recreational drug use in his descriptions of the 'Café Wisteria' (the Café Royal) and a group of habitués amongst whom a reasonably discerning reader could spot the *doppelgängers* of Augustus John, Jacob Epstein, Frank Harris, Lord Alfred Douglas and Iris Tree.

As Virginia Berridge notes, cocaine was the 'in' drug of the era.[8] Another scandal, that of the drug-induced death of Freda Kempton, a nightclub dancer, broke in 1922. As ever there was the lurid background, the obligatory Chinaman (one 'Brilliant' Chang, supposedly London's top drug-lord) and better yet, a black jazz musician, Edgar Manning, as the evil pusher. Equally titillating, and again in 1922 was the tale of three young sisters, found unconscious in the opium-filled room of Yee Sing, a.k.a. Johnny Hop, sited above a Chinese laundry in Cardiff. Quite what had brought them there was never revealed, but that failed to restrain the press. Papers wrote of a Chinese love potion based on hashish and aimed directly at white women; its antidote was based on geraniums. A film, *Cocaine*, was made the same year. It was banned by the notoriously strait-laced Board of Film Censors and the L.C.C. Applauding the censors, the *Daily Express* salivated over 'sleek young men and thinly clothed girls . . . [who] jazz and shimmy and foxtrot under the influence of late hours and excitement, nigger-music and cocktails, drugs and the devil'.[9]

Compared with opium, cannabis was rare in Victorian England and would not bulk much larger in the decades that followed, other than for occasional medical usage. In the recreational sphere a number of colonial administrators undoubtedly indulged 'on station' but once again, their drug, like that of their contemporaries at home, was more likely opium. Nor did they bring the indulgence home: cannabis was not addictive, it could be dropped as one mounted the gangplank for England. 'Bhang', as it was known, was merely another piece of Oriental exoticism, best-suited to the 'natives'. What *attention it did receive was generally as a part of the growing worries about opium. There were occasional questions in the House about cannabis use in India, and reports were written, but the government was largely unconcerned. A report released in early 1895 by the Indian Hemp Drugs Commission (IHDC) found that 'the long-term consumption of cannabis in moderate doses has no harmful effects'. In England where so few qualified as a user of any duration, let alone 'long-term', the mystics and decadents could take their own paths to hell; the majority of the country was untainted. The 1895 report gathered dust until in 1967 the Wootton Report into cannabis disinterred it.

By the 1920s, however, demands for a penal approach were increasing. Facts were ignored; what mattered was moral fervour. It focused on the opiates and cocaine and had one clear aim: to drive the addict and the drugs trade into extinction. From a pre-1914 situation where controls were established on the basis of professional self-regulation, depending on a doctor's experience and expertise, the government (impelled by the general atmosphere of the war) turned increasingly towards drug control. What had begun life as wartime expediency was elevated into long-term policy. Britain's membership of the League of Nations underpinned the passage of the Dangerous Drugs Act of 1920, but the influence of America, which had paradoxically ignored the League, soon became more important. The Harrison Narcotics Act of 1914, the culmination of two decades of American anti-drug hysteria, and a number of decisions that followed it, defined the drug user not as a medical problem, but simply as a criminal. Maintenance of a drug addiction was outlawed. The user must stop at once, or go to jail. The same went for the doctors who had hitherto prescribed such drugs. As had happened with America's contemporaneous prohibition of alcohol, the result of such legislation was not a solution to the drug problem, but a vast and immediate increase in criminality: not of the users themselves, but of those who administered and profited from the lucrative drugs black market.

Despite the obvious futility of the Act, the Home Office in Britain was impressed. The medical profession, who – 'drug panics' notwithstanding – had reasonably satisfactorily policed drug use since the Pharmacy Act of 1868, held quite different views. Throughout the early 1920s this was a source of constant conflict. In 1924 there arrived a compromise: the establishment of the Rolleston Committee, 'to consider and advise as to the circumstances, if any, in which the supply of morphine and heroin . . . to persons suffering from addiction to these drugs, may be regarded as medically advisable, and as to the precautions which it is desirable that medical practitioners . . . should adopt for the avoidance of abuse'. The result of its deliberations was the setting up of what was known as the 'British system' of drug control. It was by no means libertarian; if drug-users called for a prescription simply because they happened to enjoy the drug, knowing full well how deleterious the effects might be, 'it is the clear duty of the doctor to refuse the case.' In drugs, as elsewhere in British social policy, adults were apparently unable to make their own decisions. But if the patient posed as a sick person, then 'the physician must use his discretion.'

The result of the Committee's efforts was, surprisingly, to satisfy both the government and the medical profession. The Home Office held the ultimate sanction on drugs, but the profession's 'medical model' was the one accepted when it came to treatment and maintenance prescribing. The system lasted until 1968, when the old core constituency of middle-class, often professional people (at most maybe 300–400 individuals and which itself had dwindled through their gradual deaths) had been joined by the 'evil junkies' of the working-class. This created, as will be seen, a very different situation, and one that was faced with anything but liberal provisions. Once the 'junkie culture' evolved with its expanded numbers and quite different class orientation, the formerly humanitarian doctors, long incorporated into drug policy-making, soon embraced the more rigorous, repressive stance of the Home Office. Like the prosecution of *Lady Chatterley's Lover*, which had only been called when a 3/6d paperback – rather than the usual £3 hardback – made the book available to the proles, hard drugs were fine for the élite; once they reached the wider world opinions and legislation changed.

With the opiates and cocaine stowed away, there remained only cannabis. Here there was no real debate, even within the legislature or the medical profession. Britain preferred to lie back and embrace the regulations put forward in the 1925 Geneva International Convention on Narcotics. The main agitators for reform were Egypt and Turkey, both of whom claimed that hashish sent its users mad. (The truth was, as witnesses to the IHDC had explained, that it was easier for the authorities to write 'ganja' on a certificate of madness than to make any effort to elicit the real cause of a patient's mania.) India much preferred the *status quo*. The British delegate didn't even vote, but when the Convention duly ruled against cannabis, was happy to play the role of a responsible nation by signing it. The new measures were included in a revised Dangerous Drugs Act in 1928. It would be twenty-two years before cannabis prosecutions topped those of opium or others (in 1950 the ratio was 86:41:42) but by then the consumption, and more important the symbolism of drugs (and their users) was very different.

One last drug remains, and that one would be the most important, even if not the most widely consumed, for the Sixties to come. It would be the 'youngest' in the pharmacopoeia, and one of the most potent. THC or tetrahydrocannabinol, the 'active' ingredient of cannabis gives the drug a degree of hallucinogenic potency, but even the purest THC palls in the face of a far more powerful trigrammaton: LSD or lysergic acid diethylamide-25. The drug entered the modern world at 4.20 p.m. on 19 April 1943 when Dr Albert Hofmann, working at the Sandoz Pharmaceuticals Laboratories at Basel, Switzerland, swallowed the world's first dose. Hofmann was in charge of Sandoz's ergot project, looking at the analgesic potential of the fungus *Claviceps purpurea*, which grew on diseased kernels of rye. Ergot had been used in folk medicine for centuries. Hofmann had devoted the last seven years to ergot, synthesising a succession of ergotamine molecules, in the hope of finding, perhaps, a new treatment for migraine. On 16 April, in pursuit of his discovery, he synthesised a new batch of LSD-25. As 'acid' manufacturers would discover time and time again, he soon found that he had been affected by the simple fact of handling the hallucinogen. Very soon he began to feel odd, so odd that he went home. In bed he began to experience hallucinations, as he put it, 'an uninterrupted stream of fantastic images of extraordinary plasticity and vividness and accompanied by an intense kaleidoscopic play of colours'. Hofmann had just experienced the world's first LSD trip. Three days later, determined to check, like any disciplined scientist, that his visions had definitely originated with the LSD that he had been synthesising, he tried again. He took a measured dose of 250 millionths of a gram, 250 micrograms as it would be known, and even in so tiny a dose, the drug proved almost frighteningly powerful.

It was not long before the hallucinations began again, only much more intensely. It was impossible to stay in his laboratory, and Hofmann mounted his bicycle and began to cycle home. It was not an easy ride – what was normally an uninspiring street had turned into something resembling a painting by Salvador Dali, and usually amicable neighbours seemed grotesque, their faces covered in bizarre, malevolent masks. Not until the next morning, when the trip was over, was he able to consider what had happened. It was the birth of a new age – that which would become known as the psychedelic era – although not until it reached Harvard University, and such young experimenters as Timothy Leary and Richard Alpert, would LSD emerge from its scientific confines and take its place as one of the most powerful drugs known to humanity.

The road that would take LSD from a laboratory in Basel to the brains of millions of young people, and thence, in its most debased form, to a merchandising orgy that, in its relative absence of any actual drug, typified the triumph of commercial form over spiritual content, is long and complex. It begins in Langley, Virginia, home of the US Central Intelligence Agency. That the drug found its first fans in the ranks of the US intelligence community might have amused the hippies of the Sixties, but would hardly have surprised them, given that conspiracy theories came as second nature to their take on the contemporary world. The idea of some kind of 'truth drug', geared to the destruction of an enemy's psychological defences, had never been restricted to Hollywood fantasy; or perhaps it is that the CIA's own fantasies would continually rival those of the nation's entertainment capital. The Agency had already considered a number of candidates: mescaline (which had been pioneered by Nazi doctors at the Dachau concentration camp), THC (which offered inadequate control mechanisms), a mix of barbiturates and amphetamines (sometimes boosted by a little marijuana – known as 'sugar'), cocaine and a variety of its synthetic derivatives, and finally, heroin. None really did the trick. (They had also looked at lobotomy – seen as the surest-fire way of reducing an individual's potential as a security risk.)

Then, in autumn 1951, they discovered LSD, thanks to a paper on the drug's psychological properties written by Dr Werner Stoll, a colleague of Hofmann's and the son of the president of Sandoz Labs. At last, it appeared, the much-desired 'truth serum' was at hand. What would follow was a bizarre tale of cloak-and-dagger fantasies, of increasingly optimistic and strange schemes and experiments, and of the CIA's gradual realisation that LSD, far from being a malleable tool for interrogation and subversion (the US Army also liked the idea of dosing enemy troops with it), was in fact an untameable monster that was just as likely to make a subject unreachable as to render them open to questioning. Only in their assessment of its power were the spooks correct. And even here they were disturbingly casual. Nothing was more fun than the spiking of some innocent, a process that unbalanced a number of agents and in one case, perhaps the only one, despite all the media claims that would follow, led to a person tossing themselves from a window, believing, in that cliché of clichés, that under LSD 'they could fly'.[10]

Even in its early days LSD attracted some strange and unpredictable figures. Chief among them was Captain Alfred M. Hubbard, a rags-to-riches uranium entrepreneur, former member of the Second World War OSS (the immediate predecessor of the CIA) and a man of awesome connections and influence. He had first tried LSD in 1951 when he was given a trip by a British doctor. The experience had amazed him – he had allegedly experienced his own conception and birth – and he became one of the drug's most dedicated proselytisers. Among those to whom Hubbard talked was the young psychiatrist Humphrey Osmond, another Briton, who was currently experimenting with LSD and mescaline at the Weyburn Hospital in Saskatchewan, Canada. Osmond's speciality was the treatment of mental illness, and he had noted that under the influence of hallucinogens a 'normal' person could see the world through schizophrenic eyes. He suggested that trainee medical personnel should start using such drugs, to give them a greater insight into the thoughts of their seriously disturbed patients. At the same time, Osmond was contacted by another, very different figure, the British novelist Aldous Huxley, best-known as the author of *Brave New World*, a dystopian fantasy that tends to be bracketed with Orwell's *1984*, but offers a very different vision of a totalitarian future. Learning of these new drugs, Huxley saw their potential as agents of a new consciousness and offered himself to Osmond as a guinea-pig for further experimentation. The psychiatrist was slightly worried – 'I did not relish the possibility, however remote, of being the man who drove Aldous Huxley mad'.[11]

In May 1953 Huxley took his first trip, using mescaline. 'It was without question the most extraordinary and significant experience this side of the Beatific Vision,' he wrote. 'It opens up a host of philosophical problems, throws intense light and raises all manner of questions in the field of aesthetics, religion and theory of knowledge.'[12] Later, Huxley's meditations on this and other drug experiences, *The Doors of Perception* (its title a tribute to William Blake), would become a key work within the psychedelic community. Unlike that community, however, Huxley contented himself with that single trip until 1955 when, this time in the company of Al Hubbard, he took another, in order to help him write *Heaven and Hell*, his sequel to *The Doors of Perception*. It was Huxley and Osmond who made one further, highly important contribution to the hallucinogenic revolution. Writing to the novelist in early 1956, Osmond told him, 'I have tried to find an appropriate name for the agents under discussion: a name that will include the concepts of enriching the mind and enlarging the vision . . . My choice, because it is clear, euphonious, and uncontaminated by other associations, is psychedelic, mind-manifesting.' In other words, a hallucinogen does not produce a predictable result, as does, say, a given pain-killer, but simply brings out what is already there, deep in the unconscious. As Osmond jokily summed it up in a later letter, 'To fathom hell or soar angelic | Just take a pinch of psychedelic.'[13]

As the Fifties progressed Hubbard and Osmond became increasingly impressed by the possibilities of LSD. According to Martin A. Lee and Bruce Shlain, writing in their history *Acid Dreams*, convinced that the drug could radically alter one's belief system, they arranged LSD sessions for a number of influential figures, 'a prime minister, assistants to heads of state, UN representatives and members of the British parliament'.[14] But while Osmond still operated within the established disciplines of mental health institutions, Hubbard, who had obtained some 6,000 bottles of LSD, costing around $200,000, was busy justifying his latest nickname: 'the Johnny Appleseed of LSD'. Hubbard wandered the world, offering and administering the drug to anyone who put up a hand. As Lee and Shlain put it, 'During the 1950s and early 1960s he turned on thousands of people from all walks of life – policemen, statesmen, captains of industry, church figures, scientists. "They all thought it was the most marvellous thing", he stated, "and I never saw a psychosis in any one of these cases." '[15] Among his converts was a small group centred in Los Angeles, including Huxley, his friend Gerald Heard, the philosopher Alan Watts and the psychiatrist Dr Oscar Janiger. It was this group who could claim to be the very first for whom the taking of LSD was a social rather than a clinical experience. By the start of the 1960s LSD had become the drug of choice for a large number of Hollywood figures. Cary Grant, one of whose guides was Oscar Janiger, was an especial fan, offering what amounted to a testimonial: 'All my life I've been searching for peace of mind . . . Nothing really seemed to give me what I wanted until this treatment.' Others to benefit from Janiger's stock of acid were Jack Nicholson, Anaïs Nin, André Previn and Allen Ginsberg, who would return from his trip to hymn 'the multiple million eyed monster'.[16] Another, far less likely user was Henry Luce, a staunch Republican and president of *Time-Life*. Thanks to LSD, he announced, he was able, *inter alia*, to talk to God on the golf course

It was a piece in Luce's *Life* magazine that, indirectly, would move psychedelics into an even wider arena. The seventeen-page feature on the Mexican 'magic mushroom' or 'teonanacatl' ('God's flesh' and properly *Psilocybe mexicana*) appeared in May 1957 (as part of a series entitled 'Great Adventures') and was written by the amateur (but highly experienced) mycologist R. Gordon Wasson, another establishment magnate who worked as a vice-president of J.P. Morgan and Co., a bastion of Wall Street. Hundreds of thousands would gain their first knowledge of psychedelics through Wasson's piece. Among its readers was Albert Hofmann, who now turned from ergot to teonanacatl and extracted its active ingredient, creating a new chemical hallucinogen: 'psilocybin'. (The CIA would immediately pounce on the first available samples; they were tested on heroin addicts in the Lexington Narcotics Hospital.) The piece was also read by a young clinical psychologist, Professor Timothy Leary, then director of clinical research and psychology at the Kaiser Foundation Hospital in Oakland, California. Seen as a rising star in the world of behavioural psychology, his personality test known as 'the Leary' was widely used in business and elsewhere – the CIA included – to test prospective employees.

Leary had not actively sought out psychedelics; indeed he had yet even to experience marijuana. That was soon to change. In 1960, aged thirty-nine, he had moved from California to Harvard and that summer he took his holiday in Mexico. Here a more psychedelically experienced friend offered him a handful of magic mushrooms. Leary was slightly dubious but easily persuaded. As it had been for so many others, this first encounter with the psychedelic experience would prove unprecedentedly momentous. 'It was above all and without question the deepest religious experience of my life. I discovered that beauty, revelation, sensuality, the cellular history of the past, God, the Devil – all lie inside my body, outside my mind.'[17] Unlike those others, however, Leary didn't leave the matter there. Back at Harvard he determined to abandon behaviourism and turn instead to the pursuit of this new and wonderful chemically induced inner world. He established a psilocybin research project and took on a partner, Richard Alpert, son of a rich New England lawyer, whose 'preppie' image belied his fascination with 'magic mushrooms'. As it happened Aldous Huxley was nearby, appearing at MIT as a visiting lecturer. Leary and Huxley took psilocybin together and Leary was introduced to Osmond, who approved of the idea of introducing psychedelics to Academe, but wondered whether he wasn't 'just a little bit square'[18] for the job.

Fascinated by the links between psychedelics and religion, Leary's first experiment involved the administration of psilocybin to a group of theological faculty and students. But not all his 'magic' pills were taken in controlled surroundings. Leary made it clear that those with a genuine interest could get psilocybin for their own use and a variety of graduate students, leavened with various individuals from outside the university, joined the tripping circle. In late 1960 Leary met Ginsberg and his friend Peter Orlovsky. As it would in England a few years later, when his cheery public nakedness shocked the supposedly liberal Beatles, Ginsberg's response to the drug – to strip off and proclaim his desire to contact world leaders in order, instantly, to establish a new world of love and peace – left Leary less than delighted. But Ginsberg, as ever, was unfazed. He was convinced that psychedelics were the key to a whole new world order; not only should its leaders be 'turned on', so should everyone. What Ginsberg wanted was a psychedelic crusade and, he proclaimed, Leary was to be its Messiah. Leary was enthralled. As he wrote later, the time had come for a profound change, 'for far-out visions, knowing that America had run out of philosophy, that a new, empirical, tangible metaphysics was desperately needed, knowing in our hearts that the old mechanical myths had died at Hiroshima, that the past was over, that politics could not fill the spiritual vacuum . . . Politics, religion, economics, social structure are based on shared states of consciousness. The cause of social conflict is usually neurological. The cure is biochemical.'[19]

Not everyone loved the new experience. Neal Cassady called it 'the Rolls-Royce of dope' (and would soon be the figurehead of Ken Kesey's West Coast 'Merry Pranksters') but more austere figures were less embracing. The poet Robert Lowell responded to Ginsberg's promise that 'love conquers all' with a dour 'Don't be too sure'; Arthur Koestler enjoyed his trip, but damned the all-too-easy access it seemed to give to the infinite: 'This is wonderful, no doubt, but it is fake, ersatz, instant mysticism . . . I solved the secret of the universe last night, but this morning I forgot what it was.'[20] It was a classic intellectual's response: no gain should come without pain and if it did, then one should be suspicious. It was not, as time would show, a problem that would trouble the young. And as Lee and Shlain point out,[21] one person above all had no time for psychedelia: William Burroughs. In 1961 Leary visited Burroughs in Tangiers, where he was living and working, and handed over a psilocybin pill. Burroughs was unimpressed. Still, he was open to suggestion, and while his dealings with drugs were never in the slightest hedonistic, he was willing, when visiting Harvard, to try again. He remained unconvinced. Drugs were a useful short-cut, but, 'Remember, anything that can be done chemically can be done in other ways.' Not only that but Burroughs, paranoia always to the fore, saw Leary and his pals as possibly, even probably, no more than tools in the hands of far more sinister manipulators.

For Leary and his circle, there remained one more piece of the jigsaw. For all his crusading, for all his proselytising, the Harvard professor had still only experienced psilocybin. As the next generation of users would find, 'magic mushrooms' were a docile hack compared with the unfettered thoroughbred that was LSD itself. In September 1961 that piece of the jigsaw would fall into place. Shortly before that a young Englishman, Michael Hollingshead, working in New York for the British Cultural Exchange, had obtained himself a whole gram of LSD. He split it in half, giving the rest to an associate, and mixed his half-gram with icing sugar and distilled water, before spooning the resulting paste into an empty mayonnaise jar. Hollingshead then scooped himself a generous spoonful and sat back to follow developments. They were, as he would discover, spectacular. Hollingshead, though by no means a novice in the world of cannabis, had no conception of what was about to happen. The trip, no doubt much stronger than the usual 250 micrograms, blew him away. It left him shattered, disorientated, his normal reference points dissolved in the aftermath of this peak experience. His first reaction was to call

Aldous Huxley: what should he do with the remainder of the acid, some 4,975 trips as he estimated. Go and see Timothy Leary, advised the sage.

This he did. Leary offered him a spare attic room and a psilocybin trip, and when that was over Hollingshead opened up his mayonnaise jar. Leary began by saying no – all psychedelics were alike, in his opinion, and he was after all the psilocybin master – but a few days later he acquiesced. It was the most astounding experience he had encountered, many times more dramatic than his most intense use of psilocybin. For a while he followed Hollingshead around like a doting puppy; as supplier of that inaugural trip the man seemed godlike and Leary's friends began to think that he had finally overdone it. But Leary recovered his poise and was quickly back on the crusade. The only difference was that now the drug of choice and change was not psilocybin, but LSD.

Gradually Leary's experimentation and his on- and off-campus activities began to disturb the Harvard authorities. The CIA, who had conducted a number of their own experiments under university auspices, and monitored all LSD use very closely, began keeping him and Alpert on file. When Leary, perhaps jokingly, contributed a paper to the *Journal of Atomic Scientists* warning that the Soviets might well be planning to dose the nation's reservoirs with psychedelics and suggesting that the best defence was for the US to do it first – thus giving people a taste of what they might experience – it all seemed to be getting out of hand. Harvard's medical faculty called for his activities to be curtailed and when the story hit the local, then national press, it was clear that the establishment were intent on stopping their rebel professor's work. In May 1963 Alpert was summarily sacked, for giving LSD to undergraduates. Shortly afterwards it was Leary's turn, despite claiming that he had been 'supplying a student with the most profound educational experience'.

No matter. LSD, as he proclaimed, was 'more important than Harvard'.[22] Leary and Alpert co-operated gleefully with a rash of national media stories on psychedelics. Suddenly everyone knew about it and, equally importantly, they knew about its main populariser. For Americans young and old Timothy Leary *was* LSD. It was not an image he wished to disclaim.

In 1963 Leary and Alpert, free of academia's shackles, founded the International Federation for Internal Freedom (IFIF). Offices sprang up across the States and there were soon 3,000 members, every one dedicated to the untrammelled use of mind-expanding drugs. They saw themselves, said Leary, as 'modest heroes, an educational tool to facilitate the development of new social forms'.[23] After a short spell in Mexico, Leary and Alpert met William Mellon Hitchcock, the wealthy stockbroker son of the founder of Gulf Oil. Hitchcock gave them his estate at Millbrook, in Dutchess County, New York, for the peppercorn rent of $500 a month. It was the ideal base: a sixty-room mansion set in 4,000 acres of land. Here Leary, Alpert, Hollingshead and perhaps thirty more adepts of the new vision gathered. In a country where cults had always flourished, one might be forgiven for seeing Leary and his acolytes as one more ring on the old changes. Gurus would gather their clan, give out their messages, a few people, maybe even hundreds might follow. But this was different. Some time in 1964 Leary coined one of the most enduring calls to action of the era: 'Turn on, tune in, drop out'. It was a call that would echo not simply through the leafy acres of upstate New York, but across America, across Britain and in time across the world. Wherever there were young people, and especially where there were young people and LSD, the crusade, led by its unlikely high priest, was underway.

Chapter Ten

The Underground: In Theory

To be a member of the protesting underground, I consider, is an essentially behav-
ioural phenomenon. It is living by what you believe, with a set of attitudes shared
by, but not sacred to, a number of people intent on challenging their society to live
up to its promise . . . It is a movement of social liberation through individual libera-
tion. Everyone must be free to do their own thing. The Underground puts self at the
centre of its spectrum. That is, no form of social or political liberation, however de-
sirable, can take place unless its first priority is to allow each individual to deter-
mine his own desires, free from psychological, political or conventional pressures.
Peter Buckman *The Limits of Protest* (1970)

At the crux of any discussion of what happened during the Sixties, one inevitably comes up against the word 'revolution'. For the purposes of this discussion it seems best to divide the 'revolution' into two parts. One, the 'cultural
revolution' that lay at the heart of the 'underground' or 'counter-culture' is
best assessed at once. The political revolution, the capitalised 'Revolution',
as it were, can best be considered later in this narrative.

The use of the word 'underground' to denote a primarily cultural rather
than political alternative to establishment society emerged during the late
1950s, and made its presence increasingly felt during the next decade. Its initial stimuli were two-fold: the 'underground movie' and the small, duplicated magazine. Both phenomena seem to have originated in America, but
only the latter managed to make much headway in the UK. In some ways the
innate cultural references of this underground, as opposed to those of more
political and thus more 'genuine' undergrounds – typically those of wartime
Europe or of the post-war dissident movements that burgeoned across the
world – invalidate the term's use from the start. In the first place, if 'underground' was supposed to be synonymous with 'clandestine', then the counter-
cultural underground of the Sixties was nothing of the kind. As visible as a
neon-decked billboard, it proclaimed its credos – often transient, ill-worked-
out and quite contradictory – at top volume. Educated, almost invariably
middle-class, the children of an older élite in many cases, it could never have
consented to silence. It was often infantile; for all its loud contempt for consumerism, it was irredeemably locked into the consumer society (never more
so than in its relationship with those indispensable 'hip capitalists', the drug
dealers), and would die when the 'straight' economy could no longer give it
house-room. To persist in a negative mode, it was never more, as Charles
Shaar Murray put it, than 'a gorgeous, playful and decadent exercise in lifestyle'.[1] And looking back twenty years the social historian Jeffrey Weeks noted
in 1989 that, 'The counter-culture itself was a curious, transient phenomenon. A

rejection by largely middle-class youth of the values and avid consumerism of middle-class society, it was often largely parasitic on that parent culture. It was a mood and style, a network of interlocked cultural manifestations, which by its nature was unstable and ephemeral and which by 1972, in the context of a grimmer social and economic climate, and with the collapse of most of its "alternative press", was effectively dead.[2]

So much for the hindsight. The contemporary reality was very different. Had it not been, whence all those agonised newspaper features, those earnest discussions on late-night television, those celebrations and denunciations of 'the counter-culture' or the 'alternative society'? Something, as Bob Dylan admonished his 'straight' everyman, 'Mr Jones', was definitely happening, and if it wasn't as clear cut, as black-and-white as might have been proclaimed, then that in no way diminishes the overall event. For all the easy mockery, there was an 'underground' with leaders, institutions (however fissiparous and short-lived some of them might have been), a thriving press and, of course, a definable brand of music. It existed both in the minds of its advocates and acolytes and, equally importantly, in the eyes of the Establishment, the 'straights'.

Before moving on to the specifics – the leaders, the institutions and the like – it is necessary to try to assess just from where the 'underground', or perhaps more felicitously the 'counter-culture', emerged. Each of its chosen names bears its own nuance, but whether underground, counter-culture or alternative society, the abiding image is of a parallel, oppositional universe. There is no doubt that the counter-cultural rhetoric called for substantial change, but if the *leitmotif* is one of revolution, it is a cultural rather than a political revolution. A subversion from within rather than a full-scale overturn from outside. As might be expected from a membership characterised by its critics as little more than a bunch of spoilt middle-class brats, self-fulfilment (what critics might have termed self-obsession or simply selfishness) lay very much at the heart of the movement. This grail was tied to the pursuit of the purported freedoms and revelations offered by hallucinogenic drugs, but drugs, while central, were not indispensable. For members of the counter-culture social liberation would be preceded by individual liberation, and as the era wound down in the Seventies, it became clear that if the movement had achieved anything it was in this arena of personal space, of maximised personal freedoms, even if the larger world of Establishment power and social boundaries remained largely untouched. The personal, as the slogan would run, is the political. The politicos of the New Left may have felt little in common with the 'freaks', and despised much of their efforts as gaudy posturing, but the much-vaunted 'revolution' of the Left would never happen. Counter-cultural utopianism was equally unsuccessful, but so many of the underground's supposedly bizarre fantasies – environmentalism, sexual politics – would embed themselves in the wider consciousness and within a decade or less move from the margins into the centre.

However, the counter-culture did create a type of revolution, what the sociologist Bernice Martin, borrowing a phrase coined by Talcott Parsons, termed the 'Expressive Revolution'. Coming as the latest incarnation of a series of avant-garde styles that had progressed almost seamlessly through the century, the counter-culture believed in the primacy of 'anti-structure', of boundary-breaking, of what Martin has termed: 'a pitting of freedom and fluidity against form and structure . . . a long and concerted attack on boundaries, limits, certainties, conventions, taboos, roles, system, style, category, predictability, form, structure and ritual. It was the pursuit of ambiguity and the incarnation of uncertainty.'[3] It was, she suggests, the vanguard of a movement that would make itself known throughout the decade and throughout Western society, a movement which embraced the destruction of those boundaries, many of them relating to the way one lived one's private life, and the potential that destruction revealed. That the details of the revolution may at times have seemed absurd, and at others genuinely challenging to the Establishment is true; it is also true that within ten or certainly twenty years (whatever the new political complexion of that establishment) so much that had been terrifyingly revolutionary was now quietly mainstream. In the words of test-flight jargon, the Sixties expanded the envelope, and once expanded, it did not spring back. Some of the counter-culture's 'excesses' were not destined to last, and others would be subtly modified, but the subversives had paraded round this cultural Jericho with their trumpets and drums and the walls, once tumbled, remained down.

The bulk of those who participated in the counter-culture were either war babies or products of the immediate post-war 'baby boom'. They had grown up in the Fifties, a period when self-expression had been severely restrained. Externals, as had always been the Western, and in particular the English way, were paramount. Yet agitation for changes in such private affairs as one's sexual preference or the literature that one was allowed to read within one's home, was already appearing. The soil, however thinly fertilised, did exist for the production of change. It may be true that had people chosen to wait, those changes, however gradually, would have been made. The counter-culture was not prepared to wait. As the US hippie leader Jerry Rubin would entitle his own polemic, their credo was 'Do It!' It may be that the very stability against which its members grew up provided the counter-culture with the opportunity to tear down the walls behind which, *in extremis*, they could always retreat – the spoilt bourgeois brat thesis once more – but such theorising was irrelevant. They chanced their arms, they abandoned assumption, they 'did it', and did it now. And it is this urgency, this willingness to question the easy assumptions of the *status quo* that seemed so revolutionary, and thus so threatening and which, before the decade ended, would release forces of genuine reactionary hostility. As David Widgery, looking back on the era in a valedictory issue of *Oz*, noted, the 'Sixties' ended not through a lack of enthusiasm but because for all the absurdities, all the ephemerality, all the excess for excess's sake, the counter-culture had proved itself. The authorities could no longer laugh.

> The truth of the matter is not that the-leaders-sold-out or that something-greatly-beauteous-grew-cankered, but that the underground got smashed, good and proper by those forces of which it stood in defiance. It was smashed, because it could not, by 1968, be laughed at or ignored or patronised any longer. The underground was able to make really painful attacks on the system's intellectually based forms of power. Of all the intellectual property speculators of the Sixties, it made the most sizable incursions into capitalism's real estate, the family, school, work, discipline, the 'impartial' law courts and the British Broadcasting Corporation. Unlike previous movements of radical critics, it actually transmitted its mood of indiscipline to young people of all classes.[4]

Much of this would be reined in as the new decade moved on (a tightening that to some extent was determined by a very different, and far less optimistic economic climate). But the boundaries were broken, the limits expanded, and in daily life, if not in reactionary or ignorant outpourings that's the way it has stayed.

Whatever the phenomenon known as the Sixties may have been, and however much that era would turn out to change the world in general and Britain in particular, there was, as ever, not that much new under the sun. Aside from rock 'n' roll (then 'youngest' of the predominant 'drivers' of the period), most of the major concerns had been in place, whether for years, decades or even centuries. The Sixties did not spring, fully formed, into place. Certain elements, undoubtedly, were new; certain stimuli had not been seen before; certain individuals, the driving force of any movement, could not possibly have existed prior to that specific time (although their avatars may well have pursued their own particular trajectories). But if one looks at the bones, the skeleton upon which the time-specific events would form, there is so much that was in fact already rich with the patina of ages.

On 5 July 1969, a blazingly hot day in the last summer of the Sixties, some quarter of a million young people gathered together in the largest and most central of London's verdant 'lungs', Hyde Park, to witness a concert given by the Rolling Stones. It had been proposed some time earlier – free concerts in the Park were becoming increasingly popular – but its immediate justification was the death, just forty-eight hours earlier, of the band's erstwhile guitarist and one-time figurehead Brian Jones, whose body had been found floating and inert in the swimming pool of his country house, the former possession of A.A. Milne. The precise cause of Jones's death has yet to be ascertained – did he fall or was he, as many wondered, metaphorically or even actually pushed? – but that afternoon, as Mick Jagger stalked the stage dressed in a white frock, a large wooden cross and a bondage dog collar, replete with eye-shadow, rouge and lipstick, it was of little import. What stirred the crowd was Jagger's choice of obituary: a stanza from Shelley's poem 'Adonaïs'. 'Peace, peace, he is not dead, he doth not sleep,' intoned the befrocked lead singer, 'He hath awakened from a dream of life . . . '

Brian Jones was hardly John Keats, for whom 'Adonaïs' is a valediction, and Jones's drugged and drunken death was far from romantic, in any sense, but whether Jagger (let alone the quarter-million crowd) realised it or not, in quoting Shelley to elegise his lead guitarist he was using perhaps the most apt of all poets. Shelley (1792–1822) was Sixties-man in embryo. In a description of him by the nineteenth–century essayist William Hazlitt, it is hard to ignore the signposts of a Sixties' lifestyle.

> Shelley was indeed the most striking example we remember of the two extremes described by Lord Bacon as the great impediments to human improvement, the love of Novelty and the love of Antiquity . . . in him free enquiry and private judgement amounted to a species of madness. Whatever was new, untried, unheard of, unauthorised, exerted a kind of fascination over his mind. The examples of the world, the opinion of others, instead of acting as a check upon him, served but to impel him forward with double velocity in his wild and hazardous career. Spurning the world of realities, he rushed into the world of nonentities and contingencies, like air into a vacuum. If a thing was old and established, this was with him a certain proof of its having no solid foundation to rest upon: if it was new, it was good and right.
>
> Every paradox was to him a self-evident truth; every prejudice an undoubted absurdity. The weight of authority, the sanction of ages, the common consent of mankind were vouchers only for ignorance, error and imposture. Whatever shocked the feelings of others conciliated his regard: whatever was light, extravagant and vain was to him a proportionable relief from the dullness and stupidity of established opinions. The worst of it however was, that he thus gave great encouragement to those who believe in all received absurdities, and are wedded to all existing abuses: his extravagance seeming to sanction their grossness and selfishness, as theirs were a full justification of his folly and eccentricity.[5]

Shelley (known at Eton as 'mad Shelley' and 'the Eton Atheist') represented the whole range of Romantic preoccupations. He deplored the ritualised superstitions that were elevated into religious dogma; he was an advocate of the political radicalism of William Godwin and of Tom Paine, whose writings spurred both the American and French revolutions. He deplored monogamous matrimony, disdained royalty, meat-eating and religion. He was a self-proclaimed feminist, though observers of his turbulent private life might have argued. He was fascinated by what he saw as the exotic Orient. He advocated freedom of speech and in 1812 fly-posted a democratic broadsheet, 'A declaration of Rights', although when the authorities sought to

prosecute the author, his servant took the rap. He set up a prototype commune, but it did not prosper. In 1813 he published *Queen Mab*, a poem
which, backed up by its integral Notes, encapsulated the thoughts and philosophies that made the poem (in the cheap, pirated edition that appeared after 1821) a textbook for thousands of working-class radicals. Like his
atheistic pamphlet, and his play *The Cenci* (1819–21), a meditation on incest,
atheism and finally, the nature of evil, *Queen Mab* would face prosecution for
blasphemy. His poem 'The Mask of Anarchy' ('I saw Murder on the way |
he had a face like Castlereagh . . . '), written in response to the Peterloo Massacre of 1819 (when some 500 people, demonstrating for parliamentary reform, were either killed or wounded by the troops sent in to control them)
was an anthem of revolt.

The sincerity of Shelley's radicalism was never in doubt, but like his Sixties successors, the poet was rarely seen as a genuine threat. Matthew Arnold
dismissed him as 'an ineffectual angel, beating in the void his luminous wings
in vain' (*Essays in Criticism*) and like the butterflies that Mick Jagger would
toss into the Hyde Park audience, or indeed like that earlier 'bug with gilded
wings | This painted child of dirt, that stinks and stings', to whom Jagger
himself had been compared in the celebrated *Times* editorial of 1967, Shelley
was seen as an exotic, but an impotent one. The positions for which he stood,
whether social, political or sexual, were simply untenable. Interesting, perhaps, threatening, even, but ultimately irrelevant. Yet they would take root,
working themselves beneath the skin of national consciousness. Yesterday's
radicalism becomes tomorrow's banality and Shelley's theories were no exception. For the Sixties' 'underground', or at least those who were aware of
their existence, Shelley and his fellow Romantics provided a paradigm of a
revolutionary life.

If the Romantics represent the counter-culture's most distant ancestory,
then another, more recent group of literary rebels and intellectuals can also
be seen as part of the 'family tree'. If, as Lord Annan has suggested,[6] the two
most important influences on 'Our Age' (the 'great and good', not to mention
the social reformers of the Sixties) were modernism and pacifism, then the
nexus in which the two met was in that slightly older group known as
'Bloomsbury'.

It may seem contradictory to link the precious goings-on of a group of
well-born, well-connected hyper-intellectuals with the rumbustious adventuring of a pack of class mongrels, by no means invariably intellectual, who
took up the banner of cultural revolution forty years on. None the less in
their ways they have much in common. In the first place the role of shock was
central to them both. Given the background, given the chronology, was it
more astounding for Germaine Greer to exhibit her vagina in the avowedly
pornographic *Suck* magazine in 1969, or for the etiolated essayist Lytton
Strachey to remark in 1908, on seeing a stain on a skirt worn by Virginia

Woolf's sister Vanessa Bell, 'Semen?' Were Nuttall's sTigma or John Latham's burning Skoob towers that much more dramatic than Roger Fry's
Post-Impressionist exhibition, universally excoriated by those who dared
even visit, and was it not a novel by a Bloomsbury acolyte, D.H. Lawrence,
that would be tried in 1960, setting the whole 'obscene publications' bandwagon rolling. It seems that the thread of democratisation that runs through
'the Sixties', takes in a number of the freedoms that the Bloomsbury group,
and its espousal of modernism, had also sponsored.

In many ways Bloomsbury was more daring than their Fifties and Sixties
successors. The Fifties may have been dull, and vested interest as firmly em-
bedded in the *status quo* as ever, but the Victorian strictures against which the
Bloomsbury group rebelled were even more determinedly hidebound. However, unlike the youthful rebels of the 'counter-culture', who may have been
middle class but were far from uniformly élite, the Bloomsbury rebels had
the protection of their privileged backgrounds. The concept of classlessness,
which they too voiced, was even less substantial than when it reappeared in
the fantasies of those who came later. No one who has read Virginia Woolf's
diaries need have the slightest illusion as to her innate, unvarying snobbery,
though she defended herself with the plaint that everyone, herself included,
is compromised by what she termed 'worldliness'. Her supporters would add
that she had no illusions about her social position and saw no reason to abandon it for some prototype of self-denying political correctness. If the
counter-culture could be dismissed as scions of privilege, how much more
did the description fit these gilded protestors, chafing at their cage but ensuring that there would always be someone to keep it properly burnished. In any
case, how much was it a cage, and how much a safety fence, excluding the
outsiders as much as entrapping those within?

For those who venerate Bloomsbury, the suggestion of a link between
these aesthetic sensitives and the grubby figures who staffed the counter-
culture may seem sacrilegious. Yet Bloomsbury was not so far from what
would come later. Most important of all, they were Modernists (defined by
Lord Annan as those who valued 'Style, Experiment, Originality and Mockery' – none of which exactly alienated the 'underground').[7] They espoused
the latest trends in avant-garde European art or culture, and enjoyed the effect they had on those of staider mien. (Ironically they loathed James Joyce,
destined to become the supreme modernist: they, especially Virginia Woolf,
found him too squalid for their ostentatiously refined tastes.) Their intellectual élitism made their position even more unpopular in philistine England.
They distrusted authority of any sort, they questioned everything and respected nothing. If the Establishment fought back, one could assume that its
mouthpieces were lying. What mattered above all was the acting out of feelings;
it was what a person was, not how they were categorised by some external social ranking that actually counted. Self-expression was the root of good, self-

repression that of evil. The idea of 'duty', so cherished by the Victorians, was anathema. That quintessentially English anti-intellectual coverall – 'common sense' – was no more than a mask for the unwillingness, or inability to think and to question. Woken from a sleep during a conference of intellectuals in France, Strachey was asked what he felt to be the most important thing in the world. His response: 'passion'. They were cultural patricides: Strachey's *Eminent Victorians* and Maynard Keynes's *Economic Consequences of the Peace* poured vitriol respectively on such Victorian monoliths as General 'Chinese' Gordon or the saintly Florence Nightingale, and on the madness of the Versailles Treaty. And like the Sixties rock 'n' roll underground' they espoused an air of millennarianism that declared: we are the elect, we are the chosen ones; in a corrupt world, only we have the keys to the kingdom.

Finally, if more prosaically, they exerted a substantial influence on Lord Annan's 'Our Age' reformers, typical of whom was Roy Jenkins. Their attitudes played a vital role in forming the beliefs of those who administered the social changes that underpinned the Sixties. Not only that, but there were certain unassailable flesh-and-blood links. Aldous Huxley, whose *Doors of Perception* would accompany thousands of day trippers on their hallucinogen-fuelled exploration of their inner self, was not a fully-fledged Bloomsbury, but he was undoubtedly of their society. And Virginia Woolf, Bloomsbury incarnate, became a totem for the feminists of the 1970s.

The Romantics and Bloomsbury aside, the counter-culture had more immediate theorists. Aside from its own polemicists – Jeff Nuttall, Richard Neville and Mick Farren (and their American peers Abbie Hoffman and Jerry Rubin) – the movement was indebted to the theorising of a late middle-aged German-born professor. Had he wished, Herbert Marcuse could justifiably have cited himself 'the grand old man' of the underground. He played a similar role for the New Left, and it was through the pages of the *New Left Review* that his major works, *Eros and Civilization* (1955) and *One-Dimensional Man* (1964), would first find an audience in the UK, but his social theorising undoubtedly underpinned the counter-culture too. Marcuse was a co-founder of the Frankfurt *Institut für Sozialforschung*, better known as the 'Frankfurt School', where he and such fellow-members as Walter Benjamin and Theodor Adorno concentrated on producing a critical theory of Marxism. For them there was no point in the dogma-heavy versions of Marxism that could be seen in such monolithic societies as Stalin's Soviet Union; they believed that only through constant analysis, self-criticism and re-interpretation could the philosophy be kept relevant in the changing modern world. Concentrating on Marx's earlier works, many of which had only become available in the 1930s, they emphasised the libertarian aspects of his beliefs. It was this that informed Marcuse's own philosophising, and that in time would underpin his appeal to the Sixties' radical young.

Like many intellectuals Marcuse fled Germany following Hitler's advent to power in 1933; a year later he began teaching at Columbia University in New York. During the war he worked as an intelligence analyst for the US Army and after it headed the Central European Section of the Office of Intelligence Research. He returned to teaching in 1951 at Columbia and later Harvard, Brandeis and the University of California at San Diego, where after retirement he remained honorary emeritus professor of philosophy until his death in 1979.

A Hegelian-Freudian-Marxist, Marcuse believed uncompromisingly in radicalisation, vociferous dissent, and 'resistance to the point of subversion'. To him Western society, for all its boasts of 'freedom', was effectively anything but free; its touted liberalism merely 'repressive tolerance'. Technological advance, and the material progress it created, had simply bought off the masses with a modern form of Rome's 'bread and circuses' – what the French revolutionary 'Situationists', who also absorbed some of his ideas and would play a central role in forming the philosophies of the more radical wings of the counter-culture, decried as 'the Spectacle'. Sedated with material gain, people's intellectual and spiritual development had stultified; they remained cheerful robots, working to produce the goods they yearned to consume, then working for more of the same. 'Play' or 'leisure' was no more than another form of social control. Paradoxically Marcuse, for all his encouragement of revolution, drew the line at student demonstrations. Like many intellectuals of his generation, typically Leslie Fiedler whose 1965 essay on 'The New Mutants' (in the *Partisan Review*) is a petulant shriek of trampled liberal sensibilities, he saw the universities as sacrosanct oases of free speech and intellectual debate. They were not to be touched. Such a citadel might be changed, but only from within. The students who brandished his books even as they occupied 'the citadel' seemed not to mind the contradiction.

Writing at the height of the Cold War Marcuse held no brief for either capitalism or communism. In both systems the mass of people had become effective slaves of their governments – seduced by false liberality in the former, crushed by totalitarianism of the latter. Shelley had written, in *Queen Mab*, that: 'Obedience | Bane of all genius, virtue, freedom, truth, | Makes slaves of men, and of the human frame, | A mechanised automaton.' Marcuse would have agreed. As he puts it in *One-Dimensional Man*: ' "Totalitarian" is not only a terroristic political co-ordination of society, but also a non-terroristic economic-technical co-ordination which operates through the manipulation of needs by vested interests.'[8] The 'affluent society' was a myth. Establishments were *de facto* guilty, while the proletariat, the traditional source of revolution, had been neutered by the sticks of their work and the carrots of consumption, all backed up by the seductive cajoling of the mass media. For Marcuse the only possible saviours – a modern-day version of the Millennial belief in an 'Elect' or 'Chosen People' – would emerge from the radical fringes: students, Third World and Black revolutionaries, even the hippies of the 'counter-culture'. These groups, rejecting the stifling *status quo*, would advocate 'the Great Refusal'.

As will be seen, Marcuse had a role to play in the formulation of the stance taken by the New Left, a blanket description that embraces the most vocal of self-proclaimed 'revolutionaries', but in many ways he has a more central position in the world of counter-cultural belief. It was his work that illumined one of the great paradoxes of the contemporary world. If one really had 'never had it so good', then why was it still necessary for the majority of people to continue living and working on the same old patterns? It was as if Macmillan's line was one more advertisement, proclaiming a product as 'the best ever' even as the salesmen prepared to wheel out its 'better' successor.

A further stimulant of the counter-culture had long played an important role in twentieth-century life: the European avant-garde. There is no doubt that in its most obvious manifestations the counter-culture's greatest debts were to America, and its most immediate predecessors were the Beats of New York and California, but the input from Europe cannot be denied. It was appreciated by most of those who, like Jeff Nuttall, were processed through the art schools. That avant-garde can be seen as starting in early 1916 at Zurich's Cabaret Voltaire, home to a group comprising the Romanian poet Tristan Tzara, the German *dramaturg* and mystic Hugo Ball, the German chanteuse Emmy Hennings, the Alsatian artist Hans Arp, Richard Huelsenbeck, another German poet and part-time medical student, and Marcel Janco, a Romanian friend of Tzara. In earlier years it had been a bar, the Hollandischer Meierei, run by a former sailor; by the 1980s it was the Teen 'n' Twenty Disco. But from February to June 1916 it was the home of a new movement, 'artistic' for want of a better description, and known as Dada. Writing in a memoir entitled 'Dadaland' Hans Arp recalled the crazy improvisational anarchy that informed the performances in which the six 'musicians' played the only instrument they possessed: themselves:

> On the stage of a gaudy, motley, overcrowded tavern are several weird and peculiar figures . . . Total pandemonium. The people around us are shouting, laughing and gesticulating. Our replies are sighs of love, volleys of hiccups, poems, moos, and the miaowing of medieval Bruitists. Tzara is wiggling his behind like the belly of an Oriental dancer. Janco is playing an invisible violin and bowing and scraping. Madame Hennings, with a Madonna face, is doing the splits. Huelsenbeck is banging away nonstop at the great drum, with Ball accompanying him on the piano, pale as a chalky ghost.[9]

Eighty years on it all seems rather tame, but in 1916, the very mid-point of the First World War, its anarchy, its disrespect, its overturning of established attitudes was truly shocking. Soon, helped by Tzara's indomitable self-publicising, the movement began to influence similarly-minded groups around the world, notably in New York, in the persons of Man Ray and Marcel Duchamp, and in Paris, where it attracted among others André Breton, Louis Aragon, Paul Eluard and Francis Picabia. As far as the originals were concerned, Dada was first and foremost a protest against the horrors of the war. 'We were seeking an elementary art to cure man of the frenzy of the times, and a new order to restore the balance between heaven and hell.'[10] Inevitably those they termed 'the bandits' of the Establishment loathed Dada and the work itself 'rapidly became a subject of general disapproval'. As for the word, it had a multiplicity of origins. The *OED* goes for French: 'être sur son dada': to ride one's hobby-horse, but Greil Marcus notes, 'in German it was a dismissal "Goodbye", "Be seeing you", "Get off my back". In Romanian "Of course", in Italian "wet nurse", in Swabian slang "sex-crazed moron", in English "father" and "get ready" – a fanfare. Deep in the Indo-European substratum it meant both yes and no; it was a magic word.'[11] Its originator has never been fully proven: each of the originals laid claim, typically Huelsenbeck who claimed to have found the word in an open dictionary (fifty years on the Grateful Dead, most psychedelic of all their peers, would christen themselves by much the same method).

Above all Dada wished and intended to shock and through shock to change the world. As it gradually transmogrified into its own successors – Surrealism, Lettrism, Situationism, Fluxus – that desire did not wane. Thus, come the Sixties, it would remain an important influence, whether on the alternative culture – typically Nuttall's subterranean sTigma, an intentionally disturbing 'environmental exhibition' that attempted to lure people into the Better Books basement where they would face 'a violent involvement with . . . unalterable facts', or on the mainstream – such as Tom Stoppard's *Travesties*, a fantasy entanglement of Tzara, Joyce and Lenin (who could, just feasibly, have met in First World War Zurich).

Yet even as the cultural 'underground' sought to shock, it remained too often a prisoner of its background. Looking back, it would seem that the counter-culture, however vociferous, however shocking, however apparently 'revolutionary', was always acting, as it were, 'on licence' from the Establishment. Without the economic flourishing of mainstream society, it can be argued, the 'underground' would never have existed; as such what was it more than a rather more melodramatic version of the wider 'youth market' that had sufficed for earlier teenagers, and still provided amusement and satisfaction for the less radical (and less educated and middle-class) of the young. It is this paradox that informs any discussion of the role of the counter-culture. Once the order was: work hard, and you'll have enough goods; now it was consume hard, so as to provide a rationale for working some more and creating more goods (and of course creating the wages that would be used to pay for them). The counter-culture wanted to break the mould, but as Robert Hewison has pointed out, there was an 'intimate relationship between the counter-culture and the values it opposed. The turning towards "inner space", the anti-materialist idealism and would-be spirituality of the underground was a reaction against the excessive materialism of consumer society. But the very materialism and hedonism promoted by the official culture in the cause of consumption (overt or implicit eroticism in advertising, for instance) made that anti-materialism possible.'[12] The speed with which the more hedonistic side of the counter-culture folded with the end of that boom economy, spurred by the oil price hike that followed the Yom Kippur war of 1973, makes the relationship absolutely clear.

It can also be seen that, for a variety of reasons, the counter-culture was simply unable to form a 'proper' political revolution. As will be underlined in the context of the Grosvenor Square demonstrations of 1968, the hippie wing of the movement was deeply uninterested and, as much as their philosophies of 'love' allowed it, actively hostile to political involvement, but even those who ran some of the underground's main institutions, for instance Jim Haynes at the Arts Lab or Caroline Coon at Release, let alone Richard Neville or Mick Farren and the other main contributors to the 'underground press', were distinctly cold on orthodox politics.

On 5 January 1968 Richard Neville, whose magazine *Oz* had just celebrated a year of appearing in the UK after an already stormy career in his native Australia, wrote a lengthy letter – in essence a feature of its own and very much a forerunner of his book *Play Power* – to the *New Statesman*. It can serve as a paradigm of the underground stance on 'straight' politics. With its exaggerations, half-truths, and deliberate misinformation – 'so far there is no classic Underground Manifesto . . . although it is rumoured a sensational one exists and will soon be published' – it is a typical piece of Neville editorialising. *Oz* readers would have recognised it at once. Mainstream politics, with its 'expedient lies [and] hack betrayals' was pointless. Instead, join the Underground, form an alternative society, drop out of 'the competitive panic', experiment with 'a new way of living'. If the hippies disdain parochial politics, it is because of their greater concern for the entire world. A disciple of Marcuse, consciously or otherwise, Neville rejects conventional politics, however radical, as little more than another Establishment con trick.

Neville's diatribe was not allowed to pass unopposed. Quintin Hogg wrote from the Carlton Club to denounce Neville's letter as a 'strange flood of semi-literate verbal diarrhoea'.[13] Other, less celebrated critics defended socialism, or suggested that the 'underground', given its youthful constituency, would be better emulating such precocious genii as Mozart or Pitt. Most interesting was the response from a fellow Aussie ex-pat Clive James, then a Cambridge academic (and an occasional *Oz* contributor himself), who stood up for the liberalism that Neville had pooh-poohed and accused the *Oz* editor of a cardinal sin: ignorance of the historical background to his ideas, and the error of assuming that he and his generation had minted them. The underground press was a 'hive mind', much of its supposed novelty merely 'old hat', the creation of an older avant-garde. Finally, to abandon politics was to ensure that the Establishment would merely win the day without a fight.[14]

Neville had the last word, regretting his attempt to package the underground 'like margarine'[15] but it was an unresolved standoff. Given the oppositional position of the underground, ideological or otherwise, their stance was, inevitably, 'political' (quite anarchistically revolutionary as far as the shocked 'straight' world could see), but while they might have sung along to the Jefferson Airplane with their chant of 'Up against the walls, motherfucker!' or echoed optimistically the Doors' proclamation that, 'We're taking over!', these were lyrics they did not choose to write. The Beatles' 'Revolution' was more the underground stance: those who 'go carrying pictures of Chairman Mao . . . ain't gonna make it with anyone anyhow'. That said, the formally political New Left was hardly welcoming. Enmired in the niceties of ideology, as wrapped up in mutual recriminations as in promoting the new Jerusalem, they had no time for what were considered the innate frivolities of the counter-culture.

However, deprived of hindsight, the inter-relationship between the 'straight' and the 'freak', for instance, was by no means apparent thirty years ago. The initial reaction of the Establishment to this seditious, subversive, apparently anarchistic 'underground' was to take it at its most hysterical word. The vandals *were* at the gates. And as such they must be repelled. In time the counter-culture, or at least those parts of it that survived, would undergo the traditional cycle: hostility, familiarisation, acceptance, absorption, but not yet. The sociologist Stuart Hall, writing in *Resistance through Rituals* (1976) noted that:

> In the first flush of affluence, the guardians of the middle-class ideal first encountered the break in the shape of 'youth': first, working class, then its own. In the name of society, they resisted its hedonism, its narcissism, its permissiveness, its search for immediate gratifications, its anti-authoritarianism, its moral pluralism, its materialism: all defined as 'threats' to societal values springing from both aspirant working-class youth and malformed, badly socialised middle-class youth. They misrecognised the crisis within the dominant culture as a conspiracy against the dominant culture. They failed (as many members of the counterculture also failed) to see the cultural 'break' as, in its own traumatic and disturbing way, profoundly adaptive to the system's productive base.[16]

They also failed to notice that the 'rebels' were often as middle-class as were those who criticised them. The 'underground', whatever pieties it might offer, was no great lover of the proletariat. In the work of contemporary polemicists there is a gradual drift away from the mass. Ray Gosling, generally cited as the first homegrown writer on the UK scene and whose 'sort of autobiography' *Sum Total* appeared in 1962, is nearest to the working classes (his own background was upper-working/lower-middle class grammar- school, and later Leicester University dropout). His proles are romanticised, but they still have a place. His successor Jeff Nuttall is less sympathetic. For him the masses mean mass culture – Mods, Rockers, the like – and mass culture is no culture. His romantic fixation is on the angry rebel artist (working against a background of imminent nuclear holocaust); his heroes are Dada's children, the Surrealist anarchs whose line runs through the century, from Jarry and Tzara through to Joyce, Mailer, Ginsberg, Burroughs and R.D. Laing. There was little room here for 'pop'. By the time one reaches Richard Neville, whose *Play Power* appeared in 1970, or Mick Farren and Edward Barker, who published *Watch Out Kids* in 1972, the working class exists only as a blank hole. 'If there is hope,' wrote Orwell's Winston Smith in *1984*, 'it lies in the proles.' Such traditionally socialist sentiments were lost on the 'counter-culture'. The line most underground leaders would take was nearer to that of John Lennon's dismissive acerbity in his song 'Working Class Hero': 'You think you're all clever and classless and free – but you're all fucking peasants as far as I can see.'

In the end the counter-culture was as depressingly riven with hierarchies as was its 'straight' equivalent. It placed those with invitations to the dinner parties of the radically chic over those who lacked such an entrée, those who appeared as figureheads in the Establishment media over their lesser, if still élitist associates back toiling on the typesetter, those whose names appeared on the newspaper mastheads over those for whom they wrote, those who ran the counter-cultural institutions over those who merely queued at their doors, and for everyone, however lowly, those who lived in London over those still entrapped in the provinces. To Cheryll Park, a young woman arriving from the north to make her way into this still strange world, the underground, for all its boasts, was depressingly familiar:

> It was exactly the same as everything else: there were rich people and there were poor people and there were people in the middle. There was a kind of a decadence there and you could belong to that because you might be beautiful or you might be able to take lots of drugs or able to get lots of drugs – it was just the same as any other society. It was class-ridden. And that élitism took the whole movement over and the people who could afford to carry on living like that did and the rest dwindled away. There was no working class in the underground because nobody did any work. And the working-class people who did join the movement, if there was a movement, found their own little slot and they found that some people were still in control because they had the money. You didn't *have* to be an intellectual and you didn't *have* to be rich, but you had to have something that you could contribute. If you were an ordinary people person who lived in some suburb, you had no chance at all.[17]

However much the alternative society might stand as a parallel world; it was rarely an opposite one.

Such theories inform the 'counter-', what of the 'culture'? If the 'underground' had neither time, inclination nor ability to create a 'proper' political revolution, such commodities were in more than adequate supply when it came to setting up what would be termed the 'alternative society'. And it is that society, an identifiable if patchwork confection, that must be considered next.

Chapter Eleven

Coming Together: Wholly Communion

World declaration hot peace shower!
Earth's grass is free!
Cosmic poetry Visitation accidentally happening carnally!
Spontaneous planet-chant Carnival!
Mental Cosmonaut poet-epiphany, immaculate-supranational Poesy insemination!
Skullbody love-congress Annunciation, duende concordium, effendi tovarish
  illumination,
Now! Sigmatic New Departures Residu of Better Books and
Moving Times in obscenely New Directions! Soul
revolution City Lights Olympian lamb-blast!
Castalia centrum new consciousness hungry generation
Movement roundhouse 42 beat apocalypse energy-triumph!
You are not alone!
The 'collaged invocation' delivered at the Albert Memorial, as a prelude to
the Albert Hall Poetry Reading, 11 June 1965

In any discussion of the 'Sixties' the question inevitably emerges: when did the
period begin? The dismissal of the simple chronology is easy enough – no one
ever suggests that 1 January 1960 was some kind of seminal date – but then
what? One thing, fortunately, is clear: that 1965 – and especially 11 June 1965,
the day of the Albert Hall Poetry Reading, somewhat grandiosely known as
'Wholly Communion' (at least in retrospect and in Peter Whitehead's film of
the event) – was pivotal. Irrespective of the quality of the event – as will be
seen, this was infinitely debatable – the reading was the moment at which the
nascent underground stood up to be counted. It was a moment perfectly representative of a time when – as Peter Stanshill and David Mairowitz, whose anthology of 'underground manifestos', *BAMN* ('by any means necessary'),
begins in 1965, put it – 'the gloomy earnestness of the "protest" mentality
[was] displaced by a new "tough" frivolity and creative lunacy . . . Suddenly
the debate is no longer between Right Wing/Left Wing, but rather between
the oppressions of the external world and the desire for internal liberation, between activist commitment to the continuing social struggle and dropping out
of a cultural milieu that won't allow it.'[1]

Symbolically linking the artistic avant-garde, such as Alex Trocchi and
Jeff Nuttall, with the beat poets, led by Michael Horovitz, who were loosely
linked in the magazine *New Departures* (home particularly of Pete Brown and
Adrian Mitchell), and the 'little magazine' and bookshop world of such as
Miles and Jim Haynes, it brought together several thousand people who, for
want of any more subtle emotion, were just delighted to find that they were

not alone. Whether it stands more as the grand climacteric of one era or as the launch-pad of the next is important, but was less obviously so at the time. It was the moment that counted, and what followed, over the next five or six years would for many people represent 'the Sixties'. The reading did not, of course, spring fully-formed from nowhere. The coming together of formerly disparate groups that was perhaps the most important product of the reading had been growing in intensity for the previous half-decade. As the drawing together grew in momentum it would see assembled all the major underground players – although some, typically Nuttall, would opt to reject, or at least stand aside from, the new 'alternative' consensus, while others, such as Richard Neville, still making his way along the hippie trail from Sydney, had yet to arrive.

The groups that 'came together' in this way often overlapped – there were no bounds that restricted a given individual to a given group – but were essentially discrete entities, each working to achieve its own ends, and generally existing in its own self-absorbed world. There was often a sense of like minds, but not always a meeting. What linked them was an inchoate desire to 'change the world', but the methods they proposed and the means they had available often kept them apart. Thus at the same time one could see the beats, covering the country but leaning especially to Liverpool and to London, the privileged exquisites of swinging London's 'new aristocracy', the avant-garde artists (typically Jeff Nuttall), the acolytes of America (led by Miles, most enthusiastic of all proselytisers), and so on. And there were simply the unaffiliated, such as Mick Farren (future *IT* editor, UK White Panther and leader of that exemplar of underground bands, the Social Deviants). His voice stands for many: 'There we were, living on Ladbroke Grove, thinking, "There's something in all this shit", but we couldn't figure out what.'[2] Less central but moving towards a greater involvement was Notting Hill's black community, from a narrow point of view simply offering the primary source of grass and hash for those who indulged, but already pursuing its own agenda. The only missing ingredients were the pioneers of what would become known as 'gender politics': women's and gay liberation were for the future. There were also what one might call a group of benevolent elders, 'the grown-ups' of the party, never to be formally involved in the 'counter-culture' but always on its fringes, available to sign suitably liberal petitions, appear at the better parties and smarter openings, contribute to the chic-er magazines, to sleep with the more attractive young women and occasionally back their liberal principles with hard cash. It included such arts heavyweights as the theatre critic Ken Tynan, impresario Michael White, publisher Clive Goodwin who would back Tariq Ali's newspaper *Black Dwarf*, Tony Godwin, Derek Boshier, the painter and a tutor at Central, Colin MacInnes and Christopher Logue. The putative 'underground' itself was by no means a kindergarten: such guiding lights as Hoppy (John Hopkins), Nuttall and Haynes all predated the baby-boom as, obviously, did Horovitz and the rest of the beats.

CND, of course, had been the engine that had already brought a number of these groups together, and it was the effective breakdown of CND – however large and noisy its marches might be becoming – and its failure to make a real difference that prompted those who had been involved to search out new ways of changing in society. From approximately 1963 the lack of an immediately suitable route proved a major problem. As Jeff Nuttall put it, 'You couldn't march any more because it hadn't worked. You couldn't join the left because of Hungary and because of Gaitskell. You couldn't join in the political machine at all: so what were you to do?'[3] What 'you did', it would turn out, was to leave traditional politics to those who were happy with its hypocrisies, compromises and evasions and start looking to culture.

For the purposes of the 'underground in waiting' that culture took two forms: literary and artistic. There had been major changes in theatre: the late Fifties had seen productions of Ionesco, Brecht, Beckett, Pinter and others, all of whom were in the forefront of the theatrical avant-garde, but mainstream none the less. 'Fringe theatre' was bubbling under, but it did not yet form part of the 'underground' offensive. Only Peter Brook's *Marat/Sade*, which was premiered in 1964, might be seen as an exception, but that too was deeply indebted to Artaud, creator some years earlier of the 'theatre of cruelty', and once more part of what might be termed oxymoronically the 'mainstream avant-garde'. For the young, frustrated and disillusioned CND veterans, who could be found in such hangouts as the Peace Café in the Fulham Road, the choice was 'little magazines' and poetry readings (with or without accompanying jazz). These magazines were rarely noted by the Establishment and they were often cheaply produced and with tiny circulations – the publisher/poet's friends, a few loyal art school pals – but each one invariably brimmed with enthusiasm. Among the better known were Michael Horovitz's *New Departures* (from Oxford) and Dave Cunliffe's *Poetmeat* (from Blackburn). Miles, whose *Long Hair* would prove to be one of the most important, although somewhat distanced from the home-grown British efforts with its showcase of 'visiting' American beat superstars, started off at Cheltenham art school with *Tree*.

Horovitz was also involved heavily in the jazz-poetry nexus, in which he was invariably partnered by fellow-poet Peter Brown (later lyricist for the Cream). The pair had met at the Beaulieu Jazz Festival of 1960, where, to quote Nuttall, 'the beats ran amok with fire and water'.[4] (According to George Melly these dedicated trad fans, with their bowler hats, army boots, strategically tailored potato sacks and old fur coats – an ensemble known as 'rave gear' – had become overexcited by the unlikely figure of Acker Bilk.[5]) The festival seems to have kicked off a number of beat anabases. Johnny Byrne, later co-author of the *echt*-Sixties novel *Groupie*, but then part of a group based in Liverpool 8 (today's Toxteth) that would produce both the 'Liverpool Poets' and the Beatles (as well as the *Daily Worker*'s sour remark that, 'The Mersey Sound is the voice of 80,000 crumbling houses and 30,000 people on the dole'), recalled that after that year's festival, '[Spike] Hawkins, [Mal] Dean and I and Horovitz and Brown decided to split the country, rather like the Popes decided to split Europe between Avignon and Rome. Hawkins and Byrne would have everything north of Stafford, and Horovitz and Brown would have everything south. And we would set up these (poetry) readings. So Hawkins and I went straight back to Liverpool to set up the first of the readings at a place called Streate's. We had a couple of local jazz musicians, and us mainly reading from poems in the *Evergreen Review*.'[6] Supplies came from Better Books – the poets made regular treks to pick up the latest imports. 'The following year it was decided that we would extend our activities further because Brown and Horovitz had come up to Liverpool . . . Adrian Henri started coming and performing. He was part of the Liverpool painters. Brian Patten was a fifteen-year-old cub reporter on the local paper. Roger McGough was just coming out of teacher-training college . . .'[7] It was the same across Britain: British beat poets wandering the nation's roads, reading in student unions and coffee bars, spreading the word. Life on the British road was summed up in 'Blues for the Hitch-hiking Dead', an ever-expanding (and expandable) poem by Horovitz and Brown.

In August 1963 the writers' conference of that year's Edinburgh International Festival provided another form of impetus, albeit somewhat closer to the Establishment. It was set up by the publisher John Calder, whose list already included the cream of the European and American avant-garde and who would be central to the struggle against literary censorship over the next decade. Calder had two main helpers: one was Sonia Orwell, widow of George, and the other a young American 'cultural entrepreneur', Jim Haynes.

Mrs Orwell, very much an 'Our Age' figure, had been essentially co-opted to add a necessary element of highbrow intellectual cachet, but Jim Haynes, who would become one of the central players in the counter-culture, was of a very different background. He had arrived in Edinburgh in 1956 thanks to the USAF. Here a sympathetic CO allowed him to live off base, take classes at the university and in mid-1959 granted him an early discharge. The basis for this was the 26 year-old Haynes's plan to set up what would be Britain's first paperbacks-only bookshop. The military, apparently keen to encourage one who wished to 'better himself', gave him the go-ahead. He sold his VW, threw in his discharge bonus and bought a rundown antique shop on Charles Street for £300. The Paperback Book Shop was an immediate success. Like London's Better Books (where paperbacks played second fiddle to hard covers) Haynes carried an eclectic stock of British, American and European authors, often unobtainable anywhere else in the country, plus a regular selection of so-called 'obscene publications' (a far more wide-ranging, not to mention tame concept in the era preceding the 1959 Obscene Publications Act). He also picked up some useful publicity a year later when an ex-missionary, less than impressed by the book's recent acquittal at the Old Bailey, publicly burnt *Lady Chatterley's Lover* outside the shop. For Haynes's Edinburgh contemporaries the Book Shop provided a vital cultural centre. It was, as its owner recalled, 'a salon, it was a coffee house, it was a gallery, it was a meeting place, it very quickly became a real centre.'[8] Like Better Books, like New York's Peace Eye bookshop or San Francisco's City Lights, the Paperback Book Shop became both a focal point and inspiration of the cultural revolution. In 1962 Haynes opened the Traverse Theatre, and like the bookshop, it soon became a landmark for cultural advance and a focus for the young and intellectually inclined. It took the north-of-the-border role, noted Robert Hewison, of London's ICA.[9] Haynes found himself something of a 'cult figure for the anarcho-leftie-inclined students in Edinburgh, and acted very much as a proselytising force'.[10] The Traverse mounted plays by the European avant-garde, brought over America's Living Theater, and put on new plays by home-grown authors, typically Heathcote Williams's *Local Stigmatic*.

Calder and Haynes had already put together a conference in 1962, offering the festival-going public an array of writers that included Angus Wilson, Rosamund Lehmann, L.P. Hartley, Simon Raven, David Caute, Rebecca West, Lawrence Durrell, as well as an important US presence, notably Henry Miller, Norman Mailer (then best-known as the author of *The Naked and the Dead* but also a co-founder of the world's first 'underground' paper, New York's *Village Voice* – naturally available at Haynes's shop), Mary McCarthy and, perhaps most important of all, the relatively unknown William Burroughs, author of one of the most startling novels of recent years, *The Naked Lunch* (1959). This novel, the first sight of which had been in excerpts published in 1958 in the Chicago magazine *Big Table*, had already survived the first of a number of obscenity cases – on both sides of the Atlantic – which would dog it through the Sixties. Burroughs's appearance in Edinburgh was to talk on a panel dedicated to censorship. He also described his 'cut-up' method (a form of literary collage which he had taken from fellow-writer Brion Gysin) and suggested that this method of 'folding' texts in on each other, was the future of writing.

Haynes and Calder's second Writers' Conference, in August 1963, focused on the theatre, bringing together Kenneth Tynan (as chairman), and a range of playwrights including the orthodox J.B. Priestley and John Mortimer as well as Joan Littlewood, John Arden, Alain Robbe-Grillet and the Dutch critic Jan Kott. The high (or for some low) point of the conference came, however, outside the intellectual forum. The 'happening', defined as 'an improvised or spontaneous theatrical or pseudo-theatrical entertainment'[11] and seen as any form of unusual public event that set out to jolt the viewer from passivity in dealing with 'the arts', had originated in the US during the Fifties. Combining Dada, Artaud and abstract impressionist experimentation, its primary philosophy was the principle of 'transformation by destruction'.[12] Among its leading exponents were Allan Kaprow and Kenneth Dewey, both of whom were at the Conference. Allied with the theatre director Charles Marowitz, they decided to treat Edinburgh to its own event. It was all very quick and less than earth-shattering: a bagpipe skirled, a tape offered recordings of the conferees, and, most important, a naked female art student ('a shapely nineteen-year-old blonde' as the *Daily Express* put it) was wheeled in a wheelbarrow around the gallery that surrounded the conference hall. Tame it may have been, but the organisers could not have wished for a more dramatic response. Tynan, supposedly doyen of the avant-garde, fulminated at Kaprow and Co. as 'totalitarian' and 'apocalyptic'; the press donned their best masks of synthetic outrage. In the following issue of *Encounter* the distinguished Brechtian Martin Esslin mourned: 'Six days of intensive argument, hundreds of speeches, six Third Programme broadcasts, dozens of thoughtful press reports on the conference – all utterly obliterated by a forty-second appearance of a nude in a public place . . . Is there any significance here for our *kultur*-critics?' The immediate effect was simple: next year's conference, to be dedicated to poetry, was promptly cancelled.

Aside from Burroughs, another important influence on the future counter-culture had appeared at the 1962 conference. This was the Scot (with Italian parents) Alexander Trocchi, like Burroughs (whom he had termed 'a cosmonaut of inner space')[13] a long-term heroin user, who had recently returned from a period living in Paris, where he had combined the usual left-bank activities (in his case the magazine *Merlin*) with a spell writing for Maurice Girodias's Olympia Press. Trocchi, along with Christopher Logue and a number of other American and British ex-pats, had been the mainstays of what Girodias called his 'D.B.s' or dirty books. In this capacity Trocchi had been responsible for *Cain's Book* (devoted to heroin reminiscences), a supposed 'Fifth Volume' of Frank Harris's *Life and Loves* as well as, under the pseudonym 'Frances Lengel', such unashamed pieces of porn as *School for Sin* and *White Thighs*.

By 1963 Trocchi was very much an elder statesman (somewhat wilder, however, than the Tynans and their like), with properly Parisian credentials, not to mention his heroin habit, to lend gravitas to the role. In mid-1964 he began publishing what he called his *Sigma Portfolio*, in essence a manifesto aimed at bringing together avant-garde art and the politics of change. It would continue appearing sporadically until 1966. Typical of Trocchi's projections for a better world was what he titled 'The Invisible Insurrection; sigma, a tactical Blueprint' published in the *City Lights Journal* no.2. It lays down many of the themes that would inform the counter-culture to come. Trocchi told his readers:

We are concerned not with the coup d'état of Trotsky and Lenin, but with the coup du monde, a transition of necessity more complex, more diffuse than the other, and so more gradual, less spectacular. Our methods will vary with the empirical facts pertaining here and now, there and then.

Political revolt is and must be ineffectual precisely because it must come to grips at the prevailing level of political process. Beyond the backwaters of civilisation it is an anachronism. Meanwhile, with the world at the edge of extinction, we cannot afford to wait for the mass. Nor to brawl with it.

. . . the cultural revolution must seize the grids of expression and the powerhouses of the mind. Intelligence must become self-conscious, release its own power, and, on a global scale, transcending functions that are no longer appropriate, dare to exercise it. History will not overthrow national governments; it will outflank them. The cultural revolt is the necessary underpinning, the passionate substructure of a new order of things . . .

We must reject the conventional notion of 'unchanging human nature'. There is in fact no such permanence anywhere. There is only becoming . . .

Meanwhile our anonymous million can focus their attention on the problem of 'leisure'. A great deal of what is pompously called 'juvenile delinquency' is the inarticulate response of youth incapable of coming to terms with leisure. The violence associated with it is a direct consequence of the alienation of man from himself brought about by the Industrial Revolution. Man has forgotten how to play.

How to begin? At a chosen moment in a vacant country house (mill, abbey, church, or castle) not too far from the City of London we shall foment a kind of cultural 'jam session'; out of this will evolve the prototype of our spontaneous university.

The cultural possibilities of this movement are immense and the time is ripe for it. The world is awfully near the brink of disaster. Scientists, artists, teachers, creative men of goodwill everywhere are in suspense. Waiting. Remembering that it is our kind even now who operate, if they don't control the grids of expression, we should have no difficulty in recognising the spontaneous university as the possible detonator of the invisible insurrection.

. . . Now and in the future our centre is everywhere, our circumference nowhere. No one is in control. No one is excluded. A man will know when he is participating without offering him a badge . . .

In looking for a word to designate a possible international association of men who are concerned individually and in concert to articulate an effective strategy and tactics for this cultural revolution, it was thought necessary to find one that provoked no obvious responses. We chose the word 'sigma'. Commonly used in mathematical practice to designate all, the sum, the whole, it seemed to fit very well with our notion that all men must eventually be included.

The basic shift in attitude . . . must happen. IT IS HAPPENING. Our problem is to make men conscious of the fact, and to inspire them to participate in it. Man must seize control of his own future: only by doing so can he ever hope to inherit the earth.

Trocchi was the signatory, but he claimed a wide range of supporters: Burroughs, Ginsberg, Leary and Mailer from America; Tom McGrath (soon to be the launch editor of the underground's first newspaper *IT*), John Latham, Feliks Topolski, Colin Wilson, Michael Hollingshead, Joan Littlewood, the inevitable Jim Haynes, 'anti-psychiatrists' R.D. Laing and David Cooper. Sigma's legal adviser was listed as Arnold Goodman, an unarguably Establishment figure, usually known as Harold Wilson's lawyer and political fixer.

In January 1964 Trocchi met another struggler for change and enlisted him among the sigma's supporters. He became, as he described himself, 'Trocchi's office-boy'.[14] Jeff Nuttall, a CND stalwart and professional art teacher, had exhibited with Group H (founded in 1951 as the Hendon Experimental Art Club, by the concrete and 'soundtext' poet Bob Cobbing. Group H quickly fell foul of less progressive figures, notably the then chairman of the Finchley Art Society. Arriving at one exhibition, which featured works that Nuttall admitted were 'real filth'[15] she took one look at what was generally acknowledged to be the mildest piece on show, a white board with a white 'splash' painted on it. 'That', she declared, 'must be removed.' When quizzed as to why, Margaret Thatcher informed the incredulous artists that the 'splash' was obviously an ejaculation. Nuttall also worked with another Cobbing creation, the Writers' Forum of Arts Together (later the Writers' Forum Press). His *Limbless Virtuoso*, produced with Keith Musgrave, was the Forum's first ever publication. Heavily influenced by Burroughs, in November 1963 he started producing his own homage to cut-up, *My Own Mag: A Super-Absorbent Periodical*. Two months later he actually met the master, who repaid his compliments by a series of contributions to *My Own Mag*, entitled 'Moving Times'; Nuttall defined Burroughs's work as 'a programmed assault on reality'.

Trocchi's plans for a cultural revolution could be said to have reached some form of fruition in the counter-culture over the next few years; his idea of a 'cultural jam session' was put into practice earlier, and proved anything but the meeting of like minds he had envisaged. Best memorialised in Jeff Nuttall's *Bomb Culture*, it was a gruesome weekend in mid-1964 when Trocchi, Laing, Cooper, McGrath, Cobbing, Latham, Clancy Segal, Beba Lavrin, Adam Esterson and Nuttall himself gathered at Braziers' Park, a Quaker retreat in Oxfordshire, administered – quite coincidentally – by Marianne Faithfull's estranged father Glynn. Here the various egos clashed, bickered, immersed themselves in alcohol and dispersed, still nursing their various antagonisms. It was a disaster even if in due course the meeting would have a positive end: the Philadelphia Association, a charity set up by Laing, Cooper and Esterson, went on to found Kingsley Hall, a therapeutic community based on Laing and Cooper's 'anti-psychiatry'.

If Jim Haynes's bookshop was urging on progressive cultural developments in Edinburgh, then Better Books was fulfilling a similar function in
the Charing Cross Road. As well as the shelves of books and magazines, the
basement became a centre for avant-garde debates and exhibitions. There
were 'writers' nights' (typically a discussion between Peter Brook, John Arden and Adrian Mitchell on 'The Theatre and Its Future') and more notoriously there was, starting in February 1965, the sTigma. Jeff Nuttall had been
determined to put on some form of environmental exhibition for some time.
His first basement event was a happening, created with Charles Marowitz
and Ken Dewey. The sTigma, which followed, was 'a sort of labyrinth which
was supposed to be an indictment of society'.[16] Nuttall's collaborators were
fellow-Group H member Criton Tomazos, Bruce Lacey, John Latham, Nick
Watkins, Keith and Heather Musgrave and Dave Trace. Working from an
original plan developed by Tomazos they spent late 1964 and early 1965
working towards it. Given that each member of the team imparted a quite
different meaning to the project – the Musgraves saw it as a joke, Tomazos as
a sacred enterprise, Latham as one more weapon against the books he hated
and Nuttall as 'anger [and] ebullient sarcasm'[17] – it was not a happy experience. Still, it came together and opened in February 1965.

> The entrance . . . was through three valve-doorways lined with old copies of
> the *Economist*. The last you could just squeeze through, but not back, no re-
> turn. The corridor this led to was lined with hideous bloody heads, photos of
> war atrocities, Victorian pornographic cards, tangles of stained underwear,
> sanitary towels, French letters, anatomical diagrams; the passage narrowed
> into complete darkness – tin, glass, wet bread, plastic, sponge rubber, then a
> zig-zag corridor of polythene through which you could glimpse your goal, a
> group of figures. They were gathered around a dentist chair which had itself
> been turned into a figure, with sponge rubber breasts and a shaven head. On
> the seat of the chair was a cunt made of a bed pan lined with hair and cod's
> roe. Detergent bubbles spluttered from between the slabs of roe, which re-
> mained spluttering and stinking for four weeks. Then a corridor of television
> sets led past the window of Dave Trace's sleazy café with its festering meal,
> also left through four weeks, into a replica living room, furnished with choice
> items of ghastly ornament and with a sideboard drawer containing human
> toes. The voices of Trocchi, Burroughs, Mike Osborne's alto and the BBC
> leaked out and intermingled from concealed loudspeakers. After the living
> room a corridor of old clothes, a red cylinder, knee deep in feathers, a vaginal
> tunnel of inner tubes scented with Dettol through which the public had to
> crawl to get out, a womb-room with a plastic abortion nailed to the wall, a
> plethora of political and religious propaganda and a beaming photograph of
> David Jacobs.[18]

'It was,' added Nuttall in 1988, 'supposed to be a shocker, to drive people out of their minds' although 'it would look very tatty and very comic now.'[19] A few months later Nuttall's next show at Better Books featured performers.

> We fitted ourselves out as sculptures and prepared ourselves in various ways, wrapping stuff round ourselves, and I hid myself behind a screen and just had my belly and my prick and one finger coming through holes. People were sent invitations to a private view. So they came round and looked at the sculptures. They were served sherry, which was what you got at private views and they wandered round and said, 'They're real . . . ' and a girl touching my belly said, 'Well, it's warm.' It was called the People Show – the first People Show.[20]

The People Show, still in existence today, would provide a primary pattern for alternative theatre; the extravagances in the basement did not last. In August 1967 Hatchards, booksellers to the Establishment, took over Better Books. There would be no more happenings. It was also the beginning of the end for Nuttall's role as a pioneer of the 'underground'; however, first he, Better Books and a number of other 'counter-cultural' hierarchs would unite in what would prove one of the seminal events of the entire decade. The poetry reading at the Albert Hall.

In retrospect everyone always wants a piece of seminal action and the pretenders to the genesis of the Poetry Reading are many. Chronologically the process appears to have been triggered by the timely arrival in London of Allen Ginsberg. London was in fact the latest stop on what was proving a world tour (albeit a rather involuntary one): earlier in the year the poet had been invited to Cuba from where, on discovering his far from closeted sexual predilections the revolutionaries promptly threw him out. From Cuba he moved on to Prague – the Cold War dictating that it was impossible to get a direct flight back to the States – and thence to Moscow, before returning via Warsaw back to Prague. From here he was deported once again, but not before the local students had crowned him King of the May, and en route to New York he decided to stop over in London. Here he gravitated to Better Books and was put up by its manager Miles and his wife Sue. Miles then suggested that Ginsberg give a reading at the bookshop. For a group that was still reeling from the collapse of CND, Ginsberg's appearance would be 'the first healing wind on a very parched collective mind'.[21] The reading was a triumph, packing out the basement not only with London's poetry lovers but with a passing caravan of New Yorkers, among them Gerard Malanga, Andy Warhol (on a big promotional swing through Europe), Edie Sedgwick, Baby Jane Holzer, the creators of *Fuck You* magazine, and Kate Helecser (ex-wife of film-maker Pierre), best-known for helping put cunnilingus on screen (in a non-porno context) for the first time ever. It was one of these Americans, the avant-garde New York film-maker Barbara Rubin (cynical observers suggested that her main contribution to the avant-garde was running the stock through the camera twice) who suggested a more ambitious plan.

Sue Miles remembers, 'There was an afternoon when Allen realised that Gregory Corso was in Paris, Ferlinghetti was coming to London, Pablo Neruda and Pablo Fernandez were here, and so was Andrei Voznesensky. Major international poets, nearly all in London and this should be celebrated: there should be a poetry reading. Barbara Rubin turned round and said, "What's the biggest hall in town?" and we all went "The Albert Hall". And she got the phone, dialled the number and said, "Hi. How much is it to book the Albert Hall?" "£450." "When's the next free date?" "Ten days time." "We'll have it." Down with the phone.'[22] The money was found, from Jill Richter, wife of Dan, editor of *Residue* magazine (published in Athens) and a man better known by the cognoscenti for his appearance in the movie *2001* as one of the apes, capering before the mysterious monolith. And that, as Sue Miles puts it, was it.

But was it? If Ginsberg and Co, backed by the Better Books claque, seem to have set the ball rolling, it was another group who actually took it over. According to Christopher Logue the actual organisation was the responsibility of Alex Trocchi, as much as part of his proselytising for sigma as any desire to bring poetry to the culture-hungry London masses. And through Richter there came his flatmate John Esam, who had gained a certain éclat for visiting friends armed with a small eyedropper and a bottle of diluted LSD, part of Michael Hollingshead's original stash. Esam had faced the first ever prosecution for possession of LSD in Britain but he had escaped; in any case the drug was yet to be declared illegal (the law changed almost immediately after the trial). And alongside them came Michael Horovitz, editor of *New Departures* and perhaps England's best-known beat poet in his own right, who had already arranged a Ginsberg reading at the ICA one month earlier.

Meanwhile Allen Ginsberg achieved a small dream of his own: meeting the Beatles. It was not the most auspicious of occasions. Eight days before the reading, on 3 June, it was Ginsberg's thirty-ninth birthday. Miles, who supposedly had the right connections, was deputed to ensure their presence. And on the night, held in film-maker David Larcher's home in Chester Square, John Lennon and George Harrison, with wives in tow, duly arrived. Unfortunately, in the way of superstars, they were somewhat late, and by then Ginsberg was well into the liquor cabinet. He greeted the pair of Fabs totally naked, other that is than for a pair of Y-fronts adorning his head and a 'No Waiting' sign dangling from his penis. Lennon and Harrison were less than amused. 'You don't do that in front of the birds,' Lennon told Miles, before shepherding Cynthia and Patti to a safer environment.

Once the poetry reading started happening, everyone wanted a piece. And given the proximity of the booking, all volunteers were very welcome. Rubin began hassling the media, who responded with great enthusiasm –

June 1965 was proving a slow month, so slow that on the eve of the event the BBC News devoted a substantial piece to the story and the rest of the press followed suit. Boosted by daily press conferences, a photo session on the Albert Memorial (Christopher Logue recalls: 'Trocchi called me up and said "Why don't you come down to the Albert Memorial. There's a lot of really interesting people just hanging about." So I went down there and there were a lot of people there, quite interesting-looking people and it was fun and it was sunny and the girls were very pretty and what more could you ask for . . . ')[23] and a flood of handouts and bulletins, the event took off.

As Miles saw it,

> Everybody was going to be there: Voznesensky, Ferlinghetti and Corso who were in Paris, Simon Vinkenoog from Amsterdam, Pablo Fernandez, the Cultural Attaché for the Cuban Embassy and a poet himself, and all kinds of people. (They all promised, anyway, although they didn't all read in the end.) Ferlinghetti arrived and he moved in with Julie Felix the folk singer, who had a TV show and was hanging out with these strange people who were followers of Bart Huges, a Dutch madman who believed that the only way to really get a head was to get a hole: trepanation, which he had indeed performed upon himself. Everyone you talked to about it instantly had lots of friends who'd get involved and there was this endlessly growing constituency.[24]

The reading was, as all but the starriest-eyed noted, an event of which the importance and effect of the entirety far transcended that of its individual parts. The publicity certainly worked. Seven thousand people, an unprecedented number for a poetry reading, turned up, paid their couple of pounds apiece and crowded the galleries of the Albert Hall, gazing down on the assembled poets lounging on stage below. Most of them were young, although a few 'straight' fans turned up, one of whom shouted to Trocchi, 'When are we going to have some real poetry?' But he was as solitary as another heckler, crying out for 'naked ladies'. There was a substantial US contingent, and for no apparent reason there was Indira Gandhi, a 'strange Indian woman', given a lift by Sue Miles.

As far as the readings themselves went, starry headliners or not, quantity outweighed quality. Miles recalled it as 'one of the worst poetry readings ever'.[25] Alex Trocchi, flying on his regular heroin dosage, had taken on the role of MC but was woefully inadequate. The mix of celebrities and wannabes was inevitably volatile and all too often Trocchi seemed less than capable of corralling it. Ginsberg, the inspiration of the whole thing, was drunk and, his omnipresent finger-cymbals chiming an accompaniment, read atrociously, a fact of which even tipsy he was well aware, and suitably annoyed. The crowd, just grateful to hear 'Howl' from the lips of the man who had written it, were less worried. Voznesensky, appalled by the chaotic stage management and the increasingly restless audience, refused point-blank to make his promised contribution. The Cubans had apparently put a stop to Fernandez coming anywhere near such bourgeois decadence. Ginsberg then started reading the Russian's poetry, including a line of self-criticism which the audience, forgetting that it was Voznesensky's and not Ginsberg's comment, took badly – they didn't like what seemed like Ginsberg's arrogance. Burroughs, who was not among the readers, sent a tape, played on stage by his then boyfriend Ian Somerville – so rickety was the PA that his intonations went almost unrecognised. Corso hadn't essayed a reading in three years and managed to alienate most of his fans by reading a lengthy piece of autobiographical self-analysis that was hardly suitable for what was supposed to be a celebratory gathering. And Harry Fainlight, talking about his poem 'The Spider' but never seeming capable of merely reading the relevant verses, was actually booed off stage. It didn't help that he was wearing a pair of glasses with flowers painted on the outside of the lenses, totally obscuring his view.

As recorded by Peter Whitehead on film and in print the central readings came from Ginsberg, from Ferlinghetti, from Logue – the old pros. Aside from the obvious stars the night's hero was probably Adrian Mitchell – too simplistic for the beat purists – whose 'To Whom It May Concern' (with its menacing chorus: 'Tell me lies about Vietnam') struck chords among those for whom CND, the beats' tainted grail, was becoming *passé*. (Coincidentally for those who eschewed the poets there was another event that night: the Teach-In on Vietnam at London University. Few seem, however, to have noticed the neat symbolism of this duality.)

The main problem, however, was not the stars but the hopefuls. A number of the British poets were reasonably well-known – Horovitz, Brown, Hawkins, McGrath, MacBeth, Logue and Fainlight – but there were others who ought to have been filtered out long since. Trocchi, in charge of the bill, had been too kind to effect this necessary cull and the evening suffered accordingly. People would grab the microphone, supposedly in Trocchi's gift, and mutter or shout, wail or scream their particular piece of self-exposure to a far from enthusiastic crowd. Or there were the non-poetical distractions: Simon Vinkenoog, Trocchi's Dutch lieutenant, founder of *sigma nederland* and introduced as 'the grand old young man of Dutch letters', wandered the auditorium out of his mind on LSD; R.D. Laing and *his* lieutenant Joseph Berke appeared with a dozen patients from Kingsley Hall who wandered around the Hall, interfacing with poets and audience, pausing occasionally to burn money. Offstage there were further problems. Apart from inducing a general horror in the Albert Hall's staff, mainly British Legionnaires who had never seen anything remotely like this barbarian invasion – no one even remotely involved would ever be allowed to book the Hall again – there were certain acts of individual madness. Jeff Nuttall and John Latham had planned their own happening – their appearance was described in the *Guardian* as 'astonishing figures looking as though they had been tarred and feathered with the torn leaves of books and newspapers': the aim was to mock the printed word by tearing apart their costumes. Unfortunately Latham, who had painted himself blue, passed out shortly before the pair were due on stage: he had forgotten to leave a small patch of untouched skin for breathing purposes. The recumbent artist was then borne away to a convenient dressing room (variously ascribed to Sir Malcolm Sargent, Sir John Barbirolli or Sir Thomas Beecham) and dumped in a bath. (This too was a problem: it had been filled with some form of goo by 'Professor' Bruce Lacey, who specialised in mad robotics, and could be seen briefly in the Beatles' first movie.) Nuttall then climbed in after him and the pair began washing off the paint. At which point an attendant wandered in, saw the two en-woaded men, high and happy, apparently indulging in some homosexual excess, and staggered away. Yet even taken reading by reading, it was not an unmitigated disaster. Michael Horovitz reduced the audience to hysteria with his performance, aided by half-a-dozen fellow-poets, of Kurt Schwitters's 'Sneezing Poem'. And in an inspired gesture Trocchi called up Stevie Smith, hardly the most counter-cultural of artists. She sang rather than read her poems and received a massive ovation. The Austrian Ernst Jandl, offering wordless 'sound poems', was similarly effective, his destruction of normal communication making what Alexis Lykiard, writing the foreword to *Wholly Communion*, the book of Whitehead's film, termed 'the most extraordinary event of the evening: parody and warning, cacophony with its own logic, rational collapse of reason, and despair of communication communicating. Artaud, who understood the sanity of madness, would have relished it.'

For the poets, good, bad or indifferent, it was another world. They were used, with the exception of the stars, to small college unions or the coffee bars of provincial towns; the Albert Hall was undoubtedly their biggest arena yet. Poetry would achieve larger auditoria – in 1969 Christopher Logue read to 150,000 people at the Isle of Wight festival, though, as he was the first to point out, they were there for Bob Dylan, not for his verses – but this was one of the few occasions when it was the poets who pulled the crowd. Spike Hawkins saw the event as 'a surging thing. The place was full. It was very exciting, being led along by Pete Brown and Horovitz and I said "Where do we go?" and they took me down to this tunnel and it was very badly lit, and suddenly this lid went up and I found myself with the light of the world upon me, and thousands of people, just coming out of this little hole in the ground on to the stage. I felt this must be some sort of metaphor. I was totally astounded by it.'[26]

Then of course there was the problem of the money. At one stage the chief worry had been whether enough tickets would be sold to pay back Jill Richter her £450, but as the audience flooded in that was soon irrelevant. But, as would prove the case in a number of counter-cultural events, where did the money go? Then, and in several reminiscences, the finger pointed at

John Esam, though nothing would be proved. The most damning story is retailed by one of the participants who found himself strolling backstage with Allen Ginsberg. When it transpired that neither poet had yet been paid they went searching for the organisers, and found Richter and Esam ensconced in the box office piling pound notes into a bulging sack. 'So we said, "Are we going to be paid for this?" and they said, "Help yourself!" and we just took some money. Nobody else was paid, except Ginsberg and I! Maybe a hundred quid each and they got the rest. But a hundred quid in 1965 was serious money.' Afterwards the lucky poet treated everyone to supper at a nearby hotel, splurging the whole lot in one glorious excess. Others, rightly or not, believe it all went on paying the Americans' air fares.

Esam himself has a simpler theory. 'Truth is, simple and elegant, and brief, as ever, there was no great profit.'[27] Seats were 10/- (50p) and 7/6 (37.5 p.) which meant £3,000–£3,500, but expenses, including Ginsberg's flight, were around £2,700. Esam came away with something less than £100. It was hardly the golden hoard. For him the entire tale, first retailed in the *Observer* shortly after the event, remains a 'canard'. Only the box office knows.

None of which mattered in the face of the overall effect of the Reading. 'You are not alone', the Albert Memorial 'collage' had declared, and in that the poets had been incontrovertibly accurate. Some see the event as no more than a very large poetry-reading, but for the majority of those who would move on to help create the institutions that made up the counter-culture, it was a symbolic 'gathering of the tribes'. It may be, as Christopher Logue has argued, that few of those that attended were genuine poetry fans, and that the numbers were artificially boosted by the fortuitous BBC feature. It may also be, as few but the most besotted deny, that on pure poetry grounds the evening was a disaster, but none of that could minimise the larger importance of the event. Opinion differed (often on the basis of the speaker's age) not merely as to the quality but just as much whether it was a culmination of the old or a harbinger of the new. For a beat like Johnny Byrne, for whom poetry reading had been his life blood for the previous half-decade, it was the biggest, the best, but also the last. From thereon the 'alternative' began to wither, began believing its own myths, recycling its own propaganda. For many of the old beats the Albert Hall genuinely represented a dream come true. They had had this fantasy for years – and here it all was, actually happening. So on the one hand they saw it as the basis of endless such readings, ever bigger, ever more influential; on the other a fantasy so perfectly achieved is not usually a fantasy open to re-creation. It was better to see it as a moment, a single moment and to savour it as such. (Later, in 1966, Horovitz would try to do it all again: it was not a success. When in 1996 he tried yet again it was positively embarrassing.) It cannot be denied that for Byrne's peers such as Brown, Hawkins and Horovitz (Byrne chose to skip the event himself, disliking its grandiosity even as he acknowledged its importance) the poetry reading proved a swansong. None of them would play so central a role in the next five years as they had in those that had just concluded.

For others, and not only the younger elements, it was an unmistakable signpost to the future. Jeff Nuttall, elegiac mode turned up to its highest, wrote later of: 'all our separate audiences . . . come to one place at the same time, to witness an atmosphere of pot, impromptu solo acid dances, of incredible barbaric colour, of face and body painting, of flowers and flowers and flowers, of a common dreaminess in which all was permissive and benign. There was a frisson for us all to savour as there had been at the first Aldermaston, and the Underground was suddenly there on the surface, in open ground with a following of thousands . . . After the sick capitulation of CND it did look as though we were once again winning . . .'[28] He put a good deal of the bonhomie down to LSD and wrote to a friend, 'London is in flames. The spirit of William Blake walks on the water of Thames. sigma has exploded into a giant rose. Come and drink the dew.' And indeed there were a few signs of the upcoming world of flowers and peace. Kate Helecser and a few friends had been down to Covent Garden (still a working market) to pick up left-over flowers. With faces adorned with psychedelic colours they brought them to the reading, handing them out to any taker. There was a good deal of dope-smoking, Vinkenoog was surely not the only person on acid.

Michael Horovitz, writing with Blakean fervour in his anthology *Children of Albion* (1969) saw it as the best reading ever. 'Poem after poem resonated mind-expanding ripples of empathy – uncut and precious stones in a translucent pool. The buds of a spreading poetry internationale, the esperanto of the subconscious sown by Dada and the surrealists and the beats bore fruit.' The 'straight' world, which had been so useful when it came to publicity, was more measured. The *Guardian*'s Norman Shrapnel seemed somewhat dumbfounded by the whole event, though generally appreciative; the *Times Literary Supplement*, in a piece headed 'Stirring Times', was unimpressed by the poetry but acknowledged that the reading was a historical event, with its 'combination of flair, courage and seized opportunities'.[29] The *TLS* also noted the remarkable atmosphere created in the staid vastness of the venue and it was this, rather than the poetry as such, that was the real significance of the night.

Before the Poetry Reading even the most highly involved individuals had never seen themselves as part of any sort of mass movement. Seven thousand did not make such a movement; but it was still a good deal more impressive than the fifty or so people who believed, not so much arrogantly, but with a certain lonely desperation, that they were all there was. As Mick Farren, another non-attender, but a devoted searcher after potential peers, put it, 'We found that there were some other people who looked like us. These other people [who] represented more than just the five of us who were heartily sick of each other's company, with limited resources and limited ideas. It was like discovering survivors after this holocaust of conformity that followed the Second World War.'[30] The last mass 'alternative' had been CND and that was a gutted, irrelevant shell. This had the makings of a far more genuine 'counter' culture than ever the anti-nuclear protestors had achieved. There would be no Canon Collins, no Michael Foot, not even that most youthful of senior citizens Bertrand Russell. Ginsberg and his fellow stars were no babies, but the audience, and those who brought that audience together were generally under thirty. Born too late to fear National Service, they represented a very different generation from the Nuttalls or the Cobbings. For them 'the bomb' was not some kind of ever-present menace, but something, like National Health Orange Juice or Muffin the Mule, that they'd grown up with. There would be substantial crossovers, but, as ever, the apotheosis of one generation's hopes would prove no more than the launch-pad for those of the next.

While the Poetry Reading stands as an undeniably important event, and was quickly appreciated as such, the first reaction of those involved was to step back and admire what they had created. The sheer fact of so large a constituency was impressive. Quite how to cater for it was another matter. For a while there was talk of a 'British Poetry Renaissance' (a conceit that lasted until the end of the Seventies), but in effect that often meant no more than the sudden upsurge of interest in the 'little magazines' and their publishers by the mainstream heavyweights. For Miles there was a more immediate problem: Better Books was to be sold and with its autonomy would go its role as an avant-garde bookshop. As its manager, Miles wished to continue running some sort of equivalent. The problem, as ever, was funding. At which point came one of those fortuitous blendings of interest groups that so often drove the counter-culture forward. Paolo Leoni, who had been involved with the Reading as a friend of Gregory Corso, suggested to Miles that he should meet 'these friends of mine'. The friends in question were John Dunbar, then art critic for the *Scotsman*, and his wife Marianne Faithfull.

Dunbar, the son of a liberal family involved in film, was a well-heeled, Cambridge-educated rebel who had moved from the world of Soho coffee bars and jazz clubs into that of the new 'rock aristocracy'. A friend of the Beatles and of the Rolling Stones, it was logical that he should know Miles, himself an intimate of the Beatles. It was all highly incestuous and disentangling the facts remains difficult. Faithfull recalls the concoction of the 'Ur--Myth' 'in an espresso bar in Chelsea (just as we thought the Russian revolution was plotted on a train in Zurich). Early in 1963, John and a man called Paolo Leone [sic], a leftwing beatnik type, and Barry Miles, John's partner, put their heads together and hatched a plot. I was just a young girl watching these mad intellectuals all dressed in existential black charting the future of the globe. They had it all worked out. "It's going to be the psychic bloody centre of the world, man!" Paolo announced portentously. John and Barry thought that Paolo was a little mad, but the idea was infectious (why not!).'[31] Both Dunbar and Miles, less melodramatically, put it a couple of years on, and set the encounter not in Chelsea, but Soho.

The result of their dinner was Indica, named for *Cannabis indica* but ostensibly and publicly reflecting their first exhibition, 'Indications' – of things to come. The money ('a couple of grand' – Dunbar; '£700' – Miles, 'two thousand each to both Miles and Dunbar, to be paid back with interest' – Sue Miles) was borrowed from a friend, Peter Asher, and the holding company was christened MAD: Miles, Asher, Dunbar. Business was hardly their central concern. 'I had no understanding of business,' says Miles, 'I just thought it would be a really good idea to . . . do this bookshop-cum-art gallery and change the world.'[32] Once established they would use an old Victorian cash register, essentially a box with a handle and a till roll, borrowed from the Ashers. Years before Jane had used it as a toy for playing shops and when they sent the first year's accounts to be checked the accountant added in her childhood bills, still heading up the roll. They rented a shop in Mason's Yard, a cul-de-sac off Duke Street, St James, costing twenty pounds a week. It was next door to one of swinging London's favourite clubs, The Scotch of St James, and only yards from William Burroughs's current residence, a flat in Duke Street. Ian Somerville, whose expertise ran to wiring, did the electrics. Paul McCartney helped put up the bookshelves and designed the wrapping paper; later he would help again, offering the odd thousand or two when times got hard and finances more appallingly erratic than usual. Of all the Beatles, McCartney was always the most committed to the 'underground', although Lennon's art school background gave him the more obvious credibility.

In many ways the Beatles, for all their superstardom, represented one more small constituency in a world composed of such over-lapping, mutually interested groups. Miles, in particular, would become a close friend (capturing a number of exclusive interviews for early issues of *IT* and in 1997 becoming his biographer; so close that Mick Farren nicknamed him 'the albino Beatle').

The first time I really had a long talk was after Indica had just moved to Southampton Row in March '66. I went back home and found McCartney sitting in my kitchen in Hanson Street, eating hashish cookies with Sue, and Sue being clearly quite pissed off that I'd arrived. I guess we'd told him the recipe when we first met and he'd just dropped by one day to see if we had any. It was a small scene in those days. Now the Beatles have this legendary reputation, but it wasn't really like that. A best selling record would sell 100,000 in this country. We saw an enormous amount of them, we went to movies with them, went to concerts with them, lectures, all kinds of shit. I must have seemed terribly pompous. I thought it would be very good for the Beatles to know about avant-garde music so I persuaded Paul to come along to a lecture by Luciano Berio at the Italian Institute. We got there and sat down and almost immediately the fucking press came bursting in – the Italian embassy called them up. That was the kind of thing that happened all the time.[33]

Indica originally had books on the ground floor and the gallery in the basement. There weren't any conventional paintings; Dunbar's taste ran to Takis and Yoko Ono. Miles stocked the same kind of material that he'd specialised in at Better Books. The gallery opened in early 1966 and was a hit from day one. As ever, there was a degree of luck. The first show, the *Groupe de Recherche d'Art Visuel*, fronted by Julio le Parc, fortuitously won the Grand Prize for Painting at that year's Venice Biennale. With no effort they had the art world's hottest property. 'Guys were running in from everywhere; one guy rushes in: "I'm a big Texas art dealer!" and John Dunbar who's completely stoned says, "I'm a little English art dealer." '[34] Indica soon became an 'in' place. Other than the Marlborough Gallery, which dipped a somewhat tentative toe into such things, MAD had first refusal on the avant-garde. Indica became a venue on the Swinging London circuit and its owners were co-opted ever-deeper into the merry round. The press, naturally, loved it. In the hothouse world of the time its reputation spread to New York and Miles was asked to start writing for the city's new 'underground' paper, the *East Village Other*: his first piece was a review of Pink Floyd. Relatively unnoticed at the time, but celebrated ever after, was the meeting at Indica between John Lennon and Yoko Ono, whose 'Unfinished Paintings and Objects Show', a development of her involvement in the early-Sixties 'Fluxus' movement, was mounted at the gallery. Dunbar, according to Philip Norman, 'sent her across to "chat him up" as a potential sponsor'.[35] More consciously 'artistic', McCartney claims the credit for the meeting and recalls Ono appearing on a mission for the New York composer John Cage and asking whether he still had any original manuscripts of his lyrics. He fobbed her off with Lennon and come that night at Indica they met. (Ian Somerville, in the spirit of the times, offered yet another version: Yoko was a witch; she had waited to meet Lennon so as to secure some of his fingernail clippings; thereafter he was in her power.)

By 1967 the Mason's Yard shop had been abandoned and a new Indica, for books only, had opened in Southampton Row. Ironically the gallery had always been much more of a paying proposition – Miles's taste in books, while on the cutting edge, was all too often wildly uncommercial. He had also been breaking the Berne Convention, which forbade the import of US paperbacks. Meanwhile Dunbar had been losing interest. His marriage to Marianne, now heavily involved with the Rolling Stones, was evaporating; critics found him more interested in smoking dope than pricing art or arranging exhibitions.

Indica lasted until late 1968, when it went into liquidation, owing a relatively tiny £500, a sum that reflects more on McCartney's generosity than on any in-house business acumen. Under-capitalised, and frequently cheated or robbed (signed editions seemed to vanish almost as fast as Miles accumulated them; on one occasion a large Swede, out of his head on LSD, simply smashed through the window, grabbed a pile of books and resumed his trip), it had been fun, but never easy. With the closing of Indica Miles moved to New York.

If the poetry reading was the first occasion on which the counter-culture saw itself *en masse*, then the Bob Dylan concerts (once again staged at the Albert Hall) twelve months later cemented the experience. It wasn't Dylan's first appearance in Britain; in 1962 he had appeared in a BBC television play about the Deep South performing a song called 'The swan on the river went gliding by' and in 1965, shortly before the reading, had toured the UK. It was this tour that would be memorialised in D.A. Pennebaker's movie *Don't Look Back*. The '66 tour, however, offered a new Dylan: an electric Dylan. The first half of the concert was folk music, albeit Dylan folk music, as usual, but come the second, there were rock 'n' rollers – The Band – surrounding the star. As any listener to the bootleg album of that concert will know, Dylan's move into electronic music was viewed with almost apocalyptic terror by those, the folk music constituency, who had been religiously setting him on an ever-higher pedestal since 1963. 'Judas!' a heckler screams; 'You're a liar,' responds a laconic Dylan. A similar switch had devastated fans at America's Newport Folk festival in July 1965, and the release of the unmistakeably 'electric' single 'Like a Rolling Stone' shortly after his return from the 1965 UK tour should have left no one with any illusions. The meaning of the conversion was not lost on those who witnessed it. While the Poetry Reading had represented the climactic and last (had they known it) beat event, bringing to a head a movement that had been building since CND held every beatnik hope in its disillusioning embrace, the Dylan '66 concerts represented the new world. A world in which there was no time for hairy-sweatered folk purists.

For Mick Farren it was nothing short of a turning-point, a veritable shock of the new:

> There was this sort of phalanx of old fogies out to cause trouble, because they knew their days were numbered. There were about 700 of them and everybody else was like these strange-looking people that we'd only sort of glimpsed from the hill-tops. So, first of all there was this sort of cultural burial, when Dylan comes out. . . Folkies go 'Yeah, hooray!'. But everybody knows the fucking Band are coming on after the interval. So the Band came out, the folkies all cut loose, Dylan baits them, most of them walk out and then we all sort of closed in and there it was, the start of 'something entirely different'. Motherfucker! we cried. All these fuckers who looked like us.[36]

Chapter Twelve

The Next Stage: The Birth of *IT*

It was mainly atmospherics: two and a half thousand people dancing about in that strange, giant round barn. Darkness, only flashing lights. People in masks, girls half-naked. Other people standing about wondering what the hell was going on. Pot smoke. Now and then the sound of a bottle breaking. Somebody looks as if he might get violent. There was a lot of tension about.
'2500 Ball at *IT* Launch' *IT* 2 Oct 31–Nov 2 1966

The Poetry Reading, as everyone who had been involved acknowledged, represented some form of way-station for the counter-culture. The question was where from, and far more important, where to? The Beats may have seen it as the apotheosis of everything they'd been moving towards for the past half decade or more, but there had emerged an equally influential constituency who saw the poet-crowded stage of the Albert Hall as a launch-pad and not a victory podium. And while the most immediate development would be the launch of Indica, there was an undoubted belief that the energies channelled into that Victorian mausoleum on Kensington Gore had a potential far greater than the opening of one bookshop-cum-art gallery, wrapping paper and bookshelves by Paul McCartney notwithstanding.

The next twelve months would see the launch of a number of new enterprises whose combined effect far outweighed their individual success or failure. The most important, and the longest lasting of these would be *IT*, or the *International Times* as it was known before legal restrictions forced the abbreviation. (It was considered possible, in a year that had seen *The Times* finally deign to place news on its front page, that 'The Thunderer' might be confused with the young upstart were the name not changed.) It would be modern Britain's first 'underground newspaper' and would survive for longer than any other underground institution, officially folding only in 1974, but popping up undeterred throughout the decade. There had, of course, been many radical British publications before. *Black Dwarf*, Tariq Ali's left-wing broadsheet, for instance, would take its name from a similar publication, selling around 12,000 a week in 1817. However, like many other countercultural institutions, the paper drew its inspiration from America. There was, none the less, a slight twist on the usual pattern. The American underground press, to which *IT* owed its existence and its early inspiration had been the brainchild not of the usual coterie – the Beats or the New Left – but of an emigrant Yorkshireman, whose own arrival in America had come more than ten years before.

John Wilcock, 'that strange mixture of Gulliver, Randolph Hearst and Elsa Maxwell'[1] arrived in New York in 1954 with one aim: to start some form of newspaper. He'd already worked for the 'straight' press in Britain, now he was looking for something new. Fascinated by the columnist Walter Winchell – not for his rabidly right-wing views but for his ability to pack so much information into so small a space – he began leafleting Greenwich Village, already renowned as the natural home of the city's Bohemia, inviting any takers to join him in setting up a local sheet. The paper he eventually helped found was the *Village Voice* (a free sheet today, it is still appearing, more than 40 years on). Branded a 'Communist' paper by the critics of McCarthyite America, it was never intentionally 'underground' in the later sense. Its interests were always essentially focused on the people, politics and events of New York, its home. But as the new scene built, the *Voice* could hardly ignore it. It remains the 'godfather' of the underground press.

Once in the world of 'alternative newspapers' Wilcock would never leave. After a decade writing a column for the *Voice*, he broke with the paper in 1965 and moved to the West Coast, working for the first of a new generation of underground publications, the *Los Angeles Free Press*, better known as the *Freep*. From there he moved up the coast to the *Berkeley Barb*, then back to New York to co-found yet another paper, the *East Village Other* (*EVO*). Here he reinstituted the column, now called 'Art and Other Scenes', and soon abbreviated to a simple 'Other Scenes'. In time 'Other Scenes' would start appearing as a 'magazine' in its own right, published at random and from wherever Wilcock happened to be at a given moment. (Given his 'day-job' as one of the first reviewers for Arthur Frommer's 'XXXX on $5 a day' travel guides this could mean some of the world's more exotic locations.) Unlike the *Voice*, *EVO*, in common with many of its Sixties' peers, took a far more oppositional role to all forms of culture, politics included. Among other of his stories, Wilcock would become the first writer to note that drugs didn't just mean the weirdo beatniks – over in Vietnam 'our boys' too had discovered the delights of marijuana. Wilcock also worked in Japan and in England, where he edited issue six of *Oz* (it had an 'Other Scenes' supplement). His greatest achievement, pioneered at *EVO*, was the foundation of the counter-culture's answer to the Press Association: the Underground Press Syndicate, a co-operative organisation whereby any subscribing member was allowed, with due credit, to use any of the work appearing in any of the others. Thirty years on Wilcock is still mailing 'Other Scenes' in its various, ever-new incarnations to a vast aquaintance around the world. The founder of the underground press, he has a good claim to be its last representative.

So much of this era can be seen in terms of small groups finding first themselves and then their coevals, and the founding of *IT* is no exception. The idea of having some form of 'alternative' publication would always bubble along somewhere near the surface of any counter-cultural discussion and Miles, who would help to stablish the paper, was typical in his own creation of a variety of 'little magazines', starting from his art school days in Cheltenham. The more immediate trail that led him to *IT* began in 1964 when he and Sue Crane went to Edinburgh to get married. It was a ceremony very much of its times: one of their witnesses being 'the famous Rubber Man: he had this rubber hose that wrapped around him on one end of which there was a mouthpiece and on the other was some kind of container with hashish in it. So you'd have this enormous sucking until he got red in the face and then he'd suddenly explode in a great burst of smoke and fall over.'[2] They stayed, thanks to an introduction from the ubiquitious Pete 'the Rat' Roberts, with one of the city's best-known beats, Adam Parker-Rhodes, who was currently experimenting, according to the story you heard, with effects of LSD on monkeys or of morphine on rats. He introduced the pair to two important figures: Jim Haynes, of the Paperback Bookshop and the Traverse Theatre, and another American, an ex-patriate gay Jewish Oklahoman called Jack Henry Moore, a former member of the theatre group the Fantasticks, whose electronic expertise would underpin the underground club UFO, the Technicolor Dream and a number of other hippie *sons et lumières*.

A year later, with the Poetry Reading over, the leading players looked around for a new direction. It was a moment of tremendous optimism. In Miles's words, 'We did begin to believe that we could change the world.'[3] For him the immediate move was from Better Books to Indica, but in the heady aftermath of the Albert Hall, the over-riding emotion was: 'We've got to capitalise on this energy, we've got to use this constituency.' Some form of publication seemed the ideal way forward, and Miles founded Lovebooks (a milder predecessor of the company that would run *IT*: 'Knullar', the Swedish for 'fuck'). The board included Miles and John Hopkins plus their 'hip accountant' Michael Henshaw (whose clients included a large proportion of the fashionable artistic world and the majority of those involved in the 'kitchen sink' school of drama and who would soon be employed by *IT*). The intention was to bring out more 'little magazines' but their first 'publication' was a record, albeit spoken-word. Ginsberg, Corso, Ferlinghetti and Voznesensky were all still in London, and gave another reading, this time at the Architectural Association in Bedford Square. The reading was taped and Lovebooks released it on disc. The 'little magazines' were not far behind. In December 1965 Miles brought out *Longhair* magazine, subtitled 'NATO: North Atlantic Turn-On' (a name conjured up by Ginsberg). This excerpt gives a reliable flavour:

> North Atlantic Turn-On 1965: Watts riots, Vietnam escalation, Rhodesia White Coup, Dominican intervention. Communist homosexual schizophrenic Negroes menace all capitalist heterosexual non-neurotic White supremacists everywhere. Give me your tired, your poor, your huddled masses yearning to breathe free – I will give them Rockefeller, Ford, Rhodes, Getty, Churchill, Anslinger and Giordano, the FBI, the Mafia, the CIA, Moral Rearmament, KKK, Colin Jordan, colour television, nuclear submarines, the

Peace Corps, bombs in space. Wilson your pedestal is rotten, your democracy infested. Johnson the worm is in the apple, the rat in the manger. While your invisible governments throbbed obscenely, while you lay in bed with your wives dreaming of your names inserted into history, the premature little bastard of insurrection struggled into the world. INSURRECTION, by tobaccomen steelmen oilmen rubbermen, out of exploitation malnutrition slavery. It's too late Mr Prime Minister Mr President: run to the Stock Exchange, telephone the Pope, fill your fallout shelters with money, kill the poets with euphemisms and the lovers with napalm. Vomit obscenities in Parliament Congress General Assembly Security Council – too late. Slimy fingers fumble at the controls/no effect/unleashed generations of accumulated madness/now.

Energetic, undoubtedly, if somewhat incomprehensible. But *Longhair* still remained a magazine and not a newspaper, and as 1966 moved on the desire to create a 'real' newspaper intensified. As fantasy gradually hardened into fact one thing became clear: for all their enthusiasm neither Miles nor Hoppy actually knew how to make their dream come true. The Lovebooks board was expanded to take on the two old Edinburgh friends, Moore and Haynes, both of whom were conveniently in London. Haynes, with his vast list of connections, was the most immediately useful. He knew people like Sonia Orwell (whom he had co-opted for the Edinburgh Writers' Festivals) and Victor Herbert (the former pyramid salesman and associate of the notorious Bernie Cornfeld). Herbert duly kicked in some funds, while Orwell turned over her late husband's typewriter: it was promptly lost or possibly sold. Ever positive, the team approached a wide variety of potential backers; none seemed willing to offer funds. However one of them, Bobo Legendre, a southern version of Warhol's big-haired heiress pal and Tom Wolfe's 1964 'Girl of the Year' Baby Jane Holzer, living for the period above a fish-shop in Shepherd's Market, did supposedly name the paper. At one of the meetings that gradually served to move the new publication from theory to practice, she suggested, no doubt facetiously, 'Let's call it "it".' Her suggestion, serious or not, was taken up. 'It' could mean a good many things; the one they liked best was 'International Times'.

In the way of such occasions, there exists a certain level of disagreement about this naming. Miles opts for Ms Legendre; but others have their own take. John Dunbar: 'Some guy who was doing the *East Village Other* came over; a refugee from the *Village Voice* who had started *EVO*, and he came over and he was talking one day in Indica and the name came out and various other things. It was one afternoon, a lot of dope and joints, maybe even some acid. It all just came up.' Jim Haynes: 'I think Jack Moore thought up the name, but we all probably claim credit. You sit around in a room and everybody says about ten names out and everybody else says, "No not that!" and in the end . . . somebody said "it".' Sue Miles: 'There were lots of conversations

about what the name should be and we talked about the "IT" girl and being
from a journalistic background I said, "Well, call it 'IT'. We've got 'IT'!" And
they said, "What's 'IT'? It's got to stand for something." And I said, "Well, 'I-
nternational Times', I suppose", and they said, "Fine!" ' Of one thing there
was no doubt: when it came to designing the new logo, what better than Hollywood's famous 'It Girl'? Michael English (others claim Michael McInnerney,
but he 'swears blind' they're wrong) was commissioned. Unfortunately there
was a slight mistake: McInnerney's featured siren was Theda Bara, a different
silent sexpot; the real 'It Girl' was Clara Bow.

Choosing a site for the launch proved less controversial. The Roundhouse in Chalk Farm had been designed in 1847 for turning the locomotives
of the London and Birmingham Railway; abandoned by the railways in 1869,
it had been a storehouse for Gilbey's Gin, but by 1966 it had long since fallen
into disuse. It was the Roundhouse that (at least since 1964) had been at the
centre of one of the great avant-garde-cum-socialist projects of the time:
Centre 42. The Centre was the obsession of the radical playwright Arnold
Wesker, who had cemented his reputation with such Fifties hits as *Chicken
Soup with Barley* and *Roots*. Founded in 1960, Centre 42 had taken its name
from resolution 42, presented to that year's TUC by the television engineers'
union, in which the union, urged on by a pamphlet penned by Wesker earlier
that year, called on the TUC to recognise its responsibilities towards the arts in
an era of increased leisure. Wesker himself found that his theories were far
from isolated. By 1961 he had been joined by a number of left-inclined members of the arts (many of whom had also been front-runners in CND), and all
of whom were equally determined to narrow the gap between artist and public.
From their conversations came plans to launch a non-profitmaking company,
dedicated to the formation of a pool of artists and a network of 'people's festivals'. A Management Council was formed (four trade-unionists plus Jennie
Lee, soon to be Minister for the Arts in the Wilson government) and on 24 July
1961 Centre 42 was officially launched.

Wesker was a true utopian, as much so as any flower-brandishing hippie.
He held no brief for élite culture, but neither did he espouse the romanticis-
ing myths of 'working-class culture'. As he put it in the brochure released to
launch the project:

> Centre 42 will be a cultural hub which, by its approach and work, will destroy
> the mystique and snobbery associated with the arts. A place where artists are in
> control of their own means of expression and their own channels of distribu-
> tion; where the highest standards of professional work will be maintained in an
> atmosphere of informality; where the artist is brought into closer contact with
> his audience enabling the public to see that artistic activity is a natural part of
> their daily lives.[4]

It was a classic left-wing tract of its times, ostensibly optimistic egalitarianism mixed with an inescapable air of patronage. The more dedicated socialists resigned almost at once (later one of them, John McGrath, would assail Wesker's promotion of 'bourgeois' culture). Another valuable ally, Joan Littlewood, whose Theatre Workshop, founded in 1945 had established something of a genuine working-class audience around its base in the Theatre Royal Stratford East and which would reach its apogee with her production of *Oh What a Lovely War* (1963), also moved elsewhere. The problem, as Robert Hewison has pointed out, was that Centre 42 was running before it could walk. Its first need was a building to serve as a centre for its operations, but in 1962, before any such building had been obtained, Wellingborough Trades Council requested help with setting up a festival. This was promised, and soon there was a 'rolling festival', moving around a number of provincial towns, mixing the Centre's professionals with amateurs, gifted or otherwise, drawn from the local community. Local critics liked it, national ones, suspicious of the union involvement and the overt socialist position, and rather snooty as regards the local amateurs, backed off. All in all the project lost money and it was decided to resist any further provincial perambulations until the outstanding debts had been paid off. Instead the project would concentrate on obtaining the much needed 'head office'.

The empty Roundhouse had just been bought by Louis Mintz, a millionaire property dealer and patron of the arts. Just north of a yet-to-be-gentrified Camden Town, the Roundhouse stood in suitably proletarian surroundings, but its rundown state demanded a very un-proletarian bank balance to see it attain Wesker's desires, even after he had obtained, via Mintz, the remaing sixteen years of the Roundhouse lease. An appeal, aiming to raise £600,000 for improvements (eventually it would rise to £750,000) was launched but few donors seemed interested; by 1971, the year after Centre 42 had been officially wound up, no more than £150,000 had been offered. It was nothing like enough. Of this some £80,000 was raised at a single event, a tea-party held at 10 Downing Street, arranged by Mary Wilson. This at least would pay for the initial conversion. But by the time it was held, on 25 July 1967, the Roundhouse had moved, at least culturally, elsewhere. That day it was midway through hosting the Dialectics of Liberation, a political outpouring many lightyears from Wesker's homespun socialism.

Back in 1966 it was Jim Haynes, the connected fixer, who called Wesker to say, 'Arnold, we're having a little party to launch a paper, can we borrow the Round House? I promise we won't make a mess.' Wesker, in an act that now seems more symbolic than either party could have imagined, handed over the keys. As Haynes recognised, there was a difference between the way the two groups saw the building that underpinned a larger chasm between the old and new cultures. For Wesker, for all his socialism, immured in an older tradition, everything had to be 'just so': the People's Palace must have all the best accoutrements before ever its doors could open. For Haynes, like some escapee from a Mickey Rooney/Judy Garland vehicle, it was 'Here's a building; hey gang, let's put the show on here.'

The '*International Times* First All-Night Rave Pop Op Costume Masque Drag Ball Et Al' was held on Saturday 15 October. It cost ten shillings at the door, five for the prescient who'd bought their tickets in advance. The poster, this time featuring the correct 'It girl' (though in the most decorous of head-and-shoulders shots) offered the Soft Machine and the 'Pink Floyd Steel band' alongside 'Strip trip / Happenings / Movies'. There would be a 'Sur Prise [sic] for Shortest – Barest'.

For the bands, more used to the relatively tiny All Saints Hall in Notting Hill, it was their first major gig. The Floyd, who had a light show, got £15.00, £2.50 more than the Soft Machine who didn't; the 'Softs' however offered an amplified motorbike wired up by 'some guy called Dennis in a long cape and head-dress', which when not linked to the sound system was available to give girls rides around the venue. Neither band was helped by the rudimentary electricity supplies. On the door people handed out sugar cubes, then the acid vehicle of choice, to every arrival. They were fakes, but a large number of the audience managed to trip none the less. Paul McCartney, the eternal counter-culture fan, arrived dressed as a sheikh; Antonioni, in town to make *Blow Up*, arrived with Monica Vitti (who had turned down the lead). The poet Kenneth Rexroth was on hand to report for the *San Francisco Chronicle*. According to his story the promised bands failed to turn up; instead the audience threw together a rough and ready pick-up band which made awful squawking noises.

The Dutch fashion designers Simon Postuma and Marijke Kroger set up a small psychedelically decorated cubicle in which they told fortunes; Bob Cobbing and the London Film-makers' Co-Op showed films, including the supposedly satanic Kenneth Anger's *Scorpio Rising*; the designers Binder, Edwards and Vaughan, regulars at contemporary parties, displayed their wondrously decorated Pontiac, more recently shown at the Robert Fraser Gallery. There was a giant jelly, moulded in a bath-tub. Its glory was ruined by Pink Floyd's van, which backed into it, and someone else who rode a bicycle through the remains. The two lavatories were horribly over-used, and their sexual distinction had long since been abandoned. As well as drugs there was alcohol – and with it a good deal of throwing up. But what did it matter? It may have been filthy, it may have been dank and damp, it may have been, as the Floyd's manager Pete Jenner pointed out, a place you'd have hated to see by daylight, but the raw excitement transcended all that. For one night at least, the Roundhouse, in a way its absentee owner Arnold Wesker could never have dreamed, was indeed the 'people's palace'.

Above all, like the Poetry Reading it was another of those 'everyone you ever knew will be there' events. As Chris Rowley, later to be involved in a variety of underground institutions, recalled,

All these little groups from all over London were massing together. First of all they'd done it at the poetry reading or the Dylan concert, where they'd seen each other. But at this *IT* thing they were actually rubbing up against each other, sharing joints, talking frantically about turning on the world, everyone had mad plans of various kinds and they all babbled away furiously about either electrifying the skies so that messages of love and peace could be beamed off the clouds, or turning European universities into a vast library of worthwhile information and so on. It was remarkably optimistic. When had there been such vast quantities of raw optimism among any group? Perhaps not since 1914 when the lads went off to die.[5]

Only one major player was missing from the nascent 'underground'. Richard Neville, newly arrived from Australia, was elsewhere, in the south coast resort of Hastings to be precise, watching a re-enactment of the Battle of Hastings.

The party over, it was time to get the paper on the streets. A newspaper, even a counter-cultural one, requires some degree of hierarchy, but in *IT*'s case it seemed as if there were an abundance of Indians, all very keen and many of them highly talented, but not a single volunteer for chief. Everyone wanted to write, but no one fancied editing, let alone running the office or dealing with printers and typesetters. Fortunately Tom McGrath, who had already worked on Nuttall's *My Own Mag*, on *Ambit* and a number of other 'little magazines', had just quit as editor of *Peace News*. Summoned to London from a Welsh hideaway by a telegram from Hoppy, he announced himself willing, after some persuasion and an offer of the then astronomical weekly wage of £25, to take on the job. Four months later, after the first eight issues, McGrath would be gone; no one had noticed, apparently, that he was a heroin addict. Like John Lennon's later and more celebrated vanishing act, he 'went out for cigarettes one day' and never came back. With him went the paper's sole typewriter. Later he would re-emerge, after a painful detoxification, back in Scotland and start carving out a career as a leading dramatist.

In autumn 1966, putting together the first *IT*, the editors knew pretty much what was wanted: an international cultural magazine that would link outposts of the 'alternative' world across the globe. *IT*'s aim may have been to move the counter-culture on from the Poetry Reading but it also looked back to the sort of cross-cultural internationalism that had informed that event. Unlike a 'straight paper', which supposedly looks outside itself to report the news (in however biased a manner), the *IT* group were far more inward looking. In many ways the content reflected their own preoccupations: they wanted writers, but they also wanted to touch on the other aspects of the arts. Like *EVO*, which featured its 'Slum Goddess of the Lower East Side', *IT* offered an 'IT Girl'. Jenny Fabian, later co-author of *Groupie* and then girlfriend of Spike Hawkins, was one, posed unappetisingly in a bath, naked flesh conspicuous mainly by its absence. Jeff Nuttall drew a cartoon strip; there was a small listings section (in his first editorial McGrath called for a 'Twenty-Five Hour London'), and a variety of ads: Yoko Ono at Indica, Better Books, and so on.

(Maintaining the listings was an especially uninspiring task. When, in 1968 a young student publisher, Tony Elliott, approached the current editor, Bill Levy, with the suggestion that he absolve him of so onerous a burden, Levy agreed. John Hopkins was in jail: he might not have been so casually generous, but what Sue Miles characterised as 'this amateur, nutty, disorganised rabble that was the original underground press' simply didn't think in terms of actually making money. 'Anyone else could have seen the potential, but when Tony came into *IT* in his tennis shoes and said he wanted to do a listings magazine they just said, "Take it." ' Elliott went on to launch the London listings magazine *Time Out*, often cited as one of the underground's greatest hits, but a greater testimony to Elliott's commercial savvy than any real identification with the counter-culture.)

Those first issues took themselves immensely seriously. Heavily international, dedicatedly avant-garde, they offered among other things a piece on the Amsterdam Provos (early-model Greens, and best-known for their provision of free white bicycles in the city), the French radical Jean-Jacques Lebel's obituary for the surrealist André Breton (an underground founding father), an interview with Claes Oldenberg, a public dispute between Peter Brook and Charles Marowitz over the former's *US*, a flawed attempt to deal with the Vietnam War on stage, a piece on Yoko Ono's current exhibition, another on the Chinese Cultural Revolution. With what one must hope was innocence, they ran an interview with rock hustler Kim Fowley directly above an EMI ad for his current product. In issue two came the US poet Ezra Pound's pro-Nazi wartime broadcasts, hitherto unpublished, and defended by McGrath as a necessary read: 'We can never know what folly and what wisdom is in the speeches until we have a chance to read them.'[6] Drugs received substantial coverage. As would be the papers that followed, it was very much male-orientated. 'IT Girls' aside, feminism had no more penetrated this pace-setter of the underground press than it would any of its successors, not until *Spare Rib* arrived in 1971. It was suggested that the editorship be offered in rotation to a woman, to a black man and then back to the old guard, but like *Oz*'s 'Cunt Power' issue of a couple of years on, it was largely tokenistic.

As Hopkins would recall,

It was impossible! *IT* was impossible as a proposition and that's why it happened because we didn't know that it was impossible and if we had known it was impossible we wouldn't have done it. The first edition we put together in metal, lead type out in a printing works in what is now Hillingdon and the printers had never seen people behaving like this. I didn't know I was going to run into metal type, nobody knew about that, I'd taught myself offset litho. It was an adventure. The printers were fine but they just weren't used to people coming in with this point of view: 'What's this? . . . it doesn't fit? . . . all right, get rid of this . . . can we have one of these? . . . my God we don't usually have headlines this size' and so on.[7]

The one area that was conspicuously absent from the new paper was politics; certainly in the traditional sense, as seen for instance in the earnest (and, to *IT*'s potential readership, turgid) pages of the *New Left Review*. This anti-political stance climaxed in Hopkins's 1968 'Open letter to Tariq Ali', then masterminding the demonstrations against the Vietnam War in Grosvenor Square, but *IT*'s anti-political stand had already alarmed Jim Haynes's friend, Jennie Lee. She invited the whole board to meet her. Why, she asked, had Jack Henry Moore proclaimed that 'Politics is pigshit'? For *IT*, steeped in beat philosophising, the only ideology was that of absolute libertarianism: sex, drugs, the right to use your own body and mind as you desired. To career politicians, however self-proclaimedly radical, this was self-indulgent anathema.

It was also disdained by more traditionally radical groups. The *New Left Review* might kow-tow to the American counter-culture, which it perceived as properly 'authentic', but was far too arrogant even to acknowledge the paper. David Widgery, a member of the Trotskyite International Socialists, despised such campaigns as that for a 25-hour city as 'reformist'; he disliked what he saw as the 'Situationists manqués' who seemed to dictate such politics as the paper espoused. The 'Sits' themselves weren't overly impressed either. Members of King Mob, a London Situationist group, amused themselves by invading Indica (briefly home to the paper) and generally scaring the wits out of the *IT* staff.

To some extent their mistrust of *IT*'s 'revolutionary' stance was justified. Haynes was certainly not averse to spending an evening squiring Evangeline Bruce, wife of the then US ambassador, or one of President Johnson's daughters – he could never recall which – to the Royal Court Theatre and then to Annabel's, the most aristocratic of nightclubs and hardly a bastion of 'alternative' values. Self-publicists, like most of the more visible members of the underground, the editorial board were constantly on television or in the press; 'media manipulation' was the term of choice. The figure who came nearest to incorporation in the Establishment, or at least in its arts subsection, was Miles. In 1966 the Arts Council decided to appoint two junior members to each of its advisory panels. One of these, scheduled for inclusion on the literature panel, was Miles. Like its boss Jennie Lee, the Arts Council had always proclaimed its appreciation of 'youth culture' and, like much of the Establishment, it was happy to play groupie to the still acceptable Beatles. When Paul McCartney, thanks to Miles, attended the Luciano Berio lecture at the ICA in 1965 the event merited a mention in the Council's annual report, but as ever, there had to be 'sensible limits'. Arnold Goodman, the *eminence grise* of the Wilson government, and a fixer more impressive and definitely far more powerful than Jim Haynes, disapproved of *IT*, and especially of the paper's refusal to demonise drugs. He had already withdrawn his support from Haynes, who neither drank, smoked nor doped, but as a member of the *IT* board was tainted with the pro-drugs smear. No sooner had Miles's appointment been announced than Goodman had him bounced off, just four days after getting the job offer. It was a move that combined pragmatic politics – keeping the Arts Council free from association with the demon cannabis – with the naïvely paternalistic attitude the Establishment took to the counter-culture. Young people, Goodman believed, needed moral guidance from the great and good such as himself – a man who was reputed to have launched his own rise to power by coat-tailing the property-developer Howard Samuel in a number of deals that, it was rumoured, were not best inspected too closely. Speaking in the House of Lords in April 1967, he explained that, 'Young people lack values, lack certainties, lack guidance . . . they need something to turn to; and need it more desperately than they have needed it at any time in our history – certainly, at any time which I can recollect. I do not say the arts will furnish a total solution, but I believe the arts will furnish some solution. I believe that once young people are captured for the arts they are redeemed from many of the dangers which confront them at the moment.'[8] It was not, however, necessary that young people be actually represented amidst those arts.

Those of a less conspiratorial bent noticed that Miles's appointment had coincided with the publication of a *News of the World* 'revelations' piece, aimed variously at the underground and the rock business (specifically such visible stars as the Rolling Stones). The first of these appeared in January 1967, a farrago of ill-informed and synthetic moralising – 'I saw half naked teenagers injecting reefers as they gave themselves to LSD-addicted Negroes' as one observer summed it up. This first attack was headed 'Pop Stars and Drugs' and promised 'Facts that will shock you'; a month later on 12 February a second piece targeted Indica, soon to suffer a police raid. They attacked its posters, its book and picture stock ('browsing through the shelves was like a glimpse of a madhouse'), its apparent links to the London Free School, one of the 'most active British groups advocating LSD', itself a 'sophisticated evil . . . from America.' A copy of *IT* was analysed: Nuttall's cartoons were definitely dubious, the editorial was 'dedicated to drugs'. It was hard to see what frightened the paper most: the fear of American inspired modernity or the old fantasies of Limehouse drug dens.

For *IT*, in its early days at least, this was all part of the fun. Wasn't *all* publicity good publicity? What mattered, as it would to any young publication, was that *IT* knew it had a constituency ready and waiting for the product. They had been at the Poetry Reading, at the Dylan concerts, at the *IT* launch. *IT* tapped into their concerns and their interests and when the paper began appearing it would not be long before they started making themselves known. Whether the first issue sold 10,000 (Miles) or 750 (Sue Miles) its very existence made it a success, and that first sale began climbing until, sometime in 1968, it would peak at around 44,000 copies a fortnight. Like many of the underground papers, *IT* functioned essentially as a forum, reflecting as much as dictating its readers' interests.

And as Miles noted, *IT* somehow managed to get it right. A mix that fell somewhere between the portentousness of the *Village Voice* and the stoned craziness of *EVO*, it was right for London. People believed in *IT*, whether reading it, selling on the streets, staying up most of the night rolling up copies for distribution by post or laying out, designing and writing the newspaper. The constituency they believed in, the idea for which the time had undoubtedly come : all these factors combined to make *IT*, so long in arriving, a vitally important creation, a focal point of its period.

But the *News of the World*, pitiable and laughable though it might seem, could not easily be ignored. Where their hacks attacked, a police raid would often follow. It would be the case with the Rolling Stones and with *IT*. The first few months of publishing *IT* may have seemed idyllic, but this would not last. In the months and years to come there would be more attacks, both from the Establishment, and, equally importantly, from within the paper's own staff.

Chapter Thirteen

Institutions: An Alternative Society

Dear Mr Haynes,
We are most concerned that the matter of your outstanding account has not been
given the appropriate attention as requested in our letter of the 8th April. The hire
purchase agreement to be drawn up to cover the buying of a Kelvinator Bottle
Cooler is also causing anxiety in as much as the Banker's reference you gave us has
been returned by the Bank in question stating that your account is unknown to
them . . .
Letter from Coca-Cola Southern Bottlers to Jim Haynes, 18 April 1968

The London counter-culture of the mid-Sixties was split between the West
End and the West, from Notting Hill Gate itself to the two Groves, Westbourne and Ladbroke, and stretching at its furthest limits to Bayswater in the
West and Kensal Rise in the East. Its effective northern boundary is the Harrow
Road, that area apostrophised by Colin MacInnes as 'Napoli', 'with its railway
scenery, and crescents that were meant to twist elegantly, but now look as if
they're lurching high, and huge houses too tall for their width cut up into
twenty flatlets, and front facades that it never pays anyone to paint, and broken
milk bottles *everywhere* . . .'[1] It was the area designated by the post-war governments for the housing of the new West Indian community, lured across the Atlantic with promises of jobs on buses and in hospital wards, and turned over to
the strictly tempered mercies of such landlords as the notorious Peter Rachman.
As well as West Indians and the poor whites who couldn't afford to escape,
there was a growing population of young people, driven into the area by its low
rents and by the genuinely Bohemian atmosphere.

Typical of the young tenants was Mick Farren, who lived 'in an Irish
rooming house near Powis Square. There was a Chinaman downstairs whom
legend had it was trying to raise enough money to ship his dad's body back to
China and it was still in there. The Irishmen weren't allowed to bring women
in, but I was. It was a bit like living in a vertical bothy.'[2] Farren, as he appreciated, was an exception: until the hippies began making serious inroads towards the end of the decade, it remained very much a West Indian enclave.
Whites drank in the two main pubs – Henekey's and Finch's – both on Portobello Road but elsewhere was black. Best known to the fashionable outside
world was the Rio, a club-cum-café on Westbourne Grove. Frequented by
such chic slummers as Princess Margaret and Tony Armstrong-Jones, it had
hit the headlines during the Profumo Affair: Stephen Ward, Christine Keeler
and her troublesome black lover Lucky Gordon had all been customers. By
mid-decade that was a memory, but the Rio remained an important symbol.
As Courtney Tulloch, *IT*'s only black editor, recalled, 'The Rio represents a

lot of different things to different people. There were people who would buy a bottle of whiskey, go to the Rio, take it out of their coat pocket, sit down, pour it in a cup and drink it; there were people who sat down, smoked a cigarette, had a coffee and reminisced about when they were growing up in Trinidad; there were people who looked through the window to see which white is coming down the road and wonder what do they want and how could they con them. And for certain white kids it might have been a place where you scored drugs.'[3]

Such white Bohemia as there was was intimately tied to the black community. They had the best drugs – indeed, the only drugs as far as most people were concerned – and the best music – where else could you find ska or bluebeat? Despite the best efforts of Oswald Mosley, whose BUF, turning from Jews to Blacks, had campaigned in the area through the Fifties and the tumult of the Notting Dale race riots in 1958, the area remained multicultural. Michael de Freitas, only recently Rachman's chief lieutenant and not yet 'Michael X', ran a record store with Alex Trocchi; they specialised in import jazz. Across the street was a corner store, The Safari Tent, which sold grass to both communities. If there were white dealers they were simply those who purchased larger deals from black sources. The relations cut both ways. At least one Aldermaston march had a black contingent, many of them Rastafarians: when they took off their hats the marchers saw the first dreadlocks to go on show in Britain.

Among others who lived in or around the area was John Hopkins, then a photo-journalist working for the quality Sundays and putting together, among other pieces, the first ever feature on cannabis for *Queen* magazine. Hopkins was one of the major focal points of the emerging new world and until his arrest and imprisonment on drugs charges in 1967, was involved centrally in virtually every aspect of the counter-culture. Miles might have been more cerebral, and Jim Haynes the well-connected fixer ('the hole in the middle of the record' as he has been termed), but Hoppy, as he was universally known, was closer to being the leader of the counter-culture than either.

In his Westbourne Terrace house lived Miles and his wife Sue. Everyone who was going to be anyone passed, or claimed to have passed, through his door. Due to start work at the Atomic Energy Commission at Harwell, Hoppy had spent some time in Oxford, where he had gravitated to the student beatnik world of Mike Horovitz, Spike Hawkins and a passing Johnny Byrne. Hoppy's life at the heart of national defence lasted until 1960 when he was thrown out. He and a dozen friends, including Graham Keen who would later turn up on *IT*, had gone off to Russia in a hearse. When the tabloids sniffed out Hopkins's involvement the holiday trip turned quickly into a *cause célèbre*. Back in the UK Hopkins was splashed, barefooted, across the *Daily Mirror*: 'Atomic Scientist Propositioned' gasped the headline. Hopkins had indeed been approached, but had prudently made his excuses and left for

England. He was promptly grilled by the AEC and responded by handing in his resignation and decamping to London. Here, clutching the black and white camera he had been given for his twenty-first birthday, he gravitated via Camberwell and Pimlico to Bayswater, right on the fringes of Notting Hill. He established himself in Westbourne Terrace, began pushing his way into Fleet Street and supplementing his income with a little light dope dealing. Those who knew could score grass at £4 an ounce. Along with Miles, Hoppy helped put together *Teamwork*, the magazine of the standing conference of West Indian affairs.

The first years of the decade saw Hopkins establishing himself both as a photo-journalist and as a person whose life became more and more interwoven with what would soon be termed 'the underground'. As well as working for Fleet Street, his pictures came out in *Sanity*, the CND paper, and in *Peace News* (whence *IT*'s first editor would eventually be recruited). In 1964, around the same time as Timothy Leary was downing his first ever spoonful of Michael Hollingshead's magical icing sugar, Hopkins too met LSD. Later that year he visited America and found even more signs of a world that seemed capable of existing without the usual establishment constraints. He came back, as friends remembered, full of ideas, among which two were pre-eminent: an 'underground paper' and a 'free school'. They tried the school first.

Looking back, Hopkins has dismissed the Free School as 'a scam' which 'never really worked out'.[4] It began with a meeting in late 1965. Present were Hoppy, Andrew King and Peter Jenner (co-managers of Pink Floyd), Ron Atkins, a jazz writer, Alan Beckett (of the *New Left Review*), the film-maker Kate Helecser (who would be there at a similar meeting for the creation of *IT*), Joe Boyd and John Michell. Michell, who owned property all round the area, offered a derelict basement at 22 Powis Terrace; Michael de Freitas had his office across the road, and David Hockney's studio was on the same street. Five years later the Westway would be opened, fast-tracking its way westwards from Marylebone Road; now it was in its earliest stage and houses were being cleared. It gave the area something of a moonscape feel; for those who hoped to push towards a new society it was an ideal backdrop.

The Free School was, as Graham Keen has put it, 'an alternative social work thing . . . The initial idea was that anybody who had anything to teach would set up a class. It was fairly half-hearted. Nobody really wanted to do very much canvassing and the kind of people that came around weren't the indigenous population who naturally enough and quite rightly viewed us with a great deal of suspicion.'[5] Those who did turn up were a strange amalgam. There were old beats such as Harry Fainlight, Dave Tomalin and Neil Oram, tramps such as Michael McCavity (or that's what he called himself) and hip teenaged girls from nearby Holland Park comprehensive (where Hoppy would appear at the gates to purvey his counter-cultural 'sweeties', urging the pupils to try this alternative establishment) such as Emily Young, whose father was Wayland, best-known for his sexological study *Eros Denied*, and her friend Angelica Huston, daughter of the movie director John.

Even those who were keenest on the School seem unable to recall any 'lessons'. There was, it seems, a good deal of experimental sex between the young visitors and the somewhat older beats. There were plenty of drugs and the basement received the necessary psychedelic makeover to enhance the joints and trips. There was also plenty of talk. John Michell offered his take on UFOs, ley-lines (his book *View Over Atlantis* would become a classic of the genre), Jerusalem and Glastonbury. The world of anti-psychiatry was explained by Joseph Berke, an American who worked with R.D. Laing and who had been involved in the Free University of New York.

Perhaps the most important spinoff from the Free School – and certainly the longest lasting – was the first of the annual street processions that would become known as the Notting Hill Carnival. But if the Free School hoped to attract local support then it was sadly disappointed. As the founders of the Free School's successor, the Antiuniversity would find, ordinary people did not regard hippies and beatniks as their leaders towards the promised land. However there were exceptions. At some early stage there was an effort to drum up interest and people began knocking on local doors. One door revealed Rhaunie Laslett, a local woman who, rather than reject the Free School's advances, welcomed this potential new dimension to Notting Hill life. Very quickly she turned herself into a major local figure, fighting the council for much-needed grants and, allied to such exiled Trinidadian steel band musicians as film-maker Horace Ové, actor Stepan Califa and Michael de Freitas, set in motion Britain's first Black Carnival. For the first Carnival they needed just one lorry and they mustered about fifty people to walk and play their way through the local streets.

Carnival aside, Hopkins was right: the Free School didn't really *do* that much. Nor did it last. Courtney Tulloch, writing in an early *IT*, cheered its importance as a force for unifying the black and white communities, and called for its revival, but by early 1967 that force was spent. People had more pressing things to do, and with the basing of *IT* in Covent Garden the focus of the counter-culture had shifted 'up West'. *Oz*, the next underground paper to emerge, would be based in Notting Hill proper, but Portobello, while ever more popular, would have to wait until early 1970 for the return of a paper, in the form of *Friends*. But the importance of the Free School as a catalyst, as a momentary and necessary stage on the way to greater things cannot be denied. It was the need to fund the School that would lead to the All Saints Hall gigs – featuring Pink Floyd – and thence to UFO, and it was the energy that the School's leading figures produced amongst themselves that would help push events towards the founding of *IT*. And in moving Michael de Freitas from being a man who, as a Rachman heavy, preyed on the community, to one who seemed (if only on his own evidence) to be contributing towards it, one can see the first shoots of what would be British Black Power.

If the Free School was the first 'underground institution' to ponder the possibility of an alternative education, then the Antiuniversity was its logical successor. Other predecessors included the Free University of New York (FUNY) and the Conference for the Dialectics of Liberation, held at the Roundhouse in July 1967. Arranged by the Philadelphia Foundation, home base for such 'anti-psychiatrists' as David Cooper, R. D. Laing, Leon Redler and Joseph Berke, the Conference offered such speakers as Allen Ginsberg; Julian Beck, leader of the exiled American Living Theater; the veteran theoretician Herbert Marcuse; Lucien Goldmann; the Americans John Gerassi, Paul Sweezy and Paul Goodman; the Marxist economic historian Ernest Mandel; and Stokely Carmichael, the Trinidad-born pioneer of Black Power. It was, as James Webb has called it, 'an Intellectual Be-In'[6], mixing hardcore hippies with strait-laced politicians. This symposium, bringing together for the first time the counter-culture and the 'official' political New Left, was subtitled 'Towards a Demystification of Violence', but as audience reaction to Carmichael's firebrand exhortations made clear: violence was far more romanticised than demystified. Given its intimate relation to 'revolution', the Dialectics will be more substantially considered elsewhere. In this context it is as a source of energy for further developments that the Conference matters most. Like the Poetry Reading two years earlier, participants left feeling energised and inspired. A veteran of the Free University of New York, Berke had already been marginally involved in the Free School. The driving group behind the new institution, or 'anti-institution' as they carefully named it, were three men who had already been involved with FUNY: Berke, plus his fellow anti-psychiatrist David Cooper and Allen Krebs, FUNY's co-ordinator. They enlisted a committee, and evolved a manifesto, in which they proclaimed the bases of the anti-institution:

> We must destroy the bastardised meanings of 'student', 'teacher', and 'course' in order to regain the original meaning of teacher – one who passes on the tradition; student – one who learns how to learn; and course – the meeting where this takes place. At the Antiuniversity many of the original and radical artists, activists and intellectuals of London as well as Europe, America and the third world will have a place to meet among themselves and others to discuss their ideas and work. The emphasis will be on a diversity of approach, but we shall work to unify widely disparate perspectives. Above all, we must do away with artificial splits and divisons between disciplines and art forms and between theory and action.
>
> We raise no *a priori* barriers to membership in the Antiuniversity other than a desire to find out or relate to 'what is going on'. We prefer those who have not yet succumbed to the streaming of the state educational system.

> The Antiuniversity of London is not a university or a school. It gives no credits and grants no degrees. However, those who study full time under one or more faculty members may be given a letter from these people stating that the individual has sufficient expertise in a given subject to allow for 'higher' study.[7]

On top of this proclamation of aims, the Antiuniversity wished to end the usual divisions, both of staff and pupils and of rigidly structured and separated courses. Famous names, such as a passing Allen Ginsberg, would be courted: the Antiuniversity would provide them with a ready-made forum of hungry minds. The Antiuniversity was to become a centre of radical politics; there would be no form of political censorship and courses would include studies of guerrilla tactics and racism. It would move from the 'battery student' world of its established and Establishment peers and towards the medieval concept of a 'community of scholars'. The 'working class', still essentially excluded from tertiary education, would be especially welcome. All in all, as Alex Trocchi (who lectured on 'the invisible insurrection') put it, in *IT* 26, the Antiuniversity was designed to be 'an exploration of the tactics of a broad cultural (r)evolt'.

The aims agreed, the Committee began putting their ideas into practice. The Institute of Phenomenological Studies (in real life, Doctors Leon Redler, David Cooper, and Joseph Berke) fronted £350 for immediate expenses. Allen Krebs contacted the Bertrand Russell Peace Foundation and obtained a lease on a building in Shoreditch which was being vacated by the Vietnam Solidarity Committee. Berke began contacting potential teachers and the drive for publicity got underway. A catalogue was produced, which explained that students would be charged £8 per term (plus 10/- (50p) for every course attended) while teachers would be paid only if they needed the money. Were a student unable to afford even the relatively small termly charge, some form of barter – work for fees – could be arranged. It also listed the proposed courses. Among them were Experimental Music; Psychology & Politics; Black Power; Current Events; The Politics of Small Groups; A Happening; Demystifying the Media; Writers & Writing – the Dialectics of Ungodliness; An Anthropological Survival Kit; Psychology & Religion (with R.D. Laing); a course on *Finnegan's Wake*; Anti-Institutions Research Project; Live in a Television Set; The Connection (with Yoko Ono) – 'passivity and devitalisation in a consumption orientated society'; and Family as a Counter-Revolutionary Force. Typical of the mixture of counter-cultural concerns was 'From Comic Books to the Dance of Shiva: Spiritual Amnesia and the Physiology of Self-Estrangement', described as 'A free-wheeling succession of open-ended situations. Ongoing vibrations highly relevant. Exploration of Inner Space, de-conditioning of human robot, significance of psycho-chemicals, and the transformation of Western European Man. Source material: Artaud, Zimmer, Gurdjieff, W. Reich, K. Marx, Gnostic,

Sufi, and Tantric texts, autobiographical accounts of madness and ecstatic states of consciousness – Pop art and twentieth century prose.'

Among other teachers was Jim Haynes: his media studies course 'basically told people that anything they wanted to do they could do. Enthusiasm for whatever your dream was.'[8] Such counter-cultural veterans as Miles and Jeff Nuttall (presenting a weekend-long discussion: 'Jeff Nuttall Is Fat') also appeared. The one area where the plans manifestly failed was in attracting members of the working-class. Those who attended classes (not to mention those who taught them) were very much in the mould of those who had attended the Dialectics of Revolution: the enlightened bourgeoisie. Local people, perhaps assuming that Tariq Ali (much-vilified by the media after the Grosvenor Square demonstration of 18 March) was still in residence, smashed windows; the local pub refused to serve Antiuniversity members; in a larger world trade union leaders resolutely ignored all overtures to help out. White workers at the Barbican site merely jeered at attempts to interest them, although some of their black colleagues did turn up to hear the visiting C.L.R. James.

The Antiuniversity opened in February 1968. The offer of bartered fees soon produced what would be the first of three sequential 'communes' who, with decreasing effectiveness, and with an increasingly negative effect on the larger institution, moved into the East End premises. Here students were not privileged beings, relying on 'townees' to do their 'dirty work'; instead everyone mucked in. They lived in the same five rooms that by day were classrooms, the building offered no bathroom nor any real privacy. That this group lasted until May was remarkable in the circumstances. Among them was the intense media interest, at least initially, fanned by the pre-publicity for the Antiuniversity. Camera-crews seemed in constant attendance and as Peter Upward, the community's leader, remarked, 'You can't have everyone watch you learn to live together; this makes a spectacle of it, makes you an act rather than people.'[9]

A large influx of German and Austrian students followed, drawn partly by the chance of gaining new insights and partly, as at the Arts Lab, in the hope of finding somewhere to stay. Some chores were accomplished, but the earlier system was much eroded and began to break down. When in July the students were in turn replaced by what might best be seen as dossers, whose only real interest lay in finding a roof for their heads, the Antiuniversity effectively collapsed. The building, which had begun to look like 'a Bowery flophouse',[10] was abandoned, and although classes continued in private houses, the impetus was inevitably diluted.

The structure, or properly 'anti-structure' of the Antiuniversity provided the seeds for its own demise. It was quite unlike any 'straight' place of learning: Cornelius Cardew refused to play any of his own compositions until his very last lecture; before that students had to make their own music: each member of the class had to lead a week's session. John Latham's classes in 'Antiknow' ('Knowledge is an illusion that people have') peaked with his plunging an edition of the US critic Clement Greenberg's *Art and Culture* into a jar of sulphuric acid and returning the residue to the art school library from which it had been loaned. Berke, after asking his class, 'How can we discuss how we can discuss what we want to discuss?' and receiving only the answer, 'Maybe we don't need to discuss it', announced that he wasn't feeling very well and disappeared from the room. But to the delight of those who could never countenance the deliberate sabotage of the 'class' relations that order a 'normal' institution, the attempt to break down the roles of 'student' and 'teacher' never really worked. Writing of the first day in *IT*, Harold Norse reported that: 'the anti-university got off to an anti-start. Within an hour the room, jammed with poets, painters, sculptors, publishers, novelists, psychoanalysts, sociologists, and just people was a howling underground cell of clashing ideologies and aims.'[11] It was pointless, said Ronnie Laing, to expect anything else – the Antiuniversity, unlike say, Germany's Bauhaus or America's Black Mountain group, had no central ideological spine; the best they could hope for was some kind of ashram. To continue learning and teaching while unleashing what was in effect anarchy demanded a paradoxically high level of personal discipline. Undoubtedly the teachers were often happy to attend each other's talks – typically fifty per cent of those listening to Francis Huxley on dragons had their own classes to teach – but the systematised destruction of roles was too hard for most to sustain.

As Theodore Roszak put it, so devotedly 'anti-' was the Antiuniversity that 'seemingly nothing the adult society had to offer any longer proved acceptable. The superheated radicalism of the school was eventually to reach such a pitch that even the age-old student/teacher relationship came under fire as an intolerable form of authoritarianism. So it too was scrapped, on the assumption that nobody any longer had anything to teach the young; they would make up their own education from scratch. Unfortunately – but was the misfortune more comic or more tragic? – the school failed to survive this act of radical restructuring.'[12] What Roszak cruelly termed 'madcap brainstorming' of teachers 'barely out of their teens' degenerated 'into a semiarticulate, indiscriminate celebration of everything in sight that is new, strange, and noisy; a fondling of ideas that resembles nothing so much as an infant's play with bright, unfamiliar objects. The appetite is healthily and daringly omnivorous, but it urgently requires mature minds to feed it.'[13]

To be harsh, the Antiuniversity hardly even gained momentum, let alone showed itself capable of the long haul. Opened in February, salaries had already been abandoned – there was no more cash – by April, and as noted, the communes that occupied the building became less and less interested in the larger aim. In August the building was reclaimed by the Russell Foundation. The dossers left, but the institution they had hijacked went with them. The teachers went their own ways: anti-psychiatrists back to their therapeutic centre, Kingsley Hall, the artists back to their studios and the counter-culturalists back to *IT* and similar projects. The students, or anti-students, simply faded away. If its aim had been to tear down the boundaries that so limited a 'straight' institution, the Antiuniversity had undeniably succeeded, but in succeeding had destroyed itself.

While one underground forum might have gone, another was more than capable of replacing it. This new venue-cum-community centre would be the Arts Laboratory, universally abbreviated to the Arts Lab, founded that same year by the near-inescapable Jim Haynes. In many ways the Arts Lab would be a London version of the sort of 'energy centres' that Haynes had created so suc-cessfully back in Edinburgh. There would be experimental theatre, movie shows, a gallery, a restaurant. It would also provide, as did so many of the un-derground's institutions, community focus. And as with other institutions, the first problem would be that of funding. The name, thought up by Jack Henry Moore, was deliberately geared to tease the consciences of the liberal great and good. As Haynes noted, 'It was a name that guaranteed getting a grant. Who could refuse giving money to the "Arts Laboratory"? '[14] The answer was al-most immediate: everyone. The Arts Council, which had already abandoned the Jeanetta Cochrane Theatre (the Traverse's London home) once Goodman had taken a look at the inaugural issue of *IT* ('Mr Innocent here sent [him] a copy off, saying, "This is the *Tribune* of our generation." He didn't like that. He said "Come and see me immediately." '[15]), now blanked Haynes's new project, as did every other arts foundation. Haynes was thrown back on indi-vidual approaches. Trawling the *Who's Who of British Theatre* he sent a beg-ging letter to some 600 potential donors. Among those who sent back cheques were Fred Zimmerman, Peter Brook, Tom Stoppard, Doris Lessing, Fenella Fielding, Ken Tynan and David Frost. Tynan would be an especially keen supporter, using his 'Shouts and Murmurs' column in the *Observer* to cam-paign for the much-desired Arts Council grant. He saw the Lab as: 'culturally omnivorous . . . blessedly unsmart [with] a happy sense of work-in-progress, of new departures that may bloom into new arrivals'.[16]

There was, however, one Goodman connection that did bear fruit. Nigel Samuel, the son of Goodman's friend Howard, had inherited a vast fortune on his father's death. He was also Goodman's godson (Jennie Lee, whose at-titude to the counter-culture was far more positive, was his godmother). Eighteen years old, he had arrived in the *IT* office around the third or fourth issue. As Miles recalled, 'He came wandering in one day, wearing a long green suede coat, dragging along the ground, very fashionable, and crushed yellow velvet pants. Looking very wasted. You never knew in those days whether someone was tripping out or literally starving to death. He said he admired what we were doing and could he help distribute the paper?'[17] It soon turned out – maybe the large silver Aston Martin into which Samuel began loading bundles of *IT*s gave the staff a hint – that this was no ordinary freak. Depending on one's view Samuel was the underground's prime patsy, or a genuinely sad figure, a 'poor little rich boy', awash with drink and drugs, trying in the only way he could to push his own version of politics. It soon became clear that the counter-culture had open season on his inheritance. *IT* seems to have been reasonably reticent (Samuel, who had a controlling interest in the *New Statesman*, then a leading left-wing weekly, once threatened to incorporate that journal into the underground paper), but others, notably Michael de Freitas, by now reborn as Michael X, were quite ruthless. It was hardly surprising that the property developer's son would end up helping the counter-culture's main hustler. He went to Haynes and offered to guarantee the Arts Lab's overdraft (at least until July 1968, at which point he paid off the outstanding £2,200). Goodman was powerless to intervene.

The Arts Lab, sited in a couple of old warehouses at 182 Drury Lane, has some claim to being the very first bit of 'trendiness' in Covent Garden. The area was still a working market, although its days were numbered, developers were circling and the fight to keep its buildings on site was still gearing up. Like all such icons the Arts Lab has gained a certain nostalgic patina over the intervening years, but the focus of most memories is the enormous foam rubber mattress that substituted for seating in the movie theatre. Open all night, it soon became as much a crashpad for itinerant hippies as it was a cinema. By the early hours the smell of feet – it was mandatory to check shoes at the door – was overpowering. There were drugs, of course, and the inevitable police raid – in his innocence the non-toking Haynes had actually visited Scotland Yard days before to seek 'counselling' about the fact that most of the customers were dopers – but miraculously nothing was found. The Arts Lab was quickly colonised by the People Show, late of Better Books' basement, and saw the development of a number of other experimental troupes, notably the Pip Simmons Theatre and the Portable Theatre, fronted by Howard Brenton and David Hare. The People Show helped spread the Arts Lab's notoriety after their first performance: locking the audience in cages and abusing them horribly. On a more accessible level was Jane Arden's 'mini-musical'[18] *Vagina Rex and the Gas Oven*, with Sheila Allen and Victor Spinetti. (It played to packed houses for five weeks: the entire company were naked, plunging wildly beneath the light-show). There was also Yoko Ono, who took space to prepare her next show: a selection of quotidian household items, all carefully cut in half and painted white. Later, in 1968, John Lennon joined Ono to mount a sculpture exhibition. Upstairs was a restaurant, run by Sue Miles.

What characterised the Lab was the spontaneity that permeated its every aspect. Apart from the fact that as a major 'alternative venue' it was plagued by a near-nightly invasion of international television crews, all desperately seeking out the source of all that 'swinging' that *Time* had preached a year earlier, there was very little in the way of pre-planning. As Haynes puts it in his memoirs, 'You went there and you didn't know what was going to happen to you or what you were going to do. You might meet someone, have dinner, have a cup of tea, go and see a film, a project. You could go to a concert, see dancers.'[19] Like some freaked out town crier, Haynes would make his way through the gallery or the restaurant to announce that in ten minutes or whatever, such and such an event would be starting. People took it or left it as they pleased. Among the events was one that took place not in the Lab itself, but a few doors down the street. Entitled 'Tea with Miss Gentry' it sold only ten tickets at a time, and the lucky few – who had no idea of what experience they were to expect – would be taken to meet the eponymous star, a former hat designer for the stage who lived on Drury Lane. They drank tea (paid for by the Lab) and she talked.

The Lab attracted a huge cross-section of visitors. Maybe thirty per cent were tourists, drawn in by the products of those roving television crews, but one might see Christine Keeler, R.D. Laing, Dick Gregory and James Baldwin (who gave a joint press conference there), 'Mama Cass' Elliot and others. Angus Wilson, who gave money to *IT* and *Black Dwarf*, was another. More parochially David Bowie, still David Jones, used Arts Lab space for rehearsals (later he would launch his own equivalent in Beckenham, Kent); Donovan turned up one evening and gave an impromptu concert. The British Council were constantly on the phone, asking Haynes to give a quick cultural rundown to visiting Russians, Cubans and Africans.

All this gave the organisers at least the feeling that here at last was the much-vaunted 'multi-media experience' that seemed to run hand-in-glove with most 'alternative' media fantasising. At times it was true, but the main appeal of the Arts Lab was a good deal less cultural. It was sex. For some, like Chris Rowley (who managed the Lab's small bookshop and among whose occasional gigs was doing Yoko's slicing for her), the Arts Lab was 'one of the great makeout centres of the Western world. Jim Haynes lived at the back and he was taking innumerable young women down there and Jack Moore lived opposite and he was taking innumerable young men.'[20] Haynes backs him up: 'The Arts Lab was like a little brothel. Boys sleeping with boys, girls sleeping with girls, boys sleeping with girls, girls sleeping with boys, it was a whole thing.'[21] For some it was all a bit of a tease. You may have turned up in the hope of some foam-rubber fornication, but what you got was recumbent, snoring hippies and one more re-run of *Citizen Kane*. And for others, mainly women, it was simply repellent. Not everyone was that delighted by Haynes's self-indulgence. One man's freeing up of the sexual boundaries was another woman's unwanted groping; this was not 'sexual revolution', but, as one visitor put it, 'just these predatory elderly men, salivating around'.[22] Perhaps the most important sex-related aspect of the Lab was the Sunday evening free clinic –

the Digger Medical Service – run by Dr Arnold Linken, a friend of Haynes and a well-known, if controversial sex educator.

The preliminary problem of funding stayed with the Arts Lab, even in 1968, its peak year. Despite the procession of smart visitors, there was still very little money other than the odd fee from the camera crews and such ticket money as could be raised. This latter, at one stage a reasonably sure source of income, was sorely reduced as the ever-increasing flow of youthful hippies, desperate for a place to sleep, gradually crowded out the more afflu-ent older patrons. In December 1968 Haynes and Moore decided to make a major effort. Telling the owners that they would be presenting a Leonard Cohen concert, they managed to hire the Albert Hall (still reeling from the Poetry Reading) and mount on 18 December what became called 'The Al-chemical Wedding'. Cohen, who had visited the Lab sometime previously, didn't show (he probably never even knew the gig had been announced) but in his place came John Lennon and Yoko Ono. Or so it was believed. There on stage was a large bag; inside the bag, allegedly was Yoko Ono and with her, just after his divorce from Cynthia, was Lennon. It provided enormous fun for the press, whose love affair with the Beatles had long cooled. The audi-ence were not quite sure, their attitude epitomised in the shout, 'Everyone's gone home now, John!' More exciting was what was now becoming an inevi-table moment: the amateur (female) stripper. A decade or so later such events would be confined to sports arenas, in 1968 it was more likely involved with some form of art. In rushed the Albert Hall stewards, followed by the police. Their enthusiasm waned, however, when large numbers of the audience started to follow suit. It was bad enough to have megastars rolling around on stage in a sack; a naked audience would not improve matters. The ticket money just about covered the Arts Lab's costs.

The Lab's popularity was not boosted by Haynes's involvement with what would come to be seen as the birth of the squatting movement that would reach its climax in the 1970s. Next door to the Arts Lab was the long-abandoned 86-year-old Bell Hotel, boarded up, empty but, as Haynes dis-covered when he broke in one night in March 1969 and inspected the prem-ises, perfectly habitable. It belonged, he discovered, to the GLC, but a suggestion that it might be rented and used by some of the thousands of young people who were descending on London was rejected. Haynes in turn rejected the rejection: a few Arts Lab regulars began breaking in on a nightly basis, gradually clearing up rooms that were littered with debris. The clear-ing up went on unhindered until the workers were spotted creeping out one morning. A GLC official appeared, flanked by police, to serve a notice to quit. The situation quickly polarised. Those who had already started moving in their sleeping bags and other possessions declared themselves 'owners' of the Hotel. They were, they announced, the 'Human Rights Squatters'. The outcome was predictable, and came two weeks after the first squatters had moved in. Technically outlawed from interfering – squatting is a civil, not criminal matter – the police armed themselves with a drugs warrant and broke in on 22 March. It took more than an hour to search the 100 rooms, and as many as 150 young people were arrested. The police then systematically smashed the building's interior beyond repair.

The Arts Lab meanwhile was in crisis. There was no money, the 'arts' were being swamped by the itinerants, and the landlord, who had always stressed that any lease would be temporary, decided that he wanted his building back. Camden Council took Haynes to court for unpaid rates. Perhaps most vitally the energy that had sustained Arts Lab for two years was finally running down. 'With both sadness and a sense of relief'[23] it was closed in October 1969. Ronald Bryden, the *Observer* theatre critic, provided the obituary:

> It refused to define itself because any definition would have implied limitation. It was simply a place ... where Jim Haynes encouraged people to come, act, paint, talk, dance, drink coffee, watch or show films, or just fall asleep ... You could drift in at almost any hour of the day or night, eat a huge beef sandwich or a bowl of soup, watch the People Show or an Andy Warhol movie, buy a copy of the *International Times* or *Oz*, sign a petition about Biafra, find out where the next demo would start, sit on the floor under the branches of a lurid pop-sculpture and meditate on the Vedanta ... [The] Lab was really a kind of mission to the disaffected young, an attempt to show them that, even if the culture around them had failed on their terms, cultures are necessary and can be remade.[24]

Perhaps the greatest effect of the Arts Lab experiment was outside London. The counter-culture was in many ways a metropolitan phenomenon but the Arts Lab movement took it far from the centre. At its peak the Arts Lab Newsletter could list some fifty local clones. They rose and fell; some like that in Birmingham became major local centres. Some evolved beyond Britain, notably in Amsterdam, where the Milky Way club began life as an Arts Lab, or in Paris where at least two such creations, L'Entrepôt and La Lucinière, long outlasted the first Sixties rush.

The collapse of the Arts Lab would prove Jim Haynes's last appearance on the counter-cultural stage in London, or indeed in Britain. Determined to advance his own fascination with sex, and simultaneously to further the much-talked-of 'sexual revolution', he decided to add an 'alternative sex paper' to the ranks of underground journals. This would be *Suck* – a paper that would have been impossible to produce in Britain. Haynes, plus co-editor Bill Levy, moved to Amsterdam.

Chapter Fourteen

Drugs '67: Butterflies on the Wheel

Show me that I'm everywhere – and get me home for tea.
The Beatles 'Only a Northern Song' (1967)[1]

Whatever else may have happened during 1967, whatever other components may have contributed to the 'Summer of Love' (and however diluted that particular fantasy may have been by commercial pressures) one thing runs through the year in an iridescent, indelible line: drugs, notably cannabis and LSD. Cannabis as a badge of the 'underground' and an increasingly contentious focus for the rival forces of Establishment and counterculture; LSD, strongest of the psychedelics, as an underpinning of everything that would and could be labelled 'alternative'. The year saw the peak of the drug debate. Never was there so concerted a media attack – with rock stars bearing most of the brunt; never, one might suggest, did the consumption of cannabis and LSD escalate so rapidly. Nor, for that matter, has there ever again been instituted a full-scale Report into cannabis, as there was under the Wootton Committee, for all that its actual conclusions would not appear until early 1969.

The role of cannabis, in particular, would not be as fiercely contested until MDMA, better known as 'Ecstasy', took on a similar role for the 'rave culture' of the 1980s and 1990s – once again transmuting a source of pleasure into a political symbol. LSD was less political. Perhaps because its effects were so demanding, so intense, so unpredictable and in the end, so unknown. Unlike America, where the drug was taken by hundreds of thousands, it was never that widely consumed in the UK. Ecstasy, with its millions of weekly 'trippers' would be far more of a mass-market high. Cannabis on the other hand was categorised as a 'soft drug' and the Establishment knew – their own experts were quite capable of telling them – that it really didn't do very much harm. As is now generally known, cannabis is a weed far less harmful than such stimulants as nicotine or alcohol, but it remains stigmatised and demonised in a way those 'legitimate' drugs never were. In the late 1960s there were struggles over obscenity, homosexuality and other 'lifestyle' decisions, but they had been in place for decades and had no real generational edge. Cannabis was different: it was essentially a young person's drug and the young, as has been seen, were a threat. If this was their symbol, which is what the weed became, then it was imperative that the Establishment not kow-tow (or, as will be shown, be seen publicly to kow-tow) to its supporters. As Theodore Roszak pointed out, after noting that in 1967 the US alone consumed 10 billion amphetamine tablets, it was not merely the proclaimed health problems that had drawn a line at cannabis and LSD, but because 'these substances have gotten associated in the public mind with the aggressive bohemianism of the young . . . Unwilling to blame themselves for the alienation of their children, mother and father have decided to blame the drugs.'[2]

In the history of 'recreational' drug consumption cannabis had, until the Sixties, been something of a 'poor relation'. It lacked the romantic miasma of opium, the deadly potential of heroin or the class-connotations of cocaine. At the international conference of 1925 which saw it placed off-limits, the British delegate had not even agreed to vote for its outlawry, merely not to vote against. Even in the Fifties, it had remained basically a black people's indulgence, with a few white Bohemians joining in.

There were, of course, a few stories. They focused, as ever, on the 'alienness' of drugs, in this case 'reefers' or 'doped cigarettes'. The tabloid articles were full of their references to 'the same old sickening crowd of under-sized aliens, blue about the chin and greasy' or 'coloured pedlars' with 'the brains of children' whose 'perverted satisfaction [is] "lighting up" a white girl'. Thanks to the deliberate distortions of the American police and media – carried across the Atlantic as yet another cultural import – cannabis was positioned as far worse than the drugs of genuine addiction. By the time it came to mounting a proper debate on the drug such prejudices would have been locked into the mass mind.

As late as the early 1960s cannabis was still very much a minority taste: a low-yield hallucinogen that gave a private pleasure and represented nothing else. The authorities were singularly unworried; and it hardly impinged on the popular mind. As the report of the Interdepartmental Committee on Drug Addiction (better known as the Brain Committee) stated in 1961, neither use nor 'trafficking' in such drugs was especially widespread, a fact the Committee was happy to attribute to public opinion: 'The cause for this seems to lie largely in social attitudes, to the observance of the law in general and to the taking of dangerous drugs in particular.' Such an attitude was, of course, 'coupled with the systematic enforcement of the Dangerous Drugs Act 1951'.[3] It should be added that while that 'enforcement' may indeed have been 'systematic', the country still had very few dedicated 'drug squads'. They too, like drug mass consumption, were a creation of the mid-Sixties. Oxford, for instance, had no such unit until 1966, following the death by heroin overdose of the former Prime Minister's nephew, Joshua Macmillan. Even then their methods lacked something of sophistication: this author recalls being told with absolute sincerity by one such officer that the squad always checked people wearing trainers – an infallible mark of the pusher. It was also ironic that the most important of these squads, that based in Scotland Yard, should be the province of Detective Chief Inspector Vic Kelaher, who with five junior officers – most notoriously Detective Sgt. 'Nobby' Pilcher (the 'semolina pilchards' in John Lennon's song 'I Am The Walrus') and Detective Constable Nick Prichard, both of whom were involved in the

arrests of various leading rock stars – would prove to be among the most corrupt members of what would turn out to be a particularly corrupt era in the
Metropolitan Police.

By 1967 that mood would have changed radically. In the years 1945–59
there were rarely more than 100 convictions for cannabis in a year. From
1960 (235) the graph jerks upwards. In 1966 convictions topped 1,000 for the
first time (1,119), while in 1967 the police moved in on 2,393 people, more
than double the numbers of the previous year. (This leap forward may have
reflected vastly increased consumption, or possibly only the number of
purpose-built drug squads set up in the intervening twelve months.) At the
same time the racial pendulum had swung. As late as 1963 black defendants
still outnumbered whites (367:296). A year later the trend had reversed
(260:284) and by 1967 white dominance was well established (656:1,737).
The only area in which the graph failed to maintain quite so upward a trend
was in quantities seized: the Customs' 'best' year was 1959, when some 282
kilos were confiscated. It would be getting on for two decades before the kind
of major seizures, multiple tons rather than mere kilos, would start to hit the
headlines. The increases, however, were noted, and the government established the Hallucinogens Sub-Committee of the Advisory Committee on
Drug Dependence under the chairmanship of Baroness Wootton of Abinger,
in April 1967.

There is no single reason why cannabis had moved from a relatively minor
pleasure, to the symbol of a generation's rebellion. It had a certain 'artistic'
cachet: if they were going to take a drug the middle classes who made up the
counter-culture were less likely to follow the mainly working-class Mods into
the world of amphetamines. Cannabis had another romantic association: with
the black community and its music. The Beats, precursors of the hippies,
smoked. And inevitably there was the frisson of illegality: it may have been a
weed, but it was an illicit weed and as the slogan had it: the only dangerous
thing about cannabis is getting busted. But as was so often the case, it was less
the drug's intrinsic charms than the official reaction to cannabis – of increasingly unreasoned hostility – that gilded its image for the young.

As the statistics show, arrests and prosecutions for cannabis had risen
sharply during the previous twelve months, but 1967 would witness a new
intensity in the 'fight against evil drugs'. It was epitomised in what seemed an
orchestrated attack, combining the synthetic, sensationalist moralising of the
tabloid press with the almost groupie-like obsession of the Drugs Squad as
the hacks and heavies moved in on the Rolling Stones and even threatened
the Beatles. The campaign, for so it appeared, had been initiated on a rather
lower level, with the arrest on cannabis charges of the underground's most
prominent figure, John 'Hoppy' Hopkins on 30 December 1966. Some detected the hand of Arnold Goodman, whose personal animus against the
'alternative society' as a whole, and *IT* in particular was growing increasingly

undisguised. Certainly, when police raided Indica early in 1967 it was on Goodman's instructions: according to Tom Driberg, an MP whose own raffish lifestyle made him by parliamentary standards something of a 'counterculture' in himself, Goodman, knowing that such interference would be blocked by Home Secretary Roy Jenkins, went over the minister's head, calling on the DPP to order the raid.[4] This, however, was not a drugs raid, but an 'obscenity' one (among the books and papers carted away was Kenneth Patchen's *Memoirs of a Shy Pornographer*). But attacks on the underground and its newspaper were hardly major news. That began when the tabloids, particularly the *News of the World* and the *People*, realised that rock stars (once such anodyne figures but now increasingly linked with those wondrous words 'sex' and 'drugs') would provide infinitely more exciting headlines than the usual pederastic scoutmasters and B-list starlets. The band whom the papers chose to target was the Rolling Stones, a group whose songs – 'I Can't Get No Satisfaction', 'Let's Spend the Night Together' – were bad enough, but who had compounded their guilt with the ultimate in showbiz *lèse-majesté*: their refusal, after their appearance on the show on 22 January to join the other stars in the traditional 'happy family' sign-off that concluded TV's *hommage* to long dead music-hall: *Sunday Night at the London Palladium*. Such petulance may seem trivial, and indeed it was, but the response from the public made it into a national event. The *Daily Mail* filled a whole page with anguished readers' letters ('Who do they think they are?', 'I have never seen such a repulsive turn.') For the tabloids it was ideal: and they were determined to mine this profitable seam for even greater treasures.

As Marianne Faithfull saw it there was a serious conspiracy abroad:

> By the beginning of 1967, there were highly placed people in Her Majesty's government who actually saw us as enemies of the state . . . In selecting Mick as the target of their campaign they had fallen for the central rock 'n' roll fallacy: confusing the artist with his work. They proved no more capable than the most smitten rock fan of disentangling the two Micks, the dancing god on stage and record, and the mild-mannered, middle-class boy he actually was. Like most voyeurs, they imagined far more lurid goings on than there actually were. The idea that the Rolling Stones were about to undermine Western civilisation with drugs, rock and polymorphous sexuality was completely farcical. But having established that the fate of the nation was at stake, this revolution must needs be led by a particularly dissolute and perverted bunch.[5]

As Vernon Bogdanor has noted, 'Mick Jagger really was an Angry Young Man, beside whom the writers and dramatists who had caused such a big splash in such a small puddle in the fifties dwindled into insignificance. After all they never actually tried to put John Osborne in gaol . . . The adult world seemed to hold Mick Jagger in abject terror. He was a challenge to all that parents held sacred. Every mother who saw him realised that he was the one who would come in to steal her housekeeping, seduce her daughter, and light his cigarette, probably drugged, with the latest article by Godfrey Winn. He seemed to hold nothing sacred. He even appeared on the Ed Sullivan show in his tee-shirt.[6] But there was no chance of their fomenting a real-life revolution. As Marianne Faithfull says, while the Stones may have represented anarchy to a far greater extent than ever did their punk descendants, the Sex Pistols, the problem was that it was indeed anarchy: far too disorganised to threaten anyone.

On 5 February the *News of the World* offered 'The Secrets of the Pop Stars' Hideaway', a piece that featured an interview, in Blaises club, with Mick Jagger happily babbling on about his use of drugs. There were just two small problems: first, Jagger was talking about LSD; the journalist sincerely assumed this was one more nickname for hash. The other was that 'Jagger' wasn't Jagger; the Stone in question had been Brian Jones. Such ignorance, compounded by the fact that of all the band Jagger was the most cautious when it came to drugs, and had openly worried about Keith Richards's and Brian Jones's all-encompassing dedication to such pleasures, first astounded and then infuriated the star. On the same night as the real Jagger read the *News of the World* piece he was due to be interviewed on Eamonn Andrews's chat-show. It had all gone well, Jagger seeming to best his fellow-guest, the ferociously right-wing Tory Quintin Hogg (the Oxonian Hogg was especially mortified to find that the rock star too had been to university), and that success may have encouraged Jagger to push a little too far. Like Oscar Wilde, whose decision to sue his enemy the Earl of Queensberry for libel had opened a pit into which only he would tumble, Jagger announced that he was suing the newspaper.

The *News of the World* did not roll over. They accepted their blunders, but were determined to prove the greater point: that Jagger, as a rock star, undoubtedly did take drugs and that rock stars really were a menace to society and deserved 'outing' as such. What they needed was proof. If proof could be found the libel would collapse and unrestrained stories could follow. Their vindication came a week later. That weekend Jagger, Marianne Faithfull, Richards, George and Pattie Harrison, photographer Michael Cooper, Robert Fraser and antique dealer Christopher Gibbs gathered at Redlands, Keith's country pile. The guests also included David Schneidermann, self-proclaimed 'Acid King' and well supplied with the world's premier LSD, nicknamed 'Sunshine' and created in California by Owsley Stanley III, doyen of the acid chemists. Everyone took Schneidermann's tabs that Saturday night (Jagger finally succumbed and took his very first trip) and by Sunday evening they were just about getting up when at 7.30 some nineteen policemen moved up the Redlands drive. Armed with a warrant under the Dangerous Drugs Act (1964), they began searching the house and the guests. To the invading officers, the world of Redlands – all Oriental and North African furniture, gorgeously dressed ashen-faced young people, strange music (Dylan), a soundless TV – was one of unparalleled decadence, a fact that was merely compounded by the appearance of Marianne, clad only in a large fur rug. (Popular myth has always depicted Marianne as the sole woman at the party. However both Anita Pallenberg and Pattie Harrison were there – or at least had been. Neither was mentioned, nor indeed was Pattie's husband: the police, not yet ready to bust the nation's recent darling, seem to have waited until the Harrisons had left before moving in.) As the searches continued, the police began to realise they had struck very lucky. Robert Fraser, the old Etonian guards officer turned avant-garde art dealer was holding a piece of hash, a few amphetamines, but worst of all twenty-four 'jacks' (pills) of heroin. He told the police that they were diabetes pills, containing insulin; they believed him, but kept one back, for analysis. It would be enough to see him jailed. Keith was clean, but the police carefully packaged up some sachets of airline mustard and several matchbooks; he was the owner of the house where drugs were being taken, which was a culpable offence. Schneidermann had a small piece of hashish, but far more important was the attaché case in which he kept his drug 'samples'. As the police moved to open it he forestalled them: 'It's full of exposed film!' Miraculously they believed him and left it unopened. But the choicest find of all, the one that justified the entire expedition, came from Mick Jagger, a totemic figure whose face, as Philip Norman put it, was 'engraved like a Wanted poster on so many policemens' minds'.[7] Jagger's jacket, a green velvet one that he had last worn when holidaying on the French Riviera with Marianne, just weeks earlier, was searched; inside was a small glass bottle, containing four amphetamine tablets, known on the street as 'black bombers'. The tablets were actually Marianne's, given to her by a French DJ friend, but Jagger, ever the gent, immediately took the rap. They were his, they came with a legitimate prescription (he didn't have the paper, but named his Harley Street doctor) and he claimed that he used them 'to stay awake and work'. The police finished their search, said a polite farewell, and left, bearing their spoils. The guests took stock. It could have been worse – none had actually had, for instance, any LSD – but one thing was very odd: they were still there; normally the police would have had the lot in the cells.

Back in London both sides began preparing for battle. As the gossip had it, the Stones, through Keith's dealer 'Spanish Tony' Sanchez, were told that for a 'bung' of £7,000 all the drugs discovered at Redlands could 'go missing'. Although Keith, in particular, was enormously shocked by the idea that the police could be so hypocritical, they found the money. Sanchez passed it over in a pub in Kilburn. Whether the 'bung' would have worked will never be known; even its existence is in doubt. Marianne Faithfull, better positioned than most to know the facts, is contemptuous of the whole story. By all accounts Sanchez was ripped off: certainly the money never reached the 'swedes' down in West Sussex, whose policemen were in charge of the case. In any case, it was irrelevant. On 19 February the *News of the World* had splashed the Redlands story. It was a classic piece: no name was ever mentioned – the case was supposedly *sub judice* and thus barred to the press – but the paper talked authoritatively of 'pep pills' in the possession of a 'nationally known star', of the 'bottles and an ashtray' that had been confiscated for analysis, of another major star (presumably George Harrison) who had left the house moments before the raid and of a 'foreign national' (Schneidermann) who was on the run. This was not speculation: it was, names aside, hard fact. Someone, the Stones camp believed, had talked. The immediate assumption being that someone at the party was less than he seemed. It couldn't be a Stone, nor could it be an intimate: suspicion swiftly focused on Schneidermann and one Nicky Cramer, an upper-class layabout who, like many others, tried to gain a little reflected glory from his association with the band. Cramer's position was quickly ascertained; one David Litvinoff, another seeker after reflections, in his case those of the Kray Brothers, beat him half to death. When a battered Cramer still remained adamant in his innocence, Litvinoff had no choice but to believe him. (A year later, when shooting began on *Performance*, that fictional study of the point where rock meets the mob, Litvinoff would be hired as 'Director of Authenticity'.) Schneidermann was more of a problem. Back in London after the bust he had barely paused before vanishing. He has never reappeared. The real source for the *News of the World* material was rather more prosaic. Crime reporters and policemen had always worked hand-in-glove; it was unlikely that the tradition would be abandoned for this, one of the 'sexiest' busts-cum-news stories to date. Whether, as Marianne Faithfull suggests, there was a deliberate conspiracy, and the whole affair was orchestrated from on high, remains another unsolved mystery.

Given the publicity and their increasing sense of persecution, the defendants decided to go abroad. Mick, Keith and Brian, their girlfriends, plus Cooper and Fraser, decamped to Morocco. They were back by early March. The outcome of the raid materialised on 22 March: Richards was charged with allowing his house to be used for drug offences, while Schneidermann, Fraser and best of all Jagger were charged with possession of their respective 'substances'. At the magistrate's court in Chichester on 10 May the defendants opted for a jury trial at a higher court, scheduled for 27 June. The Stones' feeling of persecution increased when, as Mick and Keith stood in the Chichester dock, a third, Brian Jones, awoke, late that same May afternoon, to the sound of police knuckles on his front door. He, and his friend Stanislas (Stash) Klossowski de Rola, son of the painter Balthus, were searched and arrested for possession of cocaine, methedrine and hashish. Jones denied any knowledge of the coke; Stash had no drugs whatsoever on his person. Both were charged with possession: Jones with the cocaine and methedrine, de Rola with the hash.

Unlike the Redlands group they were arrested and spent the night in Chelsea Police station; they were bailed the next morning.

The Redlands trial lasted three days: 27–29 June. Jagger was tried first: his sole defence witness, Dr Dixon of Harley Street, was brushed aside on directions from the judge. He had never actually prescribed any pills and his verbal acquiescence in Jagger's claimed pill-popping was far from an actual amphetamine prescription; the star, authority's most prized defendant, was found guilty. So too was Fraser, who appeared next. Both men spent the next two nights in prison. The press particularly enjoyed the shots of their hand-cuffed wrists, but the public were less vindictive. To Marianne such a gloating exhibition was a bad move: 'When pictures appeared . . . of Mick and Robert handcuffed together, just seeing these two obviously frail people chained to each other brought out the absurdity of the situation. They weren't the Moors murderers, they weren't rapists or extortionists, they were guilty of a victimless crime. [Those] pictures also triggered a wave of sympathy.'[8]

On day two came Richards. The evidence against him would recount the entire raid, with the prosecution dwelling lasciviously on Marianne and her rug, supposedly dropped from time to time to excite the attendant law. She was not named, the court preferred 'Miss X', but the frisson was exquisite. 'At the mention of "nudity" there had been excitement enough . . . at the mention of a "fur rug" there was something close to collective orgasm.'[9] Within days a new revelation would add an extra twist: according to 'sources who knew', not only had there been drugs, nudity and fur, but at the very moment that the police stepped in, Mick Jagger had been prone between Ms Faithfull's legs, attempting to eat a Mars Bar, strategically inserted in her vagina. Such was the case that few, as the rumour mysteriously made its way around the country, saw it as anything but unassailable fact. Richards's suggestion that the entire raid might have been inspired by the *News of the World* found fewer takers. After a judicial summing-up that left no one, especially the jury, unaware of His Honour's own bias in the case, he too was found guilty. He was jailed for twelve months and charged £500 in costs; Fraser got six months and £200 costs and Jagger, the prize specimen but convicted of the least crime, three months and £200 costs. Inside the court the public gallery, crammed with teenage girls, screamed as one; outside some 600 fans mobbed the prison van – it proved to be a decoy. A day later the two Stones were free, pending an appeal, although Fraser remained inside. This had not stopped an outcry back in London. There had been demonstrations following the verdict and the next night saw the UFO club's entire audience marching first to Piccadilly Circus, and thence to the *News of the World* offices in Bouverie Street. The police retaliated with dogs and truncheons. The crowds returned on Saturday night, and there were further beatings and arrests.

That the freaks should march was hardly surprising – even given the professed apolitical stance of the average flower child. (The real Left were notably absent.) This after all was not boring old Parliament: this was the Stones, 'the greatest rock 'n' roll band in the world', this was cannabis, the sacramental high. Far more surprising was the attitude of the Establishment. In the Commons the maverick Tom Driberg spoke up for the band, even as they awaited trial. Driberg, whose own father had testified to the Indian Hemp Commission seventy years earlier, knew Jagger – their first meeting had been with Allen Ginsberg and the gay MP had embarrassed the supposedly un-shockable beat guru when he stared fixedly at Jagger's crotch and remarked, 'Oh my, Mick, what a big basket you have!' Jagger blushed 'like a little boy'.[10] John Osborne attacked the prosecution through *The Times* letters' page, but the most astounding reaction came on 1 July from *The Times* itself. In a first leader penned by the editor William Rees-Mogg, every vestige the Establish-ment man, and entitled 'Who Breaks a Butterfly on a Wheel?' (a phrase from Pope's 'Epistle to Dr Arbuthnot'), *The Times*, the mouthpiece of the Estab-lishment, came out one hundred per cent pro-Jagger.

'It should be the particular quality of British justice,' concluded Rees-Mogg, 'to ensure that Mr Jagger is treated exactly the same as anyone else, no better and no worse. There must remain a suspicion in this case that Mr Jagger received a more severe sentence than would have been thought proper for any purely anonymous young man.'

It was a piece that astounded Britain. It had its flaws: there was no men-tion of Keith Richard nor of cannabis. It was the image, as Marianne had noted, of a handcuffed Jagger that had touched his heart. None the less it was an exemplary piece of British liberalism. It was also technically in contempt of court – the case was still awaiting appeal – but the fact that the paper re-ceived no legal threats merely underlined the new official mood: the errant Stones were likely to be let off, a fact that was compounded by the announce-ment that their appeal would be brought forward to 31 July.

Meanwhile other events had been in progress. Hoppy, who had been on bail for the previous six months, was tried on 1 June, the day on which the Beatles' *Sgt Pepper* was released. His case had not been helped by his reject-ing the customary hypocrisy of such occasions and lecturing the court on the charms of cannabis. The judge dismissed Hoppy as 'a pest to society' and jailed him for nine months, depriving the counter-culture of one of its most charismatic figures. He would be back, but his influence would never be so substantial. A day later, as Hoppy began the first day of six months' imprison-ment, a number of his friends met at Indica. Obviously something had to be done, and among the ideas put forward was that of an ad in a national news-paper, probably *The Times*, being the nation's newspaper of record. It was not without precedent: Allen Ginsberg was a great believer in the idea, and barely a year earlier one Mr Matsuda, a Korean, had taken four whole pages in the paper to appeal for peace in Vietnam.

Foremost among those advocating the advertisement was Steve Abrams, then a 29-year-old research psychologist, working at St Catherine's College, Oxford. He was perhaps the most prominent figure then campaigning for cannabis law reform. His official role was as the head of SOMA, an acronym that spelt out the Society Of Mental Awareness but was obviously linked to *soma*, the peace and love drug created by Aldous Huxley in *Brave New World*. It had been launched in early 1967 and was immediately catapulted into some notoriety when the *People* picked up on the fact that Abrams had contributed a piece of 'pro-pot' research to a recently published anthology, *The Book of Grass* (ed. George Andrews). What really excited the press was his remarks *vis-à-vis* dope smoking in Oxford. There was, he suggested, plenty of it – maybe 500 smokers – and no one should be in the slightest perturbed. This appalled the University, whose senior members queued to air their anti-Abrams views in sympathetic newspapers. Privately the University was more sophisticated. A committee was summoned and quickly produced the Student Health Report. This largely echoed Abrams's findings, accepting the figure of 500 smokers, but adding that things were no worse in Oxford than anywhere else. The SHR then called for a proper investigation into the situation nation-wide. The government, less terrified of such contentious issues than those that have followed, responded sensibly. On 7 April the Home Secretary Roy Jenkins announced the appointment of a 'subcommittee on hallucinogens' to report on cannabis to the Advisory Council of Drug Dependence. It was, the activists felt, a triumph. The next step would be the Committee's report: as Abrams has put it, 'We hoped for something earth-shaking.'[11]

Before the advertisement appeared there would be one more 'cannabis' event: the 'Legalise Pot Rally', held at Speakers' Corner, Hyde Park, on 16 July. With a few thousand belled-and-beaded hippies, many of them smoking dope quite openly, plus such celebs as Allen Ginsberg and Stokeley Carmichael (both taking time out from the Dialectics of Liberation Conference), Alexis Korner and Adrian Mitchell, along with underground figures like Caroline Coon and Spike Hawkins, the rally inevitably made the press, who tended, irrespective of their audience, to rate it as a rather sweet old English event, not that far removed from village cricket or morris dancing.

Letting a little cannabis smoke swirl into the Hyde Park air was one thing. Taking one's cause to the very heart of the Establishment was another. On 24 July, readers of *The Times*, turning to page five, found the declaration that 'The law against marijuana is immoral in principle and unworkable in practice.' A lengthy quote from Spinoza advising the authorities to quit their role as Canutes, since 'he who tries to determine everything by law will foment crime rather than lessen it', was followed by an overview of use and current legislation – noting the pointlessness of a continuing ban – a list of (uniformly favourable) medical opinions and, down the lefthand of the page, a five point programme of possible reform:

1. The government should permit and encourage research into all aspects of cannabis use, including its medical applications. 2. Allowing the smoking of cannabis on private premises should no longer constitute an offence. 3. Cannabis should be taken off the dangerous drugs list and controlled, rather than prohibited, by a new ad hoc instrument. 4. Possession of cannabis should either be legally permitted or at most considered a misdemeanour punishable by a fine of not more than £10 for a first offence and not more than £25 for any subsequent offence. 5. All persons now imprisoned for possession of cannabis or for allowing cannabis to be smoked on private premises should have their sentences commuted.

Beneath this came what, for most readers, was the meat of the advertisement: the signatures of some seventy individuals. Not everyone who had been asked to sign the ad agreed. Jill Tweedie, perhaps the country's best-known feminist journalist, refused. But Abrams won over many influential names. Top of the bill was Nicholas Malleson, head of the student health system at University of London and a vital voice on the Wootton Committee. Abrams visited Malleson, promising to rewrite the ad copy until it reached the stage where Malleson, had he not been involved with Wootton, would have been happy to sign. He made similar approaches to psychologists Anthony Storr and David Stafford-Clark, and asked all three for help in canvassing further support. There were dozens of rent-a-liberal signatories, but Abrams judiciously ignored them. Instead he gathered a wider, and thus (as seen by *The Times* readers) more impressive list. Francis Crick, co-discoverer of DNA; George Kyloe, chairman of the Young Liberals; Grey Walter, then among the world's leading authorities on the brain. There was Brian Walden, a Labour MP whose interest had been stirred by the treatment of heroin addicts in his constituency; Calvin Mark Lee a Chinese-American pharmacologist; the writers Michael Hastings, John Pudney and Alistair Reid. Few of them would normally sign petitions; that they did sign this one was what mattered. In addition to these were such as the four Beatles (McCartney had guaranteed the £1,800 bill for the space), Ken Tynan, David Hockney, Graham Greene, Tom Maschler, David Dimbleby, Jonathan Aitken, Michael Abdul Malik (Michael X), George Melly, Patrick Procktor and Peter Brook.

It did not, it was noted, call for full-scale legalisation. This was pragmatism. Abrams was well-aware that such as Jonathan Aitken, despite his much-publicised taking of LSD for the *Evening Standard*, couldn't put his name to such a demand. Nor could many others. But calling for decriminalisation was subtly different. As for getting it into *The Times*, if SOMA expected a fight – and Abrams certainly did – they were pushing at an open door. Once Paul McCartney (whose identity was kept a mystery for as long as possible) had turned over the money, it was simply a matter of typesetting.[12]

The advertisement, unsurprisingly, caused a good deal of excitement. Perhaps the most important reaction was the adjournment debate on its relevance called by Paul Channon, then in opposition, later a Thatcherite minister. He was briefed by Abrams and gave a convincing case. His opponent, Labour's Alice Bacon (later Baroness Bacon) paraded the usual canards: all hash smokers turn to heroin; cannabis and LSD were responsible for importing 'negro music' and 'Indian spirituality' into England's otherwise unblemished acres; and if Beatles saw themselves above the law, they weren't: they were only pop stars, no more important than Lulu. William Deedes, now Lord Deedes, gave his opinion: hashish was far more dangerous than the very different marijuana and worried that 'if we were to end the black market in cannabis leaf by legalising it, a black market in resin would not begin. That could undermine this nation.' After this piece of wondrous unwisdom he condemned the signatories, 'unless they can back what they say with more knowledge than most of us believe we have'.[13] Deedes would have a good deal more of the same to say when it came to debate the Wootton Report.

As far as SOMA was concerned the aim of the ad was twofold: to make a statement that might improve the position of John Hopkins, and if not Hopkins himself, then future victims of the cannabis laws. And as a knock-on from that, to influence the Wootton Report. As to the first of these, it had some success; there was a tacit and partial acceptance of decriminalisation in the decades that followed – today mere possession of cannabis for 'personal use' is unlikely to end up in court. As regards the second, the proof lies in paragraph 2 (Procedure) of Wootton, where it states that among those developments that gave the study 'new and much increased significance [was] an advertisement in *The Times* on 24 July 1967 . . .'[14] And there was one more effect: on 31 July, exactly one week after the ad appeared, Mick Jagger and Keith Richards had their appeal. Richards's sentence was quashed while Jagger's was reduced to a conditional discharge. John Hopkins, however, remained in jail, as did Fraser.

But the Establishment had not yet finished with the Stones. If *The Times* leader had astounded many of its readers, then the treatment Jagger received on his release seemed even more remarkable. The night before the trial three employees of ABC television's *World In Action* current affairs programme – including director John Sheppard (who would shoot the Doors and Jefferson Airplane at the Roundhouse in late 1968 and the Stones memorial concert for Brian Jones in Hyde Park in 1969) and a trainee called John Birt – contacted Jagger. It seemed certain that he and Keith would be freed; it was also certain that the world would want to hear from them. *World In Action* proposed a plan: Jagger would make a quick appearance in ABC's London office then be whisked off by limo and helicopter to Sir John Ruggles-Brise's house in Essex. Here he would sit down with a panel of Establishment stalwarts: Lord Stow Hill, an ex-Home Secretary, the Jesuit Father Thomas Corbishley, Dr

Mervyn Stockwood, the Bishop of Woolwich, and Jagger's number one fan, William Rees Mogg. And so it went. A handwritten contract was signed in a break from recording 'Dandelion', the B-side of 'We Love You'. There may even have been a suggestion of payment, but it seems that none ever materialised. Then it was helicopters away, touchdown in Essex, a quick break for Mick and Marianne to slip upstairs to get reacquainted (a prolonged event which an embarrassed Birt finally had to break up), and on with the show. The great and good met the greater and bad and wasn't it all fun. Stockwood proved himself especially enthusiastic – 'Well, you and I understand each other, Mick . . . ' but they didn't, any more than did Stow Hill ('A crime against society should be punished') or Rees-Mogg ('Er . . . Mick, we know this has been a very difficult day for you . . . '). It was a performance of consummate skill by Jagger. The oldies, so desperate to hear just what *exactly* these difficult, strange, incomprehensible young people wanted; the young prince, trying to humour them, but all too well aware that even in their wildest dreams they'd never really know.

Meanwhile the Wootton Committee, another of that summer's attempts by the Establishment to understand their errant young, continued with its hearings. It consisted of eleven members. Wootton herself was a classic 'Our Age' figure. She was a social scientist of great repute, a Governor of the BBC, a magistrate, and a veteran of several other Commissions. Alongside her were a mixture of senior psychiatrists, pharmacologists, sociologists and the head of the CID. Whatever fantasies might be spun in a hostile House of Commons, these were neither lobbyists nor liberals. If anything, their stance had begun as generally anti-cannabis (one member had apparently dismissed the need to consult any witnesses: the Committee's sole task was 'to stop the spread of this filthy habit').[15] Only their disinterested analysis of what the expert witnesses would say changed their minds.

Those witnesses were interviewed in some of the seventeen sessions that ran from April to July. Among them were R.D. Laing, literary agent Clive Goodwin, Laing's colleague at the Philadelphia Association Joseph Berke, Dr Sam Hutt (gynaecologist, prescriber of 'legal cannabis' (THC) and now known as the cod-country star Hank Wangford), Bill Levy, the current editor of *IT* and Martin Sharp, the Australian artist whose contributions to *Oz* had helped define what was meant by psychedelic illustration. Others included Francis Huxley, signatory of the SOMA ad, the journalist Peter Laurie and Steve Abrams himself.

The printed Report was finished by Christmas 1968 and delivered on 7 January 1969. Aside from explaining its own procedure (in which it acknowledged current 'protests' against official drug policy), and running down the background and history of the drug and of its controls, it quoted from the witnesses and from relevant statistics to outline the current situation in the UK. It dealt at length with a range of popular fallacies and found that cannabis did not lead to violence, nor did it automatically create a vast constituency of junkies. It pointed out that a populist, contemporary assessment of a drug was nothing to go by: at one time or another tea and coffee, not to mention alcohol and tobacco, had all been excoriated in much the same terms as cannabis was now. Its most important conclusion came in par. 29: 'Having reviewed all the material available to us we find ourselves in agreement with the conclusion reached by the Indian Hemp Drugs Commission appointed by the Government of India (1893–1894) and the New York Mayor's Committee on Marihuana (1944), that the long-term consumption of cannabis in moderate doses has no harmful effects.'[16]

Equally vital was par. 67:

 The evidence before us shows that: An increasing number of people, mainly young, in all classes of society are experimenting with this drug, and substantial numbers use it regularly for social pleasure. There is no evidence that this activity is causing violent crime or aggressive anti-social behaviour, or is producing in otherwise normal people conditions of dependence or psychosis, requiring medical treatment.

 The experience of many other countries is that once it is established cannabis-smoking tends to spread. In some parts of Western society where interest in mood-altering drugs is growing, there are indications that it may become a functional equivalent of alcohol.

 In spite of the threat of severe penalties and considerable effort at enforcement the use of cannabis in the United Kingdom does not appear to be diminishing. There is a body of opinion that criticises the present legislative treatment of cannabis on the grounds that it exaggerates the dangers of the drug, and needlessly interferes with civil liberty.[17]

It urged that the current controversy over cannabis should be cleared up and accepted that until this was done, 'in the interest of public health' it was necessary to maintain restrictions. There was no alternative to the criminal law, but if the law was to be changed, the realities of cannabis use should be taken into account. It called for proper research into all types of cannabis use, but noted that 'the present legal position is unhelpful [to research]'.[18] While the Committee had no authority to recommend changes in law it did state that the current situation, in which there was no difference made between cannabis and the opiates was 'quite inappropriate'[19] and that 'the present penalties for possession and supply are altogether too high'.[20]

The report concludes with a list of recommendations (par. 101), including:

(2) Every encouragement, both academic and financial, should be given to suitable projects for enquiry into the cannabis problem.
(4) The association in legislation of cannabis with heroin and the other opiates is inappropriate and new legislation to deal specially and separately with canna-

bis and its synthetic derivatives should be introduced as soon as possible.

(5) Unlawful possession of cannabis without knowledge should not be an offence for which the law provides no defence. The practicability of distinguishing between possession intended for use and possession intended for supply should be examined.

(6) Possession of a small amount of cannabis should not normally be regarded as a serious crime to be punished by imprisonment.

(8) The existing law which inhibits research requiring the smoking of cannabis . . . should be amended to allow qualified workers to study its use both by observation and by laboratory and social experiments.

(9) Section 5 of the Dangerous Drugs Act 1965 (permitting premises to be used for smoking cannabis) should be redefined in scope so as to apply only to premises open to the public, to exclude the reference to dealing in cannabis and cannabis resin, and to remove the absolute nature of the liability on managers.

(10) The Advisory Committee should undertake as a matter of urgency a review of police powers of arrest and search in relation to drugs . . .

(12) Preparations of cannabis and its derivatives should continue to be available on prescription for purposes of medical treatment and research.[21]

Wootton arrived in the Commons on 23 January 1969. The Home Secretary, James Callaghan, made an initial statement on the report. A debate was scheduled for the following Monday, 27 January, but even in his brief report to the House, Callaghan, a former lobbyist for the Police Federation, made it clear that Wootton was not to his taste. For a while, it was rumoured, he had even considered suppressing the Report – so antagonistic was it to his preconceptions – but eventually he gave in. Various members had threatened to resign and Steve Abrams had even considered publishing a pirate edition.

The subsequent debate merely underlined Callaghan's position, with the Tory Quintin Hogg congratulating him on his steadfast opposition to any change, and other speakers queuing to air the worst populist fantasies. Callaghan's own speech merely emphasised the inevitable: the Report, so sensible, so balanced, so rational, had been all in vain. Unlike the reforms of the abortion law, or that of homosexuality, skilfully guided through the Commons by a sympathetic Home Secretary, there would be no hope for cannabis. After smearing Baroness Wootton and her colleagues as a 'cannabis lobby', and implying, quite against the facts, that they had called for full legalisation, he declared triumphantly, '[The pro-cannabis lobby] is another aspect of the so-called permissive society, and I am glad that my decision has enabled the house to call a halt in the advancing tide of so-called permissiveness.'[22] Wootton would reply via the press, but the harm had been done; as Callaghan himself, railing at smears directed against himelf, had noted elsewhere, 'A lie can be half way round the world before the truth has got its boots on.'

The 'quality' press stressed Wootton's recommendation of continued control and intensified research. Nothing should be changed until that was concluded. One can sense, re-reading their leaders, a definite sigh of relief.

Their news columns were less temperate, the *Daily Telegraph*[23] trumpeting the claim by a consultant psychiatrist that Wootton was no more than a 'charter for junkies', filled its story with the comments of anti-Wootton experts. Paradoxically the paper was no more tolerant of the excesses of the debate, quoting Lord Macaulay on the absurdity of Britain in its 'periodical fits of morality' and noting the number of bars, all touting unrestrainedly a per-fectly acceptable drug, on offer around the House. Writing in the *Sunday Times* Baroness Wootton's summary of the Report concluded with this opti-mistic line, 'There is no doubt that we are going to antagonise a great body of opinion who regard pot as a "beastly menace". We'd never get anywhere if we didn't make proposals that antagonised a lot of people. I'm old enough to have made what are considered outrageous proposals fairly often and lived to see them become accepted commonplaces.' Alas for the Baroness and those who backed her Report, it was not to be. The Baroness died in 1988, aged 91: her Report, which for many people was the most important (and certainly the most public) work she ever did, was not even mentioned in her obituaries.

The letter of the law, however, may point in one direction, its daily prac-tice may take singularly different paths. Steve Abrams emphasises that '[for all] his posturing the Home Secretary did not refuse to implement the Woot-ton Report. He merely refused to legislate unilaterally and immediately on cannabis at a time when new comprehensive legislation was being planned.'[24] Among the Wootton recommendations that Callaghan did support was the call for further research. It is hard to see what exactly has been done but in 1967 one organisation was actually doing something. This was SOMA itself, which had obtained a Home Office licence for supplies of tetrahydrocan-nabinol (THC), the active principle of the drug. When *The Times* ad had appeared, SOMA had still been an informal group; shortly afterwards it had been properly incorporated as the SOMA Research Association Ltd. Its directors were Abrams, Francis Crick, Norman Zinberg, a Harvard professor whose researches into cannabis (he concluded that it was essentially harmless) had been authorised by the US government, Anthony Storr, the anti-psychiatrists R.D. Laing and David Cooper, the Rev. Kenneth Leach, a cler-gyman and 'legaliser', and Francis Huxley. There were five employees, among them Dick Pountain, a chemist whose other interests lay in Situationism and the paper *King Mob Echo*:

> Everybody thought that the Wootton report was going to legalise cannabis. Steve got a licence to handle cannabis products and we had this lab behind Chelsea Football ground [438 Fulham Road] where I synthesized a whole bunch of THC. And we bio-assayed it, subjectively. Steve had these incredi-bly high-falutin ideas that after the Wootton report legalised it, we were go-ing to industrially manufacture it and we were going to make cigarettes soaked in THC. In the end I fell out with Steve over money – he wasn't pay-ing me what he'd promised and he wasn't paying on time.[25]

SOMA also linked up with two doctors, Ian Dunbar and Sam Hutt. Their surgery, on Ladbroke Grove, was hardly run-of-the-mill NHS. White-walled, with foam rubber pouffes to sit on, it offered *Zap* Comix, rather than crumpled copies of last year's *Horse and Hound*, to read. Their speciality was people attempting to withdraw from heroin, and they had discovered that, quite legally, one could still prescribe cannabis, at least in its 'tincture' form: extract of cannabis in a surgical spirit solution. It tasted disgusting, but it worked. As Sam Hutt put it, 'We were trying to give people something to get high off, not to be authoritarian. It doesn't replace the heroin experience at all but at least it's something to get high. And at least it's a connection with a doctor. We went on prescribing it, lots and lots, to prevent our patients committing illegal acts. If I found out you were going out and buying dope, of course I'd prescribe it for you, to stop you being a criminal. I didn't want my patients to be criminals, I wanted them to be within the law.'[26] Johnny Byrne was among those who visited Ian Dunbar. 'I went down to Dunbar and said, "I know you've still got this and I'd like to register and I'd like to have it." And he said, "It must be used for a medical treatment." I said, "Well I've got a medical complaint," and he said, "What's the trouble?" and I said, "I'm paranoid." He said, "Why are you paranoid?" and I said, "Every time I smoke a joint the police want to arrest me." So he said, "I can't think of a more serious case than that, I shall instantly give you a prescription." '[27]

As 1967 drew to a close Brian Jones's appeal was still pending. Busted in June, Jones had been found guilty of smoking cannabis and of allowing his flat to be used for smoking. In return for accepting the cannabis charge the coke possession, specious at best, was dropped. Stash de Rola was found not guilty. Jones was jailed for nine months, and removed to Wormwood Scrubs. However, thanks to an impressive (if depressing) psychiatric report, the jail sentence was quashed and a £1,000 fine plus three years probabtion substituted. He was also ordered to continue seeing a psychiatrist.

If the position of cannabis remained basically unchanged during 1967, then there was one positive development. The immediate result of the demonstrations outside the *News of the World* in June was the creation of one of the counter-culture's most important and most long-lived institutions. Release, which continues to help thousands of people after a drug-related run-in with the authorities, emerged directly from the angry ferment outside the paper's Bouverie Street offices. Among the demonstrators was Caroline Coon, an art student and model who had turned up because her boyfriend, a West Indian, had recently been sent down on cannabis charges (two years jail for a single joint). The Hopkins bust, while naturally highlighted in underground circles, was only symptomatic of what was happening to more and more young people, few of whom had ever considered themselves criminals nor ever expected to find themselves in court. The need to provide for these people was growing. The hat had been passed, as it were, at UFO, but the need for something more substantial was already understood. Its creation required one final shove, and the *News of the World* demo provided just what was needed. 'One met various people,' recalls Rufus Harris, then an art school drop-out, soon to become a joint founder of Release. 'The one I particularly remember is Caroline Coon. Somehow or other a number of us fetched up at Piccadilly Circus, standing around and wondering what to do, and decided to hold a meeting, which we fixed. That really was the beginning of Release. The people who were involved in these initial meetings were: Caroline, myself, Joe Boyd, Michael English, a lawyer called Dean Sargeant, Colin McInnes, who only came to one meeting, Michael X and Steve Abrams.'[28]

Not all of these would stay. Abrams, after making a number of useful introductions, left to concentrate on SOMA; Colin MacInnes appeared at one meeting, made a rather petulant speech and walked out; his friend Michael X was also otherwise occupied. It soon became clear that Coon was the prime mover. Never a flower child, and a friend of the Logues and Goodwins rather than the younger 'alternatives' she was stunningly attractive and the media loved her. (In time she would be given a column in the *Daily Sketch*, billed as the 'beautiful hippie girl who cares for drug addicts', where she offered worried parents comforting advice on their incomprehensible young.) That she was apparently upper-class yet slept with black boys and knew Michael X merely increased her 'exotic' appeal. Under her leadership Release took off very fast. There was a hole, which was expanding with every bust, and Release filled it. And unlike other underground institutions, which might gain their few minutes in the sun of 'straight' publicity, Release, hard-nosed, relatively unglamorous, getting on with a vital job, gained increasing respect, whether from those who benefited from its services, from the drug experts, who observed its progress, or, grudgingly, even from the police.

Like any institution without mainstream funding, Release had its financial problems. There were tithes taken at UFO and later the Electric Garden – sixpence off every admission – there were concerts and benefits, and there were less than usual methods of collection. One young woman, appreciating that the best way of tapping a rock star's wallet was probably by going for his fly-buttons dutifully offered herself to George Harrison and earned a crisp thousand pounds. Her next target was Mick Jagger. The Stone accepted her offering, but when asked for a little contribution in return, proved himself less amenable. Exiting from the bedroom in which the young fundraiser was still recumbent he informed his attendant claque: 'If she thinks she's getting five hundred quid for a blow-job she must be joking: She may have got a grand out of George Harrison, she won't get a penny out of me.'[29]

Release was quickly overwhelmed with work and at first the volunteers were only marginally more competent than those who queued for their services. Four hundred people a month were turning up, the bulk with drug problems, but there were others too. Without ever intending to embrace so wide a brief, Release workers found themselves dealing not just with drugs, but with pregnancy counselling, housing, runaway youngsters and psychiatric problems. There were socialising facilities, a room with no desks or typewriters, where people could just sit and have coffee and talk. There were late evening advice sessions with a solicitor and a doctor; for a while one could buy food to eat as one talked. Like many similar organisations, Release's greatest success would have been to shut down, its services no longer needed thanks to a more enlightened and intelligent drug policy, but that has yet to emerge. As it is Release is one of the most significant legacies of the alternative society.

LSD, already notorious across America, arrived in the UK via its great proselytiser Michael Hollingshead, who moved on from Timothy Leary's upstate New York estate to London's Chelsea, where in late 1965 he established his World Psychedelic Centre (WPC) in Pont Street. Leary himself had handed him a sheet of written orders, headlined 'Hollingshead Expedition to London 1965–66 Purpose: Spiritual and Emotional Development . . .' He was to gather a suitable community of acolytes, to set up some form of gallery to promote psychedelic art (known as 'tranart' for 'transcendental art') and to bombard the media with the new philosophy of a 'yoga-of-expression'. He had brought half a gramme of LSD, purchased wholesale from the Czech government labs in Prague and still untouched by British anti-drugs legislation. Alongside the drugs came thirteen cartons of books – *The Psychedelic Experience: a manual based on the Tibetan Book of the Dead* (eds. Leary, Alpert and Metzner), 200 issues of the *Psychedelic Review* and 200 copies of the *Psychedelic Reader* (ed. Gunther Weil). All these would be used to spread the 'gospel' and to help in the guidance of the hoped-for psychedelic community. Hollingshead was by no means the first Briton to take acid, but he was undoubtedly the first bulk importer. With his arrival acid 'took off' on this side of the Atlantic.

In some ways this was surprising: Englishmen seemed to have been in on the drug from its earliest days; certainly Tim Leary seemed to think so. Writing sometime later in *The Politics of Ecstasy* he declared that, 'For the last few years America has been on a Magical Mystery Trip, planned and guided by Englishmen.'[30] That autumn, on the first full moon that followed his arrival, Hollingshead assembled a dozen people, 'voyagers in search of answers to the secret of magical self-liberation'[31] as he put it. There in the sitting room at Pont Street, stripped of all furnishings but its carpet and supplied with such 'sympathetic' objects as 'hand-woven cloth, uncarved wood, flowers, ancient music, burning fire, a touch of earth, a splash of water, fruit, good bread, cheese, fermenting wine, candlelight, temple incense, a warm hand, fish swimming and anything . . . over 500 years old'[32] plus some cushions, some tapes and a few chillums of hash, he set about re-creating a scene that had become routine at Millbrook. The acid itself came in the form of impregnated grapes, each holding around 300 mics., slightly more than what would become the average trip. Hollingshead read from the *Tibetan Book of the Dead*, they heard music – Ravi Shankar, Scriabin, Bach, John Cage and some bossa nova – and watched slides of various sacred images (mandalas, the Buddha) projected on the wall. It was all very, very serious and a very far cry from what was happening on nearby King's Road, the first peacock flutterings of Swinging London.

As the WPC took off, Hollingshead began to attract a fast-expanding group of fans, 'a select group', as he put it, of 'young aristocrats and artists and musicians and writers, responsible for influencing sharply the patterns of the New Vanguard of British Culture and intellectual life'. Among them were 'my partner, Desmond O'Brien, [who] was already achieving renown as one of the most far-out LSD exponents in London . . . and our Vice-President, Joey Mellen, one of the first persons to trepan himself . . . '[33] Others included Victor Lownes, who co-founded the Playboy empire with Hugh Hefner; Julian Ormsby-Gore, the film-maker; Alex Trocchi; Julie Felix, the singer; Joseph Berke; Feliks Topolski; John Hopkins; Ian Sommerville; Roman Polanski; Bart Hughes, the high priest of the trepanation movement; Sir Roland Penrose, a director of the Tate Gallery; William Burroughs; Donovan; Paul McCartney; John Esam; Christopher Gibbs and Victoria Ormsby-Gore. It was a reasonably predictable list: a mix of new aristos, old beats (and one Beatle) and avant-gardists of one type or another. (Although despite his involvement in the relatively avant-garde ICA Sir Roland Penrose might not usually be associated with either.) Of them all, the most important in terms of LSD was John Esam. He was the 'alternative' to the WPC, much less obsessed by all the 'set and setting' mantras, and more likely to appear with a small bottle and an eyedropper and say, 'Stick out your tongue.'

The campaign against LSD emerged, like that against cannabis, largely through the circulation-seeking efforts of the tabloid press. Timothy Leary had just been found guilty of transporting not LSD but a mere three ounces of marijuana across the Laredo/Mexico border – for this he was fined $40,000 and jailed for thirty years – when London's *Evening Standard* newspaper ran a large, half-page ad. Headlined 'LSD – The Drug That Could Threaten London', it continued, 'Just for kicks, some famous artists, pop stars, and debs are taking a "trip" on LSD – one of the most powerful and dangerous drugs known to man. It produces hallucinations. It can cause temporary insanity. Kicks like this may be bought at the appalling cost of psychotic illness or even suicide. It is banned in America and elsewhere – but is still available in London, quite legally. Still more appalling – just half an ounce of LSD could knock out London . . . ' The ad promoted an investigation by *London Life* magazine, which had: 'investigated LSD fully and has uncovered a social peril of magnitude which it believes demands immediate legislation . . . to stop the spread of a cult which could bring mental lethargy and chaos.' As a piece of drug-related hysteria it lacked only the once-obligatory wily Oriental or predatory darkie; in their place *London Life* of-fered 'the man who calls himself Mr LSD'.

The story, which was especially excited by the idea that, armed with a few grammes of the stuff, 'anarchists' could take over the country, peddled the usual line: trippers flying out of windows, 'weird hallucinations', broken homes, 'young girls caught up in London's twilight club world' and victims of quite legitimate LSD therapy who went on their supervised trip *and never came back*.

As for 'Mr LSD' this was Desmond O'Brien of the WPC, the existence of which had been verified by Hugh Blackwell, another associate. Like Hollingshead, Blackwell mixed his LSD experimentation with a regular in-put of methedrine, the most advanced form of 'speed' available. Approached by the *London Life* reporters he had happily babbled of whatever came into his head. Like the *News of the World* twelve months later, mixing Jagger with Jones and cannabis with LSD, *London Life* had no time to disentangle fact from fantasy, and unquestioningly printed the whole thing. O'Brien himself consented to a lengthy interview (and a large picture). This chat, allegedly nine hours long, was notably anodyne, with O'Brien pointing out that the main reason for his consent was the demystifying of the drug.

But *London Life* with its minimal circulation, had only minimal effect. When the story broke a week later in the *People*, among the most popular Sunday tabloids, the results would be far more serious. Headlined in inch-high capitals, 'THE MEN BEHIND LSD – THE DRUG THAT IS MENACING YOUNG LIVES', it labelled 'Lysergic Acid Diethylamide' as 'by far the most dangerous drug ever to become easily obtainable on the black market. LSD, which is said to give "visions of heaven and hell" is used legitimately by psy-chiatrists to produce carefully controlled hallucinations. In the wrong hands, the hallucinations it produces can lead to utter irresponsibility, disregard for personal safety and suicidal tendencies. IT IS, IN FACT, A KILLER DRUG.' The piece talked of 'LSD parties' and called the Psychedelic Centre 'an alarming group of people who are openly and blatantly spreading the irre-sponsible use of this terrible drug'. When the *People* reporters arrived: 'The Centre was deserted and in a state of considerable chaos . . . there were used hypodermic syringes, empty drug ampoules and a variety of pills. Among the litter of papers were dozens of phone numbers, some of them of well-known show-business stars and personalities.'

Hollingshead fled London and hid out for three days, high on methedrine and quivering with paranoia. When he returned he held an ill-advised party at the Centre. In true Acid Test tradition it featured a spiked punch. By now Hollingshead's own drug use was out of control – three trips a week, usually of double the average dosage, non-stop consumption of hash or grass, and a methedrine habit that saw him shooting up seven times a day. There seemed no harm in adding another couple of hundred people to the enlightened. Unfortunately two of those who suffered an involuntary glimpse of the white light were undercover policemen. The Centre was promptly raided. Hollingshead's decision to take acid (and doubtless his usual maintenance drug cocktail) before entering the witness box turned the trial into some kind of psychedelic B-movie; it also saw him conduct a ludicrous self-defence, which resulted in his being sentenced to twenty-one months in jail. He served the bulk of it in Wormwood Scrubs, the monotony of his existence leavened only by hashish, massively available, and the occasional trip, left by visitors, one of which he passed on to a fellow-inmate, the recently imprisoned (and soon to escape) Soviet spy George Blake. Freed in 1967 Hollingshead left the UK, moving initially to Scandinavia and thence back to the US. He would re-emerge briefly in 1970, supposedly part of the UK White Panthers.

LSD's brief period of immunity ended in 1966 when an amendment to the 1964 Dangerous Drugs Act rendered it illegal. But the police had already decided to start their own campaign against the drug, targeting not the WPC itself but Hollingshead's 'alter ego', John Esam. An American visitor, passing through Cromwell Road, had brought with him several thousand trips, which were dripped on to the usual sugar cubes. When the police raided, Esam tossed a sack of impregnated sugar out of the window; unfortunately the police were already in the garden and the bag was caught. The trial went to the Old Bailey.

The prosecution hinged on whether LSD really came from ergot, which was illegal under the Poisons Act. If it were so, then Esam was guilty. In the end it all came down to rival pharmacologists. Alongside their usual forensic experts the police dragged in Albert Hofmann himself, who had used ergot in his own LSD experiments. The defence put up Ernest Chain, the co-discoverer of penicillin. Eventually, after much conferring of both sides' experts, it was decided that while Hofmann had indeed used ergot as the basis for LSD, it was a different ergot to that forbidden. Esam went free.

The prohibition of LSD, while presumably quelling the fears of those foolish enough to take the tabloids at face value, had little effect on those most likely to be take it: the young. Starting, as ever, with the inner circles, the most fashionable, the most chic, the drug would spread into a larger world. Of the élite, Keith Richards, never one to turn down a new experience, had flirted on the fringes of the Psychedelic Centre, as had Donovan, and by mid-1966 the whole 'Swinging London' clique were knocking back their sugar lumps and squares of blotter with determination.

Except, it appeared, for the Beatles, who unlike the Rolling Stones had managed to resist any public endorsement of drugs. Their 'nice boys' image, so sedulously cultivated by Brian Epstein, had always been nonsense – Hamburg's grimy leather jackets were a better indicator than the Palladium's collarless Cardin bum-freezers, and Epstein's own drug habits were hardly restrained – but it was an image that had worked well. If they did take drugs – speed at first, then cannabis – it was carefully kept from the media and thus from the fans. (They even shied from their own producer, taking care to hide their joints from George Martin as they worked in his studio.) By 1965 and certainly 1966 that image was rapidly falling apart. With *Revolver*, their 1966 album, they made it clear that they were moving into a world that transcended the usual limits of good old rock 'n' roll. According to Paul McCartney it had all begun when, sometime in January or February 1965 Lennon and George Harrison were both spiked. 'They had this dentist friend, "the Beatles's dentist", and he spiked them one evening. I think he wanted naughty sex games, 'cos they had all their wives there, and he sort of said, "Does anyone fancy a little bit . . . " and they said, "You fuck off mate! But we'll have a coffee . . . " After the coffee, because they didn't really know what would happen, they went off to the Ad Lib Club. It was brightly lit and it appeared to be on fire, so they decided they'd get away from that, and they drove back at about twenty miles an hour, hugging the kerb apparently, out to Esher, where they ended up at George's house and these huge big friendly trees were waving at them . . .'[34] Over the next twelve months the Beatles, or particularly Lennon, would encounter the drug increasingly often. The next experience came during that summer's Beatles' tour of the US, when Lennon was given a trip by Roger McGuinn and David Crosby of the Byrds.

As for McCartney himself, his admission in June 1967, just before his twenty-fifth birthday and a fortnight after the release of *Sgt Pepper*, that in late 1966 he too had ingested what the tabloids persisted in calling the 'heaven and hell drug' shocked the fans. (According to Barry Miles's 1997 biography, McCartney's initial acid mentor was the same Guinness heir Tara Browne who, a year later, would be immortalised in 'Day in the Life'.) Of all the Beatles McCartney had been the last one to lose the gentler, all-family allure that had been theirs in the days of Beatlemania. As a fan had only recently written to the pop press, 'I know that if Paul took drugs I'd be worried sick. But I know he's too sensible.'[35] McCartney chose *Life* magazine, then still an important mouthpiece, to voice his confession. Unlike the speed-crazed Hollingshead, tripping as he faced the law, or John Hopkins, who attempted to lecture the judge on the joys of recreational drugs, McCartney was very sensible, very grown up. He was also totally honest.

But as he subsequently accepted,

> I got into trouble for being honest. The option was there to say, 'What, LS what? Never heard of it, sorry.' No one had certainly ever caught me at it. But the point was that we were in a sort of group, we were a generation and really

more than anything you don't want to let each other down. You don't want to be the one who says, 'I've never had acid, sorry,' and then you go, 'Fucking hell . . . ' and you have the courage to say it. And to me, I'm not ashamed of it, this is something I've done, something Aldous Huxley had done, plenty of good precedents for experimenting in these areas amongst artists. When I did take it, once or twice I did enjoy it and once or twice I didn't. It was only ever nature and wonder and quiet when you enjoyed it, when anything else interfered it was bum.[36]

McCartney's measured peccadillo was marginal, however, compared with Lennon's growing infatuation with LSD. Before he was through with the drug, a lengthy course of near-addiction which would prove increasingly deleterious to his life and indeed his creativity, Lennon would experience at least 1,000 trips. Its influence would inform most of the music on which he worked between 1966–67, notably such songs as 'Rain' (1966), 'Strawberry Fields Forever' (1967), 'I Am The Walrus' (1967), and the gloriously climactic tracks on two successive albums, 'Tomorrow Never Knows' (from *Revolver*, 1966) and 'A Day in the Life' (from *Sgt Pepper*, 1967). Ironically, on the one occasion he took acid in the studio – during the overdubbing sessions for *Sgt Pepper* – it proved a mistake. In the first place, rummaging through the pillbox in which he kept his drugs, he was looking for speed. He picked the wrong pill. When the acid hit, McCartney had to help him on to the Abbey Road studio's roof for some fresh air. The others, as seduced by the myths as any innocent, rushed to follow: they'd realised what was happening and didn't want Lennon thinking he could fly.

With the ecstatic reception of first *Revolver* and then *Sgt Pepper* it was hard to fault Lennon's claim that the Beatles were 'more popular than Jesus', however much damage the remark did to their 1966 US tour. By 1967 Timothy Leary would be hailing the band as: 'mutants . . . prototypes of evolutionary agents sent by God with a mysterious power to create a new species – a young race of laughing free men . . . They are the wisest, holiest, most effective avatars the human race has ever produced.'[37] Leary's embarrassing effervescence was echoed around the world. Only Bob Dylan could rival the Beatles as a spokesman for a generation. Fans played their albums fast and slow, backwards and even forwards; they analysed the record covers, the New York underground paper *Rat* launched a 'Paul is dead' rumour that gained tens of thousands of true believers. And if the Beatles took LSD, legally or otherwise, the drug couldn't have a better sales pitch.

At its most superficial, LSD, like cannabis, was a badge, a statement of one's membership of a hip élite. However, taking it required, for many, a certain courage. Unlike cannabis, which might set off the odd burst of paranoia, but didn't last that long and could be counteracted with vitamin C or even a large sandwich, once you stepped aboard the acid roller-coaster, you were there for the duration. Physiologically the drug had been metabolised by the liver within fifteen minutes. The eight hours that followed, moving slowly to their peak one to two hours into the trip and starting to tail off four or five hours later, were outside one's control. The individual could exert certain pressures – the obsession with 'set and setting' fostered by Leary was intended to minimise the possibility of a 'bad trip' – but for many people the experience was that of pushing impotently on the rudder as one's boat shot through whitewater rapids.

As laid out by the Canadian Government's LeDain Commission report into the 'non-medical use' of drugs, LSD trips fall into a variety of categories, which categories can occur 'in varying degrees, in sequence or simultaneously'. They are, in what might be termed reverse order of psychosis:

> The *psychotic adverse reaction* or *freak-out* which may be characterised by an intense negative experience of fear or nightmarish terror to the point of panic, complete loss of emotional control, paranoid delusions, hallucinations, catatonic features, and, perhaps, profound depression . . . Second is the *non-psychotic adverse reaction* ['bad trip'] in which the person may experience varving degrees of tension, anxiety and fear, unpleasant illusions, depression . . . Inappropriate or disordered social behaviour may occur . . . Third is the *psychodynamic psychedelic experience* characterised by a dramatic emergence into consciousness of material which had previously been unconscious or suppressed . . .
>
> Fourth is the *cognitive psychedelic experience* characterised by an impression of astonishingly lucid thought. Problems may be seen from a novel perspective and the inter-relationships of many levels of meaning and dimensions may be sensed simultaneously . . . Fifth is the *aesthetic psychedelic experience* characterised by a change and intensification of all sensory impressions, with vision often most affected . . . (music and other sounds may be 'seen'); objects such as flowers or stones may appear to pulsate or 'become alive'; ordinary things may seem imbued with great beauty; music may take on an incredible emotional power; and visions may occur.
>
> The sixth type of psychedelic experience has been called . . . *transcendental or mystical*. Some of the psychological phenomena which are said to characterise this experience, are: a sense of unity or 'cosmic oneness' with the universe; a deeply felt positive mood of joy, blessedness, love, and peace; a sense of sacredness, awe and wonder . . . and a belief that the experience is beyond words, non-verbal and impossible to describe.[38]

The interaction of drug and human chemistry was what determined the progress of a trip; it was axiomatic that LSD put nothing in, but undoubtedly brought out what was already there. Thus the acid community was almost callously sanguine about the regular tales of freaked out 'casualties'; the assumption was always that such figures were half-crazy already: the acid had merely accelerated an inevitable decline. Dropping acid implied an act of faith, in the drug and in one's own sanity. The 'heaven and hell' fantasies of the tabloids were foolish, but the shorthand was not without validity. Sixties acid, unlike its Eighties successor, had no vacuous smileys to summarise its effects; two-faced Janus would have been a better image.

Acid, even more than cannabis, served as the perfect drug for an era obsessed with looking at things in a new way. 'Better living through chemistry' ran a teasing hippie slogan, mocking a current US advertising campaign. The simple act of taking the respective drugs involved a totally different level of commitment: the effects of a joint lasted maybe an hour, and for most people, despite a certain 'distancing' from the outside world, did little to impede one's normal activities. LSD demanded eight hours out of one's life, for most people it put 'normal life' on hold. Ken Kesey may have called on his Merry Pranksters to 'function under acid', but anything like a full dose made it near impossible to comply. With splendid understatement LeDain notes that LSD 'has deleterious effects on performance in tests requiring a high degree of attention, concentration or motivation'.[39] And it was this aspect of the drug, taken figuratively as well as practically, that the Establishment found least acceptable. Leary's 'Turn on, tune in, drop out' was less an exhortation than the map of a logical succession of psychological changes. LSD, with its world-shattering effects, led one to challenge and, quite possibly, to reject. It was also a Rubicon that, once passed, placed you in a new world, one not wholly comprehensible to one's generational peers, and quite beyond the understanding of virtually all one's elders. The writer Duncan Fallowell, then an Oxford undergraduate, saw acid as an enormously challenging, but equally enormously positive drug:

> I could see why people get hung up on religious groups and conversion. You're banded together in this great spiritual adventure . . . There was also the Alice in Wonderland aspect: this secret garden . . . Pavilions of bliss. This idea that the palace is just over the next hill, that heaven is just around the corner, and smelling it, knowing that this is true, not a fantasy. I had a very strong head. I never felt that hallucinations were to be confused with reality. They might continue but you actually knew what was going on, it was like being at the cinema in that sense. You could stand outside conceptually, even though you couldn't leave the cinema.
>
> One of the most useful things acid did was demonstrate that it is possible to view reality in various ways. This is very important: it stops you being a bigot; it enriches the way you look at the world. The dangerous thing is that for someone who doesn't have a real sense of who they are and where they want to go, this sudden dislocation, this feeling that everything is relative could loosen up someone who was usually confident about their own perceptions and make them hopelessly vague and even mad.[40]

Primacy in the counter-culture did not automatically create a happy tripper. Christopher Logue tried the obligatory trip, loathed it and decided that anyone who claimed to like the drug must be 'masochistic' at best; *Oz* editor Richard Neville held out until he was spiked and would always treat acid very cautiously; for Sue Miles, it was all far too revelatory: 'I thought my unconscious was there for a good reason. There were certain things that didn't function very well and we hid them – and I'm never going to get them out again.' For others it was truly shattering, blowing the world into pieces that would take some time to reassemble. Alan Marcuson, later editor of *Friends* magazine, and a friend foolishly licked clean a piece of foil that had held their dealer's store of pure, crystal acid. Later he reckoned he had taken a quarter gram of LSD, a monumental amount. At its peak, for maybe five hours, he simply left his body: 'I hovered above the bed, looked at myself lying there and voom! I was gone. The white light like you cannot imagine . . .'[41] It would take three days for the trip to end. He had survived, 'but only just'.

One figure who had been involved with the drug from its relatively early days was the 'anti-psychiatrist' R.D. 'Ronnie' Laing. Laing took his first trip in 1960, 'turned on' by a fellow professional who had obtained a supply for medical use. Warned that he 'was very likely to go psychotic'[42] he took it 'with a certain amount of anxiety', but all was well, and Laing saw the experience as analogous with the primary emotions of a very young baby. As he followed this trip with others he became increasingly fascinated by the way it could both bring back early memories, and mimic to a remarkable degree the experience of schizophrenia. He began using it in his therapy (usually taking a smaller dose himself, to help 'travel with' and guide his patients), treating such individuals as the US novelist and McCarthy blacklist victim Clancy Sigal, who later captured the relationship in his novel *Zone of the Interior* (1976). As his 'Laing', the fictional 'Dr Willie Last', puts it, he is all in favour of the psychedelic: 'Anything tae shake th' shackled mind loose from its moorings an' let th' soul rediscover itself.' As the decade moved on Laing's consulting rooms would become a focus for the disaffected young, who saw in him a sympathetic figure.

Like Hollingshead, but without the complexities of his multiple drug use, and with infinitely greater intelligence, Laing took LSD very seriously. Set and setting were of paramount importance; there should be no interruptions since a smooth, focused trip gave the best possibility of an untroubled return to normality. As he put it in an untransmitted interview for ABC-TV's *New Tempo* programme recorded in February 1967:

> I think that the drug is much less dangerous than it's been made out to be, though I am not on the other hand saying that people should take it lightly. It's a drug which . . . literally puts you out of your mind and no one who's got any respect for themselves will take a trip out of their mind casually. I think it requires as much inner preparation and as much sense of responsibility as deciding, say, to climb the Matterhorn, and I wouldn't stop people climbing the Matterhorn, even though some people fall off it.[43]

In all of this Laing's own role was that of companion and guide; it was one that made him, inevitably, an enormously potent figure. By 1967, at least in the eyes of the young, he was a, if not *the* British drug expert.

In 1964 Laing came face-to-face with another, even more celebrated 'Man': Timothy Leary. Leary recaptured the encounter in 'The Magical Mystery Trip', a section of *The Politics of Ecstasy* devoted to Britain ('I humbly suggest that to find God we have to learn to speak English').[44] Leary had been alerted to Laing's arrival by Allen Ginsberg. He was less than enthusiastic:

> Another dreary, platitudinous psychiatrist . . . We sat at the table, ate a sand-wich, drank wine. I told him that medical-therapeutic talk about LSD was a fake. I was interested only in the mystic aspects of the drug. His move. He said that the only doctor who could heal was the one who understood the sha-manic, witchcraft mystery of medicine . . . After a bit Laing said he knew an interesting game: 'Did I want to play it?'. . . The point of this game was to move your hands and your body without talking. We began to spar, karate style, moving in between each other's guard. 'Do we have to spar?' A shrug. Our hands changed into a dance . . . My eyes were riveted to his eyes. I was gone. Spun out of the kitchen in Millbrook, spun out of time. Stoned high in a Sufi ballet. We were two organisms from different planets communicating . . . We were exchanging the hard-core information about life, about our tribe, the mystery.[45]

By the time Laing was due to leave Leary had joined the fans: 'You will not find on this planet a more fascinating man than Ronald Laing. A pontifex. A bridge builder between worlds. Turns on that dreariest of professions with graceful strokes – an elegant hippy. Shrewd Edinburgh observations. Academic Poise. He is tuned in to Eastern philosophy, English poetry. *Magister ludi*. He weaves science-religion-art-experience into the slickest bead game of our time.'[46] Whether Laing, the tough, Marxist Glaswegian would have returned such adoration is doubtful, but they met again, six months later in Alex Trocchi's house in London. Laing also met Richard Alpert, Leary's one-time Harvard colleague making a trip to London in 1965. They tripped together, Alpert's regular 300 mics. was somewhat more than the Londoner was used to; for a change it was Laing who would be guided, and not guide.

LSD would play a role in Laing's world for the rest of his life, but his involvement reached its apotheosis with the publication in 1967 of his best-selling book *The Politics of Experience*; it made him into an international celebrity. As the journalist Peter Mezan, writing on Laing in *Esquire* (January 1972) noted, 'Runaways, street freaks and disillusioned GIs pack Laing's book in their shoulder bags as manuals for making sense of a berserk world.' Laing himself claimed that Richard Nixon kept a copy under his pillow. (Presumably, as advised by Lord Montgomery with his picture of Rommel on the tent wall, to 'know his enemy'.) But the young, who empathised

with its fiery condemnation of the contemporary world were the real constituency. There was no truth, no beauty, no absolutes, least of all those set
up by those in 'authority'. Doom overlaid the planet, epitomised in the futile
struggle in Vietnam and the omnipresent shadow of nuclear destruction. The
paperback cover featured a detail from Hieronymus Bosch's apocalyptic
'Garden of Earthly Delights'. This nihilistic assessment of modern life informs the first half of the book; in fact a collection of previously published
pieces, it was similar to the opinions Laing would put forward not long afterwards in his speech at the Dialectics of Liberation Conference. Even more
electrifying for many of his youthful readers was part two, entitled 'The
Bird of Paradise', a Blakean howl of spiritual revelation that seemed to spring
directly from the very peak of the most soul-shattering LSD trip. 'I have
seen the Bird of Paradise, she has spread herself before me, and I shall never
be the same again.' 'If I could turn you on,' it concludes, 'if I could drive you
out of your wretched mind, if I could tell you I would let you know.' Lines
like that, delivered to a receptive audience, were inevitably linked to acid.
Only Laing refused to play. The piece, he explained, was modelled on the
nineteenth-century prose poem, typically Balzac's *Séraphita* (the story of an
angel, half man, half woman, passing through its last earthly transformation)
or De Nerval's *Aurelia* (an account of the poet's descent into temporary madness). He also cited that hippie favourite Herman Hesse, a figure who Leary
had termed 'The Poet of the Interior Journey'. Nevertheless *The Politics of
Experience* joined Huxley's *Doors of Perception* in the hippie library, on the
shelf marked 'to be read before tripping'.

By 1970 Peregrine Worsthorne was telling his readers at the *Sunday Telegraph*, 'Why I would be willing to try "turning on". It is time we seniors
found out the facts ourselves.'[47] Prompted by the appearance of Leary's *Politics of Ecstasy*, Worsthorne's piece deplored the spread of drugs, but he noted
the public hypocrisy and suggested that the old had no right to legislate
purely through prejudice. They had to understand and perhaps even experience what it was they deplored. But for the most part LSD, which barely a
decade earlier had been lauded as a possible 'wonderdrug' by many therapists, continued to be reviled and feared.

Chapter Fifteen

Anti-Psychiatry: Brotherly Love

They are playing a game. They are playing at not playing a game. If I show them I see they are, I shall break the roles and they will punish me. I must play their game, of not seeing I see the game.
R.D. Laing *Knots* (1971)

Ronald Laing's involvement with LSD had given it an element of 'respectability'. However it should be noted that hallucinogens were for him a part of a far greater whole: his psychiatric work, which for its perceived revolutionary aspects became known as 'anti-psychiatry'. Laing, in partnership with a small group of like-minded professionals – Joseph Berke, Morton Schatzman, David Cooper and Aaron Esterson – would form a group of anti-psychiatrists whose influence would persist for decades. Like Release, anti-psychiatry came from the 'social work' end of the counter-culture, and like Release, it managed to survive, however diluted and adulterated, far longer than some of the movement's flashier manifestations. In an era so dominated by change it was inevitable that the mind should become a focus for investigation. The quick and dirty route was via drugs, specifically LSD, but there was no guaranteeing the results. And merely mimicking madness, which some saw as a primary role of LSD, was a far cry from tackling the real thing.

Since his first post, at Gartnaval Royal Mental Hospital in Glasgow, Laing had tried to transcend the traditional rigidity of such institutions. Here, in 1953, he had established a prototype of what was to come: 'the Rumpus Room'. He chose as its *habitués* the twelve worst patients from the female refractory ward – in which the schizophrenic inmates suffered the most demeaning and depersonalising indignities of a Victorian mental regime, together with ECT, lobotomy and insulin shock therapy. None of his group had been lobotomised, or had long-term experience of ECT. They were taken off the ward and from nine to five, five days every week, placed in a separate room – large, bright, well-decorated, furnished with magazines, knitting and drawing equipment – under the supervision of two specially chosen nurses. The effect was remarkable. By the second morning, the usually entirely passive women were newly animated, laughing and jumping, revelling in their newfound freedom. Laing saw it as 'one of the most moving experiences of my life'.[1] As he put it in an interview published in *IT* fourteen years later, there were two paths that psychiatry could take. 'Establishment' psychiatry, 'is going to become a more and more sophisticated technological means of controlling people. On the other hand, there is the sort of psychiatric stance, which is the one that I adopt, where one's client is a person who approaches one himself and one enters into some sort of understanding or contract with this person.'[2]

In April 1965 Laing and his group formed the Philadelphia Association; its name, like that of the US city, meant 'brotherly love', and its motto, taken from Revelations 3:8, stated: 'I have set before thee an open door, and no man can shut it.' Its declared aim was the relief of mental illness, 'in particular schizophrenia', and the undertaking of research into the causes, detection and treatment of mental illness. The Association was based at Kingsley Hall, a large, rundown building near Bromley-Le-Bow station in London's East End, built in 1923 by the two pacifist daughters of a rich engineer; in 1931 Gandhi had stayed, complete with obligatory goat to provide his daily milk, while attending a conference.

The aim of Kingsley Hall would be summed up by Laing in *The Politics of Experience:*

> No age in the history of humanity has perhaps lost touch with this natural *healing* process, that implicates *some* of the people we label schizophrenic . . . Instead of the mental hospital, a sort of re-servicing factory for human breakdowns, we need a place where people who have travelled further, and consequently, may be more lost than psychiatrists and other sane people, can find their way *further* into inner space and time, and back again. Instead of the *degradation* ceremonial of psychiatric examination diagnosis and prognostication, we need, for those who are ready for it (in psychiatric terminology often those who are about to go into a schizophrenic breakdown), an initiation ceremonial, through which the person will be guided with full social encouragement and sanction into inner space and time.[3]

The first person to experience life at Kingsley Hall was Mary Barnes, a nursing sister in her early forties who had suffered a major mental breakdown. She had seen Laing some time earlier and was a natural choice as an early resident. In time she would become hugely celebrated – she collaborated on a book with Joe Berke, provided David Hare with the subject of a play, and was widely interviewed and commented upon in the media.

Unlike those sent to a typical mental hospital referrals came not merely from professionals, but often from individuals who, having read Laing's books and seen their own stories within, would appear, like a disciple arriving at an ashram, seeking life at the guru's side. Whether they were allowed to stay was down to everyone at the house. Inevitably, as Laing's fame grew, the house became a magnet for counter-cultural tourists, fellow psychiatrists and therapists, international radicals, plus a cross-section of painters, dancers, actors, yoga students and members of the short-lived Antiuniversity, which later that year opened its doors a few miles away. This constant flow could be difficult; it could also be glamorous: another Scot, Sean Connery, came and argued passionately with Laing across the house billiard table.

There were very few rules. No one, for instance 'had' to work, although everyone had to turn over some form of rent money into a communal fund which could be used for food, utilities and maintenance. You didn't have to go to bed, you didn't have to get up. There was no hierarchy, no caste system, no separation between 'staff' and 'patients'. As the *Guardian* explained, reporting on Kingsley Hall in October 1966, 'It houses almost twenty people, of whom half would be diagnosed schizophrenic in any other setting. But within these walls they are not patients. They are the autonomous members of a community that is setting out to prove that the schizophrenic can find a way to meeting others and comprehending the dream-like reality which expresses his predicament.'[4] For the residents it was an on-going joke: seeing whether visitors, who always felt the need to differentiate between the two groups, could make the right identifications.

The doctors lived alongside their patients. After a day seeing his private patients at his Wimpole Street consulting rooms Laing would arrive in time for dinner, a lengthy candlelit event that would regularly stretch into the night with Laing only going to bed after everyone else had finally turned in. At dinner Laing would tell anecdotes of his past or discuss some major topic, be it politics, LSD or the *Tibetan Book of the Dead*. He was, as all attested, very conscious of his status and, like all such figures, happy to manipulate his acolytes, leading them, as Clancy Sigal put it in a fictional treatment, 'into dark, twisting mental labyrinths then suddenly abandoning you to find your own way out, which we proudly thought of as his liberating us from "th' chains o' love".'[5] For the believers Laing was: 'our sun, moon and guiding star, understanding ("standin' under") us when we didn't understand ourselves, redeeming past sins and absolving future mistakes, filling up the crack in our broken souls. We needed him.'[6]

In an era of fifteen-minute wonders, Laing was a genuinely exceptional figure and the alienated of the Sixties, for all their purported cynicism, were as keen to find larger-than-life heroes as any other era. Laing was phenomenally perceptive, he did drugs, he had revolutionised his own discipline and beyond that great chunks of the outside world. As Angela Carter saw it, Laing's books 'made madness, alienation, hating your parents . . . all glamorous. God knows what he did for people who were *really* mad, apart from making them feel smug and richly self-righteous, but he certainly set the pace for the crazy hinge of the decade, from 1968 on.'[7]

Not everyone was so tolerant of this Laing-olatry. The journalist Sally Vincent, once Laing's lover, found the set-up repellent: Laing, to her, was behaving as if he were 'the Angel Gabriel'; his colleagues, 'a collection of spectacularly physically hideous men', seemed more interested in fondling their patients, who to her seemed invariably to be 'young beautiful girls', than in any form of treatment. When, watching one of these girls being subjected to a series of particularly intimate caresses she screamed at Laing,

'What does he imagine he's doing?', the guru responded, 'Helping her down from the cross.' Vincent hit him.[8] John Clay, one of his biographers, has suggested that Laing could not be held responsible for those who followed him and he had not courted the role of guru. Others remain more sceptical. David Widgery, a doctor himself, felt that Laing had unleashed a monster. He, the guru, might have the capacity, but his followers, especially the less stable of them, gained nothing: 'People who got this idea that madness was sanity and were actually schizophrenic and thought that it was great to be schizophrenic or manic depressive in Portobello Road and drop into BIT and drop into somewhere else and take a bit of this and a bit of that. Most pernicious: those people did die because of neglect. All that watered down Laing.'[9] The filmmaker Jo Durden-Smith was more sympathetic, but had serious reservations:

> It was very interesting and very scary. It was very unsettling because what was always said about it was true: that there really seemed to be no distinction between those who were there to help, in some undifferentiated way, and those who were there to act out, go through, or whatever the current term was . . . A lot of the people who preached Laing didn't understand him and there was this idolisation of a figure who might be called 'The Holy Fool', the madman made saint. That was the most absurd over-simplification.[10]

Less tolerance still came from the local East Enders. Their initial stoicism – 'we suffered the Blitz, we can take a few schizophrenics' – faded fast. Reasonable relations were established with various local groups – old folk, a ballet class – that had used the building before the Laingians had arrived, but the main reaction was hostility, from the gangs of children who never stopped hassling the residents to the occasional 'lynch mob' of drunken, abusive adults, who turned up to hammer on the front door and demand to 'get the loonies!' Even the less aggressive neighbours were outraged, accosting him in the streets to declare, 'It's an absolute disgrace Dr Laing, these people ought to be given proper treatment.'[11]

Kingsley Hall shut down early in 1970. Between June 1965 and August 1969 some 113 people had lived there (75 men, 38 women), the longest of whom had stayed for four-and-a-half years, the average for three months. No one who had not already been in a mental hospital before their arrival entered one after they left; Mary Barnes, among others, saw the place as saving her life; many would claim their residence as a positive experience. For Laing, while he recognised the failures, it was, for the period of its existence, a success – on his terms. As he put it in a 1988 interview: 'For the time it went on, people who lived there would have been living nowhere else – except in a mental hospital, on drugs, getting electric shocks. There were no suicides, there were no murders, no one died there, no one killed anyone there, no one got pregnant there, and there was no forbidding of anything.'[12] The problem was, once again, that the ideological need to reject the strictures of the *status quo* compounded a practical need to incorporate at least some of those same strictures – if only to keep the wheels turning. To quote David Widgery once more, in a comment aimed at the larger 'underground' but pertinent here: 'If you're going to have a new society based on new values you need new social institutions. This was more like the sort of millennial movements that emerged in the English Civil War: somehow simply by the power of thought you could transcend material needs.'[13]

Chapter Sixteen

The Dialectics Of Liberation: Marcuse's Babies

*All men are in chains. There is the bondage of poverty and starvation: the bondage
of lust for power, status, possessions . . .
For the rest, terror is not masked. It is torture, cold, starvation. Death.
The whole world is now an irreducible whole.
In total context, culture is against us, education enslaves us, technology kills us.
We must confront this. We must destroy our vested illusions as to who, what, where
we are. We must combat our self-pretended ignorance as to what goes on and our
consequent non-reaction to what we refuse to know.
We shall meet in London on the basis of a wide range of expert knowledge.
The dialectics of liberation begin with the clarification of our present condition.*
Flier for the *Congress for the Dialectics of Liberation* July 1967

July 1967 witnessed a pair of contrasting events, both ostensibly geared to a
new and changing world, each in their own ways symbolic: in the first case of
the past and in the second of the future. At 10 Downing Street on the twenty-
fifth Mrs Wilson held her tea-party for Centre 42. Five days earlier, in the
Roundhouse itself, was the opening day of what was known as the 'Congress
for the Dialectics of Liberation', a two-week conference involving some of
the major figures of the international counter-culture.

The Congress was the brainchild of the psychiatrists at Kingsley Hall.
Under the banner of the Institute of Phenomenological Studies, R.D. Laing,
David Cooper, Leon Redler and Joseph Berke called together a variety of
leading British, American and French intellectuals, ranging from the political theorist Herbert Marcuse and the US Black Power leader Stokeley Carmichael, to the ecologist Gregory Bateson and the poet Allen Ginsberg. It
was an occasion, rarely attempted before and never to be re-created, on
which the two sides of the counter-cultural revolution gathered, mingled and
talked together with a single purpose. As the feminist academic Sheila Rowbotham summed it up, 'The revolutionary left . . . met the mind-blowers.'[1]
Compared to such culture-focused events as 1965's Poetry Reading it represented a huge shift towards 'proper' politics – Ginsberg and the Living
Theater's Julian Beck (a 'sinisterly charismatic' figure')[2] were the only artists
to attend. It would attract an audience of thousands in an atmosphere that,
suitably, overturned the arid rituals of Establishment conferences. Speeches
from the stage were augmented by an audience who, far from settling in
merely to receive instruction, impressed their own presence, with happenings, drugs, music and even the occasional 'freak-out'. It had, as Robert
Hewison has it, 'a characteristically carnival atmosphere'.[3] As A.M. Fearon,
reporting for *Peace News*, saw it,

We rebelled, we organised, we talked, we learned how to get high on oxygen, how to get stoned on human communication. Several people brought sleeping bags and actually lived there. The local kids, too, wandered in and made themselves at home. A huge swing had been hung from the gallery, and kids and grown-ups swung and climbed. One afternoon, when a large audience was sitting waiting for Herbert Marcuse to arrive for a lecture, the kids settled themselves on the platform; one urchin took the microphone and announced that he would now recite some of his own verses. He did so, to enthusiastic applause. Meanwhile, the grown-ups also played. A pedal organ in one corner was in constant use. Impromptu poetry recitals were held. Poems were pinned up on the wall, and were joined by a set of charcoal drawings. Someone discovered an old piano frame in the yard and began playing it with two sticks: others joined in with metal pipes, milk crates, tin cans and produced a mind-blowing sound.[4]

And he added, 'I doubt if Centre 42 will see as much real creativity in ten years as we saw in these two weeks . . . And I doubt if when the Roundhouse has become Arnold Wesker's People's Palace of Culture, the local Chalk Farm kids will come within spitting distance of it. Or if they do, it will probably be to break a window or chalk rude words on the newly smart walls, not to recite poems and hand out flowers.'

It was not the Roundhouse's first essay in counter-culturalism. Just a week earlier the rickety former gin-store had housed an 'Angry Arts Week' in support of protest against the Vietnam war. Nor was the Congress the first gathering of its type. Earlier that year the Catholic Marxist review *Slant* had organised its own Symposium, 'From Culture to Revolution'. *Slant* had emerged in the wake of the 1962 Conference of Cardinals, better-known as Vatican II. This essentially liberal gathering had brought a radical change, at least by ecclesiastical standards, to Catholicism. *Slant*'s founders 'approached the idea of a socialist revolution . . . as the central perspective within which the revolutionary message of the gospel can find articulation'.[5] Its Symposium was geared to clerics but attended by such influential leftists as Raymond Williams and sociologist Stuart Hall. Outside the Church it went largely unnoticed; it proved, however, how widespread such conversations were becoming.

The Dialectics of Liberation was subtitled 'Towards a Demystification of Violence', and as it soon became clear, the precise interpretation of this line depended very much on whose mouth was offering it. For the pyschiatric group, and for such figures as Marcuse and Ginsberg , the aim was to look at the varieties of 'bourgeois violence' – state violence, war, racism, the 'repressive tolerance' of psychiatry and education. For the revolutionary activists, personified by Stokeley Carmichael, the goal was the demystifying, even promotion of violence as something that need no longer worry the equally 'bourgeois' proponents of 'revolution'. Violence, he had once remarked, is 'as American as cherry pie'; now his intention was to make this revolutionary junk food available to all. Carmichael's fiery speechifying delighted his audience, even as he trashed the passive hippie world with its mantras and marijuana ('I've been turning on since I was thirteen, and I still haven't found my way because the structure is still oppressing me'). *IT*, which had been banned from sale at the Roundhouse, was less impressed. 'Instead of demystifying violence, the crowd cheered frenziedly at every mention of violence. Nonviolent actions were booed, racism was once again affirmed.' Carmichael's reception came in stark contrast to that of the West Indian historian C.L.R. James, author of the classic study of slave rebellion *The Black Jacobins*, but no fan of Carmichael's black nationalism. His speech, in which he demolished Carmichael's position with his own rigorous scholarship (although at no time was he anything but supportive of the larger Black cause) was received in silence.

There were also those who represented a very different mindset. Allen Ginsberg, entitling his speech 'Consciousness and Political Action', chanted a mantra, the burden of which was that the work of his friend Bill Burroughs ('the planet drifts to random insect doom') was 'politically speaking one of the best analyses of the present consciousness existing in the West'. Ginsberg's contribution would provide the Congress with an ironic coda. The entire conference had been tape-recorded, with the intent of releasing it as a set of albums. Unfortunately a woman worker at the pressing plant, listening to a test pressing of Allen's speech to check for faults, was so upset by the quotes from Burroughs she became ill and had to be sent home. The plant refused to press the record, and other means had to be found, a delay that postponed the release of the entire series.

As well as the advocates of terrorism and sabotage, such counter-cultural celebrities as Simon Vinkenoog and Emmett Grogan of the San Francisco Diggers added their voices. Especially popular was Paul Goodman, who won a standing ovation for his discussion of the dangers of excessive centralisation and regimentation of the young and noted the increasing awareness of the damage, both spiritual and ecological, being done to the planet. The greatest ovation of all, however, was reserved for the elder statesman of the counterculture, Herbert Marcuse, whose attendance was perhaps the organisers' greatest coup, and whose theme was 'Liberation from the Affluent Society'. To the disgust, no doubt, of the politicians, but to the delight of the freaks, he stated that revolution was unlikely, there existed no mass desire to have one, and in any case (as the Who would be singing in a few years), it was rarely more than another example of 'here's the new boss, same as the old boss'.[6] What was needed was a very different sort of change, a fundamental change that had to originate not in ideology – 'You have to be wrong because I am right and since I am right, you must suffer for being wrong' – but in a level of imaginative change that many would dismiss as utopian. There was required a 'total rupture' with what had gone before.

David Widgery was there: 'He was brilliant, so delicate and fragile and precise. It was the authentic voice of a recovered Marxism, a lineage that was being reconnected. It was astonishing. There he was – along with other middle-aged and quite old people – saying what I actually felt. It was very important to see those one or two figures who stood up not just in solidarity but with a welcome on their faces for us. We felt very isolated, marginal, crazy, an embarrassment to our parents and the authorities – and then we'd see old Marcuse beaming out at his audience as though we were his spiritual children.'[7]

Alongside Carmichael and Marcuse was one other major player: R.D. Laing. He remained, however, very ambivalent. He had put down his ideological marker simply by attending, but admitted that he 'really had no idea what would come of such an extraordinary conglomeration of people'. His own stance was neutral and he steered clear of overt political actions. That said, he emphasised, quoting Julian Huxley, that 'obedience' was 'the most dangerous link in the chain' that held together society. Whether between parents and children or rulers and ruled, 'Ours not to reason why' was no excuse, 'because I say so' no justification. What delighted the young, as David Widgery noted, was his ability to: 'put the subjective revolt in an allegedly political framework. He and others associated with him demonstrated that the "normality" we'd had beaten and taught and learnt into us – family life, being a man, being a woman, being sane – was an excruciatingly artificial construct.'[8] As for those who did the 'beating' and 'teaching' and 'learning', for Laing 'The people who do this are the danger, but they don't see it that way They're divorced from reality, but they think they are sane. They're the violent ones but they think that they are maintaining sanity, peace, law and order. Those of us who have seen through this to some extent can see that we have a system of violence and counterviolence.'[9]

Laing and Carmichael, both prima donnas, inevitably clashed. The flashpoint came at a grand dinner, peopled by all the top names, at which Laing remarked – ironically? 'candidly'? – 'The thing is Stokeley, I like black people but I could never stand their smell.' Carmichael promptly left.

Spats aside, the Conference was deemed a great success. Those who had been there, in whatever capacity, from the starry speakers to the local children who appeared one day to parade around the hall, giving out monster hollyhocks that had obviously been 'liberated' from some local front garden, felt that they had been in on something very important. Yet the much-debated violence seemed to have been romanticised, not 'demystified'; no questions had been answered, although many had been aired, and the 'mind-blowers' seemed no nearer the 'revolutionary left'. Still, for the contemporary counter-culture, the Congress would herald a definite new twist. The flower children would gradually shed their petals and start toughening up; many would make a definite move away from 'peace' and into the world of confrontation. As David Cooper put it, in a rabble-rousing farewell speech, 'Now is our time!' and in saying it laid down an increasingly popular belief. The next year, 1968, would have no time for 'love and peace' and it would not only be Mick Jagger who would cast aside his silks and satins and see himself, if only temporarily, as a 'street-fightin' man'.

Chapter Seventeen

Flower Power: Love, Love, Love

1. A tendency to date only members of different races and creeds.
2. A sudden interest in a cult, rather than an accepted religion.
3. The inability to sustain a personal love relationship – drawn more to 'group' experiences.
4. A tendency to talk in vague philosophical terms, never to the point.
5. A demanding attitude about money but a reluctance to work for it.
6. An intense, 'far-out' interest in poetry and art.
7. Constant ridiculing of any form of organised government.
8. A righteous attitude, never admitting personal faults.
9. An increasing absentee record at school.
10. The emergence of a devious nature, manipulating people for personal gain.
Ten counter-cultural danger signs, cited in 'How to tell if a child is a potential hippie and what you can do about it', by Jacqueline Himelstein[1]

The unpicking of any moment in history into its component strands is always hard and never more so than in a world so consciously amorphous as was the Sixties' counter–culture. Reading the contemporary press and ancillary writings – whether 'straight' or 'underground' – it is hard to draw precise lines or to define even key terms such as 'hippie' or 'flower child' (or later 'freak'?).

Like so much slang, 'hippie' originated as an African-American term of the 1940s, referring to one who poses (with little or no success) as a 'hipster' (and for this further group think Charlie Parker or, for a white, Lenny Bruce). Both terms of course stem from 'hip', another Black term, meaning sophisticated, *au fait*, aware, in tune, which reached the apex of its popularity during the 1950s. (According to some lexicographers the term comes from the Wolof *hepi*: to see, or *hipi*: to open one's eyes, although others refer to the opium-related phrase, 'on the hip'.) The '-pie' suffix, with its slight air of infantilism, is what makes the term less congratulatory. Around 1965 hippie gained its secondary meaning: a young person, preaching a philosophy of 'love and peace' and using drugs, especially cannabis and hallucinogens. By the Seventies the term was wide-ranging and relatively vague, defined by the *OED* as: 'anyone young and unkempt in appearance, who is considered to have dropped out of "straight" society, and who in general puts little premium on the values of contemporary society which he has rebelled against.' The flower-child was a later coinage, *c.*1967, and he and she, along with the much-mocked 'flower power' they espoused, withered fast.

'Flower children' were a short-lived and extreme aberration from the hippies, in many ways as much creatures of the mainstream, commercial world as of the counter-culture itself. As George Melly has noted, whatever validity the concept may have had at its outset it was soon little more than a 'national joke',[2] seized on by the same forces that a few years earlier had been mass-manufacturing Beatle wigs or pop art ephemera and a decade on would be gearing up their trivialising forces to nullify the genuine shock created by Punk. Perhaps, when the hippies of San Francisco sought to mollify and disarm their critics, especially those that came in police uniforms, with floral tributes there had been a certain sweet innocence, and the press loved those long-haired, short-skirted California beauties brandishing their roses or lilies. But by the time Scott McKenzie was urging 'If you go to San Francisco, be sure to wear a flower in your hair' and Eric Burden, once a hardarse Geordie rocker and leader of the Animals, had vanished westwards to launch a solo career and bemoan 'The cop's face is full of hate | Heavens above, he's on a street called Love', not to mention the sniggeringly labelled 'Flower Pot Men', the sweetness had turned cloying. Like all such shorthand – braburning for feminism, mini-skirts for 'Swinging London' – it was destined to define a period, but in reality it was merely one small element.

Despite this, the flower children did have a moment of real importance before the forces of triviality and commercial exploitation closed around them: the 'Summer of Love' of 1967. (This phrase, according to a recent piece in the *Guardian*, has apparently been copyrighted by the Bill Graham Organization of America, whose own genesis came in the promotion of the original psychedelic 'acid tests' of 1966.) In truth it was never that impressive: London as an *ersatz* California, filled with kaftans, beads and bells, and solemn references to such icons as the Haight-Ashbury, the iconic power of Love, the Maharishi and of course LSD. The Beatles and their peers may have reversed the usual US to UK progress of popular culture with what the pop press of 1964–65 called the 'British invasion', but by 1967 it was business as usual. The growth of psychedelia, stimulated by the ever-widening ingestion of LSD, had created the psychedelic sound – bands such as the Grateful Dead, Jefferson Airplane and various lesser clones – which started in San Francisco and made its way east. A number of major British bands, notably the Who, appeared at that summer's Monterey Pop festival (the most important such gathering until Woodstock, two years later) but it was as supplicants at the psychedelic court, and certainly no longer as trail-blazers.

You didn't have to take the drug to pick up what would have been termed the 'vibes' and the LSD culture spread far wider and faster than the drug itself. Gradually the California feel began to permeate London. The proportion of active 'acid-heads' to those who'd even heard of the hallucinogen was tiny. But as the constituency grew, knowledge, if not actual experience, became one of the badges of the 'in-crowd'. Articles began appearing in the smarter style magazines – *Queen*, *Town*, the short-lived *London Life* – most of which focused on the 'amusing' coincidence of the abbreviation of LSD in its

hallucinogenic and its more normal monetary role. As to the drug itself they
were wary: it was a foreign invention, beloved of Californian weirdos and
probably best left alone. Eventually Jonathan Aitken, boldly going where no
other hack had ventured for his column in the *Evening Standard*, did drop the
fateful tab, guided on his 'trip' by Michael Hollingshead's colleague Bart
Hughes, a Dutch acid expert and, although Aitken failed to note this, one of
the country's foremost advocates of the ultimate in 'mind expansion': trepanation. Aitken was careful to distance himself from acknowledging the
slightest pleasure, let alone self-knowledge or altered perception that LSD
might have provided, but the simple fact of running his piece in London's
best-selling evening paper ensured wide publicity for the new high. But for
the cognoscenti LSD and its 'mind-manifesting' properties went far beyond
the commercialised trappings. Taking the drug meant that one would never
see life quite the same again. The materialism of 'real life' quite simply
evaporated under the hallucinogen's power, and among the knock-on effects
was that for many who indulged in LSD the society based on that materialism seemed a good deal less appealing.

However subtle may have been the core counter-culture's appreciation of
the drug, the mass-market take was only the most banal and superficial. In the
first place there was no actual need for LSD, merely what the 'straight' world,
growing increasingly sophisticated in its appropriation and exploitation of
each successive 'youth fad', saw as its most marketable and clichéd attributes.
For Fleet Street it was ideal: a neat, easily recognisable if somewhat simplistic
piece of shorthand that implied to their readers an alluring mix of drugs, the
long-haired 'beatnik' young and 'love', a term that meant either 'loonies' or
pretty teenage girls dressed in a minimum of clothing. Whether broadsheet ('a
charming teenage creature weighed down by about half a pound of necklace and
half an ounce of dress'[3] or tabloid ('a couple lay down in the middle of the dancing throng and made love. People took no notice . . . '[4]) – they loved it.

Voyeuristic thrills aside, the 'acid' of the 1960s had much the same effect
in the wider world as did its successor, otherwise known as Ecstasy, of the
1980s and 1990s. Advertising loved its bright colours, its light shows, its 'surrealism'. Films began throwing in the obligatory 'trip sequence' – wildly
zooming camera, Vaseline on the lens. Fashion, naturally, grabbed on hard.
'Suddenly', trilled the *Daily Sketch* in a piece representative of hundreds,
'happiness is flower-shaped,' and went on to hymn 'Indian jackets and
dresses, kimonos, Victoriana dresses, elaborately patterned, beaded and
flowing twenties and thirties dresses, bell-bottomed trousers and brocade
waistcoats. Plus, of course, those beads, bells – and flowers.'[5] Or there was
eighteen-year–old 'Neville', categorised as 'a Plastic Hippy'.[6] By weekday an
unexceptional clerk, Neville dragged up in the full hippie kit at weekends,
'ready to spend forty-eight hours in the world of the Flower Children'. Still,
he 'admits to sticking chewing gum inside his tinkling Indian bells because

"the noise of them rattling all the time gets on your nerves something terrible" '. Even more characteristic was this report, run by the *People*, on a 'hippie ballet', presented at the Electric Garden, 'a scene which occurred only five minutes from . . . the heart of London'. Amid cross-heads that read 'Screams' and 'Briefs' the reporter shuddered as

> A young man stood in the centre of the crowded, sweltering club and began to recite a poem. It was normal for a few lines. The rest of it was an incredible series of swear-words. The Hippies applauded appreciatively. Then to deafening music, which seemed a deliberate distortion of all normal musical construction, they began to dance. The Hippies leapt high in the air, arms flailing – and screaming at the tops of their voices. One group walked round and round screaming in blood-curdling tones . . . Eventually the dances got more and more uncontrolled. A beautiful teenage blonde sank to the floor, groaning and head between her knees. One girl stripped off the top part of her clothing. Within minutes I counted two other bare-chested girls . . .
>
> Other hippies passed round scores of oranges. One young man deliberately put his orange on the floor and, with a faraway look in his eyes, crushed it with his heel – in time to the music. Another young man squeezed the juice of his orange over a bare-breasted girl. The blonde suddenly leapt up and rushed to a side room. She reappeared wearing a nun's habit. She went on the club stage with a youth wearing a policeman's uniform and helmet. With strange music in the background the 'policeman' dragged the girl across the stage, ripping at her clothing . . .[7]

Eventually the reporter fled after a young man told him, 'You and I are just not on the same planet.' 'It was a great relief to hear him say so.'

Flower power was especially susceptible to trivialisation and easy abuse. Yet beneath the commercial trappings, there was a core, hardish rather than hard, of political intent. One of the most potent pictures of the period, American and not homegrown, was that of a rank of National Guardsmen, rifles thrust forward, facing off against an equally determined row of hippies, who were in the process of putting flowers into the barrels of their weapons. Beneath all those hippie 'good vibes' lay a genuine anti-consumerism, a hatred of the materialism and lack of spirituality that underpinned the modern world. The phrase, after all, was 'flower power', and as one freak put it to the *New York Herald Tribune*, 'Our flower power is like gun power, fire power, man power. We spread lightness, joy and sunshine.'[8] What they also spread, as the increasingly antagonistic Establishment noticed, were drugs. This was not what the mass-market wanted, and undoubtedly helped create the suspicious atmosphere which enshrouded the freaks from the start.

For the 'in-crowd', the energy which peaked in the 'summer of love' had emerged sometime earlier. By late 1966 the acid constituency had expanded. Not massively, but enough to set the media muttering, and to provide sufficient energy to launch a club: UFO (for Unidentified Flying Object). It was not the first such attempt at a club. The 'Goings-On' featuring such beatnik veterans as Johnny Byrne, Spike Hawkins, Mal Dean (later an *IT* cartoonist) and their old Oxford mate Peter Roberts, better known, after some undergraduate excess, as 'Pete the Rat', had opened up on Sunday afternoons at the Marquee Club. They appeared jointly as 'The Poison Bellows' (an alternative name, 'Bader's Legs' was rejected as 'too strong'). This emanation of the 'Spontaneous Underground' featured a variety of improvised events – from concerts of ancient 78s to members of the audience receiving haircuts on stage and 'anti-conjuring' acts to Bach fugues on a conga-drum. As a contemporary newspaper reported, 'Who will be there? Poets, painters, pop singers, hoods, Americans, homosexuals ("because they make up 10% of the population"), twenty clowns, jazz musicians, "one murderer", sculptors, politicians and some girls who defy description.' Star of the shows was a pianola, which played such tunes as 'When the Sergeant Major's on Parade'. Pink Floyd made some of their earliest appearances, as did Donovan and legions of sitar players. There was no real audience/performer division. Spontaneity ruled: the stage was where you made it, the audience anyone not actually performing at that moment.

The relatively tiny group at the Marquee expanded first at the *IT* launch, when a far greater number arrived at the Roundhouse to celebrate the new paper, and later still at the Notting Hill Free School. UFO proper began life in All Saints Hall, a church hall off All Saints Road, Notting Hill (later in the Seventies to become the area's racial 'front line'). Like many such projects it began as an answer to another question: in this case the funding of the Free School, which while never hugely successful was still running up bills. *IT*, which had been in business barely a month, was also desperately in need of cash. There were small attempts to raise it, typically the 'Uncommon Market', a sort of freaks' jumble sale held at the Roundhouse, which might be accompanied by various performances, but there was a need for something far more substantial. Such bills devolved on the underground entrepreneur John Hopkins and it was he, together with a man called Jack Braceland, a fifty-year-old whose previous counter-cultural experience was the running of a nudist club in suburban Watford, who in October 1966 began putting on gigs at the hall. The main feature, apart from up-and-coming bands like Pink Floyd, was the light-show, a phenomenon pioneered by the artist Mark Boyle, who had worked with Mike Horovitz's *New Departures* and with a range of avant-garde musicians and composers. The aim had been to use the free-flowing lights to stimulate the musicians. When UFO moved to the West End, Boyle began working there too. Robert Wyatt, of UFO regulars the Soft Machine, recalled, 'He was burning himself to pieces doing these experiments with different coloured acids. You just saw him with these goggles, looking all burnt and stuff, high up on some rigging. He used to play tricks, he used to make bubbles come out of people's flies and things.'[9]

In December, pushed by Joe Boyd, an American ex-pat running the London office of Elektra records (primarily a folk label, but also responsible for the Doors, Love and in time the MC5) and a friend of Hopkins, the club moved to the West End, cautiously booking just two nights, one each side of Christmas at the Blarney Club on Tottenham Court Road. Usually, as its name implies, the club played host to London's Irish community.

Initially called 'Night Tripper' (UFO began life as a subtitle on the posters produced by Michael English) the club opened on Friday 23 December and, as Hopkins recalled, 'went off like a forest fire'.[10] A second night, a week later, was just as successful, and by the New Year UFO (Night Tripper had somehow dematerialised) was a fixture, opening up every fortnight. Pink Floyd were the house band, at least for the first five gigs and soon to be joined (and when their prices went up, replaced) by such contemporary stars as the Soft Machine, Procul Harum (who were providentially playing at UFO on the night they released their one real hit 'A Whiter Shade of Pale'), the Bonzo Dog Doo-dah Band and the Crazy World of Arthur Brown, featuring a singer whose last gig had been a 'novelty' act at a Mayfair supper club and whose elongated frame was topped by a flaming 'helmet', which appeared to be, and quite possibly was, a colander filled with meths. Less starry was the debut of Mick Farren's Social Deviants, punk thrashers a decade before their time.

Like the early *IT*, which still had a high proportion of European avant-garde intellectual material, rather than the dope, sex, rock and revolution of later years, UFO mixed music with movies (the Marx Brothers, Chaplin, Kurosawa), with dance troupes – David Medalla's Exploding Galaxy (whose headquarters on the Balls Pond Road had suffered so many police raids that they no longer bothered to rehang their front door), poets, prototype performance artists and others. There was also a steady supply of drugs – LSD, cannabis and amphetamine – initially purveyed by a chubby young German known only as Manfred, who gave away as many trips as he sold. It was far from glamorous, a 'dingy hole in a basement'[11] as one regular recalled it, but with the light-shows and a dose of acid, no one minded. And even the much sneered-at 'flower power' occasionally really worked. One visitor watched as

Suzy Creamcheese [Hopkins's girlfriend and later wife, properly Suzy Zeiger, a runaway Californian heiress] and two other girls love-bomb a bunch of rather uptight young Mods who got into the club. The third or fourth UFO. These mods were standing there pilled up, chewing, looking around them, semi-freaked out. And the girls noted that these mods were semi-hostile, almost lashing out at the hippies around them. So these girls descended on them semi-naked, clad in gauzy stuff with flowers and all the rest of it, and caressed them. These guys did not know what had hit them. But they calmed down and later on they were to be seen holding flowers and talking to Manfred.[12]

And like the Poetry Reading of a summer earlier, and the *IT* launch of three months before, UFO provided another opportunity for a community to come together and recognise itself.

It also provided, as had been intended, a useful source of cash for the underground. It paid the *IT* wage bill, but there was plenty left for other projects. Unfortunate dope dealers, desperate to skip bail, would be helped with an air ticket; Release took some of its startup funds from the club; other cheques went to set up a poster company, capitalising on the new interest in the world of psychedelia. It was also a major employer. At its peak, in July 1967, it was employing around sixty people and provided 'a survival amount of money' as Mick Farren saw it[13] for 200 more. Indeed, of all the underground institutions that would emerge, UFO would prove the most consistently profitable; perhaps only *Oz* in the immediate aftermath of its trial, when Soho porn-shops were queuing to buy back-copies and selling them, under discreetly plain covers as 'Schoolkids' Specials', was as generous a cash generator.

UFO had been running for six months when Hopkins was busted for possession of cannabis and jailed for nine months. His role as promoter was taken over by Joe Boyd, the 'yuppie' of the party who, unlike his predecessor, had no especial loyalty to *IT* and had little time for the constant syphoning away of the quite substantial profits. Boyd saw the venue as an ideal spot for exposing the new 'underground' bands, notably his own acts, the Incredible String Band, Fairport Convention and Nick Drake (the legendary 'lost talent' who would release three folk-orientated albums before his premature death in 1974). In financial terms he was undoubtedly successful, so much so that the local gangsters started asking for protection money, and in turn the nascent Black Power groups offered *their* protection against the gangs – as long as UFO began using one black band every gig. But the club was gradually losing its appeal – summer had arrived, tourists were starting to crowd out the regulars – and when the *News of the World* sent in its reporters to drum up a story, the party, at least in Tottenham Court Road, was over. The piece ran on 30 July, only days after *The Times* had shocked its 'top people' readership with the full-page 'Legalise Cannabis' ad. Now it was the turn of the masses. According to the paper, whose reporters joined the queue of 'two thousand' Flower Children, the club played host to an unbridled orgy of sex and drugs. In hyped-up prose the paper recounted tales of couples rutting openly amid the cannabis smoke and lurid light-shows, while dogs ran freely among the dancers and in the Ladies' men gazed as young girls combed their hair. 'Discordant music', 'weirdly dressed men and women', 'tinkling cowbells', 'obscene poetry' . . . to paraphrase the paper's own masthead, all (in)human life was there. It was the usual confection of nonsense, but it served its purpose. The police had never liked the club – they had not interfered when a very different youth group, the still emergent 'skinheads', began harassing the members as they came and went – but they'd been paid off by its owner and had held back from a major raid; now they had the excuse they wanted. The club was shut down within twenty-four hours of the story appearing. Brian Epstein, the Beatles' manager, suggested that it reopen in the unlikely surroundings of the champagne bar of the Savile Theatre, which he owned, but his lawyers were less enthusiastic. Four days later Boyd had found a new venue, the Roundhouse in Camden Town, but the old ethos was hugely diluted. By October it was all over.

Writing in *IT* 29 in a piece that cannot have much pleased Joe Boyd, Miles memorialised the club and its role in the counter-culture:

> UFO was created by and for the original 'underground'. It was a club in the sense that most people knew each other, met there to do their business, arrange their week's appointments . . . hatch out issues of *IT*, plans for the Arts Lab, SOMA and various schemes for turning the Thames yellow and removing all the fences in Notting Hill. The activity and energy was thicker than the incense . . . UFO as an institution is dead – its members live on . . . What went wrong? The film-crews, magazines and journalists killed it. UFO was killed by the establishment. It got into the rat-race of bigger groups = more people = more money, forgetting that more people = higher overheads = loss of quality – not of the music (though some still debate this) but of the club itself.

He regretted the change and the decline but offered the Arts Lab as 'the scene of this year's manifestations' and assured his readers, 'Don't be fooled, the underground exists.'

There would be other hippie clubs, notably the Electric Garden and Middle Earth, which would essentially follow the UFO pattern. But while they too had their dealers, their light-shows, their bands and even their occasional police raids, they were clones, their policies, their atmosphere and their audience of the mainstream. The counter-culture, while still providing some of those who patronised them, had moved on. One of its main venues would be the Roundhouse; another, albeit for one night only, was the Alexandra Palace. On 29 April 1967 the Palace played host to the Fourteen-Hour Technicolor Dream, an all-night hippie get-together that, both as to the performers and their audiences can be best described as the ultimate UFO. Like UFO proper it had a financial purpose: Miles, Hoppy and Jim Haynes met at the Arts Lab and decided on 'one big fund-raising event, an incredible event, which would create publicity, which would be fun in itself, and that was an end in itself, and it would produce some cash for the underground.'[14] Certainly the idea was sound, and ticket sales raised around £10,000. Very little, unfortunately, survived. As ever, no villain has ever been named, but other than a few small donations to *IT*, to Release and to the Arts Lab, the great bulk of the cash simply vanished. Posters for the 'Dream' had subtitled it 'the *International Times* Free Speech benefit' but no one at *IT* was counting on much profit. Only Haynes's fortuitous sales of the film rights brought in enough money to pay the performers, the light-show artists, hire the helter-skelter, the stages and pay the night's rent. As an event, it was very familiar to UFO regulars. The Social Deviants played first; Pink Floyd, starting their set as dawn broke over Muswell Hill, topped the bill. In between came a fair cross-section of the contemporary hip or thereabouts, including Christopher Logue, Alexis Korner, Arthur Brown, the Flies (another proto-punk band, who allegedly peed on the audience), the Pretty Things, the Soft Machine (drummer Robert Wyatt, a true avant–gardist, appeared with short-back-and-sides, a suit and a tie for the occasion), the Giant Sun Trolley, Alex Troc-chi, Michael Horovitz, the Poison Bellows (who reluctantly and perhaps sym-bolically abandoned their pianola at the gig) and the Exploding Galaxy. DJ Jeff Dexter helped compère, rushing over from Tiles where he had already dropped acid, ready for the night ahead.

Dexter, a pillar of counter-cultural rock 'n' roll, had been one of the few to make the leap from 'show-biz' to the underground. Starting off as a four foot eight inch tall Mod, who'd blagged his way into demonstrating the Twist (and all its short-lived successors) in front of a variety of big bands, he'd moved on to co-found the first ever mobile disco, following that with DJ work at the Flamingo and then Tiles. When Tiles folded after its owners lost their investment at the Woburn Abbey Festival of the Flower Children, he moved on to UFO and thence Middle Earth. Like many others he found his life changed by LSD. Tiles audiences, used to Motown or R&B, found themselves tuning in to Dylan or Pink Floyd and even (for Dexter's 21st), to the Social Deviants. There would be few major 'alternative' rock events without his presence as compère: the Doors and Jefferson Airplane at the Roundhouse; Chuck Berry and the Who at the Albert Hall (he had been offered the Stones in the Park, but the band had been to slow to confirm the gig and he chose to pass); the 1970 Isle of Wight Festival and *IT*'s *echt*-underground event, Phun City. He was a natural for the Dream.

Like some Piccadilly Circus of the alternative culture, it was a crossroads where if one stayed long enough, everyone one had ever met would eventu-ally appear. Brian Jones was supposedly there – though no one actually saw him; John Lennon certainly was. John Dunbar came with him:

> We were all down in Weybridge, at John's. It was 'No, I'm not going to mend your fucking bike, Julian,' and snorting up Owsley tabs and coke out of a kitchen pestle and mortar. And we were watching the TV and suddenly saw that this thing was on. So we thought fuck it, let's go! So we get into one of the space-age motors out there, Terry the faithful guy drives and we ended up at this place where everybody I'd ever known in my life swam before my eyes at one time or another. All eyes were vaguely on us because we were with John and I literally saw people I'd last seen at kindergarten and hadn't seen since.[15]

For those who weren't tripping it was rather aimless but for those who were – the majority – it was the nearest thing the UK could put up to compare with Ken Kesey's fabled 'Acid Tests' of a year before. It was, as Pete Jenner, manager of the Floyd put it, 'a truly psychedelic experience'.[16] Not always, however, in the conventional manner. The Technicolor Dream was the high point of a fantasy that proclaimed that banana skins, if properly prepared, could produce an hallucinogenic high. It was a mistake: the main result of burning bananas was a foul smell; it probably did nothing for one's lungs either. Undeterred, potential adepts squatted in a plastic bubble and accompanied their noisome vegetable spliffs by lighting sparklers.

The Technicolor Dream did little to fund the counter-culture's pockets. But more commercially-minded individuals saw all those hippies and started doing sums. John Crosby, two years earlier the first writer to delineate what would be 'swinging London', had been there. Writing in his *Observer* column he noted the ticket sales and remarked presciently, 'That ought to provide food for thought in showbiz circles. If 10,000 people will pay one pound a piece to entertain one another, obviously Warner Brothers is in the wrong business.'[17] Three months later on 29 July, the Alexandra Palace again played host to a hippie get-together, the International Love-In, a carbon-copy of the 'Dream', but strictly for the masses. Later still came a further clone, the 'Last Christmas on Earth', held at Olympia. Few of the 'real' underground went anywhere near it, but it was distinguished by offering Syd Barrett's final appearance with Pink Floyd. Barrett, the band's inspiration and creator of their early hit singles, had taken far too enthusiastically to the world of psychedelics. He stood paralysed on stage, clutching his white Stratocaster, incapable of playing. The band did three numbers before abandoning the set. Similarly commercial was that summer's next hippie event: the Festival of the Flower Children, a brainchild of the Duke of Bedford, a figure who continued to earn a degree of sniffy obloquy for his willingness to exploit both his title and the estate that went with it. Held over Bank Holiday weekend the festival attracted around 25,000 people, paying a pound apiece – of which the Duke, apostrophised by the *Daily Sketch* as 'Past-master of the Gimmick and Keeper of the Spoils', held on to ten per cent. It was hard not to mock His Grace, who had declared with an apparently straight face that, 'Only flower children will be allowed in. They are nice peaceful young people who like beat music and coloured lights. They are very different from hippies who take drugs and make trouble. Hippies will definitely be barred.' As the *Sketch*, which otherwise worried as to what happens when 'flower children go to seed' (answer: drugs and orgies), responded, 'How in the name of Allen Ginsberg, the Grand Guru of Hippieland, will anyone be able to tell the difference?' It must have worked, because there was a repeat in 1968, this time with Jimi Hendrix headlining.

The most glamorous of the flower children, who would certainly have avoided the festivals and were only marginally interested even in the most

élite of counter-cultural goings-on, were those who formed the current incarnation of swinging London's 'Beautiful People'. These were the same
young aristos so recently at the heart of the 'swinging' scene, now to be found
far from their usual London haunts making their way around the country in a
variety of gypsy caravans. It was hardly a novel adventure: the fictional Mr
Toad had been especially keen on caravans and Augustus John, another
well-connected Bohemian, had taken off in his caravan some forty years earlier. It was, of course, wonderful media fodder. The *Daily Mirror* offered
'The Meditations of Michael' (Rainey, the owner of Hung On You) which
offered the young master's faith in colour, due to save the world, and in
Merlin the Magician, alive and well and living in Glastonbury. The *Sketch*
preferred to drag in Rainey's wife Jane, formerly an Ormsby-Gore, baby
Saffron, and of course her father Lord Harlech, formerly our man in Washington. Lord Harlech stood by his daughter's choice of lifestyle (the three of
them had been arrested sleeping rough in a Glastonbury carpark) and assured the press that, whatever else they might choose to do, the young couple
eschewed the evils of drugs. Jane, whose day-job at *Vogue* was enhanced by a
matutinal lick of acid – 'an A-side high', as she put it to friends – might have
told him otherwise.

Maldwyn Thomas, late of Vidal Sassoon's and more recently a model at
the ultra-chic agency English Boy (founded by Mark Palmer), was one of
those who joined the upper-class gypsies.

> It just came up. I was round at Mark Palmer's flat in Radnor Walk and he
> said, 'I'm going to drop out, do you want to come?' It wasn't luxurious travel-
> ling. Quite the opposite. We caught the train to Didcot and we got off and
> walked to the Downs and we spent the first night out in the fields. Mark knew
> or found someone who was an old dealer, and we bought a dung-cart, a sort of
> tipper cart. It was perfectly clean. We put a tilt on it and wrapped it in canvas
> and it was very, very primitive. Mark bought this horse, a huge black and
> white mare. That was the start – and we set off.
>
> It was far from luxurious, but lots of glamorous people turned up: we had
> visits from Brian [Jones] and Suki [Poitier] in the Rolls, they'd drop in on us
> at Glastonbury or somewhere. People used to find us and come for weekends.
> I'd dread weekends. Some of them were really boring, and we were having to
> be really practical. 'Hey man, it's really groovy down here . . . ' and we'd go,
> 'Yes, can you chop some fucking wood for the fire?' One day someone said
> quite innocently, 'Would you like a bath?' and without thinking I said, 'It's all
> right: I had one about two months ago.' You just didn't think about it.[18]

Of all the commercial manifestations of hippiedom, the most popular, the
most successful and as such the most repellent in the eyes of the counter-
culture was the so-called 'tribal love-rock musical' *Hair*. As is the way of
commerce *Hair* was too late even for the first flush of hippie exploitation,
opening on Broadway on 29 April 1968, one year to the day, as it happened,

after the Technicolor Dream, and in London at the Shaftesbury Theatre six months later. It would be the West End's first production to open after that year's Theatres Act finally disposed of the 300-year-old censorship operated by the Lord Chamberlain; it was hardly what the long campaign to push through the Act had struggled to promote. *Hair* was the first musical to emerge from the movement (Lloyd-Webber/Rice's hippified *Jesus Christ Superstar* had yet to arrive) and while the coach parties, who would roll in for the next few years, loved it, the real hippies were repelled by its banalities. As an exemplar of mass-marketed trivialisation, of course, it was unrivalled. Politics were eliminated, as was any genuine hippie activity, especially smoking dope, and any cast member caught with a joint was automatically dismissed. Songs hymning 'The Age of Aquarius' and 'Good Morning Starshine' reduced psychedelia (let alone the political protest that was supposedly part of the show) to middle-of-the-road pap. Keen to show its cutting-edge liberalism it offered a few obscenities, and a good deal of nudity, and a song called 'Sodomy' got the press very excited. But *Hair* was a shallow simulacrum, safe enough for a teenage Princess to be wheeled in to show her supposed identification with 'ordinary' young people, and it came as no surprise that many of the cast were wearing wigs – their own hair was far too short.

Other than at the nursery level, flower power was dead. LSD was more popular than ever, but its consumers had other preoccupations. By September the counter-culture had abandoned the flowers, beads and bells. That month, spearheaded by the New Left, there would be the first demonstration against America's involvement in Vietnam. It was not an underground event, but it heralded a new mood. The summer of love had become a winter of discontent. The next summer, that of 1968, would have a very different atmosphere.

Chapter Eighteen

Hippie Trails: On the Road

The Burning Ghat
Is Where It's At
In Old Benares
Necrophiliacs
Can stain their macs
In Old Benares
. . .
It'll make you happy rapping
As the sacred cows are crapping
And freaks beg for a cup of tea.
Oh won't you drink a lassi
With me in Varanasi,
Yes, Benares is the town for me.
from *Hepatitis: The Death-Rock Eastern Musical* by David Jenkins & Duncan
Campbell, 1973[1]

The Leary mantra – 'turn on, tune in, drop out' – had many effects. As far as
the third injunction went, some 'dropped' further than others. It was one
thing to absent oneself intellectually from 'straight' society. It was something
else to leave one's country and join in a youth pilgrimage that, for its scale and
for its all too common excesses and disasters, came to be compared, and not
entirely favourably, with the Children's Crusade of the early thirteenth century. And here too, one can see the theory of democratisation. Travel abroad
may not have been hugely expensive, but it required money, and connections
never hurt. At the same time, the mass of the population simply lacked the
freedom, as well as the facilities for such explorations. The idea of the package tour, still restricted to European destinations, had only appeared in the
Fifties, and the Sixties was still witnessing its expansion. The sort of worldwide travel for everyman, epitomised by the popularity of such handbooks as
the *Lonely Planet* series or the *Rough Guides*, would be a phenomenon of the
Eighties. What links the two is the very Sixties take on the concept of dropping out, known then and now as 'the Hippie Trail'.

By the end of the Sixties the trail was very well worn. In *The Last of the*
Savages Jay McInnerney, writing thirty years on, laid out its extent:

> He'd spent a month living in a tent with a band of Pathan tribesmen who ran
> guns and drugs through the Khyber Pass and were big fans of American rock
> and roll; after a hard day of smuggling and robbing they would listen to Chuck
> Berry and Elvis around the campfire. He'd then trekked the Himalayas to
> Ladakh, where he had meditated with Tibetan monks. Rolling overland by

train and by thumb, he had lingered on a Greek island and in a squatters' commune in Amsterdam, whence he had taken a steamer to Rio. In a village in Ecuador, stoned out of his gourd on mushrooms, he was captured by a band of guerrillas, who took him to their mountain camp and interrogated him for three days as a suspected CIA agent. More than merely convincing the guerrilla leader of his innocence, Will had by his own account worked up for this charismatic warrior/scholar a New Left reading list which emphasised Marcuse and the rest of the Frankfurt school. And he had apparently promised financial and other support upon his return to the States, though, of course, he explained to me he was sure I would understand that he could not be specific about this.[2]

A little extreme but not that far from the truth. And he misses out the Balearic Islands (now Ecstasy central), notably Ibiza and Formantera, and Morocco, especially Tangier, long-colonised by the Fifties' gay and beat. Much of the trail worked by word of mouth, from the actual decision to go – what one traveller called the 'sheep effect': your friends had gone, you didn't want to be seen as lagging behind in the hipness stakes – to where you went and what you did there. In Formantera, at least in the early days, it was La Tortuga or the Fonda Pepe, in Tangier it was the Café Centrale, in Katmandu Hanumandoka, the main square, with its Matchbox Hotel and cafés like the Globe or the Cabin, which advertised itself as 'where the Jet meet the Beat' and sold hash candies at sixpence each; the Rex Hotel (invariably spelt 'Wrecks') in Bombay, in Delhi either Janpath Lane (for Mrs Colico's or Mr Jain's) or the Crown Hotel or the Rose.

Duncan Campbell, writing then in *Ink*, saw half-a-dozen varieties of tripper:

The One Way Trip: sensible, purposeful men on their way to make money in Australia. You'll recognise them by their corduroy levis, anti-malaria pills, nail-clippers, supplies of lav paper, water-bottles and all-purpose knives. They may smoke dope but they won't buy it and they'll shave off their beards when they hit Darwin.

The Dope Trip: which covers everyone from junkies to pot-heads who go to India for cheap dope, cheap living, and the absence of the West End Central drug squad . . . You can tell the dope-trippers by the holes in their arms, the holes in their nostrils or the holes in their heads.

The Wheeler-Dealer Trip: these are the student-card pushers and the rupee millionaires. They fly out to India on a charter flight, or drive out by land-rover to pick up Afghan jackets, beads, dope, boots, shirts or what have-you (or haven't, more likely). They're the hip colonialists, the screwed-on heads.

The Religious Trip: the guru-collectors, Hare Krishna folks, Divine Light cavalry, Buddhist converts and searchers after nirvana, truth, light or a cheap temple to stay in.

The Cultural trip: you don't see them around much. They're in India to study sitar or tabla or learn Sanskrit or do a sociology paper. On the whole they look down a bit on those drug-crazed, religious freaks they see around them.

The Other Trip: the general, cheerful ragbag of travellers who wear Injun clothes, eat with their hands, smoke everything, know a few words of Hindi, dabble with the odd swami and dig Ravi Shankar. They include the long-haired Californian remittance men, the passers-of-time, escapists, curry-lovers, ex-GIs on their way home from Vietnam, voyeurs, Capricorns, readers of Hesse and associated freaks.

What sent them? For most it was a phenomenon that long-preceded their wanderings, that clichéd but still potent 'lure of the East'. For the more reflective hippies, underpinning the myth of self-discovery was a turning against the Judaeo-Christian ethic, so laden with guilt and work ethics, and a belief that the religions of the East, however diluted, might be more what the seeker required. One could stay at home and immerse oneself in these new, ascetic disciplines, but how much more exotic and exciting to head out East, following one's karma. As one veteran recalled, 'Everyone was stripped bare – that was what everyone was trying to do, to eliminate culture from themselves . . . They wanted to die, in fact.'[3] India was usually the ultimate destination, with stop-overs along the way in Greece, Turkey, Iran and Iraq, in Afghanistan, Nepal and Pakistan. Only a small minority made it even further, to Burma, Thailand and, for gore-trippers, Vietnam. As the list indicates, it was a very different era: few travellers today would be able to move so casually around Iran or Iraq, Afghanistan or Nepal. Most of these countries provided a relatively uncontrolled abundance of that staple of hippiedom: drugs. There was hashish, of the highest quality and at minimal cost, there was also morphine, heroin, and a variety of 'uppers' and 'downers'. North Africa provided more of the same, only here it was Moroccan *kif* rather than Indian *charas*, while those, a minority, who chose South America for their enlightenment, found cocaine. There were inevitably those – usually the least overtly 'hippie' in style – who planned to bring or send home a supply. As the decade proceeded, European Customs grew more efficient, but for a while every traveller seems to have a tale of moving from Pakistan to Nepal or Nepal to India with a pound of hash down their trousers and a box of morphine syrettes in their rucksack. And even if one was busted, the chances are that little would happen. David Jenkins, now a journalist, was on his way from Benares to Jodhpur:

> I still had some dope and some opium and some mandies and trips and we were chugging along on the train smoking this hash, which I didn't really want to smoke because, on top of the opium, I was feeling sick. As we slowed down near Allahabad, on leaped these policemen. They came rushing down the second class coaches where all the hippies were, going 'Charas, afim! charas, afim!', meaning hashish, opium. I then shoved all my charas down my trousers but there was the most amazing smell all round us, so there I was in

the middle of the train forced to pull my trousers down, having no pants on, so I was waggling my dong for the carriage, and there they found a pound and a half of hashish. And thus I was hauled off the train with my French friend leaning out of the window saying, 'Keep cool, David, keep cool.' Thank you very much, I felt.

I wasn't that frightened, because I knew of other people who had been busted and it wasn't that bad but it was still rather unnerving. Sitting on the station platform I tried to get rid of my acid and so on, though luckily they didn't really realise what it was. They took me off to the police captain's veranda where he kept saying, 'This is very difficult, this is very difficult.' I was put into a cell on the station, on the platform, and I had this to myself, shitting and peeing in the corner and vomming a couple of times, tried to sleep until I was taken out the next morning and given breakfast on the station platform and introduced to Mr Pandy, ex-President of Allahabad Students Union and my lawyer.

Then I was driven handcuffed in a rickshaw through the streets of Allahabad to the court which was rather like the Parthenon, an open court, and of course the crowds rushed up. I was going up and down in spirits thinking well this was hilarious and a brilliant story to tell, and then feeling rather nervous and eventually getting them to take me away from the crowd and into court . . . I said I'd just come from Nepal where it was all legal and then I'd come from Benares where there were government grass shops and how was I to know that it was illegal? And the magistrate made the sharp point, 'If you didn't think it was illegal, why did you stuff it down your pants?' And I said, 'Ah, if you saw twenty policeman coming at you you'd probably think there was something fishy too.' He then pronounced sentence: 'You have to have compulsory jail for opium but since you have spent one night in jail already that will do for that and I fine you 20 rupees (£1). To complete the sentence you must stay in the dock.' Then came in a man loaded down with many more chains than me and I felt rather sympathetic and asked him 'What are you in for?' and he made these stabbing motions – he was up for murder.

After my trial I was taken to lunch by the magistrate and my lawyer who asked me, 'You have a girlfriend in England?' and I said yes. 'She lets you sleep with her?' And I went yes. And they both went, 'Nice!' Thereupon I gave them a very merry description of England, culled from the *News of the World* – all wife swapping and five-in-a-bed orgies. And he ended up with the wonderful line: 'These things you talk about – they are just for the upper classes or they are for everyone?' I said, 'Everyone,' and they said 'Nice!'[4]

Not everyone was so lucky. For a while burning one's passport was viewed as a fine gesture against Western conformity. Local government was less impressed, as were the British, French, German and American consulates, whose harassed, not always sympathetic officials would turn up regularly at local jails to extract their stoned, bewildered compatriots and deposit them on the next plane home. However seriously the freaks might have taken it at the time, it's hard to deny a certain frivolity in these travellers. For people so gloriously under-prepared what was amazing was not the rollcall of casualties, but the remarkable numbers who – while psychically and physically bloodied – remained wondrously unbowed by the experience.

The great irony of the trail was that few hippies genuinely 'saw' the countries through which they moved. Their world, from hotel to hotel, from dealer to dealer, from bus to bus was in its own way as hermetically sealed as that of any package tour. It was a tribal movement, and while some of the nomads might choose to abandon the tribe, the great majority kept well within range. There were differences – Germans were very earnest, Americans rather foolish, the British colonialists *manqués* and the French generally abused as thieves and cheats – but in the end it was a large, undifferentiated mass, moving backwards and forwards to and from the East. For the freaks the Third World (a term only coined in 1966) had no intrinsic meaning: it was a backdrop, a wonderful if occasionally scary but invariably groovy playground. Reading in *Play Power* Richard Neville's inevitably hyperbolic evocation of the trail, one sees this almost complete disinterest. Yes, the trail is wonderfully formative, yes one meets all sorts of weird and wonderful people, yes it's all dope 'n' sex 'n' rock 'n' roll but the problem remains: they're all the same – this meandering tribe of thinkalike, talkalike, lookalike hippies.

What the locals felt was often a mystery in itself. You were a novelty, you were puzzling: it was not surprising that people stared. The freaks were obviously a source of money, and the girls one of lascivious speculation. But for all the noises in the British press – gloating if usually specious reportage of gang-rapes, stonings, violence, theft, disease, madness, hippie boys begging, the girls selling themselves for a 'fix of hash' – the inhabitants of India or Afghanistan, of Morocco or Formantera, were generally welcoming. Much less tolerant were the wealthy American and European tourists who came home with horror-stories of people who might be their own children volunteering for third-class travel, for drugs, for cheap hotels and a life of effective beggary. Such people had come to these countries to avoid their creeping democracy: now it was on their trail. The underlying racism of their stance was best-echoed in the British tabloids. As the *Mirror*'s man put it in a piece entitled 'In the Hell of Hashish City' (Kabul), 'To grovel in the gutter, begging money from Afghan peasants is about as low as you can get.'[5] Yet as the much-travelled *Oz* editor Jim Anderson pondered, 'It's hard to know which Americans fuck up countries like Morocco more – the big companies pumping in false money, Coca-Cola and the tired old skyscraper dream, or the communal hippies trying to tell them that their old struggle for existence from the soil is where it's at.'[6]

Inevitably, as the decade passed and their numbers increased hippies would grow less popular – and less sensitive to local feelings. In 1968, undoubtedly spurred on by the fears of that year's potential 'revolution' on the streets of Europe and the States, the mood turned nastier. Italy, Yugoslavia, Mexico, Ibiza, Greece, Turkey, India, Singapore and Laos were among countries who, one way or another 'declared war' on the travellers. By the 1980s, with the Mullahs in power in Iran and the Russians fighting their own 'Vietnam' in Afghanistan, plus a general hardening of attitudes along most countries of the trail, the free-and-easy days had vanished.

It was not, however, mandatory to take the hippie trail for spiritual enlightenment. The tradition of fringe religiosity was well-established in Britain, and there had always been a variety of self-ordained gurus for the credulous. The Sixties, when the search for the meaning of life, or oneself, became so important, gave the whole area a new impetus. Some might see in LSD a way of tearing down the crenellated monuments of myth and superstition that represented organised religion. Far more took from their acid experiences, with their instant attainment of 'white light', a desire to delve further into the supernatural. This could take many forms, among them a fascination with magic, or earnest readings of Herman Hesse, J.R.R. Tolkien and the dubiously authentic 'Don Juan', the supposed *curandero* and product of the imaginative mind of writer Carlos Castenada. None of it was especially new; in one form or another small bands of dedicated seekers – cranks, as their opponents would put it – had always turned to one teacher or another for answers. The Sixties, with their propensity to take such causes and write them infinitely large, gave such crankery a new lease of life.

Nowhere was the phenomenon so apparent as in the popularity of what Sue Miles termed the 'Indian travelling salesmen'.[7] There was Meher Baba, known as 'The Awakener' and beloved of the Who's leader Pete Townshend; beginning on 10 July 1925, he observed silence for the last forty-four years of his life, communicating with his disciples at first through an alphabet board but increasingly with gestures. He observed that he had come 'not to teach, but to awaken', and noted that 'things that are real are given and received in silence.' Ironically the Baba was determinedly anti-drugs, which he described as 'harmful mentally, physically, and spiritually' but such admonitions didn't appear to faze his young followers.

Even more popular was Mohan Chandra Rajneesh, self-styled Bhagwan Shree Rajneesh, who preached an eclectic doctrine of Eastern mysticism and individual devotion; the hippies especially enjoyed his advocacy of unbridled sexual freedom (it would not survive the onset of AIDS) while the Bhagwan himself (it means 'God') enjoyed the fact that with his new popularity came vast personal wealth. His fleet of Rolls-Royces provoked particular comment, as did the less than gentle bodyguards with whom he surrounded himself. After lecturing throughout India, he established an ashram in Pune and by the early 1970s had attracted 200,000 devotees, many from Europe and the United States and all clad in his trademark orange robes. In 1981 the cult bought an abandoned property in Oregon, where they set up Rajneeshpuram, a community of acolytes. The Bhagwan would visit only rarely but the disciples appeared to run riot and by 1985 the community was in ruins, amidst accusations of arson, attempted murder, drug smuggling, and vote fraud in the nearby town of Antelope. Rajneesh himself was deported that year on immigration charges. He died soon after. His acolytes may have been surprised at his downfall but Rajneesh's fellow-villagers, amongst whom he had taken his first steps as a 'Godman', practising a form of far from successful hypnosis, were merely amused. Their only question was how so-called Western sophisticates could be gulled by so obvious a con-man.

For whatever reason many people felt a distinct need for some form of religiosity; with the organised Church increasingly more of a symbol than a living, spiritual entity, they looked elsewhere. As Bernice Martin has observed, what emerged was a 'kind of do-it-yourself kit of spiritual self-development (or prophylactic against anomie) passed around by word of mouth and the odd paperback book'.[8] Within this 'kit' one might find 'a generalised dabbling in the literature and history of the occult, mandalas (Jungian and other), tarot cards, astrological prediction, yoga, techniques of mystical ecstasy (with and without drugs) in meditation and expanded consciousness'.[9] Like so much in hippiedom, so keen to abandon limits and rules, it was a grab-bag into which one dipped at leisure.

Setting aside such cults as the Children of God, the Process (whose leader Robert de Grimston would leave London to turn up as a friend of Charles Manson's bloody 'Family'), the Unification Church (the 'Moonies'), the Jesus People, Maharaj Ji's Divine Light Mission, Scientology, Krishna Consciousness, the movement led by Swami Bhaktivedanta and all the similar emanations of the era, the top dog in gurudom, at least for the late 1960s, was undoubtedly the Maharishi Mahesh Yogi, the pioneer of transcendental meditation (TM). This means of self-improvement is based on the giving to each devotee of a personal mantra (a sacred sound or phrase); the subject concentrates on this mantra, gradually excluding any extraneous patterns of thought, and thus, ideally, attaining a higher consciousness. Where the Maharishi came from remained slightly mysterious. Born around 1911, he had studied physics at the University of Allahabad and worked for a time in factories. He then spent thirteen years in the Himalayas, studying under Guru Dev, the founder of TM. When Dev died in 1952, the Maharishi organised a movement to spread the teachings of TM throughout the world; his first world tour took place in 1959 and brought him to the United States. Here he held court in the Waldorf Hotel, signing up disciples and chatting up the media. His giggle, with which he would punctuate any conversation, serious or otherwise, became as well known as any of his actual pronouncements.

The power of gurus to sway the otherwise rational rich, successful and powerful is a constant of history: Rasputin, Billy Graham, the astrological know-alls who have influenced a succession of Indian governments (not to mention the Reagan White House), the Scientologists who woo Hollywood.

For the Sixties hippies, and in particular those hippie gods the rock stars, it was the Maharishi. Heralded by a series of monster ads in the London Underground (always a popular venue for optimistic gurus) the Maharishi appeared in the UK in 1967 for his first major visit. By that time at least one Beatle, George Harrison, had already 'discovered' India, especially in the person of the sitar-playing Ravi Shankar; and Indian themes could be seen in a number of Beatle compositions. It was, however, not Harrison but his wife Pattie who would bring the guru and his superstar disciples together. She had joined the Maharishi's Spiritual Regeneration movement early in 1967 and later that year heard that the Maharishi himself was due in London on 24 August. Here, at his base in the Park Lane Hilton, he was due to give one 'final' lecture; once it was given he was to retire to India for ever, and devote himself to a 'life of silence'.

The Beatles, along with less celebrated devotees, forked out seven shillings and sixpence a head to be told that TM could guarantee 'inner peace' for a mere thirty minutes' meditation a day. There was no mention of sacrifice, or asceticism or anything else that might diminish the delights of being one of the four most famous people on the planet. Apparently the Maharishi was unaware of his distinguished visitors, but when they sent a note round after the talk, requesting a private audience, he was more than happy to see them. His response to their questioning was to suggest that they join him at his retreat in Bangor, North Wales, where that very next day he was launching a ten-day course of spiritual regeneration. The Beatles agreed. Brian Jones, another rocker with an eclectic interest in the East was asked to come too; he was busy, but Mick Jagger, with Marianne Faithfull, decided to join the party. Thus on 25 August, a Friday, the rock star special set off from Paddington to North Wales. Only Cynthia Lennon failed to join the party: she missed the train, held back by guards who thought she was just a fan. 'Run, Cindy, run!' called John – but with proper symbolism she was too slow. The express moved on without her.

Crowding on even more symbolism, it was the first journey the Beatles had made without their ever-present mother hen Brian Epstein. They sat, as Philip Norman has recounted, 'wedged into one first-class compartment, afraid to venture so much as to the lavatory'.[10] During the trip the Maharishi, cross-legged on a sheet, gave them a private consultation, brandishing a flower – it was, he explained, just an illusion – and explaining that the beauty of his teachings was that Spiritual Regeneration was like a bank, ever-available (at least to the rich) for the withdrawal of dividends of peace. Arriving at Bangor the Maharishi was delighted to see frenzied crowds packing the small station. His assumption that they had assembled in his honour was somewhat diminished when the Beatles pointed out the reality. There were around three hundred other disciples and the Beatles' party, like them, were forced to spend the weekend in the spartan cubicles of the teacher training college (emptied for the summer) in which the conference was held. They were almost outnumbered by journalists, and the Maharishi addressed a press conference. The hacks, predictably, were cruelly hostile; the Beatles remarkably loyal, silencing them with the sop of a small (if mendacious) scoop: they had decided, as of this weekend, to abandon drugs.

Of all their exploits this flirtation with the Maharishi was perhaps the most mocked (other than John Lennon's solo adventures with his new friend, Yoko Ono) but the Beatles, naïvely but sincerely, felt that there really was something there. A year later, on *The Beatles* ('The White Album'), they would deride the Maharishi as 'Sexy Sadie' (a track written during the final hours of their eleven-week stay at the Maharishi's Indian bolthole of Rishikesh and, at least in its original but rewritten version, referring less than charitably to the 'special tuition' that the giggling Master had apparently offered the Beatles' wives and girlfriends); yet as Paul McCartney recalled,

> Maharishi is not a religion, don't get that wrong, that is not a religion. It is merely a system for meditation. We used to talk to him about that: 'Well, what about God?' we'd say and he'd say, 'I'll leave that up to you. What I'm offering is a system of meditation.' And it was essential at the time, with acid posing all these questions of eternity: what is the meaning, why am I doing it . . . India was suggested by the music first of all. George met Ravi Shankar . . . that kind of expanded into, 'Well, if you like the music they have all these great festivals and these guys run round naked with mud on them . . . 'cos they believe in this religion . . . ' Then you started to get the idea: one note, one concentrating, one lessening of stress, one reaching of a sort of new level did seem to get you in contact with a better part of yourself . . . If nothing else what Maharishi was suggesting was a pleasant relief from all that in order to recharge your batteries.[11]

Mick Jagger's interest was less likely. But just as the Stones' latest album, *Their Satanic Majesties Request* had payed necessary homage to *Sgt Pepper*, so had Jagger felt it politic to bow to the prevailing Eastern wind. For Marianne it was 'like we were back at school again . . . very austere and spartan for us rock hedonists'.[12] Nor were they quite so keen on the guru. 'We'd heard . . . that the word in India was that the Maharishi was suspected of certain financial improprieties and sexual peccadilloes. And also an obsession with fireworks. But we were trying to be true believers and this all seemed like rancorous hearsay. We went in separately to see him. He gave us each a mantra and a few flowers and we had brought flowers for him. He giggled a lot and had very cheerful, light vibes which was a relief . . . After we had been given our mantras and flowers, we were terribly sweet and serious about it. Nobody even asked anyone else what he'd said to them.'[13]

Then, on Sunday afternoon, a phone started ringing somewhere in the empty college. It echoed through the dusty, empty rooms until finally

McCartney, ever the practical one, went to pick it up. Brian Epstein was dead, apparently over-dosed on sleeping pills. For the vast majority of those who saw the story on television and read about it in the next morning's press, he had apparently preferred death to possible revelations of his homosexuality. For those somewhat nearer the centre there were nasty rumours of problems with his business dealings in the States, of Mafia plots, even of assassination. The truth remains undisclosed, if fascinating.

For the Beatles, trapped in a scruffy college, suddenly bereft of their father figure, preparing themselves to face the armies of the descending press, it was a nightmare. And one that was not improved by their newfound guru. As Faithfull recalled, 'The Beatles were desolate. All of them, it was as if a part of them had died. The Maharishi acted so badly and so inappropriately, in my opinion. He gave them the classic Indian thing, which is, "There was a death in the family. There are many families, there is one family. Brian Epstein has moved on. He doesn't need you any more and you don't need him. He was like a father to you but now he is gone and I am now your father. I'll look after you all now." I was appalled.'[14] The Beatles, shattered, returned to London. A year later they would move *en masse* to India, spending nearly three months at Rishikesh. (They stayed no longer, it was rumoured, because of the guru's request that they tithe him ten per cent of their earnings.) But the Maharishi's retreat, like 1968's other diversion, the creation of Apple, would do nothing to attack their real malaise: the terminal boredom of four young men who were now merely one more set of passengers, clinging on to the mighty juggernaut they had launched.

REVOLUTION

Chapter Nineteen

Introduction: Revolution for the Hell of It

A British revolutionary usually has eyes that are close together, and he wears a satisfied smirk. He has badges in his lapels and is sometimes a martyr to acne. He uses the word 'irrelevant' quite a lot, sometimes as many as ten times in a sentence. He uses the word 'fascist' nearly as often and 'imperialist' more often still. British revolutionaries are firmly against violence, except when they are being violent, and dead against hypocrisy except when they are posturing . . . Britain's revolutionaries could not organise a church bazaar.
'How to spot a real live yahoo', the *Sun* 28 October 1970

Of the counter-cultural slogan's gleeful triumvirate – dope, revolution and fucking in the streets – by far the most problematic was 'revolution'. It was a concept that tripped easily off the tongue, but which, when faced with definition, proved a far more complex creature than the simplicities of drug experimentation or (at least prior to the onset of the 'gender politics' of the feminist and gay movements) sexual liberation. The 'revo' as it tended to be termed, at least among the hippie end of the movement, was a concept that gradually gained momentum as the Sixties progressed, reached a climax in the eruptions of 1968 and then gradually petered out. For the politically minded, 1968, for all its excitements, was merely an initial step; the revolutionary impulse continued through into the Seventies, reaching perhaps its highest point with the 1974 miners' strike.

The revolution must thus be seen from two aspects, that of the politically motivated, who can best be bracketed together, for all their viciously back-biting fissiparousness, as the New Left (NL), and the culturally orientated, who remained resolutely indifferent to the hard grind of changing society, preferring the more indulgent process of tinkering with their own lives within it. With hindsight the irony is that the hippies, for all their passivity, probably engendered more substantial and more lasting changes with their jettisoning of the then 'straight' *status quo*, than did the IS, the IMG, the SLL and all the other bafflingly initialised groupuscules. But before turning to the 'hippie' version of the 'revo', its more established alternative should be considered.

According to works by the movement's sages – Marcuse, C. Wright Mills, Paul Goodman and others in America, and Raymond Williams and E.P. Thompson in the UK – the 'old Left' (OL), born in the shadow of the Russian Revolution, had come to noisy fruition in the 1930s, neared its demise first in Spain and subsequently during the Second World War, and was now effectively dead. It continued to make the right noises, but fewer and fewer listened. Once, between the wars, the likes of Bernard Shaw and Lincoln Steffens could visit Soviet Russia and return to announce that there indeed was the future – and it worked. But by the 1950s few but the Stalinist diehards could affect such optimism. The communist future, at least in the grim practicalities of the USSR and its East European subjects, was more akin to Orwell's *1984*: 'If you want a picture of the future, imagine a boot stamping on the human face forever – and remember – that is forever.' It would take until the end of the Eighties for the Cold War to be declared officially over, but for the left-wingers of the West the acknowledgement could have come thirty years earlier. Sabres would be rattled, crises flare up, cruelties and excesses committed by both superpowers for some time, but in the simple terms of daily life capitalism, not socialism had long since won. In America, in the UK, in Western Europe people of all classes were happy to accept their place at the materialist trough.

Yet the 'stamping on the human face' was hardly a Soviet monopoly, nor did the 'stamping' have to be overtly violent. For those who chose to look, Western society was no paradise. One might not be beaten to death, but one could be stroked. And it was the growing feeling among the more reflective young people that 'something must be done', that would create an alternative to what was increasingly seen as the discredited 'old Left'. In movements such as America's civil rights marches and Britain's CND (especially in its more militant wing, the Committee of 100) were the first shoots of what would become a forest of protests, all loosely unified in the label 'New Left'. As opposed to the *status quo* as were their 'old' predecessors, they saw the way forward along very different lines. Perhaps the most important of all these, as epitomised in the gender politics of the Seventies, was the concept that 'the personal is political'. Your political stance began in your lifestyle, in what you actually did, not some external theory. While the OL often generated its greatest heat in what could be termed 'ideological talking shops', the NL would always opt for action. To borrow from Nigel Young's 'typology'[1] there are a number of discernible differences. The OL was authoritarian, the NL libertarian. The OL was highly centralised, disciplined and hierarchical; the NL highly decentralised, giving primacy (especially at first) to participatory democracy. The OL believed in theory, in 'correct positions' and ideological purity, and in political training; while the NL mistrusted theory (unless based in practice) and tolerated division. The OL (especially in Britain) steadfastly maintained the myth of the organised, militant working class as the key to change; the NL knew too well how conservative were that class, opting instead for new agencies of progress: women, Blacks, Third World peasants and students. The OL believed in material and technological progress, the NL questioned the march of technology, preferring cultural change; the OL loathed the 'alternative society' or 'counter-culture', the NL were less than keen, but infinitely more tolerant of such diversity (if despairing of its ultimate use to their 'revolution'). Finally the OL were positively right-wing in their terror of drugs or unorthodox sexuality (whether hetero- or homosexual); the NL, at least on paper, rejected such puritanism. On top of these 'cultural' differences was one more: while the OL had been able to look to a single model, post-1917 Soviet Russia, and elevate that as the perfect state, the NL had no such useful revolutionary monolith. One could look to Cuba, to North Vietnam, to China, even North Korea, but none offered the same level of geo-political gravitas. One might hate one's own society, but there were only imagined Utopias to replace it.

None of this, of course, was immutable. By the late 1960s the NL was as capable of sectarian infighting as the most benighted of OL factions. And while the British NL claimed to back libertarian attitudes to sex and drugs, they remained somewhat po-faced when actually indulging, desperately searching for justification when it came to emulating the hippies' unbridled hedonism. However, America's Weatherman, the most extreme of all NL groupings, psyched themselves up with LSD-drenched orgies.

At the heart of NL belief was that the time had come to create some form of 'new man'. This ideal would refuse, unlike most of his peers, to be co-opted by what Marcuse termed the 'repressive tolerance' and what the Students for a Democratic Society (in the Port Huron statement) termed the 'civilized barbarism' of modern, western capitalism. In 1969, at the very peak of counter-cultural activity, Theodore Roszak, who defined the post-war society as 'the technocracy', explained some of the rationale behind the anger: 'The business of inventing and flourishing treacherous parodies of freedom, joy, and fulfilment becomes an indispensable form of social control under the technocracy. In all walks of life, image makers and public relations specialists assume greater and greater prominence . . . a lieutenancy of counterfeiters who seek to integrate the discontent born of thwarted aspiration by way of clever falsification . . . It is called "being free", "being happy", being the Great Society.'[2] In the face of this conspiracy of comfort, who was to act? The traditional left had been thoroughly co-opted. However antagonistic towards capitalism the big unions may once have been, one of the great financial growth industries of the Fifties was investing their pension funds in the great capitalist casino of Wall Street or London's City. American unions in particular had played no real oppositional role since the 1930s. And as the Wilson victory of 1964 would prove, a Labour government was no guarantor of socialism. Small-l liberalism was of little help. How could it be, when its bland conformity suited the prevailing consensus so well. Democrats and Republicans, Conservatives and Labourites all couched their positions in some form of liberal newspeak. Liberalism was further undermined when it was revealed that a number of supposed bastions of its position, among them America's National Council of Churches and Congress for Cultural Freedom and the British journal *Encounter* had all been funded, and to an extent infiltrated, by the CIA. As C. Wright Mills, another guru of the NL, had it, liberalism had become 'the official language of all public statement'.[3] Mills,

who died in 1962 aged only 45, was one of the main creators of the NL position. In his books *White Collar* (1951) and *The Power Elite* (1956) he pointed
up the great paradox of American life: the increasing power of the nation, and
the decreasing power of individual citizens. And while Mills might theorise,
nothing captured that desperation better than Allen Ginsberg's 'Howl', with
its incantatory repetition of 'Moloch! whose mind is pure machinery! Moloch
whose blood is running money! Moloch whose fingers are ten armies! Moloch
whose breast is a cannibal dynamo! Moloch whose ear is a smoking tomb!'
This was the modern world, a twentieth-century reincarnation of a demon to
whom children were sacrificed as burnt-offerings.

It was a feeling that was echoed in the UK, although there the state power
was in decline and only the economy seemed to boom. Mills's white collar
men (as yet there were no women) seemed robotic, working on auto-pilot, always striving, always advancing, never knowing why, never considering an
alternative. Individualism was an ideal, but the ideal had no substance; the
corporate rat-race was the reality. In other key texts, such as David Riesman
and Nathan Glazer's *Lonely Crowd* (1950), such individuals were revealed as
'alienated' (as Marcuse had it) and it was that world of alienation that the NL
saw as its prime enemy. The mass society stifled the genuine individual; conformity was the great plague that suffocated all it touched. In the absence of
effective alternatives, the role of revolutionary could devolve on one group
and one group alone: the young. What is a rebel? asked Albert Camus, another early NL inspiration, and answered 'a man who says no'.[4] The NL
were determined to do just that.

From the late Sixties to the early Seventies the NL would pursue its revolution through a variety of areas. The first, and one that would be intermin-
gled in all the others, was the student movement; there would be parallel,
linked movements against the war in Vietnam (perhaps the greatest unifier of
opposition groups in the period), in the cultural revolution of the 'alternative
society' (though given its specific agenda a rather distanced outpost of the
'real' NL), in the civil rights agitation of increasingly radical Blacks (first and
by far most importantly in the US, but by no means insignificantly in the
UK) and finally in small-scale community action projects. Taken together,
these added up to rebellion on a large-scale, and one which, whether ultimately successful or not, might be termed 'the revolution'.

As far as Britain is concerned, the NL makes its first appearance, as did
many of its international peers, in the context of a journal or journals, in this
case the *Universities and Left Review*, (founded, as was CND, in 1958) and
the *New Reasoner* (1957–60). Paradoxically, despite its name, the *ULR* soon
came to represent a position very far removed from the orthodox NL, at least
as laid out above. Its initial editors, E.P. Thompson, Stuart Hall and Raymond
Williams, did offer the requisite humanism, and a genuine devotion to community action (the *ULR*'s 8,000 readers packed out meetings and discussion

groups and the journal was heavily involved in community projects in Notting Hill and other areas) but after 1960, when a 'palace coup' saw off the old guard and renamed the journal the *New Left Review*, those aspects were quickly jettisoned. In their place, under the guiding hands of the left-wing old Etonian Perry Anderson, plus such intellectuals as Alexander Cockburn (son of the celebrated upper-class Communist journalist Claud, editor in the 1930s of the *Week*), Robin Blackburn (son of a right-wing MP and soon to be expelled from the LSE), Tom Nairn (the pioneer of the influential Italian Marxist Gramsci in the UK) and others, came an increasingly arid, doctrinaire leftism, obsessed not with hands-on activities, but with the endless theorising of European (especially French) leftism, and a preoccupation not with the situation in the UK, but in the Third World. Theirs was the hyper-intellectual world of such social theorists as Adorno, Althusser, Lukacs and of course Sartre. The old board were dismissed as 'populist and presocialist' and worse still, as completely failing to 'offer any structural analysis of British society'. Anderson especially loathed Thompson, whose writing he described as 'vacuous and simplistic'.[5] This undisguised élitism was far more OL than NL and such distancing from the everyday grime undoubtedly contributed to the long-term division between 'politicos' and 'freaks'. The journal was highly influential amongst academics and chic 'lefty' intellectuals, and ran some major pieces, typically Juliet Mitchell's ground-breaking early analysis of feminism, as well as giving space to R.D. Laing and the jazz critic Alan Beckett (who also analysed the Rolling Stones). However the overall image was masturbatory stodge; stodge of the highest calibre, no doubt, but stodge none the less.

The 'non-*NLR*' New Left, as it were, found its initial forum in CND, especially in the Committee of 100 and the Spies for Peace, but by 1963 CND was a spent force. Its members, who would reappear right across the 'revolutionary' spectrum, from the orthodox NL to the extremes of the 'underground', split up. Unlike America, where there had been no real anti-nuclear movement, but where such student groupings as the SDS or the more civil-rights orientated Student Non-Violent Co-ordinating Committee (SNCC) gave the NL a solid basis that would last throughout the period, Britain's equivalent would languish until the second half of the decade. One reason, undoubtedly, is that unlike the US, there was no great central bonding issue. British teenagers were not facing the lottery of the draft for Vietnam. It was only in the demonstrations of 1968, when Britain's homegrown opposition to the US adventure momentarily solidified, that the NL can be said to have rivalled its US equivalent in potency and (however briefly) in inclusivity. For the first time since the best years of CND, there was a feeling of tangible opposition. Otherwise the scene is one of small-scale, differentiated actions. Some, like the student activism at the LSE, and subsequently at Essex, Leicester, Hornsey and Birmingham, made a definite impact (as with everything 'the

young' were to do in this era, the press turned happily hysterical on cue),
and there were one-shot campaigns over such diverse issues as immigration,
workers' control, community action, tenants' and claimants' rights as well as
such national melodramas as the *Oz* trial. But they remained isolated incidents. Even the relatively large-scale 'Vietnam' movement, as commentators
have noted, lasted barely a year (from November 1967 to October 1968).

The 'official' left was similarly fragmented. The International Marxist
Group (IMG) was perhaps the best-known faction, thanks mainly to their
leadership. This included Robin Blackburn and Tariq Ali, who would enjoy
a media-directed demonisation as the 'foreign agitator' behind the Vietnam
Solidarity Committee (VSC) in 1968. More interested in forging links with
the Third World (Ali made reverential pilgrimages to Cuba and North Vietnam) than in the British working class, the IMG was perhaps the nearest in
spirit to the US New Left. Their involvement in student movements only
boosted that image. The International Socialists (IS) were less fashionable,
but unlike the IMG had established themselves over a decade and when the
IMG collapsed, took over their leading role as student recruiters. In addition
to these were the Socialist Labour League (SLL) (condemned by their rivals
as lots of talk and little action), a variety of Maoists (trying without much
hope to extend the Long March to the satanic mills), the Socialist Workers
Party (the renamed IS post-1969), the Anarchists (a spent force) and the
Communists (likewise). As David Widgery (himself a devoted propagandist
for IS, but capable of standing back and observing as few peers were), would
say: all these groups were no more than 'political Cassandras able only to say
"I told you so" '.[6]

All of which was largely irrelevant other than to those who pursued one or
another mini-party and read their papers: *Black Dwarf*, *Red Mole*, the *Socialist Worker*, *7 Days*. And these were lamentably few. For one glorious moment, in Paris in May 1968, the workers allied with the students and the
young, but it was a union that would not be forged in America nor in the UK.
For the average worker, who had already found CND pretty extreme, the
NL, in whatever form, was a good many steps too far. As the sociologist
Theodore Roszak was forced to accept,

> How baffling it must seem to the long-suffering and long-deprived to dis-
> cover the children of our new affluence dressing themselves in rags and tat-
> ters, turning their 'pads' into something barely distinguishable from slum
> housing, and taking to the streets as panhandlers. Similarly, what can the
> Beatles' latest surrealist LP mean to an unemployed miner or a migrant farm
> laborer? What are the downs-and-outs of Nanterre to make of the latest pro-
> duction of Arrabal on the Left Bank? Surely they do not see these strange
> phenomena as a part of *their* culture, but as curious, somewhat crazy things
> the spoiled middle-class young amuse themselves with.[7]

If it was true in the US or France, it was equally so in Britain. In any case, carefully nurtured by the media, the image of the young 'revolutionaries' was either trivialised or demonised. They were either 'a pack of students' (and as such privileged beyond the dreams of any prole and quite incomprehensible in their desire to shuck off the delights of materialism for which those same proles had to work so hard) or vicious reds, undermining Queen, country, democracy and anything else that morning's leader chose to include.

In America the New Left had long recognised that the masses would not be on their side, but the image died harder in class-obsessed Britain, and the idea of the militant working man, needing but a little political education to urge him to the barricades, had yet to be abandoned by the left. As observers noted sadly, the only time British workers marched with any real enthusiasm was to back their beloved Enoch Powell, classically-educated harbinger of racial hatred.

Given the essential stability of Western society in the post-Second World War period, for those who had faced insufficient food, inadequate plumbing and heating, and poor if any education, how could Fifties materialism not be an improvement? No amount of whingeing by the New Left would convince those who had been subject to such limitations to discard the society that had brought about these improvements. As the historian E. J. Hobsbawm, hardly a right-winger, noted, right up until the late Sixties, capitalism had been, 'by and large, a sensational success economically, technologically and . . . in the provision of material prosperity (or hope of it) for the masses'.[8] When the workers criticised the 'students' (as they categorised most of the NL and/or the hippies) as the creatures of bourgeois privilege, it was hard in honesty to reject their view. The chief of many reasons why such young idealists, however sincere, were less than likely to bring about the revolution, was their very middle-classness, their inextricable links to affluence. Despite this they assumed that were the revolution to come to pass, their role would be nowhere but in the vanguard; like children who wonder what it would have been like to live in the Middle Ages, their standpoint was invariably that of the king or queen, never the peasant. The youth of the would-be revolutionaries was another problem. The Sixties gave an increasing importance to the young, but for their elders, irrespective of their own politics, it was still hard to submit to what may well have seemed like transient youthful caprice. The likelihood was that the majority of these young 'revolutionaries' would drift off when college or university ended, and return to the security that few had ever really abandoned. For many older observers, the division between the New Left and the non-political 'youth culture' (alternative or not) was far narrower than between the New Left and 'real' politicians.

For the counter-culture – Jerry Rubin and Abbie Hoffman in America, Mick Farren and and Richard Neville in Britain – the orthodox left, new or old, held marginal appeal. As their every publication, their every institution proclaimed, they were first and foremost cultural revolutionaries. The Left, new or old, was in the end one more aspect of the *status quo*. What did lefty preaching have to do with the end-product of 250 mics of acid? As Warren Hague, writing in *Oz* 37, put it: 'One sometimes gets the impression from some socialists that socialism means a job in a factory for every worker. Ugh!' *IT*'s retrospective of the struggle at the LSE was typical: 'gloomy political masturbation that has been boring us all for so long . . . the official student left reveals its amazing boringness, its bureaucratic nervousness, its Sunday-paper emptiness . . . a drawing-room charade of internal LSE politics for which *IT* readers will be justified in feeling the greatest contempt.'[9] If the hippies found the Left boring, then the Left found them trivial. A few people 'crossed over', but most kept to their own side of the line. Reading the contemporary underground press there is of course a degree of lip-service to the political end of 'the revo', but it's hard to feel that many of the writers held out much hope of converts. 'Louis Jigsaw', writing in *Oz* 32 (Jan. 1971) urged the freaks to understand the workers, not to mention the politicos, to join in rather than lie stoned on the sidelines; but there's more desperation in the piece than conviction that anyone's listening. A year later, in *Oz* 40 the same author is still pounding the drum, trying valiantly to explain why the masses have problems with 'students' and once more urging his readers to get a job and start changing things from within. David Widgery, perhaps the only person who managed to bridge the gap between the 'counter-culture' and the New Left, adds his opinion two issues later. Full of unimpeachably right-on quotes from the likes of Lenin, Trotsky, Desmoulins and Reich, it is a reasoned plea for genuine revolutionary commitment. But *Oz*, being *Oz*, had much more fun publishing excerpts from that bible of do-it-yourself sabotage, weapons training and in-house drug manufacture *The Anarchist Cookbook*, with its slogan 'Turn On, Burn Down, Blow Up' (but then so did the *New York Review of Books* – to rather greater outrage).

Oz did occasionally provide a forum for the revolution. Amidst the psychedelic overlays and Robert Crumb posters ('Honeybunch Kaminski, 13, of L.A. What a little yummy!') there was always room for a massive rant by John Gerassi, US historian and star of the Dialectics of Liberation Congress. Bargain basement Marcuse, the piece calls upon the world to 'fight the dehumanizing society', to reject repressive tolerance, and above all to 'live the revolution'.

'No party? No ideology? No program? How in hell then, do we make this 'humanizing' revolution? By living it. By fighting for what's relevant to you, not to some theorist. You want to turn on, turn on. You want to drop out, drop out. Groove to the MC5 singing John Lee Hooker's "Motor City Is Burning" . . . or the Lovin' Spoonful's "Revelation: Revolution" . . . Live in a commune. Be faithful to your values, not your parents . . . Don't be afraid to be happy.'[10] Or, as the contemporary underground cartoon had it, 'When yer smashin' the state kids . . . don't fergit t' keep a smile on yer lips an' a song in yer heart!' Not everyone felt that way. Clive James, then an *Oz* contributor, deplored such simplicities:

> Hasn't the remarkable thing about this particular revolutionary generation been that it advances its own innocence, its own impatience and its own ignorance as positive qualities? . . . Ideology, pared down to a mood-determined minimum of 'ideas' and all the more powerful for being free of analytical determinants, attains a new spreadability, like butter left a long time in the sun. Anyone can have a go. If you feel young and all the world looks wrong, you're in . . . It's a sweet set-up. If you want a revolution, no matter how much of a bastard or idiot you are, you're part of this most popular of all popular fronts. If you don't want revolution, no matter how deep your concern for liberty, mercy and justice in individual cases and in society at large, then you are part of the system, this static system which has never really changed, until last year in Paris and of course next week here.[11]

But James's call to acknowledge pluralism had little more success than Widgery's appeal for political involvement. The underground, whether represented by the pages of *Oz*, *IT*, *Friends* or any of the others, would never really address the hard questions that came with such 'revolutionary' fervour. There were exceptions; *Frendz*, which took over from *Friends*, made a genuine attempt to tackle the increasingly violent situation in Northern Ireland. *Oz*, in its post-trial 'Angry' issue, sent a reporter to check on Glasgow's Upper Clyde Shipbuilders, then attempting to set up by themselves; the workers' interest in a leather-clad longhair, brimming with inchoate fervour, was predictably minimal. It also ran the alleged 'confessions' of one James McCann, a self-promoting IRA man, but one whose interests turned out to lie closer to cannabis wholesaling than smashing the British state. *Ink*, one of the last of these papers, and designed to take a 'serious' view on non-hippie life, proved a travesty, its first incarnation sabotaged by its own editor, a planted member of a far-left group. Later, relaunched, it would offer a more cogent view of the revolution, taking on board gender politics, black interests and a serious analysis of, among other topics, Ireland, but it would be a late flowering, and, short of cash, a very brief one.

Yet the hippies themselves were happy to give their view of this thing called the revolution. It might have been, as Ian MacDonald knowledgeably entitled his study of 'the Beatles records and the Sixties', a 'revolution in the head' but it was a revolution. Things were meant to change. For Rosie Boycott, who would move from underground journalism to feminism and thence to the heights of what was once 'Fleet Street', it was all rather hard to define, but,

> there were certain specifics: there would be no taxes, there would be no Conservative party, there would be no forcing people into doing what they didn't want to do, there would be no discrepancy between rich and poor . . . What

we were offering was a freedom to do what you wanted: to take drugs if you want, to stay up all night, to work your own hours, to not being regimented, not having to prove one's success by dressing in a particular way or catching the 8:15 to Waterloo. To prove that there was a different way of running the world. And I assumed that we'd all grow up in some way running the world. To an extent this *was* a case of 'when I grow up Mummy won't be able to tell me what to do', but it was also leading to some very good things. Very few people are total loners, totally able to stand up against the great mass of people. And it did provide people with the ability to question and give one the awareness that went with that. It had a real effect and an effect for the good.[12]

Others would say much the same. For the late Richard Trench, traveller and underground press writer,

It wasn't just dope, sex and rock 'n' roll, it was far more well intentioned, far better. Everybody would work less, everybody would become middle class like us, everybody would read poetry like us. The world would be a better place if people were educated and were peaceful. And you had certain ambitions for yourself: I was pretty certain I'd make a pretty good ambassador in a socialist country. I wanted to be of the élite although you weren't aware of it at the time and you'd have been shocked if it had been put to you, you'd deny it.[13]

Jeff Nuttall's reductionism went even further, envisaging a form of modern tribalism. As ever style won out. Che Guevara, as the cynics loved to point out, was best known as the name of a Kensington boutique. 'The Revolution', meanwhile, was a nightclub, where a graffito in the gents asked, 'If this is the revolution, why are the drinks so fucking expensive?'

But counter-cultural feelings did transcend such triviality. The ever-positive Richard Neville was in no doubt:

The anger in *Oz* and the alternative world was quite genuine, David Widgery once used the phrase 'gut radicalism'. Revolution was in the air: the very first political meeting I went to in London was held in my basement: we formed something called the Free France Committee, which was raise to money for the French students who'd been hit over the head with truncheons, and were on the run. We also went on Vietnam marches. I remember Germaine [Greer] burning an Australian flag on one of them. The very first issue of *Oz* has an incredible caricature of Lyndon Johnson, lambasting his skullduggery. The aim of the alternative culture was to shake up the existing situation, to break down barriers not only between sexes and races and God knows what else, it was also to have a good time, it was to enlarge the element of fun that one had occasionally in one's own life and to make that more pervasive – not just for you but for everyone.

   I was quite keen to abolish this work/play distinction. There is something incredibly oppressed about the mass of grey people out there. I just thought that people on the whole looked unhappy: they seemed to be pinched and grey and silly and caught up with trivia and I felt that what was going on in London would bring colour into those grey cheeks and into those grey bedrooms. We thought we were going to change the world. With a bit of sexuality and rock music and flowers, if not in their hair at least in their living rooms, that somehow the direction of society could be altered.[14]

On one occasion, however, the counter-culture did enter the activist game. The event came as response (some might suggest showing off) to the visiting *über*-radical Jerry Rubin, who with fellow New Yorker Abbie Hoffman had inaugurated the Youth International or 'Yippie Party' (specialities: nominating a pig as their candidate in the 1968 Presidential election, burning money at the New York Stock Exhange and appearing before the House Un-American Activities Committee, the once-omnipotent creature of the Commie-bashing Senator Joe McCarthy, dressed in American revolutionary uniforms). Urged on by Rubin a couple of dozen freaks, mainly underground press staffers, invaded television's *David Frost Show*. There was much shouting, much smoking of joints on camera and much huffing and puffing from Frost and the media. The world, however, did not end, nor even tremble and the event, more cut-rate Dada than revolution of any sort, was soon forgotten.

In the end, the problem would be that the young could not achieve change unaided. Setting aside their own inadequacies, their own divisions, and the fact that youthful enthusiasms cannot last for ever, the truth remained that the young, however keen, however militant, however willing, alone they remained powerless. The political revolution would not come about, however much various countries – especially America, France, Germany, Italy and Britain – briefly feared that it might. The *status quo* would survive, the trough remain unbroken, the pigs as greedy as ever. Politically, the true legacy of the Sixties was Reagan and Thatcher, with their triumphalist rightism, fed, *inter alia*, by a loathing of the Sixties. Yet for a while the world did shudder, however slightly, and before returning to the 'revolution in the head', it is worth considering some aspects of the one that tried to take place on the streets.

Chapter Twenty

Student Power: Seize the Time

These days there's only one place for an active man or woman.
JOIN THE STUDENTS AND CHANGE THE WORLD! Vietnam talks . . . non-
proliferation treaties . . . negotiations and relief in Nigeria and Biafra – the world
is threatened with peace . . . The seat of war has moved to the campus, and now,
there is a Korea for you as a Professional Student.
Look at what the new student is doing already in the first weeks of 1969, and you
will see that somewhere, somehow, there is a rewarding place for you. The year is
off to a whirlwind start. YOU as a student, can keep it that way.
From a cod-advertisement in *Oz*, February 1969

If a single sub-group of young people could be seen as the prime movers in any form of revolution, whether political or counter-cultural, then that group was the students. Whether in America, in Britain or in Western Europe, this essentially middle-class, privileged, more than averagely intelligent and highly educated section of the young tended to take the lead when it came to 'changing the world'. Inevitably, when one compares the role of students in the various countries, Britain's representatives could hardly be compared with their American counterparts, whose commitment lasted longer and who faced opposition far more vicious in its intensity, or to those in France, who perhaps more than any other group came nearest to creating an actual revolution, but the thought was certainly there, and for a while, and in various contexts, so too was the deed.

There had, obviously, been a core of student involvement in CND, and most of the pioneers of *IT* and other underground institutions had spent some time at a university, but for the first half of the decade the universities were untouched by the fervour. By the mid-Sixties, however, such equanimity, like so many other aspects of a once quiescent *status quo*, was under serious threat. There was a variety of reasons, the most obvious being that students, being intelligent and educated, were among the first to sense the *zeitgeist*. But for once quality seemed less important than quantity. Universities, once the hothouse breeding ground of a small élite, destined to run the country as their forebears always had done, had been expanded and with that expansion came an influx of new students, whose background was very different. There was not, as there was in the US, a deliberate policy of tying the universities into the military-industrial system, but British students were equally well aware of the way in which these institutions, supposedly so democratic, in fact dictated what they did. Their tutors encouraged questioning, but only of their specific subject; to question the larger principles behind the university, and beyond that the whole educational and then social system, was certainly not on the curriculum. But like young people every-where, university educated or not, the students were becoming increasingly autonomous. Increasingly aware of their power as young people, no longer willing to accept a half-life in some strange limbo-land between childhood and maturity, they claimed and then demanded new rights.

The first signs of student militancy emerged in summer 1966, at the London School of Economics. The LSE, founded by Fabian socialists in 1895 'for the study and encouragement of Economics or Political Economy, Political Science, Statistics, Sociology, History, Geography and any subject cognate to any of these', had long established itself as one of Britain's most important educational institutions, and with its large input of foreign students, came to influence a world that extended far beyond its own London boundaries. Of all the top universities the LSE, which had been deliberately created in opposition to the rigid classical training that dominated Oxbridge, was most likely to see the allure of change. In mid-1966 it was announced that the School's new Director was to be Dr Walter Adams, then Principal of University College, Rhodesia. The students, as was customary, had not been consulted, but when *Private Eye* ran a piece attacking the appointment, and linking Adams with Ian Smith's breakaway white supremacist Rhodesian government, protests inevitably followed. They appeared in the form of a pamphlet, 1,250 copies of which were sold at the start of the autumn term. A week later there appeared in *The Times* a letter from Lord Bridges, chairman of the LSE's Court of Governors, deploring the attacks. The Students Union drafted a reply, also for publication, and as the LSE's regulations required, submitted it to the current Director, Sir Sydney Caine, for approval. This was denied. Outraged, the students instructed their president, David Adelstein, to send it anyway. This was done and Adelstein soon found himself summoned before the Board of Discipline (a body that had only met once since 1945). Adelstein responded by sending a list of conditions under which he would attend, without which he felt he would not be given a fair hearing. These included legal representation, the right to cross-examine hostile witnesses and the standing down of Sir Sydney as *parti pris*. His fellow students then voted to boycott the hearing: two-thirds refused to attend lectures and demonstrated in the street, their banners including the promise, 'Berkeley 1964: LSE 1966: We'll bring this School to a halt too.' In the event Adelstein's conditions were met, and he left the hearing unpunished.

It was, however, only a first round. The Adams issue re-emerged in January 1967. A 'Stop Adams' meeting was called in the School's Old Theatre for 31 January, advertised by extensively circulated posters and leaflets. Caine, claiming such publications were libellous, banned them and proscribed the meeting. He also called for the removal of the fuses from the Theatre's electrical circuits. The two sides met in an angry confrontation outside the closed doors of the lecture theatre. Caine was asked to back down. He refused, telling the students to leave. A tense situation was then exacerbated when the Director, who had already made it clear in a number of discussions that he did not believe that students should have a say in decisions that affected their lives, declared that, 'Students have no rights.' The crowd then elected to take a vote on whether or not to defy their Director. At some stage a student hit a porter, the porter hit back and a scuffle ensued. Meanwhile a number of students entered the Old Theatre. It was then that another porter, Edward Poole, aged sixty-four, slipped, fell and dropped dead of a heart attack. Inside the theatre a few students lit candles and watched as Caine mounted the platform to tell them, 'The man has now died. Does that satisfy you?' However, he continued, no one should take personal responsibility – this was what happened if meetings got out of hand. The students, thoroughly shaken, left.

The next day Adelstein, Marshall Bloom (the American President of the Graduate Student Association) and four members of the student council, all of whom were accused of fomenting the disorder, were summoned to face disciplinary proceedings. The council members were acquitted, but Adelstein and Bloom were both suspended for the remainder of the academic year. It was not a decision taken quietly. On 13 March more than two hundred students, fresh from an angry union meeting, began 'sitting-in' all over the School. They were backed by a number of staff, including the political scientist Ralph Miliband, and received a telegram of support from that doyen of civil disobedience Bertrand Russell. Several days later, at 4.30 a.m. the night porter heard a knock on the door and a shout of 'Cleaners'. What he let in, however, was not cleaners, but sixty-five students, who occupied the School's administrative department. They were thrown out of the building, and summarily suspended for three months. This triggered a new upsurge, with students from other institutions arriving at the LSE to join a large march along neighbouring Fleet Street. One banner warned, 'Beware the Pedagogic Gerontocracy'. For reasons no one quite understood, many marchers carried daffodils. The students, a relatively sober lot, and far from the 'bearded weirdies' that the press loved to attack, sent a circular to every don, explaining their desire for communication rather than altercation, and stressing their intention to suppress any excesses. Bloom and Adelstein wrote their own letters of regret, enabling the Court of Discipline to make its own magnanimous gesture of pardon. Adelstein stayed; Bloom returned to America where he joined a hippie commune, and committed suicide in 1969. And that, for the next few months, was that. Dr Adams arrived in September 1967, and took up his post with barely a ripple disturbing the LSE's resumed tranquillity.

For many it was probably a moment of relief. A contemporary survey polled around 80% of the LSE's near three thousand students. Thirty-nine per cent had taken some part, however brief, in the nine-day sit-in (only 1%

stayed the full course), 56% boycotted at least some lectures. The rest, however, had taken no part. As for their desires: a mere 13% complained of Adams's appointment; 69% wanted greater student participation in the running of the School library, 54% in questions of discipline and 43% in teaching arrangements; only 28% actually wanted to determine their own courses. The activists, as ever, captured the headlines, but for students like Chris Rowley, who had no ideological axe to wield, there seemed far more heat than light. He attended a few meetings, but,

> The Trotskyists fought each other with venom and vituperation . . . It was hard to imagine that we were all on the same side, when someone would stand and accuse somebody of being 'a Leninist, a filthy Leninist, a splitter! an enemy of the people!' and all the rest of that stuff. Then they'd all be shouted down by the Socialist Society which would be five hundred strong; it was like something out of Orwell. There'd be this furious argument going, people yelling, and through it would come the voice of the moderator: 'It's time to vote on the motion,' and the Socialist Society would go, 'We vote!' and that would be that. There was no right wing, and the Socialists were the centrists. There were no women.[1]

Nor did it convince the waverers when a member of IS stood up to announce, 'We are sitting in because we have to protest against starvation in the Third World.' Such platitudes were plainly nonsense – if they were sitting for anything it was in the hope of gaining greater control of an institution which could influence their entire lives – yet there was no escaping the sense of moral absolutism.

The period of peace did not last. Larger events were consuming the student world. Notably in Paris. On 23 May 1968, 200 LSE students proclaimed their solidarity with their French peers by holding an all-night vigil, conspicuous for a display of the red and black flags of the left and of anarchism. The vigil was condemned by the current Union president as unfair to those facing examinations. Once more quiet descended, and once more it would not last. In June 1968 a new group, the Radical Socialist Students' Federation (RSSF) was launched (replacing its predecessor the Radical Students' Alliance), holding an inaugural conference at the LSE. It was attended by Danny Cohn-Bendit ('Danny the Red' as the press branded him) and Alain Geismar, both major figures in the French *évènements*. They called for extra-parliamentary action, demanding, 'Students of the World IGNITE'. Later that year the RSSF held its first plenary session at the Roundhouse. Among other demands was that the universities become 'red bases'; the power structure was to be revolutionised: no more hierarchy, no more *in loco parentis*: henceforth all would be shared between students, staff and administrative workers.

The RSSF, as one leading member put it, aimed to create 'an organisation which was not tied to any of the existing left organisations, that would be open to political debate and would have a clear idea of its priorities. It should create a student power consciousness to expose and destroy the authoritarian structure of education as a means of creating revolutionary consciousness.'[2] However there remained an even greater problem: most students were not really politically motivated, and most students remained highly suspicious of Marxism. The RSSF preached only to the converted, and they, in many cases, preferred the full-blown political groupings – IS, Maoists, whatever – to some junior approximation. Finally the RSSF had another problem: the NUS, reputedly so staid a body, was becoming more radical. Incredible though such a concept may seem today, its leader Jack Straw was seen as a hardcore lefty, determined to toughen up his once vapid organisation.

If one believed the media, Britain's post-war revolution was scheduled for 27 October, the day on which, for the second time that year, demonstrators were due to march on the US Embassy in Grosvenor Square, protesting against American involvement in Vietnam. To express their support some 800 students occupied the LSE. The authorities, now led by Adams, threatened to shut the school down. It didn't happen but a new figure entered the debate, Lord Robbins, chairman of the board of governors and the man whose Report (published in 1963) had done most to expand the system of higher education, offering university life to those who merited it as well as to those who could find the cash. He was unsympathetic to the students, believing that, 'you can't have a democracy paying the money for youngsters to do what they like'. He also warned the academic staff not to back the young rebels: those who advocated or took part in 'disorderly conduct' would face instant dismissal. This, apparently the first ever such warning issued in a British university, was very unpopular and seventy-six members of the academic staff (25% of the faculty) signed a letter pointing out to their charman that under LSE rules no member was to face punishment for merely expressing opinions, no matter how contentious the subject. The Students Union countered with a motion attacking Robbins's threats and promised a renewal of direct action. This uneasy stand-off persisted through to the end of term.

January 1969 saw renewed confrontation. On 8 January Adams addressed a teach-in on Rhodesia; he was faced with three demands: that the college was to reveal its interests in Rhodesia and S. Africa, that the governors should resign from the boards of any companies dealing with white southern Africa and that such companies should be banned from recruiting at the School. Two days later Adams faced the students again: he refused to make any such promises and stalked out of the meeting. He was asked to return but refused. The students, by now furious at his disdain, moved to fetch him, invading the administrative building *en masse*. They found the connecting fire doors had been locked and changed tactics, invading the senior common room. Here a vote called for the expulsion of the governors from the School, 'by force if necessary'.

The locked fire doors were not the only impediment the students faced. Far more important, symbolically as much as practically, were the newly erected iron gates and grilles that had been installed at various strategic sites by the governors in order to isolate sections of the LSE's buildings. On 23 January the Union Council voted to meet the authorities for discussions. Such moderation did not impress the more radical elements and a day later they engineered a second vote calling for the immediate destruction of these impediments to freedom. The votes had barely been tallied before militant students (plus some workers from the Barbican site, where a recent dispute had been boosted by student involvement), wielding sledgehammers, crowbars and pickaxes, smashed the gates from their hinges. Some dons attempted to stop them, but were simply pushed aside. Adams summoned the police, who arrived somewhat reluctantly since they felt this did not properly constitute a public violation of order. When they did appear a number of students were taken to Bow Street magistrates' court, immediately sparking a new demonstration. This time Adams had no hesitation: the LSE was shut down.

'The gates' were the great crux for the LSE. This was 'real' revolution. A witness, Rachel Dyne, recalled, 'It was a euphoric feeling, I felt a great sense of power. We were doing something authentic, we resented the gates, felt they were transforming the place more or less into a prison. Taking them down was a way of challenging authority.'[3] Absent gates were the very epitome of broken boundaries, but like so many other aspects of the period, student-orientated or not, the LSE witnessed a widespread breaking down of limits, both symbolic and practical. The 'Ladies' and 'Gentlemen' signs were removed from lavatories; signs indicating on which floor a lift had stopped were carefully unscrewed. As 'An LSE Student', writing in *IT* put it, 'ALL the gates have got to be knocked down: the monopolised property and power that they protect must be demystified.'[4]

The lock-out, backed by the police, lasted four weeks. The students decamped to the University of London Union, followed by sympathetic staff members who mixed their normal courses with more radical seminars. This spinoff was particularly notorious for the invasion of ULU's swimming pool. To the delight of those who enjoy such symbolism, the Marxist invaders modestly retained their underwear; the anarchists stripped to the buff. It was an American, Paul Hoch, who opted for action, rather than words. The more staid representatives of the New Left watched aghast, mingling revolutionary rhetoric with exhortations to mind the paintwork. Robin Blackburn, who was present when the LSE contingent moved in, watched as the Vice-Chancellor came to talk to this group of renegades who had suddenly appeared in his university.

He proposed to negotiate with us, the idea being to get us to leave the building. So he was sitting there negotiating and he'd actually put the keys of ULU on the table in front of him. We were arguing back quite strongly, then Paul Hoch said, 'I don't think you understand the situation. We are occupying this building. This is a building meant for students,' and as he spoke, he made a swift gesture and scooped up the keys from the table and put them in his pocket. He said, 'We now control this institution and we intend to do with it as we like. And we intend to help the students at the LSE and we don't care about the rules and regulations you've been telling us about.' That was the end of the discussion. The vice-chancellor had obviously never thought that someone would reach right across the table and snatch these keys.[5]

This occupation-cum-swimming party also signalled a small taste of the future. Among the non-LSE students were a couple who'd trekked up from Goldsmith's College at New Cross: typically impoverished art students, dirtier than the LSE activists but otherwise unremarkable. One was called Malcolm Edwards. Later he would change his surname to McLaren. The germ of what would be the Sex Pistols and the 'great rock 'n' roll swindle' had started burrowing into the body politic.

By now the politicians were weighing in, their comments inevitably negative. If the LSE authorities harked back to visits to Nazi Germany in the 1930s, where they had witnessed storm-troopers shouting down liberal teachers, the Labour Secretary of State for Education Edward Short, talked of 'squalid nonsense' and called for these 'thugs' to be 'thrown out on their necks'. To implement Short's blustering the LSE took out injunctions against thirteen individuals, including Adelstein and Paul Hoch. Internal disciplinary charges were brought against three junior dons: Lawrence Harris, an economics lecturer, Robin Blackburn, an assistant lecturer in sociology and Nicholas Bateson, who taught psychology. All three were charged with supporting the students, especially as regards calling for the tearing down of the gates. On 7 March the DPP joined the fray, officially charging eight students, plus Harris and Bateson with committing wilful damage, a criminal charge. Two days later the Union hit back, voting for a new occupation. Once again the students moved into the building, spray-painting walls and trashing faculty offices. (The IS, however, then cleaned up their mess, earning much scorn from harder-line brethren.)

Despite the efforts of Blackburn's counsel, LSE law professor J.A.G. Griffith, both Bateson and Blackburn were sacked without the opportunity of an appeal. Many of their fellow-teachers were appalled, while in Parliament Lord Balogh, a distinguished economist and mainstay of the Wilson government, declared that the LSE's academic freedom had been compromised by a coterie of conservatives. In France and Italy, where college-based clashes had been infinitely more intense, not a single teacher had been dismissed. None the less, the verdicts stood. Quizzed on BBC radio, Blackburn remained unrepentant: 'I think it was an infinitely less violent act to take [the gates] down than it was to put them up in the first place . . . We are proposing a new model of the university, in which there'd be no place for administrators who feel they have the right to monopolise decisions which affect the lives of students. It's an elementary democratic principle.'[6]

The student response was predictably enraged. A vast majority voted to boycott lectures; those dons seen as siding with the authorities were pilloried – the doors to their rooms spray-painted, locks glued shut, their lectures invaded. There was a second invasion of the SCR, where Hoch, watched by the LSE faculty, ceremonially took down a portrait of Lord Robbins. Despite the apparent mildness of such a gesture, it seemed to infuriate his witnesses more than anything else. 'The portrait symbolised authority to many of the academics there. So I moved it about two feet off the wall and put it on the floor. Within a second I was grabbed by about five people – it was almost as though I'd shot the Queen! Academics were erupting from their seats, yelling and screaming.'[7] Later the LSE attempted to have the ringleaders imprisoned, and even charged Hoch with moving the picture – the judge laughed all their efforts out of court.

And suddenly, after all the sound and fury, it was over and silence returned. The student anger seemed to have burnt itself out. The protests stopped, there were no more sit-ins, no more excited votes, no more invasions. Where did it all go? If one believes Alan Marcuson, a drop-out from Leeds and actively involved in the more extreme actions of the LSE movement, the Old Left's suspicion of their juniors had been correct: that for them 'revolution' was just one more fashion, a way of enlivening the years before one finally had to face up to real life.

Marcuson may be disparaging, but the rapidity with which student dissent went from vociferous anger to near-silent quiescence does seem to bear him out. For a while, however, revolt had seemed popular, the flavour of an entire year. The LSE, while garnering the major headlines, was not the only site of student unrest in 1968. Other universities – among them Sussex, Birmingham, Leicester, East Anglia and Hull – would add their contribution to the summer of discontent. In June sixteen separate colleges and universities were making some kind of gesture, the direct result of the dramas in Paris. But in the end, whether at Essex, where a small group of ultras would take their first steps on the road to a brief but noisy life as Britain's most sought-after urban guerrillas, or at nearby East Anglia, where a big revolutionary gesture was the burning of Union Jack-emblazoned carrier bags as the Queen drove by, the movement was always broadly the same. Student demands tended to similar desires: an end to the paternalism, to the top-down, hierarchical regimes; a beginning for greater student autonomy and participation in the regulation of their own lives. The one place where student action had a wider impact was Northern Ireland, where student agitation was highly in-

strumental in the founding of the People's Democracy Movement, the attacks on which led then to a situation that nearly thirty years later has yet to
show real signs of abating. IS put out some feelers, and gave some help, but
for the most part, then as now, Northern Ireland only concerned the main-
land when the bombs were going off. 'London, Paris, Rome, Berlin,' sang the
demonstrators, 'we shall fight and we shall win.' Belfast was not conspicuous
on the rollcall.

But beyond this there was a greater problem. Other than for the hardcore
politicos, who would follow their various factions long after they had parted
from university, the New Left as a whole had failed to deliver. The young, being young, had little patience. Like the mob in Peter Weiss' *Marat/Sade*, they
were bored with revolutionary rhetoric and demanded instant action:

> Marat we're poor and the poor stay poor
> Marat don't make us wait any more
> We want our rights and we don't care how
> Marat we want our revolution NOW![8]

It did not come 'now', nor did it come in the form the students demanded.
In his casually bitter summation of the whole decade, from which the title of
this book is drawn, John Lennon suggested that nothing had changed. 'The
class system and the whole bullshit bourgeois scene is exactly the same. The
same bastards are in control, the same people are runnin' everything, it's exactly the same. They hyped the kids and the generation.'[9] Gradually, the universities would change, but that would be when this generation of students,
revolutionaries or not, had reached the end of their courses and joined the
ranks of dons. Talking of Germany but equally applicable to Britain, Neal
Ascherson saw that,

> Instead of declaring war, the leaders of the student movement transformed
> whatever they controlled – mostly universities – into turbulent archipelagos
> of democracy in which professors and cleaners had equal status. They fore-
> saw that a cybernetic age would make traditional hierarchies irrelevant and
> would decentralise every institution. They knew that the old labour move-
> ments were moribund, and they had enormous faith in the capacity of indi-
> viduals to choose wisely and empower themselves. Their mistake was a
> hopeless underestimate of capitalism's power to adapt.[10]

It had been a revolt of the privileged, and the majority of the privileged,
while happy to let off youthful steam, are less enthusiastic at the prospect of
losing those privileges. Thus it would be for the student protestors of 1968.
The next years would see a continuation, even an escalation of revolutionary
activity, but not on a mass scale. The essence of the counter-culture, after dis-
carding the past, had been the search for an alternative future. By 1969 this

search was breaking up into a wide range of possibilities. Pursuing a political revolution would become just one choice from many. One had, the slogan read, to live the revolution. The politically-orientated would retain their obsession with the revolution, but for the majority of the 'alternative' young what mattered now would be a new emphasis on the life.

Chapter Twenty-One

Vietnam: Ho, Ho, Ho Chi Minh!

Fortunately, in England at any rate, education produces no effect whatsoever; if it did, it might prove a serious danger to the upper classes and would probably lead to acts of violence in Grosvenor Square.
Oscar Wilde *The Importance of Being Earnest* (1895)

However exciting and absorbing student revolt may have been to those involved, if Britain as a whole felt that the nation was trembling on the brink of a real live revolution it was not through the agency of a few thousand disaffected late adolescents, complaining against the conditions of their further education. It was instead a response to a far larger issue: the opposition to American military involvement in the war in Vietnam. Abandoned by France, its former colonial master, after the débâcle of Dien Bien Phu in 1954, Vietnam, once 'Indo-China' and now divided into North (Communist) and South ('democratic'), remained one of the world's 'hot spots'. For America the problem was simple: if the Communists moved down across the demilitarised zone and thus took over the South, according to the much-touted 'domino theory', each South-East Asian country would then 'fall' into far-left hands. Thus in late 1954, even before the last French forces had left in ignominy, the first American envoy, General Lawton Collins, appeared in Saigon bearing promises of financial and other support to the south Vietnamese regime, that of Ngo Dinh Diem. By the end of the 1950s US cash and promises had been supplemented by 'advisors', helping train the south Vietnamese in what was becoming an escalating battle against infiltration from the north. On 8 July 1959 two of those advisors became the first Americans to die – the victims of guerrilla attack – in what would be termed the 'Vietnam era'. It would continue until 30 April 1974, when it would be the American turn to make a dismal exit, their last representatives helicoptered from the embassy roof as North Vietnamese troops moved through the suburbs of Saigon. More than 55,000 Americans and unaccounted numbers of Vietnamese, from both sides of the political standoff, and both civilians and soldiers, died in the fifteen-year struggle.

US advisors and a variety of covert US agencies had often gone out into the field with their Vietnamese clients, but openly active troop deployment had only begun properly in 1965, when President Lyndon Johnson sent in 125,000 GIs. At the same time the scope of the draft – compulsory conscription, determined by a lottery – was to be doubled. The war continued to intensify, as did US involvement over the next three years; 1968, with 540,000 US troops 'in-country' represented the high-water mark of the American presence. It was also the year in which American confidence, once so inviolate, began to be shaken. On 31 January what was known as the 'Tet Offensive', named for the Vietnamese New Year, Tet, erupted across the country. It initiated a month of bitter fighting in which the US Embassy compound was overrun and once 'secure' cities such as Hue were taken by the North Vietnamese. As far as the successful prosecution of the war was concerned, the nation's confidence would never properly recover. America sank into a crisis of self-doubt, escalated by such hitherto unthinkable excesses as the My Lai massacre.

Opposition to the war had begun almost as soon as Johnson cranked up his country's presence. It was initiated, logically, in the US, and in many ways sprang from a rather naïve outpouring of what can best be termed injured innocence. How, asked a growing number of people, could America, with all its positive self-mythologising, have involved itself in this monstrous, seemingly one-sided war? Vietnam was the first televised war (and the lessons of that conflict would ensure that subsequent confrontations, certainly those that involved Western troops, would henceforth be carefully sanitised). The screen, omnipresent in every American home, did more than anything else to 'bring the war back home'. The coverage, like that of the newspapers, was largely supportive of government propaganda, but there were just enough dissident voices to cause unease. (When Walter Cronkite, the nation's most respected anchor, declared on the national news that, after a personal trip to Saigon following Tet, even he had finally lost faith, the country was deeply affected.) But however the anchormen presented the story, the litany of high-tech weapons, of 'tiger cages', of defoliation, of saturation bombing, and of suffering peasants – none of this fitted in with America's self-image. American boys didn't casually destroy someone's home, however far away, with a flick of their Zippo. American boys didn't wear necklaces of dried, severed ears around their necks. And most important of all, American boys didn't come home in bodybags from some distant country.

The full realisation of what happens in a war took time to filter through. The patriotism of most Americans made sure of that. But protests did begin, primarily among students. The first attempt to educate America as to what was being done in its people's name to the Vietnamese was held in spring 1965 by students at the university of Michigan, one of the strongholds of SDS. Three thousand students crowded that first 'teach-in', and within months there were hundreds of copycat events, held on campuses nationwide. These 'enemies' were not Russians but peasants, whose main desire was less to embrace communism, but to overthrow a regime of tyranny and exploitation. For those, many of them students, who had already responded to the civil rights movement, these peasants seemed all too similar to the poor blacks for whose rights they had been fighting. (American Black radicals themselves, while accepting the identification, not to mention providing a vastly disproportionate percentage of the 'grunts' who were sent to fight the war, were less obsessed with anti-Vietnam protests. For them the first war to be won was that contested on the streets of their own country; protesting the situation in Vietnam fell into the category of bourgeois luxury). The success of the teach-ins spurred SDS to a new demonstration of their animosity towards the war: a march on Washington. Some 20,000 people – a figure that surpassed the estimates of all concerned – made the trip. It was the basis from which an ever-expanding anti-war movement would develop, moving from civil disobedience to more aggressive anti-war activism, active draft resistance (whether fleeing the country or, more dramatically, burning one's draft card), the sabotage of draft boards' records and similar activities.

The story of the anti-war protests, like that of the war itself, is largely American, but, like so many other aspects of Sixties America, it inevitably crossed the Atlantic. The first European demonstration came in February 1966, organised by the German brand of SDS (*Socialistische Deutsche Studentbund*). Some 2,000 people appeared for a march through West Berlin. As far as demonstrations were concerned Britain, like France and Italy, where indigenous protest would also emerge, was slower on the uptake. But in summer 1965 there was held a seven-and-a-half hour Vietnam teach-in at Oxford University, masterminded by the then president of the Oxford Union, an expatriate Pakistani student activist, Tariq Ali. It was a major media event, featuring major Establishment players – the Foreign Secretary Michael Stewart was sent along by Whitehall, while America's next ambassador to South Vietnam, Henry Cabot Lodge, appeared at the behest of the US embassy; the critical view came from two LSE academics Ralph Milliband and Bill Wedderburn. There were no Vietnamese. According to Ali the opposition speakers tore the Establishment spokesmen to pieces (Lodge described the Vietnamese as 'laughing and happy people enjoying their bananas');[1] but when the debate, filmed by BBC-TV, was eventually screened, it had been edited to leave Stewart and Cabot Lodge as masters of the discussion.

Harold Wilson won no plaudits for his attitude to Vietnam. A celebrated cartoon by Gerald Scarfe had pictured him sliding a forked tongue deep between President Johnson's buttocks; a popular chant asked, 'Where has Harold Wilson gone? | Crawling to the Pentagon, | When will they ever learn . . . ?' While Labour's pragmatic stance on Vietnam had virtually no effect in electoral terms, it did hurt the government on a wider front. Those same young intellectuals who had supported them in 1964 were now at the forefront of those who criticised and paraded their growing disillusion. If the Left needed a single issue on which to focus the charge that Wilson had 'betrayed' their hopes, then Vietnam was it.

Of the once iconic names that still conjure up the period, Tariq Ali is undoubtedly one. Born in Lahore in 1943 to a wealthy but definitely left-wing family, he earned his activist's spurs before, in 1963, he left Pakistan to enter Oxford. The teach-in was his first appearance on the public stage, and it earned him an invitation from the Bertrand Russell Foundation to appear in Helsinki and take part in the Russell War Crimes Tribunal. He also visited Bolivia to witness the trial of the French leftist Regis Debray on charges of guerrilla activity. Just as the teach-in had put Ali on the Vietnam protest map, so did the subsequent trip to Helsinki convince him that the war had to be seen as the central issue for the contemporary left. 'There was one overriding priority for radicals, socialists and democrats in the West. We had to do everything in our power – if necessary turn the world upside down – to help the Vietnamese drive the Americans out of their country.'[2]

During the first part of 1967 Ali visited North Vietnam. Here he met the premier Pham Van Dong. His suggestion of an international volunteer force, a throwback to the 'international brigades' of the Spanish Civil War, was rejected. What was really required, he was told, was an international solidarity movement.

The result of this injunction was the founding in July 1967 of the Vietnam Solidarity Campaign, the VSC. Tariq Ali would become known as its figurehead, but the campaign actually sprang from a small Trotskyite group, led by a pair of one-time Communists, Pat Jordan (an engineer) and Ken Coates (a former miner). Their organisation, never more than thirty or forty strong, was based around the *Week*, a tiny duplicated magazine, backed by a number of Labour and trade union figures. The *Week* had one main policy: fighting against the war in Vietnam. When they approached Ali to become one of the founding members of the VSC, he agreed. There existed one organisation, the British Campaign for Peace in Vietnam, but this was known as a Communist front and, more important, was committed to gradual pressure. Ali, inspired by what was happening in the US, wanted high-profile street actions. Gradualism had never influenced the British Establishment, the brushing aside of such featherlight pressure was its stock-in-trade. Ali defused any opposition from the BCPV by cleverly contacting the three North Vietnamese officials resident in Britain and asking for their support. This he received, although the BCPV would continue to snipe at the VSC and its highly publicised stance. (That antagonism was somewhat modified at the October 1968 march, when Ali, leading the parade, found himself arm-in-arm with a pair of burly dockers; they had been sent along by the Communists to protect him.)

A week later Ali arranged a meeting at the flat of the literary agent Clive Goodwin, whose own involvement in the movement was based on a desire to found a new, left-wing paper, to which end he had contacted Ali some months earlier. Here the VSC formed its *ad hoc* committee, including such stalwarts of protest as Christopher Logue, Adrian Mitchell, David Mercer, Ken Tynan, Sheila Rowbotham and others. It was decided to start a paper forthwith and Logue was deputed to search the British Library for a suitable name. He returned with *Black Dwarf*, a name that had first been used for a radical sheet that had appeared between 1819–28. D.A.N. Jones, a veteran left-wing journalist and stalwart of the *New Statesman* was appointed editor. When it began appearing, in May 1968, it attracted, aside from the usual political polemicists, a number of celebrities from the 'youth culture' and the arts. Mick Jagger sent a manuscript of his new song 'Street Fightin' Man'; John Lennon contributed; the artist Jim Dine offered some pictures, as did David Hockney. Goodwin, meanwhile, used his connections to drum up cash.

On 22 October 1967, shortly after Ali had returned from his trip to Bolivia, the VSC staged its first demonstration, a march from Trafalgar Square, that time-honoured launch-pad for so many forms of British protest, to the US Embassy in Grosvenor Square. (The VSC had in any case been keen to hold such a demonstration, but were urged on by a letter from Berkeley, calling for a sign of international solidarity.) By the time the procession reached its destination there were around 10,000 people, sporting the NLF flags, the anti-American slogans and ideological trademarks that would typify a succession of VSC marches. Calling not for 'peace' but for positive victory to the forces of the North, the march was surprisingly successful, penetrating nearer than either of its successors to the Embassy itself. The police, vastly outnumbered, were unable to hold the marchers back as they reached the large plate glass windows behind which stood armed Marine guards. Had they wanted, they could have entered the building, but once on 'US soil', it was unlikely that the guards would have been as acquiescent as the bobbies. For those who were there, whether as participants or observers, the march represented a new style of protest: action, at last, not simply words.

Energies immediately focused on a second march, called for 17 March 1968. Once more it would proceed from Trafalgar Square to the US Embassy. The tone was far more aggressive. Fired up by its success, not to mention the rather more resonant effects of the Tet offensive in Vietnam, and the general growth across the west of anti-war feelings, the VSC was determined to make this demo bigger, better and more effective. Both sides had had their rehearsal; this would be 'the real thing'. Quite what was to happen, however, remained unresolved. Whether this time the marchers would push that extra inch and actually storm the embassy, was put on hold. A plan for Ali to announce this aim at Trafalgar Square was vetoed; he could be arrested for inciting a riot. Instead, it was agreed, tactics would depend on the situation when the marchers reached Grosvenor Square. The Establishment was also girding its loins: apart from Special Branch surveillance, which everyone assumed had been in place since the previous October, there was a degree of black propaganda, notably a leaflet, which the VSC denied, calling on demonstrators to 'Come armed'. The VSC's ambivalence over the degree of violence they wished to allow was put into perspective by the arrival of a contingent of German SDS who demanded: if the masses want to attack the embassy, where will you stand? Ali was forced to drag their leaders into a private room and convince them, through long, hard arguments, that such militancy must be adopted only *in extremis*.

On 17 March Trafalgar Square was filled with some 25,000 people, mainly students, plus a leavening of young workers. Flags, banners and slogan-covered posters turned the square into a political carnival. On the plinth of Nelson's Column Ali, Vanessa Redgrave and other speakers gave their speeches (even Richard Branson, then editing his magazine *Student*, was scheduled to have his say; memoirists claim that he 'bottled out', his revolutionary fervour overcome by stage fright). Then, suitably exhorted, the marchers began moving up Charing Cross Road and along Oxford Street on their way to Grosvenor Square. By the time of the year's second big march, in October, the myth had evolved that the March demonstration had seen neither side fully ready for what happened. This was hardly true. The rehearsal had been six months earlier, in 1967. The mere size of the demo showed how well-prepared the VSC had become; as did the substantial police presence in Grosvenor Square. What neither side did expect, however, was the ferocity of their own emotions and the response they faced. It was a very far cry from the CND marches of old. There were no jolly hats, no jazz bands, no children, no earnest, liberal priests. Whether the police had been instructed to come down extra-hard on the demonstrators remains unresolved; the fact was that they did. In turn the demonstrators, unlike the passive sitters-down of CND days, fought back.

Which side initiated the violence remains arguable. The police, no doubt, would put it down to angry demonstrators, motivated by external agitators; the demonstrators accused the police, or more specifically the mounted police, who provided the authorities' strike force, of charging the demonstrators, clubbing and truncheoning, but to their great surprise finding themselves pulled to the ground and beaten. Demonstrators rolled ball bearings beneath the animals' hooves, or simply grabbed the reins. A theory that horses were terrified of lion dung led to the planning of an incursion into Manchester Zoo to pick up supplies – it didn't materialise. Other plans included defoliating the Square's trees; unfortunately they hadn't yet come into bud; other demonstrators brought along bacon rashers on lengths of string: the intention was to induce vomiting on the Embassy steps or failing that those of 10 Downing Street. Madder theories aside, a good deal of the emotion was undoubtedly down to numbers. But whatever the details, the overall effect was one of intense radicalisation. Horace Ové, who had gone along to take pictures for *IT*, had no doubts:

> It was incredible. Grosvenor Square was packed; it was the first time I saw young people in this country, mostly middle-class, really angry, really come out into the streets and really stand up to the police, really fighting back. There were thousands of police, horses and things like that. I was running

down trying to get there in time and I was fixing my camera and a policeman saw me and he looked at me and said, 'You better go back home, curly, else you'll be in a lot of trouble.' (I've never forgotten that, those lines, 'curly' because my hair was long in those days.) Anyway I didn't go home, and I got in the middle of it and I remember there were speeches and so on and then the whole clash. There was the pushing: I push you, you push me back and suddenly the whole thing broke down. I think it was the first time a black policeman appeared on the scene, there was one black policeman there and he got a hard time from everybody, everybody. When the police started to charge with their horses and really lay into people and beat the shit out of them there was one girl that was shouting and screaming back to them and about five police really laid into her and really kicked her about on the ground and then they pulled back. And then the crowd surrounded one police that did not get away and they really laid into him and beat him to the ground.[3]

The fighting, which had begun around five o'clock went on till seven that evening. It was a vicious, bruising encounter, with plenty of casualties on both sides. As the press pointed out, some 117 police were injured; only forty-five demonstrators received medical treatment. But many more were taken away by sympathetic friends. There were 246 arrests. The media, it was also noted, expressed its quintessential Englishness by showing even more concern for the police horses; one Sampson was a source of particular worry. The demonstrators, including one badly beaten pregnant woman, had only themselves to blame. That many of the demonstrators were able to turn on the television on arriving home and see themselves locked in revolutionary confrontation with 'the pigs', in no way diminished the event, nor their bruises. For many it was an emotional blooding too, a crossing of some form of spiritual Rubicon. Yet again the middle-class young had been given notice of how tiny a distance one could push the authorities before they pushed back – and how hard they were happy to do it.

One further aspect of the demo is worth noting: the involvement of the counter-culture. *IT*, in the person of John Hopkins, had published an editorial in which the paper decried the VSC's efforts, but for many Grosvenor Square was the place to be. For once the freaks had stubbed out their joints. Mick Farren and the Deviants had just returned from a gig in Birmingham:

We were coming back down the M1 and ran into these humungous police road blocks and they pulled out all our equipment and we said, 'What the fuck do you want?' and they said, 'We're looking for weapons.' And we get back to London and plan to go to the riot the next day. So we got up about lunchtime, went downstairs and there were maybe fifty motorcycle cops at the top of Endell Street outside the Shaftesbury [Theatre] and round the corner was like buses full of these geezers who look like they feed on vodka and raw meat and don't get let out except on riots. I thought, 'Motherfucker!

what's going on here?' There weren't exactly tanks on the boulevards but . . . shit, it was like Chile or something.

So we went marching up to Centrepoint where we ran into Miles and we hooked up with the march somewhere by Tottenham Court Road and Oxford Street. We were marching along and there were reports that Mick Jagger had been seen and this was happening and that was happening and it was all very sort of aggressive. There were all sorts of Germans who were a real nuisance because they kept linking arms and getting into that run that the Japanese had invented. We didn't really want to go that fast – we'd just got up and we didn't feel too good and we didn't need a lot of mad Krauts doing the Japanese run, very disruptive, like Zulu impis getting wound up, and they kept doing these flurries of running on the spot which got people very excited to the point that somebody tried to nose his car out through the crowd and Miles kicked in his headlamps! I thought, 'Jesus!' So we got to South Audley Street and started streaming down there and everything halts and nobody knows what's going on and there's all these rumours that they're tear-gassing people here and there, in fact they weren't. We hadn't seen the US Embassy yet, although there was another rumour that there were armed marines who'd kill you if you actually got inside.

Then everything started to move and we went charging down Audley Street and it seemed like the police had given way, that's what everybody assumed. And we arrived on the grass in Grosvenor Square, where, although I didn't know it at the time we had immediately been surrounded. So there we have these thousands of people boxed in on the grass, though it's not that crowded, there's room to stroll around, except down the end by the Embassy where it's so crowded you can't see anything. Then there was a thunder of hooves and there we are in the middle of the charge of the Light Brigade, which was fucking scary. What little I knew, basically from Napoleonic history, was get under a tree, because it's very hard to swing one of those truncheons when you're on a horse and the other guy is under a tree. So the first charge goes through and they're sort of whacking people and one geezer on a white horse, who became quite notorious, whacked this girl on the head at which point everybody became exceedingly annoyed and dragged him off his horse and kicked him. He got away a couple of times but then he was surrounded and when everyone closed ranks he was just left there. And then people were hurling bits of turf and rocks and stuff and then they'd retreat, and charge again and retreat and charge and people were getting hit and hurt and injured and then we went home. Just like that. And watched it on TV.[4]

The VSC, while shocked by the Establishment response, saw their efforts as a victory. The campaign's profile had been lifted enormously and from across the country came calls for information on how the protests could be sustained. Phones rang off the hook and Ali calculated that had he said yes to everyone he would have been giving six talks every day for the next three months. His immediate response was to join Jordan and Coates's 'party', the IMG; on 15 April, on a more public level, he joined a two thousand-strong march from Hyde Park to the London headquarters of the Springer Press, the largest and most right wing of the German media conglomerates. The German SDS leader Rudi Dutschke had recently survived an assassination attempt; the Springer papers, outspoken opponents of any form of anti-authoritarianism, were deemed complicit. Notable among the members of this particular demonstration were a group of hardcore hippies, led by Sid Rawle; their banner read simply 'Cannabis Martyrs'.

The six months that would elapse between the year's first march on Grosvenor Square, and its much-heralded successor were perhaps the most dramatic of the decade. If 1963 can be seen as an annus mirabilis, with the election of Kennedy, Beatlemania, the Profumo affair and other amusements, then 1968 was its antithesis. In America Martin Luther King and Bobby Kennedy were assassinated; later, at the Democratic Convention in Chicago, Mayor Daley's police rioted, their gleeful brutalities relayed to the world via the now omnipresent television cameras; in Paris students and workers briefly united in the May *évènements*, as near to genuine revolution as any student movement would come that year and an inspiration to activists the world over; in Czechoslovakia the 'Prague Spring' vanished beneath the tank treads of the Russian invasion. In Vietnam, where in June American combat deaths passed 25,000, the war rolled on and elsewhere the protests against it continued unabated.

For the VSC the next priority was the organisation of the October demonstration. This time both sides were more than ready. With all the excitements of the summer, notably those of Paris, both Establishment and radicals genuinely anticipated revolution. And as October drew nearer it became clear that the authorities were determined to do everything in their power to frustrate the VSC plans. Special Branch surveillance, a fact of life for many left-wing groups, was stepped up. VSC mail was regularly opened, the phones were tapped; it was assumed that the Branch had infiltrated the membership. A variety of *agents provocateurs* materialised, urging the leadership to nihilistic excesses. The VSC offices were raided and the Branch showed a surprisingly acute knowledge of their layout, even including the graffito of a Molotov cocktail, drawn just a day before by some passing anarchist and judiciously hidden beneath a poster pending a more permanently disguising paint job. The VSC's caution was justified: two days later *The Times* informed its readers that,

> A small army of militant extremists plan to seize control of certain highly sensitive installations and buildings in central London next month, while 6,000 Metropolitan policemen are busy controlling an estimated crowd of 100,000 anti-Vietnam war demonstrators . . . This startling plot has been uncovered by a special squad of detectives formed to track down the extremists who are understood to be manufacturing 'Molotov cocktail' bombs and amassing a small arsenal of weapons. They plan to use these against police and property in an attempt to dislocate communications and law and order.[5]

The 'revelations' were nonsense, and *The Times* should have known it, but that was irrelevant. It was assumed that the story had been cooked up by MI5, and publicised in a fit of professional pique when the Special Branch, citing their own infiltration, rejected (sensibly) the spooks' latest piece of bugging and burgling. Both parties then faced a good deal of embarrassment: the Branch couldn't admit that they disbelieved the story, while MI5 couldn't say anything at all. Officially, the story was withdrawn, although the *Daily Telegraph* continued to suggest that it might have some real basis.

The flood of black propaganda intensified as the autumn neared. Tariq Ali received regular death threats, and a member of the VSC committee was shot at as he walked through the East End. Politicians from both sides called for the demonstration to be banned. The press were in paradise, as were the pundits. Quintin Hogg trembled for the readers of the *Daily Express*, warning them not to underrate 'this sinister threat' and affecting amazement that someone bearing the name 'Tariq Ali' could possibly be considered a 'citizen of the United Kingdom . . . with rights equal to those of anyone born in England of ancient stock'. He found it particularly odd that the 'hare-brained revolutionaries' of the VSC seemed so inimical to a police presence. Was it that such a presence might block the way, so easily accessed from Trafalgar Square, to Whitehall, the Houses of Parliament, the BBC? All of which, Mr Hogg advised, were ripe for invasion and disruption. The appositely surnamed right-wing MP Tom Iremonger was less subtle, claiming in the Commons that, 'the British people are fed up with being trampled underfoot by foreign scum' and demanding that 'alien militant agitators' be deported forthwith. He especially deplored the appearance of the German SDS in March, their chants of 'Ho, Ho, Ho Chi Minh' were in fact, he claimed, those of 'Sieg Heil!'[6]

On Sunday 27 October, the prevailing spirit was, as the *People* headlined it, one of a 'stiff upper lip'. It listed a variety of 'so British' measures, gleaned no doubt from some Ealing comedy: policemen wearing cricket boxes, the Horseguards appearing without their mounts ('whatever happens the HORSES must not get hurt'), the 'we never close' spirit of the local Lyons Corner House ('If we didn't stop our service for the Germans, why should we stop for our own people?') and the Soho strip clubs (said one [probably apocryphal] tout, 'Boy – with all those ignorant twits down from the provinces we'll make a bomb.')[7]

Reading the pamphlets that could be picked up all over London, if one had feared for one's life then it was through death by laughter rather than suspension from the nearest lamp-post. MI5 or indeed the Special Branch might have been responsible for this example (a Maoist creation), but embarrassingly, like the rest, it was probably genuine.

The Soviet revisionist clique is keeping up its pressure on the heroic Vietnamese people to surrender to US imperialism through the 'peace talks' plot
. . . While the repressive state machine is busy polishing its police truncheons
and gas grenades, the prostitute press and the spokesmen of the reactionary
political parties . . . are threatening dire consequences if the youth persist in
their militant march to Grosvenor Square. The double-faced Trotskyite
clique of the VSC and the revisionist YCL renegades, who have the bureaucratic control of the *ad hoc* committee for the October demonstration are using dual revolutionary tactics, also to divert the militant youth from the US
Embassy, the lair of the aggressors . . . DENOUNCE THESE POLICE AGENTS
AND THE DEFENDERS OF THE US AGGRESSORS! TEAR OFF THEIR
FRAUDULENT REVOLUTIONARY MASK!

The *Sunday Telegraph*'s Peregrine Worsthorne, under a headline that
told his readers 'No Need for Panic', was positively balanced, if disdainfully
patronising. 'What we are faced with . . . is not a revolution. It is in large part
a perfectly respectable and legitimate attempt to express the depth of youthful dissent over Vietnam.' It was neither 'unhealthy' nor 'sinister'; in his
opinion it was foolish, but 'by no stretch of the imagination can the student
agitators be said to be revolutionaries . . . nor, even if they were, would they
have the slightest chance of success. Indeed, their hatred of the present system arises precisely from their knowledge that it cannot be overthrown because it is too deeply rooted in mass apathy and acquiescence.' What most
worried Worsthorne was the inevitable hysteria that would follow the
equally inevitable television screening of the most violent clashes. People
must not fall prey to such images. 'There is a combination here of juvenile
idealism and juvenile delinquency, along with a touch of straight hooliganism, which should certainly be met by the *smack* – that for once really is the
right word – of firm government.'[8]
    What, to borrow from the *People* was really 'so British' was this mixture
of paranoia and patronage which extended throughout the media. Not a revolution, no fear of that, just foolish young people letting off steam, probably
misled by foreigners, give them their head, but not too much, no tolerance of
genuine hooligans of course . . . The list lacked only the usual dismissal:
'they're going through a phase'. Perhaps the most intelligent assessment appeared in the *New Statesman* where Mervyn Jones pooh-poohed the promises of 100,000 marchers, but acknowledged that March had heralded a new
style in demonstrations, that this new movement was 'indeed significant' and
that 'something remarkable is going on'.[9] In a lengthy piece he suggested
three causes. The first was a breakdown in confidence in 'the entire system of
party politics' and a conscious movement away from such organisations; the
second an increased awareness of and sympathy with revolutionary movements in the Third World; the third, and 'this is what is called militancy',

'the belief that real social change can be secured only through determined struggle'.[10]

Setting out the major participants in the march (some eight groups: the RSSF, Trotskyites [IS and IMG], the Anarchists, the CP and YCL, the Maoists, the Young Liberals and groups of ex-pat Americans, Australians and New Zealanders opposed to the war), Jones noted the march's route and wondered why, once one had discounted the melodramatics of both sides, a clash was still so profoundly feared. His answer was the VSC tactic (as opposed to that of the CND which had obeyed all police injunctions) of 'taking over the streets', i.e. moving with linked arms down the entire width of a street, thus making traffic flow impossible and ignoring traffic lights and other signs. Their proclaimed intention, to reach Whitehall and 'maintain a presence there' for at least an hour, during which a teach-in was to be held, would obviously intensify the paralysis of central London. The question was, was this in fact illegal? In Britain's unwritten constitution there was, lawyers noted, no actual right to march; but nor was there a prohibition against it. In the event, it was up to the police: if they acted, then there was a plethora of laws (starting with the Public Order Act, under which an entire march could be banned, and moving from the genuinely serious 'riotous assembly' to such petty offences as 'insulting behaviour' and 'obstruction') that could be used to justify any arrest. If a clash was on the cards, suggested Jones, it was less to do with the Maoists' 'militant youth' than the way Britain policed its demonstrators. Treating adults like a primary school crocodile, shepherding them along, jumping on anyone who dared break the conformist ranks: these were the best ways of exacerbating a tense situation. The CND marchers might have stood for such treatment, those of the VSC were less amenable.

Jones also noted the intractability of the police, especially in the person of Scotland Yard's Commander John Lawlor, who was in charge of the day's policing. Lawlor refused to be interviewed, offered answers only to written questions and then refused to deal with the majority of such questions since they were either 'too specific' or impinged on 'operational thinking'. The idea that proper consultation, with both sides made aware of what the other was planning, could have defused much of the incipient panic was never considered. But the rank-and-file police were no more inclined to compromise. After March, when, for all the media sympathy, they were (thanks to television) perceived as brutal but ineffective, they were looking for revenge. On a pettier, but absolutely human level, it was a Sunday, a day off, and few fancied the overtime. Nor was the VSC innocent. They too scorned proper negotiations; they had no desire (or ability) to police the marchers and while they claimed to have no wish for violent confrontation, there was no doubt that their supporters were not about to lie down beneath the police truncheons. Those leaders who were appearing in the media rarely seemed to espouse anything but the most blood-curdling predictions. Jones ended his piece on a pessimistic note. All sides, he felt, were hell-bent on confrontation, on 'the most ferocious, most appalling and undoubtedly most unnecessary spasm of violence seen in London in our times'. Only one hope remained, the most 'British' of all: 'it may rain.'

It didn't rain, but neither, in the event, did the gutters run with blood. Later Tariq Ali would claim that the idea of a genuine revolution had never crossed the VSC's mind, and that what the march represented was 'a show of the anti-imperialist left's strength'.[11] One thing was undeniable: the movement against the war was not some crackpot bunch of isolated idealists. The march was hugely popular, the 100,000 that Mervyn Jones had found so inflated a projection really did make the trek, but it was largely peaceful. A relatively small group, perhaps 6,000 led by Abhimanya Manchandra and the 'Britain-Vietnam solidarity front', appeared in Grosvenor Square and tangled with Commander Lawlor's massed policemen, but they were exceptions. There were only forty-two arrests, only four policemen injured and perhaps another fifty demonstrators. Stuart Christie, who had been among them, saw the clash as: 'the only bit of liveliness in the day that saved it from utter collapse into a pleasant Sunday afternoon walk to Hyde Park to hear the interminable speeches exhorting us to join one or another of the Marxist groups and ensure working-class salvation'.[12] But such jokiness belied the overall tone: to reverse the old protestors' standby, it was the Establishment that would be singing 'We shall overcome'.

The press, having spent the previous weeks winding up all concerned to a frenzy of twitchy anticipation, now indulged in an orgy of nationalistic self-congratulation. 'Well done us,' trumpeted the *Evening Standard*,[13] and the rest of the popular press followed suit. *The Times*, so enthusiastic a disseminator of black propaganda, now informed its readers that the 'calm wall' of police had 'won the day against a militant few'. 'The system', added that day's leader, had won. Sensible demonstrators could have their bit of drama, the police could thump anyone who got out of line, freedom of speech and assembly had been preserved. In an ineffably smug conclusion worthy of the most benighted of headmasters, the writer affirmed, '[R]adical youth . . . must be allowed to demonstrate the strength of their feelings and the extent to which they are shared, so long as they keep within the tolerant rules of order of their society. Whether their methods help the causes they have at heart is a matter for them. They certainly put the other members of their society to inconvenience and try their forbearance. But forbearance is the distinguishing civic virtue of a free democracy. And the events of yesterday justify a feeling of pride and confidence that free democracy is of mature and hardy growth in Britain.'[14]

So, it had all been a storm in a teacup, after all. Hadn't the demonstrators and police gathered after the march to sing 'Auld Lang Syne'? There you are. Equanimity was restored and whatever might happen in alien lands all was for the best in democratic Britain, the best of all possible worlds. It was galling, but the triumphalism was underpinned by a degree of truth. The *NLR's* Alexander Cockburn, among others, wrote to *The Times* to protest the newspaper's skewed treatment of the demonstration, both in their happy acquiescence with the most grotesque of rumour-mongering before and their self-satisfied reporting after the event, and his complaint gained pride of place on the letters page. But no one could honestly deny that the police had shown a remarkable degree of sophistication. The decision of the VSC to redirect the march to Hyde Park, thus diverting the bulk of the marchers from the far greater likelihood of confrontation in Grosvenor Square (which for all its proximity to the Embassy would, inevitably, have favoured the police, given its relatively small dimensions) also helped. There might even have been a sense of subconscious surrender: Hyde Park Corner, after all, was a synonym for outlandish crankery.

What was perhaps more interesting was the breadth of representation among the marchers. Only 50%, it was noted in a survey published soon afterwards, were actually students, and of these 10% were still at school; 12% were non-student manual workers under 25. It was also noted that 70% of the marchers felt themselves to be demonstrating not just against the Vietnam War, but against the structure of capitalist society in Britain.

In the end the determination of the VSC to pursue the single issue of Vietnam would be its undoing; the movement simply 'ran out of steam'. It was, as Tariq Ali admitted to Ronald Fraser, 'a tragedy'.[15] Tens of thousands had been radicalised, and now their energies, lacking a focus, simply dissipated. The workers returned to work and the schoolchildren to school. The politicos focused once more on each other's backs and fragmentation and sectarianism prevailed. The students retreated to their individual universities, and while sit-ins, occupations and other forms of protest would continue, they couldn't offer the same kind of impact as the VSC. In time the energy would evaporate on campus too. There was also one more factor to be noted. As the 'underground' would find with the trial of *Oz* magazine in 1971, there was only so far the authorities allowed themselves to be pushed.

Chapter Twenty-Two

The Angry Brigade: A Really Wild Bunch

The Angry Brigade is the man or woman sitting next to you. They have guns in their pockets and hatred in their minds. We are getting closer. Off the system and its property. Power to the People.
Communiqué 9. The Angry Brigade (22 May 1971, following the bombing of Tintagel House)

Of all the political groupings so far noted in a necessarily brief overview, one, a vital ingredient of the larger phenomenon of the Sixties left, has been missed. The Situationist International, which has come to be filed alongside such political/cultural 'isms' as Futurism, Dadaism, Surrealism and Lettrism, played a major role (if perhaps a subconscious one) in the thinking that led to the most important (if ultimately unsuccessful) outpouring of British revolutionary fervour: the Angry Brigade.

Situationism emerged from the Lettrist International, an avant-garde, existentialist art group, based in Paris in the early 1950s, and itself a more radical breakaway of the earlier Lettrism, founded by the Paris-based Romanian writer Isidore Isou in 1946. His aim, as he put it, was to 'revolutionise every aesthetic discipline of its time, from poetry to the theatre, by way of painting, and then to renovate the other cultural domains, whether philosophical or scientific'.[1] It was a cultural makeover for the world. Lettrism was short-lived, as were such contemporaneous movements as COBRA, founded in 1948 and named for the main centres of its operations: *C*openhagen, *B*russels and *A*msterdam. A new movement, dedicated to the 'overthrow of situations' emerged on 27 July 1957 when eight representatives of the European avant-garde met in the Italian town of Cosio d'Arroscia and formally amalgamated under a new name: *L'Internationale Situationiste*: Situationist International. They rejected the old, élitist concept of art, preferring to maximise the links between art and politics that had been growing ever since Dada. Committed left-wingers, they rejected orthodox Communism, opting for workers' autonomy. Their thesis was articulated by a pamphlet 'As We See It', issued by the British Solidarity group (a breakaway faction of the SLL) in 1961.

> Meaningful action, for revolutionaries, is whatever increases the confidence, the autonomy, the initiative, the participation, the solidarity, the equalitarian tendencies and the self activity of the masses and whatever assists in their demystification. Sterile and harmful action is whatever reinforces the passivity of the masses, their apathy, their cynicism, their differentiation through hierarchy, their alienation, their reliance on others to do things for them and the degree to which they can therefore be manipulated by others – even by those allegedly acting on their behalf.[2]

For the Situationists the world had become a place where the rulers – governments, capitalists – conspired to rob the individual of freedom, substituting 'entertainment' for genuine leisure. Although his name would not be cited, their analysis reflected that proposed by Herbert Marcuse, with his concepts of 'repressive tolerance' and 'alienation' and of a world in which the work existed only to tie the individual to purchasing the very products that he worked to create, in an unfulfilling, endless circle of self-delusion. 'Freedom', the much-touted cornerstone of the liberal democracies, was nothing but a sham: the 'freedom' to do only what the larger society determined was acceptable. The ultimate result of such programmed amusement was inevitably boredom, the most all-encompassing product of the 'leisure society'. Modern society, based on this programmed, delusive freedom, was apostrophised as 'the Spectacle', a term coined by SI's best-known theorist, Guy Debord and developed in a variety of writings through the 1950s and 1960s, culminating in *The Society of the Spectacle* (1967). 'The spectacle', he declared, 'is the moment when the commodity has achieved the total occupation of life . . . [it] is both the result and the project of the existing mode of production . . . it is the heart of unrealism of the real society.'[3]

What the Situationists desired was to cut through this mass-produced illusion, to counter the pervasive tedium, to range against boredom the excesses of the unfettered sociopath: better the man who slashes the Old Master than the mandatory adoration of the Old Master; better the spontaneous riot than the well-policed demonstration, better unmitigated chaos with all its risks than sanctioned, if comfortable, order. Freedom must be differentiated from licence, intoned the Establishment. Bollocks! replied the Situationists: true freedom *was* licence, and take it as far as you dared. Situationism was not an ideology, it was a style, a stance. If freedom was, as Debord saw it, practised in a closed circle, then what the Situationists wanted was to smash open this circle and offer real freedom to all. They wished, as the first number of the journal *Situationiste Internationale* put it in June 1958, 'to wreck this world . . . Everyone must search for what he loves, for what attracts him.'

The SI were, as the writer Greil Marcus has noted, primarily critics, judging (and condemning) every aspect of contemporary society, but they acted too. As Debord put it, 'Where there was fire, we carried gasoline.'[4] Much of the action came in the form of writing – the SI journal, an outpouring of pamphlets from various Situ stars – but there were 'scandalous activities' too. The first of these came in 1961 when members of the Scandinavian branch beheaded Copenhagen's best-loved image, the statue of the Little Mermaid. Five years later they returned to the headlines, but this time their role was less 'artistic' and a good deal more 'political'. In 1966, when students took over the University of Strasbourg five Situs infiltrated the student union and set about antagonising the Establishment. Their supreme success was a pamphlet: 'On the Poverty of Student Life', the work of a Tunisian Situ, Mustapha/Omar Khayati. If the students, self-ordained 'revolutionaries', had been hoping for a cosy piece of congratulatory propaganda, they were sorely disappointed. Their 'bohemian' stance was decried, their espousal of revolution dismissed as 'rent-a-crowd militancy for the latest good cause'; their freedoms no more than those permitted by the Establishment; their only real interest was status and their awareness of real, rather than synthetic culture, was as a voyeur.[5]

As for the university, it was no more than a 'society for the propagation of ignorance; high culture has taken on the rhythm of the production line. Without exception university teachers are cretins, men who would get the bird from any audience of schoolboys.' The pamphlet admired 'the young thug', who at least had begun to exhibit some signs of revolt against the stagnation of his existence. For him there were two choices: surrender to the lure of the Spectacle ('clothes, discs, scooters, transistors, purple hearts all beckon him to the land of the consumer'), or he can 'attack the laws of society itself', either by turning to robbery or to 'revolutionary consciousness'. Student rebels, on the other hand, were irrelevant, their successes transient; if they did achieve a breach in society, then the Establishment could easily 'recuperate', i.e. repair the damage. Students, like every other revolutionary, had to move to the bigger stage: 'We must destroy the Spectacle itself, the whole apparatus of the commodity society . . . We must abolish the pseudo needs and false desires which the system manufactures daily in order to preserve its power.'[6]

Strasbourg, in the end, was a storm in a provincial teacup – the students were punished, a judge, summoned by the authorities to restore order, pontificated, life returned to normal – but within a year more than 300,000 copies of Khayati's pamphlet had been absorbed into the French university system. Readers appealed to the SI for instruction: the only advice they received was to act autonomously and to promote an insurrection that would mean something to themselves. One of these groups of pro-Situs named themselves *les Enragés*, the 'furious' or 'angry ones', a name taken from a synonymous group, founded by the radical priest Jacques Roux during the French revolution. It was the original *Enragés* who in June 1793 infuriated the Convention, the contemporary revolutionary government, with a petition which attacked the persisting inequalities of the so-called new order, in which 'liberty is just a vain illusion when an entire class of men has the means of starving the people with impunity'.[7] The descendants of these original *Enragés* were among the front-runners of a student uprising in early 1968 at Nanterre University, a soulless campus of the main University of Paris situated in the city's suburbs.

Among the many students voicing their discontent was one Daniel Cohn-Bendit, soon to be named 'Dany the Red' by the popular press.

Cohn-Bendit jumped into fame with a single confrontation, when the Minister of Sport appeared on campus to open the college's new swimming pool. According to popular myth the minister was on his way out, carefully averting his eyes from the anti-government graffiti bespattering his route, when Cohn-Bendit suddenly appeared. 'Minister, you've drawn up a 600-page long report on French youth but there is no mention of our sexual problems. Why not?' 'I'm quite willing to discuss this matter with responsible people,' responded the Minister, 'but you are certainly not one of them. I myself prefer sport to sexual education. If you have sexual problems, I suggest you jump in the pool.' 'That,' replied Cohn-Bendit, 'is what the Hitler Youth used to say.' Cohn-Bendit moved on to found the 22nd March Movement, an ultra-radical group that would keep the pressure on Nanterre and spearhead the expansion of discontent across the university system.

The Nanterre eruption was still at its height when on 2 May the Dean closed the college and summoned Cohn-Bendit to face a disciplinary tribunal. His fellow-students promptly marched in protest, calling for a revised curriculum and for higher State expenditure on education. A day later their action was echoed at the Sorbonne, France's most prestigious university, in Paris. Frightened by reports that a group of right-wingers were planning to attack the students the Sorbonne rector called in the CRS – France's riot police. There were no right-wingers, but the CRS were quite happy to move in, beating students and bystanders without discrimination. The rioting engulfed Paris's Latin Quarter, home of the Sorbonne; by the end of the day there had been 600 arrests and hundreds of injuries. 'CRS = SS' read one graffito.

From thereon matters escalated, reaching their first climax a week later at the 'Night of the Barricades' on rue Gay Lussac. Once again the CRS demonstrated their brutality and a day later Prime Minister Pompidou, assailed by those who resented seeing their children beaten, was forced to withdraw the riot squads. The convulsions spread. On 13 May the majority of France's trade unions came out on strike in sympathy with the students; by 21 May nine million strikers were out, most factories were occupied and the vast majority of French public opinion appeared to support the young rebels. President de Gaulle broke off a state visit to Romania. Eight days later the *évènements* were over. On 28 May de Gaulle had taken a secret flight to meet his army C-in-C General Massu. The army, he was assured, would remain loyal. The next day de Gaulle addressed the nation, offering a simple (and mendacious) assessment of the situation. Whatever people might believe, France was on the verge of falling into the hands of a 'Communist dictatorship'. Surely this was not what the people desired; and in any case, if things did not calm down, he would have no hesitation in calling out the troops. He also announced an immediate general election. The 'revolution' evaporated. In the end the workers and students, that supposedly unbeatable combination so eminently desired by revolutionaries in America and Europe, had too little in common. Their alliance, while momentarily threatening, had insufficient substance. For the rest, the stick of Communist threat and the carrot of French nationalistic fantasy saved the day for the government. When the election was held, de Gaulle won the largest majority in recent French history. The factories reopened, public transport returned to normal, the students went back to their campuses and the 'revolution', briefly so near, retreated.

The role of the SI, keen to move from pamphleteering to action, was as central members of the Council for the Maintenance of the Occupation, their aim to move the 'revolution' off the campuses and into factories and workplaces. As Debord informed his Situationists, 'The SI must now prove its effectiveness in a subsequent stage of revolutionary activity – or else disappear.'[8] In the event they found themselves condemned to the latter option. Their Council suffered the same disintegration of enthusiasm following the abrupt collapse of the 'revolution' as any of the other groups who just days before had been manning the barricades. In the years that followed, for all their disdain of the orthodox Left and its auto-cannibalism, the SI fell into the same rancorous divisions. By 1972 there were but four accredited members. Their ideas, however, would not be lost, and in the aftermath of Paris took root in new soil: that of England.

While *les évènements* were primarily a French phenomenon, the idea of an actual revolutionary situation, where student power had moved from the limitations of campus protest to the streets and factories of whole nations, electrified Europe's radical young. Thousands began making their way to France, and especially to Paris, in the hope of joining the party before it was all too late. Among them was David Robins, mixing university life with a job at *IT*:

> I didn't have any political affiliations but I'd got pissed off with the non-politics of the underground, wanking on about drugs and stuff, and I was now proud to be a student. We arrived at night. Loads of people around, flames, no cops, water everywhere and the most appalling pong of tear gas. And none of the shops had any glass in their windows. The aftermath of the day's riots . . . When we got to the Sorbonne the strike was in progress, the *quartier* was full of workers, arguing . . . We introduced ourselves and we had names of other people to prove we weren't cops. The worst thing to be was a revolutionary tourist so you enrolled in one of two services for the revolution. So we enlisted in the *Service d'Ordre*, in the Beaux Arts in rue Bonaparte. This was one of the places where visitors were billeted. The whole college was filled with beds: but nobody slept, everybody talked . . . The days passed just like a blur. There was a fantastic demonstration one day when the cops chased us down this street and the people dragged us in off the street and gave us shelter. This very smart gallery owner just said, 'Come in here.' The adrenalin was flowing. I'm not a hero but you didn't actually feel fear.
>
> As it went on things became nastier. It wasn't so much the cops, there were also these people who would emerge out of the walls, criminals, the

barbousses, the scumbags, and they'd be these dangerous-looking guys wandering around, it was very lawless . . . The one event that I took part in particularly was the occupation of the British Council. Opposite the Sorbonne, and it remained open throughout the revolt. Some Brits thought that was ridiculous – we should do something. We all went over to the British Council and there was this amazing scene where we occupied them. But it was a truly British occupation: 'Should we occupy the library?' 'No, no – that's stealing . . . ' 'We should speak in French.' 'No, this is the British Council occupation', and so on. It lasted till we lost interest and pissed off. And we went across the bridge into the rich area of Paris and when we came back we found there was this ring of steel. So at seven o'clock in the morning we walked back through them. There were lorries of CRS on all the bridges all along the Seine. Military trucks, guys with guns, tear gas and so on. Then the word went around that they were looking for the foreign students, 'cos they were seen as the trouble-makers. We had twenty-four hours to get out.

At the Gare du Nord there was a mass meeting taking place. The Tannoy was saying 'Bon voyage' and the first train took off and there was applause and I was on it. There were a lot of French comrades came with us, many of whom were wanted, and when we got to the other side we did the very criminal thing of starting singing and causing a big distraction as they tied up and meanwhile two comrades leapt off, over a big gap on to the quay, over the railway sidings with a British bobby after them . . . Got back, Hornsey College [in north London] was in revolt and I went to meetings and told them what was happening in Paris and nobody believed us.[9]

Robins was one among many. Amongst those who also made the trek to Paris were John Barker, from Cambridge University, Christopher Bott, from Strathclyde, and Anna Mendelson from Essex. They would meet in person soon after, and four years later, along with five others, star in the century's longest ever political conspiracy trial, officially billed as 'Regina vs [James] Greenfield, [Ann]aMendelson, [John] Barker, [Hilary] Creek, [Stuart] Christie, [Christopher] Bott, [Angela] Weir and [Kate] McLean', better known as the 'Angry Brigade Trial'. Four would be acquitted; Greenfield, Barker, Creek and Mendelson would be found guilty, and sentenced to ten years' jail apiece. In a decade which had seen Weatherman in the US, Baader-Meinhof in Germany, the Red Brigades in Italy and variations on the same theme in a dozen other countries, both in and out of Europe, the Angry Brigade would be Britain's contribution to that late-twentieth-century phenomenon: the student urban guerrilla.

Thirty years on from the time when their alleged conspiracy supposedly began the identity of the Angry Brigade is still in doubt. If one believes the prosecution, then the guilty four were indeed the Angry Brigade, a solid corpus of individuals who from early 1968 to mid-1971 exploded some twenty-five 'infernal devices' (as the forensic experts summoned by the bomb squad apparently still termed the subjects of their investigations) of which nineteen actually exploded in and around the homes or offices of a number of senior politicians, captains of industry, and other 'political' targets. As listed at the trial, the bombings began on 3 March 1968, with explosions at the Spanish Embassy in Grosvenor Square and the American Forces Columbia Club in Lancaster Gate. There would be a number of Spanish targets (the Bank of Bilbao, the Bank of Spain, Iberia Airways, the Spanish Embassy for the second time) as well as Italian ones (the Italian Trade Exhibition, two Italian Consulates) – which evidence led the police to believe that the Brigade was linked in some way to European terrorist groups. These however were merely a preface to a second tranche of attacks, aimed at the British Establishment and what were deemed its business allies. The first of these, on 18 August 1970 came at the Putney home of Sir John Waldron, Commissioner of the Metropolitan Police. This was followed on 8 September by an attack on the home of the Attorney-General Sir Peter Rawlinson, and on 12 January 1971 on that of Robert Carr, the Tory Secretary for Employment and Productivity and, more importantly, the chief advocate of the highly controversial, and supposedly 'anti-union' Industrial Relations Bill. There was one more attack, on 31 July 1971, on an Establishment figure: John Davies, the Secretary of Trade and Industry. Allied to these were the bombings of a BBC camera van, stationed at the 1970 Miss World competition (later that day Women's Liberation members would disrupt the annual parade of swim-suited 'beauties'), at the Ford Motor Company in Gant's Hill, Essex (19 March 1971) and of the home of its managing director William Batty (22 June 1971), of Biba's boutique in High Street Kensington (1 May 1971), of the Metropolitan Police computers at Tintagel House, Lambeth (22 May 1971) and of a Territorial Army Drill Hall in Holloway. There were a number of smaller incidents and, to the delight of those who claimed that the eight on trial were not *the* Angry Brigade, an attack on the home of a Birmingham building contractor, Christopher Bryant – two months to the day since the arrest of the supposed 'Brigade'. A further high-profile bombing, of the GPO Tower in London, was generally attributed to the group.

All in all there had been 120 bombings in England and Wales since mid-1968 – the majority still unattributed – and while the IRA campaigns that would soon be getting under way in the wake of the renewed 'Troubles' would be far more spectacular, this outbreak of what looked like a low intensity urban guerrilla war was disturbing enough. The authorities reacted accordingly. At first, given the predominance of European and especially Spanish targets, it was assumed that some form of Spanish Republican cell had established itself in the UK. It was also noted that these bombings were often linked to simultaneous explosions, also aimed at Spanish targets, in other European cities. As investigations proceeded, it was claimed that the bombers in question were the so-called 'International First of May Group', a spin-off of the Spanish anarchist movement. That assumption was shattered with the attack on Sir John Waldron. Not only did the senior Met man have no 'Spanish' connection, but for the first time the attack came accompanied by a communiqué. 'DEAR BOSS,' its hand-written capitals read, 'YOU HAVE BEEN SENTENCED TO DEATH BY THE REVOLUTIONARY TRIBUNAL FOR CRIMES OF OPPRESSION AGAINST MANY WHO ARE OPPOSED TO THE CAPITALIST REGIME WHICH YOU KEEP IN POWER. THE EXECUTIONER HAS BEEN SEVERELY REPRIMANDED FOR FAILING. HE WILL MAKE NO FURTHER MISTAKES. BUTCH CUSSEDLY THE SUNDANCE KID p.p. THE TRIBUNAL.' With its 'Just William' level of melodramatic prose, and its signature, a reference to a recently released hit movie, the message might have been written off as some kind of joke, had it not been accompanied by a very palpable bomb. The police were confused; perhaps it was some form of retaliation for the recent imprisonment of six Cambridge students for the 'Garden House Affair', when they had broken up a dinner honouring the Greek Colonels' repressive regime, and to the shock of those university authorities who had turned them over to the police, received not the expected slap on the wrist, but custodial sentences. When another bomb, this time targeting the Attorney-General, went off nine days later (this time the note – 'You can dream up all the law and order you like. But remember you are subject to OUR justice. He who liveth off the people – by the people shall he die' – was signed by another gang of movie cowpokes, 'The Wild Bunch') this seemed even more likely. Once again illusions were shattered by experience: attacks on the BBC van, on the Spanish Embassy (a 'drive-by' shooting) and on the Department of Employment and Productivity in St James's Square, seemed to have no real common theme.

The authorities were definitely worried. Desperate to hide their own confusion they imposed a press blackout, a move that was countered on 5 December 1970, when the underground paper *IT* received its own communiqué. It cited a number of attacks, railed against the blackout and was signed, for the first of what would be more than a dozen times, 'The Angry Brigade'. Quite where the name emerged remains debatable. The popular view suggests a loose translation of the French *Enragés*, with a nod to the International Brigades of Spain. Stuart Christie disagrees. In his memoirs he suggests that it was probably intended no more seriously than were the film references of the preceding communiqués; the difference was that, unlike them, it gained publicity and therefore stuck.[10] Certainly that 'Angry' does tend to trivialise the whole image. The real change came in the new year. On 12 January, a day on which thousands struck against the Industrial Relations Bill, two bombs exploded at the home of Robert Carr, its chief advocate. This time the 'straight' press were included in the mail-out: 'Robert Carr got it tonight. We're getting closer. Communique 4. The Angry Brigade.' The authorities' response was simple: the Brigade was, in the words of Home

Secretary Reginald Maudling and on the instructions of the Prime Minister Edward Heath, to be 'smashed'.

Led by DCI Roy Habershon, deputed to the task by his boss Commander Ernest Bond, the bomb squad began trawling their files, talking to the few contacts they had, and dragging in on one pretext or another a variety of 'usual suspects' on a series of 'fishing raids' (few of which were reported, and a number of which were only marginally legal). 'Faces' did not immediately materialise, although Bond, who had taken over the hunt in June 1971, the month of the attack on Ford's UK managing director, was not entirely without insight when he suggested that the Angry Brigade was not so much an identifiable group as an idea or philosophy. If you agreed with it then, *faut de mieux*, you were a 'member'. The aim of this philosophy, he added, taking his evidence from their targets and the tone of their communiqués, was an 'armed working-class revolution'.

There would be six more major explosions in 1971 before the Angry Brigade, or at least the eight people who would be charged with being the Brigade, were finally arrested. When police arrived at 359 Amhurst Road in Stoke Newington, they found Barker, Creek, Greenfield and Mendelson and arrested the lot. They also found a quantity of guns, explosives and reams of paper, covered in lists, what seemed to be plans for future attacks, and attempts at political pamphleteering. Perhaps most damning of all was the discovery of a John Bull Printing stamp, still bearing the incriminating words 'Angry Brigade'. Within forty-eight hours all eight had been grabbed and were facing lengthy interrogations.

Before their case began, there would be another, linked accusation to be dealt with. In February, in the wake of the Carr explosion, Jake Prescott, a petty criminal not long out of prison, was arrested in Notting Hill. He seemed to be drunk and was taken to the local police station; here he was found to be holding some cannabis and, more importantly, three presumably stolen cheque-books. Nothing special, and he was sent on remand to Brixton Prison. Here, however, matters altered when Prescott, it was alleged, began talking openly of his involvement with this revolutionary 'Angry Brigade', whose exploits were filling the papers. What he didn't realise was that his cellmate (later known as 'Prisoner A') was an informer; a second informer ('Prisoner B') would also materialise. 'A' was paraded in front of Habershon, who decided to take his allegations seriously. It was a major breakthrough. Habershon was able, via Prescott's address book, to get some much desired names. He was also, through a series of raids, notably that on a commune at 29 Grosvenor Avenue, Islington, to get his first real idea of the sort of world in which the Brigade seemed to move: a fluid circle of community activists, squatters and libertarians. Prescott denied any involvement in the bombings, but Habershon was unconvinced; he charged him with conspiracy to cause explosions. Prescott had also dropped enough names, notably the otherwise

unidentified 'Hilary', 'Chris' and 'John' to alert Habershon to further investigations. Among them was one Ian Purdie, who had recently shared another
cell with Prescott – in Albany Prison on the Isle of Wight. On 7 March he too was
arrested and charged with the same conspiracy.

The arrests of the alleged Angry Brigade on 20 August followed Habershon's dedicated analysis of what he could learn from Prescott and his pursuit of the leads that this unearthed. But the eight defendants of that trial
were still languishing on remand when Prescott and Purdie ('Jake' and 'Ian'
as the underground termed them) faced *their* trial in November 1971. By
now there were no doubts as to names. None of the Stoke Newington Eight
would appear, but their names appeared on Prescott's and Purdie's charge
sheet, and were frequently mentioned in court. (Such open identification of
individuals yet to be tried and thus still innocent in law might have seemed
somewhat injudicious, let alone *sub judice*. Indeed, at the very outset of their
trial, some of the eight defendants called for a two-year moratorium before
their trial so that such possibly adverse publicity might fade from public
memory; the motion was denied.) The Crown case rested chiefly on the evidence of Prescott's handwriting, found on three of the envelopes sent out
with communiqués after the Carr bombing. Purdie was seen as his evil mentor, a man heavily involved in the Brigade, and who had, during their joint
stay at Albany, indoctrinated the hitherto apolitical Prescott. As for links between him and the bombs, there were none and no evidence was offered that
altered that fact. It was unsurprising, therefore, when Purdie was acquitted
and Prescott convicted; less predictable, indeed wholly shocking, was Prescott's sentence: fifteen years' jail; five years, it was noted, per envelope. The
judge, the unashamedly right-wing Mr Justice Melford Stevenson, talked of
'an evil conspiracy' and suggested that Prescott had been 'chosen as a tool by
people more sinister than you'.[11]

The idea of an 'enemy within', of 'sinister forces massing behind the
scenes' dominated the atmosphere behind both trials. Typical was an *Evening
Standard* leader, in the aftermath of the first 'Angry Brigade trial'. Headlined,
'The red badge of revolution', it wilfully cranked up the paranoia:

> These guerrillas are the violent activists of a revolution comprising, workers,
> students, trade unionists, homosexuals, unemployed and women striving for
> liberation. They are all angry . . . Whenever you see a demonstration, when-
> ever you see a queue for strike pay, every public library with a good stock of
> socialist literature . . . anywhere would be a good place to look. In short there
> is no telling where they are.[12]

Aside from the Angry Brigade, London boasted one more group of urban
guerrillas in those last years of the decade, though they preferred pyschologi-
cal bombs. These, more a loose affiliation of like-minded souls than a cogent
group as such, took the name King Mob, an abbreviation of the graffito 'His

Majesty King Mob' which had been written on the walls of Newgate Prison, when it was burnt down by the insurgents during the Gordon Riots of 1790. For a 'subtitle' they preferred 'a street gang with analysis'. They had emerged from Heatwave, England's one group of accredited Situationists, whose perceived 'deviance' from the official SI line had soon seen their affiliation cut short. Heatwave was also heavily influenced by the American group Black Mask, supposedly real-life gangsters, toughened up in the prison system and now preaching revolution. Their credo elevated 'the Idiot/Madman/Guerrilla in life . . . the man without aims or prospects, the "lowest" of all, the shit of America'.[13] Black Mask, later reformed as Up Against the Wall Motherfuckers, specialised in disruptive actions: invading élite cultural events, releasing starving dogs into exclusive restaurants, 'trashing' the financial centre of Wall Street. Like Black Mask, if King Mob had any ideology it was nihilism, but like the Situationists, from whose ideas they drew some of their inspiration, they liked to mix action with sloganeering. And like the Situs they saw the need for a new take on revolution: 'Any strategy for the coming civil war has to abandon the assumptions of the old revolutionary movement, which has engendered such monsters. It has to find the weak links in the chain of modern repression, and fight the temptation to rejoin battle at the traditional points of confrontation: ideology and economic infrastructure. Capitalism's most intractable crisis in the advanced industrial states is the crisis of socialisation.'[14]

Their main target, the Establishment and its acolytes aside, was the orthodox Left, whether Old or New, and the posturing that they felt accompanied its humourless pronouncements. Such orthodox revolutionaries, in King Mob's opinion, were utterly spurious, and it was King Mob's genuinely revolutionary duty to undermine them. Thus, on the first march to Grosvenor Square, as the ranks of demonstrators intoned their chant of 'Ho, Ho, Ho Chi Minh!' up popped some of King Mob chanting derisively 'Hot chocolate, Drinking chocolate', a popular advertising catchphrase of the period. For King Mob nothing was too excessive. Bourgeois society was so repellent, how could one possibly outdo it. Thus the nihilists set on pedestals such hate-figures as Jack the Ripper, Mary Bell (the ten-year-old child killer) and John Reginald Christie: King Mob decorated his old house in Rillington Place, Notting Hill with the line 'Christie Lives!' (In a nice irony, on the night of the Carr bombing there was not a single senior policeman available to answer the hysterical calls for action: every one was off duty, at a special showing of the film of Christie's exploits, *10 Rillington Place*.)

Urged on by Chris Gray, best-known as the pro-Situ author of *Leaving the Twentieth Century* (1974), King Mob came up with a bizarre menu of possible actions, all designed to infuriate, enrage and above all disgust the bourgeoisie. A waterfall in the picturesque Lake District was to be dynamited and the slogan 'Peace in Vietnam' sprayed on the rubble; Wordsworth's house, a shrine for literary tourists, was to be blown up; in this case the caption would read 'Coleridge lives' (a tribute to the Romantics' opium-addicted genius); back in London they planned on hanging the much-loved peacocks of Holland Park ('Peacocks is dead'). Perhaps the most interesting was Gray's own contribution: the idea of the ultimate in repellent rock bands. No talent, no charm, a gob for every hand that fed them – how they'd coin the cash. Their main achievement, however, was rather less dramatic, although its benefits were much appreciated. King Mob opened up the hitherto fenced off Powis Square, in the heart of Notting Hill, establishing it as a children's playground. The attack was led by Dave Wise, a King Mob regular, clad in a gorilla suit. Children always benefited from King Mob. In what some see as their finest hour a team appeared in Selfridge's over Christmas 1968. Led by their own 'Santa Claus' they proceeded to hand out free gifts to the queuing children. The store called the police and the children were forced to return their presents.

It was also King Mob who saw to the decoration/desecration of Notting Hill with such slogans as 'The Tygers of Wrath are Wiser than the Horses of Instruction', 'The Road to Excess leads to the Palace of Wisdom' and 'Crime is the highest form of sensuality'; the Situs (borrowing largely from William Blake) may have thought them up, but King Mob wielded the spraycan. They were also far more drug-orientated than the rather strait-laced, if hard-drinking Situs. At the Notting Hill carnival of 1969 King Mob's float featured 'Miss Notting Hill', a junkie girl with a monstrous syringe attached to her arm. They also saw the commercial potential of 'illicit substances'. One former activist recalls:

> We had this idea to make funds by making drugs. I made a bunch of this drug called TMA, which at the time wasn't illegal. Its real name was Paramythoxyamphetamine: based on essence of aniseed. It was totally disastrous because nobody liked it except us. It was sort of like psychedelic methedrin – I'm not even sure that Ecstasy isn't the same thing, rediscovered fifteen years later. Very, very speedy . . . As a money-making scam it was a total waste of time, we never sold any of it at all. When you actually shot it up the rush made everything go black and white and the sky went like the set for a Wagner opera and you had this certainty that you were about to die but you didn't care. This didn't exactly endear it to the punters in Notting Hill Gate.[15]

King Mob faded, leaving the revolutionary field to more serious, if less inventive people. They did, however, have one lasting effect: knocking down fences and similar hands-on community activities appealed greatly to activist students, and *King Mob Echo*, their paper, was popular in both Cambridge and Essex. Thus the scene in Notting Hill drew together a number of such students, among them John Barker and Jim Greenfield, both fresh out of college and keen to see what King Mob was up to and perhaps join in. In the event they moved on, unimpressed by what they dismissed as a trivial, compromised scene, setting up a new home in Manchester. That self-imposed exile would lead to their involvement in Claimants' Unions and a meeting with Hilary Creek, Kate McLean and Chris Bott, all of whom were living temporarily in the city. Others saw the link as even more binding: for the King Mob stalwarts Dave and Stuart Wise, writing in their pamphlet 'The End of Music', the Brigade *is*, to all intents, a spinoff of King Mob. As George Robertson has suggested, Barker and Greenfield, who in Cambridge had founded the Kim Philby Dining Club (named for the spy whose efforts at undermining British society seemed to epitomise all that they admired), 'took seriously these words of Vaneigem: "From this moment, despair ends and tactics begin. Despair is the infantile disorder of the revolutionaries of everyday life." These 'revolutionaries of everyday life' became the Angry Brigade.'[16] A version of that same Vaneigem quote would appear in the Communiqué ('The Brigade Is Angry') that accompanied the Bryant bombing in October 1971.

As 1972 passed by those 'sinister' people, the butt of Melford Stevenson's judicial wit and the absentee co-defendants at the Prescott-Purdie trial, were in Brixton and in Holloway awaiting their own tussle with the law. On 30 May, the trial began. The complexities of the case, which would last for six months and run to some three million words of transcript, require more space than is available for an exhaustive rehearsal here. They hinged variously on forensic expertise, on the possibility – fiercely attested by the defendants, equally fiercely rejected by those officers concerned – that the weapons and explosives had been planted and that supposedly damaging statements by the defendants had been made up (as well as whether or not Barker and Greenfield had been beaten up shortly after their arrests), and on whether the trial was merely criminal, as the prosecution suggested, or whether it was, as the defendants averred, a political clash, one more aspect of the class warfare that dominates English life. It was this, claims Stuart Christie, that made it so vital to vet the jury: 'The case revolved around our politics and the nature of class justice. We were not prepared to disown the Angry Brigade [throughout his memoirs he maintains the absolute innocence of all eight accused], which was doing something, however small, to fight back against repression. On the other hand we didn't want to take the responsibility for actions carried out by others, just because we happened to be the ones who were picked up.'[17] Finally, and perhaps most important of all, there was one question: whether the eight accused really did make up 'the Angry Brigade'. In all, the 'central issue' of the trial, as the *Sunday Times*'s Tony Geraghty put it, 'was one of integrity: police integrity, integrity of forensic science, even the integrity of the counsel in the case.'[18] And above all, it might be added, of the eight people in the dock.

Given that in no case was a single defendant positively tied to any of the explosions, but that a large amount of 'bomb-making equipment' had undoubtedly been removed (planted or not) from Amhurst Road, forensic evidence was at the heart of proceedings. For the police, there was the sheer weight of material. All in all the jury would be shown 688 items, ranging from a Beretta sub-machine gun to 'an unidentified substance from foot of tree in garden rear of door'; they included letters, batteries, political literature, a vehicle licensing application, a cache of gelignite, the detonators to ignite it, address books, letters, counterfeit US dollars, Angry Brigade communiqués and much more. If quantity and circumstance were all, the police seemed on solid ground. But as the rival experts went through their paces, cracks appeared. In the first place none of the weapons or explosives had a single identifiable fingerprint; in the second none of those arrested tested positive for traces of the explosives; nor did their clothes. Given that a trace of nitroglycerine can survive on a person's hands for seventeen hours (and this despite six washings of those hands) there were absolutely no traces. This hardly gibed with the prosecution's claim that the explosives had arrived in the flat, fresh off the Boulogne ferry, just one day before. It was with this in mind that the four Amhurst Road defendants pushed so hard to embed the theory that the police had arrived *with* their incriminating booty. In the event they would fail: in bringing a conviction the jury had presumably discarded such pleas. But a paradox remained: Stuart Christie, an avowed anarchist and the one alleged member to have actually served time for political activity – he had been jailed in Spain for his involvement in an attempt to assassinate the fascist dictator Francisco Franco – was not convicted. Yet, so the police attested, in the boot of his car were found several detonators. He too claimed that they had been planted, and this time, in finding him not guilty, the jury must have agreed. But as Neil Ascherson and Colin Smith put it in a piece for the *Observer*, 'far more questions were raised during the . . . trial than were ever answered.'[19] This remains one of them.

Summing up the case the Judge, Mr Justice James, made it absolutely clear that in his opinion: 'This is not a political trial. Political trials are of people for their political beliefs which happen to be contrary to those in government . . . We do not have them in this country.'[20] If this was his belief, then it was most likely his alone. And even he seemed, in a trial which all but the most hard-nosed agreed had been administered with a minimum of prejudice or judicial interference, to make some acknowledgement of what others perceived. In what was a very rare instance in a British court, he permitted the polling of the jury by the defence. The grounds on which this was conducted – no middle-classes, no members of the Tory party, no links to anyone who might be judged a potential 'Angry Brigade target' – ensured that the 200-strong panel would be whittled down to a staunchly working-class dozen. The defendants had no doubt that theirs was a wholly political trial, their hope was that at least they had engineered a jury who might understand them. Mr Justice James showed himself to be scrupulously fair; if anything he erred to liberality. He helped the three defendants who represented themselves (his allowing their lengthy cross-examinations was one of the main causes of the protracted trial), he permitted them their 'Mackenzie' lawyers (legally knowledgeable but unqualified 'amateur lawyers' who were allowed to appear alongside their friends), perhaps most significantly, he allowed a good deal of 'politics' to enter both cross-examination and personal statements. He was also strict in adjuring the court that whatever they might feel about the defendants' 'communal' lifestyle it was totally irrelevant as regarded their culpability or otherwise. Later all the defendants would comment publicly on his fairness. The police, at whatever level of seniority, may have been unabashed in their hostility, but the judge was not the problem.

That there was a trial at all was, to the defendants, the real issue. To them, as they would all attempt to prove, the reason for their being in court, rather than some other group, was that the Establishment was frightened, and that in the 'smashing' of the Angry Brigade any means were justified. Certainly the police had not bothered over-much when it came to arrest or search warrants, the granting of access to solicitors, or the odd thump when no one who might care was watching. Commander Bond, whose refusal to unveil himself during the search for the bombers had delighted the press, which promptly christened him 'Commander X', suggested that, 'I cannot see how getting innocent people arrested is going to help stop the bombing.' In other words, we've caught them, they must be guilty.[21] It is hard to see how he would reconcile this assurance with those bombings that followed immediately on the arrests. Within a very few years the police would be steam-rollering through the trials of a variety of alleged IRA bombers, using very similar tactics. The arrests, interrogations, trials and sentencing of the Guildford Four or Birmingham Six (all of whom would come to be declared victims of deliberately miscarried justice) come from much the same mindset. The need to act, the pressure from political masters and professional superiors, the cavalier attitude with raids and 'verbals' (the record of the police/prisoner conversations), the arrests of people whose actual involvement could not be proved – all factors that link the hunt for and the trial of the Angry Brigade to these IRA-related successors. Nor should one overlook the most telling development: the same forensics experts whose evidence was found to be so overwhelmingly flawed in the reassessment of those later trials, had (despite staunch opposition from a professional rival called by the defence) worked to convict the Amhurst foursome.

Looking at all accounts of the Brigade, one cannot avoid a feeling of frustration: for all the 688 exhibits, for all the three million words of transcript, the story doesn't hold properly together. One minute there is an entity, otherwise unidentifiable, that terms itself the Angry Brigade: they plant bombs, they send communiqués. Then, at an address in north-east London, four people, admittedly far to the left of the average, admittedly involved with what are seen as 'extremist' attitudes and individuals, but in no way whatsoever proven terrorists, are raided, charged and suddenly they and no others *are* the Angry Brigade. They are, as the police say, 'in the frame'. And yet there is no evidence finally to tie one to the other.

If one trusts the defendants, while they admitted to knowing the Brigade (or at least the two members whom they claimed had visited their flat, but whose names would never be revealed), they were not the Brigade itself, merely members of some form of unspecified outer circle, fellow-travellers, perhaps, but hardly in the front line. After the trial, as the media, which had remained silent on the bulk of its six-month progress, sought to pin down just who they were and what had happened, there were attempts to link the Brigade to some form of identifiable political grouping. Yet for all the efforts, it didn't work. One could see, from John Barker's masterly summing up of his position – worthy, said watching lawyers, of a top-rank QC and a political apologia by any name – where, as the idiom had it, they were 'coming from', but where, one might ask, were they going? While the 'Brigade' may have flirted with student uprisings, with trips to Paris in May '68, with Claimants' Unions and what they termed 'counter-sociology' (the sociological study of an upper-middle-class area, in this case Kensington), but there were no useful, easily categorised tie-ins to the usual Marxist or Trotskyite groups. Indeed, one of the Defence Committee's main complaints was the way in which the 'proper' Left ignored the trial. The resentment of the orthodox, it would appear, was as much territorial as ideological. Guerrilla activities in the Third World were admirable; those in the London suburbs, it turned out, were 'fascist propaganda'. The Left couldn't face a couple of simple facts: they weren't leading the 'revolution' and, worse still, they hadn't a clue who was. The 'underground' on the other hand was very keen, but the 'underground' was hardly a viable political creature. The nearest the defendants came to self-categorisation was the phrase 'libertarian revolutionaries', but that, were one to exclude the explosions, could have gone for most of the 'underground'. The press preferred 'anarchists', with its overtones of bearded, be-cloaked figures tossing fizzing bombs at the upper classes, but other than in the case of the undeniably anarchist Stuart Christie, whom the police tried hard to brand the evil genius behind the whole campaign, that failed too. And Christie, after all, was found innocent. The one group to whom they might have been tied were the Situationists: the term 'spectacle', used in a communiqué, was the first alert to the police that they might be dealing with far-left politics and Situ-originated phraseology bespattered Brigade communications. But however much its tenets may have influenced the defendants in the longer term, 'Situationism' does not play a role in the trial. If any of Vaneigem's empty

'–isms' is pertinent, it was 'anarchism' that was the focus of courtroom debate.

Nor did their backgrounds offer any particular clue. John Barker, aged twenty-three, who would be categorised as 'the ideologue', and undoubtedly the brightest of the four, was the son of a North London journalist. Working-class, he was drawn to orthodox Labour politics, canvassing during the 1964 election. But Labour in office was a grave disappointment and Harold Wilson a trimmer. Student life at Cambridge was no better. Like James Greenfield, the son of a lorry-driver and another bright schoolboy, he found it class-ridden and anachronistic. The pair met, and together they mounted a number of political plays. In London they began running a bookstall in Camden Market before moving on to take part in a variety of activist groups. Their main interests were in the nascent squatting scene, and in Claimants' Unions.

Anna Mendelson, then twenty-four, had been born into a politically active family in Stockport; her father was a Labour councillor and the family had come over as refugees from Russia. She arrived at Essex University in 1967 to read comparative studies, including sociology and politics, but she was yet another who found university unrewarding. She was asked to leave. By 1970 she was a mainstay of a variety of community action and protest movements in London. Hilary Creek, who was twenty-three, was the bourgeoise of the party. She had met Mendelson at Essex and, like her, was an active feminist and politician. And like her too, she was asked to leave the university: both girls had fallen too far behind in their neglected studies. They had lasted long enough, however, to take part in the occupations of 1969, an exciting period and a formative one. A daughter of the Home Counties, she alone had some sort of private income, which was used by the group for communal purchases.

Amongst the four who would be found not guilty, the 'makeweights' as Christie calls them, one sees similar situations. Christopher Bott, something of a political firebrand at Essex, where he was a graduate student, stayed only one year before failing his examinations and leaving. Kate McLean, another member of the middle-class (but with radical credentials: her father had fought with the International Brigades in Spain), had failed to gain a university place. Instead she spent a year at art school and then moved from Kent to London where she immersed herself in Women's Liberation. Angie Weir was the academic highflier, with degrees from Bedford College, Cambridge and the LSE. A lesbian, she had been involved in Gay Liberation since its early days. Only Stuart Christie, the genuine revolutionary with jail time to prove it, differed from the rest. Otherwise they would hardly stand out from the great mass of their leftish, self-declaredly radical contemporaries or seem any more likely than the next rebellious young person to pick up the bomb and gun. Yet, it was alleged, that's just what they did, even if Paul Lewis, then editor of *IT*, and an early recipent of communiqués, gave this dismissive analysis: 'Nobody can say who or what they are. But there are plenty of people who are potential Angry Brigade material. Basically they are concerned with lifestyle rather than philosophy or theory. They are freaks getting together to combat capitalist oppression: people who have tried to drop out and found nowhere to go.'[22]

A decade later Stuart Christie suggested that,

> It seemed that ... a lot of the left who wanted to participate in what was clearly a revolt against conformism and the accepted rules of the political game were joining in: the manifestos accompanied fresh attacks but they were not necessarily coming from the same people. It was this that made the police task of solving the problem well nigh impossible, and drove them into agitated confusion; they were trying to find an organisation that did not exist, and in furtherance of whose cause different people were acting both legally (for there is nothing criminal in drafting a manifesto, even for the Angry Brigade) and illegally. Not only this but the massive police action was rapidly fanning the flames of discontent among a wider section of the left. Even people who thought it was all going a bit too far didn't like being turned over for nothing.[23]

With or without a proven ideology, it was vital for the police to conjure up some unifying factor. Other than the physical proximity of four people in a flat and another four who had been found trying to pay them a visit this had proved hard. The catch-all embrace of a 'conspiracy charge' (similarly levelled at the *Oz* defendants) suited the situation perfectly. For the jury to bring a guilty plea they had simply to believe – on the evidence – that there had been one large conspiracy to cause explosions. They might not accept that every one of the cited twenty-five explosions were relevant, nor that all the defendants were involved in all the attacks, but no matter: as long as two or more defendants could be seen as involved, and a number of the explosions linked, then that was good enough. As the defence counsel Ian MacDonald put it, it seemed that if the Crown, having failed to make all the links required to prove a conspiracy, was now back-pedalling: maybe they couldn't link every explosion – but apparently it no longer mattered. In the ends of a conviction, any combination would do.

Later, during his lengthy summing up (250,000 words in itself), the judge returned to the topic. The law, as he expounded it (and there would be no successful appeal), was remarkably wide-ranging: 'As long as you know what the agreement is, then you are a conspirator. You needn't necessarily know your fellow conspirators, nor need you be always active in the conspiracy. All you need to know is the agreement. It can be effected by a wink or a nod, without a word being exchanged. It need have no particular time limit, no particular form, no boundaries.'[24] As far as the charges went, all eight were charged with all twenty-five bombings. If all could be proved, so much the better for the prosecution. But even if they could prove only that there had been a single agreement to which each of the defendants had been party, for any period of the three-and-a-half years under consideration (from January 1968 to August 1971), then that made them just as guilty. This was further complicated by an additional fact: had there been more than one agreement to conspire during that same period (the defence claimed that there had been six separate ones) then these defendants were not guilty as charged.

The jury were out for thirty hours before returning to inform the judge that try as they might, they could not reach a unanimous verdict. 'Having regards as to the passage of time,' he told the foreman, 'I am prepared to accept a majority verdict.' At five o'clock on the evening of 6 December they returned. Four of the accused – Barker, Greenfield, Mendelson and Creek – were found guilty of the major charge, conspiring to cause explosions for the entire 44-month period. The others were to go free. The foreman added a rider: the jury had requested 'I believe the word is leniency or clemency'.[25] Later it would transpire that the verdict had been very much a compromise. Two jurors, the hold-outs, made it clear that they were utterly opposed to conviction; three more were definitely sympathetic, the remaining seven wanted to convict the lot, on all charges. The eventual verdict, including the plea for clemency, was a deal engineered by the foreman. It had taken him 52 hours.

In giving his verdict the judge continued to demonstrate his impartiality. He threw out the first fifteen incidents, in other words those that preceded the first 'Angry Brigade' communiqué, and dealt only with the last ten. This obviously focused on those in which prejudicial evidence was strongest, but it also reduced the extent of the conspiracy. He noted that they had not set out to kill or maim (though one person was injured by a bomb and others undoubtedly might have been) and that had they desired they could have been far more ruthless; he resisted the usual lecture from the bench and regretted seeing 'such educated people' in their situation; he did however put down their ideas – based on their objection to an 'orderly way of society' – as the fruit of a 'warped understanding of sociology'; he acknowledged that they had 'sought to do good' in many of their non-Brigade activities, and, acknowledging the jury's recommendation, reduced the sentences from a potential maximum of 15 years to that of ten. A number of concurrent sentences – for possession of explosives and of the various weapons – were then handed out. Mendelson, Barker and Creek all thanked those members of the jury 'who had faith in us' as they were taken down. It was noted, however, that the problem of linking the supposed 'Brigade' to the bombs remained unresolved: in no case was any of them found guilty of actually committing explosions.

The press, who had found better things to occupy their readers as the lengthy process dragged on, notably the peculations of the Home Secretary Reginald Maudling, swarmed to offer their own version of events. The pops reached their apogee in the *Sun*, which claimed that the Brigade's next 'job' was the kidnapping of Lord Hailsham, and re-created a supposed 'conversation' between one member and a Belfast Provo (' "F—off!" a Provisional

IRA chief told him, "F—off, nigger-lover!" '). The paper also regaled its readers with a glorious (if sadly spurious) account of what they termed 'Sex orgies at the cottage of blood', a tale of 'sinister goings-on' at a small cottage in Wivenhoe, Essex. It was here that the Amhurst foursome were wont to congregate 'for drugs, and conspiracies and sex. Most revolting of all their activities was the ritual slaughter. Turkeys stolen from a local farm were torn and slashed to pieces. Afterwards the revellers, drunk and exhausted, collapsed on the kitchen floor to sleep off their orgy in a ghastly mess of blood and fragmented flesh.' A next door neighbour talked of 'sacrifices', and the local publican of 'Communists'; his wife, inadvertently, came a little nearer to what had been happening: they were, she explained, 'a real wild bunch'.[26]

The heavies acted predictably. The liberals wondered why such bright young people seemed so alienated, the conservatives rejoiced that once more all was right with their world. The anomaly was the *Guardian* who decided, belying its 'liberal' image, that the Brigade were 'polyannas' who had no right to sully that fine word 'revolution'. The acquittal of four, far from the actual fudge that it had been, was lauded as a tribute to the jury's absolute fairness; they had resisted, despite all temptations to the contrary, to consider that long hair and communal living represented *de facto* the gateway to hell. The judge was exemplary and as for the police, well, hadn't the peerless Commander Bond said that they would hardly be going around arresting the innocent. And from them all came a faint sense of disappointment, of Romans cheated of their bloodthirsty spectacle. Only one injury, no deaths: it was all very amateur compared with 'proper' revolutionaries. Fortunately for the front pages the IRA would be remedying that shortfall all too soon.

Creek and Mendelson both served less than five years. Prison life undermined each woman's health and they were freed before the damage became irreparable. Barker and Greenfield served their entire sentence, with remission: they were freed in 1978. Prescott, who received the longest sentence of all (although it would be reduced in line with the Brigade's ten-stretch), emerged twelve months later. In 1985 Barker and Greenfield joined a couple of Israelis, quite possibly renegade Mossad agents, in a massive dope deal. It failed and Greenfield was jailed for six years. Barker managed to escape but in 1990 was recaptured trying to enter England on a false passport.

As for the Angry Brigade, if 'smashed' meant no more bombings, then 'smashed' it was. (That said, the chronology that runs through Tom Vague's study *Anarchy in the UK* offers a number of explosions, continuing through 1972 and beyond.) The emotions that informed the Brigade did not die, but for all that there were 'Angry Brigade Resistance Movement' communiqués dispatched to the Tory party in both 1983 and 1984, it would be hard to see an extensive legacy of urban guerrilla activity running on through the eighteen years of Conservative rule. The most notable example was the emergence of Class War in the mid-Eighties, loudly touted as the return of 'anarchism' to Britain's peaceful shores. Its main orientation was 'Bash the rich', and it made some headlines in its efforts to do so. But Class War, for all that it briefly excited the more impressionable media, was the most minuscule of phenomena. By 1987 it had all but vanished. Given the infinitely harder-line positions taken by the Thatcher and Major governments than had ever been espoused by Edward Heath, one might ask why was the 'revolution' so muted? Perhaps the state had improved the machinery of repression, perhaps the press were more effectively muzzled in their reporting of what did happen. And in the end perhaps it was simply chronology: above all the Brigade was of its era, the Sixties. The right place, the right time, the right opportunity. Only one question remains, was it also the right people?

Chapter Twenty-Three

Black Power: RAAS

In the heyday of the whole Black Power movement when people had started taking Michael serious, somebody called a meeting with him – some MPs, people high up in society – to discuss what they can do about the problem. And everybody had an idea and gave a speech and everything and Michael was quiet as usual and sitting at the end of the table and they asked, 'Well Michael, what do you think will solve the problem?' And he pulled his beard and then he says, 'I think that the way we going to solve this problem is that a black man fucks the Queen and they have a half-caste child,' and everybody started to choke on their brandies and the dessert came out of their mouth and the whole thing came to a close.
Horace Ové, film-maker and friend of Michael Abdul Malik[1]

In 'revolution' as in other areas, the Sixties remain essentially monochrome: rock 'n' roll may have started off black, white-boy blues bands yearned to be black, and large parts of the much-emulated American culture had been rooted in black, but the individuals were primarily white. Immigration had been going on for centuries, but even with the surge in arrivals over the Fifties, England, and even London, remained white. But in imitating so much else of American life, it was inevitable that England's far smaller black community would emulate a central aspect of the American 'revolution'. This was Black Power, a concept minted by Stokeley Carmichael, and propounded in their various ways by such figures as Malcolm X, the Black Panthers, Elijah Muhammad's Nation of Islam and even Martin Luther King. Its implications were spreading around the world's black ghettos. London would be no exception.

After the Second World War successive governments began looking outside England for new workers to help the steadily improving economy of the 1950s, which could no longer be serviced by the indigenous population. They began recruiting in the Commonwealth, notably in the islands of the West Indies, and found that the black populations were more than willing to make the journey. England was 'the mother country', many of them spoke its language, worshipped in the same church, experienced a similar education. At home the population was increasing, and with it the levels of unemployment and poverty. England beckoned and the boat-trains began arriving from Southampton, disgorging their passengers, many still in the summer clothes in which they had left home, on to the platforms of Victoria Station, where some, undoubtedly, would soon be at work. The flow of West Indians was still restricted until 1953, but thereafter it increased dramatically, governed directly by Britain's labour needs, reaching its first peak in 1956, slowing slightly for the next three years, then taking off again from 1959. In 1954

10,000 people arrived, 24,000 a year later, and 26,000 in 1956. By 1959 36,000 more had arrived. In 1961, a second peak, some 75,000 made the trip. Concentrated in London, they began carving out their own centres: north of the river around Notting Hill, Paddington and North Kensington, south in Brixton and Stockwell. At the same time enclaves developed in all the major provincial cities. The government, keen to house its new labour force, created a new breed of landlord, usually white, whose substantial incomes depended directly on putting the often rickety roofs over the heads of these new ghetto-dwellers. Whatever one's qualifications back home, much the same jobs were on offer. In fairness many immigrants were merely swapping one labouring job for another (at a higher rate), but those with higher aspirations and qualifications fared no better, forced to take menial jobs, manual labour, some work in hospitals (as porters and orderlies), on London Transport and in the Post Office. The immigrants were predominantly male, although the flow of women and children slowly increased as more men became established and sent for their families. These women also worked in hospitals (but as nurses) as well as in the service industries.

The first white versus black race riots had occurred as early as 1919 in Cardiff, Liverpool and a number of other ports where there existed a noticeable black population. They were allegedly inspired by white working-class fears that immigrant blacks, recruited during the First World War, were taking their jobs. New outbreaks followed the next war, notably in Birmingham, Liverpool and Deptford. In 1954 there were two days of racial warfare on the streets of Camden Town. Hostilities sputtered on through the Fifties – for many immigrants their first experience was the landlady's defiant proclamation: 'No Blacks' – until August 1958, when riots in the Chase, the black centre of Nottingham, and across parts of West London (notably the run-down Notting Dale area) made racial disturbance into a national preoccupation.

Race would never retreat far from the front pages. Racism, that 'safe hatred' as Colin MacInnes put it, was and remains an integral part of the nation's culture. For those who cherish such fantasies, the decline of an Empire where 'natives' supposedly 'knew their place' has been made even more bitterly poignant by the arrival in England of those same natives, hell-bent on equality. Tougher immigration controls appeared in 1962 and 1968, limiting the influx of foreign workers, but the mood of the Sixties was fundamentally liberal, offering a degree of new racial self-awareness to the coloured, and particularly the black community. England's blacks echoed their counterparts in America with calls for the raising of black consciousness and the setting up of indigenous black institutions. A new generation of blacks began to emerge: the children of the original 'newcomers'. Their parents had used a passport to assert their rights of entry, these children needed only their birth certificate.

For Miles, 'The hip society in Notting Hill in those days was basically very involved with the West Indians. They were the only people around who had good music, they knew all about jazz and ska and bluebeat. They also smoked rather good dope. That was the classic excuse in court in those days, if anyone got busted: "Where did you get it from?" "I bought it from a black man in Notting Hill." And the magistrate agreed: "How can you possibly ever recognise them again, they all look the same." "[2] For those who knew, and those included Mayfair slummers as well as Notting Hill's embryonic hippies, the Rio on Westbourne Grove was the place to score. In you went, white boy or girl on black man's territory; down the stairs and round the back through a grimy basement replicated ten thousand times within half a mile, and eventually out would emerge some guy, take your thirty shillings (£1.50) and hand over a newspaper-wrapped bundle of grass. The Rio was all things to all men.

Among those who used it was the one individual who was (and for many remains) synonymous with the concept of Black Power in its UK context: a former Trinidadian sailor, born half black, half Portugese and an exile in London since his arrival in 1958, Michael de Freitas. In 1965, when he began to move into the limelight, acquiring the image that would, for a while, make him the darling of the capital's liberal establishment and the ever-vocal figurehead of black rebellion in the city, he was busy remaking himself for the delectation of his new audience. But for those who knew him around 'the Gate' and 'the Grove', the Black saviour was somewhat less appealing. The de Freitas of the late Fifties had moved in the world of hustling and small-time gangsterism, most notoriously as an enforcer for the area's major landlord Peter Rachman, like de Freitas a refugee in England. Rachman, whose friendship with Mandy Rice-Davies and Christine Keeler would make him one of the central figures in the Profumo Affair, has become a full-time bad guy in Sixties mythology. In truth he was probably no worse than many of his peers, but his involvement with the sordid evasions of the Profumo scandal damned him then and forever. Like Stephen Ward he was a necessary scapegoat. He had his defenders, but for most people his flats were squalid, their rents high, his treatment of those who attempted to stand in his way either violent or criminal. He was an extortionist and a pimp. Yet he fulfilled a role that had been sanctioned by a government who, desperate to import the immigrant labour it needed, was less keen on following up what became of these 'newcomers'.

Michael de Freitas, who joined Rachman's band of rent-collectors soon after his arrival in London in 1958, was similarly vilified, but once again, by no means universally. Like Rachman he had a job to do, and not everyone in the black community found him so reprehensible. The film-maker and photographer Horace Ové, who took the pictures for de Freitas's 1968 autobiography, appreciated the realities:

Now he's branded as a gangster, but in those days it was hard hustle to survive. There was no black power, there wasn't anything, everybody was out there hustling. Michael was used as a sort of heavy to sort of get people to pay up. But also the government had created a huge avenue for Rachman to move into. Because nobody wanted to house all these black workers that they'd brought over from the Caribbean to do the dirty work for them; nobody wanted to put them up. So Rachman provided very cheap, dirty sort of housing in the most down-beaten areas that you can find and charged a lot of rent. He exploited the situation: people were living in shit. But at the same time that Michael was getting people to pay their rent, he was part of the community, he knew the community, he was a spokesman for it, and he was brave enough to stand up for it. So when the race riots took place and blacks were getting beaten up, Michael was the one who organised and went to the police station and said, 'Listen, if you don't stop this shit, we'll put a stop to it and we'll fight back!'[3]

The tranformation of hustler to community hero was hardly novel. Malcolm X, born Malcolm Little, was the exemplar, transforming himself from pimp and hood to liberation saviour. Michael de Freitas, who by the mid-Sixties had rechristened himself Michael Abdul Malik and would go on to mimic Malcolm with his final apotheosis as Michael X (gullible journalists liked to believe his claim that they were related) was of an identical mould. Of all the blacks who found some degree of common interests with the counter-culture he would be the most important, the most active and ultimately the most manipulative and alienating. If on his best days he seemed the living bridge between the two worlds, then by the end he did as much as anyone to demolish it.

Black-white relations had started, perhaps inevitably, through drugs – even if what for blacks was essentially a form of relaxation had been upgraded to a noble badge of rebellion in white hands. Places like the Rio provided a crossover point, with both parties meeting for mutual benefit. Thirty years on it's easy to decry the relationship: romantic white bourgeois weaned on beatnik fantasies encounters black hustlers who need an 'in' to the larger world, but at the time there did seem to be a genuine meeting of interests. Much of it was predicated by fantasy: the white boys saw themselves as rebels and assumed that the blacks, many of whom were utterly respectable, aspirant figures, whether or not they smoked the occasional spliff, were of their number. The world was to be changed through a happy combination of sex and dope and music (though one can't deny the implicit racism, however subconscious: the happy, laughing darkie of old, but with a gun and a joint). For the West Indians the charm of the counter-culture, in a world in which so many doors were closed to them, was its openness. These were whites who seemed friendly. The initial bond may have been marijuana, but for a while there would be more.

This meeting of minds was further developed in December 1964 with the founding of CARD, the Campaign Against Racial Discrimination; it was inspired by the recent visit of Martin Luther King to the UK. Two months later, in February 1965, CARD was replaced in the popular consciousness by another black 'liberation' organisation: RAAS, the 'Racial Adjustment Action Society'. A harder-edged organisation, with minimal if any white input, this too followed the visit of a major US figure, this time Malcolm X. It was the brainchild of Michael de Freitas. At some time de Freitas must have realised that in this over-lapping world of middle-class 'drop-outs' and working-class blacks lay an environment in which a good hustler could undoubtedly profit. And as Frank Critchlow, owner first of the Rio and then of the Mangrove Restaurant which succeeded it, had noted, Michael wasn't just a hustler, he had to be the biggest of all hustlers.[4] He wanted nothing less than to be the most famous black man in the country. His celebrity began with a lengthy piece in the *Observer*, detailing the creation of RAAS. As one journalist remarked later to V.S. Naipaul, 'Michael took the press for a ride and vice-versa. And out of it grew a monster'[5] – never more so than in this piece, which reported enthusiastically on this militant black organisation, with its alleged 4,500 members (sometimes the figure aggrandised to 45,000 – in truth there were rarely as many as 200), which had been put together, 'in near-secrecy' by de Freitas and which, according to the writer, combined 'revolutionary fervour . . . formidable professionalism . . . [and] underground technique . . .' Finances had apparently come from the leader's own pockets, while his volunteer helpers, 'in the best revolutionary tradition', accepted only a pittance in return for their efforts. De Freitas himself was 'a shy, gentle and highly intelligent man . . . the authentic voice of black bitterness.'[6]

RAAS lasted until 1970, eliciting a string of adulatory pieces. Writing, once more in the *Observer*, Colin Smith came out with a similarly positive account; the main difference was that de Freitas was now Michael Abdul Malik, 'perhaps better known as Michael X', the self-styled 'Chief Servant' of the Society. Smith focused on the Black House, a building in Holloway Road that had housed RAAS since early 1969:

> At the moment it is a maze of passageways and interconnecting rooms like a badly designed hotel. The conversion work has been done by volunteer labour, and this sometimes shows . . . But the brothers and sisters of the Society (everybody is brother or sister and goes in peace) are happy with their work and have already produced a well-illustrated brochure showing what everything is going to be like . . . As befits the Chief Servant . . . his office . . . is an impressive affair. New desk, big and wide. Three telephones. Comfy chairs for visitors. Spears, masks and other tribal bric-a-brac around the walls and in a book case, an iron slave collar . . . Mr Malik, in rust-coloured silk shirt and high-buttoned dark suit, said he hoped we weren't going to write a spectacular story full of urban guerrilla warfare and such nonsense. A moment later the

telephone rang and he was busy explaining to somebody that people from Birmingham and Manchester had asked him to become military head of the organisation, but that he had declined their offer because such posts were completely unsuited for guerrilla warfare. He talked about the rules of his society. 'No fornicating. No white girls here, just our own women. No card playing. No shooting dice. No going into betting shops. No drugs. No alcohol.' Instead there are lessons in African language and history.[7]

It was an idyllic picture, and while Smith might be ridiculed as gullible, he was hardly alone. The underground press, in particular, was swamped with pro-Michael pieces. *Friends* offered a lengthy interview ('I've heard myself described as a gangster. Well . . . it is possible that I am a gangster. I've seen myself described . . . as a thief. I have to provide for a number of people, for their very special needs . . . needs that black people will have in a hostile environment. And it is necessary for me at times to steal some of the things we want . . . ')[8] with nary a doubting syllable; *Oz* gave him ample houseroom. The Establishment was equally welcoming. Colin MacInnes proved especially useful. The author of *City of Spades* (and the lover when possible of gay black 'rough trade'), and one of the best-known whites in the black community, he was one of the few whites who seemed capable of crossing the wall that inevitably separated the two worlds in the aftermath of the 1958 Notting Dale race riots that shattered the superficial harmony of his West London 'Napoli'. After those riots MacInnes had joined the jazz critic Max Jones, publicist Les Perrin, 'Francis Newton' (the pseudonym the historian Eric Hobsbawm used for his jazz column in the *New Statesman*) plus such stars as Humphrey Lyttleton, Cleo Laine, Johnny Dankworth, Tommy Steele and Lonnie Donegan in the Stars' Campaign for Interracial Friendship. The campaign was short-lived: there was perhaps one month of laudatory coverage (although the local *Kensington News* asked 'Will Too Many Do-Gooders Pave the Path to Notting HELL?') and one of decline. They managed a multi-racial Christmas party, but that was it. MacInnes, unlike his showbiz colleagues, took it all very seriously. If nothing else he managed to raise some decent cheques.

By 1965 MacInnes had established himself not merely as 'the best off-beat journalist in London'[9] but, more importantly, one of the most consistently outspoken advocates of racial harmony, especially between West Indians and whites. Thus his decision to take Michael seriously, whether in a piece in the *New Statesman* in 1967 or a major interview-analysis in *Encounter* (where he had recently written in depth about James Baldwin) in 1965, influenced the larger world of white liberals. To him Michael had certainly been a hustler, but then so had Malcolm X. Michael, on perhaps a smaller stage, had the same potential. 'Is Michael a racialist?' he asked, and answered with proper liberal self-abasement, 'What . . . he hates is what we do, not what we are.'[10] For MacInnes, quoting from James Baldwin's grimly prophetic essay *The*

Fire Next Time, England's race problem was what mattered; Michael X might not be the agent one would have chosen, but he was the one that had emerged. What was vital was change, and if this reinvented enforcer, pimp and thug was at its heart, then MacInnes was not about to pronounce a premature judgement on what might be a genuine potential for good. MacInnes also represented the white world on another Malik organisation: Defence, formed in 1966 as a counter to increasing police hostility in Notting Hill. Its laudable aim was to help blacks through the maze of the British legal system; its failure was that once set up and publicised, no one, however enthusiastic, could quite turn their hand to the tedious practicalities.

The problem was that for all the hope that a figure like Michael could conjure up, he didn't deliver. As Tony Gould, MacInnes's biographer, noted, Malik was a creature of the media: 'he struck the right poses and the newspapers did the rest.'[11] The name RAAS was a perfect example. Writing in his ghosted autobiography *From Michael de Freitas to Michael X* (1968) Malik dignified it:

> We eventually came up with Racial Adjustment Action Society, whose initials form the word RAAS. This abbreviation has great appeal as a sound and it also has various interesting connotations. In the first place RAAS is a West Indian word for a menstrual blood cloth. It has some symbolic significance in view of the way the black man has been drained of his life blood for so long. In the second place there is the similar African word ras (from the Arabic ra's – head) meaning Ruler or Leader. The Committee thought it very suitable.[12]

This was nothing if not disingenuous: 'raas' means 'arse', nothing more; and as for 'menstrual blood cloth', this is 'raasclat', literally 'arse-cloth'; it refers to a used sanitary towel and is seen as one of the most obscene terms in the West Indian vocabulary. A more relevant colloquialism, and one used by the knowledgeable MacInnes in his *Encounter* piece, was 'mamagai': to fool or trick. That, as events would prove, would be the kindest description of what Michael Abdul Malik/Michael X was up to.

Whether one believes, as did MacInnes, not to mention those blacks who were associated with RAAS, the Black House or the Black Eagles, the so-called 'military wing' of RAAS that flourished briefly in 1968–69, that Michael's supposed potential for good outweighed his undoubted capabilities of evil, or whether, like the unremittingly hostile V.S. Naipaul, one sees him as just one more vicious hustler on the make, what is clear is that the honeymoon period was a short one. His peak years fell between 1965 and 1967. For two years he rode the wave of his own fantasies, happily supported by an obeisant media. Like every hustler he was an actor, relying heavily on the credulity of his audience; that the era's white liberals found themselves emotionally paralysed in the face of an articulate, 'revolutionary' black man, unable to essay the slightest criticism, merely boosted his success. Yet it was

soon clear that the old thuggishness that had stood him in good stead in his
Rachman days had not entirely deserted him. To those, such as the Notting
Hill dope dealers whose trade he ripped off – stealing their stock, taking their
cash, breaking their heads – or the *IT* staffers who stood by as the machete-
wielding X walked off with their typesetter, or those who, for whatever
transgression, were beaten up in the secluded security of the Black House,
the falsity of his image was clear. His defenders still see another side. Michael,
they suggest, was into 'psychodrama', what Tom Wolfe termed the 'ma-
umauing' of the do-gooding liberals by 'right-on' blacks. Courtney Tulloch
saw it all as part of the larger game:

> He was a poet, a very, very sensitive man. He was a dramatist. And when peo-
> ple were talking he'd sit there and think, 'I wonder what would freak these
> people out.' And he'd go and act it out. He said, 'You make everything work
> for you. You make your clothes work for you, your looks work for you, you
> think where you're going, what you're doing. . .' Mike worked up everything
> that he ever did, and if he's going down to *IT* and he wants something, he's
> going to go there and dramatise it, and if it takes a machete, then he's going
> to take a machete and slap it down, because he knows that this is a frightened
> little hippie who's out of his depth in the first place. So that's what he's going
> to do. He's everything, he's an actor, he's an artist.[13]

The 'frightened little hippies' were less impressed. To an extent, of course,
it *was* a game, the same one those same hippies were putting over on their
'straight' parents when they turned up with waist-length hair and brandishing their 'exotic' cigarettes. The problem for Michael X, as it is for most
demagogues, is the moment when he started believing his own publicity. It
came in 1967. Fired up by the visit of the genuine Black Power activist,
Stokeley Carmichael, to the Dialectics of Liberation, he appeared at a meeting in Reading on 24 July. But when he announced to the seventy-strong
audience, 'If ever you see a white man laying a hand on your black woman,
kill him immediately,' someone took the speechifying seriously. With studied irony Michael Abdul Malik, self-proclaimed messiah of Black activism,
was charged with contravening the Race Relations Act. In court he played his
part right up to the cell door, telling the recorder to 'cool it', swearing on the
Koran (which had to be wiped with warm water before he was willing to
touch it) and performing 'Islamic' ablutions prior to giving evidence. It
didn't save him. He was jailed for twelve months.

Once out of jail it was business as usual, but by then he had lost much of
his liberal constituency. He managed, on the other hand, to pick up a new
and very useful supporter, perhaps the saddest victim of his accomplished
'soft-soaping': the poor little rich boy, Nigel Samuel. Destined to bale out a
succession of counter-cultural entrepreneurs, Samuel, who also invested in
IT, in Jim Haynes' Arts Lab and in the Social Deviants' debut album, was a

natural target for Michael X. Samuel, who on one occasion was taken to Trinidad by his new mentor (on another trip, on a chartered aircraft presumably financed by Samuel, the incongruous plair flew to Timbuktu and later Guinea, where they visited Stokeley Carmichael), seemed to most witnesses to be a mere puppet. Tales abounded: Nigel grovelling to Michael at the *IT* office, Nigel and Michael, plus a carload of henchmen, careering into Downing Street to demand an appearance by the Prime Minister (Wilson did appear, and Samuel was swiftly extricated from the car and dragged inside Number 10). Malik's greatest coup was enlisting the young millionaire as a director of the Black House, for which he paid out the £4,000 a year rent. Later he boasted that he had mulcted Samuel of £250,000; investigative reporters put the figure nearer £15,000. The pair split in time – the alliance, like Michael's 'Black Power' efforts had been one of convenience; it was noted that on 16 May 1975, on the day that Michael Abdul Malik was hanged in Port o' Spain, Trinidad for murder, Nigel Samuel was getting married.

By 1970 it seemed that Michael X was fast disappearing into his own ever more grandiose fantasies. In March 1970, after a visit to Trinidad during which he made plans for his eventual return home, he launched what would be his final throw in England: the Black House Building Programme. He contacted a PR firm (but backed off when they raised the question of payment), and wrote widely to the nation's leaders ('Dear Brother. . .') touting a programme of peace and love ('The men of culture are true apostles of equality'). No one wanted to know. Further afield he sounded out the Emir of Kuwait and his role models, the Black Muslims in America, abandoning equality but appealing to their presumed anti-Semitism. Still no luck. Even with Nigel Samuel's donations, cheques drawn on Black House accounts began bouncing. Worse still there were new legal problems: an altercation with a local Jewish businessman (Michael had explained to some of his correspondents how 'we must get the Jews off our backs') had ended with the man allegedly being brutalised and led around the Black House on a dog's lead. Despite Malik's attempts to dismiss the event as 'a farce', he and five followers were charged.

Even as the pressure intensified, and the need to escape became ever greater, he continued with the pose. He gave interviews and appeared on television, explaining that he was abandoning his involvements with Black Power and moving on to 'constructive work'. The Black House was handed over to an associate, Stanley Abbott; Malik wrote to the Trinidadian Prime Minister to announce his imminent return and tout his reputation as a pimp ('I ran the most successful string of Gaming houses and Whore houses that any Black person ever did in England') and of his new role as the country's best-known black man. He left in March 1971, never to return. His legacy was marginal: the last few weeks of the Black House had seen it collapse into chaos and eventually looting. The Black Power movement seemed irrelevant;

like so much Sixties optimism it had failed its initial hopes. Michael X, defended as one who, if nothing else, always offered hope, had quit, leaving
nothing but disillusion.

The loss was, in the end, that of the Black community. For all of Michael's hyperbole, and a programme that maximised his own interests far
above those of the larger community, British racism was as strident and ugly
as ever. If one area of the Sixties, so clamorous with the changes wrought by
enlightened social engineering, seemed mulishly resistant to change, then it
was the national attitude towards its immigrant population.

In 1968 Enoch Powell, ironically an MP from that area of Britain known
(from its post-Industrial Revolution landscape) as 'the Black Country', was a
Tory front-bencher, one of the more intellectual members of Edward
Heath's shadow cabinet. Known for his classical education, and his espousal
of the free market ('Often, when I am kneeling down in church, I think to
myself how much we should thank God, the Holy Ghost, for the gift of capitalism'),[14] his recent pronouncements had focused on a new area: race. Always a supporter of stricter controls on immigration – as a minister in the
Macmillan government he had pushed for such controls prior to the Commonwealth and Immigrants Act of 1962 – he returned to this issue in 1967,
reviewing for the *Daily Telegraph* a major study of immigration in Birmingham Sparkbrook, not far from his own constituency, Wolverhampton
South-West. In a piece that mourned the way in which 'the substitution of a
wholly or predominantly coloured population for the previous native inhabitants' had transformed areas 'as completely as other areas were transformed
by the bulldozer', he claimed that such changes were tantamount to war –
only worse.

> Acts of an enemy, bombs from the sky, they could understand; but now, for
> reasons quite inexplicable, they might be driven from their homes and their
> property deprived of value by an invasion which the Government apparently
> approved and their fellow-citizens – elsewhere – viewed with complacency.
> Those were the years when a 'For Sale' sign going up in a street struck terror
> into all its inhabitants.[15]

That no one was 'driven' anywhere, but left only when impelled by their
own grubby prejudices, and that no value was lost other than as a result of
that selfsame racism, was omitted from the Powell thesis. Instead, presumably
desiring the re-creation of *Kristallnacht* on the streets of the West Midlands,
he voiced his 'astonishment' that local people had permitted this 'shattering'
alteration 'with no physical manifestations of antipathy'. This *Telegraph*
piece was but a forerunner of what was to come. As the year passed his racism
became increasingly outspoken: in a minute to the Shadow Cabinet he noted
the 'breeding by past immigrants'; in another newspaper article, for the *Sunday Express* on 9 July, he asked, as the headline read: 'CAN WE *AFFORD* TO

LET OUR RACE PROBLEM EXPLODE?', a question he answered not with a policy for educating people out of racism, but by a desire, reiterated in a variety of environments in the months that followed, for the repatriation of those 'not fitting in' to British life.

All of which was as nothing in the face of the speeches he gave in early 1968. By then the country had begun absorbing the influx of Kenyan Asians, thrown out by their own government and eligible, as Commonwealth citizens, to gain entry to Britain. On 9 February, speaking to a Tory party dinner in Walsall, he spoke of the isolation of those who were suffering the black invasion, of which people in the rest of the country 'know little or nothing and . . . care little or nothing'. And he went on to tell how a fellow–MP had been 'dumbfounded' to hear that a constituent, a little girl, was the only white child in a class of immigrants. That the local paper was unable to find such a child did not diminish the impact of his words. In early April 1968 Roy Jenkins, the Home Secretary, introduced the new Race Relations Bill. As well as proposing new controls on Commonwealth immigration, it also urged an extension of the laws governing racial discrimination, especially in housing and the workplace. Many Tories, including the shadow Home Secretary Quintin Hogg, found themselves wrong-footed. Their instinctive desire to control the 'aliens' was balanced by the pragmatic knowledge that voting against the Bill would be to appear racist. The Shadow Cabinet therefore created an amendment in which they underlined their desire for racial harmony, and called for laws to help it, but declined to back Jenkins's bill. When they were polled no one, including Enoch Powell, disagreed. They disbanded, promising to consider the matter again after the Easter recess, on 22 April.

Powell, however muted he may have been in the Shadow Cabinet, had his own agenda. Scheduled to give a speech in Birmingham on 20 April (coincidentally Hitler's birthday), he spent the Easter holiday tidying it up and preparing for its delivery. In the immediate aftermath of what followed, he continued to assert his innocence as to its impact; but, as noted by Richard Shepherd, he was hardly being frank: a couple of days before the speech he had boasted to a friend that it 'would go up like a rocket, and stay up'.[16] The media, both local and national, had been alerted, and the meeting's chairman noted with surprise that what would usually have been a relatively unimportant event seemed to have attracted not just national journalists, but television crews as well. 'The supreme function of statesmanship,' declared Powell as he began speaking, 'is to provide against preventable evils.' And with that, made doubly portentous by the general appreciation that when an overtly religious figure such as Powell used 'evil' he genuinely meant it, he set out his anti-immigrant stall. Taken as a whole it was the usual agenda: the mounting numbers, the need for inward controls and outward repatriation, the feeling that the country 'must be mad' to let such a revolution in nationhood proceed unopposed, the idea that the feelings of 'discrimination and deprivation, the sense of alarm and of resentment' lay not with the immigrants, but with the urban whites whose feelings he enunciated. But it was his inclusion, as in Walsall, of anecdotal evidence that ensured that his speech hit the bulletins and the front pages. There were a number of these, typically the 'middle-aged quite ordinary working man' who was desperate to emigrate since very soon the 'black man will have the whip hand over the white man'.

The ultimate tale, however, and that which propelled Powell's speech into unforeseen prominence came when he turned to the beleaguered white city-dwellers, their lives allegedly blighted by this alien influx: strangers in their own land, suggested Powell, forced to accept changes that they neither wanted nor understood. Then came his *tour de force*: the elderly widow of Wolverhampton, the sole white in her street, a prisoner of fear and anti-social blacks. This old lady,

> is afraid to go out. Windows are broken. She finds excreta pushed through her letterbox. When she goes to the shops, she is followed by children, charming, wide-grinning piccaninnies. They cannot speak English, but one word they know. 'Racialist', they chant. When the new Race Relations Bill is passed, this woman is convinced she will go to prison. And is she so wrong? I begin to wonder.

Integration, he added, was useless: after all, why should the growing immigrant population care about integration when soon they would dominate the native British, 'to agitate and campaign against their fellow-citizens, and to overawe and dominate the rest with legal weapons which the ignorant and ill-informed [Labour government] have provided'. It was then that Powell, reaching into his bag of classical tags, declared in words that would brand him forever, 'As I look ahead, I am filled with foreboding. Like the Roman, I seem to see the River Tiber foaming with much blood.'

Contrary to popular myth, Powell did not receive a standing ovation, if anything his speech won only limited applause, but the wider world was devastated. His Tory colleagues were appalled; only Margaret Thatcher, who in a decade would be noting that while the neo-Nazi National Front were extreme, they were not without worthwhile points, 'sympathised strongly' with what Powell had to say. His departure would be 'a tragedy'. Nor, in her opinion, was he in the slightest racist.

Edward Heath was less tolerant. For him the decision was simple: Powell must go, and he was sacked before the next day. As for the media, of the forty-five editorials on the speech, twenty-eight attacked it, ten equivocated and only seven offered support (these last however included the *News of the World* and the *Daily Express*, both with massive circulations). It was noted that 'his own' *Express and Star* was less than enthusiastic, condemning the 'extravagance' of his speech. The public, who sent Powell 100,000 letters and 7,000 telegrams, were largely in favour. Only a little over ten per cent were overtly racist, but a large majority had something negative so say, even if it was no more than their attempt to articulate their essential unease at the way the country seemed to be altering under the pressure of immigration. The crackpot racists wrote to cheer Powell on, but their real excesses were saved for Heath, whom they attacked viciously and in great numbers. Whether or not the widow of Wolverhampton had received excrement through her front door, Heath undoubtedly did through his, albeit packaged and stamped. Lord Prior, then Heath's PPS, wondered whether Powell 'really knows or understands . . . the filth he collected to his side'.[17] Filth or not, Powell's speech generated a substantial response among the working classes: on 23 April there were marches, most notoriously that of 4,000 London dockers (backed by a group of Smithfield meat porters), to demonstrate solidarity with the man whose name they chanted, like some gang of football supporters menacing their rival 'frogs' or 'krauts', 'E-noch! E-noch!' The National Front were impressed; that a man of Powell's stature could air such opinions naturally made it easier for them – and their membership picked up accordingly. Only the immigrant community were united in their condemnation. For them, Powell's 'outing' of his racist credo had immediate effects: Paul Boateng, black but born in Britain and later a politician himself, was for the first time ever abused and spat at in the street within days of the speech. He was undoubtedly not alone.

As for Powell, he pleaded innocence. Confronted on radio or television by his critics he posed as a simple man who had never expected such a frenzied response to his unexceptionable comments, and enjoyed, as his biographer Richard Shepherd has noted, the paradoxical position of being a pariah in Parliament, yet a darling for large sections of the country. (His sole regret, it would transpire, was that for the 'rivers of blood' he hadn't prudently stuck to the original Latin.) Not everyone was so kind: students, the most vociferous of his critics, were united in their efforts to give him the hardest possible time. His media appearances were often picketed or even broken up; attempts to address students directly were invariably opposed; a large swastika was hung from the railings outside his London home. None of which, while unpleasant, deterred him from what he was convinced was the rightness of his cause. Nor even did the refutations of his supposed 'facts'. The media sought assiduously to track down the Wolverhampton widow, she of the excreta-laden letterbox and the constant abuse by 'piccaninnies': she did not exist. As for his role as a racist, that was never a problem. As he informed the journalist Michael Cockrell in 1995, 'What's wrong with racism? Racism is the basis of a nationality.'[18] In any case, he had been at pains to repeat, he loved eating in Indian restaurants. In the end the speech destroyed Powell as an effective politician. 'E-noch' may have delighted the unreconstructed proles, but while he would remain an MP until 1987 (but now an Ulster Unionist and not a Conservative proper), he would never regain his status. He died in 1997, his lasting memorials confined to the reference books: the 'rivers of blood' entering those of quotation, his eponym an entry in the *Oxford English Dictionary*: 'Powellism: The political and economic policies advocated by J. Enoch Powell; spec. one of restricting or terminating the immigration of coloured people into the United Kingdom.'

But if Powell retreated to the footnotes, the attitudes he promoted certainly did not, and nowhere more so than in the streets of Notting Hill. The relations between police and local blacks, never good, would plumb new depths in the Seventies, and sputter on unpleasantly until the housing market boom of the next decade would see the invasion of the old black areas by moneyed yuppies and 'trustafarians'. The first, and most celebrated flashpoint came in 1970, with the trial of the 'Mangrove Nine'. The police had long since hated the Mangrove restaurant, a fixture on All Saint's Road, W11. They had portrayed it as a home to drugs, pimping and worst of all 'Black Power' ever since Frank Critchlow had opened it up in 1968. They had raided it twice in 1969 – failing on both occasions to find the drugs they sought (uncharacteristically they neglected to bring any with them) – and in spring 1970 Critchlow was charged with serving food after eleven at night. Colin MacInnes, who had been called in by Scotland Yard to make his suggestions on the possible improvement of police-black relations, noted the charge and suggested that one way of improving matters might be to extend rather than curtail the Mangrove's opening hours. That, to no one's surprise, was rejected. The Mangrove remained the area's top target for over-zealous policing.

It was in response to this that in August 1970 a group of blacks determined to make a demonstration against West London policing. The group marched to the three major police stations in the area, giving a speech at each one and then moving on. For a while the protest went as planned, but gradually the numbers built up, emotions intensified and inevitably clashes between the two parties began. A major fight broke out in Portnall Road W9, once briefly home to a young V.S. Naipaul, and still heavily West Indian. As the press fulminated and the police licked their wounds, it became clear that the authorities, as wilfully blind as ever to the real situation, were determined to find a scapegoat. That, it turned out, would be the Mangrove, or more properly Frank Critchlow and eight of his customers, who had been singled out as the alleged 'ringleaders' of the march and the subsequent street battle.

The trial would be one of the longest since the war, and certainly a landmark in black/white relations. In the end the Nine would be acquitted – the jury found it impossible to give credence to the procession of police witnesses, each offering his own lies and evasions. MacInnes appeared as a character witness for Critchlow, noting how, far from some ravening revolutionary, he was invariably 'a perfect gentleman'. The judge, like his equivalents at the *Oz* trial and that of the Angry Brigade, refused to acknowledge the slightest 'political' aspect to the proceedings, but no one else was fooled. Unlike the defendants in those other landmark events, the Nine were representing a community that really was oppressed. Sadly the trial proved nothing, other than the depth of anatgonism between the black and white communities. The arguments, the clashes and the demonstrations continued, reaching a new height of hostility in the riots that accompanied the Notting Hill carnival of 1976, echoed in the following two years. The racism, espoused ever more openly by the Conservative governments of the Eighties, has of course remained.

FUCKING IN THE STREET

Chapter Twenty-Four

Introduction: Civilising Society

On the whole range of issues where much progress remains to be made – hanging, Wolfenden [homosexuality and prostitution], the licensing laws, betting reform, Sunday observance, divorce, theatre censorship, police control, the abortion laws – there is immensely more to be hoped for from a Labour Home Secretary than from the most liberal Conservative Minister.
Roy Jenkins, MP in the *Spectator* 14 August, 1959

Despite Philip Larkin's oft-quoted stricture, sexual intercourse, that generic for a concern with private morality and all its ramifications and controversies, began long before 1963. Feminist agitation was hardly a product of the Sixties, though the style and the philosophies were some distance from those propounded by Mary Wollstonecraft in the early nineteenth century and the Pankhursts and their suffragette followers of the early twentieth. The campaign to set the realities of homosexual life above the prejudices and fantasies that informed the usual stereotyping was newer, but there had been determined agitation, however frustrated, all through the 1950s. Similar attitudes had been emerging *vis-à-vis* abortion and divorce. As for censorship, a product in which, if in nothing else, Britain consistently outperformed (and indeed continues to surpass) virtually any contender in the so-called 'progressive' West, that had been under assault for decades.

The moral world of 1950s Britain, at least as far as the statute book was concerned, was barely altered from that of a century earlier. The concept of 'Middle England' had yet to emerge, but as an entity it dominated such discourse with its tawdry prejudices, its tedious fulminations and its overriding terror of almost literally unspeakable, but hugely potent horrors. As the decade drew to its close it was still impossible to procure a legal abortion, to obtain a divorce without a grubby charade that often involved private detectives and elaborately staged 'proof of adultery', for one man to have a sexual relationship with another without fear of prosecution, to see a play without its first having been blue-pencilled by the Lord Chamberlain, to read a book if its contents were seen as contravening a century-old act, and much more in the same vein. And still, despite a growing trend against it elsewhere, those who were convicted of premeditated murder would end their days hanging in what jails still termed the 'topping shed'.

The concept of what became known as 'permissiveness' has been looked at earlier. Seen in the popular and right-wing mind as some kind of free-for-all, with hippies, gays, feminists and foreigners all locked together in some kind of ghastly orgy, it carries in fact a far heavier burden. What matters is the word permissive, and its root 'permit'. For all the campaigning, for all the slogans and banners, during this crucial period 'permissive' was not what was taken, but what was handed out. 'Seize the time!' demanded one of several contemporary slogans and the time was about all that ever really was 'seized'. The campaigner remained a supplicant, and the gentlemen in Whitehall (who, as a former Labour minister Douglas Jay had once suggested, 'really do know best' as regards what the nation's electorate receive) plus their parliamentary masters, still cracked the whip.

None of the legislation that made up the background of what became first lauded and in due course excoriated as 'the permissive society' was simply handed over as demanded. The laws that changed society did not come in a single package, and for all that the same Home Secretary was involved in them all, and had openly professed his desire to see a more 'civilised Britain', there was no directed, focused agenda. Nor did any of the legislation, except perhaps the simple reversal of that which governed capital punishment, fully resolve the problems they addressed. The new laws were fudges, compromises, and in many ways the fact of their being so left 'unfinished business' that would be debated almost as soon as the initial euphoria of legislation had passed by. Writing thirty years after the event, it is hard to say that arguments over censorship, over abortion, over large areas of gay sexuality have exactly vanished. The 1970s, a decade of reversal, saw the first and fiercest attacks, but what might be called the 'counter-revolution' of the repressive society has yet to falter, for all that those same 'Jenkins laws', however battered, remain in place.

All the new laws affected the counter-culture, although it is interesting to note that the topic that touched on the hippies most directly, the possible reassessment of the law on cannabis, was (perhaps inevitably) the place where the liberal tide finally broke. Jenkins, alas, had been replaced by a regulation issue Home Secretary and the breadth of vision that had typified his regime was not sustained. When considering when 'the Sixties' ended, surely one date is January 1969, when James Callaghan made it clear that, despite overwhelming evidence to the contrary, he had absolutely no intention of abandoning a foolish and divisive law.

As the various 'case-histories' make clear, each piece of legislation was strictly *sui generis* but, with the exception of capital punishment, licensing and Sunday observance (which latter pair survived any suggestion of change), all pertain to a single topic: sex. How one did it, in the case of homosexuality; in what context one was permitted to do it, in the case of divorce; and how one portrayed it or to what extent one was allowed to read about or view it in the case of film and theatre censorship and the control of so-called 'obscenity' on the printed page. Space does not permit a full discussion of every 'Jenkins law', but given the furore that surrounded these changes then and later, and the massive effect this social engineering would have on the whole of British society, these 'sex-related' areas deserve proper coverage. However, prior to looking at the laws themselves, and the effects they would have, it is worth looking at the larger topic, hymned then and now, rightly or wrongly, as the Sexual Revolution.

> Fucking was very popular. It was very sexually free, loose and easy. Sex was sex for everybody. Fucking's such a good way of making friends. Everybody was just happy to walk into someone else's room, 'Hi, how are you?' and you'd go to bed and you'd just fuck them. There was a girl staying in a flat I had in Redcliffe Square: I got up, took her a cup of tea, climbed into bed and we screwed. Just like that.[1]

Like so much that happened in the Sixties, the revolution in sexuality, such as it was, began at least a decade earlier. There had been, in the 1920s and 1930s, a far more free-and-easy attitude to intercourse, at least of a heterosexual variety, and the urgencies of wartime inevitably led to many brief encounters, few of which lasted longer than that particular period of leave. But what went on behind closed doors was one thing; the airing of sexuality as a mainstream topic of discussion, a change that continues to advance today, is very much a development of the late 1940s, the creation in fact of two works of research: Alfred Kinsey's *Sexual Behavior in the Human Male* (1948), known as the Kinsey Report, and its follow-up *Sexual Behavior in the Human Female* (1953).

In 1938 Kinsey, then professor of zoology at Indiana University, was approached by a group of his students with some questions regarding marriage. At first he gave no answer, fearing that his own knowledge was too limited, then he began reading everything available and, appalled by how limited that 'everything' proved to be, determined to establish his own course on sexuality and marriage. It was hugely successful and soon began to dominate his life. As his wife Clara innocently remarked, 'I hardly see him at night anymore since he took up sex.'

Kinsey began by interviewing his own students, some 400 of whom had signed up for his course by the end of the first year. He sent his assistant elsewhere, locked the door, and started asking questions. By 1939 he had declared his efforts, 'a scientific gold mine' and had expanded his researches into neighbouring towns and cities, setting out every weekend to find new subjects. Inevitably, as news of the course and of his researches spread beyond the university, there were complaints. Moralists were appalled by both his lectures and his case-histories. His refusal to denounce extra-marital sex was apparently especially threatening. In 1940 the president of Indiana University, who on the whole backed Kinsey's work, gave him a choice: give up the histories or abandon teaching. It was assumed that Kinsey would opt for the course; in the event he stayed with his research. In 1942 he was appointed director of the university's new Institute for Sex Research. As a good Middle American, Kinsey remained acutely sensitive to the prejudices of the small-town ethos. His interviewers, often hired out of his own small salary, were impeccably neutral figures. Nothing must disturb an interviewee: there were no Blacks or Jews, nor indeed anyone whose name did not seem acceptably Anglo-Saxon.

All too conscious of the frisson that would, inevitably, attach itself to his work, Kinsey went out of his way to present himself as a paradigm for the old-fashioned values of Middle America. When his books appeared the ranks of interviewers dutifully reported on what Kinsey termed his 'monotonously normal' life, an image that, by necessity, was the squeakiest of clean. It was also pure fabrication. He and his wife may have started married life as virgins, but they soon made up for that. Kinsey's own appetites tended to the voyeuristic but Clara Kinsey bedded a succession of partners, all for the sake of research. Kinsey may have deplored extramarital affairs, but his researchers joined in regular 'swinging' parties, all under the Master's unsmiling gaze. Kinsey himself perfected elaborate masturbation rituals, inserting anything from a straw to the bristle-end of a toothbrush into his urethra as he tugged on a cord, fast around his scrotum. On top of this he led an active gay life, his hands-on research giving him the excuse to cruise the cottages of New York and Chicago in search of new statistics.

None of which came out. Instead the Kinsey image was one of a serious researcher, working with dedication rather than with the slightest vestige of enjoyment, a man who was apparently unable even to write the word homosexual and who labelled his files on the topic the 'H Files'. He rarely drank and, when he attempted to take up smoking – believing it might put his interviewees more at their ease – he never quite managed to avoid seeming like a child essaying an illicit, and distasteful puff.

Kinsey published his first book in 1947; choosing a conservative medical publisher and charging the then high price of $6.50. Any royalties would go back into the Institute. In order to minimise any possible impact on the University, publication was carefully postponed to avoid any clash with the sessions of the Indiana state legislature. Inevitably hindsight does him little service. Fifty years on his findings seem less than dramatic: healthy sex meant a healthy marriage; extramarital sex (on the part of both men and women) was infinitely more widespread than anyone wished to admit; petting and premarital sex tended to produce better marriages; masturbation did not cause mental problems whatever the old wives might proclaim and finally homosexuality, like extramarital sex, was infinitely wider spread than people wanted to admit. The *Report* was an instant success: within ten days of publication there had been five reprints, making 185,000 copies. To the embarrassment of the *New York Times*, which initially neither reviewed nor accepted advertising for the book, it topped the paper's bestseller list. Not only that, but the critics seemed to approve, noting Kinsey's research, his generally sensible judgements and approving of the sobriety of his tone. Polls taken around the country found that the mass of Americans were equally positive. At which point, like some delayed-action explosive, the negative critics appeared. They queried his research, they denied his findings, refusing to accept such threatening information; above all they loathed his scientific detachment: his failure to judge and, more importantly, to condemn.

Kinsey, so scrupulous in his refusal either to trivialise or sensationalise what he had done, was shocked by the attacks, and then increasingly defensive. The support of the Rockefeller Foundation, his main paymasters, began to wane. A new head of the Foundation, Dean Rusk – who in time would be known as one of the major backers of America's foolhardy involvement in Vietnam – was less than supportive. None the less Kinsey was able to publish his second volume, *Sexual Behavior in the Human Female*, in 1953. It was another bestseller. Once again the critics began in a positive mode, and then found themselves swamped by the moralists. Neither result was surprising: this book, with its discussion of those supposed madonnas of American life, one's wife and daughters, was even more explosive. It was also the last straw for Dean Rusk. Responding to such comments as the bible-thumping Billy Graham's: 'It is impossible to estimate the damage this book will do to the already deteriorating morals of America', he dumped the Kinsey Institute. Its latest request had been for $80,000; instead Rusk directed that $520,000 be sent to the Union Theological Seminary.

If Kinsey, to the fascination of some and the terror of others, had revealed the nuts and bolts of American (and, it might be assumed, Western) sexuality, then another scientist was contemporaneously working towards a discovery that would impinge on the very mechanics of that side of human life. The advent of penicillin in the 1930s had seen off that oldest of anti-sexual bugaboos, venereal disease. But the likelihood of pregnancy following a sexual encounter, remained a major constraint on the freedom of couples married or not, to enjoy their sex life. By the late nineteenth century the demand for birth control, or 'neo-Malthusianism' as it was termed, had become a central pillar of a wider demand for female liberation, itself a subset of a wider movement for socialist, communist or even more radical social change. America's 'Red Emma' Goldman was the first of many women who stressed the link between woman-controlled contraception and wider liberation. Of these, two stand out as the most influential: Marie Stopes in England and Margaret Sanger in America.

Marie Stopes (1880–1958) was among the most important of Britain's sex educators, whose campaign to disseminate knowledge on what for many women was still something of a forbidden and slightly embarrassing mystery, was spearheaded by her book *Married Love*. Qualified as a palaeobotanist, Stopes abandoned her studies in fossils for those concerning sex after she was forced to consult volumes in the British Museum before realising that her marriage to fellow academic Reginald Gates, already several months old, had yet to be consummated. After extricating herself from this marriage, she wrote *Married Love* (1916), a 'strange amalgam of purple prose, suffragist philosophy and sage advice on lovemaking'.[2] It was this latter which made the book both a vital sex guide and a source of notoriety for its author. The book outraged many, and in 1931 was tried as 'obscene' under America's Tariff Act, but it survived all such attacks and by 1939 had sold over a million copies in America alone.

In 1917 Stopes married again, and finally lost her virginity. With money from her second husband Stopes, already in demand as the purveyor of marital advice, and author of a second book, *Wise Parenthood* (1918), founded in 1921 Britain's first birth control clinic. She became an international figure, contentious, flamboyant and arrogant. She attacked the Catholic church's antipathy to contraception, became a fanatical proponent of eugenics, and fought what she called the 'perversion' of homosexuality with the same fervour as she advocated contraception. She died of cancer in 1958, still feeling, so she claimed, as young as ever.

Stopes's peer, and lifelong rival, was America's Margaret Sanger, the coiner of the phrase 'Birth Control'. Sanger, who had been influenced by Emma Goldman, and by a visit to France in which she marvelled at the sexual sophistication of French women, had come to public notice when in 1912, she wrote a number of frank pieces about the dangers of venereal disease. The magazine which published them was promptly banned from the US mail (though not from news-stand sale), and Sanger responded in the next issue with the headline: 'What Every Girl Should Know: NOTHING! By Order of the Post Office Department.' In 1916 she opened a birth control clinic in Brooklyn. It appealed directly to the poor immigrants of New York, printing its circulars in Italian and Yiddish as well as in English. (Despite this, like Stopes, Sanger was an élitist and eugenicist, advocating, 'More children from the fit, less children from the unfit – that is the chief issue of birth control.') After being arrested and serving thirty days in jail. Sanger hit back with her film *Birth Control*. This was in effect a documentary, largely autobiographical, charting her struggle against censorship. It ends with its heroine in jail, still proclaiming, 'No matter what happens, the work shall go on.' The New York authorities fought to ban the movie but the courts found for Sanger. A second film, *The Hand That Rocks the Cradle*, a similar attempt to use the medium to pioneer the knowledge of birth control and sexual hygiene, was also prosecuted in 1917. This time the censor won. Sanger's written work was also widely suppressed. Her own newspaper, *The Woman Rebel* (its masthead proclaimed 'No Gods, No Masters') was in constant trouble. Her book *Family Limitation* (1915) was prosecuted by the Society for the Suppression of Vice and found to be 'contrary not only to the law of the state but also to the law of God'; Mrs Sanger was imprisoned, as was her husband William, for distributing her pamphlets on birth control. In 1923 the book was suppressed in England. In 1929 the New York police raided the Sanger clinic, arrested the staff and seized vast quantities of records. Sanger was completely acquitted and the authorities were warned off similar raids.

The rest of Sanger's life would be punctuated by such attacks, every one challenged and often overcome, and gradually her cause gained both support and respectability. By 1950 she had in many ways won. Despite the opposition of such institutions as the Roman Catholic church, contraception was very big business, and her opponents, once the majority voice, were gradually being exiled to the ranks of crankery. Then, in that same year, when she revived an old friendship, she reached what might be seen as her pinnacle: as co-pioneer of the ultimate expression of her lifelong campaign, the development of the oral contracepive, 'the Pill'. The friendship was with Katharine McCormick, a venerable grandee whose fortune was such that, according to one acquaintance, 'she couldn't even spend the interest on her interest.'[3] McCormick's own fascination for contraception came from her marriage to Stanley McCormick, heir to the International Harvester fortune and diagnosed a schizophrenic. Believing that the illness might be hereditary, she determined that there should be no children. Instead her energies went to her social preoccupations: the study of schizophrenia and the campaign for unrestricted contraception.

McCormick's perception of contraception was twofold. On the one hand she saw it as a woman's right, the inalienable control of her own body; on the other it was a matter of population control: like many others, she feared the results of unchecked human growth. In early 1952 she wrote to Sanger, asking if there was anything she could do to turn her dreams into practical progress. Sanger responded by telling her of a researcher, one Gregory 'Goody' Pincus, who was working on the possible contraceptive value of steroids and of injections of progesterone, which, it had been proved, could fool the body into thinking it was pregnant. Once McCormick had heard of Pincus's efforts she opened her cheque-book. An initial donation of $10,000 was soon upped to a massive $150,000 per year, a gift that was maintained to the end of her life. The immediate result of her munificence was the recruitment of an important new researcher, Dr John Rock, a gynaecologist whose expertise lay in the application of discoveries in endocrinology to clinical gynaecology. That he was a Catholic, not to mention extremely good-looking, and thus mitigated the 'Jewish' image that Pincus gave to the project, was an added bonus. Along with Rock came two more important members of the team: Carl Djeraasi, who had used progesterone to regulate menstrual disorders, and Min-Chueh Chang who was using progesterone on rabbits.

Starting in late 1954 the team began testing not rabbits but human beings. Tests on a small group of women were encouraging and Pincus coined a new shorthand for their work: 'the Pill'. In 1956 tests began on a hundred poor women in a suburb of the Puerto Rican capital, San Juan. There were no problems obtaining volunteers: hundreds of disappointed women were turned away. The Pill was Enovid, although its maker, Searle, was less than keen on publicising its association with what still seemed a very dubious enterprise. (Later, when market research showed how popular Enovid would become, Searle totally reversed its position, even pondering the possible copyrighting of the name 'the Pill'.) The tests were outstandingly successful: not a woman fell pregnant and such side-effects as there were – a little nausea – were soon removed by the inclusion of an antacid.

The success of the new contraceptive snowballed. In 1960, a year after Pincus and Rock had announced that Enovid was absolutely safe for long-term human use, the FDA approved it as a regular contraceptive device (although of the thousands of 'guinea-pigs', only 123 had taken it for more than a year). That the tests were, to quote Linda Grant, 'the poorest-conducted, most cursory trials of any pharmaceutical ever licensed by the Food and Drug Administration'[4] was ignored. (Barely a decade later feminists, supposedly 'liberated' by its introduction, would be at the forefront of those demanding a reassessment of its effects.) It was not simply a case of rampant capitalism burying complaint beneath triumphalist balance-sheets; like other great developments of the period – typically the wholesale destruction of inner cities, the good buildings cleared willy-nilly along with the slums – the impetus for change *qua* change was paramount. Women *wanted* the Pill.

By the end of 1961, 408,000 American women were regular users; a year later it was 1.187 million and a year further on 2.3 million and fast rising. By the 'summer of love' in 1967 there were six million users in the US alone, and by then the Pill was a worldwide phenomenon. In the words of the diplomat and writer Clare Boothe Luce, one of the nation's most celebrated women, 'Modern woman is at last free as man is free, to dispose of her own body, to earn her living, to pursue the improvement of her mind, to try a successful career.' Luce, whose own life had been an especially privileged paradigm of female success in a man's world, might have been a little optimistic, but the point was made. The Pill would revolutionise female life.

Britain, as usual, followed on from America, and as usual, a little late. Just as in the States, where the vast majority of those using Enovid and its peers were married, so was it consistently hard for young unmarried women to get the Pill in the UK. Not until the first Brook Clinic arrived in 1966 was there a large scale breakthrough, and even then the majority of general practitioners and family planning clinics refused to prescribe the Pill to unmarried women for a further three years. Only at university health clinics were the rules relaxed, although this may have sprung less from any pioneering liberality, than from the pragmatic need to get female students through their courses without pregnancy.

It wasn't just students who wanted easy, foolproof contraception. The Pill had so much going for it: it was so easy to take, it maximised what Americans termed the 'daintiness factor' – good girls were taught never to touch, let alone penetrate their own vagina and thus eschewed a diaphragm or cap – but most of all it was about *control*. The anonymous 'Jane', interviewed by Sara Maitland in 1988, found it 'completely wonderful':

> It changed my life. I don't mean overnight. I can't remember now how I felt at first. But soon, I felt in control, I felt free, if I had known then what we know now about how dangerous and so on it is I don't think I would have cared. Before I'd been on it a year I had an affair; not because I was in love with the man, nor because I hated [my husband] – I think now I did it just because I could do it and get away with it. I felt so wonderfully clever. Women say now that the Pill was just a man's plot so that women would be more available, but they can't be serious . . . for provincial married women like me it was wonderful. They would have to be women who can't remember what it was like before: worrying all the time and all that messing about. Sex belonged to me, not to [my husband] and to the children. It wasn't just the Pill of course.
>
> But the Pill did something else too, it made sex news. There were other things that happened about then, the Christine Keeler business and the *Lady Chatterley* case; suddenly you could talk about sex at dinner parties, because it was in the newspapers. So then you could talk about it; ordinary, respectable, married women could sit round dinner tables and talk about it. It wasn't the Big Secret. But it was the Pill, I think, that made it possible for things to change, for women to find out about fun . . . I never really got involved in women's lib, but I do feel sympathetic to lots of those things; and I do think it was the Pill that made it possible. All the things that have happened for women since . . . I think they wouldn't have happened without the Pill.[5]

Yet even the Pill, like a number of other socio-sexual changes that are seen, erroneously, as having sprung fully formed from the Sixties, had its antecedents. The Pill itself had, obviously, not been available, but a general consciousness of the need for contraception had been there throughout the preceding decade. The report of the Royal Commission on Population (set up after the war) had stimulated some growth in family planning clinics in the late 1940s – in 1948 there were 65 clinics, attracting 30,000 new users per year – but the real boom came in the 1950s. By 1963 there were 400 clinics. However quantity as ever did not automatically equate with quality. Of those couples who married during the Fifties a mere 20–25% actually practised formal birth control. Nor did the sort of methods recommended in the clinics always come easily to working-class people. For many, legal or not, abortion remained the main way of avoiding unwanted babies. The NHS provided 2,300 abortions in 1961, rising to 9,700 in 1967; private abortions ran at around 10,000 per year and estimates of illegal operations range between 15,000 and 100,000.

However the desire for something, especially in the UK, had little bearing on its being given. The permissive society, one cannot overstress, was one of receiving, not taking. If the 1958 Anglican Lambeth Conference chose to give its imprimatur to contraception, declaring that it was 'a right and important factor in Christian family life and should be the result of positive choice before God',[6] then this was as much a reflection of a growing fear of overpopulation as any turnaround in theology. In any case, it was not home-grown overpopulation that was a problem, it was the perceived fecundity of the ever-expanding immigrant community, supposedly poised to 'swamp' Anglo–Saxon Britain. Those same politicians were also drifting towards eugenics, a pseudo-science much disgraced after its enthusiastic adoption by the Nazi party. Nor was it only clerics and politicians who pursued contra-dictory paths. Of the men who pioneered the pill – Pincus, Rock and Chang – none had any great brief for the 'liberating' effect of their researches. Like many scientists their interest was in the task before them, the effects were immaterial. The cause of their revolution was science, the wider effect was not something they had considered.

The Pill was no cure-all for the problems attendant on sexuality. For a start its acceptance was far from universal. As Jeffrey Weeks has pointed out,[7] even when it did hit the UK, its use varied widely as to class and geography and, paradoxically, sexual adventurousness. Middle-class women were keener than their working-class sisters; there were many more users in London and the Home Counties than in the north-west; those in stable relationships were far more likely to take it than their more promiscuous peers. Men, especially working class, were often anti-pill: they wanted to maintain control of this most fundamental of relationships. A further problem emerged in the 1970s: the possibility of negative side-effects. In 1977 alone half a million British women would abandon oral contraception. Ironically the sheath (which would of course gain an even greater return to favour in the Eighties) retained its position as the main means of contraception, as popular in the early 1970s as it had been fifteen years before. Equally important was the fact that those most at risk – the young – were the least likely to get the Pill. Either they were ignorant or their local GP refused to issue the necessary prescription.

But, as 'Jane' noted above, the fact of the Pill was that for the first time women had the means to control their fertility and through that their wider life. This in turn had important effects: in the first place it meant that the end of the (once practical) taboos on pre-marital sex meant that couples would begin their married life in a far more sophisticated manner than had most of their parents. In the second the overall image of the female body and of female sexu-ality changed: VD had been largely banished (or at least subjected to reliable cures), now unwanted pregnancy was on the way to joining it. Female sexual-ity remained largely male-defined, at least through the Sixties, but like talk of sex itself, it would enter the arena of public discourse, a change that could be seen in magazines like *Nova*, and in the sort of material, once shocking, now unexceptional, that was found regularly in advertising. The culture, it was noted, had been eroticised, and there is no doubt that without the Pill, such a change would have remained, quite literally, inconceivable.

The Pill, however, was not infallible, nor was it ubiquitous. It was used primarily among the middle classes, women who might anyway have had a good idea of the best means of contraception. For thousands of other women an unwanted pregnancy had only one, far from safe and often expensive solution: an abortion. Stigmatised by Christianity, which saw it as the destruction of an immortal soul, abortion had been rendered illegal since the early nineteenth century when, in 1803, any form of termination was made an offence. In 1828 an attempt to procure an abortion became a capital offence, although it was repealed in 1837. In 1861 the Offences Against the Person Act laid down the law as it would stand for just over a century: 'Every woman being with Child,' it stated,

> Who, with Intent to procure her own Miscarriage, shall unlawfully administer to herself any Poison or other noxious Thing, or shall unlawfully use any Instrument or other Means whatsoever with like Intent and whosoever, with Intent to procure the Miscarriage of any Woman whether she be or be not with Child, shall unlawfully administer to her or cause to be taken by her any Poison or other noxious Thing, or shall unlawfully use any Instrument or other Means whatsoever with the like Intent, shall be guilty of felony.

By the 1930s there were increased worries amongst the medical profession regarding the precise interpretation of the law, and what seemed to be a disturbing rise in maternal mortality due to miscarriages. In 1937 Norman Birkett, QC was appointed as head of a government committee, charged 'to enquire into the prevalence of abortion, and the law relating thereto, and to consider what steps can be taken by more effective enforcement of the law or otherwise, to secure the reduction of maternal mortality and morbidity arising from this cause.' The report was published in March 1939, but it was as a private publication and not as an authorised parliamentary one. Its price, at 11/- four times the usual price for such a publication, was geared to discourage casual purchasers. Its main findings were that a declining rate of reproduction, with its effect on population growth, would only be accelerated by an easing in the law; neither rape nor incest were grounds for an operation, nor was a child conceived by a girl below the age of consent. The idea of helping the situation by offering better access to contraception was rejected: according to the Committee those who used it but still became pregnant would be even more likely to search out the amateur surgeons of the back-streets.

By the 1950s the situation was very different. A small groundswell had been building, aided by the founding in 1938 of the campaigning Abortion Law Reform Association (ALRA) by Dorothy Thurtle (a dissenting member of the Birkett Committee who had submitted her own minority report). In

1955 the Magistrates' Association called for urgent reform of the law; in 1958 a book, *The Sanctity of Life and the Criminal Law*, by Glanville Watkins, came out unequivocally for change; in 1959 Roy Jenkins's Penguin Special, *The Labour Case*, apostrophised the current abortion law as 'harsh and archaic'. On top of these, the whole socio-political climate had changed. Contraception was no longer a taboo topic, and even the Catholic Church, once so implacable, was giving hints that contraception was at least a lesser sin than abortion; the incidence of extramarital intercourse, while never encouraged, was increasingly acknowledged as part of many lives. The publication in 1965 of the pamphlet *Abortion: an Ethical Discussion*, in which the Church Assembly Board for Social Responsibility showed itself in tune with the demands for change, was highly influential in showing that theology was no longer implacably opposed to termination.

Perhaps the most important factor, and one that was denied campaigners against censorship or in favour of gay rights, was that in no way did the reformers' plans seek to reverse current beliefs or established social policy. Abortion, under certain circumstances, was already accepted. The *status quo*, with its one rule for the rich and quite another for the poor, was obviously unsatisfactory: what needed to be done was to ascertain how far reforms should go, and how to eliminate the possibility of abuse.

The parliamentary campaign began in 1965 when Renée Short introduced a bill under the Ten-Minute Rule. Such bills never produce legislation, but its provisions laid down the outlines of what would come. 'It permitted a medical practitioner to terminate pregnancy in good faith on four grounds: to preserve the life of a patient; where giving birth or caring for a child would involve grave risk of serious injury to a woman's physical or mental health; where there was grave risk of a child being born gravely deformed or severely abnormal mentally; where the pregnancy was the result of a sexual offence. Termination under the last three grounds was to require the concurrence of a second medical practitioner and was not to be performed after the thirteenth week of pregnancy. The burden of proof in any prosecution that the operation was not performed in good faith was to rest with the Crown.'[8]

In November 1965 Lord Silkin introduced a similar bill into the House of Lords. It echoed Short's medical provisions, but added a 'social clause': if a medical practitioner believed that a patient's health or social conditions (which included those of her living children) made her unsuitable to take on the legal or moral responsibility for caring for the unborn infant, then a termination could be justified. He also extended the permitted limitation to sixteen weeks of pregnancy. The bill, carried by 67 votes to 8 at its second reading, passed through the Lords just prior to the General Election of March 1966.

With the election out of the way, and the knowledge that were a bill to be espoused by a private member the long, post-Election session would give it every chance to succeed, the search was on, as in similar 'social' bills, for a suitable sponsor. David Steel, then a young MP and an enthusiastic reformer, drew third place in the ballot. He was approached by both the Homosexual Law Reform Society and the ALRA and he chose the latter. Backed by Roy Jenkins, he would put forward a Termination of Pregnancy Bill. The Steel bill reflected earlier measures. As drafted it allowed for therapeutic and eugenic abortions, and modified the social clause to permit an operation were the mother's capacity to perform as a mother to be severely overstrained. Short's inclusion of rape as grounds for termination was dropped. Two medical practitioners would have to agree on the abortion, other than in an emergency, and all operations were to be carried out in an NHS hospital or an approved private equivalent.

The second reading passed by an impressive 223 votes to 29, but the Committee stage that followed proved this to be wildly illusory. It lasted four months, initially postponed while another private member's bill, which had priority, was dealt with. Then it was found that a number of members who had hitherto abstained, turned out to be determined opponents of all or some of its clauses. When the bill finally returned to the Commons in June for its report stage, it was obvious that the specified single day of debate would not be enough. In the event, as it would with the debate on homosexuality, the government was forced to allot extra time. More divisions followed before the third reading vote, 167–83, ensured that the reforms were still on target. Back in the Lords there were further problems. Although Lord Silkin's bill had prepared a reasonably positive reception, there were more debates over specific amendments. The passage of two of these, quite contradictory to the Commons' decisions, threatened a constitutional crisis. Would the non-elective upper chamber frustrate the will of the democratic Commons? In the event the Lords backed down and in October 1967 the bill, now rechristened the Abortion Act, became law. Jenkins noted the 'exceptional courage' with which Steel had stuck by his bill, forcing it through despite the bitter opposition of the Committee and Report stages.

Like so many of the 'Jenkins Acts' the Abortion Act was less than wholly satisfactory. It did not provide what the activists of Women's Liberation would call for: 'abortion on demand'. That service has never been made available. A woman might have a greater right to control her own body, but she still remained subject to the decision of a doctor, all too often a man. Nor were all such practitioners generous in their assessments. Some GPs seemed to delight in saying 'No'. There was also a shortage of doctors who were sufficiently skilled in the operation and far too few NHS facilities to ensure that every woman would get her abortion as soon as possible. (In late 1969 there was a six-week waiting list for non-emergency operations.) The real

beneficiaries were the private abortionists, who could charge substantial fees
for their services. None the less, the Act gave women a degree of choice that if
exercised before 1967, would, but for the fortunate, wealthy minority, have
led to court or even death. (Not that Harley Street was especially kind. Many
abortionists took a sadistic pleasure in humiliating the women they treated,
brandishing their own moral codes even as they pocketed their inflated fees.)
Much to the horror of the anti-abortion campaigners – spearheaded by the
Society for the Protection of the Unborn Child (SPUC) which had been
founded in January 1967 with the express purpose of defeating Steel's efforts
– the number of abortions seemed to rise within days of the Act. In 1968
there were 35,000, in 1975 141,000, but the statistics may have partially depended on the fact that for the first time they could actually be tabulated with
some accuracy. It was true that a growing number of foreign women began
arriving in London to get an abortion, but that resulted less from liberality in
the UK and more from its absence in their own countries. But the battle, if
only in part, could be seen to have been won and most women would agree
with Irma Kurtz when she wrote in *Nova*: 'The only time abortion ought to
be scandalous and sordid is when it is denied.'[9]

Oral contraception and abortion were seen very much as female concerns,
and were central to the re-evaluation of female sexuality that played so central a role in the era, but the changes in attitudes to sex impinged, naturally,
on men as well. These changes were hardly revolutionary, indeed they
seemed to legitimise what had been hitherto a somewhat shameful activity –
the enjoyment of 'dirty books' – but they too made a difference. Thus, absurd as it might appear today, one has to factor in one more contributor to the
new sexuality, a man who, unlike the academic Kinsey, or the scientific Pincus saw sex as hedonism, no holds barred. In December 1953, a couple of
months after Kinsey had published his study of female sexuality, Hugh Hefner produced the first edition of what would become the world's best-known
and best-selling 'men's magazine' from his kitchen table in a Chicago apartment. *Playboy*, as he called it, was loosely modelled on *Esquire* (where Hefner
had worked in the promotions department), and Hefner too offered cheese-
cake alongside more literary efforts. There was one big difference: *Esquire*'s
pinups were illustrations; Hefner's flesh, while modestly displayed by later
standards, was real. He had also been enormously astute in buying up Tom
Kelley's hugely popular 'calendar shots' of a new starlet, Norma Jean
Mortensen, better known as Marilyn Monroe.

Issue one was a barnstorming success. Looking for 30,000 sales to break
even, the magazine sold almost 54,000. That was merely the beginning: over
the next few years Hefner went on to found what for a while was an unrivalled and apparently boundless sex empire. *Playboy* paraded the fantasies of
America's contemporary male yuppies, with its key clubs, its bunny girls, its
hip bachelor lifestyle and above all, the magazine itself, touting unashamed

consumerism: of food, drink, technology, pleasure and of course, pneumatic girls. By 1956 it was outselling *Esquire* itself and by 1972 peaked at over seven million copies. Hefner celebrated his good fortune by taking over a forty-eight room Chicago mansion, former property of a millionaire, and fitting it up as a hedonistic pleasure palace. It was the epitome of his own 'Playboy Philosophy', the turgid, seemingly endless ramblings, dutifully published in the magazine, of a man who lived in pyjamas on a circular bed, consumed endless glasses of Pepsi-Cola and videotaped his own copulations. He filled it with visiting celebrities and complaisant, resident bunnies. Above the door, in dog-Latin was the message 'Si Non Oscillas, Non Tintinnare', loosely translated for the star-studded guests as 'If you don't swing, don't ring'. A second mansion, in Los Angeles, was opened in 1971.

From Hefner's point of view *Playboy* was Kinsey with a more interesting variety of statistics. Certainly he shared the older man's Mid-Western earnestness, bringing to the selling of sex the same kind of joyless fanaticism that his own grandparents had doubtless offered religion. For him the *Reports* justified his own belief: that sex was not some grubby hole-in-the-corner preoccupation, but a motivation that drove virtually everyone. The 'Playboy Philosophy' set sex at the centre of the universe. It was summed up in the deliciously pretentious editorial of the very first issue: 'We like our apartment. We enjoy mixing up cocktails and an hors d'oeuvre or two, putting a little mood music on the phonograph, and inviting in a female for a quiet discussion on Picasso, Nietzsche, jazz, sex.' Details might change, but the essentials were set in stone: faux sophistication for Mid-Western squares. Whether the acned teens, lonely servicemen, horny truckers or banged-up convicts who, like it or not would always make up his primary audience, were that big on Nietzsche remains debatable: but they certainly liked Hef's choice of flesh. Compared with what would come it was wonderfully wholesome – Monroe was an exception, the usual centrefold was definitely the 'girl next door' – but *Playboy*, banal or not, helped bring sex into the mainstream. It also underpinned a greater social change: the decline of Puritanism as a major force. If a *Playboy* could flourish, then hedonism, once the pleasure of a relative few, had entered the mass-market. 'Play' and 'boy': he couldn't have put it better.

All these things, of course, impinged on the UK, but for many people the signpost of the changes in Sixties sexuality was seen not so much in the appearance and appurtenances of a new morality, but in revelations as regarded the decline of the old. The grubby imbroglio which would become known as the 'Profumo Affair', mixing Tory grandees, a stable of call-girls, a society osteopath who doubled as an upmarket pimp, allegations of possible espionage, plus forays into the world of Notting Hill's West Indian community (not to mention the involvement of the area's most notorious landlord) was yet another of those events by which the 'start of the Sixties' may be marked.

The Affair had dominated the early spring of 1963 and would reverberate on well beyond, adding spice to Labour's electoral denunciation of 'the thirteen years of Tory misrule'. What in many ways would turn on the imbalance between a gentleman's avowed words and his actual deeds represented as much as anything the decline of the 'old order'. There had been scandals before, but few so symbolic. The élite had always appreciated their own fallibility, but the secret had been maintained. Now the whole country could enjoy the hypocrisies of those who for so long had styled themselves 'our betters'.

Space precludes any detailed account but the bones of the Affair are these. After months of rumours in high places, and the gradual spreading of the story amongst what would now be called the 'chattering classes' it was alleged that John Profumo, then the Conservatives' Defence Minister, had been involved in an adulterous affair with an eighteen-year-old 'model', Christine Keeler. This affair, while distasteful to many, gained further notoriety when it was suggested that the 'model', a word that for a season became a synonym for 'call-girl', was simultaneously involved with a Russian diplomat, one Ivanov. A number of Labour back-benchers had already brought the matter up in the Commons, albeit without naming the Minister concerned, and it was stressed that it was not just the sex that worried the Opposition, although it certainly shocked still strait-laced Britain, but the idea that such entanglements might lead, or even had already led to spying and government corruption.

On 22 March Profumo attempted to brazen out the gathering allegations, rising in the House of Commons to aver that there had been, 'no impropriety whatsover' between him and Miss Keeler. Few insiders were impressed. The Minister's speech did nothing to scotch the rumours, and it became clear, as Profumo's affair escalated into 'the Profumo Affair', that 'impropriety' was the least of it. On 4 June Profumo backtracked, admitting that he had misled the house; he resigned forthwith. A report by Lord Denning would prove that for all the brouhaha there had been no risk to national security, but the press had the story by now and, as revelation followed revelation, cataloguing a delicious farrago of sexual shenanigans in high places, the British public, pruriently moralistic, lapped up every detail.

The excitement culminated in the trial of Stephen Ward, a society osteopath whose patients had numbered dozens of eminent figures, for living on immoral earnings. Ward was accused of using his properties in London and Cliveden to arrange rendezvous between public figures and call-girls, such as the notorious Mandy Rice-Davies (the one-time girlfriend of Notting Hill's equally notorious Peter Rachman) and Christine Keeler (whose entanglement with Profumo had originated while she was staying with Ward) and of taking a commission for making the arrangements. It began on 23 July, would last only a week, and would lose its defendant. Appalled by the weight of evidence against him, and convinced (many would come to feel rightly) that he was being used as a scapegoat to save the reputations of more influential figures, Ward took a drug overdose on 30 July, the night before he was due to hear his sentence. He died three days later.

The Affair proved too much for the Tories, moribund and increasingly unpopular after twelve years in power. A procession of party bigwigs queued up to condemn their former friend, but their promises that Profumo, however reprehensible, was but a single bad apple, did not impress. A *Times* leader, headed 'It *Is* a Moral Issue', equated the country's growing affluence with what it saw as moral decline, declaring that Conservative policies had brought the nation 'spiritually and psychologically to a low ebb'. The Affair was obviously a gift to Labour, but Harold Wilson's playing of his cards was exemplary. Rather than trumpet his delight, Wilson kept Labour low-key, concentrating on security aspects (and keeping aloof from the supposed squalor of Profumo's private life). The party image was promoted as one of probity and dignity; the Tories might be digging themselves ever deeper into a pit of their own devising, but Labour's interests were those of the country at large. Thus the probing of security matters. As the rumours gathered – naked peers in S&M get-up, Stephen Ward's supposed 'brothel' on Lord Astor's Cliveden estate, a possible link to President Kennedy – Labour remained determinedly distant. When the House debated Profumo's resignation, on 17 June, Wilson cleverly noted that he was all too well aware of the facts, but that Labour would not exploit so sensational a situation to score a few party points. As a responsible Opposition they had simply handed over their dossier – a catalogue of blackmail, sex, drugs and corruption in high places – to the Prime Minister. Unfortunately, he added, the Prime Minister had not shown similar responsibility, but had attempted to wash his hands. He was, said Wilson, 'playing poker' with the nation's security. It was consummately skilful and left Macmillan, his trouper's charm for once rendered impotent, squirming. He could only turn the whole affair over to a Judicial Enquiry under Lord Denning, and listen as his own back-benchers began to murmur for his resignation.

Reduced to its grubby facts the Affair was of no great import – a scandal of 'puzzling triviality' as Ben Pimlott has put it[10] – but the image and the aftershocks it promoted undoubtedly were. As the *Washington Post*, one of many international papers to editorialise on what seemed yet another indicator of the national decline, remarked, 'a picture of widespread decadence beneath the glitter of a large segment of stiff-lipped society is emerging.' And while Profumo would not be mentioned and would certainly not take part, that picture was undoubtedly one of those that underpinned the whole American creation of 'Swinging London'.

Far more important, however, were the effects on Britain's self-perception. However banal the details, there were few, in the first place, who doubted its wider importance. Britain, or more properly England, was changing, and Profumo was a glaring symbol of that change. For Bernard Levin, looking back from 1970, the entire affair was 'a massive exercise in hypocrisy, perhaps the most staining episode of the entire decade'.[11] But, he added, it was: 'one which . . . was perhaps inevitable; if, in the Sixties, the past was letting go of Britain, its grip was not to be prised loose without a struggle, and the Profumo affair can therefore be seen as the last struggle of the old, false standards (or, as some would have said and some would still say, the old, true standards) before a new attitude emerged.'[12] Profumo was a victim, arraigned by the old order, and martyred that a new one might take its place. For those of a more cynical bent, it was all rather obvious, but for the wider public, clinging desperately on to the myths by which they lived their lives, the idea that a supposed 'master' should sink so low was devastating. Or at any rate so it was proclaimed by the press that served that public. A decade later, when Lord Lambton would be found, unashamedly, to have enjoyed the favours of not one but two whores, the scandal, for what it was, passed by to relative indifference. Thus the changes the new order had created.

For the counter-culture Profumo was an amusing side-show, the end of an era rather than anything more progressive. For those who promoted a more enterprising version of the sexual revolution its apotheosis appeared in 1969, in the form of Jim Haynes's 'sexual freedom' sexpaper *Suck*. Its long-term inspiration was the American alternative pornzine *Screw*, launched in 1968 as a response, according to its editor Al Goldstein, to the left's 'fucked up' attitudes to sex, but its genesis came when two bored veterans, Jim Haynes, at a loose end after the decline of the Arts Lab, and former *IT* editor Bill Levy decided that it was time to set up something new. Initially there were plans to base it in London, but even the broadest interpretation of the Obscene Publications Act was unlikely to countenance the kind of thing Haynes and Levy had in mind. *Suck* was quickly relocated to Amsterdam, where the authorities had a more tolerant attitude to what Haynes termed 'the pain and problems caused by sexual repression and frustration and ignorance'.[13] Apart from the two *IT* veterans the *Suck* editorial board included Germaine Greer, still twelve months from *The Female Eunuch*, and the playwright Heathcote Williams, then associate editor of the *Transatlantic Review*. Williams's current girlfriend Jean Shrimpton, the era's supermodel, came along too. Acording to Haynes the first editorial meeting – at Williams's flat – was interrupted when the pair vanished into an adjacent bedroom to put sexual theory into practice. As Haynes recalled later, that was the big mistake: given the paper's intentions, 'We should all five have made love together.'[14]

Suck started appearing in late 1969. Unlike *Screw*, defined by Haynes as 'primarily a male heterosexual humour magazine',[15] its European cousin was deliberately geared as widely as possible to the polymorphously perverse. '*Suck* was primarily a sexual liberation newspaper which represented the

entire pendulum of sexuality. We had as many women editors as men editors
... Any way of expressing one's sexuality was represented ... and *Suck* was
funny.'[16] Unlike *Screw*, which at times was hard to distinguish from orthodox
porn. Nor was *Suck* exploitative. 'It was not a male chauvinist paper ... I was
very aware of sexism and I was very aware of women's liberation and I always
said that I was a feminist. I have a one-sentence definition of women's liberation; it's the same as men's liberation and children's liberation: women's liberation is the recognition by both men and women of the need and the right for
each and every woman to assert herself. Realising that you have the right to
have a dream and to execute your dream, that is human liberation. Also the
male input was 50:50 hetero/homo. So the only male heterosexuals were Wil-
lem de Ridder, Heathcote Williams, Bill Levy and myself.'[17]

Suck lasted for three years, reaching a circulation of around 30,000, and
read, according to Haynes, by tens of thousands more, including Salvador
Dali, Indian cabinet ministers and a supposed 2,000 Hungarians who allegedly shared the single copy they'd been able to obtain. It shut, as the founders
had always intended, while it was ahead. Before that, however, the paper
generated a couple of *causes celèbres*. The photographer Keith Morris, who
had worked for a number of underground papers, was sitting quietly in the
Speakeasy club one night in autumn 1972:

> Germaine Greer wandered up to me and this was at the height of *The Female
> Eunuch* and says, 'Keith, I want you to take some pictures of me.' 'What sort
> of pictures?' I said. 'I want them stark naked, and I want a close-up of my
> cunt. Because it's got to be for *Suck* magazine. And at the same time I also
> want some pin-ups for my boyfriend back home.' So she came round at nine
> in the morning. It was a pretty revolting experience, photographing
> someone's sweaty cunt at nine in the morning. Not the ideal way to have break-
> fast and it was after a long hot night. So I did them. Bending over, lips apart,
> anus: the whole bit. She didn't design it. Knickers! She said she wanted a pic-
> ture of her arse and her cunt – how can you design that? It was a light-bulb
> shot. A close-up, degrees of zooming in and out, maybe move the light a frac-
> tion, then into the pin-up stuff. I do these close-ups and I do these pin-ups and
> then I say, 'Germaine, I've got to ask you: why me?' And she says, 'Because
> you're the only fucking photographer I can trust who won't sell them.'[18]

Greer's essay into the world of readers' wives was not, in theory, an exhibitionist *acte gratuite*. Sometime earlier the editorial board – Haynes, Levy,
Williams, Shrimpton, the office manager 'Purple' Susan Janssen and Greer
herself, had decided that what could show their commitment to the paper's
policy more perfectly than to display themselves naked in its pages. Some
pictures were indeed taken, but on the day only one appeared: a full-page
shot of the world's most celebrated feminist icon. Haynes, in his memoirs,
admits that the layout gave 'perhaps undue emphasis to Germaine as the ma-

jor world media star' and accepts that the subsequent furore, much enjoyed by the international media, was 'difficult for her'. Greer, unsurprisingly, resigned, sending Haynes a blast of invective which was, as she explic*DITLy* demanded, reprinted in the paper. Her chief complaint was against *Suck* as a whole. 'I have always criticised the degree of sadism that has appeared in *Suck* . . . the only thing that's genuinely exciting to most people is the sadism. Therefore I regard the whole paper as counter-revolutionary.'

For all its pretensions *Suck*, like *Screw*, remained at heart just one more stroke book. *Suck* was no more likely to change its readers' hearts as the latest revamp of any other men's magazine, with a pious claim that the revised version would be not porn, but tasteful erotica. Greer, in her belief that *Suck* would be read not for its pictures but for its philosophising, was for once naïve. What she, with Williams and Haynes, had wanted was a paper that promoted the ideals of a genuine sexual revolution: no exploitation, no smut, no stereotyping, something that would break once and for all the Judaeo-Christian hang-ups that ruined sex in the West. It was a brave hope, and a futile one.

For Greer the photo was the last straw: she had already begun to feel uneasy in 1970, when *Suck* had mounted the first of what would be three 'Wet Dream Festivals', dedicated to the world's porn film industry. Like any such festival there was a jury, the first of which comprised Greer herself, the publisher Jay Landesman, Richard Neville, the journalist Michael Zwerin, Didi Wadidi (a German model, real name Fatima Ingram) and Al Goldstein. The only hiccup came when Neville, letting journalistic enthusiasm outweigh juridical gravitas, snipped half-a-dozen frames from an out-take of *Performance* and featuring Mick Jagger's penis. They appeared in *Oz*, much to the consternation of Haynes and of Sandy Lieberson, the producer, who had let the footage get out in the first place. Neville's apologetic letter was perhaps tempered by his own experience of the movies: a cameo role in Ken Loach and Tony Garnett's film *The Body*, in which Neville and his girlfriend Louise made love for the camera.

More dramatic, however, was a piece of theatrical excess that showed that even sexual revolutionaries had their limits. According to Craig Sams, who had pioneered macrobiotic food in London and went on to run the successful Whole Earth Foods,

> The Wet Dream festival was held in Amsterdam in November 1970. It was just three days of showing of various soft-core and hard-core [movies] . . . just about everything pornographic that had been put on film. It was a convention of the sexual revolution but it was the most sexless event imaginable. We were camped three or four to a room in various people's houses. But we didn't all fuck away enthusiastically. None of that happened. The climax of the thing was the final evening. Otto Muëhl and his AA Kommune people had the Rolling Stones on very loud and were dancing around naked on stage and cavorting lewdly and the climax of his show came when he took this

goose and was stroking it and obviously had it very calmed, despite the loud music and everything else, and the plan was that he would violate the goose and then cut its head off. Suddenly there's an eruption from the audience: Heathcote Williams brought him down, grabbed the goose and passed it to someone else. Otto and his team had a tantrum on stage, continuing to dance around shaking their fists at the audience and eventually crapped on the stage and went off. Downstairs Heathcote had collapsed in the arms of Jean Shrimpton. Various people argued about whether it was right or wrong that he should have done it. Being vegetarian and macrobiotic, I took the view that how hypocritical it was to make such a fuss over one goose, when thousands of people were being killed in Vietnam and thousands of animals were being killed in slaughterhouses all the time. The countervailing argument was 'Well yes, but you've got to draw a line.'

Greer and Williams, in a belated effort to save the day, stripped off, mounted the stage and began rolling around, 'knotting and unknotting like sea creatures'.[19] More and more people joined in and the resulting cluster-fuck presumably took the edge off Muëhl's excesses, but for Greer *Suck* would never be quite the same again.

The sexual revolution happened, most certainly, and at the same time failed. It bore tangible fruits: major legislative changes in the administration of obscenity, of abortion, of divorce and of gay sexuality. But if one recalls the optimistic philosophising of the counter-cultural press with its calls for an end to all the repressive hypocrisies that surrounded sex and an embracing of the full range of human sexual possibilities, then the end of the era left most people in the same state as it had found them. Sex gained a higher profile, no doubt, and for those who so desired it was easier to pursue one's own predilections, but it remained primarily heterosexual and monogamous sex. Certainly the media, who were quick to promote the new 'permissiveness' did not extend their pages or screens to anything but mainstream imagery. For the counter-culture sexual experimentation was undoubtedly one more signpost along the path to self-discovery, but for the majority it was simply sex. Furthermore, even for the counter-culture the old masculine supremacy was barely ruffled, for all its revolutionary pronouncements.

What did change was not so much sexuality, but the determination of hitherto neglected or demonised sections of society to break out of the heterosexual or male-dominated stereotype and make themselves felt. This came in what are perhaps the most lasting legacies of the period: the gender politics of women's and gay liberation. 'The personal is political,' proclaimed these new advocates, and what could be more personal than one's sexuality? On the most basic level, the new politics was centred on simply taking control of one's own body; the longer-term developments stemmed from that. Gay men, in particular, would define themselves through their sexuality –

and how their unreformed detractors delighted when that same sexuality was seen as bringing them to sickness and death – but the greater revolution was not in the quantity of copulations, but in the fact that the quality of gay life was proclaimed as of equal value to any other. Unlike other aspects of Sixties liberalism, gender politics did not fade in the harsher climate of the new decade, but if anything became more intense. Sexual experimentation as represented by *Suck* magazine did take a back seat, gradually cheapened into the world of 'swinging' (Sixties wife-swapping by any other name), of singles bars, and of sexclubs like New York's Plato's Retreat. The liberation struggles fought on and despite a world that claims to be post-AIDS and post-feminist, have yet to relinquish their efforts.

In the end one is left, as Jeffrey Weeks has noted, with many more questions than answers. Loking at society ten years on from the vaunting enthusiasms of the Sixties, he found that 'by the 1980s the most striking feature is the absence of an agreed moral framework'.

> On the most basic level individuals cleaved to fundamental values, of love, honesty, faithfulness. But what these values meant in the real social world was far from clear. Did adherence to these values mean, for instance, that one had to adhere to the traditional values of family life? Or could they be realised in less formal, less binding, even less monogamous, frameworks? Did the new emphasis on sexual pleasure involve a commercialisation of sex, as the moralist believed? Or did it imply a healthy demystification of the sacredness of sex? Was sex being debased and trivialised, or was it being freed from the shackles of tradition and prejudice?[20]

Chapter Twenty-Five

Obscene Publications: Gelding the Censors

There are in this book thirty 'fucks or fuckings', fourteen 'cunts', thirteen 'balls', six each of 'shit' and 'arse', four 'cocks' and three 'piss'.
Mervyn Griffiths-Jones, QC, prosecuting *Lady Chatterley's Lover* 1960

Of all the 'Jenkins Acts' that would turn out to impinge most immediately on the counter-culture, the Obscene Publications Act of 1959 actually predated the Home Secretary's years in office, and Jenkins was enlisted not as a minister but as a private member. It was, however, an excellent signpost for what would follow.

English literary censorship has a long and bitterly contested history. Its first appearance was as a subject for the ecclesiastical courts – in an age of minimal literacy there was no 'obscenity', let alone 'pornography', but in their place a good deal of blasphemy, sedition and even heresy. Not until the mid-eighteenth century was the offence of 'obscene libel' (literally a 'dirty little book') in place. It was now illegal to 'publish [a] lewd, wicked, bawdy, scandalous and obscene libel . . . to the manifest corruption of the morals and minds of the liege subjects of our said Lord the King, and his laws, in violation of common decency, morality, and good order, and against the peace'.

Obscene libel might have served for a less widely literate age, but the onset of mass literacy, and of publications geared to satisfy it, ensured that the nineteenth century would require new legislation. This came in 1857, in the form of the first Obscene Publications Act. It created no new offence, and made no attempt to alter the current definition of what was obscene under Common Law, but concentrated on attacking the sale of obscene books by empowering the authorities to raid suspected stocks of such books and destroy them. It was then the responsibility of the owner of that material to prove why it should not be destroyed. The bill met vehement opposition in both Houses of Parliament where critics realised that such a law would lead inevitably to the arbitrary destruction of whatever could be found to offend a conservative magistrate, irrespective of any actual worth. As the twentieth century joke would put it, 'Obscenity is whatever gives an elderly judge an erection.' As feared, the main effect of the Act was the creation of a mass of arbitrary censors: the various societies dedicated to the prosecution of 'vice' and the untutored but opinionated local magistrates. Nothing, however, much a classic, was immune.

Even more important than the Act itself was the new definition of obscenity promulgated eleven years later by Lord Chief Justice Cockburn, presiding over the case of *Regina v. Hicklin*. In 1867 Wolverhampton justices of the peace had seized, citing the Act, 252 copies of a scurrilous, possibly obscene pamphlet entitled 'The Confessional Unmasked: shewing the depravity of the Roman Priesthood, the iniquity of the Confessional and the questions put to females in confession', a deliberate attack on the Catholic church. The Wolverhampton authorities ordered that they be burnt, but the distributor appealed to the Quarter Sessions where the Recorder, one Benjamin Hicklin, found in his favour. The Catholic hierarchy then appealed to the Queen's Bench. It was at this point that the Lord Chief Justice defined obscenity as follows: 'The test of obscenity is this, whether the tendency of the matter charged as obscenity is to deprave and corrupt those whose minds are open to such immoral influences and into whose hands a publication of this sort may fall.' It would be enshrined as 'The Hicklin Rule'. The onus of this definition was that henceforth a book would be judged not upon its effect on the likely readership, the literate bourgeoisie, but by that on more susceptible individuals: women, children, psychopaths and the lower classes. It was an all-embracing catch-all and both great literature and scientific advance at once came under threat. As the American Judge Curtis Blok commented later, 'Strictly applied, this rule renders any book unsafe, since a moron could pervert to some sexual fantasy to which his mind is open the listings of a seed catalogue.' Cockburn's definition was not even binding as law – being only judicial *obiter dicta* – but it was swiftly incorporated into text-books and stood as the accepted test of obscenity for the next ninety years.

By the early 1950s the Act of 1857 and the Hicklin Rule that followed it, had led to what many felt was a grossly unsatisfactory situation. Philistine Home Secretaries, more than usually obscurantist back-benchers, wilfully blinkered 'vice crusaders' and their supporters might have rejoiced in the *status quo*, but few others would join them. It was deemed vital to draw a line between 'serious' literature and the products of the pulp pornography factories. The 1857 Act may have sought to control pornography; its sucessor was intended to protect art. (That pornography might have its place, distasteful or otherwise, was never acknowledged; as in the other social reforms that would follow, a sop, in this case that of 'taste', had to be found for repressive Cerberus.) In 1954 a Committee drawn from the Society of Authors, and chaired by Sir Alan Herbert (himself an MP), submitted its opinions to the Home Secretary. Its formation followed directly on the prosecutions of a number of novels earlier that year. None were remotely pornographic, but sections were undeniably sexy by contemporary standards: under Hicklin they 'depraved and corrupted' and as such were condemned. The findings of this Committee formed the basis of the first attempt to change the law: a Private Members Bill, the Obscene Publications Bill, 1955. It was introduced by a Labour MP, Roy Jenkins, but it achieved nothing. Neither did a subsequent bill backed by Lord Lambton. This however did obtain a second reading and was referred to a Select Committee of the Whole House, which in 1958 was asked 'to reconsider whether it was desirable to amend and consolidate the law relating to Obscene Publications'. The Committee submitted its findings – advocating reform – but once more, the government preferred to do nothing.

In 1959, basing his proposals on the Committee's report, Roy Jenkins espoused a second Private Member's Bill, the Obscene Publications Bill, 1959. When this too was ignored, widespread parliamentary pressure was aimed at the government. Sir Alan Herbert threatened to resign and seek re-election as an Independent. Eventually, the government set aside time to debate Jenkins's bill. After a variety of amendments, compromises and delays, the Obscene Publications Act, 1959, 'an Act to amend the law relating to the publication of obscene matter; to provide for the protection of literature; and to strengthen the law concerning pornography', became law on 29 August 1959. The Act, which for better or worse has governed the position of obscene publications in Britain ever since, contains the following provisions and definitions. The old offence of publishing an obscene libel is abolished and the new one of publishing, for gain or otherwise, an obscene article is substituted. An 'article' includes anything that can be read, and includes sound records and films. A person who 'publishes' an article is one who distributes, circulates, sells, hires out, gives or lends it, or who offers it for sale or for hire. Publishing covers playing records and exhibiting films, and showing artworks that are meant to be viewed. (Videotape would join the list in 1980.) The act included a new test for obscenity: 'An article shall be deemed obscene if its effect or . . . the effect of any one of its items is, if taken as a whole, such as to tend to deprave and corrupt persons who are likely, having regard to all relevant circumstances, to read, see, or hear the matter contained or embodied in it.' The legislators did their best, but ambiguity remained: there were no exact definitions of the words 'deprave' or 'corrupt'.

Writing in the aftermath of his successful campaign, Roy Jenkins noted how prolonged and painful the fight had been, but added that for all the obstacles it might face, 'Private Members' legislation on a highly controversial subject is clearly still occasionally possible in the British Parliament. But it requires the following combination of circumstances. First, a certain amount of luck; second, a great deal of time and even more patience; third, some all-party support; fourth, a Minister who will be personally sympathetic at crucial times; fifth, some well-organised and determined allies both inside and outside the House of Commons, and sixth, an articulate and impressive body of extra-parliamentary support.'[1] Such conditions would be a blueprint for the social legislation that was to come, the underpinnings of the future Home Secretary's 'civilised' society.

Between October 1926 and January 1928 D.H. Lawrence wrote three versions of a novel in which he described the affair of the fictional Lady Constance Chatterley, wife of Sir Clifford Chatterley, an intellectual, writer and Midlands landowner who has been confined to a wheelchair by war wounds, with the estate gamekeeper, Oliver Mellors, the son of a miner. While the book itself, which ends with the lovers each awaiting divorce and looking forward to their new life together, does not stray conspicuously from Lawrence's general moral and philosophical attitudes, his use of taboo language far exceeded anything acceptable in contemporary fiction. In his attempt to convey the passions of sexual intercourse, he included the sort of 'Anglo-Saxon' vocabulary that scandalised most of society.

Although the third version, which had the most lurid language, was unpublishable in England, Lawrence offered it to the publishers Jonathan Cape, Secker & Warburg and Chatto & Windus and mocked their rejections as hypocrisy. Thus satisfied, he turned to Giuseppe Orioli, who ran an internationally famous bookshop in Florence, near which city the author was living. Lawrence considered his book 'far too good for the . . . gross public', suggesting rather that subscriptions should be solicited from 'the right sort of people in the Universities'. The first, Florentine, edition of 1,000 copies sold out in 1928, even at the high price of two guineas (£2.10). As Colin MacInnes pointed out at the book's British trial in 1960, despite any ban, those who wanted the book and who were clever enough to appreciate it, would always find a way of obtaining it. None the less, while a variety of bowdlerised, pirated or otherwise ersatz editions continued to appear, *Lady Chatterley* 'proper' remained in literary purdah.

In 1957 the US Supreme Court had allowed that a defence of 'redeeming social importance' would henceforth be permitted in literary obscenity trials. Two years later, in order to test the repercussions of this on the publication of what had previously been condemned as 'obscene material', the relatively radical Grove Press deliberately issued an unexpurgated version of the 1928 edition. This was distributed through a book club called Readers Subscription and seized by Post Office authorities. In a trial before the US Post Office department the book was found obscene, but when Grove Press brought a counter-suit to restrain the Post Office ban, Judge van Pelt Bryan of the US District Court found in favour of the book. He found redeeming social merit in it and praised Lawrence's 'descriptive passages of rare beauty'. In America at least, 'Lady C' was free.

The news of Grove Press's success made it clear that a similar attempt should be made in Britain. Both aesthetic and commercial considerations, backed by the belief that the Obscene Publications Act of 1959 had offered wider latitude to 'obscene publishing', made an uncut edition alluring. On 9 January 1960 Penguin Books announced that, along with seven other Lawrence titles, a complete edition would be published to mark the thirtieth anniversary of the author's birth and the twenty-fifth of the imprint's. In July, when Penguin sent the Director of Public Prosecutions sample copies of the 200,000 they had waiting in their warehouse he was unable to resist the challenge. A trial under the 1959 Act was scheduled for October. Penguin froze their stocks in anticipation. There was undoubtedly an increasingly liberal atmosphere in the UK: Nabokov's *Lolita* had been published unscathed, but it lacked 'four-letter' words and, in an age when paedophilia made few headlines, its sensuality was less overt. The real reason for the prosecution, it was opined, was that Penguin were offering the book at 3/6 (17.5 p) a copy, a price that put the acceptable delights of the connoisseur's locked bookcase into the grubby hands of the great unwashed. The paperback had long been seen as a source of corruption. In 1952 America's House Select Committee on Current Pornographic Materials pronounced that, 'Some of the most offensive infractions of the moral code were found to be contained in low-cost, paper-bound publications known as "pocket-size books" . . . which . . . have . . . degenerated into media for the dissemination of artful appeals to sensuality, immorality, filth, perversion and degeneracy.' Nor was this exactly hard-core material: the titles in question included works by Dreiser, Huxley, Sartre and indeed Lawrence.

Unlike the US trial, which was short and to the point, the five-day proceedings that opened at the Old Bailey on 21 October 1960 were a veritable circus. The defence lawyers had mustered seventy expert witnesses, of whom thirty-five were called. They included academics, the great and good of literature and the arts, a film critic, some teachers, clergymen and politicians. Their 'expertise' was less important than what Charles Rembar, who had defended the book in America, called their role as 'lobbyists . . . (who) were not so much offering evidence as putting prestige into the claim that the book was innocent'.[2] The defence was substantially helped by the prosecution counsel, Mervyn Griffiths-Jones, who suggested to a jury, five of whose members had stumbled over reading out the oath, that it was not a book fit for 'your wife or your servants'. The essentially patronising tone of his pronouncements certainly helped alienate the jury – Griffiths-Jones's alleged concern for the morals of the proles was matched only by the obvious contempt in which he held them – although to what extent they were impressed by the procession of the liberal intellectual establishment is debatable. The most successful of the experts was the resolutely working-class Richard Hoggart, author of *The Uses of Literacy*, who taught at a provincial university. It was not only the jury who were impressed; for Ken Tynan, summing up in the *Observer*, Hoggart was 'the stubborn, uncompromising voice of the radical English moralist. Its volume and assurance grew as the cross-examination proceeded; and before long both jury and audience knew that the real battle had been joined – between all that Hoggart stood for and all that Griffiths-Jones stood for; between . . . contact and separation; between freedom and control; between love and death.'[3]

On 2 November, after a trial which had had to be adjourned for them to read the book, the jury retired for three hours before finding Penguin Books innocent. Penguin responded by dedicating the next edition to them. (It would sell two million copies in the next year.) Their verdict reflected the era: what Philip Larkin would call 'the end of the Chatterley ban' influenced far more people than CND or a bunch of youth cults, however vociferous. 'Banning the Bomb' remained a theory, however sincerely felt; the Obscene Publications Act and this, its great test case, were a tangible opening up that affected the whole of society. In its detail and and its wider implications 'the end of the Chatterley ban' presaged the new era of social engineering. (Although as Hoggart has also noted, 'The objectors' fear would have been realised, though, if they had seen the stream of miners, coming off shift at Eastwood on the afternoon of the acquittal, heading for the local bookshop or newsagent's and asking where the really dirty bits were."[4]

However, for all the trial's importance, it still failed to see off the efforts of those who found themselves unable to curb *their* most obsessive lust: interference in the private leisure activities of their fellows. As Richard Hoggart noted, looking back from 1992 in a piece for *The Times*, the trial showed not so much a consensus, but 'a deeply divided society [in which] both sides sought the same moral high ground'. The successes of what he termed 'Left culturalism' (the Jenkins Acts) were by no means universally welcomed.[5] The Cambridge critic F.R. Leavis, Lawrence's leading academic apostle, saw the trial as a misguided farce, ushering in a new and repellent form of orthodoxy: that of the liberal Left. Over in Oxford John Sparrow, the Warden of All Souls', informed the readers of *Encounter* that the parading experts were either stupid or hypocritical: they had united to acquit Lawrence of 'perversion' but how could anyone, expert or not, have failed to observe that in one episode Mellors was unarguably engaged in buggering his mistress. The experts fought back – the lawyers arguing that no barrister (and Sparrow had been one himself) would deliberately undermine his own case by spotlighting unfavourable facts, and the literary figures claiming that what mattered was Lawrence's overall vision of love. In either case Sparrow was generally derided; 'Warden of All Holes' was among the kinder nicknames.

The decade, and that which followed, would witness a series of trials. As *Lady Chatterley* was followed by John Cleland's *Fanny Hill* (1963, perhaps the only 'dirty book' to reject even a tinge of overt obscenity), by Alex Trocchi's *Cain's Book* (1964), by William Burroughs's *The Naked Lunch* (1964), by Herbert Selby Junior's *Last Exit to Brooklyn* (1966/8) and by the anonymous Victorian philanderer's chronicle *My Secret Life* (1969), the Old Bailey, not to mention the public, grew used to the regular procession of tweed-jacketed littérateurs mingling with bewigged barristers as they thrashed out the literary merits of one text or another. On the whole liberalism won the day – none of the titles listed would be banned, however keenly such diehard opponents as the MP Sir Cyril Black might fight for suppression. But by the time, in 1976, when the infinitely tacky *Inside Linda Lovelace* (the alleged confessions of a porn starlet, best known for her bringing the practice, and indeed the concept, of 'deep throat' fellatio to the public notice) found itself subject to the same literary ministrations, it had all become rather foolish. The experts, as Mary Whitehouse, in a moment of uncharacteristic wit had put it, had become a 'travelling circus', available on demand but no longer providing anything very new. However the authorities had alternative lines of attack. In 1961, in the case of *Shaw v. DPP*, the prosecution of *The Ladies' Directory*, a prostitutes' contact sheet, the House of Lords revived the old common law offence of 'conspiracy to corrupt public morals', developed *c*.1600 and last activated in the eighteenth century. The law had been created to punish those who, traditionally, might have hoped for the less severe justice of the ecclesiastical courts; three centuries on, it was redeployed to outflank not the Church, but the Obscene Publications Act. Shaw was convicted, but the 'conspiracy charge' would have a greater resonance: in the attacks, through censorship trials, on the counter-culture, and specifically the 'underground press'.

Before moving on to the travails of *IT* and more importantly *Oz*, it is worth looking at another 'opening up' of British culture: the end, after four hundred long years, of theatrical censorship. The control of literature would not properly enter its maturity until, logically enough, there were sufficient readers and sufficient books to make it – in Establishment eyes at least – a necessary function of government. That of theatre, however, which required no such attainments as personal literacy, had been a matter for the authorities since the mid-sixteenth century. The first official 'theatre censor' appeared when in 1545 Henry VIII established the office of '*Magister Jocorum, Revelorum et Mascorum omnium et singulorum nostrum, vulgariter nuncupatorum Revelles et Maskes*' (better known as the Master of the Revels). His career as the regulator of drama lasted until 1688, when the Lord Chamberlain, to whom he had always been responsible took over. By 1692 it was acknowledged (by Dryden) that the Lord Chamberlain's powers embraced 'all that belongs to the Decency and Good Manners of the Stage' and that he could 'restrain the licentious insolence of Poets and their Actors, in all things that shock the Publick Quiet, or the Reputation of Private Persons, under the notion of "Humour" '. In the Stage Licensing Act of 1737 and its successor the Theatre Regulation Act of 1843 this random collection of powers was codified and given statutory authority. The Lord Chamberlain was an absolute censor. He was responsible neither to Parliament nor to the courts of law. Every script had to be submitted to him and there was no appeal against his rulings, other than to the Sovereign. By the same token, once he had passed a play, no other authority might seek to ban it. His office dealt only with theatre managers; the actual dramatists did not, in official eyes, exist. The only way of avoiding censorship was by presenting one's work at a 'theatre club', a development of the twentieth century, which, with its ostensibly restricted membership, made for a 'private' performance.

Lord Chamberlains were rarely malicious; their supporters, among whom were managers who felt that someone had to state what was acceptable on stage, and actors who had no desire to suffer the caprices of some provincial magistrate, accepted them as a necessary nuisance. Their views, it might be argued, represented those of the great British public. But for those, notably the writers, for whom any censorship was otiose, the Lord Chamberlain represented philistine, irrelevant interference. Individuals who had suffered at the Chamberlain's hands had never been happy, but the wider movement against stage censorship started with the emergence of such 'modern' writers as Shaw and Ibsen.

In 1909, acknowledging this growing opposition to stage censorship, Parliament established a Joint Select Committee on Censorship. The Committee's creation had been particularly stimulated by a letter signed by seventy-one representatives of the theatrical establishment following the banning in 1907 of Edward Garnett's *The Breaking Point* and Harley Granville-Barker's *Waste*. It condemned 'an office autocratic in procedure, opposed to the spirit of the Constitution, contrary to justice and common sense'. The Lord Chamberlain declined to appear, but his assistants were called and showed themselves inconsistent and muddled as to their precise role. Among the witnesses was a wide range of theatrical luminaries. The Committee decided that the Lord Chamberlain should stay in authority, but that it should be optional to submit plays to him for licensing. It would be legal to stage an unlicensed play but one must accept the risk of prosecution by the Director of Public Prosecutions (acting against indecency), or the Attorney-General (acting against graver offences). There were a number of detailed proposals as to what should be banned (plays that were 1. indecent, 2. contained offensive personalities, 3. represented in an invidious manner a living person or a person recently dead, 4. did violence to the sentiment of religious reverence, 5. were conducive to crime or vice, 6. impaired friendly relations with any foreign power, 7. caused a breach of the peace) but the overall image was one of confusion. The Committee, the last major enquiry into censorship before its abolition in 1968, was, as Shaw put it, 'a capital illustration of . . . the art of contriving methods of reform that will leave matters exactly as they are'. Its efforts generated much debate but no action. The government refused to act, but merely let the furore die away. The censors, appreciating this apathy, indulged in a period of particularly crass interference that was curtailed only by the fact that during the First World War they received no challenging material to mutilate.

In the late 1950s, after John Osborne's *Look Back In Anger* began the revolution in the English drama, many critics felt that the Lord Chamberlain might as well, for all his anachronistic powers, be tolerated. He might ostensibly maintain his control, but few producers, playwrights or actors, let alone intelligent audiences, seemed to care. However the forces of liberalism were not so easily deterred. Tolerance was fine; abolition was infinitely preferable.

Like many other of the cultural campaigns that would revolutionise Sixties Britain, that which would overturn the Lord Chamberlain's archaic powers was no overnight success. And like the Obscene Publications legislation, it involved the future Home Secretary Roy Jenkins who in 1958, alongside such liberal luminaries as Noel Annan and Wayland Young (author of the ground-breaking *Eros Denied*, the best-known essay into sexology of its era) helped launch the Theatre Censorship Reform Committee.

The Committee's first move was to approach the subject of their enquiries: the Lord Chamberlain responded by stating that it would be improper for him to talk to an unofficial body. The advent of a new Labour government, and the example of the still recent Obscene Publications Act led to a new, more antagonistic mood. By 1965 the subject was back in Parliament, and the Prime Minister, while noting that there were as yet no plans for legislation, accepted 'the strong feeling that exists on this question' and that 'this aspect of our national life needs some degree of modernisation'.[6] It was in 1965 that the text of *Saved*, a play by Edward Bond in which, in a horrific central scene, a baby is stoned to death in its pram, was submitted for reading. To avoid the inevitable cuts, the play was staged at a theatre club, the Royal Court Theatre reinvented for the relevant nights as the 'English Stage Society'. For a change, the Lord Chamberlain refused to turn a blind eye. The police joined the audience and in January 1966 the directors of the Royal Court were charged under the 1843 Act with presenting an unlicensed play. They were found guilty and fined fifty guineas. The clubs, supposedly sacrosanct, were as vulnerable as any other theatre. It was a blunder the censors would regret.

In 1958 the Lord Chamberlain may have been able to shoo away his questioners; by 1966 it was no longer feasible. Of the leading lights of the Theatre Censorship Reform Committee, Annan and Young were now members of the House of Lords, while Jenkins was a singularly liberal Home Secretary. Jenkins, true to his policy of encouraging others to advance reforms that he could then tacitly support without fully involving the government until absolutely necessary, urged Annan to put forward in the Lords a motion calling for a Joint Committee of both Houses to review the position. Annan then contacted the Lord Chamberlain, Lord Cobbold, who admitted that he too was less than happy about the *status quo*. Almost every peer acknowledged the need if not for change, then at least examination. The General Election of March 1966 held back the motion from the Commons, but when Parliament reconvened it was accepted there as well. A committee was appointed, calling upon among others Lords Annan, Goodman, Scarborough (a former Lord Chamberlain) and Lady Gaitskell, plus MPs Michael Foot, Andrew Faulds (an ex-actor) and Norman St John Stevas.

The Committee heard a wide range of evidence. Members of the League of Dramatists (among them John Osborne and John Mortimer) were at the forefront of the reformers. In their submission they stated that, 'We feel this is a *moral* issue . . . We only wish to be subject to the same controls as our fellow writers and citizens.'[7] They were backed by the Royal Shakespeare Company. Lord Cobbold, the current censor, opted for passing his responsibilities on to the Arts Council; Lord Goodman, the Council's boss, rejected this: the Arts Council was supposed to promote the arts, not censor them. (The case of *Saved* was especially pertinent: the Lord Chamberlain may have weighed in to prosecute, but the Arts Council, a government-sponsored body, had given the playwright £1,000 to help with its production.) Only the Society of West End Theatre managers was completely happy, although it suggested some form of graded listing of plays, like movies, with 'A', 'U' and even 'X' productions. The Committee's report came down firmly on the side of reform. It was not, they stated, that the Lord Chamberlain had exceeded his powers, it was more that such powers were incompatible with the modern world. They had pondered the possibility of an alternative form of control, but none presented itself: the best and simplest remedy was outright abolition.

Of all the 'Jenkins Acts' this one had by far the smoothest passage. Unlike the legislation on literary censorship, abortion or homosexuality, the 'Act to abolish Censorship of the Theatre and to amend the law in respect of Theatres and Theatrical Performances', which became law on 26 September 1968, enjoyed one vital bonus: it was passed virtually unopposed. Cynics suggested that once again this was a case of élitism: the theatre remained a middle-class pleasure, for all the efforts of the 'alternative' and 'fringe' companies that emerged during the decade, and the middle-classes could be trusted with a little obscenity. There were other possible explanations, often fortuitous. The presence of Roy Jenkins was first among these: his influence as a Minister was minimal, but his involvement 'off-stage' was of immense importance. Lord Cobbold, the incumbent censor, was more than happy to abandon the post; had he fought he might have changed the whole atmosphere. Perhaps the most important factor was that there simply was no alternative. It was the Lord Chamberlain or nothing; and nothing was what was wanted. Finally there was the simple matter of timing and of *zeitgeist*: 'Left culturalism' was on a roll. By now the status of homosexuality and of abortion had been radically changed; and if those bastions of controversy could fall, that the theatre would follow was a foregone conclusion.

Based on the deliberations of the Joint Committee the Act repealed the Theatre Regulation Act of 1843 and abolished the Lord Chamberlain's role as censor. Following from the Obscene Publications Act (1959) the Act accepted a test of obscenity which held that 'a performance of a play shall be deemed to be obscene if, taken as a whole, its effect was such as to tend to deprave and corrupt persons who were likely, having regard to all relevant circumstances, to attend it.' Parts of a script may be charged with being obscene; if so, the same defence of 'public good' as exists in the OPA of 1959 may be offered. Expert witnesses may be called to prove that a performance is in the interest of 'drama, opera, ballet, or any other art, or of literature or learning'. The same test of indictable obscenity exists as in the 1959 Act, and anyone who presents or directs, for gain or not, an obscene performance of a play given either in public or in private (other than as a domestic event in a private dwelling) may be prosecuted. The play's author, however, is not liable; although he or she technically 'publishes' the play by offering it to a producer, the play does not become an 'obscene article' unless it can be proved to corrupt those who have to read it – the cast – rather than those who merely attend the theatre – the audience. Any proceedings against a play must be initiated by the Attorney-General, or by someone authorised to do so by him. Prosecutions of plays on charges of seditious libel, criminal libel and blasphemy were still feasible.

As the League of Dramatists had requested, playwrights were now treated to the same controls as any other artistic creator (other than film-makers). The theatre as a whole had achieved freedom of speech – a basic human right that had been denied it for four hundred years. As with the OPA, the new liberalism did not guarantee quality – the first 'first night' to follow the Act's passage was that of the execrable *Hair* – but that was a secondary problem.

No flood of gratuitous excess followed the passage of the Act, but it was inevitable that at least one production would provide the necessary frisson. This came in 1970 when the theatre critic Kenneth Tynan, a veteran *enfant terrible*, mounted what *The Times* disdainfully apostrophised as 'Mr Tynan's Nude Review', *Oh! Calcutta!*, (it had been aired in New York six months earlier). Tynan was a hardly a novice at stirring up controversy. A dandy at Oxford in the 1940s (not for nothing was his middle name 'Peacock'), in the 1950s he had been the main advocate of those playwrights, spearheaded by John Osborne, who smashed their way through the comfortable world of 'Loamshire' (as he termed it, 'a glibly codified fairy-tale world, of no more use to the student of life than a doll's-house would be to a student of town planning').[8] He was one of the older generation of career liberals whose support in the 1960s would lie behind a number of counter-cultural activities. It was Tynan who defined a playwright as 'a congenital eavesdropper with the instincts of a Peeping Tom . . . Would you know the shortest way to good playwriting? Pause on the stairs.' On 13 November 1965, as a guest on one of BBC TV's post-*TW3* 'satire' shows, *BBC-3*, he momentarily abandoned his 'Shouts and Murmurs' column in the *Observer* to unleash a positive screech of Loamshire loathing. As the conversation, with American writer Mary McCarthy, turned on censorship and the nature of 'obscenity' Tynan offered his opinion: 'I doubt if there are any rational people to whom the word "fuck" would be particularly diabolical, revolting, or totally forbidden.'

In 1965, with *Lady Chatterley's Lover* barely five years legal, and such pressure groups as Clean-Up TV desperate to turn back the clock, the word's appearance on television, and especially on the BBC, caused widespread outrage. What followed was a reflection, and by no means a flattering one, on the national psyche. Out in the adult world there was the Vietnam War, Rhodesia's Unilateral Declaration of Independence (proclaimed that very day) and the abolition of capital punishment (which had come into force only two days earlier). Yet in England there was but a single topic of apparent import: '*L'affaire du mot*', as a French paper, marvelling at the pitiful absurdity its correspondent was witnessing, summed it up. Tynan would receive more than one thousand press clippings; the BBC's switchboards were jammed, the correspondence columns of Fleet Street foundered beneath the 'outrage'. Tynan's own feelings were summed up in a press release: 'I used an old English word in a completely neutral way to illustrate a serious point, just as I would have used it in a similar conversation with any group of grown-up people. To have censored myself would, in my view, have been an insult to the viewers' intelligence.'

He would have been more sensible to have been less tolerant. Certainly those who believe that 'the Sixties' were some paradise of unbridled licence need look no further to find proof that for the lumpen middle classes and their representatives (elected or otherwise) how little had changed. There were questions in the House, fevered back-benchers desperate to leaven their own obscurity, crying out for one punishment or another. There were personal letters, most of them hostile, although one 'ordinary Housewife and Grandmother' derided the 'manic prudes' and expressed her affection for 'the sweet word fuck'.[9] Mary Whitehouse emerged on cue. Sadly the BBC refused to dismiss the outcry with the contempt it deserved; the Corporation did not apologise as such, but still issued an 'expression of regret', admitting that *fuck* (not that they spelt it out – nor had any of the papers who reported the story) was not a word to be used on air. To their credit Ned Sherrin, the show's producer, and arts supremo Huw Weldon both defended Tynan, but their voices were lost among the hysteria. Even the liberal press, who might have been expected to weigh in for free speech, stayed firmly on the fence, bearing out the poet Robert Frost's definition of their timorous equivocation: 'the liberal – a man too broadminded to take his own side in a quarrel'.

The idea of staging an 'Evening of Erotica', 'nothing that is *merely* funny or *merely* beautiful should be admitted: it must also be sexy'[10], came to Ken Tynan during a meeting with William Donaldson (producer of *Beyond the Fringe*) in 1966 and drew its title from a painting by the French surrealist Clovis Trouille. Depicting a naked odalisque, her buttocks to the viewer, it was entitled 'Oh Calcutta! Calcutta!', a French pun that could read '*Oh, quel cul tu as!*' or, 'Oh what an arse you have!' His idea was to dispense with a script and to use a theatre club, thus circumventing the Lord Chamberlain;

there would be female dancers and male comedians, and the sketches would take in representations of Trouille paintings, a tribute to Paris's Crazy Horse Saloon, to American burlesque, and a variety of 'semi-documentary items', such as a history of underwear, and tableaux representing national sexual stereotypes (Italy was a nun raped by her confessor, England a St Trinian's schoolgirl enjoying the birch). For all Tynan's canvassing of such theatrical heavies as Peter Brook, Harold Pinter and Michael White, the concept looks remarkably like the contents list of a reasonably sophisticated 'men's magazine'. Not that such *lèse-majesté* would have been acknowledged as Tynan pursued his talented acquaintances on both sides of the Atlantic, specifying 'no crap about art or redeeming literary merit: this show will be expressly designed to titillate in the most elegant and *outré* way'. Gay sex was out, but fetishes were in. Royalties, Tynan assured his potential writers, would be to the usual revue scale.

Over the next couple of years *Oh! Calcutta!* came gradually together. The US director Jacques Levy was recruited after Tynan met him in London with a production of the satirica *America Hurrah*. Writers were approached for sketches, among them John Lennon, Roman Polanski, the cartoonist Jules Feiffer, Joe Orton, Edna O'Brien and David Mercer (neither of whose piece survived), comedian Elaine May, Sam Shephard and Kurt Vonnegut. Keen to capitalise on the Lord Chamberlain's prophesied demise, Tynan had wanted to open in London but moved the show to New York when the agent Hillard Elkins persuaded him that he was the only suitable person to mount the show. He would also put up the money.

Rehearsals began in New York in March 1969. The big problem was nudity. The actors went through a vast range of exercises to break down their natural timidity, and Levy created all sorts of rules and regulations (notably the rule that barred the actors from fraternising outside the theatre – known as the NFL or 'no-fucking law') to govern what was an undoubtedly novel situation. When Tynan arrived to assess progress, in May 1969, he was appalled. The acting was fine but the sketches, on which he lavished far more interest, were lamentable. The best possible taste was far outweighing the *outré* elegance. As the forty-one previews helped put the show through its paces, Tynan became increasingly worried. By June he was ready to remove his name from the show. It was no longer his elegant erotica, it was Levy's fantasy, a very different creature. At the end of the show the actors appeared, stark naked under direct white light, to voice what might be seen as 'typical' audience reaction. 'If they're having fun,' asked one thesp rhetorically of the male talent, 'why don't they have erections?' Indeed. On 17 June the celebs appeared, dedicated theatre-goers paid scalpers $45 a pair for their tickets, and the show garnered what Kathleen Tynan recalls as 'decent applause and some cheering'.[11] The critics were less enthusiastic. The downmarket *Daily News* predictably condemned its 'hard-core pornography', the *New York*

Post managed to savage 'the most pornographic, brutalising, degrading, shocking, tedious, witless ... concoction' on record, but also found it the 'most shatteringly effective'. The most important critic, the *New York Times*'s Clive Barnes was probably the most accurate. He dismissed the show as innocent and sophomoric, 'the kind of show to give pornography a bad name'. (A view supported by *Screw* magazine which noted that the city authorities, while happy to permit such high-priced tosh as Tynan's review, were simultaneously conducting their 'anti-smut' war on the downmarket patrons of 42nd Street.) As for Tynan, for whom Barnes professed enormous respect, 'what a nice dirty-minded boy like him is doing in a place like this I fail to understand.' As Woody Allen would Socratically note, 'Is sex dirty? Yes, when it's done right.' *Oh! Calcutta!* was not 'done right' and soon the audiences would be made up not of Tynan's fantasy sophisticates, but of the same coach parties who were already trooping in to see *Hair*. Financially it was hugely successful: there would be 250 different worldwide productions, and by the late 1980s the box office grosses totalled $360 million. Tynan, foolishly profligate with the rights, made a mere $250,000. Its main artistic success came in spinoffs: Jules Feiffer's sketch 'Dick and Jane' would become the movie *Carnal Knowledge*; Gore Vidal's attempt to conjure up *his* fantasy led to the book then film *Myra Breckinridge*; Bob Fosse's backstage drama *A Chorus Line* has always been seen as reflecting in some ways the gestation of *Oh! Calcutta!*

The London opening of *Oh! Calcutta!* came in July 1970. Most of Fleet Street had already run reviews of the New York original, so few people needed to be ignorant of what was on offer. The authorities, however, sat up and performed right on cue. Opening in the Roundhouse, with its Arts Council grant, meant that the first whinges inevitably objected to the state giving out cash for filth. As in New York there were plenty of previews, ensuring that not only the press but the usual parade of self-appointed moralists would gather to add their condemnations. A busybody factotum of the GLC tried to get the police excited – they were not – and, thus rebuffed, attempted to invite the Archbishops of Canterbury and Westminster to see the show. The prelates rejected the suggestion. Lady Birdwood, the London organiser of Mary Whitehouse's Viewers and Listeners, an anti-Semitic pamphleteer and opponent of all things liberal, demanded the chance of a private prosecution: she was refused. Next it was announced that the DPP might be readying himself for an attack. As John Sutherland has pointed out, this would not be easy.[12] It would be simpler, for instance, to charge Tynan with running a brothel – the offence covering strip and live sex shows – or, had the play been a film and originating elsewhere, to ban it from entering the country. Similarly a book could have fallen foul of the OPA. None of these options was available: the show did go on.

What really enraged the public was Tynan's refusal to submit to the prevailing hypocrisies. The sex in *Oh! Calcutta!* was anodyne, untitillating and very far from sophisticated; if this was the much-vaunted sexual revolution, it was a singularly bloodless, flaccid event. But Tynan's undaunted insolence was another matter. As self-proclaimed 'leaders of society' queued to fulminate against this latest episode in the decline of modern civilisation, Tynan teased and provoked and gave not an inch. Whatever the reality of *Oh! Calcutta!* may have been, its creator never ceased parading the commercial sensibilities that lay behind the production. His aim was, and always had been, unashamed titillation. (The only problem was the degree to which in this the show so patently failed, but this was not the concern of its opponents.) Writing to *The Times* he remarked, 'Lord Drogheda joins several of your other correspondents in ascribing to me the phrase "tasteful pornography". Whatever his lordship may have read, I have never used this expression to describe *Oh! Calcutta!* or anything else. I have a horror of the word "tasteful".'[13]

Given the relative unimportance of *Oh! Calcutta!* the furore it provoked, orchestrated no doubt by its main progenitor, was still astounding. The letters pages of *The Times*, albeit in an era when August still represented a 'silly season' for journalism, focused on this single topic to an extent unrivalled since the Suez Crisis of 1956. Not until the *Oz* trial would moralists find so alluring a soapbox. Politicians, churchmen, the censorship advocate David Holbrook who, with a singularly inapposite image, compared the revue to 'the storm troopers who made Jewesses dance on the tables at Treblinka', all joined in. The Bishop of Peterborough spoke for many who feared the new world: 'So there is to be complete freedom of expression . . . What used to be called blasphemy or indecency or savage violence or public insult, overt or veiled, to the living and dead are to be hailed as signs of an enriching liberation.'

The Times itself weighed in on 6 August, taking up space for two normal-sized leaders. Its headline read 'Law and Morals', and it began by recalling that, 'Moralists of the ancient world were in no doubt that lewd spectacles debauch public morals.' But for all its sound and fury, the Thunderer, like the public at large, was forced to come to a regretful conclusion: *Oh! Calcutta!* may have been raunchy stuff, but it lay beyond the law. All the paper could suggest was a boycott of Tynan's revue. But the British public, like their American peers, were no longer swayed so easily by the posturings of a *Times* editorial. *Oh! Calcutta!* filled the Roundhouse for a month, then transferred to the West End, where it continued to wow the coach parties for another year.

The importance of *Oh! Calcutta!*, as is so often the case, lay not in its intrinsic qualities, but in its effects. These can be seen on two levels. The first is that of the impossibility of Tynan's fantasy of 'elegant erotica'. As the critic, himself an unashamed devotee of what the kiosk ads call 'S&M' or 'B&D' and the working girls call 'fladge', should have known, sex doesn't work that way. The caricatured dirty old man (more often an otherwise 'respectable' commuter), clutching his copy of *Razzle* or *Readers' Wives* is a much better clue to what commercial sex needs to provide. Tynan's essentially cosmetic sex-show was very much a Sixties myth: titillation without masturbation. What did work, and Tynan undoubtedly enjoyed this, perhaps even more, was the wonderful effect it had on bourgeois sensibilities. Lenny Bruce, whose scabrous sermonising had been championed by the critic, might have preferred to send his children to a strip show rather than a movie about Christ – who gets crucified in a strip show? – but the great British public were less hip. What amused Tynan had a devastating long-term effect on the freedoms he espoused. The apparent freedom of the revue not merely to appear, no matter how incensed the moralists might be, but in addition to escape the slightest legal constraint may be said to have set in motion the moral backlash that gathered energy over the next few years and has yet to abate. The Archbishop of Canterbury called upon Christians to fight back against porn; Lord Longford began gathering evidence for his Report (a glorious sideshow which climaxed with the visit of the noble researcher, accompanied by Fleet Street's finest, to Denmark's live sex clubs), cinemas were picketed, the liberal film censor John Trevelyan was dumped in favour of a more repressive successor, and Mary Whitehouse's 'misty millions' set about making themselves even more than usually intrusive into other people's pleasures. Most important of all was the formation of the 'Festival of Light'.

This evangelical crusade to clean up Britain was founded in March 1971 by a Baptist missionary, Peter Hill, as a vigilantist body working to combat 'moral pollution'. Hill had been in India working for Operation Mobilisation 'a militant inter-denominational youth group' and returned to London determined to bring its sinners to Christ. Assisting him were the Rev. Eddie Stride of Christ Church, Spitalfields, an ally of Lady Birdwood, Malcolm Muggeridge (the born-again radical journalist who suggested the name), Lord Longford, Mary Whitehouse, right-wing MP Sir Cyril Black, pop singer Cliff Richard, media 'personality' David Kossoff and the usually radical Bishop of Stepney. The Festival of Light was suitably apocalyptic, declaring in 1971 that were the country not purged according to its dictates, the world would end in five years. It claimed, in putting forward its 'Savonarola-like programme of social purification'[14] that it represented the views of 'ordinary people'.

The Festival called, together with NVALA, for a Nationwide Petition for Public Decency. This was to entail the reform of the Obscene Publications Act (1959) 'to make it an effective instrument for the maintenance of public decency'; the extension of the Act to cover sound and visual broadcasting; and the introduction of extra legislation aimed directly at protecting children; the petition also called for State directed film censorship and a boycott of shops selling 'indecent' material. After enjoying its initial burst of publicity in 1972, the Festival of Light became blurred with the NVALA and has played second fiddle to that leading anti-pornography pressure group. At its peak the movement, launched as the 'Nationwide Festival of Light' attracted much media coverage and allegedly some 215,000 people gathered in various meetings. One of these at Westminster Hall, went somewhat awry, when it was infiltrated by saboteurs, notably a group of 'nuns' whose costumes had been hired with funds from Graham Chapman of *Monty Python*.

It was good street theatre; similar events took place at a Hyde Park rally (where eggs were thrown at Cliff Richard and gay men openly embraced), but the Festival was undeterred. They were especially pleased to gain an endorsement from Prince Charles. But lower-middle-class evangelism was only a part of the counter-revolution. Pamela Hansford-Johnson and David Holbrook announced the formation of a movement, 'The Responsible Society', and Professor George Steiner, usually the most magisterial of academics, wrote in his essay 'Night Thoughts' that unfettered pornography is the first step to Auschwitz. On it went, with perhaps the most pitiable figures being those *bien-pensant* liberals, often veterans of one or another of the Jenkins Acts, who now claimed to deplore the flesh-and-blood results of their measured, judiciously compromising social legislation.

Thus by the end of the decade the backlash was in place. Morality had never really gone away – although for the past ten years it had been defeated over and over again, whether in literary trials or in the passage of hard-won new social legislation. The avant-garde publisher John Calder, founder in 1968 of the Defence of Literature and the Arts Society, believed that that victory would be permanent. Speaking in 1969 he suggested that within five years there would be no such thing as censorship in the UK. Sadly, his optimism had little foundation. 'Literature' might temporarily have escaped the forces of repression, the so-called counter-culture, lacking such respectable support, was a different matter. Far from celebrating the end of censorship, the Seventies would see its return, focusing firmly on the alternative society and its media. Within its first three years the country would see the trials of *IT*, of the undergound comic *Nasty Tales*, of the *Little Red Schoolbook*, a Danish originated 'manual of children's rights', and most important and most pivotal of all, of *Oz*.

Chapter Twenty-Six

The Underground Press: Up Against the Wall

1. To warn the 'civilized world' of its impending collapse.
2. To note and chronicle events leading to the collapse.
3. To advise intelligently to prevent rapid collapse and make transition possible.
4. To prepare . . . for the wilderness.
5. To fight a holding action in the dying cities.
Objectives of the Underground Press, Underground Press Syndicate 1967

The first attacks on the underground press were aimed, logically enough, at its first manifestation. *IT*, amusing enough when it was launched amid fancy-dressed Beatles and giant jellies, had not gone away, as the Establishment had presumably believed that it would. Nor could it be sidelined as just one more version of what could be safely dismissed as the 'little magazines'. Those magazines, the creation of small, intellectual coteries, had never appealed all that far beyond their own writers. The counter-culture was another creature: a far more substantial and far noisier one and *IT*, its newspaper, had to be acknowledged. By early 1967 *IT* had established a presence in the counter-culture. The first dozen issues had offered readers an ongoing mixture of avant-garde art and literature, drugs information, rock 'n' roll interviews and plenty more. Other papers, notably *Oz*, had begun making inroads into those newsagents that would carry them, and weighing down the increasingly omnipresent street-sellers, but for most potential readers *IT* remained the counter-culture's fortnightly of choice. It was selling well enough to include a page of small ads, often offering the kind of services that, like many of the articles that preceded them, could and would not have appeared elsewhere. And it would be these small ads that brought the paper its first major clash with the authorities.

Unsurprisingly, once they had registered its existence, the authorities began looking at the new paper with a less than sympathetic eye. The first bust came, as Miles recalls, on 9 March, just after the publication of issue eight:

It was after an interview we did with Dick Gregory in which he talked about 'white motherfuckers' or something like that. Somebody complained to the DPP and we had the full-scale police raid. By this time we'd accumulated quite a bit of paper work – subscription lists and so on – and they came and they seized everything, every single piece of paper in the entire office including the phone books. Every single back issue. Staff members' personal address books. It was a piece of classic intimidation. They kept it all for about two months then returned it saying they weren't going to bring any charges. They completely disrupted our cash flow, taking uncashed cheques, we had no idea who our subscribers were, who owed us money, anything, they just wanted to close us down. The Establishment were very, very paranoid about it. That bust is what you expect in South America or some Third World country . . . We told all the press, but the press did fuck all. Didn't even write an article. The next issue was read aloud at UFO. It was miraculously recreated and it was on the streets only a week late.[1]

And if the 'straight' world refused to take notice, *IT* could always thrust itself forward. On 11 March the paper staged 'The Death of *IT*', a piece of street theatre that focused on a small march down Whitehall to the Cenotaph, much-revered memorial to the dead of two world wars. Here, as the thirty-odd 'weirdly-dressed beatniks and their girlfriends'[2] looked on, Harry Fainlight, of Albert Hall poetry reading fame, climbed into a scarlet coffin. Chanting began and daffodils were piled on to the recumbent poet. The police appeared and the group moved on, taking the coffin, *sans* Fainlight, to Westminster Underground station where the crowd began four hours of travelling round the Circle Line, still chanting, playing flutes, guitars and bongos. Only after the LT police threw them off did the procession reemerge, at Notting Hill, to march down Portobello Road, coffin shouldered, instruments blaring on. The tabloids reacted as required. The *Sunday Mirror*'s man, quitting El Vino's for the occasion to write as '14182973 Lance-Corporal Geoffrey Ross', was especially incensed, and talked of a 'Cenotaph Sacrilege'. Surprisingly he recanted somewhat a week later, after a letter from Mick Farren, foremost among the marchers, noted that his own father had died during the Second World War and that if alternative views could not be voiced, what had been the point of the whole 'struggle for democracy'?

Low-intensity police harassment became a staple of *IT*'s life. It was as if the Establishment needed to keep its alternative permanently off-balance. Then, in early 1969, the paper faced something more serious. It may be, as was suggested at the trial, that *IT*'s decision to run the ads in question (they were to be found in *Oz* and other underground papers too), was on altruistic lines: that just as nowhere else would one find a major piece by William Burroughs or Allen Ginsberg, nor could one find, other perhaps than on the walls of selected 'cottages', freely displayed gay contact ads. On the other hand neither *IT*, *Oz* nor the rest were exactly inundated with advertising revenue. They took what they found and were grateful. *IT* made its 'personal columns' as open as possible, and as such offered a marketplace to many whose demands could not be satisfied elsewhere. Given the lack of a mass-circulation homosexual press, in which such advertisements would be carried later, it gave space to a variety of gay contact advertising which they listed as the 'Gentleman's Directory' in a column headed 'Males'. All of which was academic to Scotland Yard's 'dirty squad', who made their way to *IT*'s Covent Garden offices in April 1969.

The fuzz came in one day, showed their warrants and said they wanted to take copies away. They had a warrant under the Obscene Publications Act. The sergeant who did us kept saying, 'Nothing personal lads, all in the line of duty.' (Later he got six months himself for taking bribes from Soho pornographers.) It was months later that they decided they were going to prosecute . . . There was this amazing scene: the whole of the foyer was packed with gays who had been dredged from the box numbers.[3]

Graham Keen, along with Peter Stanshill and Dave Hall, all three directors of *IT*'s publishing company Knullar, went on trial in January 1970. In what was seen in retrospect as a dress rehearsal for the *Oz* trial, they faced the government's catch-all assault: conspiracy to corrupt public morals and conspiracy to outrage public decency. The Obscene Publications Act was bypassed; there would be no opportunity for defence experts to confuse a jury. A simple case of judicial queer-bashing was much simpler and far more likely to gain the desired conviction. In the words of the charge, the material was intended to 'debauch and corrupt the morals as well of youth as of divers other liege subjects of the Lady the Queen'. Neither Keen, Hall nor Stanshill were Richard Nevilles. There had been thoughts of staging something dramatic, but in the end discretion won the day. The trial, a scant six days long, ended in mid-November: the defendants were found guilty. Their counsel had argued that since homosexual acts were no longer illegal (subsequent to the Sexual Offences Act of 1967) nor should gay advertisements be. The Court rejected this, stating that irrespective of such niceties, the conspiracy to corrupt public morals had still taken place if a jury believed that the defendants' actions had indeed undermined the nation's morals. Each director was fined £100 and sentenced to twelve months jail on the first charge and eighteen months on the second. The company was fined £1,500 on both charges with £500 costs.

Despite so punitive an attack, *IT* survived and had its appeal heard in May 1972, a relatively low-key event in the aftermath of the previous summer's *Oz* trial. Facing the defence claim that the 'conspiracy to corrupt morals' was not a statutory offence, the Court admitted that the *Ladies' Directory* case (the last to use the conspiracy charges) might have been 'an unfortunate mistake'. They upheld the 'morals' conviction, but reversed that on the 'decency' charge, accepting that a small ad, buried within a paper, could hardly corrupt a decent person unless they were determined to find offence. This compromise satisfied no one. Questions were asked in the House of Commons and the *Times* columnist Bernard Levin (in 1971 a champion of *Oz* and now definitely pro-*IT*) and the Attorney-General swapped antagonistic opinions through that newspaper. Levin claimed that the Attorney-General, Sir Peter Rawlinson, had made an assurance in 1964 that there would be no attempt to deny any plaintiffs a 'public good' defence, and that it had also been promised that at no time would the offence of 'corrupting public morals' be used to bypass the OPA. In both instances the authorities had back-tracked. Levin suggested that 'the *IT* defendants should have a free pardon and that 'justice in this country has not been covered in glory'. Sir Peter, breaking with tradition to address the issue through the columns of a newspaper, claimed that small ads were not literature and thus had no claim on a 'public good defence'. Instead they were part of an 'apparatus of liaison'; in other words, he inferred, *IT*, in effect, was pimping for its gay advertisers. The Home Secretary then announced that the 'morals' charge was being considered by the Law Commissioners.

IT did not have the field to itself for long. It was barely four months old when in February 1967 there appeared its first rival. And if *IT* had owed much of its impetus to passing Americans, this new paper was similarly driven by 'colonials': in this case Australians. *Oz* had established itself in Australia, where it had been launched on April Fool's Day 1963, as 'a monthly magazine of satire and opinion'. The paper, an attempt at a down-under *Private Eye*, emerged from the relative insignificance of university journalism, to render itself sufficiently irritating to the authorities for them to mount a pair of trials against it for alleged 'obscenity'. The crimes in question included the portrayal on the cover of issue one of a chastity belt, while the second, which made somewhat larger headlines, featured the editor Richard Neville and a couple of friends pretending to pee into a newly un-veiled sculpture (strangely reminiscent of a urinal) outside the P&O building in Sydney. The caption explained in a gruesome pun: 'For the convenience of passers-by, and despite a nominal charge you don't have to pay immedi-ately. Just P&O.'[4] (That the picture was shot from behind, and was far from a close-up, only underlined the general absurdity.) On top of this a satire, 'The Word Flashed Round the Arms', written in the gung-ho slang of a typical beer-and-bonking ocker, was considered quite unacceptable. So too was a cartoon of a clergyman squatting doglike by a gramophone with the caption 'His Master's Voice', and a piece stolen from New York's *Realist* (it had been originally written by comedian Lenny Bruce), entitled 'Ta Ra Ra Boom Te Ay'. Another piece featured the pun 'get folked', giving rise to one of the most blissful moments of the trial: an eminent defence witness attempting, straight-faced, to declare that indeed, this was a common and harmlessly en-thusiastic phrase beloved of, yes, folk singers.

And as was so often the case in such prosecutions, the court found obscen-ity where none had ever been meant. Not a page, it was claimed, had been free of corruption. The 'dirty little rag with filth in it', as a right-wing radio com-mentator (and victim of its satire) put it, was duly condemned, for all that the Sydney press noted that in its defence *Oz* had 'mustered the most formidable gathering of intellectuals to appear at one time in an Australian court'.[5] The editors, Neville, Richard Walsh and Martin Sharp, were sentenced to six months' hard labour. The presiding magistrate declared that, experts notwithstanding, 'the publication would deprave young people or unhealthy-minded adults so injudicious as to fancy it as literature and so misguided as to cultivate the habit of reading it.'[6] Freed on bail, the defendants spent the next two years in and out of courtrooms, television stations and colleges, protesting their 'purity of motives and quality of character'.[7] In February 1965 the conviction was appealed and quashed, although prosecution counter-claims would not permit a final ratification for another twelve months.

Like virtually every hip contemporary Neville left Australia for London, summoned by *Time* magazine fantasies and the fact his girlfriend Louise Ferrier was already there. Moving in reverse along the hippie trail, he arrived in London in September. The journalist Mary Kenny, reporting for the *Evening Standard* on the arrival in London of the 'notorious satirist from Sydney', asked Neville what were his plans? 'Start *Oz* of course – this town needs a bomb under it.' As the *Standard* headlined the story: 'Rebel Aussie Whiz-Kid to Publish Here'. It was a typical piece of Neville bravado: right off the top of the head but, more vitally, just realistic enough substance to be sustainable. In any case, as the rumour mill grabbed Mary Kenny's diary piece and started running with it, he had little choice but to match his mouth with *Oz*'s money.

The first issue appeared in February 1967, poised nicely to ride the waves of the oncoming Summer of Love. The psychedelia for which the magazine would be celebrated was yet to appear. Neville had condemned *IT* – 'stodgy letterpress layouts, drug-sodden jive-talk and uncritical embrace of the avant-garde' – but the first *Oz*es were far from 'revolutionary', in any sense. *Through Private Eye*'s business manager Tony Rushton, with whom they had been discussing a potential distributor, Neville and Sharp had paid obeisance to its editor Richard Ingrams, a devotedly right-wing figure who showed minimal interest in their plans and a horror-tinged loathing for any concept of a counter-culture. His sole question was 'Are you pooves?', a theory naturally encouraged, he explained, by their below-the-collar hair. His one piece of advice was 'upset your betters'.[8] As Neville noted in his book *Play Power*, those early issues were 'an uncomfortable hybrid of satire, Sunday journalism and pirated underground tit-bits'. The cover of issue 1 offered, *inter alia*, 'Theological Striptease: Turn On, Tune In, Drop Dead; Why *New Statesman* Editor Paul Johnson Is So Bloody Successful; In Bed With . . . the English; LBJ Playmate Foldout; Colin MacInnes and Michael X.' It also savaged *Private Eye*, dismissing it as a reactionary rag, whose supposedly 'hard-hitting' satire was constrained by the endless flow of writs. Neville's still ambivalent attitude to the 'alternative society' could be seen in the photo-story of the fictitious 'Mervyn Limp', a mild-mannered bank clerk who visits Indica, tokes on a joint and is instantly transformed in 'Frisco Ferlinghetti', all-purpose repository of hippie absurdity whose fate, after trepanning and the hippie trail, is a squalid death amidst the dope-dens of Kathmandu.

All in all a pot-pourri of trends, rip-offs, downright lies and the odd flash of genius. As Auberon Waugh put it, looking back for the Fifth Anniversary Issue ('To Have Reached Five Is To have Failed In Life'), the magazine was 'a bastard and rather an unnatural one'. On that level, at least, *Oz* would never really change, for all that psychedelia would overwhelm the staid letterpress, the respectful interviews (Alexander Cockburn to Paul Johnson: 'The *Statesman* seems to have gone for a jauntier, more personal style recently. Is this part of a general policy?') and the sub-*Private Eye* barbs, as Neville, encouraged by Sharp, abandoned his distanced toe-dipping and dived head-first into full-on craziness. Issue 2 ('Bite-Sized *Oz*': interview with Malcolm Muggeridge and US lawyer and major-league conspiracy theorist Mark Lane, Greer on breasts and brassieres . . .) was an even greater disaster and in issue 3, when the magazine listed a variety of 'Magnificent Failures' 'the first two issues of *Oz*' were among them. (Listed too, with the exquisite bad taste that has always characterised the magazine, was the LSE's dead porter: 'attempts to quell a scuffle in a passageway'.)

Every issue, however, would see the counter-culture lapping harder at Neville's satirical sandcastle. Issue 3 reprinted a piece on Tim Leary and Ken Kesey from New York's *Ramparts*, while 5 offered one of the classic hippie posters – 'Plant a Flower Child Today' – featuring a flower-bedecked (and otherwise naked) hippie princess. Looking at the covers, which from issue three were outpacing the content in their acknowledgement of the new consciousness, one can see the extent to which Sharp, as much as Neville, dictated the magazine's style. Today, in an age when form has long since seemed to outpace content, *Oz* might seem commonplace; in 1967 it did not. Pearce Marchbank:

> When those early *IT*s came out they looked awful, the end of an era. But when [issue 2 of] *Oz* came out, which was printed in litho and designed by Martin Sharp on white cartridge paper with beautiful thick black ink and bright red ink and a huge pair of lips on the front, it was like the sun had come out. It really was fantastic. I went out and bought about ten copies and gave them out. It was like the first time you hear stereo as opposed to AM radio. You could see the possibilities of print. *IT* was content, whereas *Oz* was form.[9]

Sharp was *Oz*'s and indeed the counter-culture's greatest illustrator. As Jamie Reid's cut-out 'ransom note' style would provide visual shorthand for punk, so did Sharp's living colour interpretation of LSD provide an instant in to psychedelia. Marchbank again:

> He was brilliant. A rich Australian, very urbane, very handsome, tall, wore beautiful clothes, very much the King's Road figure. He had this beautiful drawing style: very original and very clean. His vision of psychedelia was

clean and pure and dayglo. Rather than that muddy, tie dyed T-shirt, mixed up liquid slide look. Sharp had wit, he was visually witty.[10]

Never more so than in *Oz* 16, better known as 'The Magic Theatre' and arguably the greatest achievement of the entire British underground press. Sharp's multi-paged collage, in which, as Neville has put it, each page is 'textured with multi levels of meaning. All the stars in the cultural political firmament – from Lennon to Loren, Lee Harvey Oswald to Edgar Hoover, Primitive Man to Nixon, Middle Earth to Outer Space, Hitler to Buddha are mixmastered into a galaxy of pop.' The cover warned purchasers: 'The price of admittance your mind . . . not for everyone'. The art critic Robert Hughes, once a fringe member of the Australian *Oz* team back in Sydney, declared that, 'Sharp has assembled one of the richest banks of images that has ever appeared.'

But it was with issue 6, which paired *Oz* with an issue of a visiting John Wilcock's ever-peripatetic *Other Scenes*, that the magazine can finally be seen to have cast aside its pretensions to satire and fully embraced the counterculture of which it would become the leading journal. Wilcock came hard-wired into the American underground and Neville, an instinctive editor ever aware of the real source of what might best excite and impress his readers, tapped in enthusiastically. There were other influences. Martin Sharp's wit was not confined to his art. As Sharp and Whitaker put together the 'Plant a Flower Child' photo session (the girl in question was one of a pair of twins, both of whom were sharing the artist's bed), Neville passed by to check on progress. Sharp gave him a cup of tea. As Neville recalled in *Hippie Hippie Shake*, it proved rather stronger than it seemed:

> Giggles floated from the bed. The twins had become quads, no, sextuplets, lying in each other's arms, flecked with petals, nibbling at each other's ear-lobes. Bob Whitaker bounded from the dark-room with a pile of twin-prints and dumped them on to the desk – why did he look like a chimp? I felt a chump. Sharp handed me [a copy of *IT*], pointing to a para, the words springing to life like a singing telegram: 'The new thing is people just coming together and grooving. If you don't know what grooving means then you haven't understood what's going on . . . ' My heart was racing . . . The walls of the studio started to breathe, inflate, shrink, along with the pop-surrealist artworks. Everything roared. Finally, it hit me. 'WHAT DIDYA PUT IN MY TEA?'[11]

Like many other new converts to the psychedelic gospel, Neville had entered the doors of perception via another's friendly, if mischievous hand. *Oz* followed suit, embracing acid with cheerful fervour. It was not, however, quite as besotted as *IT*. *Oz*, to its enduring credit, would never wholly embrace the simplistic philosophies that made the hippies such easy targets of ridicule. 'We are still old-fashioned enough to try to evaluate,' said Neville, 'I think the underground should try to be more self-critical.' Issue 5, as well as its flower child, marked out another trend. For the first time *Oz* fell foul of the authorities. The issue, on Sharp's urging, had been designed not as a magazine but as a poster. Posters, unlike magazines, were liable to purchase tax. The Customs, in charge of such things, demanded their cut. The editors fought back: 'If you have seen other issues . . . you will be aware that we consistently attempt originality . . . not merely in textual material . . . but also in typographical and pictorial design.' They then promised that the next issue would be a single sheet of paper in a paper bag. The argument seems to have faded away.

By now Neville and Sharp were not alone: a nucleus of *Oz* personnel had gathered. Sharps's artistry was set in place by the designer, and former English Boy model Jon Goodchild. *Oz* writers tended to be regulars rather than actual staff. The late David Widgery, still a teenager, his left-wing credentials noisily prominent, wrote for the first issue and remained a stalwart throughout the magazine's life; after the trial he was appointed one of the three temporary co-editors.

> I met the *Oz* people in '67. I was very angry about Swinging London. I said it was all a hoax and had nothing to do with reality and I was writing articles like that once every three months. I'd written something for the *New Statesman* on Swinging London, angry young man type of thing, and somebody told me there was this guy from Australia and he was publishing some sort of student magazine and he wanted articles, why not go and see him. So I traipsed off somewhere and there was this strange man sitting with his girlfriend surrounded by the memorabilia of his recent trip to Nepal; and wearing a little Afghan vest, embroidery on the outside, fur on the inside, absolutely hilarious in this flat somewhere in west London. So he asked what I'd like to write about and I said I'd like to write an attack on swinging London and Martin Sharp virtually resigned over the issue because he thought swinging London was so wonderful.[12]

Felix Dennis, whose role in *Oz* would move from street-selling, to advertising manager, to sometime designer and thence, in another life, to extreme, if somewhat reclusive wealth, was next to arrive. A rock drummer at the time, he had impregnated a girlfriend, an event that called for drastic action. Paying for an abortion meant farewell to his drumkit and a prized tape-recorder.

> Just before I sold this kit I'd seen this kind of pilot issue of *Oz*. I thought what a pile of rubbish! God almighty, these people are useless! I can see what they're trying to do but they're completely hopeless. So as a kind of last gamble I recorded a tape, sitting in my bedroom that night and I sent this editor, whose name I saw in the magazine, the tape. It was a very amusing tape, 'cos it was done very late at night and I was a bit smashed. This was Richard Neville.

Giving him lots of hints and tips about what was wrong with his magazine and how he ought to get his act together and what life was like living the way I was living and all that stuff. Anyway, I thought no more about it and I just put it in the mail, 'cos I knew that if you just get a tape with nothing else attached to it there's one thing for sure as hell you've got to do – you've got to listen to it.

I was living with these people, Fulham Road, somewhere, a bunch of girls, seven of them, and all of a sudden, I was in the loo and one of them screams, 'You're on the television!' and I rushed in, expecting to see this film of the band. Instead of that there was this picture of this guy I didn't know. I said, 'What do you mean, I'm on the television?' and she said, 'Listen,' and bugger me – it's my voice coming out. Over the BBC on this documentary. And they ran the whole bloody tape virtually, it had been edited a bit and Richard had sold them my tape as background for this documentary on hippies! So I thought fuck this, there must be some money in it. So I called him up and said, 'I sent you this tape in confidence, you know and I didn't send you this tape to send to the BBC, you must have got money for that – where's mine?' And he said, 'Look, I haven't got any money as it happens, but come round to [my flat] and meet up.'

So I went round there in high dudgeon and he said, 'The truth is we haven't got any money but I could give you some magazines . . .' So I said, 'What fucking use are magazines to me?' and he said, 'No, no, you go out on the street and sell them.' So I took this bundle of magazines, went back to Fulham, woke the girls up, told them to put a short skirt on and I got about three of them out there on the King's Road. I was like a sort of hippie pimp. And bugger me! as soon as you'd go up to people and shove them in front of their face, they used to give you half a crown! It was amazing! Half a crown! So we sold about a hundred, the first day, hundred half crowns was a lot of money in those days. So I went back the next day and I said, 'I think you owe me a few more of those,' and he didn't say anything and let me have a few more bundles. And I sold those, and the next time I went round he said, 'We've got to do fifty-fifty, you've got to give me the money.' So then we had an operation going.

(Richard Neville tells a somewhat different story. 'Felix sent this tape in and I played the tape and there was this very emotional voice saying this was "the greatest thing, the greatest magazine that I have ever read and I will give my life for this magazine . . . ", it was all that sort of stuff. Then this kid arrived and the only thing I could think of doing was to give him *Oz*es to sell in the street.')

Last of what would become the '*Oz* Three', was Jim Anderson, a dropped out Australian lawyer who had moved to London hoping to make it as a writer. He taught in secondary moderns, travelled voraciously, and in June 1967 met Neville at the Legalise Pot Rally in Hyde Park. They talked briefly, but Anderson was unimpressed by journalism: his goals were more serious. Two years later he sought out Neville, and started work, not on *Oz*, but on Neville's forthcoming book, *Play Power*. And when *Play Power* was finished, in late 1969, Anderson stayed, becoming incorporated into the *Oz* team. He both designed and wrote, both on his frequent forays out on the hippie trail and, since Anderson was gay, on what was still a new topic: gay liberation.

Stripped from its mad background the copy one found in *Oz* was not so far removed from that in *IT*, or indeed in any of the underground papers that would emerge in its wake. If it seemed superior then one could pay tribute to Neville's editorial skills. His range of contacts was impressive: he could enlist such figures as Clive James, Germaine Greer or Robert Hughes, none of whom would have thought of appearing in, say, *Friends*. Sharp was worth thousands of copies alone, while such staples of the American underground press as 'Dr. Hip Pocrates' (the underground's 'agony uncle') gave the magazine a cutting-edge, cosmopolitan feel. Nor did he forget his promise to be more self-critical. David Widgery ensured a steady drip of scepticism, while many visiting celebrities were recruited to offer their own slanted take on what was rapidly becoming an alternative gospel.

Writing of the new magazine Colin MacInnes, himself a contributor, had suggested that, 'the visual elements are more successful than the writing' which was 'a bit old-hat and priggish' and urged the writers to become sharper and deeper.[13] In time that wish would be to some extent fulfilled, but the visuals would always retain their pre-eminence. What made *Oz Oz* was not the copy, but the artwork. As issue followed issue, each one, it seemed, less legible than its predecessor, the magazine became something akin to a work of art. Golden poster covers you could put on the wall, covers made of perforated gummed paper, each section bearing a crazily designed slogan, an issue divided by dotted lines – cut along and read it anyway you desired – covers by such hippie artists as Michael English or Nigel Waymouth (who worked in tandem as Hapshash and the Coloured Coat).

For those who wanted an overview of what Hugh Hefner might have termed 'the *Oz* Philosophy', 1970 saw the publication of just that: Richard Neville's first book, *Play Power*. The genesis of this 'gaudy mosaic of anecdote, quotation, prophecy and wild unsupported assertion', as Ken Tynan described it in the *Observer*, was a meeting between Neville and Ed Victor, today a major literary agent, then editorial director of publishers Jonathan Cape. Malcolm Muggeridge had just written a piece for the *New Statesman* in which, true to his born-again persona, he had generally set about the contemporary world. Neville counter-attacked, but the editor, a still left-wing Paul Johnson, found himself unable to publish it. His directorial board, apparently, couldn't deal with the upset such a piece might cause. He would, however, run it as a letter, and pay Neville for his effort. Its appearance triggered a massive, often splenetic correspondence. It was, Neville suggests, the first time the public had had a chance to debate the whole idea of a counterculture. Victor saw the commercial potential of so much passion and phoned Neville, 'You should do a book.' Thus the letter became a synopsis, Victor's kite-flying became an advance of £3,000 and in time, with substantial help from Jim Anderson, *Play Power* appeared in early 1970.

One of the peculiarities of the counter-culture is that it produced very few books of any significance. Jeff Nuttall's *Bomb Culture* had appeared in 1968, and dealt very much with times past; Mick Farren and Edward Barker's *Watch Out Kids* came in 1972, in a period when the world of which Farren wrote was markedly on the wane. *Play Power*, massively flawed, offering in many ways the same combination of the hip, the hysterical, the downright embarrassing and the occasional razor-edged *aperçu*, was (at the time) the best of a hardly considerable lot. With its combination of a hippy *tour d'horizon*, offering a brief overview of anything remotely 'alternative', its heavy propagandising, the mythologising that such gung-ho optimism invariably entails and the constant elbow-jabbing presence of its author's overweening ego, it is not easy to read today.

If *Play Power* has an intellectual underpinning it is the theory of 'homo ludens': man the player, as advanced by the Dutch intellectual Johan Huizinga in his eponymous book, published in 1938. For Neville the world is divided into generational rather than national camps, and across that world the underground of 'hippies, beats, mystics, madmen, freaks, yippies, crazies, crackpots, communards and anyone who rejects rigid political ideology' had combined into a 'youthquake', a word apparently coined by *Vogue* magazine. Youth, flawless, idealised youth is Neville's obsession: long-haired boys do drugs, underage jailbait fuck like stoned bunnies; how he regrets being born too soon. Even the dull politicos have some input, since both they and the 'cultural' underground were united in opposition to the war in Vietnam. The only equally angry group are the 'militant poor', but they 'require another book': it was not one Neville or his peers were likely to undertake.

Having laid out the lines of this youthful underground, Neville takes his readers on a trip around the psychedelic theme park. The bullet points roll by: the development of the British underground, the birth of the LSD culture, Yippies, squatting, *Sgt Pepper*, the LSE, alternative theatre, Grosvenor Square, Edward de Bono, Brion Gysin. Eyes firmly on the likely readers, not so much the lumpen hippies but rather the current manifestation of the chattering classes – pretty straight but desperate for hippie cred – the sexual revolution gets substantial coverage. It's recruiting poster stuff: join the freaks and get your ashes hauled. Aside from his own indulgences (who needs the New Lad when you have the Old Hippie and his 'hurricane fuck' with a 'moderately attractive, intelligent, cherubic 14-year-old girl from a nearby London comprehensive school . . . ' during the Heinz Souperday commercial; 'a farewell kiss and the girl rushes off to finish her homework') he explains that the 'ancient rituals of courtship' are so much 'flashy paraphernalia'. 'Underground sexual morality is, in its own way, as direct as the Old Testament. If a couple of kids like each other, they make love.'

And uninhibited hippie sex is of course a million miles from the squalid fantasies of a Soho clipjoint. There's no pornography (for hippies 'fuck' is a statement of love), no prostitution, and hey, show me the Guinevere clone who isn't up for a playful, guiltless gangbang. As for feminism, it's certainly important and in fairness, when it comes to sex 'not all the problems have been solved'.

After revolution and sex, rock 'n' roll, which in Neville's view is essentially the rise of the pigeon-chested guys who used to get sand kicked in their face and now get the pick of the girls. And after music, drugs, their mysteries probed through pages of catechistic Q&A. 'Is marijuana addictive? Yes, in the sense that most of the really pleasant things in life are worth endlessly repeating.' The underground press gets a lengthy outing and the narrative ends – in a section that, no doubt unconsciously, has all the thoughtless arrogance of a Victorian memsahib – with a lengthy trip along the hippie trail.

The final thirty pages return to theory. Play is paramount, the doctrinaire left irrelevant. Despite his earlier sop to the lefties – we're all together against Vietnam – Neville set the pranksters vs. the politicians, 'the sober, violent, puritan New Left extremists vs. the laughing, loving, lazy, fun-powder plotters'. The real workers aren't impressed either: they find students and lefties equally repellent, they 'know the revolution's done for fun . . . ' In any case the underground doesn't acknowledge work. Creatives are *de facto* 'nonworkers', media work is 'substitute play'. The counter-culture has three tasks: to transfer work (i.e. to make work equal play), to sow its own wild oats and, gleefully, to undermine the system. 'Play Is Fun', he proclaims with worrying shades of *1984*, 'Play Is Freedom'. (Not for nothing did the *Sunday Times* reviewer Bevis Hillier claim to detect 'the germs of a new fascism'.) And in a final paragraph that merely compounds the ironies, Neville looks ahead to: 'The politics of play: the international, equi-sexual, inter-racial, survival strategy for the future. The laughing-gas to counteract tomorrow's Mace. Onwards to the Eighties, Motherfuckers'.

Reduced to its essentials, suggested the journalist Charles Shaar Murray, whose own career began as an '*Oz* Schoolkid', *Play Power* declared that 'if everybody listened to pop music, wore funny clothes, took drugs and screwed a lot, the millennium would come'. It was wish-fulfilment 'on a gigantic scale' and whether consciously or not, ruthlessly élitist. It offered cultural revolution for the materially and socially comfortable; 'the line', adds Murray, talking in 1987, 'from hippie to yuppie is not nearly as convoluted as people like to believe. A lot of the old hippie rhetoric could well be co-opted now by the pseudo-libertarian right: get the government off our backs, let individuals do what they want – that translates very smoothly into *laissez-faire* yuppyism, and that's the legacy of the era.'

In the only review Neville claimed to care about, David Widgery, given two pages in *Oz* to play, as he put it, the 'scolding lefty'[14] worried over Neville's apparent lack of (and indeed disdain for) the tarnished grail of socialism. He sees Neville and his élite coterie as a modern salon, and *Play Power* as the distillation of the salon's table-talk. What *Play Power*, and the underground worldview it represents, needs is a dash of historical awareness essential for a proper ideological viewpoint. Then, and only then, could the fantasy 'revo' become a genuine Revolution. Within his own political limitations Widgery was right – even if few in the underground would agree. As for the 'straight' press, they reacted predictably. The hipper broadsheets loved it, the career lefties despaired, the right-wing inevitably protested. Perhaps the cruellest comment came twenty years later, a throwaway line from Angela Carter, looking back for Sara Maitland's *Very Heaven*: 'Do you remember a dreadful book by Richard Neville, *Play Power*? Tacky, tacky, tacky.'[15]

In many ways, as was so often the case with *Oz*, form outplayed content. Overwhelmed by media invitations as *Play Power*'s publication drew nearer, Neville sent Widgery to be 'Richard Neville' for the benefit of Harlech TV in Cardiff. Widgery, who had dutifully practised his accent on the train down, was faced with five inquisitive MPs. When one asked why the supposed 'Aussie whizkid' didn't sound as Australian as one might have expected, he fell back on Barry McKenzie: 'Where can I point percy at the porcelain, mate?' The MP appeared to be satisfied. Back in London Neville leaked the story to the Atticus column of the *Sunday Times*. Widgery was pictured, stripped to the waist, his crew-cut hair prominent. 'If the media can't tell the difference between a skin-headed British Trot and an Australian druggy,' he told the paper, 'it's not surprising that they can't tell an imperialist war from a peace probe.'[16]

Richard Neville's own Sixties' memoir, *Hippie Hippie Shake*, passes over *Play Power* with a certain alacrity. One must draw one's own conclusions. But talking a decade earlier he saw it this way:

> There is some stuff in *Play Power* that today I would repudiate – such as the sexism, and in a world of AIDS you are not saying we should all sleep with each other as much as possible. Time has overtaken some of the *Play Power* ideas. On the other hand I think the spirit of questioning and dancing on the table is something that is still pretty relevant today. Having moved away from a belief in angry left-wing politics I would be more sympathetic to consciousness-raising techniques than I was then. There was a faith in the power of the movement that was not really borne out.[17]

It was, however, in the immediate aftermath that he sat down, shortly before setting off to take a holiday in Ibiza, and composed the ad which, as he put it, 'made history of a sort'.[18] It appeared in the next issue of *Oz*, number 26, and read as follows: 'Some of us at *Oz* are feeling old and boring, so we invite any of our readers who are under eighteen to come and edit the April issue. We will choose one person, several or accept collective applications from a group of friends. You will receive no money, except expenses. You will en-joy almost complete editorial freedom. *Oz* staff will assist in an administra-tive capacity.' Interested youngsters were to present themselves at the *Oz* office on Friday 13 March 1970. The resonance of so taboo a day went unno-ticed. *Oz*, the ad concluded 'belongs to you'.

It is axiomatic that the work that faces the wrath of the censor is rarely that which the creator would have chosen to defend as the best and most rep-resentative example of their work. Lawrence, it is generally agreed, would not have chosen *Lady Chatterley's Lover* upon which to base a defence of his philosophies of love and sex; similarly the editors of *Oz*, Richard Neville, Jim Anderson and Felix Dennis, would probably have preferred to make their stand upon any number of issues of the magazine, rather than the 'Schoolkids Issue' (number 28), an issue produced, it should be stressed, not *for* children, but *by* them, or at least by the crew of adolescents who re-sponded to Neville's ad. As invited, some thirty 'schoolkids' materialised for the first meeting, and maybe twenty made it through to the 'school photo' (the assembled kids lined up around their genial 'headmaster', Neville). Among them were Peter Popham, later of the *Independent*, Deyan Sudjic, founder-in-waiting of the architectural journal *Blueprint* and Charles Shaar Murray, destined to join one of the more creative generations of rock jour-nalists. Twenty years on he summed up the general feeling for the Sunday Times: 'I was simply fumbling around in a darkened room trying to find a light switch. *Oz* was it.' Neville, basking in adoration, remarked to Anderson, 'You know, they're much more intelligent and articulate than I was at that age. Come to think of it they're much more intelligent and articulate than I am at this age.' As in many previous issues, Neville was the generator, the fa-cilitator: that done he vanished back to the delights of Ibiza while Dennis and Anderson were left to do the work. Or at least advise, since both did their best to let the kids get on with the job.

The issue appeared in April 1970. It cost four shillings, sixpence up on the last four, and, in the words of today's memorabilia catalogues offered, 'Profile of the contributors. THE RETURN OF KING KONG Guerrilla Babes Wipeout! Jailbait of the Month SCHOOL ATROCITIES British Hitler Jugens. Rupert Finds Gypsy Granny – cartoon. Let it all hang out. HIGH SKOOL CONFIDENTIAL. Rehearse for the Apocalypse. BROWN SHOES DON'T MAKE IT. *Oz* Sucks – Letters. Dear Dr Hippocrates. HEAD BOOKS – Char-les Shaar Murray. Jeff Beck Truth Is Blue. COUNTER CULTURE – Bob Hughes. LP reviews . . . ' It also offered a 'Back Issue Bonanza' and the usual small ads, colonised, as were those in *IT*, by a variety of porn advertisers, both straight and gay. There were also, as the catalogue concludes, 'Front and back p. black nudes'. It was, in the end, an unexceptional issue. No more 'way-out' than its immediate predecessor 'Acid *Oz*', a counter-blast to the current Establishment hysteria as regarded LSD, and certainly far less important than its successor, 'Cunt Power *Oz*', which featured Germaine Greer's major essay 'The Politics Of Female Sexuality', a dry run for *The Female Eunuch*. The schoolkids had put together a good deal of the material, both written and pictured, typically Vivian Berger's collage of Rupert Bear and Robert Crumb's 'Gypsy Granny', but the review of Theodore Roszak's *The Making of a Counter-Culture* came from the relatively elderly Robert Hughes (commissioned by the *Spectator*, it had been turned down by a splenetic Nigel Lawson, then its editor, as 'mindless ranting'), and a number of pieces, typically 'High Skool Confidential', plus the regular appearance of Dr Hippocrates and Gilbert Shelton's *Fabulous Furry Freak Brothers*, were plucked as usual from the UPS. The cover remained the sole problem. The first attempt, the office secretary dressed as a bare-breasted schoolgirl, brandishing a machine gun and peering across a barricade, was abandoned. The final choice, initially earmarked as a centre-spread, was a picture taken from a French album, *Desseins Erotiques*. It showed eight images of a naked black girl, each offering a different erotic image. There is a dildo laced around one, a vibrator poised at the anus of another, a third grasps severed male genitals, a fourth has a tail – a rat? a lizard?– protruding from her vagina, one kisses another's breast, another enjoys her partner's cunnilingual tongue. It was pure fantasy, subtly drawn, if a little demanding for the strictures even of the 'top shelf'. The picture wrapped the issue, providing both front and back covers. For safety's sake the front cover half was slightly censored – the 'blow-job' was judiciously hidden with a picture of the most obviously 'hippy' of the children, although the tail was quite visible; the remaining images conveniently appeared on the back. Above them was printed '*Oz* School Kids Issue'.

Looking back at what followed, it might be suggested that it wasn't just the chronological schoolkids who were still in the classroom. Anderson and Dennis, freed from Neville's slightly more judicious hand, had also, some might say, entered a second childhood. But there was another side. As Anderson put it later, in an unpublished memoir: ' "So many of the revolutionary young," wrote Colin MacInnes, "are political cockteasers. With no idea that a radical attitude involves sacrifice . . . and perpetual self-discipline." I suppose I saw myself as some sort of revolutionary. Was insistence on pushing our luck revolutionary? That feeling of being a media terrorist, a psychedelic gangster, a sexual freedom raider out there in frontier country, each issue of *Oz* a home made bomb exploding with mock ferocity in the battle zone, making the enemy retreat a little in outraged, red-faced confusion? Revolutionary cockteasing, maybe that was it.'[19]

The issue had been on the streets for two months – despite the cover it hadn't sold especially well, when on 8 June 1970 the Obscene Publications Squad, led by DS Frederick Luff, arrived at the *Oz* offices at 52 Princedale Road, off Holland Park Avenue. Locking doors and disconnecting phones, (other than that on which, with uncanny timing, Neville chose to call the office, was told of the on-going bust and judiciously cut himself off before Luff could grab the line) they began carting off everything they could, stripping the office of not just *Oz* 28s, but of its files, records, phone-books and any other material considered, however tenuously, 'relevant'. Three days later they were back, this time to strip the production offices, a few doors down the road. From there, over the next few days the police proceeded to harass every known printer, binder and distributor, looking for plates or artwork that might have been used for the Schoolkids Issue. They also made it wholly clear that if further raids were not desired, continued links with *Oz* might not be seen as overly judicious.

On 18 August *Oz* was served with a summons for 'publishing an obscene magazine'. On 1 October the three defendants-to-be, clad 'satirically' in over-sized school uniforms, appeared at Marylebone Magistrate's Court. Despite their solicitor David Offenbach's strenuous demands that the whole case be dropped there and then, the magistrate was unimpressed. Faced by a folio of allegedly spontaneous public complaints, plus one expostulating south London head-teacher, the magistrate passed the trial on to the Crown Court. As the year went by, and *Oz* followed *Oz* as near to schedule as the magazine had ever managed, the editors' general attitude was casual. The last thing they wanted was to feel that their efforts had no impact; harassment at least acknowledged their existence. And in any case, none of them really believed that any jury could possibly find the magazine obscene. It was easy, especially when operating from what might be seen as its very heart, to take the whole permissive society rhetoric at face value. It would prove an oversight.

The imminence of the trial, however, did not go unnoticed. In what may have been the first move of its kind, *Oz*, rather than hire a PR company, created their own: Friends of *Oz*, run by Sue Miles and Stan Demidjuk, yet another Australian, who had moved from working for Richard Branson, to *Friends* magazine and thence to a somewhat amorphous relationship with John Lennon. Friends of *Oz* was a front organisation; with the full co-operation of the *Oz* defendants it created press kits, held benefits, staged a march through the City, launched a record 'Do The *Oz*' / 'God Save *Oz*' which combined a variety of *Oz* irregulars with John Lennon, sold prints of a David Hockney drawing of the trio (there was much consternation, at least from Neville, at the relative sizes of his and Dennis's penises) and generally worked to keep the on-coming trial in the public eye. Sue Miles recalls,

> I had come back from America with nothing particularly to do. I didn't know anything about the trial and anyway I'd never been able to read *Oz* 'cos I can't read cerise on chartreuse. Then Richard Neville asked me in early spring '67 if I would do the publicity for Friends of *Oz*. I'd never done anything like it, but I said to Richard, yes, if you clear it with everyone else. I didn't have the foggiest what to do. I knew about getting the press interested; I knew that if you've got any good tips, Saturday night about 7 o'clock anyone will buy it. I

knew the form. So I went into the *Oz* office . . . and of course it's terribly illegal. You are not allowed to run this kind of publicity about trials. Stan [Demidjuk] and I could have been held at what's called the Queen's Pleasure – we didn't have to be tried and we could have been held for good. They would do anything: you could dress them in gymslips, bikinis, anything. I went off to see the chief constable at Bow Street to get permission for a parade with four elephants and a camel. At the end of the negotiations we got down to three chickens and a duck! The press took it up. They loved Richard and he was a great media entrepreneur.[20]

There was also a less obvious source of support: from the International Socialists, among whom, of course, was David Widgery. As the trial progressed IS launched a countrywide speaking tour on behalf of the magazine. 'There were only five or six meetings, but they were very big: one in Liverpool, another in Leeds, and a huge one in Basildon. The local organiser would put up a sign saying "Defend *Oz!*" and two or three hundred people, mainly the young, turned up.' It aroused mixed feelings in IS stalwarts such as Widgery: 'The bright working-class kids that we were desperate to get to know for IS and there they were in force . . . far from seeing *Oz* as being a bunch of dilettantes who had no significance, it mattered a lot to ordinary kids who could see the issues at stake.'[21] Widgery also wrote for the left-wing press, comparing the underground newspapers to the seditious, unlicensed publications of the past and calling for support.

By the end of the year it became clear that the Establishment, now gratified by the election of Edward Heath's Tory government, had decided to move somewhat more aggressively. On 19 December Luff, now a Detective Inspector, paid a visit to Neville. He appeared early and unannounced, accompanied by half a dozen detectives and strangely, given that the raid was made under the Obscene Publications Act, a pair of sniffer labradors. The dogs found nothing; the policemen did. Neville, plus Louise Ferrier, whose admission to taking a shower every day plainly astounded the policewoman who subjected her to a strip-search, was taken to Notting Hill police station, there to be charged with possession of cannabis. He spent the night in the cells and at the Magistrate's Court the next morning was refused bail despite the offer of sureties from among others Ken Tynan, George Melly and Colin MacInnes. Instead he was removed to Brixton prison. As he put it later, writing up the experience in *Oz* 32 ('Granny's *Oz*'), it was the first time for many years he had felt frightened; not so much of the grubby horrors of London's main remand prison, but because it was now apparent that the authorities were out for blood. He was sprung, thanks to a judge in chambers, a day later, in time to attend the Release Christmas party (as he entered the Roundhouse the Who, coincidentally no doubt, were playing 'I'm Free' from their rock opera *Tommy*).

Writing in that same *Oz* Germaine Greer suggested that in some ways the oncoming battle was just what the underground needed. 'We've always known', she wrote, 'that the shit would eventually hit the fan.' The current situation revealed two points: in the first place anyone who felt that there had been too great a gap between the underground's élite and its lumpen need worry no more. The drug bust and the refusal of bail was just what happened to the great mass of hippies, 'inarticulate grubby kids who look as if they just might not have any fixed abode'. 'At a stroke, Inspector Luff reintegrated the Underground.' In the second it was noted that crushing the underground was impossible: it 'cannot be isolated and attacked'. They could attack only the underground press, the 'underground establishment'. And Greer ended on a high:

> The really exciting thing about all this unlooked-for manuring is that shit is an underground medium. It is doubtful whether the virgin prime minister and his ten thousand sainted followers can handle it as well as we can, arse-fuckers that we are. At last they've stopped laughing at us, which means we can go back to laughing at them. We don't have to thrash ourselves into a revolutionary frenzy any more ... We can be illegal. We can conspire. We can come closer together again as the space around us closes. There are more of us now, but that's nothing compared to how many of us there'll be tomorrow. Eradication means plucking up by the roots – but our roots are where they'll never get at, they're sunk down somewhere inside of every family in the British isles.[22]

The trial of *Oz*, the longest ever 'obscenity trial' to be staged in a British court, began at the Old Bailey on 22 June 1971. There were five charges, the most important of which was that the editors had 'conspired with certain other young persons to produce a magazine [which would] corrupt the morals of young children and other young persons [and had intended] to arouse and implant in the minds of these young people lustful and perverted desires'. The second charge dealt with 'an obscene article', to wit *Oz* 28, while the remainder dealt with sending *Oz* 28 through the post and with the defendants' possession on two occasions (the police raids) of 252 and 220 copies of the magazine.

The Judge was Mr Justice Argyle, a former recorder of Birmingham and a man who, according to his wife, was perfectly charming in the privacy of his home (which rejoiced in the name of 'Truncheons'), but tended to abandon such moderation as he mounted the bench, where he became a severe, punitive figure. His judgements had been overturned by the Appeal Court on more than one occasion. He also had an odd take on those before him: interviewed years later by an Australian paper he revealed that he had been sure throughout the proceedings that Neville was a 'card-carrying communist', while 'one of the others' (presumably blond long-haired Jim Anderson) was a

'Jesus freak'. Later still, in 1995, he foolishly informed the readers of the *Spectator* (quite friendly to *Oz* in 1971, rabidly right-wing two decades on) that behind *Oz* lay 'a conspiracy of criminals who were selling [*Oz*] together with soft drugs at the entrances to state schools and youth clubs'.[23] He also claimed that the defendants had been behind death threats, which occasioned him to have Special Branch protection. Felix Dennis proved less than forgiving and the *Spectator* was forced to print a satisfyingly grovelling apology and donate £10,000 to a pair of charities.

For the prosecution the crown was represented by Brian Leary, a senior Treasury counsel. A man of impeccable politeness, though prone to shout at witnesses when he felt they were not responding with sufficient immediacy, he would prove a worthy opponent. Of the seventeen professional witnesses only one would emerge unflustered by Leary's unrelenting questioning. The defence was more complex. The first QC to take the case was Tom Williams, but suddenly, just eleven days prior to the case, he claimed involvement in 'another matter' and vanished. Other QCs were tried, notably Basil Wigoder, QC, but all withdrew; 'nobbled' as Felix Dennis put it. Finally, fortuitously, John Mortimer, well known as a playwright (and later as creator of television's 'Rumpole') as well as a QC and for many the very model of a 'champagne socialist', agreed to defend Anderson and Dennis. He noted, however, that he would initially have to finish a parallel obscenity case, that of the Danish-published guide to children's rights, *The Little Red Schoolbook*. (The case of the vanishing briefs, as it were, made clear the extent to which the government was determined to 'get' *Oz*. Only Mortimer, whose extra-legal income absolved him from the need to kow-tow to those who appointed judges, could take the case in the knowledge that his career would not be affected.) The magazine, which had been charged as a business, was represented by Keith McHale.

Neville chose to abandon the professional bar and defend himself. According to David Offenbach this was less dramatic than it seemed; the intention was to get in one more defence speech to the jury. While Mortimer, known for his exquisitely tortuous legal arguments, would be speaking the judge's language, it was hoped that Neville would best be able to put across the *Oz* ethos to the jury. He was assisted both by 'Mackenzie' lawyers (legally experienced amateurs: in his case Tom Fawthrop, David Widgery and the Canadian gay activist Warren Hague) and by Mortimer's junior Geoffrey Robertson, now among the country's leading liberal QCs. The jury, ostensibly of one's peers, was very far from that. The defence challenged many of the panel, but in 1971 jury service was still limited by a property qualification and the bulk of those who would try *Oz* were in their fifties or even older.

The prosecution fielded only two witness: DI Luff, plus one 'schoolkid', Vivian Berger, who had been co-opted to attack the very magazine he helped edit. He was hardly a good choice: he came from a strenuously liberal family, he had been the most right-on of all the schoolkids, and his evidence was unlikely to harm his heroes. The defence riposted with a parade of experts, including George Melly, Anthony Smith, Professors Richard Wollheim and Ronald Dworkin, Arnold Linken, Caroline Coon, Edward de Bono, Marty Feldman, Michael Schofield, Hans Eysenck and Leila Berg. (There were, in all, thirty-six volunteers, but even then not all those asked proved so keen: among the refuseniks of the liberal Establishment were Jill Tweedie and Alan Brien, Stephen Spender, A.J. Ayer and Alex Comfort.) The nature of any trial is that of a game: truth has little relevance. One plays by the rules laid down by the law and from that standpoint attempts to offer a selective, biased version of the facts that will best impress the jury. That this can be absurd is irrelevant; one still faces prison. When applied to an obscenity trial such as this one, the absurdity is made even more manifest. The task of the prosecution, most conscientiously and ably carried out by Brian Leary, is to take every damning line and construe it with the utmost literality. Neither nuance nor context nor intent – all so pertinent to any work of creativity, even one so tenuous as *Oz* 28 – has a place in such a prosecution. Instead Leary would proceed to eviscerate each contentious paragraph or image, demanding black and white, yes or no answers from people whose entire careers were based on demonstrating that such easy simplicities were otiose to any sophisticated analysis.

The advantage lay consistently with the prosecution. Of the experts few came away unscathed. George Melly was persuaded to say that dirty stories and obscene language were a regular part of his family life, and thus was painted as a virtual child-abuser; the comedian Marty Feldman, quite out of his depth, was dismissed as a hyped-up fool; even an academic such as Ronald Dworkin was reduced to a bit-player, almost contemptuously dismissed from the stand. In almost every case the experts found themselves rattled by Leary's plodding literalness and however hard John Mortimer's friendly questioning might strive to redress the balance, the jury was all too often left with the impression of a succession of smart-arse liberals, glorying in their own eloquence but incapable of understanding the simple concerns of 'ordinary people'. The best of the experts proved to be Leila Berg, journalist, author of many books for children, as well as of a 'Charter of Children's Rights'. Leary bullied, patronised and quoted, as ever, selectively, but Ms Berg remained admirably unrattled. What apparently especially annoyed the prosecution was her demure lilac dress: it looked too middle-class, too straight. The Court, resplendent in its own sanctioned fancy-dress could deal with Warren Haig's appearing in a frock and the defendants donning a variety of garments many degrees removed from the Establishment norm, but for a defence witness to look like 'one of us' was intolerable.

As for the defendants themselves, Anderson and Dennis were only able to make their case as witnesses. For Anderson, despite his legal training, it proved a nightmare. In his summing up John Mortimer borrowed from Sherlock Holmes the image of 'the dog that didn't bark'; he was referring to the fact that at no time had the prosecution produced a witness who would state, unequivocally, that *Oz* 28 had depraved and corrupted them. But for Jim Anderson there was another species of dog. As *Oz* readers, and presumably the majority of the Court were well aware, Anderson was homosexual. He was over twenty-one and thus sanctioned in his affections by recently passed legislation, but it was clear that if the combination of straight sex and drugs and rock 'n' roll with children was troublesome enough, then to factor in gay sex was simply intolerable. According to Felix Dennis, Anderson was not alone: Leary, whose Acapulco holidays were significantly bereft of wife and family, was also homosexual – or so the defendants were convinced – and 'what was made known to Leary beyond a shadow of a doubt was that if he raised this issue with Jim Anderson I was going to fire John Mortimer and ask him the question. It was hardball.' Whether this was the case remains unproven, but certainly Anderson was never quizzed directly on his own sexual tastes. Instead Leary baited him.

> It was terrifying: if they'd actually asked him, 'Are you a homosexual?' Jim was going to say, 'Yes, and I'm proud of it and I've been a homosexual for many years.' And that would have sent us to prison for fifty years probably. And to watch Leary asking questions of Jim and dancing round the main question, the guy was a fucking sadist – he absolutely adored it. He walked the line, he walked round it, up to it, had a look over the edge, walked back, didn't ask it, and Jim is standing there shaking like a leaf 'cos he knows any minute this bombshell that is going to put his mates in prison for fucking years is going to be asked. And Leary walks up to it and walks back and walks round it and did everything he could except ask the question.[24]

Anderson believed unreservedly in what *Oz* stood for and in his part in its creation. The Schoolkids Issue was provocative, but what else should an underground magazine be? Faced by a prosecutor who, sexuality apart, was adamant in his refusal to entertain such concepts, Anderson was lost. It did not matter what he felt, it mattered only how he responded to his cross-examination and on the day, unprepared and terrified, it was not a happy experience.

Felix Dennis, on the other hand, had no such problems. At sentencing the Judge would contemptuously refer to him as 'the least intelligent of the three', but for Dennis there was no point in posing as an intellectual, a fault that he saw in Neville and in Mortimer. The jury didn't want that sort of thing. Questioned for nearly two days, Dennis never wavered from his role: 'the honest yeoman, brought here, bemused, against his will trying to give honest answers to twisted slippery snakes who couldn't put a decent question to an honest man if they tried'.[25] Later John Mortimer told him it was one of the best performances he'd ever witnessed. At the time even Leary, so insinuatingly successful in his undermining of those who sometimes seemed as interested in parading their own IQs as actually giving useful evidence, was forced to give ground. So well did he play Mr Average that it even worked outside the court: the absurd, but undeniably vicious Lady Birdwood, parading outside the Old Bailey to protest against the magazine, was unaware that the man who posed with his arm around her for the press photographers was in fact her arch-enemy.

Of the '*Oz* Three' the most important in terms of the case was Richard Neville himself. If he came over as excessively intellectual to Felix Dennis and perhaps ultimately to the jury, his performance for those who were ostensibly his peers, the assembled lawyers and those of the chattering classes who witnessed the trial, was impeccable. Seven years earlier, in Australia, he had allowed a lawyer to act in his place; this time he chose to voice his own beliefs. Growing in confidence as the trial went on, he engaged in spats with the judge and the prosecution and cross-examined witnesses (including himself) with commendable credibility. Like many others he faltered in the face of Leary's attack, but his final speech, summing up in his own defence and co-authored by Geoff Robertson, would be a *tour de force*. John Mortimer, the professional, had spoken for six hours, leaving the defendants at least, as Neville put it, feeling 'secure in the knowledge that the best team would win, the goal was truth, the stake was civilisation and all our parts would be played within the finest British traditions of justice, fairness and freedom'. Now Neville, the amateur, rose to commence his two-and-a-half hour speech, one which, despite the accepted practice that a summing-up is allowed to proceed unbroken, was regularly interrupted by Argyle. Interruptions or not, the speech was a triumph. It was an apologia not merely for his own beliefs and for *Oz* magazine, it spoke for the entire counter-culture. Later a lawyer suggested that were Neville to abandon *Oz* for the bar he could look forward to a highly lucrative career.

None of which mattered once, on 27 July, the Judge began his summing up. As would be noted at the Appeal, it was a grossly misleading piece of work: there were some seventy-five discrete errors. If Argyle, who frequently turned his chair away from the witnesses and was seen to be planning his holiday from a selection of travel brochures, had been barely able to mask his biases while the trial was in progress, he abandoned all pretence now the stage was his alone. Like Leary, whose summing-up had been a mass of selective quotations and sneering smears, he attempted to devalue the whole defence case, focusing particularly on the experts. In his opinion, it was clear, his one regret was the absence of a black cap. Predictably he bespattered his comments with Biblical quotes, usually with reference to 'the little ones'. The jury (which had been reduced by one member due to illness) retired at shortly before one o'clock. After some problems with the precise definition of obscenity and the statement that the desired unanimous verdict would not be forthcoming, they returned at five. The conspiracy charge was thrown out, and here there was total agreement (a major relief, since this charge carried a potential life sentence); but the other four charges were proved, each by a 10-1 majority. (In each case, it was noted, the stand-out was the only juror who appeared to be aged less than forty.) To turn the screw a little more Argyle refused to pass sentences: all three were to be held in Wandsworth, awaiting 'social, medical and mental health' reports. As the trio were hustled down the stairs the court erupted in hisses and boos. Outside, what the *Daily Express* termed 'a wailing wall of weirdies'[26] pressed themselves against the Old Bailey's walls, in a piece of street theatre characterised, once more by the *Express*, as 'mouthing frenzied protests about justice, freedom, love and the Fuzz'.

Two days later an appeal for bail was rejected; the trio would continue to languish in Wandsworth – where the celebrated reports took a mere twelve minutes to complete and where, quite against regulations, their hippie locks were cropped short. A limit was set down however: Argyle would have to sentence them after seven days. This he did, on 5 August. Neville was to serve fifteen months and then be deported; Anderson twelve months and Dennis nine. The company was fined £1,000 plus £1,250 costs. Once more they were 'taken down'. Outside the court hundreds of supporters burnt an effigy of the judge, sat down, and when the police attempted to clear the street engaged in running battles that led to eleven arrests.

The press, unleashed after a week's mandatory silence, let out a burst of unrestrained hatred. The *Daily Telegraph*, as might be expected, led the way:

During the past few days much drivel has been spoken and written about the 'alternative society.' This drivel implies that there is, already existing in our midst, another and arguably better society, complete and self-sufficient, capable of performing for its members all the functions which we expect society to perform for us. This is, of course, utter nonsense.

This so-called alternative society is no more what it purports to be than a cancer is an alternative body. It is entirely parasitic on our society; it flourishes and grows at our expense. We feed it, clothe it, protect it, yet without the protection of the law, which they so obscenely abuse, how long would these drop-outs survive, for the most part so manifestly weak and weedy as they are? Many of them, incidentally, including two of the *Oz* defenders, wear spectacles – a visible mark of their dependence on the normal world they despise, as ludicrous in its way as false teeth in the mouth of a noble savage.

No, this is not an alternative society but a disease, potentially very grave, afflicting our society. Its means may appear puny, hysteria about it therefore misplaced – let us hope it is so. But its ends seem almost boundless. Whatever distinguishes Man from the animals, whatever has lifted him from the primeval slime, it derides and denounces. Reason and calculation; foresight; justice; patience, prudence and hard work; all existing standards of taste and morality, perhaps all such standards; respect for the past, the family and perhaps even love itself, except in the crude sense of random copulation: all these it ferociously attacks or undermines. Triumphant, it would produce at first anarchy and then the dreadful tyranny which follows anarchy as surely as night follows day; first chaos, then wrath and tears.[27]

There were, however, more rational voices, not merely from among the 'socialists' (whose 'ludicrous' support of *Oz* the same leader had gone on to excoriate), but from other broadsheets, notably *The Times*, where Bernard Levin, previously less than sympathetic, began by quoting Hamlet ('Young men will do't, if they come to't | By cock, they are to blame') before suggesting that it was not the defendants who were in need of mental reports, but the DPP, for bringing the case, the jury, for convicting on such flimsy evidence, and the judge, for his sentencing. His first thought, on reading *Oz* 28, was that this must be an incomplete copy: where in these pages was the source of such hysteria, the justification for so vindictive a prosecution? 'Those who think such stuff pornographic quite literally do not know what pornography is.' He noted that the sexual content of the magazine was a mere seven per cent. To Levin, society was shamefully deaf to adolescent protest; *Oz* had provided a 'harmless, and indeed admirable forum in which young people might shout aloud what they felt'. Wasn't the result of the *Oz* trial more or less likely to provoke in young people exactly those emotions and actions that it had ostensibly been brought to restrain? If this was authority, had it altered its position in the eyes of the young, other than to appear ever more absurd and uncaring? And he concluded:

> The *Oz* trial was a national disgrace. It served notice on the young that we will listen to them, but not hear; look at them, but not see; let them ask, but not answer. We must not be surprised then, if they break off relations with us and cleave instead to the false gods who offer them all the kingdoms of the earth if only they will fall down and worship. Is it to be supposed that young, vital and intelligent people would for long take the editors of *Oz* as true guides, if it were not for the authorities who have insisted on including them in a new Book of Martyrs to ease their own guilt and hide their own shame? 'The fathers have eaten sour grapes, and the children's teeth are set on edge.' So the fathers have now taken, it seems, to knocking the children's teeth down their throats. A fine day's work.[28]

As Richard Neville had pointed out in his opening speech: 'If you convict us at the end of this trial, you are in reality convicting schoolchildren. And if you convict schoolchildren then you yourselves must accept some responsibility for their guilt. So far from debauching and corrupting the morals of children . . . *Oz* . . . intends the very opposite. It sets out to enlighten and to elevate public morals.' Even *Private Eye* buried its hatchet with a 'Judges' Issue' featuring a cartoon of Argyle by Ralph Steadman, captioned THIS JUSTICE SHOULD BE SEEN TO BE DONE; Argyle's face was obscured: as the accompanying note explained, 'to avoid prosecution the obscene part has been blacked out.' A regular '*Oz* industry' developed: on the Lyndon Johnson principle ('better have them inside the tent pissing out than outside pissing in') Neville was given a column – the 'Alternative Voice' – in the *Evening Standard*; there was an *Oz* musical (premiered in New York's Fillmore East rock auditorium, but hardly the most lasting of successes), a book by filmmaker Tony Palmer (who had been allowed to tape proceedings, other than the judge's summing-up, as the trial went by) and much more. And as the *Daily Telegraph* had noted, sales of *Oz*, 28 if possible, but any *Oz* would do, rocketed. The office, usually brimming with piles of back copies, emptied as the Soho 'bookshops' sent round their vans.

What happened next remains not so much in dispute, but otherwise unattested. In the long run the trio spent three days in jail, this time West London's Wormwood Scrubs, before being granted bail pending appeal. In the short run, things were more interesting. Neither of the other defendants, nor any of the lawyers back him up – but in 1988, when it appeared in *Days in the Life*, neither did anyone contest it.

As Dennis tells it the trio had gone to bed when they were summoned from their cells, handcuffed and driven through London to the Inns of Court. Here, utterly bemused and each escorted by a warder, they were decanted into a room wherein sat a man whom none of them immediately recognised. He had their cuffs removed, dismissed the guards and before making any further statement asked his attendant butler to pour the trio a sherry. It was then that Dennis, so he recalls, recognised their host: Lord Widgery, then Lord Chief Justice of England. And it was from him that there came, if Dennis is still to be believed, 'the deal':

So he says, 'Well, this is a fine mess we've managed to land ourselves in, haven't we. I've had several discussions with a person who doesn't live very far away from Downing Street, and we're in a fine pickle aren't we . . . Good god,' he says, 'I used to write better stuff than this when I was in bloody college. Look at the state of it, it's terrible isn't it. But I've got to have something, I've got to have something, I can't let you out, I must have something. And you know what it's got to be.' And Richard's much faster than me at this sort of stuff and he's saying, 'Well, what is it?' and I'm saying, 'You can fuck off I'm not giving you . . . ' and Richard's saying, 'Shut your mouth you bastard.' So Widgery says, 'You're going to win the appeal; at least I can't say that but I am going to be the lead judge on the appeal and I do have in front of me seventy-five complaints against Argyll, and a fat mess he managed to make of it . . . ' So he said, 'You can't work on the magazine.' I said, 'That's how I earn my living.' 'Shut up,' says Richard. So of course in the end we agreed and he said, 'You'll be out tomorrow morning and not a word about this meeting because no one will ever believe you, now get out. And leave those sherry glasses behind you.' And we were out the next morning, too. It was [Michael] Foot and [Tony] Benn that got us out, no question. Every time

Heath used to walk in to Question Time Benn would get up and say, 'I was wondering whether the Prime Minister had incarcerated any other young persons for writing on lavatory walls? Whether we're all safe from this abuse?' He couldn't take it.[29]

Whatever the ultimate truth there is little doubt that the Establishment, having ordained the trial, found it elevated to an importance far beyond anything they (or indeed the defendants) could have imagined. And despite the fact that Lord Widgery appeared to have let them out to save the government's face, there was not the slightest acknowledgement that *Oz* was in any way 'innocent'. As Richard Neville put it, writing in *Oz* 39, 'The meaning of Lord Widgery's Appeal judgement . . . is that if Argyle had been a bit brighter, we'd still be in jail. The three judges fully endorsed Argyle's sentencing policy [but], with obvious reluctance, were compelled to over-rule the conviction on technical grounds.'

The trial, as Geoffrey Robertson has suggested, was not merely that of three editors and their magazine, but of an era, of 'the Sixties'. The emotions behind the *Telegraph*'s triumphalist leader may seem over-heated, but they were without the slightest doubt absolutely sincere. The liberal great and good may have encouraged, even supported *Oz*, and might even have had the occasional issue adorning the coffee table, but as would be seen not simply in the impotence of the seventeen experts but more importantly in the decades that followed, such figures have little real power in a country so fundamentally suspicious of their very nature and of the philosophies they espouse. Even Roy Jenkins, who masterminded so many important changes in English society, appeared invariably as an *éminence grise*; the Establishment could not be seen to advocate such contentious reforms. In any case, by the time of the trial, Jenkins was long gone. Heath's government prosecuted the case, but in fairness, it was Wilson's, notably James Callaghan's Home Office, that set the process in motion. And Jenkins was anomalous. The Establishment did not like *Oz* or the counter-culture it represented; they had tolerated it for so long, but when Neville naïvely, injudiciously combined 'children' with the usual irritants of drugs and sex and rock, they saw their chance. What was freedom of speech compared with the potent, if spurious fantasy of youthful purity?

The trial displayed its own anomalies. As Robertson has pointed out, 'The magazine was read out in court as though it were an ambiguous contract. It was gone through letter by letter.' The nature of such a process is that the defence was constantly hamstrung by the need to prove that *Oz* – however lurid its words and pictures might have been – had not the slightest real effect, and at the same time, as creative individuals, to assert that what they were doing was not some kind of throwaway, irresponsible trash. In the end they were forced to opt for the 'zero effect' defence, even as a parade of experts – their defenders – dwelt portentously on every line. The other contradiction, and a far greater and more ironic one, could be seen in the role of the police, or more properly of the Obscene Publications Squad. Writing in his *Times* piece, Bernard Levin compared the anodyne, if sometimes grubby pages of *Oz* with the real thing, available in the 'bookshops' of Soho or Praed Street. What neither he nor any other writer (nor indeed any defendant) appreciated was the dirtiest little joke of all: the extent of corruption that riddled the aptly-named 'dirty squad' from top to bottom. The defendants couldn't know, but the Old Bailey hacks (who would happily collude with the police in ensuring that virtually no one other than the *Guardian* printed Neville's final speech) must have been aware that many of the Squad, although apparently not Luff (who would reach his professional apogee as the senior officer overseeing the Brixton riots of 1981), were as bent as the proverbial nine-bob note. Like their colleagues in the drug squad many of the OPS would face their own trials, in their case for extracting hundreds of thousands of pounds from the real pornographers, the 'porn barons' of Soho. Commander Wallace Virgo, the boss of both squads, was jailed for twelve years; his deputy, Chief Superintendent Bill Moody, received a similar sentence. Between them the pair were pulling down payoffs from fifty shops, using the occasional well-telegraphed 'bust' merely to provide free blue movies for the regular Friday night Squad stag parties. Mr Justice Mars-Jones, jailing them and the smaller fry, termed their efforts 'corruption on a scale which beggars description'. On a rather smaller scale, it transpired that in the case of *Oz* the Squad had also involved themselves in a little jury tampering: quite against any legal rule, a number of back-copies had been provided to the jury as they made their deliberations. It had apparently been these, featuring an on-going strain of craziness and excess which reinforced the jury's nagging doubts about 'suitability', that led irrevocably to the four convictions.

The *Oz* Trial was not the last of the period's obscenity prosecutions and the remainder of the Seventies would witness several more, notably that of *IT*'s comic *Nasty Tales* in 1973 (an *Oz* Trial diminuendo, although in this case the defendants escaped scot-free). In addition the unlikely offence of blasphemy would be disinterred from its ecclesiastical past by Mrs Whitehouse in her successful attack on a poem – 'The Well-hung Christ' – printed, in 1976, by *Gay News*. None the less the twenty-seven-day extravaganza, costing, it was believed, some £100,000 of public money and dismissed by the *New Law* Journal as 'an unmitigated disaster',[30] signalled the end of an era.

Oz folded in 1973; it had £20,000 worth of debts and no readership worth the name. It lingered on after the trial, but it had little more to say. Felix Dennis launched *Cozmic Comics*, and then moved into the world of Kung Fu with the Bruce Lee craze of 1974. From there to TV tie-ins and computer magazines and thence to his annual appearance (ever-nearer the top) in one of 'Britain's Richest People' lists. Neville retired to Australia, to become a media pundit and occasional memoirist; Anderson to California and novel-writing and in time back to geographical Oz in his turn.

'What killed *Oz*', wrote the *Guardian*, 'was that dissent became fashionable and then a cliché. People got tired of it.'[31] It wasn't commercial rivals that finished *Oz*, but the simple march of time. In the end *Oz*, like the alternative society it represented, had done its job and had its day. As this author suggested in *IT*'s 'obituary' for its one-time rival,

> *Oz* was more than simply another hippie rag; it was a vital force, a force which, coupled with *IT* and the papers that followed it, both helped create and managed to reflect the alternative culture that was emerging. But by the end of the decade both the culture and the press it had spawned were showing distinct signs of diminishing impetus. The people who had formed it were growing older, their enthusiasms were waning. For the [underground] press the propagation of new ideas, of news stories on topics which had formerly been their own province, of the dope/sex/rock and roll and cheap thrills philosophy, was no longer enough. The Establishment press were catching up. With infinitely greater finance and facilities, with a desire, born of the swinging sixties, to maintain a position much hipper, or even hippier than thou, they steadily took over roles that had formerly been virtually the sole preoccupation of their alternative contemporaries.[32]

Above all by 1973 the counter-culture, if such a thing existed, had moved on, far from the old, post-Beatnik premises. Fucking in the street was one thing; sexual politics, the flavour of the Seventies, was something else besides. Neither side really won the *Oz* trial. And even as the trial moved through those hot July days, there was a new agenda, one to which *Oz* with its Gay Power and Cunt Power issues had perhaps pandered, but which now, flexing its own muscles, had no need of help.

Chapter Twenty-Seven

Gay Liberation: Queer Nation

If a man lie with mankind, as with womankind, both of them have committed
abomination: they shall surely be put to death; their blood shall be upon them
Leviticus xx, 13

Male homosexuality, as these lines from the Bible make clear, has always
been abhorred. Whether as a result of the superstitions, fears and prejudices
codified as religious belief or through some visceral terror of 'unnatural' relations, the gay man has been a traditional object of hatred. In Britain Laws
against 'the abominable Vice of Buggery' were first laid down in 1533 and
have been on the statute book ever since. Like other such campaigns – typically that against the Obscene Publications Act – the impetus for change followed somewhat tardily on the institution of the injustice. The law against
which the campaigners of the Fifties and Sixties were struggling had been
passed in 1885, as section II of the Criminal Law Amendment Act. The initial aim of the law was to deal not with men, but women, 'to make further
provision for the protection of women and girls, the suppression of brothels
and other purposes'. In fact, when introduced there was no mention whatsoever of homosexuality. Then late one night, after the law had been
passed by the Lords and was making its way through the Commons,
Henry Labouchere, a noted radical whose own rackety youth had given way
to a grim, conservative puritanism, threw in his amendment. There were few
sitting members and those that were attending were less than keen to debate
so sordid a topic. As ever, no politician, faced with so contentious a subject,
wished by challenging the amendment to render himself liable to an accusation of actually condoning or even advocating 'the love that hath no
name'. It stated that,

> Any male person who, in private or in public, commits or is a party to the com-
> mission of, or procures or attempts to procure the commission of any male per-
> son of any act of gross indecency with another male person, shall be guilty of a
> misdemeanour, and being convicted thereof shall be liable . . . to be imprisoned
> for any term not exceeding two years, with or without hard labour.

The 'Labouchere amendment' took the persecution of homosexuals into
a new league: prior to 1885 the act of sodomy had to be proved, now homosexuality *tout court* was enough to bring a man to court. There were few if any
dissenting voices: *The Times* hinted at doubts in its suggestion that 'there
may be some changes made lately in the Bill which exceed the limits of sound
policy and prudent legislation', but acknowledged that, 'it is better to accept
some questionable provisions than imperil the passing of the measure.'[1]

(Whether or not this was a reference to the amendment was not in any case stated.) Correspondents to a number of papers noted one other, perhaps unforeseen effect: the act, with its all-encompassing attack, was virtually a 'Blackmailers' Charter'. This too was deemed acceptable: only frightened (and of course guilty) men need fear such a thing.

As far as the popular attitudes to homosexuality went, the tenor of the early 1950s was set by the Sunday pops, typically the *News of the World*, with its weekly litany of errant scoutmasters, straying clergymen and others convicted of what was usually typified as 'improper behaviour'. In May 1952 the *Sunday Pictorial*, piously claiming to make 'a sincere attempt to get to the root of a spreading fungus' ran a major series on the topic. Its headline: 'EVIL MEN', somewhat undermined the *Pictorial*'s claims, as did the text, which talked of 'an unnatural sex vice' and refuted suggestions of legalising homosexuality as 'quite intolerable . . . the chief danger of the perverts is the corrupting effect they have on youth . . . Most people know there are such things – "pansies"– mincing, effeminate young men who call themselves queers. But simple, decent folk regard them as freaks and rarities.'[2] Legalisation, the paper declared, would mean national decadence. The rest of the popular media followed suit.

In that same year, 1952, the Church of England Moral Welfare Council set up a study of the problem, drawing on a committee of clergymen, doctors and lawyers. Intended as an internal document, it would be published in 1954 and surprised many with its measured, liberal tones. Parliamentary and Establishment concern was also on the increase, albeit for primarily selfish reasons: in January 1953 Labour MP William Field was arrested in Piccadilly Circus and charged with persistently importuning men for immoral purposes. Found guilty, he appealed, but on losing that appeal resigned his seat. Later that year the author Rupert Croft-Cooke was jailed for nine months, after being convicted of offences with two young sailors (his account appeared in 1955 as *The Verdict of You All*), the actor John Gielgud was arrested and charged with 'importuning male persons for immoral purposes' after an incident in a public lavatory, and most notoriously of all, Lord Montagu of Beaulieu and his friend, the movie director Kenneth Hume, were charged with 'serious offences', as Scotland Yard put it, involving a pair of boy scouts. When the jury threw out one charge, and failed to reach a verdict on another, a retrial was ordered. Nor did the attacks restrict themselves to cottaging: in June 1952 Colin MacInnes published a novel, *June in Her Spring*. An innocent enough love story it had one flaw in censorious eyes: it touched on homosexuality. Such paragraphs, however brief, were enough: a number of Public Libraries promptly banned the book. (MacInnes's own attitude to homosexuality, his own and others', was predictably relaxed: 'It is an ancient, timeless, permanent human situation, rooted in nature with a

million other natural phenomena.'⁴ But for a genuinely fulfilled sexual life he
had only one prescription: bisexuality.)

On 1 November 1953 the *Sunday Times* weighed in, in a piece pinned to
what it saw as an alarming increase in these prosecutions. The bulk of the
piece rehearsed the old shibboleths, but the paper did not deny that public
opinion as a whole, 'moves on two contrasted planes. The great majority of
ordinary people view male inversion as an abomination which ought to be
stamped out' while 'sophisticated circles are apt to treat homosexuals with
amused tolerance, to regard such inversion as mere aberration, to argue that
its practitioners are cases for the psychiatrist rather than the courts, if one
need bother about them at all.' The best thing for all concerned, added the
paper, was self-control and moral rectitude.

On 9 January 1954 Lord Montagu was arrested again, this time for alleged misbehaviour with a couple of airmen, an event which had supposedly
taken place in 1952. His friends Michael Pitt-Rivers and Peter Wildeblood,
Diplomatic Correspondent of the *Daily Mail* (who would later write a best-
selling memoir of the case: *Against the Law*, 1955) were also charged. It became clear, as the case proceeded, that allegations of homosexuality appeared
to give the police *carte blanche* to exceed any normal restraints. Flats had been
searched without warrants, the men had been denied access to their solicitors, Montagu's passport had been tampered with while in police custody.
Furthermore the two airmen, who had admitted several other gay affairs, had
been promised immunity from prosecution were they to turn Queen's Evidence. Moreover the huge publicity that had accompanied the earlier trial
made an impartial jury unlikely. The trial concluded on 24 March with guilty
verdicts for all three defendants. Montagu was jailed for a year, the others for
eighteen months. Yet despite the supposed public abhorrence of their sexual
preferences, it was noted that on their conviction the public response was
very different to that envisaged. The turncoat airmen were booed as they left
the court, but not so the convicted men. The whores may have danced in the
streets when Oscar Wilde was condemned, Lord Montagu and his friends
heard only shouts of encouragement and support.

Once more the *Sunday Times* offered its views, its leader 'Law and Hypocrisy' voicing its unhappiness with the verdict and noticing that since the
law and public opinion seemed to differ so widely, that same law could only
fall into disrepute and that 'the case for a reform of the law as to acts committed in private between adults is very strong'. It called for an authoritative enquiry and cited the recently published Moral Welfare Council Report as a
possible blueprint. This report, entitled *The Problem of Homosexuality*, was
enormously influential. It suggested that homosexuality was a matter for individual conscience – as were fornication, adultery and lesbianism – and not
for the courts; it advocated a common age of consent for both hetero- and homosexuals of seventeen and that only when homosexual acts were combined

with violence, assault, fraud or duress should the law be called into use. With increasing impetus, the movement for reform gathered energy. As well as the Moral Welfare Council, the Howard League for Penal Reform called for an urgent enquiry. These essentially liberal bodies were not alone. Such usually hard-line moral pressure groups as the Public Morality Council and the National Vigilance Association (more usually associated with the prosecution of such authors as Zola, Balzac and Rabelais and for their campaigns against a variety of 'immoral' topics such as sex education, striptease and 'What the Butler Saw' machines) demanded changes in the law, albeit to assuage their worries over declining morality and not as a result of any sympathy for gay rights. Surprisingly the NVA had even taken on board the recently published Kinsey Report, with its acknowledgement of a far greater experience of male homosexuality than had been hitherto believed to exist, and called for the 'fullest investigation by experts in the light of the new knowledge now available'.[5]

While, as the Wolfenden Committee would attest, homosexuality as such was not on the increase, its prosecution most certainly was. Celebrity trials such as that of Lord Montagu were but the tip of a substantial iceberg. Worries about 'declining morality', backed by the urging of a quintessentially conservative and rigidly homophobic Home Secretary, David Maxwell-Fyfe and a devoutly Roman Catholic DPP, Sir Theobald Mathew, had led to vastly increased police activity. The average annual arrests for street offences had risen from 2,000 in the early 1940s to over 10,000 by 1952, and to almost 12,000 by 1955. During the same period indictable male homosexual offences had gone up by a factor of five. In 1938 there were 134 cases of sodomy and bestiality known to the police in England and Wales; in 1952, 670; and in 1954, 1,043. Indecent assault had increased from 822 cases in 1938 to 3,305 in 1953, 'gross indecency', which had registered 316 cases in 1938, stood at 2,322 in 1955.[6] Add to that the daily activities of the Metropolis's estimated 3,000 working prostitutes, and it seemed to those who found such things disturbing, that the streets were rampant with vice. The imminence in 1953 of the Coronation made some form of clean-up even more urgent. More specifically the fact that Burgess and Maclean, the 'Missing Diplomats', had carried their public school dabblings into adult life, helped intensify the increasing paranoia as regarded gay men in high places. It also appeared that the US State Department, earnestly purging itself of gay employees at the behest of Senator McCarthy, had told its clients across the Atlantic to start dealing with their own infestation of inverts. For whatever reasons, homosexuals, in terms of popular visibility if not in actual self-declaration, were fast moving far from the old closets.

Most important of all, as far as possible legislation was concerned, a number of MPs, including Robert Boothby, Desmond Donnelly and Kenneth Robinson all added their voices to those demanding an enquiry. In

August 1954 the government acceded: a Committee to enquire into homosexual offences and prostitution was announced. Its chairman was to be Sir
John Wolfenden, former headmaster of the public school Uppingham and
now Vice-Chancellor of Reading University. Wolfenden had one secret of
his own: his son Jeremy had himself 'come out' barely two years earlier. The
fact was never revealed, although Jeremy was hardly discreet as to his own
pursuits. According to Sebastian Faulks, his father had only two requests.
Writing in a letter in which he alerted his son to his new appointment he
asked, '1. That we stay out of each other's way for the time being; 2. That you
wear rather less make-up.'[7] Wolfenden was no reformer: he deplored homosexuality, but similarly saw no justification in a government interfering in
what was essentially a private matter, however abominable such practices
might be. His attitude, to quote Faulks again, was 'a victory for intellectual
process over personal distaste . . . a vindication of . . . disinterested mental
disciplines'.[8]

Sitting in the pleasingly Orwellian Room 101 of the Home Office,
Wolfenden was accompanied by a variety of his peers, including two MPs, a
judge, a Marquis and three OBEs. Their brief was to consider '(a) the law
and practice relating to homosexual offences and the treatment of persons
convicted of such offences by the courts; and (b) the law and practice relating
to offences against the criminal in connection with prostitution and solicita-
tion for immoral purposes'. For the next two years, over sixty-two meetings,
they would hear evidence from some 200 different organisations and individuals. Among these, certain groups stand out. The Church of England
Moral Welfare Council submitted its report, with its de-emphasis of sin, its
rejection of the principle that the state could interfere in private morality and
its ultimate conclusion that the law as it stood was completely unjustified.
The Catholic Church followed suit, although it was unable to overlook the
innate sinfulness of homosexuality. The British Medical Association, dealing with the medical aspects, bypassed any recommendation as to the law and
its reform, but did note that prison was hardly the best place to send gay offenders. It deplored the current situation, however, and wondered whether
the simple fact of such punitive legislation might not make homosexuality
more rather than less attractive, since 'forbidden fruit is always sweeter'. A
variety of youth organisations were also canvassed, typically the Boy Scouts
who were quite happy to back reform, as long as young people were still pro-
tected. All in all the witnesses came down in favour of change. There were no
major calls for upholding the law, although the more conservative bodies, for
example the Baptist Union and the Episcopal Church in Scotland, refrained
from meeting the Committee.

The Report of the Committee on Homosexual Offences and Prostitution
was published on 4 September 1957. The idea that homosexuality menaces
national stability and had led to the decline of once-mighty empires was re-

jected out of hand; that it might undermine family life was accepted, but then so too did adultery or lesbianism, and both of these were outside the law; as far as the role of paedophiliac homosexuality was concerned, this was strictly fenced off from adult/adult liaisons. The Committee had no intention of condoning let alone encouraging homosexuality, but given that 'we do not think that it is proper for the law to concern itself with what a man does in private unless it can be shown to be contrary to the public good' the Committee declared that there was no justification for maintaining the law as it stood. It recommended the decriminalisation of all forms of consensual homosexual behaviour between adult males in private. (It also acknowledged that legislation, however punitive, probably made little difference to the extent of homosexual activity, and that reform, however well-intentioned, was unlikely to reduce the gut homophobia of a large number of people.) 'Private' was defined under the existing Public Order legislation as anywhere that was not likely to offend members of the public; 'consent' was defined by the rules as were used for heterosexual relations; only 'adult' proved a problem. Some members wished to see sixteen, the heterosexual age of consent, adopted, but others, obsessed with the supposed corruption of youth, refused to accept it. The definition was settled at the age of twenty-one, being the wider definition of 'adult' as regards making contracts and being legally responsible. Only one member of the Committee, James Adair, a former Procurator Fiscal of Glasgow, challenged the report, producing a minority opinion of his own, in which he stood wholeheartedly against the slightest change in the current law.

The press, whose pages were bespattered with the Report – putting a dramatic end to decades of squeamishness as regarded the 'unnatural vice' – tended to reflect the Committee. The *Daily Mirror*, for instance, called it 'sensible and responsible' and headlined its coverage 'Don't be Shocked by This Report, It's the Truth, It's the Answer, IT'S LIFE'; the *Daily Telegraph* called it 'clear, conscientious and courageous'. The Beaverbook press, notably the *Sunday Express* (where the ineffable John Gordon reviled the 'Pansies' Charter'), remained hostile. Scotland was generally anti, backing its champion James Adair. However even the supporters had no doubt that a Report was one thing, public acceptance and possible legislation were something else again. It was best summed up by a letter in the *News Chronicle*, which had commissioned a Gallup Poll that revealed that while 38% were in favour of decriminalisation, 47% remained against: 'Alas! not a dozen such sensible, powerful and honest reports will convince a people whose minds are choked with aspidistras. It is like talking metaphysics to a goldfish.'[9]

Outside the media opinion was largely in favour. Those Church and secular organisations whose pro-reform views had formed the background to the Report unsurprisingly supported Wolfenden's conclusions. Lawyers were, predictably, divided. Many agreed, but Lord Devlin, speaking in spring

1959 in the second Maccabean lecture on jurisprudence made it clear, as reported by *The Times*, that 'no society could do without intolerance, indigna-
tion and disgust; they were the forces behind the moral law, and if the
genuine feeling of ... society ... was that homosexuality was a vice so abominable that its mere presence was an offence he did not see how society could
not be denied the right to eradicate it'.[10] (Devlin's reasoning was questioned a
few days later by a correspondent who noted that 'we once burnt old women
because, without giving our reasons, we felt in our hearts that witchcraft was
intolerable'.)[11]

As Jeffrey Weeks has pointed out, Wolfenden is a paradoxical document,
expressing at the same time '1950s moral anxieties and [giving] a blueprint
for the "permissive" legislation of the 1960s'.[12] At no time was Wolfenden
looking for liberal reform: homosexuality was still to be controlled – the debate was to what extent the current law effected that control efficiently. Thus
while the Report moved to safeguard an individual's private sexuality, it
strengthened, whether in dealing with homosexuality or prostitution, the legal controls over public sexual display. Thus prostitutes were to be removed
from the public gaze, and homosexuals were restricted both as to age and environment. By no stretch of the imagination could this be construed as liberal: as Wolfenden put it, 'It is important that the limited modification of the
law which we propose should not be interpreted as an indication that the law
can be indifferent to other forms of homosexual behaviour, or as a general licence to adult homosexuals to behave as they please.'

The immediate result of the Report was equally paradoxical. On the one
hand the recommendations on prostitution were taken up without demur, embodied in the Street Offences Act of 1959. The girls, once parading in an almost unbroken line from Mayfair and Piccadilly through to Bayswater,
vanished overnight. A new phenomenon, the call-girl, appeared with equal
speed; there were no fewer working girls, maybe even more, but now at least
they were out of sight. Homosexuality, however, was a different matter. The
law might be unworkable, and need reform but the public lagged far behind
the campaigners. As the *Belfast Telegraph* headlined the story on 5 September
1957: 'NO EARLY LEGISLATION ON VICE REPORT. TIME FOR PUBLIC
OPINION TO FORM'. A general election was only two years off and the new
Home Secretary, R.A. Butler, had no desire to undermine his party's unity by
throwing so contentious an issue into the debating chamber. Homosexual law
reform was placed firmly in abeyance, although a full scale debate in the House
of Lords showed a remarkable degree of liberality. It would take another ten
years before that reform, however diluted and compromised it might turn out
to be, would finally gain royal assent. In the meantime those who backed reform had one all-important task: the education of public opinion. Only then
could the Report, which provided the ideal foundations for legislation, actually
move from a document of debate to the statute book.

On 7 March 1958 *The Times* published a letter calling for immediate implementation of Wolfenden's proposals. It was signed by thirty-three leading figures, among them Sir Isaiah Berlin, Robert Boothby, C.V. Wedgwood, Bertrand Russell and J.B. Priestley. A month later a follow-up letter, saying much the same thing, was signed by fifteen eminent married women. Behind this nascent campaign was A.E. Dyson, a university lecturer who, with a friend, the Rev. Andrew Hallidie-Smith, established the Homosexual Law Reform Society (HLRS), amongst whose founders were a number of those who had written to *The Times*. They wrote again, to the Home Secretary. His reply offered nothing immediate but he did claim to welcome the fullest discussion, noting that public opinion was of the greatest importance in determining the government's final decision. Thus inspired, the HLRS registered itself as a charity, the Albany Trust, and appointed a Chief Executive, the young barrister Antony Grey. It published a pamphlet, 'Homosexuals and the Law' and set about campaigning. It was not alone. As 1958 passed, the press and a number of major figures, including John Wolfenden himself, were becoming increasingly frustrated and ultimately annoyed by what one paper termed Butler's 'shameful' refusal to act. On 26 November, he gave in. The House of Commons finally debated the Wolfenden Report.

Butler's opening speech made the government's position clear. The Committee were to be congratulated on their efforts, but 'there is at present a very large section of the population who strongly repudiate homosexual conduct and whose moral sense would be offended by an alteration of the law which would seem to imply approval or tolerance of what they regard as a great social evil.' There might be a good deal of suffering attendant on the current law, but the government had no intention to repeal it. The rest of the debate ran through the usual arguments, with the Tory back-bencher Cyril Black proving especially ludicrous in his fears for the 'death to souls' of homosexuals and the decline and fall of 'great nations' that tolerate them. His suggestion that a sinister coterie of well-connected perverts lay behind the whole establishment of Wolfenden was equally predictable – and sadly backed up by a large number of his peers. The most honest speech probably came from one member who admitted candidly that were he or any fellow MP to come out for reform, their constituents would be less than supportive. Civil rights, yet again, came a poor second to self-interest. A day later Butler was praised in the *Daily Express* for promoting a 'Victory for Public Opinion'[13] but the *News Chronicle* showed a greater sophistication in its suggestion that there had been 'too much emphasis . . . on appeasing popular prejudices and not enough on reform and justice . . . It is regrettable that Mr Butler should pay so much deference to an unpleasant aspect of our national character – the valuing of respectability above reform.'[14] Or as the *Spectator* had it, 'The *Vice Anglais* . . . is not buggery but humbuggery.'[15]

For the HLRS and others who sought reform, the next few years went agonisingly slowly. Gradually their efforts did begin to impinge on the public's consciousness – the press became more rational and somewhat less hysterical, and as the new decade dawned homosexuality became an increasingly popular topic for plays (both stage and televised) and films – but Parliament remained unmoved. In June 1960 Kenneth Robinson moved a Private Member's motion calling for action on Wolfenden; it was defeated by 213–99 votes. (The 99 were primarily Labour supporters, among them, inevitably, Roy Jenkins.) In 1962 the issue re-emerged when Leo Abse, the flamboyant MP for Pontypool, introduced a Private Member's Bill, its aim to legislate on the less contentious aspects of Wolfenden, while bypassing the difficult topic of decriminalisation. This too failed, a situation exacerbated by the hostility of Lord Kilmuir, a Cabinet member who promptly rose from the Cabinet table if ever the subject were even to be mentioned. Abse himself, while a veteran campaigner on social issues, was no great advocate of homosexuality. Such men should no longer be blamed, but they should be pitied. If, he explained in a debate on 19 December 1966, legal reform might overturn the national obsession with punishing homosexuals, the country could turn to a more important task: 'preventing little boys from growing up to be adult homosexuals. Surely, what we should be preoccupied with is the question of how we can . . . reduce the number of faulty [sic] males in the community.'[16]

The election in October 1964 of the Labour government was no more encouraging. It was assumed that Harold Wilson, whose government held the flimsiest of majorities, would soon be calling a second election. The HLRS, appreciative of where its support lay, accepted that this was no time to rock Labour's boat. Others were less restrained. Early in 1965 the journalist and Liberal peer Lord Arran, better known as 'Boofy' Gore, approached the HLRS to tell them that he intended to raise the whole topic in the House of Lords. He canvassed some 200 fellow-Lords and on 11 May 1965 there appeared in *The Times* a letter backing reform and signed by five bishops and three peers. Among them, it was noticed, was Lord Devlin, who only six years earlier had been so adamant in his defence of the repressive *status quo*. A day later Arran kept his promise, calling in an eloquent and impassioned speech for the end, as recommended in Wolfenden, to the legal persecution of homosexual men. Of the twenty-two peers who spoke in the debate, no less than seventeen backed his stance, including the Archbishops of Canterbury and York.

And while the Home Office spokesman reiterated the government's neutral stance, it was clear that a Labour government would be far more willing to support reform than was its predecessor. Two weeks later Arran proposed a Sexual Offences Bill. It contained but a single sentence: 'A homosexual act in private shall not be an offence provided that the parties consent thereto and have attained the age of twenty-one years.' The bill received a second reading by 94 votes to 49, a division that the *Guardian* termed 'a splendid palindrome'.[17] Not every peer was so tolerant. To quote Lord Annan,

> The bill now went to committee and the fight began in earnest . . . The Chief Scout feared the country would go the way of Greece and Rome; the Field Marshal [Montgomery] favoured the age of consent being fixed at eighty; the sometime attorney general, Lord Dilhorne, taunted the Archbishop of Canterbury by asking whether he favoured legalising the act of buggery; a former lord chief justice, Rayner Goddard, warned the House of the existence of buggers' clubs and another peer declared that he had seen a member of one of them 'shamelessly flaunting the club tie'.[18]

Though as Annan adds, 'Goddard was not without a certain grim sense of humour. A week later he told Arran that though none of the letters he received gave him support all asked for the addresses and telephone numbers of the clubs.'[19] Among Arran's staunchest defenders was Lady Wootton, soon to have her own cause, cannabis, to assess. 'I ask myself, what are the opponents of this bill afraid of? They cannot be afraid that these disgusting practices will be thrown upon their attention because these acts are legalised only if they are performed in private . . . I can only suppose that the opponents of the bill will be afraid that their imagination will be tormented by visions of what will be going on elsewhere. Surely, if that is so, that is their own private misfortune and no reason for imposing their personal standard of taste and morality on the minority of their fellow citizens who can find sexual satisfaction only in relations with their own sex.'

Arran's efforts were soon followed in the Commons where Leo Abse used the Ten-Minute Rule to put forward a bill that essentially replicated that put before the Lords. (The rule, used to 'test the water' on the Commons' opinion of possible legislation, permits a single ten minute speech in favour and one in opposition. There is then a vote which if successful ensures that the bill will get the chance of a fullscale debate.) The Commons were less impressed, although the vote was close: Abse was defeated by 178 votes to 159.

The Arran Bill, however, was still making its way through the Lords and on 28 October, by a vote of 116–46, moved through its third reading and was formally passed to the Commons. Here it foundered. No MP was willing to take up the bill, the parliamentary session ended and the unsponsored bill, as is customary, lapsed. In the new session, in February 1966, there was some progress in the Commons: Humphrey Berkeley, the Tory member for Lancaster, chose to take up the Arran measure and at the second reading on 11 February, by a vote of 166–109 the Commons voted for homosexual law reform for the very first time. (This was not, however, the major sea-change it might have appeared: only three members changed their minds – two in favour of reform, one against – but the actual turnout was radically skewed in the reformers' favour.) Once again the end of a session, this time to permit the General Election of March 1966, put an end to possible legislation.

The new Parliament would prove more fruitful. Apart from anything else the new Labour majority was now one hundred; of the Tory MPs who had lost their seats some twenty-one had voted against reform. Almost immediately Lord Arran was back with his bill in the Lords. It successfully passed its three readings and was passed to the Commons, by 78 votes to 60, on 16 June. The reluctance to sponsor it through the lower house remained at first; none of those who scored high in that session's Private Members' ballot wanted to be involved. The cause regained momentum however, when Jenkins discovered that Leo Abse intended to reintroduce his bill, once more under the Ten-Minute Rule. He promised Abse that if his submission was sufficiently successful the government would provide time for a proper debate. Abse acted on 5 July: the vote was 264-102, quite enough to justify Jenkins in keeping his promise. For the next five months Jenkins campaigned in Cabinet to persuade his colleagues off the fence and into the reformers' court. While some, such as Harold Wilson and James Callaghan, remained obdurate, Jenkins recruited an important ally in Richard Crossman, leader of the House and as such responsible for setting up the legislative programme. Crossman persuaded Wilson that given the votes of both Houses in favour of reform, it was better to have a major debate now, rather than let so contentious a subject re-emerge nearer an election.

On 19 December 1966 Abse's Sexual Offences Bill passed its first reading. For a while it seemed that the antis might trip up the bill, with their demand that the Merchant Navy be exempt from any reforms; Abse judicially backed down, and with his acquiescence removed his opponents' plank of complaint. It was further accepted that a homosexual act was no longer 'private' if it took place in the presence of a third party – there would be no approval of gay orgies. The bill returned for the all-important second reading on 23 June. This time the traditionalists, who had made no real impact on the Standing Committee, had regrouped, attempting through lengthy speeches and a vast range of new amendments to talk the bill to death. Only another Jenkins intercession saved the reform. As the atmosphere grew increasingly bitter and division followed division – each a narrow victory for reform – the opposition began to falter. At 5 a.m. on US Independence Day 1967 the Sexual Offences Bill was finally passed, by 101 votes to 16. On 21 July it was approved in the Lords and six days later it was a statute. Paradoxically the press, for so long so exercised by the mere thought of reform, barely noticed.

Speaking to the Lords on 21 July in what would be his last speech on the bill, Lord Arran was at pains to stress that the Sexual Offences Act would not initiate some kind of free-for-all. After paying tribute to such figures as Sir John

Wolfenden and the HLRS's Antony Grey he turned to the newly liberated gay community, warning them severely to resist any excessive joy.

> Homosexuals must continue to remember that while there may be nothing bad in being a homosexual, there is certainly nothing good. Lest the opponents of the Bill think that a new freedom, a new privileged dais, has been created, let me remind them that no amount of legislation will prevent homosexuals from being the subject of dislike and derision or at best of pity. We shall always, I fear, resent the odd man out. That is their burden for all time, and they must shoulder it like men – for men they are.

And he added, 'Any form of ostentatious behaviour, now or in the future, any form of public flaunting, would be utterly distasteful and would, I believe, make the sponsors of this Bill regret that they have done what they have done.' For such figures as Grey, for whom the Act was the culmination of nearly a decade's campaigning, Arran's sermonising may have been acceptable. A married man, not in the best of health, Arran had taken on a topic that still has the power to elicit the most savage, unreasoning of responses, and at the time had only recently emerged from decades of taboo. As he put it later, his espousal of the gay cause rendered his life 'a little private hell'. He received a nonstop postbag of hate mail; so terrified was he of possible blackmail that he would never see young men in his office without the presence of his secretary; in November 1965 the walls of that same office, as well as of his club and of every railway and tube station in London proclaimed the smear ARRAN HOMO. His own response, understandably enough, had been to up his drinking: it was far from heavy consumption, but it took the edge off the constant pressure.

Others, younger men, infused with the spirit of 1960s nonconformity, were not so acquiescent. And it was in their hands that the struggle for homosexual rights took on a new and far more militant character. The reformists of the old guard had been willing, at the cost of much compromise, to take what they were given. The new generation of homosexual campaigners, the revolutionaries centred on the Gay Liberation Front, had a new agenda: no more handouts, no more sermons. The catchword now was rights. 'Last time,' declared the writer Ray Gosling, speaking at a GLF rally, 'it was done by an élite who did it by stealth . . . This time it has to be done by us, brothers and sisters.'[20]

Gay Liberation was born on 29 June 1969 when New York police raided one of the city's best-known gay bars, the Stonewall Inn in Greenwich Village. As the *Village Voice* put it,

> The forces of faggotry, spurred by a Friday night raid on one of the city's largest, most popular, and longest lived gay bars, the Stonewall Inn, rallied Saturday night in an unprecedented protest against the raid and continued

Sunday night to assert presence, possibility, and pride until the early hours of Monday morning. 'I'm a faggot, and I'm proud of it!' 'Gay Power!', 'I like boys!' – these and many other slogans were heard all three nights as the show of force by the city's finery met the force of the city's finest. The result was a kind of liberation, as the gay brigade emerged from the bars, back rooms, and bedrooms of the Village and became street people.[21]

What the *Voice* didn't mention was the background. The raid was unexceptional: the police, as ever, needed to fill a few more arrest quotas, but they chose the wrong day. Judy Garland, the gay icon of the period, had been buried that afternoon and the drag queens were in mourning. When the police arrived it all became too much. Their heroine was defiled even in death and for once the 'sissies' fought back. The police may have triggered the riot by their presence, but it was the drag queens who threw the first punches. The Stonewall riots were a rallying cry for gay men and women across America. By the end of the year they were talking of 'Gay Liberation', adding their arguments and demands to the long roster of those – women, Blacks, Native Americans, Chicanos – who were demanding a radical reassessment of their civil rights. And it was people who had already been involved in civil rights who spearheaded the movement. The drag queens may have sparked the gay revolution, but more restrained, more consciously political figures took it up. It was, like so many similar movements, essentially American. Britain could never have initiated so outspoken a movement. But for Americans who had already embraced the slogan 'Say it out loud, I'm Black and I'm proud', it was not so hard a step to move from Black to gay. Nor was the adoption of the word 'gay' without resonance. It had been a part of the clandestine vocabulary of the homosexual world since the 1940s, but, like those it described, had not 'come out' until the advent of liberation. The word, so easily mocked by those who try to pun on its standard use, is important not as vocabulary but as a self-description. The old slang – 'queer', 'pansy', 'nelly' and the like – had been imposed from the outside. Gay was the community's own choice.

But Britain, as it did in so many other ways, could embrace what America had created. Inevitably the mood and the movement spread across the Atlantic. As it had with the supposed, if rarely demonstrated, equality of women, the counter-culture had paid lip-service to the concept of equal rights for homosexuals, but in reality gays were as much marginalised in the 'underground' as they were in the mainstream. That quickly changed. On 13 November 1970 two students at the LSE, Aubrey Waters and Bob Mellors, both of whom had been spending their summer in America and had been enthusiastic converts to the new world of 'gay consciousness', held a meeting to launch a British GLF in one of the School's classrooms. It attracted just eighteen men and one woman but within a month the audiences for subsequent meetings had swelled to over 200. Waters, a committed Marxist, went on to launch the Gay Men's Press, Britain's biggest gay publishing house.

Andrew Lumsden, a Fleet Street journalist at the time and one of the first gay men to come out in public, recalls the period.

> GLF came out of the ethnic melting pot of New York and Los Angeles, where people identify themselves as Italian-Americans, Chinese-Americans, Jewish Americans and so on. It's not much of a jump to say, 'I'm a gay American.' Whereas in Britain we didn't, and we don't think like that. We'd probably have called ourselves 'Dorothys', from Dorothy in *The Wizard of Oz*. Early GLF meetings were attended by people who'd worked on the Campaign for Homosexual Law Reform in the '50s and were horrified by the blatancy, the dangers, the backlash and so on. Nobody so straight as I was ever joined a revolutionary movement. What struck me was that I had never seen such roomfuls of wholly different looking people as those who met at the LSE at the time. The counter-culture was there, drag queens were there, a minority of lesbians, heavy-duty political people.[22]

The veterans of the HLRS were indeed horrified. In March 1969 Antony Grey (with criminologist D.J. West) had written a piece in *New Society*[23] deploring the fact that for homosexuals reform had meant a 'new law but no new deal'. It was a generally depressing piece, emphasising the way in which legal changes, however praiseworthy, had not changed social attitudes, neither among the wider, prejudiced heterosexual world nor in the generally negative self-image of gay men themselves. But Grey offered no positive solutions. The idea that gay men (women were not mentioned) might move from the passively grateful to the aggressively demanding remained unvoiced. The weight of Lord Arran's sober remonstrance determined the mood for many older homosexuals. GLF was quite another ball-game. The days of self-denial were over. Writing in *Oz* 32 (January 1971) under the headline 'Let's put a real Queen in the Palace', the GLF's Graham Hunt wound up a diatribe against heterosexual prejudice, 'The first task of the GLF is to help all gay people get back their self-respect . . . We cannot let our demands be just a part of some more general revolutionary group's programme. We are gay, and we are proud of it. We want to turn all gay people on to the fact, not that "gay is all right" or "gay is permissable", but that GAY IS GOOD.'

Jeffrey Weeks summed up the beliefs that motivated the movement: 'a sense of the absolute validity of homosexuality as a sexual orientation ("Gay is Good"); a belief in the vital importance of being open about one's homosexuality ("Coming Out"); and an emphasis on the importance of collective endeavour, self activity and selfhelp.'[24] Thus, as Lord Annan put it, 'What had been a tragic handicap became a glorious alternative.'[25]

This was not the case for everyone. Many gay men, especially from the traditionally discreet and self-effacing upper and middle classes, those very people who had cautiously and indeed bravely lent their efforts to the campaign for reform, saw the very outspokenness of GLF as the worst move imaginable. For them such in-your-face activity would create not further progress, but simply guarantee a terrible backlash. Nor did they like its politics, which were definitely left-wing. The Campaign for Homosexual Equality (CHE), which had succeeded the reformers of HLRS, were especially unhappy.

The early GLF was very much a working-class phenomenon but gay liberation, at least at first, had been no more embraced by the majority of the New Left than it had by the underground. As will be seen in its dealings with the emerging Women's Liberation, initially dismissed as 'pussy power', the left's heroes, like those of the underground, were strictly macho: rock stars, urban guerrillas, Third World revolutionaries. Theorists could posit links to the counter-culture's proclaimed desire to break down bourgeois sexual stereotyping (usually seen in the use of violent, often sado-masochistic sexual imagery in the underground press) but such associations were largely cosmetic. They may have preached 'polymorphous perversity' but such sophistication was less than whole-hearted.

David Widgery acknowledged that:

> The gay movement came quite late to the student and political worlds. It didn't really get accepted in the SWP, which was what IS developed into, till the mid to late '70s. I remember being absolutely horrified myself reading Richard Neville's book *Play Power* to see in the preface, 'Thanks to Jim Anderson whose new book will be *Gay Power*.' I thought, 'Jim isn't a queer, is he!?' I didn't know that Jim was gay, I didn't really know what gay was. Then I thought, 'Mmm, I suppose he is a bit funny . . .' Although there were quite a lot of gay people involved in IS, the policy was the traditional Stalinist one: after the revolution there won't be any problem because we'll all be heterosexual. When I wrote a piece on a gay liberation pamphlet for *Socialist Worker* they just wouldn't publish it. There were excuses and so on but basically they just didn't want to know.

Nor did Neville's dedication extend any further into the book. *Oz*, to its credit, ran a Gay Issue, but in *Play Power* gay sex was conspicuously absent. Even in 1972, when the Californian psychiatrist David Reuben's travesty of sexual advice, *All You Really Wanted to Know About Sex . . . But Were Afraid To Ask* appeared in England the 'Alternative Voice' used his *Evening Standard* column to excoriate not the negative, alarmist and effectively homophobic Reuben but the GLF, whose members had petitioned W.H. Allen, the publishers, not to issue the book. GLF themselves invaded Allen's offices. It made no difference, but as Andrew Lumsden has said, for all the consciousness-raising sessions, the declarations of one's own sexual fantasies and similar moments of self-revelation, there was nothing like a good demo for bonding.

   As was so often the way, the new movement was best, or at least most vo-
cally represented by a newspaper, in this case *Gay News*, mooted in late 1971
and first published in mid-1972. It was not, however, the first such journal.
Peter Fuller, better known as an art critic, produced the short-lived *Synthesis*
in 1969, while the same year saw the appearance of *Jeremy*, a rather glossier,
not to mention camper, effort. Published perhaps fittingly in Carnaby Street,
Jeremy offered pretty boys, fashion, cooking, celebrity interviews and arts reviews. Such politics as were included were very much of the HLRS brand,
with Antony Grey a regular contributor. Edited by Dennis Lemon, who had
formerly worked in a record shop and gained his journalistic experience as he
went, *Gay News*, like the movement it represented (although it was never a
GLF paper as such), was symptomatic of the new era. The first thoughts had
been more in terms of a simple propaganda sheet, peddling GLF ideology, but Andrew Lumsden, a proper Fleet Street hack, called for a 'real
newspaper'. The movement was no longer a London phenomenon, any more
than the larger gay scene was restricted to the Metropolis.

> The paper came out in summer '72. The Campaign for Homosexual Law Re-
> form subscription list was opened to us, so we could ask for advance subscrip-
> tions. Someone put up some money. Dennis and I went to see David
> Hockney. He said, 'If you want to bring out a nice magazine with lots of pic-
> tures of men, then I might be interested, but I don't want anything to read.'
> Graham Chapman did send some money, either right at the beginning or not
> long afterwards; I'd known him at Cambridge. But mainly we were scratching
> around, no substantial amounts were put up. Many monied gay men were ap-
> palled by GLF. They saw it as a socialist revolutionary enterprise, and thought
> a connection with GLF would ruin them. So far as money is class, it was a class
> thing. The first few issues of the paper were hand-distributed, taken round the
> pubs and so on. The first issue came out for Gay Pride Week, held in Hyde
> Park. And very good it was, the pace and energy of it. The early issues were
> nearly all editorial, that's why they looked so smashing. It was not a GLF pa-
> per, but rather one that came out of GLF. It dealt mainly with what was going
> on in the straight world: what the police were doing, or the media, what
> somebody had said, what the Church was up to. It started off selling about
> 6,000 and reached a ceiling [in 1976] of 20-23,000 a fortnight.[26]

Gay News was generally much more serious and focused than the rest of
the underground press. As well as the usual interviews and reviews it dealt
widely with the vicissitudes of the law, with any issue that affected the gay
community, and advocated every campaign that served to advance the cause.
Its columns offered confessionals, *cris de coeur*, anguished and angry letters; it
also had some provincial coverage, especially of Scotland. Issue 1 set a pattern for what followed. Twelve pages long, its editorial ran down the genesis
of the paper, and promised that it 'is not our paper, but yours; it belongs to
the whole of the gay community. It's for gay women as well as gay men, for

transsexuals and transvestites, for anyone with a sexual label but who we like to call "gays of all sexes".' It acknowledged the 1967 legislation, but like Antony Grey in *New Society*, felt bound to confess that:

> despite legal reform and a certain relaxation in people's attitudes to sexuality, nothing much has really changed. It is clear that many gay people are still extremely isolated, many still live restricted lives. [The aim of the paper was to create] a medium which could help us all to know what we were all doing, which could put us in contact, and be open evidence of our existence and our rights for the rest of the people to see, [which] could help start the beginning of the end of the present situation.
>
> There is still a need to dispel and counteract much ignorance and misinformation. So far we seem to have accepted society's definition of us as something that's not very nice, to be seen perhaps, but not heard. Isn't that a little crazy? We are all people with our lives, our hopes, our fears and expectations for what life has in store for us . . . to be isolated from what goes on in the world around us is not only wrong; it shows up some dangerous cracks in the society we live in.[27]

The news coverage centred on GLF's problems with the disc jockey Jimmy Savile's religious chat show 'Speakeasy', with 'queer-bashing' in London and elsewhere, and on a Manchester gay club that discriminated against women. It reported on the latest GLF dance, held at Kensington Town Hall and on Gay Pride Week, on *IT*'s unsuccessful appeal against the paper's conviction for running gay small ads and on gay life in Scotland (subtitled, 'Och yerra naffie big jessie, jimmah!'). Among the letters was one from Lord Arran, offering his conditional approval. The rest of the paper included a 'Trouble Shared' column (angst in the provinces), a movie review (the campest thing on offer: 'a sailor film, *Sink the Bismark*, where those brave, virtuous, strong and well-built boys in navy blue battle those nasty Germans and their big boat . . . ') and one on theatre (of a Dietrich show and of *Cabaret*: 'Judy Garland's daughter makes good'). There was a piece on 'The Homosexual and VD' by 'a Consultant in VD at a large London clinic' ('A more tolerant attitude by the public to private homosexual acts between adults would be a great step towards the eradication of venereal disease from the whole community, since it would undoubtedly encourage more carriers of the disease to come forward for treatment'). There was a small piece on the discrepancy between the 'straight' age of consent and that allowed gay men, small ads headlined 'Love Knoweth No Laws', the page filled with provisos about not using them for 'immoral purposes' and avoiding relations with minors, and finally the paper's 'Het of the Month': Cliff Richard.

Ironically GLF itself barely survived the arrival of *Gay News*. It succumbed, like so many other 'revolutionary' movements and institutions, to the growing chilliness of the Seventies, an increasingly harsh decade for those whose ideals had been nurtured in earlier years. As the writer Duncan Fallowell, a determined opponent of any form of categorisation, whether sexual or otherwise, saw it: however politicised gay lib attempted to be, 'they all ended up wanking each other in gymnasiums – which doesn't get you very far if you want to change the world.'[28]

But the struggle was far from over. Spearheaded by *Gay News* and a variety of pressure groups the fight to raise the gay profile, to reform public opinion (not this time for the passage of a compromised act but to change for ever the perception of the homosexual lifestyle) continued through the decade. The quality of life within the homosexual community – no longer a cowering, closeted 'gay ghetto' – was also changed enormously. If much of the outside world remained obdurately antagonistic, then within the gay world the advances were astounding. The period saw the burgeoning of a wide range of self-help organisations: community services, telephone helplines, professional and trade union groups, gay theatre groups and gay cinema, all underpinning the idea of a new and vibrant gay community. If politics as such seemed to fade, and perceptions of homosexuality remained stubbornly retrograde, the gay community, a frightened, covert phenomenon just a decade earlier, had been completely revolutionised. In this, however, there remains a paradox. For all that early campaigns sought to integrate the homosexual into society, as just one more normal person, albeit with a different sexual orientation, this had not happened. The gay world remained isolated, other than in those traditional fields such as fashion or the creative arts, which had always welcomed and indeed celebrated the homosexual (even if Hollywood, on the whole, preferred them to keep such proclivities well hidden). The difference was that for the first time a group existed that defined itself in terms of sexuality: a group that had its own politics, its own economy and its own wide subculture. And, perhaps most important of all, it had abandoned that feeling that it had feared might never quite disappear, even at the height of the hedonistic Sixties: guilt.

Tony Whitehead, one GLF's earliest activists, was typical.

> Coming out was absolutely wonderful. A marvellous experience. I'm glad I did it so quickly. It was immensely liberating: sexually, politically and emotionally. You'd made that break, you'd cast off all that tat that had oppressed you as a teenager. In getting rid of the concept of norms within human sexual behaviour, you also get rid of the norms in other forms of behaviour. Not in the sense that you became anarchists, but you became questioning . . . Gays had been meeting socially for years, but would never dare to identify themselves, or give themselves a label. So we decided you had to be public about it, put your face forward, stand up and be counted.[29]

Such unabashed revolution had its enemies, none more dedicated than Mary Whitehouse and her fearful, fundamentalist supporters who saw the self-assertive gay community as the unleashing of the Antichrist. In summer 1976, after years of sparring (notably in the short-lived excitements of the Festival of Light) the two sides clashed – not on the street, but in court. In issue 96 of *Gay News* there appeared a poem by the academic James Kirkup, entitled 'The Love That Dares to Speak Its Name'. The poem, in which a Roman soldier and Christ have sex, suggests that with the growth of gay liberation the traditional Victorian euphemism (used most notably by Lord Alfred Douglas in a sonnet about homosexual guilt) can be abandoned, since homosexuals need no longer feel any shame in declaring their sexual preference. It was illustrated, by Tony Reeves, with a picture of Christ being taken from the cross. Although the scene is conventional enough, this Christ has unmistakably larger-than-average genitals. Critics were not particularly impressed with the poem, which takes the form of a dramatic monologue interlarded with such slang as 'well-hung' to imply both the crucifixion and Christ's sizable genitals. But neither was it found especially offensive.

Whitehouse was less sanguine. The evangelical Festival of Light had been largely laughed to extinction, but she remained as determined as ever to impose her own superstitions upon a more sophisticated world. In November 1976 she initiated a private prosecution for blasphemous libel against *Gay News*, its editor Dennis Lemon and its distributor (although this last charge was dropped). When the trial commenced at the Old Bailey in July 1977 the usual liberal forces were in disarray. Casual blasphemy had become so intrinsic a part of modern life that the idea of it actually disturbing anyone seemed bizarre. Whitehouse, although lacking the support of the Director of Public Prosecutions, cleverly capitalised on the general resentment against 'uppity' gays who dared to emerge from their traditional role as 'queers' and 'pansies' to make the charge of blasphemy infinitely more dramatic. She also chose to centre her attack not on Kirkup himself, a respected academic and Fellow of the Royal Society of Literature, but on the newspaper and its editor as less respectable and thus softer targets.

Nor was this an *Oz*-style trial. In a blasphemy case no experts were permitted, merely two character witnesses who defended Lemon. The prosecution case was simple: such a filthy poem was self-evidently blasphemous. The defence mocked the anachronistic charge and claimed that poems could not be treated like lavatorial limericks. Such sophistication, further undermined by Judge King-Hamilton's summing up (King-Hamilton had shown himself equally partial to repression in 1973 when overseeing the case of the IT comic *Nasty Tales*), failed to persuade the jury who found against the defendants. The Judge asked the jury to ask themselves the following somewhat simplistic questions: 'Do you think that God would like to be recognised in the context of this poem? Did it shock you when you first read it? Would you be proud or ashamed to have written it? Could you read it to an audience of fellow-Christians without blushing?' Lemon was fined £500 and jailed for nine months, suspended for eighteen months. His newspaper was fined £1,000 and faced costs of £20,000. Casual blasphemy in England seemed little affected, but so great a victory launched Mrs Whitehouse on several years of unprecedented agitation. Six years later she would receive a firm rebuff, when her attempt at another private prosecution – of Howard Brenton's play *The Romans In Britain* – was thrown out of court. But by then the reactionaries would be enjoying a victory sweeter than anything they, or the gay community, could have ever conceived.

That same year a new acronym had entered the medical dictionaries: Acquired Immune Deficiency Syndrome or AIDS. It was occurring across the world, but primarily among certain groups: intravenous drug users, haemophiliacs, and, most prolific of all, gay men. Cases had begun appearing in 1980 if not earlier, but the word, and the worldwide appreciation of what would for a few years acquire all the terrifying, hysterical response that betokened some new eruption of a Medieval plague, did not appear until 1982. Earlier names had been GRID: Gay-related Immune Deficiency and ACIDS: Acquired Community Immune Deficiency Syndrome, both of which were intended to reflect what was seen as the uniqueness of the problem to the gay community. In the end AIDS won out, although the press, with kneejerk insensitivity, preferred the demonology of a 'Gay Plague'. The gay community, whose ten years of liberation had included an increasingly abandoned promiscuity, was in every sense devastated. For the conservatives, whether in the tabloid press, amongst their unforgiving followers and especially amongst the Whitehouses and their cohorts, there was no doubt. In those tones of ripe hypocrisy that come so naturally to the truly pious, they lamented the onset of the disease, regretting that gay excess had brought about so terrible a destiny. They even hoped for Godly mercy. The subtext was obvious, and it was not only the fundamentalists who quietly voiced it: gay liberation was through. Unnatural vices brought unnatural death: the uppity nancy-boys had finally got exactly what they deserved.

Chapter Twenty-Eight

Women's Liberation: The Personal is Political

Probably the only place where a man can feel really secure is in a maximum security prison, except for the imminent threat of release.
Germaine Greer, *The Female Eunuch* 1970

Like a number of the period's other social phenomena, feminism, which reached its noisy, truly revolutionary apotheosis in the 'Women's Liberation' of the late Sixties and Seventies, was hardly an overnight invention. The canonical texts go back at least as far as Mary Wollstonecraft's *Vindication of the Rights of Woman* (1792), and, a century later, take in the Suffragette era and its knock-on effects on the position of contemporary women, then shift to Simone de Beauvoir's *The Second Sex* (1949). Others would extend the tradition further, back to Aristophanes's *Lysistrata*, concerning a 'libber' (a word that originally, if coincidentally, meant gelder) of the fifth century BC. But as the label 'Women's Liberation' underlines, it was a very modern movement. It emerged, as had other liberation struggles, whether by blacks or students or those who took part in the Paris events of May 1968, from the clash between media-fostered rising expectations – in this case as regarded job opportunities, child care, and above all the need for a radical shift in male-female relations – and the less satisfactory reality.

The immediate post-war decades, far from promoting the role of women in society, had actually worked to drive back such advances as had been made. In both America and the UK, for instance, the war had seen a huge drive to recruit women, giving them the jobs in factories and elsewhere that their men had been forced to forgo. Within months of the war's ending, that trend had been comprehensively reversed. America, where the iconic 'Rosie the Riveter' and her peers had done such sterling work, sacked two million women almost overnight; similar layoffs could be seen in Britain. In place of the dungarees came the pinafore. The whole *leitmotif* for Fifties women was the home, and the 'making' thereof. The media, and especially women's magazines, preached the gospel of conformity, spinning a confectioner's sugary web of unattainable domestic fantasy. Writing about the US example – and what went for the US would invariably come to stand for Britain too – David Halberstam notes how the over-riding fantasy was 'togetherness', a term used to describe the supposed happy life in a 1954 issue of *McCall*'s magazine, for women readers one of America's most influential periodicals.

> A family was one, its ambitions were twined. The husband was designated leader and hero, out there every day braving the treacherous corporate world to win a better life for his family; the wife was his mainstay on the domestic side, duly appreciative of the immense sacrifices being made for her and her children.

There was no divergence within. A family was a single perfect universe – instead of a complicated, fragile mechanism of conflicting political and emotional pulls. Families portrayed in women's magazines exhibited no conflicts or contradictions or unfulfilled ambitions. Thanks, probably, to the drive for togetherness, the new homes all seemed to have what was called a family room. Here the family came together, ate, watched television, and possibly even talked. 'When Jim comes home,' said a wife in a 1954 advertisement for prefabricated homes, 'our family room seems to draw us closer together.' And who was responsible ultimately for togetherness if not the wife?[1]

According to Mrs Dale Carnegie (wife of America's self-helper supreme, the man who told his insecure readers *How to Win Friends and Influence People*), 'The two big steps that women must take are to help their husband decide where they are going and use their pretty heads to help them get there. Let's face it, girls. That wonderful guy in your house – and mine – is building your house, your happiness and the opportunities that will come to your children.' Split-level houses, she added, might be fine in architectural terms, 'but there is simply no room for split-level thinking – or doing – when Mr. and Mrs. set their sights on a happy home, a host of friends and a bright future through success in HIS job.'[2]

And Halberstam glosses: 'Those women who were not happy and did not feel fulfilled were encouraged to think that the fault was theirs and that they were the exception to blissful normality. That being the case, women of the period rarely shared their doubts, even with each other. If anything, they tended to feel guilty about any qualms they had: Here they were living better than ever – their husbands were making more money than ever, and there were ever bigger, more beautiful cars in the garage and appliances in the kitchen. Who were they to be unhappy?'[3]

It was *I Love Lucy* and a dozen other vapid sit-coms made flesh. God help the non-conformist, let alone that man-hating harridan, the hard, dessicated, loveless career girl. When a contemporary magazine headlined a piece on such women, 'Half the Women in *Who's Who* Are Single' it was a consciously Awful Warning. As a best-selling volume of pop psychology, *Modern Woman: the Lost Sex* (by Ferdinand Lundberg and Marynia Franham), made clear, 'The independent woman is a contradiction in terms'; feminism, worse still, was a 'deep illness'.[4] The educated, working woman was the neurotic woman – since the more educated she was, the more sexually 'disordered' she must be and of course, by working she proclaimed the ultimate female neurosis: the rejection of motherhood. The snappy, wise-cracking gals of Thirties or Forties cinema, epitomised by Eve Arden in *Mildred Pierce* or Rosalind Russell in *His Girl Friday* were anathema; what the Fifties wanted was anodyne slop: a Doris Day or a June Allyson.

Nor did the growing daughters of those fluffy-pinafored Fifties 'home--makers' fare much better. 'The position of women in the Revolution,' declared Black Power leader Stokeley Carmichael, 'is prone,' although he conceded that, given an adequate supply of envelopes, they might be good enough for 'the licking and the sticking'. Carmichael's many epigones felt much the same. And if the women disliked their position, there were still few who felt themselves capable of articulating any effective resistance. In the words of the artist Nicola Lane,

The important thing to remember about the '60s is that it was totally male-dominated. You had to be an awful lot of things: you had to be sexy, you had to be game for anything, there was pressure for taking drugs, and you had to be an old lady and have the brown rice ready. A lot of girls just rolled joints – it was what you did while you sat quietly in the corner, nodding your head. Looks were very important. Looks were of primary importance. What really filled me with fear and loathing were these little hippie girls in long frocks, tiny little things who were always sort of wisping around the room. The dolly bird is definitely a hippie motif as well as a Carnaby Street one. Hippie dollies wore different clothes to Biba dollies, but they were still dollies. They just wore long dresses instead of little ones. People would say, 'Wow, she's so far out, she's so cool, she never makes any waves . . . ' And she never speaks.

You were not really encouraged to be a thinker. You were there really for fucks and domesticity. The old lady syndrome. 'My lady': so Guinevere-y. You had to fill so many roles: you had to be pretty and you had to be 'a good fuck', that seemed to be very important. I think it meant mostly that a) you would do it with a lot of people, and also b) that you'd give people blow-jobs. It was paradise for men in their late twenties, all these willing girls. But the trouble with the willing girls was that a lot of the time they were willing not because they particularly fancied the people concerned but because they felt they ought to. There was a huge pressure to conform to nonconformity, which left very little room for actually finding out what your preferences were. These predatory, elderly men, salivated around the Arts Lab. Endless nights sitting in rooms with the men smoking joints and talking about mighty things. The women never really being included. It pissed me off but I didn't really do anything about it – I didn't really know what to do about it. There was a lot of misery. Relationship miseries: ghastly, ghastly, jealousy, although there was supposed to be no jealousy, no possessiveness. What it meant was that men fucked around. You'd cry a lot, and you would scream sometimes, and the man would say, 'Don't bring me down, don't lay your bummers on me . . . don't hassle me, don't crowd my space.'

It's quite extraordinary how straight the overall culture was. And in all the underground newspapers and magazines there was the first stirrings of what is now a full-blown business: pornography. The nudity and all that. All those pictures in the underground press contributed to the pressure in a way on the girls to be those sort of girls. It was like the underground *Vogue*: instead of leafing through *Vogue* and seeing models in the way that models are, they were leafing through *Oz* and *IT* and seeing wonderful girls with long hair doing unspeakable things with pigs. I can say it now, with post-feminist consciousness, but I felt it then and the way I felt it was the pressure.[5]

As a record review in one early issue of *Rolling Stone* put it, summarising the role of the average 'hippie chick': 'Put on the Dead, get on the bed, and spread.' What the magazine's editor Jann Wenner called the 'chick work'. A housewife like any other, as Charles Shaar Murray has observed, except they had to sleep with strangers too.

The underground press, from a feminist perspective, was especially culpable. The theory, with much brandishing of William Reich, was that it was vital to break down the constraints of the bourgeois attitude to sex and the best way to do this, when one wasn't engaging in screwing as many young women as possible who could be conned into helping 'make the revolution', was to extend one's pages to a wide and often violent type of pornography. *IT* went for garter-belts and the occasional whip; *Oz*, cutting-edge as ever, was especially entranced by one Bodil, a heroine of Danish porn, whose preferred partners were recruited from the farmyard, field and pigsty. It might have amused the boys, but one didn't have to step back that far, irresepective of one's gender, to note that printing a few S&M pictures, let alone anything more lurid, was hardly striking a blow for the revolution. Occasionally there was a gesture at change: Richard Neville, fresh from an harangue by his girlfriend Louise Ferrier and *Oz* girl Marsha Rowe, arrived at the office to lecture the male staff on the evils of sexism. It fell, unsurprisingly, on deaf ears. The culture of *Oz* was hardly egalitarian – male names were printed in full on the masthead, women were merely 'Virginia' or 'Louise' – and in any case there was another cause deemed as equally if not more worthy of espousal: the fight against censorship, no matter how ideologically admirable might be its grounds. It was not overlooked that the May 1970 issue of the magazine, ostensibly labelled a 'Female Energy Issue', was invariably known as the 'Cunt Power *Oz*'.

But *Oz* was hardly unique: *IT*, whips and chains aside, worked on the usual two tiers, with men in the editorial version of the missionary position, as did *Friends* and, in its first incarnation, *Ink*. These two last however, when relaunched as *Frendz* and as a more libertarian, properly political *Ink* now under the control not of the smarter end of the *Oz* group but such committed figures as Dave Robins, John Lloyd, Alison Fell and Dick Pountain, did attempt some change. *Frendz*, for instance, ran in late 1971 an all-female issue, an event that would give among others Rosie Boycott her first glimpse of feminism and associate her, albeit quite innocently, with the Angry Brigade, two of whose alleged members, Angie Weir and Hilary Creek, were involved in production. The next time she saw them would be from an Old Bailey witness box to which she was summoned to give evidence at their trial. As for *Ink*, letting feminism have its say was at one with the general drive for genuine revolution, which meant a new concentration on such hitherto excluded issues as gay liberation, the struggle in Ireland, labour relations, squatting and similar less than overtly glamorous causes. Simply enlisting Alison Fell, a no-nonsense Glaswegian and the antithesis of the wispy Guineveres of the old underground, guaranteed a harder edge.

But such advances were a matter for the early Seventies and feminism had been making inroads into the mass consciousness for some time already. It had begun, as yet another import, in the States. Once again, it was hardly a Sixties construct, but the Sixties gave the movement a new impetus. The conformity of the Fifties had become increasingly irksome, and more and more women, educated, intelligent, frustrated by their enforced domesticity in the suburbs of small towns, were determined to move on. Their emotions were captured in the publication, in 1963, of Betty Friedan's book *The Feminine Mystique*, a book that looked at their plight, with its spurious holy grail of 'togetherness', and tore it conclusively apart. Friedan was typical of those frustrated women. Educated at Smith, one of the Seven Sisters (America's female Ivy League), she had enjoyed a thriving wartime career as a journalist in New York, living in Greenwich Village and working for a progressive labor paper. It did not prove that progressive: with the war over the job went too. Married, she moved to the suburbs, raised a family and found herself wondering why she felt, for all her material satisfactions, so very stunted. She returned to journalism, as a freelance, and soon came to face a simple fact: anything that transgressed the prevailing domestic fantasy went straight on to the spike. The profile of a major woman painter was rejected: unless she would consent to be pictured painting a baby's crib; a piece on natural childbirth was too graphic; on it went. In 1957 came an event that changed her life. Asked to compile a report on her Smith contemporaries, the Class of '42, she drew up a questionnaire and set about tracking down her old acquaintances. What she found astounded her: every one seemed as frustrated and alienated as did she. What made things worse was that as she walked the Smith campus, talking to the current crop of students, she found that they, to a woman, seemed perfectly happy, Stepford Wives in waiting: the pervasive conformism seemed fine by them. It appalled her: this was Smith, in her day one of the most intellectually active colleges, how could such passivity have taken over?

The resulting piece – 'The Togetherness Woman' – faced a raft of rejections. *McCall's*, the home of togetherness, rejected it outright, as did the *Ladies Home Journal*. *Redbook*, the third of the country's major women's magazines was equally hostile: 'only the most neurotic housewife would identify with this,' declared its editor.[6] Friedan decided to turn her piece into a book. This time she was luckier: book publishers were not in thrall to the home appliance advertisers whose whims dominated the magazines. Commissioned in 1958 she promised the manuscript in a year – it would take five. When it did appear, now entitled *The Feminine Mystique*, it was a revelation. The 'togetherness woman', it showed, was about as substantial a being as the sit-coms and magazines that worked so hard to promote her image. What was really happening in the 'burbs was a major crisis, centred on thousands of bright but strait-jacketed women. Their husbands were not enough, nor were their children; 'labor-saving' devices only made more labour – all those gadgets had to be used. Friedan, who went on to found America's National Organization of Women (NOW), struck a chord, and the movement for Women's Liberation, at least in its modern guise, took off fast.

The situation in Britain was not quite the same – the sort of wealth that created this world of affluent but empty suburbs had yet to arrive – but the desire for a reassessment of female roles was equally intense. By the end of the decade the same kind of women's groups, with their consciousness-raising sessions, that had burgeoned in America were beginning to emerge in Britain. In 1968 Sheila Rowbotham, a socialist historian, wrote an important piece, 'Women's Liberation and the New Politics'. Looking coldly at women's position, that of another oppressed minority and exhibiting all the classic aspects of the oppressed, the piece makes no cry for action, but the subtext screams from every paragraph: Act, and act now!

The first question is why do we stand for it? The oppressed are mysteriously quiet. The conservative answer is 'because they like it like that'. But the revolutionary can't afford to be so sure. He has learned to be doubtful about the 'happiness' of the exploited. He knows that containment cannot be directly related to quietness. The subordination of women only achieves perspective when it is seen in relation to the mechanism of domination. The way in which we are contained only really becomes comprehensible when it is seen as part of the general situation of the oppressed. In order to understand why those in control stay on top and the people they use don't shake them off it is necessary to trace the way in which the outward relationship of dominator to dominated becomes internalised.

'But they are happy like that.'

'Can't you see they enjoy it?'

Superficially there is a complicity between the subordinated and the authority figure. But this is in fact the mutuality of whore and pimp. They associate because of the way the game is rigged. She continually keeps back a percentage, he continually steals her clothes and beats her to survive. Deceit and violence are the basis of their relationship, and continue to be so until the external situation is changed. However the conception of change is beyond the notions of the oppressed. They are confined within the limits of their imagination of the possible . . .

The oppressed in their state before politics lack both the idea and practice to act upon the external world. Both coherent protest and organised resistance are inconceivable. They do not presume to alter things, they are timid . . . They play dumb and the superior people assume they have nothing to say, nothing to complain of. Those in power conclude their 'inferiors' must be a different order of people. This justifies their subjugation. The impression is confirmed by their inability to take the advantage offered to them, by the shrugging off of responsibilities, by the failure to take initiatives. They refuse to help themselves, they are their own worst enemy . . . Like Br'er Rabbit they lie low.

Women have been lying low for so long most of us cannot imagine how to get up. We have apparently acquiesced always in the imperial game and are so perfectly colonised that we are unable to consult ourselves. Because the assumption does not occur to us, it does not occur to anyone else either. We are afraid to mention ourselves in case it might disturb or divert some important matter he has in hand. We are the assistants, the receivers, the collaborators, dumb, lacking in presumption, not acting consciously upon the external world, much given to masochism. We become sly – never trust a woman – we seek revenge, slighted we are terrible; we are trained for subterfuge, we are natural creatures of the underground. Within us there are great gullies of bitterness, but they do not appear on the surface. Our wrapped-up consciousness creeps along the sewers, occasionally emerging through a manhole. After death, hag-like spirits roam the earth, the symbols of frustrated unfulfilled desires. But in life our spirits are contained.[7]

Rowbotham, whose path had led from Methodist boarding school, to Oxford and thence, via Fifties protest, to feminist politics, was among the first to turn the New Left on to this nascent movement. Recruited in 1968 as a founder-editor of Tariq Ali's *Black Dwarf*, she suggested that after 1968, designated the 'Year of the Heroic Guerrilla', 1969 should be the 'Year of the Militant Woman'. The first paper of the new year would underline the fact, being dedicated to 'Women, Sex and the Abolition of the Family'. It was more easily said than done. The war in Vietnam, the Middle East, the exploits of such as Che Guevara were front page news every day; the women's movement had barely taken off even among activists. It would be necessary to run through the basics even before essaying anything more sophisticated. The paper's editorial, written by Fred Halliday, did just that, and as Tariq Ali recalled, was perhaps 'the first serious attempt by a radical paper in this country to discuss hitherto hidden agendas'.[8] Its premise was simple: there was no genuine 'alternative society' without the discussion of gender relations and the hitherto unspoken oppression of women. 'Political, juridical and economic inequalities between man and woman could be solved within the existing order, but the transformation of sexual relations was not possible without social revolution.'[9] The centre spread was given to Rowbotham, whose piece, 'Women: The Struggle For Freedom', was a passionate explication of the cause. It climaxed with a call not to women, but to men:

Men! You have nothing to lose but your chains. You will no longer have anyone to creep away and peep at with their knickers down, no one to flaunt as the emblem of your virility, status, self-importance, no one who will trap you, overwhelm you, no etherealised cloudy being floating unattainable in a plastic blue sky, no great mopping up handerkerchief comforters to crawl into from your competitive, ego strutting alienation, who will wrap you up

and SMOTHER you. There will only be thousands of millions of women people to discover, touch and become, who will understand you when you say we
must make a new world in which we do not meet each other as exploiters and
used objects. Where we love one another and into which a new kind of human
being can be born.[10]

If Rowbotham's clarion call failed to register as widely as she might have
wished, she remained in herself a major player; her books, *Women, Resistance
and Revolution* and *Hidden from History*, are acknowledged classics of the
genre.

In the last week of February 1970 the action that Rowbotham urged took
tangible form at a conference held at Ruskin College, the trade union-
affiliated college in Oxford. The conference had emerged, logically enough,
from women's discontent, in this case with the History Workshops that had
been established in 1967, as an attempt to encourage men and women to
'write their own history'.[11] In 1970, to voice their frustration at the increasing
male domination of these workshops, the women held the first National
Women's Conference. Like a number of important counter-cultural events it
was initiated by various American ex-pats, somewhat further down the feminist path than their British sisters, but it attracted an impressive number of
women, plus a minority of men. In total there were nearly 600 delegates.
Around twenty groups were represented, coming from trade unions, from
middle-class London, from Socialist groupuscules and working-class council estates. Like any other conference it operated around general sessions and
smaller workshops. These latter were closed to men, and indeed those men
present tended to remain silent even when the session was open. Michelene
Wandor, the soon to be divorced wife of Ed Victor (publisher of both *Play
Power* and of the initial incarnation of *Ink*) was there:

> We went to the Ruskin Conference as a group. I didn't see going to those
> meetings [in London] as a political act, but it soon was. What we saw our-
> selves as doing was consciousness-raising, for which there wasn't any real
> blueprint. The excitement of the idea of the workshop – which I'm afraid has
> long worn off – certainly at the time it was terrifically exciting that you could
> have a workshop with a whole lot of other women. That you could actually be
> in a room with a large number of women, all of whom would have their right
> to speak . . . in the event you get a small number of very vocal articulate peo-
> ple dominating, but the feeling was that in principle this was the most demo-
> cratic thing that there had ever been. That was very exciting: it was people
> who were discontened with their lot and did want to change the world and
> believed that it was going to be possible tomorrow.
>   What I was picking up was an enormous amount of the enthusiasm and
> political energy that '68 had generated . . . So there was this energy and here
> was something I could finally identify with because I was a woman and things
> were being talked about that related very directly to my experience. There

was a lot of naïveté but there always is in political newness. You thought, 'This is the first time anybody's noticed this and by God, it won't be there tomorrow, it's going to be different tomorrow.' It was about the conviction that if you changed people's consciousnesses they would have a different attitude to each other and the world changes.[12]

Sheila Rowbotham, naturally, was present too. 'I'd never seen women in that mood before, hearing people speak who'd never spoken before, seeing people inspired to do things they wouldn't have done in the past – the atmosphere was very much, any woman who wants to do anything must do it, and it was really exciting.'[13] The Conference gave women the opportunity to be as wholehearted, as committed as they wished. Even the activists of the student movement had always felt slightly constrained: the discourse was invariably centred on the men. Ruskin put an end to all that.

The Conference was a major turning-point: where before there might have been tens of women's groups, now there were scores, springing up across the country. London boasted fourteen, with at least 300 active members and another 1,000 keen to join. A national co-ordinating committee, a loose network of women, was set up, and put forward four demands: free 24-hour nurseries; equal pay now; equal education and job opportunities; and free contraception and abortion on demand. (These would remain the mainstays of the Movement: none would be achieved.) Among the main decisions taken had been that of creating a Women's Liberation movement that was not monolithic and centralised, depending on London and an élite of superstars to drive it forward. Instead there would be a loose confederation of local groups, based on women who lived in the same area getting together and organising themselves. Michelene Wandor joined the Tufnell Park group; her experiences were typical:

> What we did ... was talk about what we experienced as our oppression ... And we also talked about changing the world and how the world should be. Things should be in such a way that children are never neglected and insecure but that you have the freedom to do the things that you want to do, whether that involves working and just the unfairness of the division of labour that means that you get lumbered as a woman with the kids and the house and the cooking and he gets lumbered with the world – and there are disadvantages in both, but basically women come off worst. And that should be different.[14]

And in the way of the counter-culture, it was immediately understood that while consciousness-raising might help internally, the movement as a whole needed something a little more dramatic to get that all-important attention: the media. Thus on 20 November 1970, as the swim-suited lovelies of that year's Miss World competition at the Albert Hall strutted their stuff and vouchsafed their desires to better the world, thirty feminists, hitherto sitting anonymously in the more expensive seats, arose to add a very discordant note to the usually anodyne proceedings. Another transatlantic import, it echoed a recent US demonstration, against that year's Miss America, in which a leaflet variously condemned the proceedings as 'The Degrading Mindless-Boob-Girlie Symbol . . . Racism with Roses . . . Miss America as Military Death Mascot . . . The Consumer Con-Game . . . The Woman as Pop Culture Obsolescent Theme . . . The Unbeatable Madonna-Whore Combination . . . The Irrelevant Crown on the Throne of Mediocrity'. Finally Miss America was 'Big Sister Watching You: the Pageant exercises Thought Control, attempts to sear the Image into our minds to further make women oppressed and men oppressors; to enslave us all the more in high-heeled, low-status roles; to inculcate false values in young girls; to use women as beasts of buying; to seduce us to prostitute ourselves before our own oppression'.

As the film-maker Laura Mulvey remembered, 'It seemed a challenge that one couldn't overlook.' There had been a small demo at the previous year's event and the organisers were on their guard. Entry was arranged carefully and surreptitiously, with a number of small groups of women obtaining tickets independently. The important thing was not to look 'feminist', but as unobtrusive as possible.

One problem about the demonstration was how to avoid seeming to be demonstrating against the women on the stage, rather than against the organisation. That problem was solved magically for us by Bob Hope. At that time Bob Hope ran a circus, as it were, taking entertainers out to Vietnam to give rest and entertainment to the troops. And he had a tradition of taking the annual victor of the Miss World competition out with him. So when Bob Hope started addressing the audience about Vietnam, that was the moment when the hidden women gave the signal by waving their football rattles and we all rushed forward with flour and things and managed to pelt Bob Hope with flour and drive him from the stage. That was quite an achievement in itself, but it also blacked out the television – for probably all of about thirty seconds – which was quite something.

It did indeed make its splash. That demonstration was a gesture. You can't say that it would have attracted people to the movement particularly. It might have got it much more widely known, since people who wouldn't have heard about it would suddenly have found it on the front page of the *Sun*, described in very unflattering terms. After I escaped I went with a couple of other people in a state of great over-excitement and drove round London with some photocopies of pornographic pin-up pictures of men – which someone had done to throw in the Albert Hall but it hadn't seemed appropriate, because we were trying to keep our demonstration quite principled and respectable – but we did want to do something with them, so we drove into the West End and threw them in at the door of the Atheneum.[15]

Neither the organisers, an increasingly hostile audience, nor the successful Miss World, a Grenadan, were amused. 'I do not think women should
ever achieve complete equal rights,' she told the press. 'I do not want to . . . I
still like a gentlemen to hold my chair back for me.' Nor were the police. Five
women were arrested, charged with assaulting the police, having such weapons as smoke and flour bombs (not to mention one whistle, four plastic mice,
a stinkbomb and an over-ripe tomato), and even using indecent language.
They went to trial in February 1972. After a stormy session in which the division between authority and revolution was seen to be as clear as ever, the
women were fined. Before that, however, there had been another major demonstration, this a march from Hyde Park Corner to Trafalgar Square on 6
March 1971. Around 1,500 women made their way through a snowstorm to
hear a variety of speakers call for equal pay and job opportunities, free contraception, abortion on demand, and round-the-clock nurseries. Though the
mainstream press mocked, it was noted that among the marchers were a
number of respected women journalists. The rest, it was suggested, were
mainly lumpen middle class, with a decidedly Bloomsbury tinge: 'girls from
colleges, sad bed-sitters in North London or the smarter, liberated areas like
Hampstead'.[16] Some, the writer pointed out had bosoms 'defiantly if awe-
somely pendulous'; whether their missing brassières had been burnt was not
explained – it was the only cliché the *Standard* man resisted. The *Daily Telegraph*, employing a woman to do its dirty work, offered no jokes, only a recital
of sneering distaste. If she accepted that not all the 'nags' that the women put
forward were completely devoid of merit, she deplored the 'tone of voice' in
which they were posed, 'the *way* they want them'. And concluded fearfully:

> I may be wrong but the overriding impression that Woman's Lib with all its
> Socialist-orientated frenzy suggests is of a deep sexual unhappiness among its
> members. ('Can you wonder,' said a friend of mine. 'Don't bother to write an
> article – just print their photographs!') Couldn't this energy, I wonder naïvely,
> perhaps be used, as the hippies advocate, in making love and not war. After all,
> the activity does lead in many people's view to rather a better end. As it is, the
> danger exists that a male liberation movement might arise out of retaliation
> and, funny as Thurber was, the battle of the sexes has gone on long enough.
> Can't we drop it? Morbidly interesting though it may be I shall not attend the
> flop of the year. I shall stay at home and with my children watch 'Dr Who'. It's
> far more exciting – to this thrill-seeking female anyway.[17]

Cliché-mongering, vituperation, trivialisation, hysteria: all the linea-
ments of hostility would continue to greet the Women's Movement for years
to come, but that movement in turn, had already thrown up the doughtiest of
champions. Activists may have preferred such theoreticians as Kate Millett,
Shulamith Firestone, Juliet Mitchell, or Sheila Rowbotham, but for the mass
around the world feminism was equated with one name: Germaine Greer.

Born in Melbourne in 1939, the daughter of a Catholic newspaper executive and his wife, Greer had been a leading member of that Bohemian, libertarian group known in the late Fifties and early Sixties as the 'Sydney push'. Like fellow-Australians Richard Neville, Martin Sharp and others, she gravitated to the UK, though in her case for academic reasons. Completing a Cambridge PhD in 1968, she was taken on by Warwick University as an assistant lecturer in English literature. It was not her only job: she worked for some time on DJ Kenny Everett's TV show *Nice Time*; more importantly, recruited to the *Oz* team, she became one of the leading lights of what was a group of highly talented educated people, whose pretended illiteracy hid a degree of intelligence and enquiry that belonged far more to the traditional society than the new one they promoted. Greer's leap beyond academe and the underground came in March 1969 when *Oz* 19 featured a piece entitled 'A Groupie's Vision (The Universal Tonguebath)'. Written by 'staff writer Germaine' it allegedly recounted the thoughts of one 'Dr G', 'the only groupie with a PhD in captivity'. The cover featured Greer apparently unzipping the fly of Vivian Stanshall, leader of the Bonzo Dog Doo-dah Band, while inside shots revealed the author's unclad breasts and, as the *News of the World*, first to pick up on what the paper headlined 'The Not So Nice Time Girl', breathlessly described her, 'she is shown with a blouse undone and nothing underneath, playing the guitar.'[18]

The piece itself was no big deal, for all the fuss the tabloids tried to make. There was plenty of name-dropping, a few cracks at the music biz, and a good deal of cod-hippie musings. That the object of Dr G's immediate attentions was Stanshall, hardly number one in the rock sex-god stakes, should have been a pointer to the degree her tongue was en-cheeked, but the idea of a university lecturer fucking rock stars was too good to miss.

The papers weren't looking, or perhaps with modesty affronted simply averted their eyes, when a year later, in *Oz* 29, the 'Female Energy' or 'Cunt Power' issue, Greer printed what would prove to be a dry-run for her worldwide success. 'The Politics of Female Sexuality' examined the deliberate reduction of women to sex objects and the glorification of men as their masters. In a paragraph that could only have appeared in the free-for-all pages of the alternative press she exalted the one true revolution, more potent and more necessary by far than all the rantings of a million libbers:

> Revolutionary women may join Women's Liberation Groups and curse and scream and fight the cops, but did you ever hear of one of them marching the public street with her skirt high crying, 'Can you dig it? Cunt is beautiful!' The walled garden of Eden was CUNT. The mandorla of the beautiful saints was CUNT. The mystical rose is CUNT. The Ark of Gold, the Gate of Heaven. CUNT is a channel drawing all towards it. Cunt is knowledge. Knowledge is receptivity, which is activity. Cunt is the symbol of erotic science, the necessary corrective of the maniacal conquest of technology. Skirts

must be lifted, knickers (which women have only worn for a century) must come off for ever. It is time to dig CUNT and women must dig it first.[19]

Three months later, in October 1970, there appeared Greer's magnum opus: *The Female Eunuch*. As much a brilliantly wide-ranging collage of history's writings on the subject of woman as a revolutionary tract, the book demanded that women become autonomous. Before changing the world, the task that so many feminists claimed to have taken on, the individual woman should reassess and change herself; such a life would not be 'easier, or more pleasant . . . but it is more interesting, nobler, even'. Women were to reject the feminine stereotype, refuse to be passive consumers and acquiescent sex objects: instead they must liberate themselves as individuals. Like Neville's *Play Power* its range of topics is impressive, taking in vaginal perfumes, medieval sex neuroses, romantic novels and clitoridectomy. But unlike her *Oz* editor's effort, the *reductio ad* hippie-level *absurdum* of Marcuse and Huizinga, a titillatory peep-show for the gullible tourists of 'straight' society, *The Female Eunuch* was the best explication yet of the need for female (rather than purely feminist) autonomy, and a pointer, in the eyes of women worldwide, to what needed be done.

The reviews varied. Clive James, another Sydney veteran and a friend, wrote eulogistically in the *Listener*. The book was 'very considerable . . . a brilliant attack on marriage and on the psychological preparation for it, and on the nuclear family which is a result of it'.[20] James's sole problem, albeit a substantial one, lay in the solutions Greer proposed for the problems that her earlier chapters had laid out so well. There was little that she said, he suggested, that had not been enunciated far earlier, typically in the Fabian-influenced work of George Bernard Shaw. If it all seemed newly-minted it was only because the current generation had forgotten their history. There was one difference: when Shaw wrote of the pernicious nuclear family and of the desirability of a new brand of unfettered emotional and sexual relationships, the era was simply unattuned to what it dismissed as crank theorising. It would never happen. Now, in 1970, things had changed. Socio-economics were vastly different: fantasies might come to pass. Now the problem lay not in the outer world but in the abilities of individuals to confront the potential of their own lives.

Not everyone was so convinced. *New Society*'s reviewer, while generally favourable, noted that 'as often with hastily-written polemic there is a good deal of nonsense' and deplored such generalisations as 'that most virile of creatures, the buck Negro', a phrase that reveals that Sappho as well as Homer can nod.[21] Above all it was Greer's 'tone' that was most rebarbative: the hectoring self-belief, the dismissal of alternative views. Had she read more of the alternative press she might have recognised the style. The *Observer*, where Penelope Mortimer gave her opinion of the book, was equally ambiva-

lent. Mortimer acknowledges the truth that underlies some of the analysis
but dismisses the book at large as 'salutory nagging . . . finally unsatisfactory'.[22] Like many others who had not been inured to the delights of
unworked-out fantasy, that hallmark of the counter-culture's wilder theorising, she could accept what was rooted in academic background, but rejected
almost entirely the conclusions that rounded off the book. At her cruellest
she avers, after quoting Greer's thoughts on how best to relate to a lover, 'I
began to suspect that I was reading a very contemporary manual on How To
Get Your Man.' None the less, it is 'the most intelligent piece on the subject I
have read' and a book that all should read.

For more overtly political feminists, such as Sheila Rowbotham, who
reviewed the book for *Oz*, there was one basic flaw: Greer was not a joiner.
Secure in her own beliefs, with no need of the props of mutual support, she
resolutely stood aside from the self-analysing (but at the same time self-con-
gratulatory) workshops and consciousness-raising sessions. For an orthodox
left-winger such as Rowbotham (or Michelene Wandor, whose report on the
Ruskin College conference was headlined: 'Where was Germaine?') this was
unpardonable. For her, Greer's comments 'lack both the passion and the
self-criticism which women who have experienced working within the
movement write . . . There's a danger too when you're just writing on your
own that you start to throw out alternative stereotypes of the liberated
woman. These are just gags on other women. You reduce what is a unique
dialogue for every individual woman, between her, the movement, and the
world outside, into simply new ways in which she ought to behave.'[23] This
was a politically correct socialist, even Stalinist view: there could be no time
for bourgeois individualism. For Rowbotham, Greer was a 'scare crow radical . . . they can look very impudent but they can't do anything'. Resist the
dull side of the communal revolution at your peril: that way lies no more than
performance for a male audience, and a sophisticated brand of titillation for
the media.

It was the eternal plaint of the 'traditional' New Left against the alleged
frivolity of the counter-culture. Yet again the flashy rock star was enthusing
the fans in their thousands, while the earnest socialist meeting could barely
fill ten chairs in the parish hall. Feminists, in their struggle against patriar-
chal systems, deplored leaders or those who seemed to be setting themselves
up as such. They could not and would not accept the idea that for real success
any movement needed some visible public face on which the mass could focus. For the collectivists, locked into the New Left philosophies from which
they had sprung, Greer's very success, reinforced by a daunting intellectual
arrogance that cut through much of their more earnest rhetoric, rendered her
suspect. But for the wider audience, unfettered by the constricting demands
of ideology, *The Female Eunuch* was a world-shaker. Within weeks of publication, as the world's media clamoured for her attention, 'Dr G' had become

an international celebrity, *the* face of feminism. Only Erica Jong, whose *Fear of Flying* (with its 'zipless fuck') did for fictional feminism what Greer did for fact, would gain a similar, and far less lasting, renown.

For a while it was hard to open a paper, turn on the television or radio without finding Greer. Like Neville, but in her case thanks to the *Sunday Times*, she received a weekly column, discussing *inter alia* abortion, VD, her own love-life and the iniquities of freeloading hippies. A promotional trip across the US was retailed in a documentary all of its own. In New Zealand and her own Australia she was attacked for her supposedly foul language, while men attended her appearances to throw rotten fruit and vegetables. Her husband of a mere three weeks in 1968, one Paul du Feu, displayed naked but far from full-frontally in *Cosmopolitan*, was courted for his opinions. He explained how she demanded sex on the first night and how the query 'Can I have a cup of tea?' was invariably interpreted as a summons to bed.

Sheila Rowbotham was right: the media was indeed titillated. As were those who consumed them. The *Sunday Mirror*, hardly a feminist soapbox and unable to resist the obligatory reference to 'burning bras', ran three weeks of extracts in March 1971 ('a series to challenge the woman who thinks she's feminine – and the man who likes her that way'); *Nova* ran a lengthy piece, effectively a condensation of her published theories, headlined 'Single Women Must Never Marry'. Greer did chat-shows, arts shows and a question-and-answer session for Radio 4. The circus was unrelenting and sales across the world substantial. Women, everyday women who couldn't face the theorising, were fascinated. The painter Nicola Lane was typical of those who, uninspired by the politicos, was instantly drawn to what Greer had to offer. For her *The Female Eunuch* was an introduction to a new way of self-awareness. The ideologues might have deplored her motives, but the effect was surely what they desired.

> It was *very important*. I picked it up because of the cover, it was by Mike McInnery who did the cover for the Who's *Tommy*. It was a good merchandising job. You'd heard of her, she was a wild figure. And she could talk to those of you who'd been through that scene in some way and you'd feel, 'She knows.' There's very little ideology, it's all description. Of the way men treated you. The exhortations are very interesting: in a way they're the precursor to Shirley Conran's *Superwoman*. But in fact it's a book about how to keep your man. For example she says if you aren't possessive, if you don't demand that your man stays with you all the time he's much more likely to sleep in your arms all night. Very old-fashioned in that. Very unlike the politicos.[24]

Whatever the hardcore may have felt, the prevailing culture, with its obeisance to celebrity and its disdain for collectivism, could only be penetrated by a Greer, a woman who could be public and loud and flamboyant, a person who could make feminism, burdened with the media's nonsensical and negative caricature of hairy-legged, saggy-breasted, sexless, dungaree-clad lesbians into something appealing, something fun, something, most important, that tens of thousands of women were happy to espouse. She had, as Rosie Boycott notes, 'wit and style and intelligence and beauty and guts [which] made her impossible to ignore. There were loads of people writing equally serious works who you could just dismiss because they looked depressing and they were hangdog and they wouldn't partake of certain things.'[25]

For Boycott, and a number of the other women working in the underground, the immediate result of the upsurge in feminist consciousness was to take a new look at their own position. What they saw was nothing if not unsatisfactory. The men, for all their talk of equality and some inchoate revolution, were as unredeemably sexist as ever. The result would be the creation of *Spare Rib*, the country's first nationally noted feminist magazine. That said, there was in place a mainstream magazine that at least acknowledged the new consciousness. This was *Nova*, which had been launched in 1965 and appeared for the next decade. Its masthead declared 'A New Kind of Magazine for a New Kind of Woman'. Its first editorial laid out its basic principles: 'This is a magazine for women who make up their own minds. It is dedicated to the startling proposition that women have more to think about than what to do about dinner.'[26] That *Spare Rib* was still addressing that issue seven years on was frustrating, but also reflected how important the issue was. To a feminist like Michelene Wandor, who had attended the early meetings that led to *Spare Rib*, but had drifted away before things really took off, *Nova*, for all that it essentially embodied 'consumer' rather than 'political' feminism, was very important. The sort of pretty girls celebrated in its glossy pages, with their short skirts and long hair, 'were a version of the emancipated girl, a slightly more advanced emancipated girl, which is why when feminism struck some of them were able to take it up. It's true that they were a dolly, but they were another form of dolly, they weren't just a decorative dolly, they were a dolly who could make their own choices and not be lumbered with the consequences, not in the old-fashioned way. If you'd been at art school in the '50s and a bit careless you might have ended up as a single mum, You didn't in the '60s.'[27]

The new magazine was created by Alma Birk (now a Baroness), the daughter of a wealthy, liberal Jewish immigrant family, a JP, a Labour candidate and by the early Sixties a columnist on the *Daily Herald*. Her husband, Ellis, was a lawyer and director of the publishing conglomerate IPC, publishers of the vast majority of the country's women's magazines. In 1964 she had been asked to create a house magazine for the cosmetics company L'Oréal. What she put together was far superior to the banalities required by the client and became, instead, a blueprint for what would become IPC's new magazine: *Nova*. Birk was listed as 'editorial consultant', but her influence was substantial. With the appointment of Dennis Hackett, then magazine journalism's hottest property, plus such fledgling stars as the fashion editor Molly Parkin, designer Harry Peccinotti and art director Derek Birdsall, and such writers as Kenneth Alsopp, agony aunt Irma Kurtz and, for food, Elizabeth David, the magazine took on a positively revolutionary character.

No one would pretend it was a political revolution, but in terms of what could be presented as a 'woman's magazine' it was remarkable. Features included pieces on the whole range of Sixties' issues: racism, childbirth, women's liberation, sterilisation, revolutionary children, drugs and all the rest. Sex, especially in the world of relationships and their travails, featured heavily: it was to be efficient, 'civilised'. As the September 1968 cover put it, alongside a scarlet-trouser-suited, fag-clasping model: 'I have taken the pill. I have hoisted my skirts to my thighs, dropped them to my ankles, rebelled at university, abused the American Embassy, lived with two men, married one, earned my keep, kept my identity and frankly . . . I'm lost.' (A solution was offered on page 38.) And for all that the magazine was an adman's wet dream and a showcase for every art director's wildest fantasies, it offered more than style *per se*. It was, as Linda Grant suggests, a far cry from the relatively stodgy colour supplements: '*Nova* was excavating the foundations for a radical restructuring of the lives of middle-class women.'[28] They were the very group who would be the seedbed for the flowering of the women's movement.

In December 1971 Louise Ferrier hosted the first meeting of Women in the Underground. Among those who turned up were Michelene Wandor from *Time Out*, Rosie Boycott, fresh from the Women's Issue of *Frendz*, Marsha Rowe of *Oz*, Cassandra Wedd of *Ink*, Caroline McKechnie of *IT*, Sue Miles, Tessa Topolski and a few others. Feminism, it might be argued, didn't even need the counter-culture. It was at best a parallel movement, but the discrepancy between the underground's preaching and its practice enraged those women whose lives were involved in both. Rosie Boycott:

> It was a sensation: everybody was talking at once about all the things that they didn't like and it was as though all those vague feelings, right back to having tried to hack it across Middle Earth on your own at the age of seventeen, trying to look cool on drugs, trying to pretend you were part of something, wondering if in fact you were going to get picked up by someone you didn't like and feeling that actually it would be worse if you weren't picked up, because then you'd have been rejected – a whole lot of things that had been bubbling for everybody for a long time then became something that was shared and was obviously very dynamic and was obviously very real.
>
> What was insidious about the underground was that it pretended to be alternative. But it wasn't providing an alternative for women. It was providing an alternative for men in that there were no problems about screwing around or who you wanted. There was still a power game going on: women were typists, men were the bosses, men were the ones who decided what wages people

got, whether people had jobs – people even got fired. Women were dependent on men. The fact that this was happening in an alternative society gave it
its punch and gave it its kick. Women came into the undergound expecting to
get a liberal world and became more embittered when they did not. For people who moved in the established world and were living in the established
way: this was just how things happened, honey. The point about the underground was that this was not the way things were supposed to happen.[29]

The upshot of that and subsequent meetings was *Spare Rib*, not the first
but undoubtedly the best-known feminist magazine of its time. A major force
in the gender politics of the Seventies, it would last into the new decade and
beyond, before collapsing through an excess of sectarianism, a lack of money
and, in the end, of sufficient readers in the new 'post-feminist' world. The
prime movers, and subsequent editors, were Marsha Rowe and Rosie Boycott. Rowe, twenty-eight, had worked for Australian *Vogue*, for *Oz* (in both
Australia and the UK), for the literary agent Deborah Rogers and for *Ink*.
Boycott, twenty, had worked for *Frendz* for barely a year. The initial idea,
however, had come from neither woman: it was put forward by an American
publisher, Bonnie Boston, who was, ironically, working for that far from
feminist imprint, Maurice Girodias's Olympia Press, which, in alliance with
the New English Library, had briefly set up shop in London. (The nearest
Girodias had come to feminism was in 1967, when he befriended a fellow-
resident of New York's Chelsea Hotel, one Valerie Solanas, one-woman
creator of SCUM – the Society for Cutting Up Men – whose manifesto he
published. Solanas won notoriety as the near-assassin of Andy Warhol, but it
was widely believed that she had another target in mind: Girodias himself.
He had apparently failed to publish fast enough, an omission he quickly
remedied as Warhol's injuries hit the news.) Boston had given Rowe a copy
of an Olympia book, *The Story of O* and soon afterwards suggested that
rather than simply 'speaking bitterness', as the old Maoist jargon had it, the
women in the underground might be best occupied in producing an independent paper of their own.

Rowe told Boycott and the pair grasped the challenge. They were, given
their relative inexperience, 'foolhardy', as Rowe recalls,[30] but what mattered
was their willingess to try. Rowe had that Australian self-belief: it can be
done; Boycott, indefatigably positive and educated at Cheltenham Ladies'
College in the virtues of self-sufficiency, simply assumed that were one to
push steadfastly ahead, things *had* to happen. Money came from a variety of
sources; the producer Michael White, Caroline Younger of the beerage,
Christopher Logue, the agent Clive Goodwin, FeliksTopolski. There were
bank loans and a contribution from Boycott's father. Sometimes the fund-
raising went somewhat awry. On one occasion the pair visited a rich Arab in
his Park Lane penthouse. One of Boycott's upper-class friends was financing
her heroin habit by prostituting herself at £100 a time and suggested, despite

the patent absurdity of such a gentleman wishing to invest in a feminist magazine, that he might be good for a few thousand. Predictably he failed to bite, but the pair escaped unmolested.

An attempt to summon up a different form of help – female solidarity – had a more ambivalent result. The new editors went to a number of Women in Media meetings, a much grander Fleet Street version of the women in the underground. Here they met a mixed response. There were those, typically the *Guardian's* Jill Tweedie who proved invaluable allies and occasional contributors. Others were less friendly. There was, as Boycott, felt, 'a slight feeling of "What right do you have to do it?" I don't think that we imagined this in any way. Some people . . . were sympathetic and terrific, but at the same time there was that – it seems to me – inevitable feeling of being a bit patronised by it, because there they were all very successful media women. They had all done exotic and glamorous things and had earnt money and were seriously respected in the world. So they wanted to know: how would we do this, how would we do that. I had never stopped to think.'[31]

The *Spare Rib* that emerged later that year owed its style to a number of sources. Inevitably there was a large 'underground' input. It also owed a considerable debt to *Nova*. There were substantial differences, apart from anything more cerebral, *Spare Rib* simply didn't have the funds, but the two magazines shared in their determination to bring something genuinely original to women's publishing. And while it had some vestiges of underground ethos – at times it seemed to be riding a tricky line between tradition and the earnest stylelessness of a political pamphlet – it looked very conventional: glossy stock, good design, anything but messy. The first edition contained Antonia Raeburn on the suffragettes, Sheila Rowbotham on women of the Middle Ages, Juliet Mitchell on the movies and Angela Phillips on breasts. Richard Neville assessed another new women's magazine – *Cosmopolitan*, an American import best described in the title of its founder Helen Gurley Brown's 1962 best-seller *Sex and the Single Girl*. There were beauty tips, a cookery column, letters, a children's page and 'Man's World', in which macho soccer star George Best offered his take on liberation. Its editorial set out the stall:

> Liberation, the lady said. Rubbish we thought. Then we thought some more. Then we talked some more. Then we came together. That was it. *Spare RIB* is the result.
>
> We are not attempting the impossible. To try to explain Women's Liberation in one quick, easy lesson would be both ludicrous and wrong. Its basis is small group meetings and a magazine cannot achieve that necessary personal communication. What we can do is reflect the questions, ideas and hope that is growing out of our awareness of ourselves, not as a 'bunch of women' but as individuals in our own right.
>
> It was startling to realise that we could not buy any publication which discussed what we felt to be vital issues and so *Spare RIB* is a beginning. We

have tried to create a magazine that is fluid enough to publish work by contributors who have not written before as well as by women and men who are
successful journalists and writers.

 We are waiting with bated breath for your reactions.

Its attempt at the middle way, however, was not always successful. Neither editor saw *Spare Rib* as 'anti-men', but it seemed that anything so dedicatedly female had to take on that role. Thus the editors' single-minded
dedication to the magazine soon disposed of their current relationships. (The
newly discarded boyfriend, rendered surplus to requirements by the demands of feminist progress, became a stock figure of the period.) Greater
problems, the product of clashing ideologies, emerged even as the magazine
enjoyed its launch party. The staff may have envisaged a magazine that could
straddle a variety of horses; the more heavily politicised members of the
movement, along with those of Gay Liberation, felt otherwise. Halfway
through the party the 'Rad Fems' of the GLF erupted into the otherwise unremarkable gathering. They attacked the editors, deploring the lack of radicalism, the presence of men at the party and their appearance in the editorial.
It was all too middle-class. Verbal fights broke out, which escalated to physical ones. The Rad Fems vanished, clutching the last eight bottles of wine. (A
week later they struck again, this time targeting *Gay News*, whose Paddington office they comprehensively trashed.) Tempers calmed – and next week
Gay News carried an apologetic piece by Dennis Lemon, plus a justification
by the invaders – but the point had been made. If *Spare Rib* was to be a genuinely feminist creation, just what sort of feminism should it espouse?

 Such debates would play an increasingly important part in the magazine's
progress, but by then both Rowe and Boycott had gone – Boycott left in 1974,
Rowe two years later – and a collective, a far cry from the essentially middle-
class women who set things rolling, had taken over. At first however, like
many of its readers, it promoted easily assimilable issues – abortion, equal
pay: the original liberation demands – and people responded. The magazine
sold 20,000, which meant a readership of around 50,000. However much the
ideologues might carp, not all of them wanted to turn the world wholly upside down. What mattered was the volume of support from 'ordinary'
women, women who understood what was needed, women who might have
read *The Female Eunuch*, or at least paused to read the excerpts reproduced in
their Sunday paper, but for whom the harder-edged theorising of a Rowbotham or a Mitchell would prove simply too off-putting. As Nigel Fountain
recognised, *Spare Rib*, 'born out of persistence and what some imagined to be
a naïve confidence, effectively became the national magazine of the women's
movement'.[32]

Chapter Twenty-Nine

Rock: Sounds Like Fun

Music is now the primary weapon used to make the perverse seem glamorous, exciting and appealing. Music is used to ridicule religion, morality, patriotism and productivity – while glorifying drugs, destruction, revolution and sexual promiscuity.
Gary Allen 'That Music: There's More to It Than Meets the Ear'

When the mode of the music changes, the walls of the city shake.
IT slogan, loosely translated from Plato, *The Republic*

Looking back thirty years, the Sixties, for the vast majority of people, means essentially music. The counter-culture, while noisy, embraced relatively few people; neither dope, sex, nor revolution impinged, other than through the pages of the tabloid press, on the great majority of lives. Hippie fashions, in a diluted, mass-market form, filtered from the pioneers to the knock-offs, but the great unifying factor, especially for the young, was music. There were different musics, of course – 1967, the year of *Sgt Pepper* was also the year in which the execrable crooner Engelbert Humperdinck was actually the public's number one artist – but for most people it is songs, not LSD, that promote the most vivid flashbacks.

This is not a history of rock, and the subject is too vast, and too massively analysed and memorialised already, to permit or require further consideration here. One cannot ignore, however, the vast influence it had on the counter-culture and how, to a lesser extent, that counter-culture gave back its own mores to rock. For many the two were inseparable. Rock 'n' roll was the music of revolution, although ironically the counter-culture would emerge at a time when most of the veteran rockers were reduced to 'revival shows' and wowing the oldies at pier-ends or holiday camps. At the same time the cognoscenti could trace bloodlines from the Fifties to the Sixties, and where had such contemporary favourites as Eric Clapton or Keith Richards found their influences but in the work of ageing bluesmen. None the less, while the music moved on in an unbroken line, for ordinary hippies the musicians and their lifestyles appeared revolutionary. Showbiz had not died, and stars, however successful, remained creatures of predictable mien, their public appearance, if not their private lives, constrained by carefully manufactured imagery. But with the arrival of the Beatles, and even more so the Rolling Stones (whose manager Andrew Loog Oldham positively promoted those 'anti-social' characteristics that the Beatles' Brian Epstein fought so assiduously, and in the end so vainly to restrain) the pop star (now rock star) took on a completely new role. Always an icon of youth, such stars had hitherto been made in the image of the adult world's concept of what youth needed: hence the saccharine mouthings of a Cliff Richard or a Tommy Steele. With the new regime, the grail of 'family entertainer' was blithely discarded. The refusal of the Rolling Stones to mount the revolve at the end of *Saturday Night at the London Palladium* was definitely symbolic, even as the gesture itself could be dismissed as petty. Now bands like the Stones ('Would You Let Your Daughter Marry a Rolling Stone?' asked Maureen Cleave in the *Evening Standard* on 21 March 1964) set out the paradigm for the ideal life. They would pay for such excesses with vilification and police raids – at times Jagger's 'Sympathy for the Devil' seemed like a genuine *cri de coeur* rather than a piece of demonic irony – and in due course vanish into the gossip columns with the rest of the jetset, but as the decade ended, such bands were inescapable in their influence.

What they were preaching, unlike the Cliffs and Tommys, was a form of revolution; at least of the adolescent variety. The slogans were plentiful: live fast, die young, leave a good looking corpse; if you ain't part of the solution you're part of the problem; up against the wall motherfuckers; they've got the guns, but we got the numbers; do not adjust your brain, there is a fault in reality; give peace a chance . . . You didn't have to be a right-wing paranoid to appreciate what was going on. Once bands began to write their own music and lyrics, rather than taking on the latest catchy efforts of the Brill Building or Denmark Street, the mode of the music did indeed change. The lyrics of Dylan, Lennon (and McCartney), Lou Reed or Pete Townshend really seemed to mean something. The nature of rock lyrics, of course, had always been to appeal to youthful emotions, as much in the High School fantasies of Chuck Berry or the down-and-dirty romancing of the early Elvis, but the consciously cerebral efforts of 'Desolation Row' or the junk-fuelled madness of 'Sister Ray' went so much further. Phil Spector's fantasy of 'little symphonies for the kids' still shifted units, but for the devotees of the 'underground', such relatively easy listening had long since given way to more demanding and more pertinent alternatives.

Love, in its varieties, still dominated, but it was distinctly less idealised, typically in such titles as the Stones' 'Under My Thumb', 'Out of Time' and 'Play with Fire' (those cynical anthems of the 'new aristocracy'). Teen angst, always a staple, was expanded from its autopilot banalities to a world in which one's tussles – with the opposite sex, with drugs, with family, with society – were articulated with a new finesse and subtlety that ran far beyond the old moon/June certainties. To what extent the revolution was genuine is another story. Jagger's 'Street Fightin' Man' was inspired by the Grosvenor Square demonstration of March 1968, but the emptiness of such proclamations was underlined eighteen months later, at the Altamont Raceway when the Stones' response to the mayhem and murder taking place within yards of their stage was Keith Richards's plaintive cry: 'If you don't stop that, man, we won't play.'

Rock remained staunchly male-orientated and heterosexual. It would take a decade or more before Tom Robinson could proclaim that he was 'Glad To Be Gay', or women, other than the occasional songbird such as Sandie Shaw or Lulu, could approach the world of rock stardom other than on their knees. The old madonna/whore dichotomy remained firmly in place: as Charles Shaar Murray has pointed out, as far as women were concerned there was the pedestal and there was the gutter[1], although to paraphrase the movie critic Barry Norman, the only reason bands like the Stones might be willing to place a girl on a pedestal was to look up her skirt. No wonder the feminists of the early Seventies so enjoyed Carly Simon's 'You're so vain', a song whose target was said to be Mick Jagger.

The most obvious new ingredient was drugs, whether in the foolish nomenclature of the Flower Pot Men (nudge nudge, wink wink), the soppy clichés of 'Let's Go to San Francisco' or the less penetrable, acidulated mythologies of the Grateful Dead or Jefferson Airplane. There were gradations of course. The Byrds's gentle 'Eight Miles High' was a whole distance from the Velvet Underground's dark but still anthemic 'Heroin', and the Airplane's hippie-trippy 'White Rabbit' offered a very different perspective on illegal substances than did Lennon's agonised 'Cold Turkey', but the point was that drugs, via rock, had been propelled slap-bang into the mass consciousness. You didn't need to play the records backwards, or analyse the sleeves for arcane subtexts to know that. Rock had always proclaimed the joys of escape – what else did you do in your 'Little Deuce Coupe' – but this was pushing the envelope infinitely further. Cars and girls had been replaced by 'weed, whites and wine' and a mass of more variable substances. The connection went both ways: the Beatles' 'Strawberry Fields' was co-opted the name of a brand of LSD, as was Blue Cheer, the name of an American band. It was all a long way from 'Teddy Bear' and even 'Blue Suede Shoes', though, as it gradually transpired, the King himself was not averse – for all his signing up as an anti-drug crusader with the Nixon White House – to a little unconventional medication himself.

The drug input didn't merely amuse the kids; it could be blissfully, wildly misinterpreted by the more foolish members of the conservative community.

'Yellow Submarine' has been one of the Beatles' biggest hits and has been called . . . 'a beautiful children's song'. Those who are a little more hip . . . know that in drug terminology a 'yellow jacket' is a submarine-shaped barbiturate, seconal, or 'downer' (a 'downer' submerges you). Among other Beatle songs generally interpreted as referring to drugs are 'Norwegian Wood' (British teenagers' term for marijuana), 'Strawberry Fields Forever' (marijuana is often planted in strawberry fields, in order to avoid detection, because the plants are similar in appearance), and 'Magical Mystery Tour' ('Roll up, roll up [your sleeve] for the mystery tour . . . The Magical Mystery Tour is waiting to take you away'), and 'A Day In The Life' (I'd love to turn you on) . . .

Furthermore, reported the author, one Gary Allen,[2] 'a "trip" to your local record shop will reveal that there are now literally hundreds of drug-related songs.' Among them, claimed Allen, whose listing reveals certain fundamental failings as a discographer, were:

'Colored Rain' (Methedrine), the Wichita Falls; 'Mary Jane' (marijuana), Willie and the Rubber Band; 'Jumpin' Jack Flash' (when Methedrine, taken intravenously, hits the brain it is known as a 'flash'), 'Lady Jane', 'You Turn Me On', 'Eight Miles High' and 'You've Got Me High' – all by the Rolling Stones; 'Rainy Day Women', (a marijuana cigarette), and 'Mr Tambourine Man' (drug peddler), Bob Dylan; 'Mainline Prosperity Blues' (mainlining is shooting drugs directly into the vein), Richard Farina; 'Puff the Magic Dragon' (smoke marijuana) by Peter, Paul, and Mary; 'You Turn Me On' by Ian Whitcomb; 'Yellow Balloon' (drugs are often carried in a balloon so that they may be swallowed and later retrieved in the event of imminent arrest) by the Yellow Balloon; 'Up, Up And Away' (which sold 875,000 copies, won a Grammie Award, and was adopted by Trans-World Airlines as its theme song) by the Fifth Dimension; 'Along Came Mary' (marijuana) by the Association; 'Bend Me, Shape Me' by the American Breed . . .

Allen, who in the same article ('That Music: There's More to It Than Meets the Ear') had noted the Communist propaganda that lay behind the Beatles' 'Back in the USSR' and typified Dylan as 'this crimson troll' (another lengthy list cites the many songs calling for revolution), was undoubtedly to the crazier side of the critical spectrum, but his larger point can't be denied. In rock 'n' roll the medium, as Marshall McLuhan had dinned into the citizens of his global village, was indeed the message. Not, of course, that it should be proclaimed too loudly. The predictable descent of the press (and its attendant rent-a-quote politicians) into spasms of implausible overexcitement when a Beatle or some lesser rock panjandrum admitted to their experience of LSD or cannabis was then, as it has remained, tediously risible.

In terms of hands-on involvement with the counter-culture, rock was less immediately involved. As can be seen in the inception of Indica, *IT* and other early institutions, Paul McCartney, via his friend Miles, was a definite presence, offering money or merely DIY skills. George Harrison's involvement with Ravi Shankar undoubtedly helped spread the Indian influence into hippie culture, but neither Harrison nor Ringo Starr felt it necessary to get any further involved. The Beatles' filmed *homage* to Ken Kesey's 'Bus Trip', the *Magical Mystery Tour*, was a gruesome parody – amusing no doubt to the happy trippers, but a tedious waste of footage to almost everyone else. John Lennon presents a more ambiguous case. By the end of the decade, as his involvement with the artist Yoko Ono drew him ever further into what George Melly dismissed as the 'clapped-out avant-garde',[3] Lennon was the most openly identified with the counter-culture, with his 'bed peace', 'baggism'

and especially the song 'Give Peace a Chance'. His involvement in 1972 with
Arthur Janov's Primal Scream therapy both resulted in his best solo album
and in his identification with what would be termed New Therapies. Lennon
also involved himself with the *Oz* Trial, and in 1971 set up the Freedom
Foundation, a nebulous creation that employed Stan Demidjuk of 'Friends
of *Oz*', and was aimed in some way at bringing together rock, the underground and the New Left, but achieved nothing concrete. Like many
other liberals he professed himself taken with Michael X. At the same time,
as a composer he managed both 'Revolution' ('Count me out') and 'Woman
is the nigger of the world'. Both, presumably, were sincerely meant in context. Certainly the Establishment believed him: the FBI considered John
Lennon and Yoko Ono a sufficient threat to US security to maintain surveillance on them.

The Beatles, of course, did make one (relatively) united play for what
must, if only by default, be seen as their own form of counter-culture: Apple,
founded in 1968 and effectively dead two years later. Apple's aim, it was
loudly announced, was essentially charitable. The Beatles' money would be
on offer for the right sort of applicants. People who had something new,
something interesting, something alternative to offer. The idea had begun
with the creation of a shop which itself formed part of a larger plan: the need
to use up some two million pounds in revenue, which might otherwise be
decimated by the demands of the taxman. In September 1967 they turned
over some £100,000 to a trio of Dutch hippies – Simon Posthuma, Marijke
Kroger and Josje Leeger – whose clothes, manners and general aura made
them into exemplars for the most demanding of 'beautiful people'. They
were in London working as stage designers, creating extravagantly beautiful
sets that were equalled only by the clothes they wore. Among their commissions were the costumes for the Beatles' 'All You Need Is Love' broadcasts of
earlier that year, a painted piano and gypsy caravan for John, and a fireplace
for George's bungalow. They styled themselves The Fool, a name which
Posthuma was at pains to tell the media, bore not the usual, derogatory definition, but represented 'Truth, Spiritual meaning and the circle which expresses the universal circumference in which gravitate all things'.[4]

What the Beatles, especially Paul the dandy, now wanted from The Fool
was the creation of the ultimate in boutiques, 'a beautiful place where you can
buy beautiful things'.[5] Their previous retailing experience had been in Amsterdam, where they had opened Trend, a briefly popular boutique. That it
had folded in some financial chaos was quietly – and it would prove mistakenly – overlooked. Paul named the new venture, established somewhat surprisingly in the less than freaky surroundings of Paddington Street, W1,
'Apple', taking his inspiration from a newly purchased Magritte. It opened
on 7 December, staffed by such swinging dollies as Jenny Boyd, Patti's
equally glamorous sister, and crammed with The Fool's most glorious vel-

vets, silks and satins. Lighting, so vital to a shop, was provided by 'Magic' Alex Mardas, an inventor of electronic knick-knacks, whose father was a member of the current Greek government and whose only introductions on arrival in the UK had been to Mick Jagger and Prince Philip. (Mardas wowed the Beatles; others, especially professional inventors, were less impressed. It appeared that for all his talk, and there was plenty, usually appended to a demand for new development funds, there was a distinct lack of protoypes.) Apple, the shop, soon proved a ghastly blunder: thousands trooped through, gazed, fingered and priced the profusion of glorious garments – then left, their wallets defeated by the ludicrous markups. It lasted but eight months before vanishing in a one-off giveaway. It was not, however, without issue. In the offices above the showroom there developed a variety of 'Apple' business: Apple Music, Apple Retail and the like. Soon there would be a whole empire: Apple Films, Apple Publicity, Apple Records, Apple Books; in January 1968 Epstein's old company Beatles Limited, was renamed as the punning Apple Corps. It soon outgrew Paddington Street, moving first to Wigmore Street and thence, where it stayed, to 3 Savile Row.

The aim of Apple, and especially the latest creation, the Apple Foundation for the Arts, announced McCartney, was 'a controlled weirdness . . . a kind of Western Communism'. He told the media, 'We want to help people, but without doing it like a charity.' The Beatles knew what it was like endlessly to be begging for money in order to indulge their dreams. Those days were over for them, and they wanted others to benefit. 'We're in the happy position of not needing any more money, so for the first time the bosses aren't in it for profit. If you come to me and say, "I've had such and such a dream," I'll say to you, "Go away and do it." '[6]

It might have sprung from a tax dodge, but there was no denying the element of genuine idealism. For Derek Taylor, their old PR man and now established as the Apple Press Officer after a spell in the California rock business, where he had been the organiser of the Monterey Pop festival,

> There was this general disposition to be nice to anyone who seemed to be on the trip. Anyone who wanted a small amount or who could give us a service for a reasonable sum. So if someone came in off the street with an idea and they looked right and felt right and had a nice manner they would get money given to them. It was naïve, it was idealistic, but that's how it was. It's all in that song 'Baby, you're a rich man too'. We're all beautiful people, what do we want to do? What do we want to be? We want to help save the world. And that was the message and to make sure that people knew about it they went on the Johnny Carson Show and said, 'Come to us, we'll give you a cup of tea or a drink . . . ' And they did come.[7]

If one aspect of the counter-culture was wide-eyed *naïveté*, then the Beatles, and Lennon and McCartney in particular, had never shown themselves

more 'alternative'. Presumably they had issued their invitation on the premise of quality applications; what they received was quite the reverse. Apple
became a magnet for every hopeful who'd ever made a tape, written an unpublished, unproduced book, play, movie or poem, every painter, every
model-maker, gadget-concocter and scores of others. Many, as advised, sent
in their efforts; these at least could be filed for rejection. Many others turned
up in person, bearing whatever piece of crankery they thought would work,
happy to hang around and wait for what they presumed would be the speedy
disbursal of Beatle largesse. Often the supplicants had nothing to offer: just
themselves, with a hand open for cash. They were usually disappointed.
Apart from anything else, the real *schnorrers* were in-house. A variety of new
people augmented the hometown Liverpudlian loyalists, and while the
original 'family' remained on relatively short commons, these arrivistes
chose to write their own inflated cheques.

It didn't take long for disillusion to set in, though nearly twenty years on
Paul McCartney preferred to see it less as disillusion, than as a step too far:

> We weren't disenchanted but there was more required than we could bring to
> it. The theory was what we could bring to it, the music, the vibes if you want
> to call it that, the good will as it would be known in business – it's worth an
> awful lot of money. We could bring all that to it and actually did and on that
> side the company was quite successful. It did something for one or two artists
> and we managed to do quite a few things ourselves through it. But it couldn't
> exist on that alone. It needed business expertise. Our idea was to create an al-
> ternative: by our good will we would be saying to people, 'Look, we've got
> this really great little company, you won't be hassled by any of these business
> heads who are always hassling you . . . all you need to do is just flourish in this
> garden that we're going to provide for you, and we, as artists ourselves, will
> sympathise with what you're going through.' We will provide these things
> and then the businessmen will merely structure it all for us and will make
> sure that we don't overspend or we don't do this when things are looking
> dodgy. But they actually didn't do that. Our slogan at the time was 'business
> with pleasure'. We wanted to work very hard, but we wanted it enjoyable:
> this was how we worked and we felt sorry for all the plebs who didn't have
> that luxury and we wanted to bring that to everyone. Why Apple failed was
> that it wasn't set up well enough on a business level. So we just had pleasure
> with pleasure.[8]

The symbolic heart of that pleasure was the press office, where Derek
Taylor had established himself in unmistakable style. For visitors, whether
of the underground press begging an interview or a full-page ad to stave off
the next issue's print bills, or musicians and their entourage, or fellow members of the rock industry, or simply passing liggers, there seemed to be a permanently open house. Long lunches, longer afternoons, the endlessly
revolving light-shows, champagne, joints, the occasional trip. It couldn't

last, as McCartney was the first to appreciate, and for a while Taylor's indolent generosity would be scapegoated, but in truth, the blame lay with the whole set-up. If Taylor gave away the odd unnecessary ad, if his bar and stash-box were always open, then so too were the cheque-books brandished by all four Beatles. As circumstances would prove, the band would not survive their Savile Row empire. It was more than fitting that their final public performance would take place on its roof. For Taylor, there were simply too many conflicting agendas. At the top were the Beatles, who had their group fantasy, on top of which they had individual, often conflicting demands. But they were not alone:

> There was Neil [Aspinall] who was the keeper of the conscience, the keeper of the files, the man who had some sort of hand on the Beatles. You had Peter Brown running his own adventure. He was their personal assistant. Peter would lunch, it was a feature of Apple. Then there'd be some MP around and you'd have Hardy Amies coming in perhaps, and Andy Williams and 'Perhaps George may come in today, Andy, who knows. Keep a place for George ...' So we'd all sit down and have lunch and champagne and then in the afternoon Lauren Bacall would appear by the request of Lord Bernstein on the off-chance that she might meet all four, but with a promise of Ringo. Or sometimes one of my friends who had drunk too much, or Dominic Behan or a Hell's Angel would find his way down to that floor downstairs and there'd be this culture collision which wasn't with the straight world, but with the elegant world of David Hicks interiors which was Peter Brown's room. Then there was the I Ching. There was a special I Ching thrower – Caleb. He wore all white and his white blond hair parted in the middle. He got fifty quid a week. We couldn't have gone on and on like that running around. Apple was like Toytown and Paul was Ernest the Policeman. We had to have a demon king. Who was Klein.[9]

Allen Klein, a hard-headed New Yorker, had already taken charge of the Rolling Stones' wayward finances; as Apple slipped further into chaos, he had been hired by John Lennon to do the same job for the Beatles. In pantomime the 'demon king' is generally vanquished, however vile his previous disruptions. In Klein's case he was perceived as the victor, but his role was more of a sweeper-up: Apple had already moved into serious self-destruction long before his arrival. He cut back expenditure, saw off the endless procession of hippie importunates, and generally cleaned house. By this stage, other than Apple Records, which was still pouring out dependable Beatles hits, the remainder of the empire was pretty much an empty shell. However convoluted the last days of the Beatles might become, with the agonising, bitter lawsuits between McCartney and the rest, and the mish-mash of warring emotions engendered by John's alliance with Yoko Ono and Paul's with Linda Eastman, Apple as 'controlled weirdness', was already dead. It had proved true for the counter-culture, and it was equally inescapable for the icons of the age: there was weirdness, there was control, there was no happy in-between.

If, taken at its simplest, Apple was the Beatles' attempt to do good, then the Stones, whose role had always been portrayed as a counter-point to the merry Mop-Tops, made sure that their, or certainly their leader's contribution to popular culture, was doing, or at least portraying, 'bad'. And in so doing, via the Donald Cammell-Nic Roeg movie *Performance*, they came nearer to creating what Mick Brown has termed 'the quintessential record of Sixties London hedonism, amorality and violence'[10] than any contemporary or indeed subsequent evocation. *Performance* tells the story of a gangster, Chas (James Fox) and his encounter with a reclusive rock superstar, Turner (Mick Jagger). It co-starred various East End wideboys, notably John Bindon, a thug turned thesp whose real life party-pieces included hanging a number of pint beer mugs from his erect penis, and who would eventually be jailed for beheading a rival in a pub, plus rock's dark queen Anita Pallenberg and the waif-like Michele Breton as Jagger's concubines. In the movie Chas, a psychotic enforcer ('I like a bit of a cavort, I don't send them solicitor's letters'), possibly bisexual, oversteps the line after he is tortured by a gangland rival and, turning the tables, savagely beats and then kills him. Such excesses displease his boss ('united we stand, divided we're *lumbered*!') and he is forced on the run. He ends up in Powis Square, Notting Hill, where he bluffs his way into Turner's house. Here he enters a bizarre world of, quite literally, sex, drugs and rock 'n' roll, a miasma of mind-games and role-swapping, accentuated by hallucinogens and blurred, polymorphous sex. In the end the gang hunt him down and the film ends with Fox – or is it Jagger – vanishing to his death in their Rolls.

The plot, however, was secondary: what came across to those who saw *Performance* was its unassailable realism. As 'Turner' says: 'The only performance that makes it, that really makes it, that makes it all the way, is one that achieves madness.' *Performance*, a strange, compelling and disturbing movie, managed that in spades. With the memories of the recently jailed Kray Brothers still fresh, there was no doubt on whom the gangsters were based; as for Jagger's ménage, no one would ever again capture that atmosphere of drugs and what could only be termed decadence that ran through the lives of rock's contemporary élite. Anyone who moved around the London scene recognised that here, in its drug-fuelled intensity, its elliptical, opaque communications, its sense of a locked-in, hothouse world cut off from the mundane, was the real thing. It was, to quote Marianne Faithfull, 'truly our Picture of Dorian Grey. An allegory of libertine Chelsea life in the late sixties, with its baronial rock stars, wayward *jeunesse dorée*, drugs, sex and decadence – it preserves a whole era under glass.'[11]

Donald Cammell, whose father had written one of the first biographies of Aleister Crowley, the self-styled 'Great Beast' and 'Wickedest Man in Britain', had already scripted one film with Fox, *Duffy*, when in 1967 he put together his story of gangland and rock 'n' roll. After convincing Jagger, a Chelsea neighbour, Fox, the cinematographer Nic Roeg and the interior designer Christopher Gibbs (more than anyone responsible for introducing the rock aristocrats to the real thing) in the excellence of his script, Cammell took the idea to Warner Brothers. Warners noted Jagger's interest, checked the massive profits engendered by the two Beatles' hits *A Hard Day's Night* and *Help!* and gave Cammell the go-ahead. Presumably they expected a jolly little romp, with plenty of songs and pretty girls. There were songs, the girls were undoubtedly attractive, but jolly . . . As Marianne Faithfull has noted, 'They were making a film out of what the public imagined our lives to be. It was voyeurism . . . Warner Bros., I should think, envisioned a "Hollywoodised" version of our circle complete with moral and retribution.'[12]

As every memoir makes clear, the line between fact and fiction soon blurred. Many of those involved were friends, already involved in some version of the Turner world. The real-life prelude to *Performance* had been an acid-fuelled orgy, involving Fox, Jagger and Fox's then girlfriend. Turner's ménage came straight from Cammell's own predilection: threesomes. In Paris he and his girlfriend, the model Deborah Dixon (enlisted as the movie's costume designer), had lived with Breton; a couple of years earlier it had been Pallenberg. Not only that but the androgyne Breton resembled Fox's girlfriend, Andee Cohen, while the blonde rock goddess Pallenberg had overtones, if only visually, of the equally blonde Faithfull, Jagger's inamorata. Their 'Director of Authenticity', David Litvinoff, known as Litz ('a PhD with honours in street-savvy,' recalled Nigel Waymouth[13], was a suitably shady character, part of the Stones' inner circle and a reputed friend of the Krays (and possibly Ronnie's lover), straddling in real life, as the movie did in fantasy, the nexus between artistic Bohemia, élitist rock and hardcore gangland. It had all seemed, as Faithfull says, 'auspicious'. Wasn't everyone essentially 'playing themselves'?[14]

In which, it would transpire, lay the problems that seemed to bedevil the shoot from day one. Jagger might have thought he could waltz through the role of jaded rock star, but, as his later, disastrous appearance as 'Ned Kelly' would make amply clear, genuine acting requires something more than playing rock aristo mind-games. In the end, tutored by Faithfull, who prudently removed herself to Ireland, he thought not of his own life, but of that of his fellow-band members. One was Brian Jones, though Jagger dyed his hair not blond, as was Jones's, but shiny black, more reminiscent of Elvis. And if Jones represented the tormented, paranoid world, then there was a second model in Keith Richards, that epitome of strength and cool. Except that Richards was far from cool in this context. Deeply suspicious of Jagger's on-set couplings with Pallenberg (supposedly simulated, they were the real thing, a fact proved by a short film of outtakes submitted to the first Wet

Dream Festival), and banned from the set on Cammell's orders, he could be found sitting in his car, jealousy emanating from every pore.

The professional actor senses the line between fact and fiction, and draws it, but the *Performance* cast had no such protection. Even Fox, a genuine pro, was sucked into the chaos. He had, it was claimed, mixed all too enthusiastically with the parade of flesh-and-blood gangsters to whom Litz introduced him; Jagger and Pallenberg failed to induce him to trip, but the druggy mood – the hash joints circulated without cease – was all too smothering. Of all the human rats in what Marianne Faithfull has termed Cammell's 'psychosexual lab' James Fox became 'the prime experimental animal'. Cammell, she felt, 'had set out to confront everyone with their worst nightmare. One of the sub-plots to [the movie] is this: what would happen if you took a repressed upper-class Englishman and loaded him up with a bunch of psychotropic drugs, played mind games with him, buggered him and then put him in a film that recapitulates all this (but with genuine gangsters). James Fox was, to say the least, slightly out of his element.'[15] Breton was equally unhappy, her paranoia reaching such heights – she thought Jagger and Pallenberg were plotting against her – that a doctor had to be summoned, bearing a tranquillising syringe. Even the set was ill-fated: a house in Lowndes Square (known to Cammell as an illicit gambling club) which belonged to the former MP Captain Leonard Plugge: it was his daughter, Gale Benson, who four years later would be murdered in Trinidad by Michael X.

It was truly scary stuff and, when they viewed the finished article, none were as scared as the Warner Brothers board. The film was promptly put on hold; it would take two years, and a drastic edit, before it was released in early 1970. It would become a cult classic, voted in a *Time Out* poll of directors and critics the twenty-eighth most important film of the century (sharing the place with *Battleship Potemkin* and *It's a Wonderful Life*) and listed among the *365 Treasures of World Cinema* by the National Film Archive. Most reviews were favourable, although the *New York Times*'s John Simon suggested that, 'You don't have to be a drug addict, pederast, sado-masochist or nitwit to enjoy it – but being one or more of these things would help!'

The stars, or at least some of them, were less fortunate. Fox did not, as many suggested, go mad (although none could doubt the increasing pressures he was suffering) but a year later he turned to fundamentalist Christianity, abandoning his career for a decade; Pallenberg became increasingly involved with heroin while Breton would turn first junkie, then heroin dealer and finally destitute, telling Mick Brown in 1995, 'Nobody wants me.' Cammell would never have such a success again – though Nic Roeg would go from strength to strength, notably with *Don't Look Now* – and killed himself in 1995, an increasingly disturbed figure, still searching for a hit. Only Jagger seemed to emerge untouched, if anything stronger. 'He didn't have a drug problem and he didn't have a nervous breakdown. Nothing really touched him.' Instead, as Faithfull notes, he had 'a new, shining and impenetrable suit of body armour . . . In the same way that some actors get to keep their wardrobe, Mick came away from *Performance* with his character. This persona was so perfectly tailored to his needs that he'd never have to take it off again.'[16]

Whatever the fate of Apple, at least the Fabs had tried. Few other bands paid more than lip-service. The Stones provided the paradigmatic lifestyle, epitomised in *Performance*, but while Jagger would appear for the ritual interviews in *IT*, the stars had little to do with the freaks. As Stan Demidjuk, briefly involved with Lennon's Freedom Foundation, saw it, the bands, even the major stars, 'were negative, bitter, [and] contemptuous . . . They were singing about it, they were writing about it, but they were not living it.'[17] The so-called 'underground' bands – most notably Pink Floyd, Soft Machine and Arthur Brown – put in their time at UFO and its successors, and would turn up at a variety of rock festivals, but had no real involvement, other than that their music seemed better orientated to the counter-culture than to a more mainstream world. They did not, on the whole, get on BBC playlists. In the view of Andrew Bailey, an ex-*Variety* reporter (his best headline, penned for Allen Klein's takeover of the business: 'Lennon Bites Apple and Finds Worm') and later editor of *Rolling Stone* UK,

> All their managers were professional music business or entertainment business people. They knew all the angles, there was nothing ever, ever remotely underground about Pink Floyd or the Soft Machine, ever. They were always well-managed, they always had their publishing deals together. Probably even when they were regulars at UFO. I always saw the underground and the whole scene in terms of business, in terms of record sales and column inches. I might have seen that as a cynic, but I think the bands saw it that way naturally. Every band knows that to be successful you've got to get publicity and these were no different.[18]

Jimi Hendrix, perhaps the most successful performer to come out of what began at least as an underground milieu, and whose lifestyle put even the Stones to shame, was the same. Chas Chandler, the former Animal who managed him, and Track, Chris Lambert and Kit Stamp's record label, were no hippies. Track may have been somewhat unorthodox by the standards of, say, EMI, but it certainly wasn't preaching peace and love.

How much the bands felt any genuine fellowship with the freaks is debatable. There was lip-service, undoubtedly, and for a while even the top stars liked to see themselves as part of the underground. But there was a real gulf, and as the bands became increasingly famous and rich, it could only widen. Perhaps the worst aspect of the increasing deification of such stars was epitomised by the rise of *Rolling Stone* and its peers. Freed in such journals from the constraints of the old litanies – what's your favourite colour? what's your fa-

vourite food? – the rock gods came to believe that they had more to say than
might be encapsulated in a three-minute song. Encouraged by a fawning press
they said it: taking themselves, and worse still, being taken, very seriously. Not
everyone sees rock as a particularly positive force. The old guard, those who had
seen the Poetry Reading of 1965 as a climax rather than a launch-pad, were less
than impressed; some, for whom jazz not rock had always been the revolutionary
music, were positively hostile. Jeff Nuttall saw the advent of rock as enfeebling,
the dilution of fine ideas by crass materialism.

> Because of drugs and rock 'n' roll nobody seemed to spot the authorities can
> cut off the juice. If you've pivoted the whole operation around stuff that has
> to be bought and provided, then you've lost your integrity and you've lost
> your revolutionary power. Unless you make sure that there's something you
> can do with your hands, with your brain and with anything else to hand –
> that's what an alternative is. The alternative society hippies didn't grow their
> own cabbages – they lived out of the dustbins of supermarkets. They re-
> mained parasitic communities, not alternative communities. And parasitic is
> not alternative. There was a shift between '66–'67 from poetry and art and
> jazz and anti-nuclear politics to just sex and drugs, legalise pot. It was the ar-
> rival of capitalism. The market saw that these revolutionaries can be put in a
> safe pen and given their consumer goods. Electronically amplified music and
> narcotics. You had rock 'n' roll, which is the most unchanging, conservative
> popular music that there has ever been, under the banner of perpetual revo-
> lution. I thought we had to invade the media, but what we misjudged was the
> power and complexity of the media. The media dismantled the whole thing.
> It bought it up.[19]

George Melly felt much the same. Rock to him and his fellow jazzers was
no more than 'a contemporary incitement to mindless fucking and arbitrary
vandalism: screw and smash music. To us in the jazz world it seemed a meaningless simplification of the blues with all the poetry removed and the emphasis on white, and by definition, inferior performers.' They could just
about tolerate Little Richard or Fats Domino, even Presley in his earliest incarnation, but as for what followed . . . Yet Melly, unlike Nuttall, appreciated
rock's immense power, and its symbolism for the young. Rock was a conduit
for youthful emotions: 'What we failed to recognise was that the whole point
of rock 'n' roll depended on its lack of subtlety. It was music to be used rather
than listened to: a banner to be waved in the face of "them" by a group who
felt themselves ignored or victimised . . . Rock 'n' roll, crude and emotionally
limited as it was, established an important principle: the right of the underprivileged young to express themselves with a freedom and directness which
until then had been considered the prerogative of their elders and betters.'[20]

That, indeed, was exactly how the young saw it. Not that Nuttall's take
isn't valid, never more so when one observes the cynicism that lay behind a
CBS ad campaign that headlined itself 'The Man Can't Bust Our Music' and

featured a bunch of hairy freaks, apparently locked behind bars and waving placards that bore not slogans but CBS album covers. If anything justified the underground's denunciation of big business 'vamping on the people's culture' this was surely it. As Charles Shaar Murray put it, 'This equated buying a Big Brother, Electric Flag or Moby Grape album with burning a draft card, marching in solidarity with the Black Panthers or demonstrating against the decision of the Democratic party to withhold political legitimacy from opponents of the Vietnam war . . . It exploited the most urgent social and political issues of the time simply in order to shift units, and . . . it enabled large numbers of American kids to get as close to the Revolution as they wanted to be: a chance to bug their parents, a little sex, a joint or a tab of acid and a *bitchin'* new album.'[21] The sharks may have been a little younger than their predecessors, and as such swapped Cecil Gee suiting for kaftans, beads and bells, but that was the extent of any change.

On the whole the exploitation didn't have to be that crass. The underground *needed* the music industry. If it was a victim, it was a generally acquiescent one. Whether they liked it or not, the underground, or certainly its press, could not have existed without the income they derived from music business advertising, usually geared to what was described as the 'progressive' end of the market. Dope dealers, perhaps the underground's leading business people, preferred not to advertise; other than a few clubs, the freakier clothes shops or publishers flogging some book that might appeal to the hippies, there was only one dependable source of income: the music business, whether in the form of the promotion of records, of the space taken by individual record shops or for the announcement of upcoming gigs and festivals. Whether you were *Oz* or *Time Out*, *Rolling Stone* or *Gandalf's Garden*, you looked the same way to the entrepreneurs of rock 'n' roll.

Ironically, the underground was all too complicit. When what might be conceived as a genuinely alternative label was attempted, they were less than welcoming. John Peel, whose late-night slot on what the BBC termed 'Radio One-derful' plus his 'Perfumed Garden' column in *IT* made him into the most authoritative of 'underground' DJs, came up against the gap between rhetoric and reality when in 1968 he initiated his own Dandelion Records:

> It was all very idealistic: the chap who started it and myself were taking no money out at all. We had a vegetarian reception for the music business, without any alcohol at all: all these case-hardened old drunks turned up and were absolutely speechless with fury. We had a special presentation box: just a wooden box with about 4 singles in it, a paper dandelion and a few other bits and pieces – bars of soap, I can't remember. We had Mike Hart who had been with the Liverpool Scene; then there was Principal Edwards Magic Theatre who were a real pain in the bum actually when it came right down to it. They did a lot of prancing about without very much clothing on, playing guitar rather badly and singing half-baked songs. But I thought it could turn into something – as it

happened I was entirely wrong. So I rushed round to *IT* and *Oz* and *Gandalf's Garden* and so on – but none of them would review the records because there was no advertising involved in this. I was very downcast and that was when the process of disillusion in the hippie thing began for me.[22]

Disillusioned or not Peel (born Ravenscroft in Liverpool and educated, like another but far more mainstream DJ Simon Dee at the public school Shrewsbury, prior to learning his trade on the radio stations of the US) remained one of the most important voices in the expanding world of progressive music. Like a number of his less venturesome peers he had emerged from the world of pirate radio, a short-lived phenomenon, based mainly on boats moored just outside British territorial waters. The most popular were Radio Caroline, run by the Irish entrepreneur Ronan O'Rahilly, and its rival Radio London ('The Big L'), Peel's own 'home'. Freed of the stifling conformity of the BBC, and blithely ignoring such professional bodies as the Performing Rights Society (who extracted royalties from every record played on air) the pirates delighted the young. As Peel recalled for the *Listener* in September 1968, 'You had a remarkable two-way dialogue with the audience which it's not possible to simulate on land. You put the show out completely on your own in the bowels of a rotten ship three miles out at sea. You knew the audience felt a little bit daring even listening to you.'[23] But Peel, who perhaps more than any of his peers bought wholeheartedly into the whole hippie fantasy, was something of an exception, albeit an influential one. Daring audiences and DJs or not, the pirates' own playlists were far from revolutionary (it was only when the government began moving against them that they espoused an image of revolt), but they had advertising – given a paradoxical allure by its very illegality – and the sort of transatlantic style that would never have been permitted by 'Auntie' BBC. The DJs, slipping in and out of the UK, would turn up at clubs to enormous acclaim, setting the trends and wowing the punters. It was perhaps inevitable that the government, few of whose members echoed the liberal spirit of Roy Jenkins, sought to shut such stations down. The agent of such censorship was the Minister of Technology, Tony Benn, whose puritanical socialism recoiled in the face of such genuinely popular entertainment. Add to that the fact that broadcasting was a state monopoly and that the pirates were stealing airwaves vital to the smooth organisation of North Sea shipping, and they hadn't a chance of survival. Their DJs were recruited to the BBC's emasculate offering – Radio One – and with the exception of Caroline, which limped on for a few months more, they died with the imposition of the Marine Offences Act, 1967.

Perhaps the most direct involvement of the rock business in the underground press was in the launch, in early 1969, of a British edition of the then increasingly successful US magazine *Rolling Stone*. *Rolling Stone* had been launched two years earlier by a San Franciscan, Jann Wenner who, like his peers in the British scene, Tony Elliott of *Time Out* and Richard Branson of what would become the Virgin empire, saw the counter-culture not so much as a social phenomenon, but as a commercial opportunity ripe for maximum exploitation. Cleverly, he chose as the first issue to appear in the UK number 27, the first major study of groupies, a topic that had nothing to do with changing the world but focused instead on that ever-alluring topic, sex with the stars. By 1969 'the *Stone*' was sufficiently popular in the UK to convince Wenner that a local edition could make the grade. It was never successful, though the kudos was unmistakable. Backed by Mick Jagger, its headquarters in Hanover Square, W1 – far distant, both geographically and spiritually from the underground's traditional haunts of Portobello Road or Covent Garden – it fell miserably between all available stools. It lacked the cachet of the US edition while avoiding, in its obsession with rock, the wider concerns of the counter-culture. It was old-fashioned, ill-designed, rigid in every way. But Wenner was right: like CBS and their shameless exploitation of youthful fantasies of revolution, he knew that all the average youngster wanted was not change but escape. *Rolling Stone*, in its US version, would become the publishing sensation of the period, going from strength to greater strength with every issue. As for the British version, Jagger was tolerant of its failings, but Wenner the control freak grew increasingly frustrated. The climax came in September 1969, barely six months after the launch, when drinkers at a celebrity-packed office party were spiked with a liberal dose of tainted LSD. As the stars (notably Marc Bolan who for all his 'flower child' image had yet to taste a psychedelic) and record company flacks vomited their way down the stairs, visions of hell vibrating through their brains, *Rolling Stone* UK effectively kissed goodbye to its future. A few weeks later and the staff arrived to find men from Jagger's office changing the locks. By the end of the year they had reassembled, launching *Friends* (a gruesomely 'hippie' title, by no means excused by the fact that it had started, prior to a threatened injunction from Wenner, as the ironic *Friends of Rolling Stone*).

Not every band fell neatly into place. Those most widely identified with the counter-culture might have ridden the popular tide no more than was necessary, but there were exceptions. Most notable of these was the Social Deviants, later the Deviants and later still, somewhat reorganised and bereft of its founder, the singer and underground journalist Mick Farren, the Pink Fairies. As much as anyone else, the Deviants can be numbered among the claimants to that much-disputed title: 'godfathers of punk'. To their one-time manager Peter Jenner of Blackhill Music, better known for his involvement with the early Floyd, they were 'working-class boys who couldn't play: what more do you want for punk. Lots of energy, lots of enthusiasm, loads of bottle, and they articulated anger very well.'[24] The problem for the Deviants, who had begun life as prototype pub rockers bawling out a mixture of Irish rebel songs, Woody Guthrie folk and Howlin' Wolf blues to an audience of

Guinness-drinkers off the Portobello Road, and became in due course what Farren termed 'this amphetamine shriek band', was that, unlike the Sex Pistols, they lacked the necessary Malcolm McLaren. They had the attitude, they had the excess, the audience abuse, the insatiable appetite for drugs (less psychedelic than energising: Methedrine, the *über*-speed, was especially popular) and even some arguably good lyrics (Farren had problems singing, but his writing was fine). But somehow they never really took off. Their finest hour came in summer 1969, performing in Hyde Park a few weeks after the Rolling Stones. For once it all came together, but the trip to North America that followed broke the band. Abandoned by management, deserted by fans, out of cash, lost in personal chemical chaos, the band collapsed. Farren was expelled and came back to London; the remainder moved on to San Francisco where the Deviants became the Pink Fairies.

The Deviants were not wholly alone. There was Quintessence, very much the trippy, hippie trail end of the spectrum; there was the Edgar Broughton Band, whose leader's mother doubled as their roadie, and whose gigs were invariably enlivened by their chant of 'Out Demons, Out!' and more importantly Hawkwind, true scions of Notting Hill, who were, perhaps, the most consciously representative of hippie music. In time they moved into genuine stardom, and Lemmy, one of their guitarists, went on to found heavy metal stars Motorhead, but in 1969 they were freaks pure and simple.

Of all the era's many manifestations of rock perhaps the supreme example is in the plethora of festivals that came on stream as the decade died. They were not the first such get-togethers, the Beaulieu Jazz Festival was a long-established event, and jazz fans enjoyed a similar display at Richmond which in time moved to Windsor, and then, as numbers continued to escalate, to Reading. But what the more romantic scribes of the underground press like to typify as the 'gatherings of the tribes' were a new phenomenon. The first and best was, as might be expected, American: Monterey Pop, held in California, and which showcased Hendrix, Joplin and provided the Who with their first taste of real American fame. There would be few events to equal it. But Britain soon mounted the bandwagon. The first hippie festival was 1967's gruesomely named Festival of the Flower Children, hosted by the Duke of Bedford at Woburn Abbey and mounted by the owners of the mod club Tiles, the Sellers Brothers, among whose other interests was Carmen Rollers. Another Woburn festival followed a year later, and 1969 saw Blackhill's development of concerts in London's Hyde Park. There would be a number of these – the first featured Pink Floyd, another showcased the first of the 'supergroups', Blind Faith, but all would be subsumed in the most important: the 'Stones in the Park', an event that became a memorial for the recently dead Brian Jones.

The concert was very much the creation of TV, notably the Manchester-based Granada, best known for its current-affairs coverage and a company which more than any of its peers had already appreciated the appeal of rock. It had been the first to offer a television piece on the Beatles and more recently had filmed the American bands the Doors and Jefferson Airplane at their Christmas 1968 Roundhouse gig. For 1969 the initial idea had been to hold a massive superstar jam session. Jo Durden-Smith and John Sheppard, who had worked together on the Roundhouse film (Sheppard had also filmed the meeting between Jagger, William-Rees Mogg and a variety of clergymen that followed his notorious bust), approached a number of major figures: Jimi Hendrix, Janis Joplin, individual members of the Who, the Stones and the Beatles, as well as Spencer Davis and Cream. Many said yes, provisionally, but there was a problem. Granada executives, less hip than their directors, had never heard of most of the musicians. The idea foundered until early summer when Durden-Smith received a call from the Rolling Stones' office. Durden-Smith: 'Out of the blue Jo Bergman [a Stones aide] called up and said, "Mick wants to talk to you," and Mick said, "Do you want to do a film? We're thinking of doing this concert. The only big expenditure is the stage – do you think you can get Granada to pay for that?" The stage cost £3,000, the film was £9,000 and that was seen as a very big budget indeed.'[25] Sheppard had been preparing to leave for Eritrea, where he was scheduled to meet the Eritrean Liberation Front. Instead he found himself running the team that brought the Stones, and their quarter-million fans, to the nation's screens.

I spent the day with Mick. We had six or seven directors working, covering different aspects, and I followed Mick. Which boiled down to my flat in Chelsea, just around the corner from Mick's house. Granada hired a suitably bloated limo. Some time in the late morning I went round to Mick's place and chatted with him for a while, waking him up really, gently bringing him towards the day. Then we got into the limo and drove round to my flat, where Nick Knowland (who later became John Lennon's cameraman) was waiting. He and the soundman were set up in my main room and my wife had cooked . . . some easy to eat oriental type of thing. Mick sat in a chair and toyed with one of our exquisite little cats . . . and you'd hardly know the camera was running.

Then back into the limo, pick up Marianne and Nicholas, her son, round the corner and from now on we're filming, all the way to the suite in the Inn on the Park. Stones lounging about, Mick looks at self in mirror, Mick winks at camera in mirror and leaves shot – all nice freeform hippie stuff, Sixties stuff. Down in the lift to the armoured van. The crew didn't go in the van but we were right up its arse all the way into the Park. Then the van arrives, the door opens and the Stones do a rat run into the luxury caravan, as quite brilliantly did Nick and his soundman so you have scenes from inside the caravan. Charlie passes an apple to the fans, the Stones tuning up . . . and away we go. And then up on stage and a good time was had by all.[26]

It wasn't an especially good concert – *IT*'s reporter deplored 'Chicks holding balloons painted with golliwogs hand you one and ask for 2/6 . . . ice cream cones at 2/ – and all at a free concert' and noted that no one seemed very cheerful and 'the beautiful idea of free concerts in the park has been taken over by the mass media freaks with *Evening Standard* special editions',[27] but it was an epochal event. As well as the Stones there were Family, King Crimson (that season's much-hyped flavour of the month), the Battered Ornaments and Screw. Followed later that same day by the climax of the Pop Proms, a double bill that featured both Chuck Berry and the Who at the Albert Hall, it remains one of the great days in Sixties rock. But above all it was the Stones. People recall Jagger's white dress, the boxful of butterflies that died before they could be released, the eulogy to Brian Jones and the presence of the London chapter of the Hell's Angels, acting as a remarkably affable security team. It was this affability that would, three months later, cause the Stones such misery. Setting up for their concert at California's Altamont Raceway, Jagger suggested to their tour manager Sam Cutler – who at Hyde Park had been the first man to declare the Stones 'the greatest rock 'n' roll band in the world' – that since the Angels seemed such a pleasant bunch of guys, why not hire their Californian counterparts to do the same job. It was a mistake that ended in murder and mayhem, with the distraught Stones fleeing their besieged stage. California's Angels were more than just geographically removed from their London chapter.

But while Altamont, excoriated then and now as the grim symbol that ended the era of peace and love, may have been a disaster, it was not a paradigm. That had been provided some weeks earlier, by Woodstock, held in a small town in upstate New York and host to hundreds of thousands of American freaks, whose unbounded enthusiasm transcended all the rain and mud the elements chose to throw at them. It encouraged hyperbolic assessments, not least of which was the characterisation of 'Woodstock Nation': a generic for the love and peace tribes and much embraced by their members. (It also made clear, in one incident, the precise relationship of even the most 'underground'-sympathetic musician and those who sought to exploit his visibility. When the hippie revolutionary Abbie Hoffman attempted to interrupt the Who's set Pete Townshend, with a deft flick of his guitar, simply knocked him into the crowd.) Woodstock represented all that, in hippie eyes, seemed right about their fantasies of an alternative culture. Even Burroughs, no hippie, believed that 'it portends a new mass consciousness.'[28] It combined the requisite ingredients of dope and sex and rock 'n' roll, of love and peace, of self-sufficiency and vegetarian cooking. It was the supreme counter-cultural feelgood event and unsurprisingly it spawned a number of clones.

John Peel, as befitted his role as what he termed 'a minor princeling among the hippies', was at a large proportion:

I did the very first Isle of Wight, in 1968, which wasn't very big. Jefferson Airplane played there. It was organised by a bloke who was a bit of a scoundrel: Rikki Farr. I compèred that, but I can remember nothing about it except that it was extraordinarily cold and in the true hippie spirit I gave my socks to a girl who hadn't got any and my feet were absolutely frozen. I spent the rest of the night regretting it bitterly. The Shepton Mallet festival [Bath, 1970, the *Friends* report was headlined 'Angels Rampage As Garbage Mounts'] was very nasty: I got threatened by Hell's Angels, and they kept picking on my wife and eventually I just cleared off – I thought bugger it, what's the point in this. Then I did the Wheeley festival in Essex. That was awful: they'd provided straw bales for everybody and people built themselves igloos out of them and the Angels set them on fire. I'd volunteered for ambulance duty and we were dragging out people with burns.

There were so many festivals: Hollywood with the Grateful Dead, Mungo Jerry and Traffic; extraordinary ones at Buxton, at one of which the local paper announced that John Peel the Radio 1 disc jockey was seen using heroin; it never occurred to me to sue. Festivals were always gruelling, putting up with constant indignities at the hands of Hell's Angels, and various power-mad people of one sort or another. I said very, very early on that they reminded me of nothing so much as National Service. I seriously suggested that medals should be struck for people who had survived various festivals so that they could wear them with pride when they were stupid enough to go to other festivals.[29]

And there were others: Bickershaw, more a mud slide than a festival; Trentishoe, on a huge cliff in Devon, free events at Windsor, the very first Glastonbury. Everyone aping Woodstock as best they could, with their bonhomie, their bravado as England's weather proved itself all too English, their announcements of babies born, freakouts decanted via ambulance, their arrogantly tardy bands, their MCs gleefully, belatedly, informing the happy trippers, 'If you've got any of that brown acid, then don't take it, and if you have done, then sorry, it's a real bummer.' The biggest, if not the best, however, were the trio of festivals that were held in 1968, 1969 and 1970 on the Isle of Wight, an area hitherto best known for its status among the nation's less than counter-cultural yachting community. The first, a relatively minor affair, brought over Jefferson Airplane, en route to their appearance at the Roundhouse; the second featured Bob Dylan and the third Jimi Hendrix. Massive affairs, they had emerged from a series of gigs promoted in 1965 at the Sandown Town Hall, and featuring such Mod bands as Jimmy James and the Vagabonds, the Clique, the Action, Chris Farlowe and the Thunderbirds. They were enormously successful, for their time, and it was when the Town Hall bouncer told a friend of his, a promoter named Rikki Farr, the son of the boxer Tommy, that the monsters of the late decade were conceived. Farr was the only non-family member of Fiery Creations, a local firm of rock promoters run by the three Foulk Brothers (and their wives). When in 1968 they decided to put on the first festival, Farr, a veteran of the Crawdaddy in Richmond (birthplace of the Stones) and the Marquee, as well as the National Jazz and Blues festival, was duly roped in. A year later it was he who brought Bob Dylan from New York. Dylan, declared Farr, 'was all right, he didn't want any bullshit and neither did we.'

They didn't get it. Of the three 'Isle of Wights' the 1969 event was a relatively quiet affair. On 30 August Bob Dylan, who had abandoned the snappy Mod suits of yesteryear for something in white, played what was quietly admitted to have been a less than standout set to an audience of 150,000 devotees. Alongside Dylan, who was paid £35,000 for the set, were the Who, soon to appear at Woodstock proper, Free, the Bonzos, Marsha Hunt, the Nice, the Third Ear Band and many others. Jane Fonda and Roger Vadim, the Beatles, the Stones and Terence Stamp were among the celebrities who helicoptered or Rollered in. The police were happy, the organisers were happy, the fans, who had paid £2.50 apiece, were generally happy, the locals, who were charging vastly inflated prices for barely edible food, were happy, the couple who plunged into a sea of bubbles to have sex amidst a crowd of laughing freaks were definitely happy, even the prisoners at nearby Parkhurst jail, getting an earful of what was supposedly the world's most powerful sound system, were happy; only the security man who stepped in to cover up the obligatory naked girl ('I just want to be free!') seemed to miss the point of the proceedings. Christopher Logue, who read his poetry and wrote the event up for the *Daily Telegraph* ('If I didn't bring the field down at least I made the *Guinness Book of Records*'), was impressed by the crowd's behaviour, and wondered why the rest of the press, deprived of bloody chaos, found it so necessary to dismiss the entire event as a three-day flop.

Twelve months later it would all be a very different story. Perhaps because this year's headliner was Jimi Hendrix, widely advertised as a major-league degenerate whose sexual exploits, for the mass-market, far outweighed his guitar genius, the burghers of the Isle of Wight having sat quietly through two festivals decided that they would not countenance another. A 25,000-signature petition was arranged and the pressure groups, spearheaded by the Vectis Nationalists (UDI for the IOW), challenged Fiery Creations, the organisers, to abandon their plans. What they achieved, after a number of public meetings had degenerated into shouting matches (Rikki Farr: 'This festival comes in the spirit of youth . . . you fought a war for us, now let us speak, let's discuss our fears'; his choleric opponents: 'These festivals are the start of the catching and contamination of the young'), was to have the festival site moved from West Wight to East (where the site was supposedly superior anyway), but little else. Fiery Creations saw themselves as honest promoters, caught in the middle: 'The islanders think we're a Communist plot and some people called the White Panthers think we're a capitalist plot.' Whereas all they wanted was for people to 'plod around and have a really good time'.[30]

Like the second of the Grosvenor Square demonstrations, the 1970 festival was hyped as a potential flashpoint: hippies vs. straights, apocalypse vs. Establishment. To an extent the prophesy came true, but the reality was slightly different: Fiery Creations clashed not with outraged admirals but with 'some people called the White Panthers'. The original White Panthers, named for their Black Panther predecessors, had been formed in Ann Arbor, Michigan some years previously. Their leader, John Sinclair, busted with a single joint, had been jailed for ten years and risen at a stroke to the top of the counter-culture's martyrology. It was inevitable that Britain would see some form of homage; it appeared in the person of Mick Farren. It was, if one is honest – and even at the time most people were, cruelly – something of a joke. As Richard Neville, reporting for *Friends*, put it: 'The White Panthers, actually that should be singular, but no one dared reveal that Mick Farren is a one-man tribe'.[31] But there were others. Michael Hollingshead, the acid pioneer, resurfaced at the Festival, claiming to be the Panthers' Minister of Propaganda. Chased by patrolling dogs he assaulted a guard and was removed by police. Steve Mann, the self-proclaimed 'Marcus van der Lubbe' of a number of underground attacks on *Hair*, was swept into the enthusiasm:

> I think we were pretty serious at the time. I forget what Micky's title was – Grand Vizier or something – but I was Minister of Information – everybody had to be Minister of something. We didn't really do an awful lot, apart from try to cause trouble. We did try to get things going in the Grove. We went off to all these neighbourhood councils, trying to organise soup kitchens or blankets for the hippies or whatever. It never really came to much. The Panthers at the Isle of Wight were very effective, but then again it wasn't really our doing: it was this huge tribe of people camped out on the hill with their sign saying 'Desolation Row'. They were well into the idea of a free festival – it only needed a couple of people to shout a bit and they were well into the idea of storming the fences. And Micky shouted. We did do a newssheet, a White Panther call to arms: 'Come on brothers! Storm the barricades!'[32]

And indeed they did. In resiting the festival Fiery Creations had made a foolish and costly mistake. Adjacent to the fenced-off site, guarded by dogs and security heavies, was a hill, conveniently overlooking the stage and well within hearing distance. While the 200,000 plus who had paid for their £3 tickets helped boost the Foulk Brothers' turnover, some 10,000 others, camped out on what they quickly christened 'Desolation Row', enjoyed the spectacle for free. (Even the paying fans had a couple of days' free music: the Foulks mounted two pre-Festival concerts on the days prior to the official launch; their attempts to charge an extra pound for each of these were simply ignored.) Despite the organisers' attempts to fence off the hill as well, people power emerged triumphant. A bizarre alliance of White Panthers, some 300 French and Algerian anarchists (led by Jean-Jaques Lebel, one of the stars of Paris '68; another '68-er, Dany 'The Red' Cohn-Bendit was also there, but only for the music), Hell's Angels and Young Liberals made constant assaults, and several days before the gates were due to open, managed to smash through a number of holes. When security men and maintenance crews moved in they were showered with missiles by sympathetic paying fans – and the gaps remained. Later the organisers would brief the press on dark, if quite unfounded tales of gun-toting Americans, murdered dogs and similar agents of chaos.

By the end of the week, with the festival underway, the security men refused to confront the freaks. It was a victory. Rikki Farr mounted the stage to give a personal appeal: 'You people, you fucking listen. Listen good. You people come to this country and we have to charge you three pounds to get in here. If you don't like it, don't fucking well come . . . You bastards . . . we work for a year for a festival of love, you just want to destroy it so, so you just go to hell, you pigs!' The only interest Fiery Creations had, he added, was to break even. This was somewhat undermined by Fiery's own figures, released shortly before the event. To break even, after a variety of expenses, the heaviest of which was £250,000 for the artists – among them Hendrix, the Doors, Leonard Cohen, Miles Davis, Donovan, Sly and the Family Stone, Moody Blues, John Sebastian and Emerson, Lake and Palmer – would require 170,000 fans. On Saturday, the penultimate day, it was announced that some 600,000 had turned up, a figure that even by the predictably inflated standards of such announcements, was well over the necessary mark. Even so, few acts, other than those who had judiciously demanded cash payments on the night, would be paid and Fiery Creations would vanish into a sea of bankruptcy litigation, claiming total losses of £92,000. For them it really was, as a petulant Ron Foulk had told anyone who would listen, 'the last festival'. He promised (though would never deliver) a movie of the whole disaster; billed as 'better than *Woodstock*', its title, predictably was *The Last Great Event*.[33]

As for the music, the *raison d'être* after all of the whole thing, it varied. The Who, still coasting on *Tommy*, were the undoubted superstars. The Doors, in the opinion of more than one critic, were abysmal, bored and apathetic. Leonard Cohen received five encores. Jimi Hendrix, the top of the bill, was a problem. Jeff Dexter was emceeing:

I went out to introduce Jimi Hendrix and he said, 'Hang on, I'm not ready.' It took him about 40 minutes to get himself together, he was in a state. He didn't want me to introduce him. I was to say 'This is Blue Angel music' – the Blue Angel was the parachute division he was in in the US Army. He went to go on, in his new gear and said, 'Hey man, I can't play my guitar . . . ' – the sleeves were too big and got in the way of the strings. So I put another record on, went to one side and I sewed up his sleeve. By this time the audience had

been waiting seventy minutes, so I said 'Better get on, Jimi,' and I just ran on
and said, 'Here's the man with the guitar!' and he was about to come on and
his trousers split. So I pinned him up – I'd trained as a tailor at school, which
was why I was so into clothes. And he went on stage all pinned and stitched up.[34]

And played well enough, but not as well as many had hoped. It didn't help
that the stage amplification was rocky, or that his backup band seemed less
than committed; the problem was Hendrix himself. He was, as the *Friends*
reviewer recalled, 'nervous or very stoned, thinking about it, both'. Barely a
month later he would be dead. Germaine Greer, writing his obituary in *Oz*,
was unsurprised; if stars had failed to relate to the counter-culture, then
hadn't that counter-culture failed them too?

> He dropped down into the Isle of Wight like the sick man lowered through
> the roof of the house to be cured, hopping from his helicopter minutes before
> he was due on stage, slipping into his psychedelic minstrel-clown's gear,
> freshing up his gum and walking out on stage into nowhere. Nothing had
> changed ... The police were still there. The crude drugs were still there and,
> as always, the brutish adulation. In front of the stage all he could see were the
> film cameras, the press, the bedraggled groupies with their blank, hungry
> faces, and the politicos as ruthless in jockeying for position as the camera-
> men. Where was it to come from, the feedback that would turn him on in
> reciprocity for all the turn-ons he gave us? His guitar pleaded for resonance
> from the people, but in the vast stormy darkness there was not so much as an
> echo ... 'Hell, I just ain't came,' he kept saying. What was there for him to
> come on to?[35]

For the counter-culture, irrespective of one's position on the barricades,
this third Isle of Wight was another of those points that mark the end – or at
least its beginning. Woodstock may have promoted itself as three days of peace
and love, IOW III could not. The numbers had grown too many, the hip capitalists, who however self-declaredly hip remained ultimately capitalistic, were
too keen on profit; the stars were still stars, as cocooned, as élitist, for the most
part as blithely uncaring of their fans as the most hidebound dinosaur of the
world of 'legitimate' show business. As Alan Marcuson of *Friends*, who had
been busted by the ever-zealous police as he drove the magazine's van off the
ferry (busts were frequent, with instant justice: £40 or thirty days; Marcuson
paid up), told the *Sunday Telegraph*: 'They aren't human events any more.
People go along as audience. Extras in someone else's movie.' Anthony
Haden-Guest, writing his piece – 'Was This the End of Rocktopia? Peace and
Love Becomes Hippie Capitalism' – talked of 'Stalag Woodstock'.[36]

Charles Shaar Murray, who a few months earlier had been helping edit
'Schoolkids' *Oz*', despaired with all the intensity of a shattered teenage
crush. He blamed not Hendrix, but the overall atmosphere, be it the rapacious
promoters or the mindlessly anarchic revolutionaries. As for the underground

press, who put out a regular news-sheet for the duration, they seemed far too
ambivalent, enjoying the privileges of the press enclosure (although that too
would be 'liberated' by the end) while touting the glories of Desolation Row.

> People would be standing up to get a better view, then go down because a
> full can of Coke caught them in the back of the head. Also there was the
> Jean-Jacques Lebel wing: storm the barricades, music should be free! I got
> the impression that they didn't want the music to be free, they just wanted to
> disrupt the event, and I thought they were less than honest about their mo-
> tives. The vibes were so bad at the Isle of Wight that Hendrix came on stage
> and couldn't do anything. Pretty good by anyone else's standards, but for
> Hendrix it was dreadful. I got quite upset, because I was very stoned, and I
> went up to Richard [Neville] in tears and said: 'You realise this thing's over.'
> I felt: fuck all this brotherhood shit, there were people getting concussed just
> standing up to get a better view and getting in someone's way. For me that
> was the beginning of the end of hippie. I'd been to the Woodstock movie,
> read all the stupid books and I thought life could be an endless free rock festi-
> val. At the Isle of Wight I realised that it couldn't be and that it was dishonest
> to carry on claiming that it was feasible. I had bought the whole package, as
> much as I could swallow. It had just seemed so exciting.[37]

For the next few years, indeed for the next few decades, the Isle of Wight
would provide the basic model of the paying festival. The ticket prices might
be higher, the catering might be better, the merchandising more sophisticated
and security more iron-clad, but today's Reading or Glastonbury are not that
far removed, whatever the different trappings of the Nineties version of
counter-cultural requirements. But the Isle of Wight was not the only way to
go. Two months earlier, from 21–23 June, the counter-culture had made a stab
at its own festival: Phun City. No capitalists, hip or otherwise, no international
megastars, no bullshit. Phun City may have started out as a money-making effort, but such hopes were soon abandoned. If the Isle of Wight set the pattern
for the pricey get-togethers that followed, then Phun City, in its anarchic freedoms, can be seen as the first of the free festivals.

The initial idea was to run a benefit for *IT*, whose legal fees for the
'Males' small-ads trial had been considerable. The problem was that *IT* itself
was thus hardly in a position to mount such an event, however limited it
might be. They had, at a generous estimate, 2/9d. Led by Mick Farren they
tried Alexandra Palace and parks and football fields and movie studios but
they all wanted money. At which point Farren suggested: 'Why don't we
have a rock festival in a field?'

> To do this one has to know a farmer and I knew a farmer and we said, 'Will
> you rent us your field?' and he said, 'Sure'. And then we had a field, which
> was our first asset. It was just outside Worthing, in a village called Clapham
> which was where I grew up and this was the horrible vengeance I took on

these bumpkins. Then we started parlaying the field into various other things and we got a caterer who gave us an advance and we got an enormously wealthy dope dealer who gave us some money and we started generating money. We started running up credit on the bill, the attractions. We were bringing the MC5 over, which was quite a radical idea and other bands came in and then we hit the crunch: we had to set up this rock festival. We actually contacted everybody in the world who had light shows and inflatables and odd towers that they'd stolen from a Rolling Stones concert and as much of that stuff as possible was erected but it required massive amounts of money so we eventually went to Ronan O'Rahilly and Ronan started sort of paying the bills. And brought down a huge film unit, and Friday night there was a rock festival.

It did get very strange. I was literally raising money while down at the site they were there waiting to pay off the scaffolding man. But eventually it came. Meanwhile 2,000 hippies had moved down to this little clump of woods that was at the side of the field and had built Narnia in there. Except that they were recalcitrant and nasty and there were some kind of ugly rumblings and they were going to have their own festival. Anyway in the middle of the night I turned up and went into the woods with various people carrying axe handles and I made a long speech – 'Listen motherfuckers this festival is going to be and I don't want no shit' – and they all cheered.

At that point we'd decided that the bands weren't going to be paid and that the money wasn't going to be collected because what we weren't ever going to be able to do was put up security fences to get the money. Then after we'd filled the hippies with revolutionary spirit we went up the local pub and filled ourselves with more commercial spirit. Then I stayed awake for a week. It was great fun at times and at one time I wanted to shoot myself, telling all these bands we weren't going to pay them. Saturday night when the MC5 played was really quite magical. It was a nice feeling to have created all that. It definitely wasn't Woodstock, it was much more peculiar. There was William Burroughs wandering about with his tape recorder, doing instant cutups. It rained most of the time. Later on it ended and the stage sagged down with Mungo Jerry and 900 other people and it was over. The next morning the police brutality squad came in and beat everybody up. I wasn't there by then, because they were chasing me all over Worthing because I had to tidy up various things and pay people for stuff . . . We got the fuck out of town and never went back. It didn't seem very prudent – they wanted to put somebody in jail. And no money was made from this benefit, absolutely none. We ended up with 2/9d as well.[38]

The locals were satisfactorily outraged. The rector sent the *Daily Telegraph* his on-the-spot revelations. Psychedelic music until four or five a.m., drug taking 'hardly concealed', naked men dancing to an 'orgy of music' in front of parents and children, the police openly called 'pigs', local girls taken into the neighbouring woods for love-making . . . When would the government act? he demanded, and suggested, in a little bit of personal sedition, that were they to fail to answer the prayers of the 'multitudes', those same multitudes might perhaps consider withholding their annual taxes.

'Carnage!' screamed the *Friends* headline, and added 'Phun City Rave: But Then It Was Chaos'. Aside from the bands, whose attitude to Farren's withdrawal of funds was quite admirable (other than in the ironic case of Free who immediately packed up and vanished before playing their set), the whole festival was as near the much vaunted counter-cultural togetherness as could be imagined. The Hell's Angels, who had always extended a degree of grudging friendship to *IT*, dealt with any potential rip-offs by the caterers (vastly overstocked in the expectations of 30,000 fans) by simply ripping them off first. Their tent was cut open, supplies 'liberated' and turned over to the contingent from *Friends* magazine, who concocted a vast stew. On Jeff Dexter's announcing this to the audience the cooks were amazed to see the entire audience seized as one by some seismic lurch as they stood, then began moving, ever faster, across the arena and towards the food. Dexter was also involved in a more contentious moment: the local drug squad had carefully mingled with the crowd, ostensibly in plain clothes but as ever all too obvious. Dexter, who had spotted a pair from the stage, announced their presence to the assembled hippies. A vast cordon formed round the police, encircling them with dancing, jeering freaks who climaxed this psychedelic war-dance by dragging off the hapless 'pigs' and tying them to nearby trees. As Farren noted, they would take a brutal revenge, returning the next day *en masse*, entering the woods where dozens of freaks were still encamped and, with a mere three minutes' warning, smashing their way through tents and benders, beating and destroying as they drove the hippies out.

In a way, for those who seek symbols, it was Phun City, not the Isle of Wight, that proved the 'end of rocktopia'. And not just of rocktopia but of the larger hippie ideal. Like the underground itself it had been capable of a brief period of unanimity, of a genuine alternative society, but for how long? The forces of authority, rebuffed and even humiliated, were never vanquished. At Phun City and in the larger arena, they would regroup, and when they returned would smash without reserve the new society that had been, so optimistically, but in the end so impotently created.

Aftermath

It was the best of times, it was the worst of times, but it was our time, and we owned them with our youth, our energy, our good will, our edginess. So let's party.
Ed Sanders *Tales of Beatnik Glory* 1990

So, Alfie, what *was* it all about? Did the earth, or even the streets of London, move? Was it just a gaudy flash in a Le Creuset pan, a middle-class chat-fest with wonderful background music and a few trips around the psychic bay? We have lived for so long with the Tories' (and now New Labour's) 'big lie', portraying the era as some kind of amoral hell on earth that it has become, as such lies of course intend, almost impossible to discern the reality and isolate it from the clouding myth. Looking back, two strands seem discernible: one is a short-lived, but vibrant period in which the country escaped its usual domination by the hierarchy of class and deference, and the other, still resonant today, is the onset of a degree of social democratisation, bringing to the mass what had hitherto been the exclusive property of the élite.

The 'underground', the 'alternative society' and the 'counter-culture', three synonyms, but in a way they reflect the fate of the movement for which they all three served as shorthand. If an underground summons up visions of secretive revolutionaries plotting behind closed and hidden doors, then no such thing existed in Sixties Britain. One might make an exception for the Angry Brigade, but they, paradoxically, had little time for what they dismissed as the meaningless world of middle-class revolt. Otherwise, who could have been less clandestine than the relentlessly self-publicising Nevilles, Farrens or Haynes. For those who called for a 'revolution' in the traditional sense, there would be no satisfaction. The energies released in 1968 would decline rather than intensify. Those primarily middle-class activists would for the most part fade back into the conventional woodwork. The miners would break the Heath government in 1974, but theirs was a different, older movement. For all the turbulence of '68, there was no class war. The uprising, as many have noticed, was one not of the oppressed, but of the privileged. The brief alliance of students and workers in Paris was an anomaly; it was never echoed in the UK. The question in the Sixties often was: how far can you push the boundaries? When the answer came – so far and definitely no further – the ranks thinned fast.

As for an alternative society: there were, undoubtedly, a number of institutions that paralleled the mainstream: the underground press, the Arts Lab, a variety of clubs, but it is in the world of what one US commentator christened as 'Das Hip Kapital' that the major players thrived. The small beginnings of the Sixties would graduate, under the guidance of such figures as Richard Branson or Tony Elliott, and later in a de-*Oz*ified Felix Dennis, into substantial fortunes. What was the preserve of a tiny minority in the Sixties

has become part and parcel of mass culture. *Time Out*'s listings, once requiring but a fortnightly update and appearing on a single, folded sheet, have
flourished as that kind of alternative moved inexorably into the mainstream.
What is the chain of Body Shops but those tiny 'natural products' stalls at the
unfashionable end of Portobello or tucked away in the Kensington Market,
writ internationally large. Rock 'n' roll, once so threatening, has become as
stolid and safe – for all its synthetic, manufactured 'rebels' – as the blue-chip
companies to which so much of the business is tied. As the writer Fred
Goodman has observed, 'The question is no longer "Will rock 'n' roll change
the world?" but "How did the world change rock 'n' roll?"'[1] That said, it
wasn't so much the world as the hippies themselves. The swift trajectory of
punk from (briefly) shocking novelty to merchandising opportunity showed
just how well the freaks had learnt the game, and adopted it to their own requirements. Hip consumerism has become mass consumerism and the seeds
of change that emerged in the period have come to dominate the modern
world, from the ageing baby boomers who were there at the start, right down
through successive age groups.

The word which seems most pertinent then is counter-culture. If there
was any revolution in the Sixties then it was a social or 'cultural revolution'.
Where the political revolution failed because of the limitations of its essentially bourgeois personality, the cultural/social one succeeded for the very
same reasons. The demands of the middle-class 'revolutionaries' may be dismissed as selfish – self-expression gibes badly with ideological purities – but
their development can be seen across the society that has developed since. It
may ultimately have been thanks not to some cabal of toking hippies, but to a
Home Secretary whose own taste ran rather to vintage claret, that the great
legacy of the Sixties is the huge expansion of personal choice. Rejecting the
stifling institutions of traditional society, the counter-culture pushed for
new freedoms in the arts, in personal expression, in the concept of family,
and above all in sexuality. Battered by AIDS, mocked by 'post-feminism',
the gender politics that began evolving as the decade ended remain utterly
central, the other, non-commercial legacy of the period. The revolution of
the left, old or new, did not emerge – the forces of the *status quo*, briefly dis-
countenanced, closed ranks and hit back, with increasing intolerance as the
Seventies moved on. The revolution that took as its slogan 'the personal is
political' is still underway. It may have been, as some would suggest, a revolution within a narrow Anglo-American cultural narcissism, but that, for
better or worse, is still the dominant discourse.

It seems, and it has been the intention of this book to promote such a
theory, that for a brief time the country – or at least its younger, more
liberal-minded citizens – basked in a degree of self-confidence that it had
rarely enjoyed. The aftermath of a war may promote substantial feelings of
pride, but for all but the blindly jingoistic it is a pride tinged with sorrow.

The Second World War, less cruelly attritional, at least in British corpses, than its predecessor, heralded an enormous social change, but the optimism was submerged in the grim struggle of a near-bankrupt country, plunged into necessary austerity. The Labour landslide of 1945 failed to create the desired New Jerusalem: instead the Tories returned and for all the thirteen years of 'misrule', could still claim that, if only on material grounds (the grounds that as ever satisfy the vast majority of voters) they had brought home a better world. It is hard to deny the increased prosperity, and it was that prosperity, vilified though it was, that underpinned what has been defined as 'the Sixties', whether as portrayed by 'Swinging London' or by the 'alternative society'.

As I suggested in my introduction, what the Sixties represent above all is a period of 'growing up', a period when so many of the old hierarchical givens were, momentarily it would turn out, tossed aside. The idea that Nanny might have taken a decade off offered her charges an unrivalled opportunity to stand up for themselves. Aided by a visionary Home Secretary, who turned his office's usual function – repression, narrow-mindedness, conservatism – on its head, the country gained a level of freedom that had never been vouchsafed before. For a while, for a change, an infantilised population, subject to a range of social constraints that had long been abandoned in many of the disdained countries of Europe, took enormous strides forward. It was, of course, quite ludicrous that in the mid-twentieth century a country might be restricted as to its reading and viewing matters, that a sixteenth-century court official could determine the nation's choice of plays, that sexuality and sexual choice was deemed so terrifying that it must be hedged about with laws which had no justification other than in myth and superstition. It was time for change, and change came, to a substantial and lasting extent.

The Sixties can be seen both as determining the progress of the last part of the century, and at the same time as the last gasp of another, much older, world. Culturally the period represents the climax of the modernist dream that was launched at the turn of this century and which in turn could find its roots in the Romantics of the turn of the previous one. It was perhaps the last era when a belief in open-ended progress still held sway, a belief that the social and economic graph would maintain its upward movement. Hindsight renders such optimism naïve, but one cannot underestimate the extent to which what would now be termed the feelgood factor permeated so much of society.

It could not, of course, last. Humankind, it would appear, really cannot bear too much reality, and while some might see an unfettered world as one of infinite possibility, many more saw only an abyss of nameless horror. As the Sixties turned into the Seventies it appeared that freedom had proved too much. People preferred the rules, preferred, as would become patently clear, Nanny's grim strictures, her 'cruel to be kind' philosophising, her mix of menacing moral tales and nationalist fantasies that had not held water for half a century. Marcuse's repressive tolerance has not vanished, it has merely become smarter, its spin doctors more subtle, its damage limitation more acute. People seem to want to be told how to live. Being given options, being offered their own choice was too much. Modern democracy creates as suffocating a prison as does open totalitarianism, the difference being that the walls are so distant that we can forget them; occasionally we even delude ourselves that there are no walls at all.

People for a while had not 'known their place'; then Thatcher, lower middle-class to her very chromosomes, rushed forward to reclaim the *status quo*. Destroy the universities and grammar schools, the source of all that liberal thought, destroy London, the great sinful swinging wen, destroy wit, sophistication, the belief that adults should and could be treated as such. Bring back 'values' (but whose values, one might ask) and smash 'cultural relativism', an ostensibly egalitarian attitude to life which supposedly demolished hierarchy then and still serves as a bugaboo for those whose vision of the period is wholly negative. (Its successor, post-modernism, was already appearing in the period, especially in architecture and art, but the Sixties were highly conscious of the received past, for all that it served as a platform for quite contradictory theories. The post-modernism that has informed the last twenty years is an ultimately plagiaristic form of creativity, a mix 'n' match recycling of periods of real originality, as if no one has the energy or talent for genuine advance.)

'If the Sixties were truly "about" anything, it was the notion of a decisive shift of power away from its traditional centres and towards people who had been historically excluded from any significant degree of control over their own circumstances and history'[2] The succeeding decades have seen a desperate struggle for a return to 'normalcy'. Back to knowing one's place, back to all the repressed appurtenances of a dull, conformist petit-bourgeois fear. A country that for a while had looked outward, buried once more beneath the terror of its own fantasies, all bolstered by a heritage culture based on a version of Anglocentric history that would have seemed excessive in the Victorian era. And underpinning so much was the most mythical narrative: the bad old days. The Jew is our misfortune, intoned Hitler, and repeated *ad nauseam* it came to be believed. Thus for Thatcher and her cohorts the Sixties were Britain's misfortune – and everything they represented was due for extinction.

The campaign against the Sixties, so beloved of the Tory and now New Labour governments, is no more than censorship writ large and extra-paranoid, the fruit, like all censorship, of fear. The supposed desire to save the world from its baser instincts, so touted by the apologists of the New Right, and more recently by the prigs and puritans who represent the current hegemony, is nonsense. The urge to save the world, as has been observed, is rarely other than the disguised desire to rule it. Nor is Conservatism the sole culprit. What could be more symptomatic of Nineties Britain than the tsunami of sentimental pap that followed hard on the death of 'the people's

Princess' Diana, promoting yet more Disneyfied fantasies of this supposedly 'softer, kinder, less deferential' country; a country in which those who dared venture a sceptical word faced near-universal opprobrium and possibly a fist lashed out 'for Britain'.

Norman Mailer, writing about the twentieth century, has noted how often the reverberations that follow are out of all proportion to the presumed smallness of the original event. Thus so much of what has followed, especially since 1979, has been a reaction to a fantasy of the Sixties as the fount of all evil. Reactions differ as to the age of those reacting. The period has been scapegoated by the older reactionaries who seem to have believed (in hindsight) all that hippie sloganeering. To them it really was a world of 'dope, revolution and fucking in the streets'. Gore Vidal once noted that 'law and order' is simply a codeword for 'Get the niggers'; similarly 'the Sixties', in some mouths, means no more than 'Get the liberals'. Their younger peers, the bright young twenty- and thirtysomethings are equally disdainful. To them the period smacks of weakness, of airy-fairy, wishy-washiness, of an ascendancy of the cranks. The question remains: how much is this pose, how much belief? Are the Nineties simply the Sixties in post-modernist drag? Were the bright young things of the 1980s and early 1990s any more genuinely committed to reaction than were the bulk of the hippies (rather than the members of the New Left and its acolytes) genuinely committed to 'revolution'? Had their roles been reversed in time, would each have taken the other's position, their impetus not ideology but that age-old desire (and since the Sixties, duty too) to *épater les parents*?

Everyone's youth is of course a golden age; those who grew up in the Sixties are moving past fifty now: how can they not look back with nostalgia? (Those who took part, that is; it is of course those who failed to come to the party who have subsequently taken their revenge.) At the same time there is much to criticise. While this book is a deliberate reaction to the smears of the last two decades, it has attempted to show the foolishness alongside the good. Much of what went on was élitist, hedonistic and solipsistic. The belief that the world could, should and above all would be changed was all too often a substitute for actually getting on with changing it. What lay on the other side was non-specific, other than for the manifestoed ideologues, but the trip was half the fun.

Not everyone, then and now, believes the concept of youth as a social powerhouse to be a wholly positive development. But it was a genuine novelty, and dominates the period, as it has the decades that have followed. Cyril Connolly's theory of 'perpetual adolescence' – which he had envisaged as the perquisite of Eton-educated exquisites – became mass fodder, one more aspect of the social democratisation that typifies the era. And again that democratisation can be seen in the way the young, mainly middle-class, adopted what had hitherto been the perspective of the upper and upper-middle class:

the move to stand outside mass society. For all the pious intonations of a revolution, the proles were almost invisible, other than as rock stars or drug dealers. What confused outsiders, however, was that just as the counter-culture took on the 'stand-aside' privileges of their 'betters', they chose to embody their revolt in the language of the working class.

The dream is over, to quote John Lennon. It has been for twenty-five years, but the dreamers are still alive. For the veterans the problem has always been what comes next. As Nik Cohn, in the music context, asked, 'When you've made your million, when you've cut your monsters, when your peak has been passed . . . what happens next? What about the fifty years before you die?'[3] A question echoed by the French critic Jean Baudrillard who notes, 'If I were asked to characterise the present state of affairs, I would describe it as "after the orgy". The orgy in question was the moment when modernity exploded upon us, the moment of liberation in every sphere. Political liberation, sexual liberation, liberation of the forces of production, liberation of the forces of destruction, women's liberation, children's liberation, liberation of unconscious drives, liberation of art. The assumption of all models of representation, as of all models of anti-representation . . . We have pursued every avenue in the production and effective overproduction of objects, signs, messages, ideologies and satisfactions. Now everything has been liberated, the chips are down, and we find ourselves faced collectively with the big question: WHAT DO WE DO NOW THE ORGY IS OVER?[4]

Tomorrow, fortunately or otherwise, never knows.

Selected Bibliography

Abrams, Steve *Hashish Fudge: Soma and the Wootton Report* (n.p., pamphlet 1993)

Aftel, Mandy *Death of a Rolling Stone: The Brian Jones Story* (London, Sidgwick & Jackson 1982)

Aitken, Jonathan *The Young Meteors* (London, Secker & Warburg 1967)

Ali, Tariq *Street Fighting Years: An Autobiography of the Sixties* (London, Collins 1987)

Annan, Noel *Our Age* (London, Weidenfeld & Nicolson, London 1990)

Armytage, WHG *Heavens Below: Utopian Experiments in England 1560-1960* (London, RKP 1961)

Baudrillard, Jean *The Transparency of Evil* (London, Verso 1993)

Berke, Joseph (ed.) *Counter Culture: The Creation of an Alternative Society* (London, Peter Owen 1969)

Berridge, Virginia 'Drugs and Social Policy: The establishment of Drug Control in Britain 1900-30' (*British Journal of Addiction* 79 [1984], 17-29)

Berridge, Virginia *Opium and the people: Opiate Use in 19th century England* (London, Yale U.P. 1987)

Berridge, Virginia 'The Origins of the English Drug "Scene" ' (*Medical History* 1988, 32:51-64)

Blanchard Sean & Matthew J. Atha 'Indian Hemp and the Dope Fiends of Old England: A Sociopolitical History of Cannabis and the British Empire 1840-1928' (San Francisco, Last Gasp 1994)

Bockris, Victor *Keith Richards: The Biography* (New York, Poseidon Press, 1992)

Bogdanor, Vernon & Robert Skidelsky *The Age of Affluence 1951-64* (London, Macmillan 1970)

Booker, Christopher *The Neophiliacs* (London, Collins 1969)

Boycott, Rosie *A Nice Girl Like Me* (London, Chatto & Windus 1984)

Bradbury, Malcolm 'All Dressed Up and Nowhere To Go' (1962)

Brecher, Edward M. et al (eds.) *Licit & Illicit Drugs: The Consumers Union Report* (Boston, Mass., Little Brown 1972)

Campbell, John *Roy Jenkins: A Biography* (London, Weidenfeld & Nicolson 1983)

Camus, Albert *The Rebel* (London, Penguin 1962)

Carr, Gordon *The Angry Brigade* (London, Gollancz 1975)

Caute, David *Sixty Eight: The Year of the Barricades* (London, Hamish Hamilton 1988)

Charters, Ann (ed.) *The Penguin Book of the Beats* (London, Penguin Books 1992)

Christie, Stuart *The Christie File* (Orkney, Cienfuegos Press 1980)

Clay, John *R.D. Laing: A Divided Self* (London, Hodder & Stoughton 1996)

Cohen, Stanley *Folk Devils & Moral Panics: The Creation of the Mods and Rockers* (London, MacGibbon & Kee 1972)

Cohn, Nik *Awopbopaloobopalopbamboom* (London, Paladin 1969)

Cohn, Nik *Today There Are No Gentlemen* (London, Weidenfeld & Nicolson 1971)

Connolly, Ray (ed.) *In the Sixties* (London, Pavilion 1995)

Cooper, David (ed.) *The Dialectics of Liberation* (London, Penguin 1967)

De Quincy, Thomas *Confessions of an English Opium-eater* (*London Magazine*, 1822)

Eisen, Jonathan (ed.) *The Age of Rock* (New York, Vintage 1969)

Eisen, Jonathan (ed.) *The Age of Rock 2* (New York, Vintage 1970)

Eisen, Jonathan (ed.) *Twenty-Minute Fandangos and Forever Changes* (New York, Vintage 1971)

Elliott, Michael *The Day Before Yesterday* (New York, Simon & Schuster 1996)

Fabian, Jenny & Johnny Byrne *Groupie* (London, NEL 1969)

Fabian, Jenny & Johnny Byrne *A Chemical Romance* (London, NEL 1971)

Faithfull, Marianne *Faithfull* (London, Michael Joseph 1994)

Farren, Mick & Edward Barker *Watch Out Kids!* (London, Open Gate 1972)

Faulks, Sebastian *The Fatal Englishman* (London, Hutchinson, 1996)

Fiedler, Leslie 'The New Mutants' in *Partisan Review* Fall 1965

Fountain, Nigel *Underground* (London, Pluto Press 1988)

Fraser, Ronald *1968* (London, Chatto & Windus 1988)

Friedenberg, Edgar Z., 'Adolescence as a Social Problem', in Howard S. Becker (ed.) *Social Problems: A Modern Approach* (New York, 1966)

'Fury, Nick' *Agro* (London, Sphere 1971)

Gibbs, David (ed.) David Hillman & Harry Peccinotti (compilers) *Nova*: THE style bible of the 60s and 70s (London, Pavilion 1993)

Goode, Eric & Nachman Ben-Yehuda, *Moral Panics: The Social Construction of Deviance* (Oxford, Blackwell 1994)

Goodman, Arnold *Tell Them I'm On My Way* (London, Chapmans 1993)

Goodman, Fred *The Mansion on the Hill* (London, Jonathan Cape 1997)

Gould, Tony *Inside Outsider: The Life and Times of Colin MacInnes* (London, Chatto & Windus 1983)

Grant, Linda *Sexing the Millennium* (London, Harper Collins 1993)

Green, Jonathon *Days in the Life* (London, Heinemann 1988)

Green, Jonathon *The Encyclopedia of Censorship* (New York, Facts on File 1990)

Green, Shirley *Rachman* (London, Michael Joseph 1979)

Greene, Sir Hugh Carleton *The Third Floor Front: A View of Broadcasting in the Sixties* (London, The Bodley Head 1969)

Greer, Germaine *The Female Eunuch* (London, McGibbon & Kee 1970)

Halberstam, David *The Fifties* (New York, Villard Books 1993)

Hamblett, Charles & Jane Deverson, *Generation X* (London, Tandem Books 1964)

Haynes, Jim *Thanks for Coming* (London, Faber 1984)

Hayter, Alethea *Opium and the Romantic Imagination* (London, Faber 1968)

Herman, Gary *The Who* (London, Studio Vista 1971)

Hewison, Robert *In Anger* (London, Methuen 1981)

Hewison, Robert *Too Much* (London, Methuen 1986)

Hewison, Robert *Culture and Consensus* (London, Methuen 1996)

Hoggart, Richard *The Uses of Literacy* (London, Chatto & Windus 1957)

Hoggart Richard *The Way We Live Now* (London, Chatto & Windus 1995)

Hollingshead, Michael *The Man Who Turned on the World* (London, Blond and Briggs 1973)

Home, Stuart, ed. *What is Situationism? A Reader* (Edinburgh, AK Press 1996)

Home, Stuart, *The Assault on Culture: Utopian Currents from Lettrisme to Class War* (Edinburgh, AK Press 1991)

Hughes, Robert *The Shock of the New* (rev. edn. London, Thames & Hudson 1991)

Humphrey, Derek *Police Power & Black People* (London, Panther Books 1972)

Irving, Clive, Ron Hall & Jeremy Wallington *Scandal '63: A Study of the Profumo Affair* (London, Heinemann 1963)

Jenkins, Roy *The Labour Case* (London, Penguin 1959)

Jeffrey-Poulter, Stephen *Peers, Queers and Commons: The Struggle for Gay Law Reform from 1950 to the Present* (London, Routledge 1991)

Kerouac, Jack *On the Road* (New York, Viking 1956)

Kohn, Marek *Dope Girls* (London, Lawrence & Wishart, 1992)

Leary, Timothy *The Politics of Ecstasy* (London, Paladin 1970)

LeDain et al. *The Non-Medical Use of Drugs: Interim Report of the Canadian Government's Commission of Inquiry* (London, Penguin 1971)

Lee, Martin A. & Bruce Shlain *Acid Dreams The Complete Social History of LSD, the Sixties and Beyond* (New York, Grove Press 1985, 1992)

Lester, Anthony (ed.) *Roy Jenkins Essays and Speeches* (London, Collins 1967)

Levin, Bernard *The Pendulum Years* (London, Jonathan Cape 1970)

Lippard, Lucy R. *Pop Art* (London, Thames & Hudson 1966)

MacCabe, Colin *Performance* (London, BFI 1998)

MacInnes, Colin *Absolute Beginners* (London, MacGibbon & Kee 1959)

MacInnes, Colin *England, Half-English* (London, MacGibbon & Kee 1961)

Mailer, Norman 'The White Negro' in New York *Dissent* 1957; reprint in *The Penguin Book of The Beats* (London, Penguin 1993)

Mailer, Norman *Advertisements for Myself* (London, André Deutsch 1961)

Mairowitz, David Zane & Peter Stanshill *BAMN* (London, Penguin 1971)

Maitland, Sarah *Very Heaven: Looking Back at the Sixties* (London, Virago 1988)

Mandelkau, Jamie *Buttons: The making of a President* (London, Sphere 1971)

Marcus, Greil *Lipstick Traces: a Secret History of the Twentieth Century* (London, Secker & Warburg 1989)

Marsh, Dave *Before I Get Old: The Story of The Who* (London, Plexus 1983)

Martin, Bernice *A Sociology of Contemporary Cultural Change* (Blackwell, Oxford 1981)

McInnerney, Jay *The Last of the Savages* (London, Bloomsbury 1996)

Melly, George *Owning Up* (London, Weidenfeld & Nicolson 1965)

Melly, George *Revolt into Style* (London, Allen Lane/The Penguin Press, 1970)

Miles, Barry *Ginsberg* (London, Viking Books 1990)

Miles, Barry *McCartney* (London, Secker & Warburg 1997)

Moraes, Henrietta *Henrietta* (London, Hamish Hamilton 1994)

Motion, Andrew *The Lamberts* (London, Chatto & Windus 1986)

Murray, Charles Shaar *Crosstown Traffic* (London, Faber & Faber 1989)

Naipaul, V.S. *The Return of Eva Peron with The Killings in Trinidad* (London, André Deutsch 1980)

Neville, Richard *Play Power* (London, Jonathan Cape 1970)

Neville Richard *Hippie Hippie Shake* (London, Bloomsbury 1995)

Nisbet, Robert 'Has Futurology a Future?' in *Encounter* Nov. 1972

Norman, Philip *Shout!: The True Story of the Beatles* (London, Elm Tree 1981)

Norman, Philip *The Stones* (London, Elm Tree 1984)

Norman, Philip *Everyone's Gone to the Moon* (London, Hutchinson 1995)

Nuttall, Jeff *Bomb Culture* (London, McGibbon & Kee 1968)

Obst, Linda Rosen (ed.) *The Sixties* (San Francisco, Rolling Stone Press 1977)

Osborne, John *Look Back in Anger* (London, Faber 1956)

Parssinen, Terry *Secret Passions, Secret Remedies: Narcotic Drugs in British Society 1820-1930* (Manchester, Manchester U.P. 1983)

Pimlott, Ben *Harold Wilson* (London, Harper Collins 1992)

Podhoretz, Norman 'The Know-Nothing Bohemians' in *Partisan Review* Spring 1958

Polan, Brenda 'Fab, Gear and Very Groovy' in *RA* magazine no. 31 special Pop Art issue Autumn 1991

Report on Cannabis to the Advisory Committee on Drug Dependence (The Wootton Report) (London, HMSO 1969)

Richards, Peter G. *Parliament & Conscience* (London, Allen & Unwin 1970)

Richardson, Perry (ed.) *The Early Stones: Legendary Photographs of a Band in the Making 1963-73* (London, Secker & Warburg 1995)

Rigby, Andrew *Communes in Britain* (London, RKP 1974)

Rigby, Andrew *Alternative Realities: a study of communes and their members* (London, RKP 1974)

Robertson, George 'The Situationist International: Its Penetration into British Culture' in *Block* no. 14, London 1988

Roszak, Theodore M. *The Making of a Counter-Culture* (London, Faber 1970)

St. Jorre, John de *The Good Ship Venus: The Erotic Voyage of the Olympia Press* (London, Hutchinson 1994)

Shepherd, Robert *Enoch Powell* (London, Hutchinson 1996)

Sinclair, Andrew *In Love and Anger – a view of the Sixties* (London, Sinclair-Stevenson 1994)

Sinclair, Iain *Lights Out for the Territory* (London, Granta Books 1997)

Spear, H.B. 'The History of the British Drug Scene' a paper given at St Anne's House, Soho on 27 Jan. 1970

Stone, C.J. *Fierce Dancing* (London, Faber 1996)

Sutherland, John *Offensive Literature: Decensorship in Britain 1960–82* (London, Junction Books 1982)

Tracy, Michael & David Morrison *Whitehouse* (London, Macmillan Press 1979)

Tynan, Kathleen *The Life of Kenneth Tynan* (London, Methuen 1988)

Vague, Tom *Anarchy in the UK: The Angry Brigade* (Edinburgh, AK Press 1997)

Vidal, Gore *Palimpsest* (London, André Deutsch 1995)

Webb, James *The Occult Establishment* (La Salle, Ill., Open Court Books 1976)

Weeks, Jeffrey *Sex, Politics & Society* (London, Longman 2nd edn 1989)

Weeks, Jeffrey *Sexuality and Its Discontents* (London, Routledge 1985)

Wesker, Arnold 'The Secret Reins' 'Centre Fortytwo' in *Encounter*, March 1962

Wesker, Arnold *Fears of Fragmentation* (London, Jonathan Cape 1970)

Wheen, Francis *Tom Driberg: His Life and Indiscretions* (London, Chatto & Windus 1990)

Wheen, Francis *The Sixties* (London, Century Publishing 1982)

Whitcomb, Ian *Rock Odyssey: A Musician's Chronicle of the Sixties* (NY, Doubleday 1983)

Whitehead, Peter 'Wholly Communion' (Lorrimer Films Ltd 1966)

Williams, Raymond *Communications* (Harmondsworth, Penguin 1962, rev. ed. 1975)

Wilmut, Roger *From Fringe to Flying Circus* (London, Methuen 1980)

Wolfe, Tom 'The Noonday Underground' in *Mid-Atlantic Man* (London, Weidenfeld & Nicolson   1969)

X, Michael *From Michael de Freitas to Michael X* (London, André Deutsch 1968)

Young, Nigel *An Infantile Disorder? The Crisis and Decline of the New Left* (London, RKP 1977)

Ziegler, Philip *Diana Cooper* (London, Hamish Hamilton 1981)

Frendz
Friends
Gandalf's Garden
Gay News
Ink
IT
New Left Review
Oz
Spare Rib

Notes

Chapter 1.
1. MacInnes, *Absolute*, pp. 10-11.
2. Bradbury, p. 185.
3. ibid., p. 181-2.
4. ibid., p. 181.
5. ibid., p. 183.
6. ibid., p. 184.
7. ibid.
8. MacInnes, *England*, p. 47.
9. Roszak, p. 30.

Chapter 2.
1. MacInnes, *Absolute*, p.9.
2. Cohn, *Gentlemen*, pp. 29-30.
3. Bogdanor, p. 304.
4. ibid., p. 301.
5. q. in Bogdanor, p. 301.
6. Cohn, *Gentlemen*, p. 28.
7. Friedenberg, pp. 37-8.
8. Bogdanor, p. 317.
9. ibid., p. 300.
10. Cohn, *Gentlemen*, p. 33.
11. Melly, *Revolt*, p. 50.
12. ibid.
13. q. in Bogdanor, p. 312.

Chapter Three.
1. q. in *Queen* 22/5/62.
2. Bogdanor & Skidelsky, p. 12.
3. ibid.
4. Nuttall, p. 21.
5. q. in Annan, p. 81.
6. q. in Annan, p. 75.
7. address to CND
8. Collins, *Faith Under Fire* (1966) p. 298.
9. Green, *DITL*, p. 6.
10. q. in Bogdanor & Skidelsky, p. 232.
11. q. in Bogdanor & Skidelsky, p. 243.
12. Young, p. 26.
13. Nuttall, p. 55.
14. Green, *DITL*, p. 25.
15. unpub. interview for *DITL*.
16. Green, *DITL*, p. 24.
17. Widgery, *The Left in Britain*
18. Fraser, p. 30.
19. Young, p.28.

Chapter Four.
1. *Dissent*, 1957.
2. q. in Charters, p. xviii.
3. q. in Miles, p. 47.
4. q. in Miles, p. 47.
5. q. in Charters, p. xix.
6. q. in Charters, p. xix.
7. q. in Charters, p. xix
8. q. in Charters, p. xx.
9. Halberstam, p. 300.
10. *Dissent*, 1957.
11. ibid.
12. ibid.
13. Whitcomb, p. 244.
14. Halberstam, p. 295.
15. *Partisan Review* pp. 305-18.
16. Sinclair, *In Love* p. 18.
17. unpub. interview for *DITL*.
18. Green, *DITL*, p. 16.
19. unpub. interview for *DITL*.
20. Hewison, *In Anger*, p. 195.
21. Green, *DITL*, p. 8.
22. ibid.
23. *People*, 24/7/60.
24. *Observer*, 11/6/61.
25. Green, *DITL*, p. 16.
26. Webb, p. 433.
27. ibid.
28. Green, *DITL*, p. 23.
29. *Dissent*, 1957.

Chapter Five.
1. Green, *DITL*, p. 36.
2. MacInnes, *Absolute*, p. 66.
3. ibid.
4. Wolfe, *Mid-Atlantic*, p. 101.
5. Green, *DITL*, p. 38.
6. Wolfe, *Mid-Atlantic*, p. 104.
7. Cohn, *Gentlemen*, p. 66.
8. Nuttall, p. 33.
9. Melly, *Revolt*, p. 35-6.
10. Mandelkau, p. 21.
11. Cohen, p. 33.
12. Hamblett, p. 20.
13. *Daily Telegraph*, 31/8/65
14. Cohen, p. 191.
15. Marsh, p. 6.
16. Obst, p. 124.
17. Green, *DITL*, p. 48.
18. Cohen, p. 189.
19. Cohn, *Awopbop.*, p. 179.
20. Marsh, p. 188.

21.   copyright © 1965 Fabulous
      Music Ltd; copyright © 1965
      Seven Music Inc.

Chapter Six.
1.   Annan, p. 412.
2.   q. in Pimlott, p. 267.
3.   Pimlott, p. 266.
4.   ibid., p. 200.
5.   q. in Wheen, *Sixties*, p. 64.
6.   Pimlott, p. 320.
7.   Hewison, *Culture*, p. 105.
8.   Jenkins, p. 135.
9.   ibid., p. 136.
10.   ibid., pp. 136-7.
11.   ibid., p. 146.
12.   Weeks, *Sex*, p. 268.
13.   q. in Weeks, *Sex*, p. 238.
14.   Weeks, *Sex*, p. 250.
15.   Greene, p. 99.
16.   ibid., pp. 99-101.
17.   ibid., p. 103.
18.   ibid., p. 104.
19.   q. in Hewison, *Too Much*,
      p. 29.
20.   Wilmut, p. 60.
21.   Greene, pp. 133-4.
22.   Wilmut, p. 71.
23.   Greene, pp. 135-6.

Chapter Seven.
1.   Levin, p. 44.
2.   Wolfe, *Mid-Atlantic*, p. 106.
3.   Green, *DITL*, p. 86.
4.   q. in Aitken, pp. 270-1.
5.   Levin, p. 362.
6.   ibid.
7.   Grant, p. 88.
8.   q. in Maitland, pp. 37-8.
9.   MacInnes, *Absolute*, p. 212.
10.   Melly, *Revolt*, p. 146
11.   ibid, p. 147.
12.   ibid.
13.   *Guardian*, 4/12/65.
14.   *Guardian*, 10/10/67.
15.   Polan, p. 62.
16.   Maitland, p. 39.
17.   Green, *DITL*, p. 220.
18.   ibid., p. 220-1.
19.   Faithfull, pp. 78-80.
20.   Richardson, p. 22.
21.   Norman, *Moon*, p. 22.

22.   Levin, pp. 186-7.
23.   Green, *DITL*, pp. 90-1.
24.   Vidal, p. 270.
25.   Green, *DITL*, p. 90.
26   Polan, p. 62.

Chapter Eight.
1.   Green, *DITL*, p. 63.
2.   Melly, *Revolt*, p. 13.
3.   Hughes, p. 342.
4.   ibid. pp. 342-4.
5.   Green, *DITL*, pp. 32-3.
6.   ibid.
7.   Melly, *Revolt*, p. 11.
8.   Hughes, p. 346.
9.   Melly, *Revolt*. p. 103.
10.   Marsh, p. 168.
11.   Melly, *Revolt*. p. 103.
12.   q. in Marsh, p. 170.
13.   Marsh p. 170.
14.   Melly, *Revolt*, p. 133.

Chapter Nine.
1.   Ziegler, p. 55.
2.   De Quincey, p. 26.
3.   Berridge, 'Origins', p. 53.
4.   ibid., p. 56.
5.   Berridge, 'Drugs', p. 20.
6.   ibid., p. 24.
7.   Ziegler, pp. 54-5.
8.   Berridge, 'Origins', p. 62.
9.   *Daily Express*, 4/5/22.
10.   For the full story of the CIA's
      involvement in the world of LSD
      read Lee & Bruce (details in the
      Bibliography)
11.   q. in Lee & Shlain, p. 46.
12.   Huxley, *Moksha*, p. 42.
13.   q. in Lee & Shlain, p. 55.
14.   Lee & Shlain, p. 50.
15.   ibid., p. 51.
16.   Ginsberg, 'Lysergic Acid' in
      Kaddish (1959).
17.   q. in Lee & Shlain, p. 73.
18.   q. in Lee & Shlain, p. 75.
19.   q. in Lee & Shlain, p. 79.
20.   q. in Lee & Shlain, p. 81.
21.   Lee & Shlain, p. 81-2.
22.   q. in Lee & Shlain, p. 88.
23.   q. in Lee & Shlain, p. 96.

Chapter 10.
1. Murray, p. 20.
2. Weeks, *Sex*, p. 282.
3. Martin, p. 26.
4. Widgery, *Oz* 45 (1973).
5. Hazlitt, 'The Spirit of the Age' (1825).
6. Annan, p. 52.
7. ibid.
8. Marcuse, *One Dimensional Man*, p. i.
9. Arp, *Dadaland*, p. 234.
10. ibid.
11. Marcus, p. 207.
12. Hewison, *Too Much*, p. 149.
13. *New Statesman*, 19/1/68.
14. ibid., 12/1/68.
15. ibid., 6/1/68.
16. q. in Hewison, *Too Much*, p. 149-50.
17. Green, *DITL*, p. 167.

Chapter Eleven.
1. Mairowitz & Stanshill, p. 13.
2. Green, *DITL*, p. 50.
3. unpub. interview for *DITL*
4. unpub. interview for *DITL*
5. Melly, *Owning Up*, p. 222.
6. Green, *DITL*, p. 20.
7. ibid.
8. Haynes, p. 41.
9. Hewison, *Too Much*, p. 105.
10. Green, *DITL*, p. 116.
11. *Oxford English Dictionary*.
12. Nuttall, p. 127.
13. q. in Hewison, *Too Much*, p. 102.
14. unpub. interview for *DITL*
15. ibid., p. 58.
16. ibid., p. 60.
17. Nuttall, p. 235.
18. ibid. pp. 235-6.
19. Green, *DITL*, p. 60.
20. ibid., p. 59.
21. Nutall, p. 238.
22. Green, *DITL*, p. 66.
23. ibid., p. 68.
24. ibid., p. 66.
25. ibid., p. 71.
26. ibid., p. 72.
27. letter to JG 18/2/89.
28. Nuttall, pp. 192-3.

29. q. in Hewison, *Too Much*, p. 113.
30. unpub. interview for *DITL*.
31. Faithfull, pp. 25-6.
32. Green, *DITL*, p. 75.
33. ibid., p. 78.
34. ibid.
35. Norman, *Shout!*, p. 238.
36. Green, *DITL*, p. 83.

Chapter Twelve.
1. Neville, *Play*, p. 125.
2. Green, *DITL*, p. 115.
3. ibid., p. 114.
4. q. in Hewison, *Too Much*, p.19.
5. Green, *DITL*, p. 114.
6. *IT* 2, p. 2.
7. Green, *DITL*, p. 120.
8. q. in Hewison, *Culture*, p. 150.

Chapter Thirteen.
1. MacInnes, *Absolute*, pp. 48-49.
2. Green, *DITL*, p. 50.
3. ibid., p. 51.
4. ibid., p. 96.
5. ibid., p. 101.
6. Webb, p. 477.
7. Mairowitz & Stanshill, p.94.
8. unpub. interview for *DITL*.
9. q. in Berke, p. 239.
10. R. Elzey 'Founding an Anti-University' in Berke, p. 243.
11. q. in Hewison, *Too Much*, pp. 155-6.
12. Roszak, pp. 45-46.
13. ibid., p. 46.
14. Green, *DITL*, p. 169.
15. ibid., p. 170
16. Haynes, p. 193.
17. Green., *DITL*, p. 213.
18. Haynes, p. 154.
19. ibid., p. 153.
20. Green, *DITL*, p. 172.
21. unpub. interview for *DITL*.
22. Green, *DITL*, p. 420.
23. Haynes, p. 168.
24. q. in Haynes, p. 214.

Chapter Fourteen.
1.   copyright © Northern Songs,
      London
2.   Roszak, p. 172.
3.   q. in Wootton Report, p. 3.
4.   cited in Abrams, p. 9.
5.   Faithfull, p. 130.
6.   Bogdanor p. 327.
7.   Norman, *Stones*, p. 177.
8.   Faithfull, p. 160.
9.   Norman, *Stones*, p. 199
10.   Wheen, *Driberg*, p. 355.
11.   Abrams, p. 8.
12.   ibid., pp. 10-11.
13.   q. in Abrams, p. 14.
14.   Wootton, p.1.
15.   Abrams. p. 13.
16.   Wootton, pp. 6-7.
17.   ibid., pp. 16-17.
18.   ibid., p. 19.
19.   ibid., p. 20.
20.   ibid., p. 21.
21.   ibid.
22.   *Hansard*.
23.   *Daily Telegraph*, 29/1/69.
24.   Abrams, p. 21.
25.   Green, *DITL*, p. 192.
26.   ibid., p. 284.
27.   ibid.
28.   unpub. interview for *DITL*.
29.   unpub. interview for *DITL*.
30.   Leary, p. 87.
31.   Hollingshead, p. 150.
32.   ibid.
33.   ibid., p. 159.
34.   Green, *DITL*, p. 182.
35.   q. in Norman, *Shout!*, p. 289.
36.   Green, *DITL*, p. 181.
37.   q. in Lee & Shlain, p. 179.
38.   LeDain, p. 95.
39.   ibid., p. 97.
40.   Green, *DITL*, p. 184.
41.   ibid., p. 180.
42.   Clay, p. 79.
43.   ABC TV *New Tempo*:
      Stimulants.
44.   Leary, p. 98.
45.   ibid. pp. 94-5.
46.   ibid.
47.   *Sunday Telegraph*, 15/2/70.

Chapter Fifteen
1.   q. in Clay, p. 55.
2.   *IT* 59, 4-17/7/1969.
3.   Laing, *Politics*, p. 107.
4.   *Guardian*, 4/10/66.
5.   q. in Clay, p. 135.
6.   ibid.
7.   Maitland, p. 215.
8.   Clay, p. 96.
9.   unpub. interview for *DITL*.
10.   Green, *DITL*, p. 209.
11.   Clay, p. 132.
12.   q. in Clay, p. 139.
13.   Green, *DITL*, p. 436.

Chapter Sixteen.
1.   q. in Clay, p. 144.
2.   Hewison, *Culture*, p.148.
3.   Hewison, *Too Much*, p. 134.
4.   *Peace News*, 25/8/67.
5.   q. in Hewison, *Culture*, p.148.
6.   copyright © 1971 Fabulous
      Music; copyright © 1971 Reswot
      /Towser Tunes Inc.
7.   q. in Fraser, p. 144.
8.   ibid.
9.   Laing, *Politics*

Chapter Seventeen.
1.   Melly, *Revolt*, p. 107.
2.   *Sunday Telegraph*, 30/7/67.
3.   *News of the World*, 30/7/67.
4.   *Daily Sketch*, 22/7/67.
5.   *Daily Mail*, 23/9/67.
6.   *People*, 30/7/67.
7.   *New York Herald Tribune*,
      31/7/67.
8.   Green, *DITL*, p. 138.
9.   ibid., p. 131.
10.   ibid., p. 135.
11.   ibid.
12.   Farren, n.p.
13.   Green, *DITL*, p. 161.
14.   ibid., 163.
15.   ibid.
16.   *Observer*, 7/5/67.
17.   Green, *DITL*, p. 216.

Chapter Eighteen.
1.   *IT* 155, pp. 11-14.
2.   McInnerny, p. 105.
3.   unpub. interview for *DITL*.

4.   unpub. interview for *DITL*.
5.   *Daily Mirror*, 9/8/71.
6.   *Oz* 30, Oct. 1970.
7.   Green, *DITL*, p. 232.
8.   Martin, p. 217.
9.   ibid.
10. Norman, *Shout!*, p. 297.
11. Green, *DITL*, pp. 159-60.
12. Faithfull, p. 187.
13. ibid., pp. 187-8.
14. ibid., pp. 188.

Chapter Nineteen.
1.   Young, p. 310.
2.   Roszak, pp. 15-16.
3.   q. in Halberstam, p. 532.
4.   Camus, p. 19.
5.   q. in Hewison, *Culture*, p. 144.
6.   *Oz* 42, 5-6/72.
7.   Roszak, pp. 69-70.
8.   Hobsbawm, p. 253.
9.   IT 51; 28/2–13/3/69.
10. *Oz* 21.
11. *Oz* n.d.
12. Green, *DITL*, p. 257.
13. ibid., p. 129.
14. ibid., p. 128.

Chapter Twenty.
1.   Green, *DITL*, p. 247.
2.   Fraser, pp. 249-50.
3.   ibid., p. 254.
4.   *IT* 51, 28/2-13/3 1969.
5.   *Listener*, 20/01/69.
6.   Fraser, p. 255.
7.   Peter Weiss, *Marat*, Act 1:5.
8.   interview in *Rolling Stone*, 1970.
9.   *Independent on Sunday* 19/5/96.

Chapter Twenty-one.
1.   Ali, p. 51.
2.   ibid., p. 61.
3.   Green, *DITL*, pp. 244-5.
4.   ibid., pp. 242-3.
5.   *The Times*, 5/9/68.
6.   *Daily Telegraph*, 24/10/68.
7.   *People*, 27/10/68.
8.   *Sunday Telegraph*, 20/10/68.
9.   *New Statesman*, 4/10/68.

10. ibid.
11. Fraser, p. 251.
12. Christie, p. 174.
13. *Evening Standard*, 28/10/68.
14. *The Times*, 28/10/68.
15. Fraser, p. 253.

Chapter Twenty-two.
1.   *Times Literary Supplement*, 6/8/64.
2.   q. in Robertson, p. 115.
3.   q. in Robertson, p. 117.
4.   q. in Marcus, p. 176.
5.   q. in Carr, pp. 21-22.
6.   q. in ibid., pp. 22-3.
7.   q. in *Chronicle of the French Revolution* (1989), p. 347.
8.   q. in Robertson, p. 119.
9.   Green, *DITL*, pp. 252-5.
10. Christie, p. 227.
11. q. in *Daily Telegraph*, 2/12/71.
12. q. in Bunyan, *The Political Police in Britain*, (1977).
13. *King Mob Echo*, q. in Robertson, p. 122.
14. ibid.
15. Green, *DITL*, p. 185.
16. Robertson, pp. 124-5.
17. Christie, pp. 310-11.
18. *Sunday Times*, 10/12/72.
19. *Observer*, 10/12/72.
20. q. in Carr, p. 200.
21. q. in *Guardian*, 7/12/72.
22. q. in *Sunday Telegraph*, 27/1/71.
23. Christie, p. 245.
24. q. in Carr, p. 200.
25. q. in Carr, p. 203.
26. *Sun*, 7/12/72.

Chapter Twenty-three
1.   Green, *DITL*, p. 352.
2.   ibid, p. 10.
3.   ibid., p. 344.
4.   q. in Gould, p. 195.
5.   Naipaul, p. 35.
6.   ibid., p. 36.
7.   *Observer* n.d.
8.   *Friends*, 14/4/70.
9.   q. in Gould, p. 177.
10. *New Statesman*, 18/8/67.

11. Gould, p. 193.
12. *X*, p. 150.
13. Green, *DITL*, p.349.
14. q. in Shepherd, p. 324.
15 Shepherd, p. 345.
16. q. in Shepherd, p. 354.
17. q. in Shepherd, p. 365.
18. BBC-2 interview.

Chapter Twenty-four.
1. unpub. interview for *DITL*.
2. q. in Green, *Censorship*,
    p. 181.
3. q. in Halberstam, p. 287.
4. Grant, p. 57.
5. q. in Maitland, pp. 150–2.
6. q. in Weeks, *Sex*, p. 259.
7. Weeks, *Sex*, p. 259.
8. Richards, p. 98.
9. *Nova*, 9/69.
10. Pimlott, p. 285.
11. Levin, p. 62.
12. ibid.
13. Haynes, p. 217.
14. ibid., p. 218.
15. ibid., p. 223.
16. ibid.
17. unpub. interview for *DITL*.
18. Green, *DITL*, p. 422.
19. q. in Grant, p. 212.
20. Weeks, *Sex*, p. 288.

Chapter Twenty-five.
1. q. in Lester, pp. 108–9.
2. *Observer*, in 11/60.
3. q. in Hoggart, *The Way We
    Live*, p. 253.
4. q. in Hewison, *Culture*,
    p. 123.
5. q. in Richards, p. 124.
6. q. in Richards, p. 126.
7. 'West-End Apathy' by
    Kenneth Tynan, 1954.
8. q. in Tynan, p. 238.
9. q. in Tynan, p. 277.
10. Tynan, p. 284.
11. Sutherland, p. 97.
12. *The Times*, 7/8/70.
13. Sutherland, p. 100.

Chapter Twenty-six.
1. Green, *DITL*, p. 158.

2. *Sunday Mirror*, 12/3/67.
3. Green, *DITL*, p. 327.
4. Oz 6, q. in Neville, *Shake*,
    p. 34.
5. q in Neville, *Shake*, p. 42.
6. q. in Neville, *Play*, p. 138.
7. Neville, *Play*, p. 138.
8. q in Neville, *Shake*, p. 75.
9. Green, *DITL*, p. 152.
10. ibid.
11. Neville, *Shake*, p. 87.
12. unpub. interview for *DITL*.
13. *New Statesman*, 26/1/67.
14. Oz 26, 2–3/70.
15. Maitland, p. 212.
16. q. in Neville, *Shake*, p. 184.
17. Green, *DITL*, p. 341.
18. Neville, *Shake*, p. 188.
19. unpub. ms. by Jim Anderson:
    'Arseholes on Your Pad, Darling.
    The Story of a Conspiracy Trial'
20. Green, *DITL*, pp. 389–90.
21. unpub. interview for *DITL*.
22. *Oz* 32.
23. *Spectator*, 20/5/95.
24. Green, *DITL*, p. 394.
25. unpub. interview for *DITL*.
26. *Daily Express*, 29/7/71.
27. *Daily Telegraph*, 7/8/71.
28. *The Times*, n.d.
29. Green, *DITL*, pp. 397–8.
30. q. in Sutherland 125.
31. *Guardian*, 25/5/73.
32. *IT* 155, May 1973.

Chapter Twenty-seven.
1. *The Times*, 11/8/1885.
2. *Sunday Pictorial*, 25/5/52.
3. q. in Gould, p. 99.
4. q. in Weeks, *Sex*, p. 242.
5. figures q. in Weeks, *Sex*, pp.
    239–240.
6. Faulks, p. 242.
7. ibid., p. 243.
8. *News Chronicle*, 10/9/57.
9. *The Times*, 19/3/59.
10. ibid., 24/3/59.
11. Weeks, *Sex*, p. 242.
12. *Daily Express*, 27/11/58.
13. *News Chronicle*, 27/11/58.
14. *Spectator*, 28/11/58.
15. q. in Jeffrey-Poulter, p. 85.

16. q. in Jeffrey-Poulter, p. 71.
17. Annan, p. 134.
18. ibid.
19. Weeks, *Sex*, pp. 285-6.
20. *Village Voice*, 3/7/69.
21. *New Society*, 27/3/69.
22. Weeks, *Sex*, p. 285.
23. Annan, p. 151.
24. Green, *DITL*, p. 381.
25. *Gay News* 1.
26. Green, *DITL*, pp. 378-9.
27. Weeks, *Sex*, pp. 116-7.

Chapter Twenty-eight.
1. *McCalls*, 1954, q. in Halberstam, p. 591.
2. *Better Homes and Gardens*, 4/55, q. in Halberstam, pp. 591-2.
3. Halberstam, p. 592.
4. q. in Halberstam, p. 590.
5. Green, *DITL*, pp. 403-4; 419-20.
6. q. in Halberstam, p. 596.
7. *New Left Review*.
8. Ali, p. 233.
9. ibid.
10. *Black Dwarf*, Jan. 1969.
11. Hewison, *Culture*, p. 181.
12. Green, *DITL*, p. 407.
13. q. in Fraser, p. 308.
14. Green. *DITL*, p. 406
15. ibid., p. 413-14.
16. *Evening Standard* 7/3/71.
17. *Daily Telegraph*, 6/3/71.
18. *News Of The World*, 19/6/69.
19. *Oz* 29, n.d.
20. *Listener*, 22/10/70.
21. *New Society*, 22/10/70.
22. *Observer*, 11/10/70.
23. *Oz* 31, n.d.
24. Green, *DITL*, p. 410 plus unpub. interview.
25. Green, *DITL*, p. 411.
26. *Nova*, March 1965.
27. Green, *DITL*, p. 404.
28 Grant, pp. 103-4.
29. Green, *DITL*, p. 409.
30. ibid., p. 415.
31. ibid., p. 415.
32. Fountain, p. 174.

Chapter Twenty-nine.
1. Murray, p. 64.
2. q. in Eisen, *Age of Rock* 2, pp. 203-4.
3. Melly, *Revolt*, p.228.
4. q. in Norman, *Shout!*, p. 315.
5. ibid.
6. ibid., p. 321.
7. Green, *DITL*, pp. 225-6.
8. ibid., pp. 278-9.
9. ibid., p. 280 plus unpub. interview.
10. *Daily Telegraph Magazine*, 3/6/95.
11. Faithfull, p. 219.
12. ibid., p. 211.
13. *Daily Telegraph Magazine*, 3/6/95.
14. Faithfull, p. 211.
15. ibid., p. 215.
16. ibid., p. 219.
17. Green, *DITL*, p. 335.
18. unpub. interview for *DITL*.
19. Green, *DITL*, p. 223 plus unpub. interview.
20. Melly, *Revolt*, p. 50.
21. Murray, p. 20.
22. Green, *DITL*, p. 275 plus unpub. interview.
23. *The Listener*, 5/9/68.
24. unpub. interview for *DITL*.
25. Green, *DITL*, p. 292.
26. ibid., pp. 292-3.
27. *IT* 60, 13-31/7/60.
28. *Friends* 5, 14/4/70.
29. Green, *DITL*, p. 318 plus unpub. interview.
30. *Friends*, 13, 17/8/70.
31. *Friends* 15, 15/9/70.
32. Green, *DITL*, p. 333.
33. *Friends* 15, 15/9/70.
34. Green, *DITL*, pp. 335-6.
35. *Oz*, 10/70.
36. *Sunday Telegraph*, 30/10/70.
37. Green, *DITL*, p. 336.
38. ibid., pp. 328-30.

Aftermath.
1. Goodman, p. x.
2. Murray, p. 16.
3. Cohn, *Awopbop*.
4. Baudrillard, p. 3.

Index